AFRICAN HISTORICAL DICTIONARIES
Edited by Jon Woronoff

Historical Dictionary of Kenya

Second Edition

Robert M. Maxon
Thomas P. Ofcansky

African Historical Dictionaries, No. 77

The Scarecrow Press, Inc.
Lanham, Md., & London
2000

SCARECROW PRESS, INC.

Published in the United States of America
by Scarecrow Press, Inc.
4720 Boston Way
Lanham, Maryland 20706

4 Pleydell Gardens, Folkestone
Kent CT20 2DN, England

British Library Cataloguing in Publication Information Available

Library of Congress Cataloging-in-Publication Data

Maxon, Robert M.
    Historical dictionary of Kenya / Robert M. Maxon and Thomas P.
Ofcansky.
        p.   cm. — (African historical dictionaries ; no. 77)
    Includes bibliographical references.
    ISBN 0-8108-3616-5 (alk. paper)
    1. Kenya—History—Dictionaries.   I. Ofcansky, Thomas P., 1947–
II. Title.   III. Series.
    DT433.215 .M39   2000   98-50070
    967.62'.003—dc21   CIP

Contents

Editor's Foreword

When Kenya became independent in 1963, it was one of Africa's most promising new states. The country was endowed with a vast territory, some of it rich farmland, and sparsely enough populated not to make it overly crowded. There were few serious conflicts between its ethnic groups, and none that could dominate all the others, and even much of the remaining European and Asian populations cooperated with the new government. The colonial power had left behind a reasonable transportation and communications infrastructure, and there were a fair number of schools and many educated Kenyans. The economic potential was good, and tourism a sure foreign currency earner. Yet, looking back, we see that little of the promise has been realized. The economy is doing poorly, and urban blight and pollution affect many parts of the country. Shortly after independence, the nascent democracy was replaced by a one-party state. There is no cause to exaggerate, however. Kenya has done better than most other African states, as witnessed by recent efforts to establish a genuine democratic form of government. The pity is that it could have done much better still.

The *Historical Dictionary of Kenya* contains entries on both the past and present, the older precolonial period, the colonial era, and the several decades since independence. It covers many aspects of the Kenyan experience: historical, political, economic, social, cultural, and others. Of particular interest are the entries on people, from those who founded the colony, to those who turned it into an independent state and ruled it, to those who may take over in coming years, whether within the establishment or opposition. Naturally, it has no entries on the future, but it does provides some basis for looking ahead and answering the question of whether Kenya *can* do better, if not whether it actually *will*. While the chronology, introduction, and dictionary offer a broad overview, they cannot go into all the details. But those can be uncovered readily by consulting the books and articles in the exceptionally comprehensive bibliography.

This volume was written by two longtime specialists on East Africa. Thomas P. Ofcansky, who is presently with the Department of State, originally went to Kenya as a traveler and then as a student conducting research. Since then, he has visited the country frequently. He has published several books and numerous articles on East Africa and is the coauthor of the *Historical Dictionary of Tanzania*. Robert M. Maxon has spent many years teaching about Kenya to Kenyans, first as a high school teacher, more recently and presently as visiting professor of history at Moi University. He, too, has written extensively on Kenya and East Africa. Thanks to this experience, Drs. Ofcansky and Maxon have produced an excellent guide to what remains one of Africa's most promising countries.

Jon Woronoff
Series Editor

Abbreviations and Acronyms

ADC	African District Council
AEMO	African Elected Members Organisation
AIDS	Acquired Immune Deficiency Syndrome
AIC	African Inland Church
AIM	Africa Inland Mission
APM	Alliance of Protestant Missions
APP	African People's Party
CCK	Christian Council of Kenya
CGS	Chief(s) of the General Staff
CMS	Church Missionary Society
CO	Colonial Office
COTU	Central Organisation of Trade Unions
CPK	Church of the Province of Kenya
CSM	Church of Scotland Mission
DP	Democratic Party
EAA	East African Airways
EAC	East African Community
EACM	East African Common Market
EACSO	East African Common Service Organisation
EAHC	East African High Commission
EAINC	East African Indian National Congress
EALB	East African Literature Bureau
EAP	East Africa Protectorate
EATUC	East African Trade Union Congress
ESAF	Enhanced Structural Adjustment Facility
FO	Foreign Office
FORD	Forum for the Restoration of Democracy
FORD-A	Forum for the Restoration of Democracy–Asili
FORD-K	Forum for the Restoration of Democracy–Kenya
FORD-P	Forum for the Restoration of Democracy–People
GBM	Green Belt Movement

GDP	Gross Domestic Product
GEA	German East Africa
GEMA	Gikuyu, Embu, Meru Association
GMS	Gospel Missionary Society
GSU	General Services Unit
HIV	Human Immunodeficiency Virus
IA	Indian Association
IBEAC	Imperial British East Africa Company
IMF	International Monetary Fund
IPK	Islamic Party of Kenya
IPPG	Inter-Parties Parliamentary Group
KA	Kikuyu Association
KADU	Kenya African Democratic Union
KANU	Kenya African National Union
KAF	Kenya Air Force
KAR	King's African Rifles
KASU	Kenya African Study Union
KAU	Kenya African Union
KCA	Kikuyu Central Association
KCB	Kenya Central Bank; Kenya Commercial Bank
KDF	Kenya Defence Force
KENDA	Kenya National Democratic Alliance
KFL	Kenya Federation of Labour
KFP	Kenya Freedom Party
KLFA	Kenya Land and Freedom Army
KLP	Kikuyu Loyal Patriots
KPA	Kalenjin Political Alliance
KPA	Kikuyu Provincial Association
KPU	Kenya People's Union
KSC	Kenya Social Congress
LEGCO	Legislative Council
MP	Member of Parliament
NBI	National Bank of India
NCCK	National Christian Council of Kenya
NCEC	National Convention Executive Council
NDEM	National Democratic Party
NDNC	Nairobi District National Congress
NDP	National Development Party
NFD	Northern Frontier District/Province
NFDLF	Northern Frontier District Liberation Front

NKCA	North Kavirondo Central Association
NPCP	Nairobi People's Convention Party
NPPPP	Northern Province People's Progressive Party
OAU	Organization of African Unity
PCEA	Presbyterian Church of East Africa
PICK	Party of Independent Candidates of Kenya
RAF	Royal Air Force
RPP	Release Political Prisoners
SDP	Social Democratic Party
UEA	University of East Africa
UKENYA	Movement for Unity and Democracy in Kenya
UMA	Ukamba Members Association
UMCA	Universities' Mission to Central Africa
WHO	World Health Organisation
YKA	Young Kavirondo Association; also, Young Kikuyu Association

Chronology

Second millennium B.C.E.: The Stone Bowl culture emerges in the Kenya highlands. These Stone Age agriculturalists flourished during the first millennium B.C.E.

500 B.C.E.–first century C.E.: Bantu-speaking agriculturalists take up residence in various parts of Kenya.

First millennium C.E.: People speaking Highlands Nilotic languages move south into the western Kenya highlands.

Second millennium C.E.: People speaking Plains Nilotic languages move south into the western Kenya highlands.

C. 1450: Ancestors of the Luyia people begin to move from Uganda into western Kenya.

C. 1490: The first wave of Luo ancestors arrive in western Kenya.

1498 7 April: The Portuguese explorer Vasco da Gama lands at Mombasa.

C. 1510: The southward migration of Oromo-speaking peoples into Kenya begins. By the early 17th century, some had arrived at the Kenya coast.

C. 1580: Kamba people begin to move from the Mount Kilimanjaro region toward the Mbooni Hills.

C. 1610: Kikuyu people begin to move south and east into the region of central Kenya that they would occupy over the next three centuries.

C. 1625: A second, and more substantial, wave of Luo movement into western Kenya begins.

C. 1820: The Gusii move toward their present homeland in the southwestern highlands after defeat by Maasai neighbors.

1824 9 February: Captain William Fitzwilliam Wentworth Owen, R.N., of H.M.S. *Leven*, proclaims a British protectorate over Mombasa two days after arriving.

1826   25 July: Owen's Protectorate officially comes to an end.

1877   24 March: The sultan of Zanzibar grants a 50-year concession of the 10-mile coastal strip between the River Umba and Kipini to Sir William Mackinnon.

1886   1 November: An Anglo-German agreement is signed, dividing a portion of the East African mainland between Great Britain and Germany. Most of the territory that would become Kenya falls within the British sphere.

1887   25 March: The sultan of Zanzibar grants a 50-year concession of the 10-mile coastal strip between the River Umba and Kipini to Sir William Mackinnon. **25 May:** Sir William Mackinnon, together with other British humanitarians and capitalists, establishes the British East African Association.

1888   18 April: The British East African Association becomes the Imperial British East Africa Company. **3 September:** The Imperial British East Africa Company receives royal charter.

1890   1 July: Anglo-German Treaty cedes Heligoland island to Germany in exchange for Berlin's renunciation of all claims to Witu, Uganda, and other adjacent territories and recognition of a British protectorate over Zanzibar, Pemba, and parts of the mainland.

1895   1 July: The Foreign Office assumes responsibility for the Imperial British East Africa Company's territory. This includes the 10-mile coastal strip, technically the domain of the sultan of Zanzibar. Sir Arthur Hardinge is appointed first commissioner of the East Africa Protectorate.

1896   5 August: Construction begins on the Uganda Railway on the Mombasa mainland.

1901   20 December: Uganda Railway reaches Port Florence (now Kisumu) on Lake Victoria.

1902   1 April: Acting on orders from British Secretary of State for Foreign Affairs, Lord Lansdowne, Uganda transfers its Eastern Province to Kenya. The transferred territory eventually became the Nyanza and Rift Valley Provinces of the East Africa Protectorate.

1904   10 August: First Maasai Treaty signed.

1905   1 April: The protectorate is transferred from the Foreign Office to the Colonial Office.

1906   4 April: Colonial government publishes Report of the Land Commission, which affirms that the highlands "should be reserved for the support and maintenance of a white population." **17 April:** Secretary of State for the Colonies Lord Elgin accepts the principle that land lying between Kiu and Fort Ternan should be granted to European settlers only.

1907   17 August: LEGCO holds its first meeting.

1908   19 March: Secretary of State for the Colonies Lord Elgin accepts that as a matter of "administrative convenience" grants of land in the highlands would not be made to Indians.

1911   19 April: Second Maasai Treaty signed.

1915   10 May: LEGCO gives final approval to the Crown Lands Ordinance, 1915. **19 August:** The Colonial Office approves an ordinance to initiate a system of registration of African men but orders that it be suspended until the end of the war.

1916   27 September: The Colonial Office accepts the principle of electoral representation in LEGCO for Europeans though details as to voter qualifications, electoral areas, etc. were left to be resolved after the end of the war.

1919   24 February: Electoral Representation Bill introduced into LEGCO, envisaging a franchise limited to adult males of European descent. LEGCO subsequently passes an amendment extending the franchise to European women. **16 August:** The London selection board for the Soldier Settlement Scheme completes its work. **23 October:** Governor Northey issues his Labour Circular, which calls upon administrative officials and African chiefs to take an active role in labor recruitment for European settlers. **1 November:** The registration of African males is begun in Nairobi with the issuing of the *kipande*. For the rest of the colony, the system was inaugurated in 1920.

1920   3 May: The first European elected members take their seats in LEGCO. **11 June:** The East Africa Protectorate is renamed Kenya Colony. The coastal strip, formally the domain of the sultan of Zanzibar, becomes Kenya Protectorate. Until independence the territory is officially known as the Colony and Protectorate of Kenya.

1923   23 July: British cabinet approves the white paper to be published as *Indians in Kenya*.

1925   29 June: Jubaland Province is formally ceded to Italian Somaliland.

1926 **1 February:** Rudolf Province is transferred from Uganda to Kenya.

1930 **13 April:** LEGCO passes the Native Lands Trust Ordinance.

1934 **14 May:** The report of the Kenya Land Commission is made public.

1938 **28 July:** Three thousand Kamba organized by the Ukamba Members Association arrive in Nairobi demanding to see the governor to protest against compulsory destocking.

1940 **30 May:** The colonial authorities ban the Kikuyu Central Association.

1943 **10 April:** Governor Sir Henry Moore submits a secret plan to London for the union of Great Britain's East African territories. It sought to create a Kenya province within which the colony's European settlers would be given self-government.

1944 **1 October:** The Kenya African Union is formed in Nairobi. **5 October:** Eluid Mathu is appointed as first African member of Legislative Council.

1947 **1 June:** Jomo Kenyatta is elected president of the Kenya African Union.

1948 **1 January:** East African High Commission established.

1950 **12 August:** Colonial government proscribes Mau Mau as an "unlawful society."

1952 **7 October:** Kikuyu chief and strong government supporter Waruhiu wa Kung'u is assassinated on his way home from Nairobi. **20 October:** Sir Evelyn Baring declares state of emergency, imposes martial law, and orders the arrest of Jomo Kenyatta, Paul Ngei, Achieng Oneko, Bildad Kaggia, Fred Kubai, and Kungu Karumba for directing the Mau Mau revolt. **3 December:** Trial opens at Kapenguria for Kenya African Union leaders suspected of organizing the Mau Mau Revolt.

1953 **26 March:** "Mau Mau" fighters successfully raid the Naivasha police station and kill 97 Kikuyu loyalists at Lari. **8 April:** Judge R. S. Thacker sentences Jomo Kenyatta, Paul Ngei, Achieng Oneko, Bildad Kaggia, Fred Kubai, and Kungu Karumba to seven years' imprisonment with hard labor for "managing" and "assisting in the managing" of Mau Mau and three years for belonging to Mau Mau. **8 June:** The colonial authorities proscribe the Kenya African Union.

1954 **10 March:** The Lyttelton Constitution is announced.

1957 **8 November:** In Nairobi, Secretary of State for the Colonies Alan Lennox-Boyd announces new constitutional arrangements.

1959 **3 March:** Eleven "hard-core" Mau Mau detainees perish at the Hola detention camp. **13 October:** Colonial authorities issue a sessional paper that announces the White Highlands will be open to farmers of all races.

1960 **12 January:** Governor Sir Patrick Renison signs a proclamation officially ending the State of Emergency. **18 January:** The first Lancaster House constitutional conference opens in London. **14 May:** At a meeting in Kiambu, the Kenya African National Union (KANU) is founded. **25 June:** Following a conference in Ngong, the formation of the Kenya African Democratic Union (KADU) is announced.

1961 **27 February:** Polling ends in the "Kenyatta election." **14 August:** Jomo Kenyatta is released after serving his sentence for complicity in the Mau Mau Revolt followed by a period of restriction. **8 October:** Jomo Kenyatta becomes president of the Kenya African National Union.

1962 **6 April:** The second Lancaster House constitutional conference concludes in London.

1963 **26 May:** Voting concludes in Kenya's first universal suffrage general election. **1 June:** Kenya achieves internal self-government as Jomo Kenyatta is sworn in as first prime minister. The date has subsequently been celebrated as a public holiday, *Madaraka* Day. **8 October:** The sultan of Zanzibar cedes 10-mile coastal strip to Kenya, effective from Kenya's independence day. **19 October:** The third Lancaster House conference concludes with agreement between the British and Kenyan governments to amend the independence constitution. **12 December:** Kenya achieves independence. **25 December:** Governor-General Malcolm MacDonald declares a state of emergency in the North Eastern Province after an escalation of attacks by Somali *shifta* raiders.

1964 **24 January:** The 11th Battalion Kenya Rifles mutinies at Lanet, Nakuru. The Third Royal Horse Artillery Regiment subsequently arrests those involved in the mutiny. **20 October:** Kenya celebrates Kenyatta Day to mark the anniversary of the arrest of Mzee Kenyatta and others in 1952. **3 November:** The Constitution of Kenya (Amendment) Bill is passed by a 75 percent majority in the House of Representatives. **10 November:** The Constitution of Kenya (Amendment) Bill passed by the Senate. It provides for a republic with a powerful presidency. Leader of the Opposition Ronald Ngala announces the dissolution of KADU in the House of Representatives. KADU members join

KANU. **10 December:** Last British troops depart Kenya. The first republican cabinet is announced. Oginga Odinga becomes vice president and minister without portfolio. **12 December:** Kenya becomes a republic. Jomo Kenyatta takes the oath of office as the country's first president. The public holiday is hereafter known as *Jamhuri* (republic) Day.

1965 27 April: Sessional Paper No. 10 is published. The document, *African Socialism and Its Application to Planning in Kenya*, sets out economic and social goals for the new republic.

1966 13 March: The conclusion of the KANU Delegates Conference at Limuru approves the abolition of the position of party vice president and its replacement by eight vice presidents, one drawn from each region plus Nairobi. **14 April:** Oginga Odinga resigns his position as vice president and resigns from KANU. **29 April:** Parliament approves a constitutional amendment requiring that any MP who resigns from the party that supported him or her at his or her election must resign from Parliament and stand in a by-election. **3 May:** A cabinet reshuffle is announced to replace the ministers and assistant ministers who resigned. Joseph Murumbi becomes vice president. **23 May:** Kenya People's Union (KPU) registers as opposition political party under Oginga Odinga's leadership. **19 June:** Polling is completed in Kenya's "Little General Election." **20 September:** Joseph Murumbi announces his intention to step down as vice president and retire from politics. **22 December:** The constitution is amended to provide for a single-house Parliament. The Senate is abolished and the 45 senators merged with the House of Representatives. These and other new constituencies give Kenya a 175-member Parliament. The possible life of the new Parliament is extended to June 1970.

1967 5 January: Daniel arap Moi becomes Kenya's third vice president. **28 October:** President Jomo Kenyatta and the Somali prime minister sign a Memorandum of Understanding aimed at restoring normal and peaceful relations at Arusha, Tanzania.

1968 25 June: The constitution is amended to allow for a popular election of the president. Candidates for the presidency will have to be members of a political party. The changes also stipulate that should the presidency fall vacant for any reason, the vice president would succeed but only for a period of 90 days, during which elections must be held to choose a new president.

1969 21 February: Kenyan government agrees to lift emergency regulations in the North Eastern Province. **5 July:** Tom Mboya, minister for economic planning, is assassinated in Nairobi. **27 October:** Oginga Odinga and the other KPU MPs are detained, following an incident in Kisumu when police fired on crowds that had given President Kenyatta a hostile reception. **30 October:** The KPU is banned. **6 December:** First general election since independence. Jomo Kenyatta is elected unopposed as president. Almost half the sitting MPs, including five ministers and 14 assistant ministers, lose their seats.

1974   14 October: A general election is held. Jomo Kenyatta is reelected unopposed.

1975   3 March: Josiah Mwangi Kariuki, a prominent MP and ex-Mau Mau detainee, is found dead at Olosho-Oibor, a settlement near Ngong Township. No one was ever charged with the crime. **3 June:** The parliamentary committee set up to probe the murder of J. M. Kariuki presents its findings. Its report alleges that high-ranking police officials were implicated in the crime. **12 June:** Minister of Works Masinde Muliro and two assistant ministers are dismissed after voting against the attorney general's motion to "adopt" the Kariuki committee report that the house defeated. **15 October:** Martin Shikuku and John Marie Seroney are arrested in parliament buildings and subsequently detained without trial. **11 December:** A constitutional amendment is approved that empowers the president to pardon anyone convicted of election offenses. It is immediately applied to the case of Paul Ngei.

1976   15 February: Ugandan President Idi Amin claims part of western Kenya, saying that it had historically been part of Uganda. The Kenyan government rejects the claim.

1977   19 May: Kenya bans all big game hunting and cancels all big game hunting licenses. **30 June:** Kenya, Uganda, and Tanzania announce the dissolution of the East African Community. **31 December:** Kenyan authorities arrest the noted dissident novelist and playwright Ngugi wa Thiong'o. He spent the following year in a maximum security prison.

1978   22 August: Jomo Kenyatta dies. Vice President Daniel arap Moi succeeds. **11 October:** Mwai Kibaki is appointed vice president. **14 October:** Daniel arap Moi is installed as the second president of Kenya and commander in chief of the armed forces. **28 October:** The first Kenya African National Union elections in 12 years are held. Daniel arap Moi is elected party president. **12 December:** President Daniel arap Moi releases all political detainees.

1979   8 November: A general election is completed.

1980   **25 April:** Charles Njonjo resigns as attorney general. Within a week, he is elected MP for Kikuyu unopposed. **31 December:** Bomb blast at Nairobi's Norfolk Hotel kills 20 people and injures another 85. The Kenyan government subsequently accuses Muradi Aksali, a member of the Popular Front for the Liberation of Palestine, of planting the bomb.

1982   **25 February:** In a major cabinet reshuffle, President Moi moves Mwai Kibaki to Home Affairs with Charles Njonjo retaining responsibility only for Constitutional Affairs. **9 June:** Parliament amends the constitution to make KANU the only legal party, thus making Kenya a *de jure* one-party state. **1 August:** The Voice of Kenya, which had been seized by 12 Kenya Air Force personnel, announces that President Moi has been deposed. Later in the day, loyal elements of the Kenya Army retook the radio station, thereby ending the coup attempt.

1983   **8 May:** President Moi claims there is a "traitor" in his government whom some foreign countries are grooming to take over the presidency of Kenya. **29 June:** President Moi suspends Charles Njonjo, minister of constitutional affairs, from the cabinet until a judicial inquiry into his loyalty is completed. **29 August:** Daniel arap Moi is reelected as president of Kenya for a five-year term. **26 September:** A general election is held. Nearly 1,000 candidates stand for parliamentary seats.

1984   **14 September:** KANU expels Charles Njonjo along with other senior politicians associated with him, G. G. Kariuki and Stanley Oloitiptip. **12 December:** President Moi pardons Charles Njonjo, former minister for constitutional affairs, after the commission of inquiry found him guilty of corruption, involvement in the illegal import of firearms into Kenya, and an attempt to overthrow the government of the Seychelles.

1986   **20 August:** A KANU delegates conference approves queue voting for preliminary elections. **2 December:** Parliament approves the third reading of a constitutional amendment that abolishes the office of chief secretary, raises the number of parliamentary seats, and removes the security of tenure for the attorney general and auditor general.

1987   **18 February:** Exiles in London form the Movement for Unity and Democracy in Kenya. The organization, the visible version of Mwakenya, opposed the presence of the British and American armed forces in Kenya and supported the creation of a democratic society in Kenya.

1988   **21 March:** The secret ballot portion of the general election is held. Voter turnout is the lowest in the history of independent Kenya. **24 March:**

Mwai Kibaki is dropped as vice president following the elections and is demoted to be minister of health. Josephat Karanja is appointed vice president. **2 August:** Parliament passes a constitutional amendment, in a single sitting, which eliminates security of tenure for judges and Public Service Commission members and raises the maximum period that a person charged with a capital crime can be held without trial from 24 hours to 14 days.

1989 **27 April:** Parliament votes an expression of no confidence in Vice President Karanja. **1 May:** Jospehat Karanja resigns as vice president and minister for home affairs. President Moi accepts the resignation and appoints Professor George Saitoti, minister of finance, new vice president. **18 July:** President Moi burns 12 tons of ivory at Nairobi National Park as an indication of his commitment to eliminating poaching that had reduced Kenya's elephant population from about 65,000 to an estimated 17,000.

1990 **16 February:** Kenyan authorities find the burned and broken body of Foreign Minister Robert Ouko. Riots subsequently break out in Nairobi and Kisumu. Those responsible have never been identified. **12 April:** President Moi rules out multiparty democracy, saying political parties would cause disunity and create chaos. **21 June:** President Moi appoints the KANU Review Committee under Vice President George Saitoti. **4 July:** Kenyan police arrest multiparty advocates Kenneth Matiba and Charles Rubia. **7 July:** Saba Saba pro-democracy riots break out in Nairobi and other major cities. Twenty-three people died over four days of rioting. Unofficial accounts maintain that more than 100 people died during the riots. **13 August:** U.S. ambassador to Kenya, Smith Hempstone, announces that the United States has cut Kenya's military aid by half to demonstrate its displeasure with that country's human rights record. If no improvement occurred, the U.S. ambassador indicated the United States would cancel the remaining five million dollars. **9 October:** The Kenyan government announces that it has arrested Koigi wa Wamwere, a former member of Parliament, who had founded the antigovernment Kenya People's Front.

1991 **12 April:** Kenya government releases former cabinet minister Charles Rubia, who had been detained for nine months without trial for supposed antigovernment activities. **9 June:** Kenyan government releases former minister Kenneth Matiba from detention. **21 June:** President Moi announces the release of Raila Odinga, the country's last political detainee. Odinga had been involved in pro-multiparty activities. **2 August:** Former Vice President Oginga Odinga announces creation of the Forum for the Restoration of Democracy (FORD). The organization's purpose is to fight for the restoration of democracy and human rights.

19 November: President Moi sacks Minister of Industry Nicholas Biwott, who had been named as the prime suspect by a British detective investigating the murder of Foreign Minister Robert Ouko. **3 December:** Special Delegates Conference of the Kenya African National Union recommends that Parliament repeal section 2 (a) of the constitution, which stipulates that KANU is the only political party. **10 December:** Kenyan Parliament repeals section 2 (a) of the constitution, thereby legalizing opposition parties for the first time since 1969. **26 December:** Minister of Health and former Vice President Mwai Kibaki resigns from the cabinet, citing President Moi's closing the official commission of inquiry into the death of Foreign Minister Robert Ouko.

1992   8 January: Mwai Kibaki establishes the Democratic Party. **8/9 March:** Press reports of ethnic clashes on the border of Nyanza and Rift Valley Provinces appear. This marks the beginning of ethnic clashes in Nyanza, Rift Valley, and Western Provinces that cause injury, death, and displacement of thousands of Kenyans over subsequent months. **5 August:** Parliament passes the Constitutional Amendment Act, 1992, which provides that in order to be elected president a candidate must win a majority of votes as well as at least 25 percent of the vote in five of eight provinces. **12 October:** The split in Kenya's main opposition party, the Forum for the Restoration of Democracy (FORD), becomes permanent as Oginga Odinga announces that the faction he leads will be registered as FORD-Kenya. The following day, the Matiba–Shikuku faction of FORD announced it was taking the name FORD-Asili. **29 December:** Kenya holds its first multiparty election in 26 years. President Moi wins reelection with 36.4 percent of the vote and 25 percent in five provinces.

1993   23 November: International donors that suspended aid to Kenya two years earlier to press for democratic reforms pledge new money. However, the donors made such aid conditional on curbing corruption and halting ethnic violence that had killed at least 1,500 people and displaced 250,000.

1995   7 May: Richard Leakey and opposition politicians, including Paul Muite, announce the formation of a new opposition political party. When applying for registration in June, the party adopted the name SAFINA (Swahili for Noah's Ark). **9 May:** Winifred Nyiva Mwendwa is appointed minister of culture and social services. She is Kenya's first female cabinet minister.

1997   3–6 April: A conference is held at Limuru, resulting in the formation of the umbrella group of opposition elements called the National Convention Executive Council. **7 July:** Kenyan security forces break up pro-democracy rallies in Nairobi, Thika, Mombasa, and several other cities. During the clashes, nine people were killed and hundreds injured. **8 August:** Further protest demonstrations and an abortive general strike, called by the National Convention Executive Council, occur in Nairobi and other Kenyan cities. **13 August:** A gang of approximately 100 armed men assaults Likoni police station near Mombasa, kills at least 13 people, and injures scores, if not hundreds, of others. The attackers also captured some guns and ammunition. **17 September:** Parliament gives overwhelming approval to the constitutional and administrative reforms proposed by the Inter-Parties Parliamentary Group. **30 December:** Parliamentary and presidential elections are extended a second day as a result of difficulties with the electoral process. After delays in counting, President Moi is declared winner with 40 percent of the vote.

1998   **5 January:** President Moi is sworn in for his last term as president of Kenya. **8 January:** President Moi announces his new cabinet. The vice presidency is left vacant. **7 August:** Bomb explosions rock Nairobi, destroying the American Embassy. More than 200 people are killed and some 5,000 wounded by the blast, allegedly the work of Islamic extremists.

1999   **18 February:** Finance minister Simeon Nyachae resigns from the cabinet rather than accept demotion to the Ministry of Industry. **24 March:** Kenya's police commissioner releases to the public the report of Scotland Yard detectives called in to investigate the murder of Dr. Robert Ouko that had been submitted to the government in 1991. **3 April:** At a roadside *baraza* in Limuru, outside Nairobi, President Daniel arap Moi announces the appointment of Professor George Saitoti as vice president, ending a period of almost 15 months during which the office was vacant.

KENYA

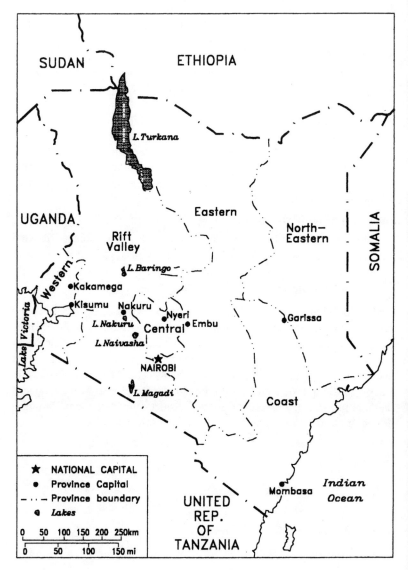

Introduction

Kenya has a long and complex history that began thousands of years ago. Indeed, some archaeologists contend that the country was the "cradle of mankind" or, at the very least, one of the places that was home to the earliest humanoids. In later centuries, Kenya's strategic location astride the Indian Ocean and the East African littoral attracted numerous foreign peoples, some of the most significant of which have been the Americans, Arabs, British, Chinese, French, Germans, and Portuguese. Additionally, Africans from throughout the subcontinent have settled in Kenya to escape conflict or political persecution, while others wanted an opportunity to begin a new life. As a result of being a gateway to the world, the country traditionally has been one of the most important business, cultural, diplomatic, and political centers in Africa. Although it has maintained this reputation during the postindependence period, Kenya, like most African countries, has been plagued by an increasing array of complex economic, political, and social problems. This dictionary provides a starting point for those interested in any of the phases of Kenya's historical evolution.

Kenya was a British colony from 1 July 1895 to 12 December 1963. Until 1 July 1920, it was known as the East Africa Protectorate; the name Kenya was officially adopted as part of the change of status from protectorate to colony. On 12 December 1964, Kenya became a republic on the first anniversary of its independence.

GEOGRAPHY

Kenya is bounded on the north by Sudan and Ethiopia, on the east by Somalia and the Indian Ocean, on the south by Tanzania, and on the west by Lake Victoria and Uganda. Kenya has an area of 582,646 square kilometers (224,960 square miles). This total includes 2.3 percent water surface. Kenya's coastline is 536 kilometers (332 miles) in length. Split by the equator, Kenya is located approximately between latitudes 4 21' north and 4 28' south and between longitudes 34 and 42 east.

Within these boundaries, Kenya comprises several topographical zones extending upward from the Indian Ocean to mountain ranges that reach elevations of more than 3,050 meters (10,000 feet) above sea level. The coastal plain is narrow and rises gradually to a series of low plateaus that stretch from the border with Tanzania over the entire northern half of the country. The region west of these plateaus, known as the Kenya highlands, is a series of higher plateaus and volcanic mountains ranging from 915 meters (approximately 3,000 feet) to 1,520 meters (about 5,000 feet) above sea level, characterized by great physical diversity. Bisected by the Rift Valley, a massive depression as much as 50-65 kilometers (31-41 miles) wide, the highlands are marked by numerous extinct volcanoes, the highest of which are Mount Kenya (5,199 meters/17,057 feet) and Mount Elgon (4,321 meters/14,176 feet). In the far west of Kenya lies the Lake Victoria basin. This includes lower plateaus near the lakeshore and highlands to the north and south of Nyanza Gulf.

Lake Victoria forms one of Kenya's major bodies of water, though only a small portion of it actually lies within Kenya's present boundaries. Lake Turkana is also a major body of water, while smaller lakes, such as Baringo, Nakuru, Elmenteita, and Naivasha, lie in or near the Rift Valley. The nation's major rivers include the Tana and Galana-Sabaki (known as the Athi in its upper course) in the east and the Kerio, Turkwell, Nzoia, and Yala in the west.

The coastal plain enjoys a largely humid and wet environment. Mean sea level temperature is 26 C (78.8 F) while average annual rainfall varies from 1,194 millimeters (47 inches) to 660 millimeters (26 inches). The low plateau is the driest part of Kenya, with mean annual rainfall below 500 millimeters (20 inches) and mean annual temperatures at 27 degrees C (80.6 degrees F) or higher. Most of the highlands receive an annual average of at least 800 millimeters (31 inches) rainfall, with much higher amounts on the highland slopes. Mean annual temperatures fall below 25 C (77 F). The Lake Victoria basin is slightly warmer, particularly at the lakeshore, while annual rainfall ranges from 760 millimeters (30 inches) at the shore to slightly over 1,930 millimeters (75 inches) in the higher elevations adjacent to the lake. For most of Kenya, rainfall is seasonal. At the coast, the lake basin, and the eastern highlands there are two rainy seasons, roughly March to June and October to December. The western Kenya highlands have a single rainy season, March to September. However, all regions are subject to periodic droughts or delays in the start of the rainy seasons.

Rainfall has had a powerful effect on Kenya's settlement pattern, since agriculture has historically been the means by which the majority of the people has made a living. Of Kenya's land, only about 11 percent is suitable for agriculture. Almost all of this land is situated in the south of the country, as the northern two-thirds of Kenya is mostly desert or semidesert.

PEOPLE

Kenya's population at the 1989 census was 21,443,636. By 1998, the country had an estimated population of 29 million. Though Kenya has a diverse population, the overwhelming proportion is made up of Africans. Other groups include Arabs, Asians, and Europeans (who constitute less than one percent in the last census). Despite experiencing one of the world's highest population growth rates for the period stretching from 1960 through the mid-1980s, population density is only about 50 persons per square kilometer (19 per square mile). Still, due to the high birth rate, at the end of the century slightly more than 50 percent of the population will be less than 15 years of age. In addition, Kenya's population is overwhelmingly rural, as more than 75 percent live in rural areas.

While the population may be divided along racial lines, as noted above, the most significant divisions recognized at the end of the 20th century are based on ethnicity. Kenya's African people are divided into more than 40 ethnic groups belonging to three linguistic families: Bantu, Cushitic, and Nilotic. Prior to the 20th century, the social formations known now as ethnic groups were fluid rather than static. Language is the primary characteristic of ethnic identity in Kenya. Among the Bantu-speaking people, a main division may be made between the western group (Luyia and Gusii), the central or highlands group (Kikuyu, Embu, Meru and Kamba), and the coastal Bantu (the Mijikenda). For the Nilotic-speakers, the divisions are the River-Lake or Western (Luo), the Highlands or Southern (Kalenjin), and the Plains or Eastern (Maasai, Teso, Samburu). The Cushitic-speaking groups comprise the Oromo- and the Somali-speakers. The Kikuyu, who made up 21 percent of the population at the 1989 census, are Kenya's largest ethnic group. Next largest are the Luyia (14 percent), the Luo (12 percent), the Kamba (11 percent), the Kalenjin (11 percent), and the Gusii (six percent).

Colonial rule solidified ethnic identity and associated it with certain areas of the country (provinces, districts, and smaller territorial entities known as locations) where only people with a specific ethnic identity were supposed to reside. While such ethnic engineering was never completely successful, the colonial government created a system under which, for example, the majority of the Kikuyu live in Central Province and the Luo reside in Nyanza. However, modern economic and political development has brought many Kenyans to urban areas and other parts of the country far from what was presumed to be the traditional areas of residence for their ethnic groups. As a result of such policies, ethnicity has long been an important factor in Kenya's politics.

In addition to the languages associated with ethnic groups, Kenya's official languages are English and Swahili. Thus, at the end of the century, the majority of Kenyans are trilingual. Kenya's people are also divided along religious lines. As a result of missionary work, largely during the 20th century, some 70 percent of the population is Christian, with Protestants (40 percent) outnumbering Catholics (30 percent). Muslims make up six percent of the population, while the remainder of the people are largely followers of traditional religions together with a small number of Hindus, Jains, and Sikhs.

HISTORY

Precolonial Period

The territory that is today Kenya was the site of some of the earliest human settlements on the African continent. These, such as Koobi Fora near Lake Turkana, indicate hominid habitation dating back some 2.5 million years. From that time until the dawn of the common era, hunting and collecting peoples inhabited portions of Kenya. In the Kenya highlands, food-producing communities, utilizing stone tools, established residence by the end of the second millennium B.C.E.

However, it was not until the last centuries B.C.E. that other food-producing peoples, using iron tools, began moving into Kenya. These were peoples ancestral to the Bantu- and Nilotic-speaking groups of Kenya. Bantu-speaking peoples entered Kenya from the west and south, eventually occupying land at the coast, the eastern highlands, and areas to the east of Lake Victoria.

The earliest Nilotic group to enter Kenya spoke languages ancestral to Highlands Nilotic. They moved from the north to take up residence in the highlands to the west of the Rift Valley. Later, groups ancestral to the Plains Nilotes moved from the area to the north of Lake Turkana into the Rift Valley and the plains to the east. Later still, during the second millennium C.E., River-Lake Nilotic-speaking people moved through present-day Uganda into the lower-lying regions around Lake Victoria. Eastern Cushitic-speakers ancestral to the Oromo moved into northern Kenya from the northeast and were followed by Somali during the present millennium.

This general description of migration patterns conceals a complicated process of large, but mostly small, population movements and population interaction spanning many centuries. From this process emerged the various social formations that existed at the inauguration of colonial rule. These groupings were fluid, representing a process of ongoing social change. The traditional way of life for those peoples included not only movement and interaction but also combined stock raising with agriculture, though some were pastoralists. No centralized states or empires emerged in Kenya.

The history of the Kenya coast, on the other hand, differed from that of the interior. The former region was long part of the Indian Ocean world, and the Bantu-speaking peoples resident there felt its impact. By the ninth century, the Swahili-speaking people had taken up residence at sites that became towns and cities. Most were located on islands close to the mainland, such as Mombasa, Lamu, or Pate.

Their towns became trade centers. Commerce led to contact with traders from Arabia and the Persian Gulf and other parts of the Indian Ocean. Thus, by the 11th and 12th centuries, many Swahili inhabitants of the towns had become Muslims. Some towns, like Mombasa, grew wealthy, controlling territory on the mainland as they developed into city-states. The cities' wealth came from their position as middlemen in trade with the interior of Kenya for ivory, timber, and other raw materials. Several such Swahili city-states dotted the Kenya coast at the time the Portuguese arrived at the start of the 16th century. Portuguese dominance did not last long, as the city-states struggled to maintain an independent existence until the 19th century, when Omani Arabs gained control of the coast. Commerce in slaves expanded, but as the century wore on, greater contacts with Europe, which included commerce and British attempts to stamp out the slave trade, took place. These commercial and humanitarian interests merged with a strategic concern to keep the Nile Valley under British control and culminated with the takeover of Uganda and Kenya at the end of the century.

British Colonial Period

The resultant British colonial rule in Kenya was formalized by diplomatic agreements between Britain and Germany, Italy, and Ethiopia and later by conquest. The colonial conquest was gradual and incremental. In fact, it took second place to the building of the Uganda Railway from Mombasa to Lake Victoria, completed in 1901. The following year, the then Eastern Province of the East Africa Protectorate's neighbor to the west, the Uganda Protectorate, was transferred to the former. Only then was the conquest begun in earnest, and by 1908 the British had brought the southern half of Kenya under their control, while the drier north, inhabited largely by nomadic peoples, did not come under British rule until well after World War I. In the conquest, the British followed a policy of divide and conquer, allying with some groups against others. From the earliest days, the colonial administration was based on what the colonial rulers discerned as ethnic identity; "tribes" were created in a form that had not existed previously.

The Uganda Railway's construction had a significant impact on Kenya's colonial history. To make the railway pay, the colonial government encouraged the settlement of European farmers. After 1902, Europeans (mostly from Great Britain and South Africa) took up land (for plantations, mixed farms, and ranches) in the highlands region, in the process creating Kenya's White Highlands. European settlement meant loss of land for some of Kenya's peoples, notably the Kikuyu and Maasai. European settlers successfully pressed the colonial government for aid in their farming endeavors, and by the end of World War I, the state had raised African taxes and used a variety of coercive measures to force Africans to work on settler farms. By the same time, the European settlers had achieved considerable political influence in the territory. The political and economic predominance of the Europeans continued through the interwar period.

Nevertheless, protests against European settler supremacy and many of the colonial government's policies emerged following World War I. One of the more important issues concerned demands by Kenya's Asians for rights (mainly political and economic) equal to those of the European settlers. Other protests emanated from missionary-educated African men who objected to labor coercion, high taxes, state labor control policies, low wages, and a general lack of opportunity for themselves. The East African Association was one of the first protest organizations to emerge, but it was violently suppressed and banned in 1922. For the remainder of the interwar years, African protest focused on local issues within the boundaries of the ethnic units recognized by the colonial government. The protest organizations sought improvement for their members within the colonial system rather than its removal.

Following World War II, African protest eventually took the form of nationalism, demanding self-government and then independence. In 1944, Kenyan nationalists formed a colonywide political party, the Kenya African Union (KAU), to achieve these goals. However, Jomo Kenyatta, who headed the party from 1947, made little headway with such demands as European settlers continued to enjoy substantial political influence. Nevertheless, economic and political discontent built up during the postwar years, particularly among the Kikuyu, and this produced increasing militancy and some violence. In October 1952, the colonial government proclaimed a state of emergency, arrested Kenyatta and several of his followers, and charged them with managing an organization called Mau Mau. Kenyatta's arrest, later conviction, and the banning of KAU provoked the Mau Mau Revolt. Thousands of Kenyans, the majority of whom were Kikuyu, fought a guerrilla war to end European political supremacy and colonial rule. The rebellion proved also to be a civil war. Those Kikuyu who fought in the forests against British colonial rule were drawn from the poorest segment of Kikuyu society, while those who had profited most from colonial rule fought with the colonial state against the rebels.

Although it eventually suppressed the Mau Mau Revolt, the colonial government quickly provided greater economic, educational, and political opportunities for Africans. Such concessions failed to stem the growing tide of African nationalism. Therefore, during the 1960-61 period, Britain moved to end European settler supremacy and to lay the groundwork for independence with the African majority in control. Colonywide political parties, banned since 1953, were formed in 1960, and when Kenyatta was freed from detention in 1961, he became the leader of the Kenya African National Union (KANU).

Postindependence Period

In 1963, this party won the first universal suffrage elections and took Kenya to independence in December of that year. In December 1964, Kenya became a republic, and Kenyatta was chosen president, a position he held until his death in 1978. The Kenyatta era was one of considerable economic growth and social change. The dissolution of opposition parties during the first year of independence meant that Kenya was, de facto, a one-party state. However, Kenyatta's capitalist policies and pro-Western orientation provoked division within KANU, which led to the resignation of the nation's first vice president, Oginga Odinga. He formed an opposition political party, but Kenyatta dealt with this challenge by the use of state power (e.g., detention without trial), increased patronage to supporters, and appeals to ethnic solidarity. Following Odinga's detention and the banning of his party, Kenya was once again a de facto one-party state. After 1967, Kenyatta rejected all attempts to remove the Kalenjin Daniel arap Moi from the vice presidency and the position of successor.

As a result, Moi assumed the presidency after Kenyatta's death in 1978. The new president adopted the Swahili word *nyayo* (footsteps) for his leadership motto as assurance that he was true to Kenyatta's legacy. Initially, Moi was a populist president, traveling among the people in marked contrast to Kenyatta's leadership style. In the 1980s, however, Kenya's economic growth began to slow, and Moi's rule became increasingly authoritarian. In 1982, for example, Kenya became a one-party state by law. In the same year, Moi survived a coup attempt by air force personnel.

Nevertheless, strong pressure for reform of the political system, sparked by growing economic discontent and ethnic hostility, emerged from many quarters by the end of the 1980s. Moi at first resisted calls for political reform as violent ethnic clashes rocked Kenya during the 1991-1992 period. At the same time, Moi's government was under pressure from donor groups, such as the World Bank, the International Monetary Fund (IMF), Germany, and the United States, to implement political and economic reforms. In December 1991, Moi finally bowed to these pressures and agreed to legalize additional political parties. However, the several opposition parties that sprang into existence in 1992 failed to unite for the elections held in December. As a result, Moi won the presidential race, though with a minority of the votes cast, while KANU won a majority of the seats in Parliament. Continuing economic difficulties and donor and domestic calls for further reform marked the new multiparty era. These culminated in demonstrations in favor of constitutional change in 1997 that were violently dispersed by police. Faced with pressure for change, a slate of political reforms was agreed to by both KANU and the parliamentary opposition and was followed almost immediately by national elections in December 1997. Moi again won the presidential race to set the stage for what would be his last term, though KANU's parliamentary majority was greatly reduced.

ECONOMY

Prior to the 20th century, Kenya did not constitute a single economic system; the country was made up of a number of economies consisting of an overlapping patchwork of cultivating, herding, and hunting peoples exploiting varied ecological realms and linked by regional trade networks. With the start of colonial rule, Kenya was brought into the world capitalist economy in a dependent role as the new colonial territory developed an economy oriented toward the export of agricultural produce. The colonial government encouraged the settlement of European farmers as a means of providing such exports. From World War I through the mid-1950s, produce from European settler farms and estates (coffee, sisal, and tea) held the leading places among exports. African households were encouraged to produce commodities for their subsistence and the market and to engage in wage employment to support the European settler sector.

During and after World War II, Kenya's economy was altered by the initiation of import substitution manufacturing. The 1950s also witnessed an important change in the agricultural sector as the state adopted measures to stimulate greater production from African households, including land consolidation, permission to grow high-value cash crops, and the expansion of extension services. This helped to unleash peasant production over the next two decades. Consequently, despite the departure of most European farmers after independence, agricultural exports rose markedly, with the majority coming from the peasant sector.

These factors, together with influxes of foreign capital and technical expertise, produced one of the highest economic growth rates for any country in tropical Africa for the period 1963-80 (cumulative 6.8 percent) with Kenya choosing to follow a more open, capitalist path than her neighbors. In the 1980s, Kenya's booming economy weakened as a consequence of deteriorating terms of trade, among other reasons. Kenya's slowing growth rate and balance of payments deficits caused the government to turn to the implementation of structural adjustment policies, which were advocated by the World Bank and IMF as part of their economic assistance to Kenya. Nevertheless, the Kenyan government set itself the ambitious target of achieving the status of an industrialized economy by 2020. In the short term, the Kenyan economy has continued to face severe difficulties, including expanding internal and external debt, decaying infrastructure, and corruption.

At the same time, agriculture remained a major sector of the economy, employing some 73 percent of the working population, and contributed approximately 27 percent of GDP (1963 = 38.4 percent). Kenya's principal food crops are maize, millet, sorghum, and cassava, while the leading cash crops are tea, coffee, pyrethrum, and sisal. Since the 1970s, horticulture (flowers, fruits and vegetables) has made up an increasing share of agricultural exports.

After 1963, the number of foreign tourists who visited Kenya expanded dramatically. To maximize the country's reputation as a leading tourist destination, the Kenyan government augmented the number of national parks and game reserves. As a result, since 1989, tourism has been Kenya's leading earner of foreign exchange.

Manufacturing, which contributed 12 percent of GDP in 1997, has played an increasingly important role in Kenya's economy as the 20th century draws to a close. The nation's chief manufactured products are food, beverages and tobacco, textiles and clothing, rubber products, transport equipment, printing and publishing, and petroleum and other chemicals. Mining, on the other hand, is a relatively unimportant part of the Kenyan economy. Petroleum is Kenya's major energy source, but the country relies entirely on imported oil. This is one of several factors that suggest that the Kenyan economy has remained dependent on foreign trade.

Since 1980, Kenya has usually run a substantial trade deficit with countries outside Africa and a surplus with those in the East African region. The main exports, in order of importance, are tea, coffee, horticultural produce, petroleum products, cement, soda ash, and pyrethrum extract (used in insecticides). The chief imports are industrial raw materials, crude petroleum, and machinery and other capital equipment.

FUTURE PROSPECTS

Kenya faces a daunting future. Some of its more pressing problems include a national and local leadership that is plagued by corruption, cronyism, and criminal behavior; the failure of job opportunities to keep pace with a growing population; the near collapse of its internal transportation infrastructure; rapid urbanization; and deteriorating health care. However, despite its many political, economic, and social difficulties, Kenya will remain East Africa's most important nation, at least for the near future. However, should it fail to resolve these problems, the country will continue to deteriorate, making it only a matter of time before it relinquishes its regional leadership position to another country, possibly Ethiopia or Uganda.

In contrast, there are some hopeful developments in Kenya's national life. The struggling multiparty political system, while far from perfect, reflects some movement toward a more open society. Also, next to Uganda, Kenya has the freest press in the region. Nairobi, despite its many problems, is still eastern Africa's diplomatic, economic, and political capital. In comparison to the region's other nations, Kenya also has a very good educational infrastructure, which will help to prepare at least part of the population for the challenges of the next century.

Over the coming years, Kenya faces two paths of development. The first is a continuation of politics as usual in which society is dominated and manipulated by ethnic favoritism and privilege. In this scenario, ethnic conflict similar to that which occurred in the months prior to the 1992 and 1997 general elections, and following the latter, will become increasingly commonplace as ethnic groups compete for access to land, wage employment, and educational opportunities. The second possibility is a gradual emergence of a national leadership and identity that will afford all Kenyans the opportunity to prosper in a pluralistic society where each ethnic group will have equal access to the nation's economic resources. As the new millennium approaches, most Kenyans remain divided over which path to pursue. Without a firm conviction about its future, Kenya will continue to be a society at war with itself.

The Dictionary

-A-

ABERDARE MOUNTAINS. Kenya's third highest mountain range after Mount Kenya and Mount Elgon [qq.v]. In 1884, Joseph Thomson [q.v.] named the range after Lord Aberdare, then president of the Royal Geographical Society. The Aberdares, also known as the Nyandarua range, are located in the eastern Rift Valley [q.v.]. Some of the more significant peaks in the Aberdares include Lesatima (3,999 meters; 13,120 feet), Kipipiri (3,349 meters; 10,988 feet), Table Mountain (3,971 meters; 13,028 feet), the Elephant (3,590 meters; 11,778 feet), and Kinangop (3,906 meters; 12,815 feet). The range confronts the Indian Ocean's easterly winds and drains them of moisture. The subsequent rainfall, which falls on fertile volcanic soil, has made the highlands one of the world's richest agricultural regions.

ACQUIRED IMMUNE DEFICIENCY SYNDROME (AIDS). In 1984, physicians diagnosed the first AIDS case in Kenya. Since then, the disease has spread throughout the country. Initially, some Kenyan government officials, including President Daniel arap Moi [q.v.], maintained that reports about AIDS in Kenya were alarmist and untrue. However, growing public concern prompted the Kenyan government to take action. In 1985, for example, it established a National AIDS Committee, which created a National AIDS Control Programme for the control and prevention of the disease. With support from the World Health Organisation (WHO) and several donor nations, the National AIDS Control Programme launched an education and information campaign, introduced blood screening at major Kenyan hospitals, and financed various research and health care programs.

Despite these and other efforts, the number of AIDS cases in Kenya has continued to rise. By June 1995, WHO reported that Kenya was behind only the United States and Brazil in the number of reported AIDS cases with 56,573, or 5 percent, of the world's total number of 1,109,811 reported cases. According to a 1995 statement by an Assistant Minister of Health an estimated one million Kenyans were infected with the HIV-AIDS virus.

On 25 September 1997, a *Daily Nation* newspaper report estimated that AIDS had caused the death of 230,000 Kenyans aged 15 to 39 and that more than 1.7 million Kenyans might be infected by the HIV virus. Additionally, the article predicted that AIDS deaths will rise to one million by the year 2000. At approximately the same time, the National Assembly [q.v.] passed a Sessional Paper on AIDS to help the government curb the spread of the disease over the next 15 years and beyond. As of early 1998, Great Britain, Belgium, Japan, Finland, the United States, the European Union, the United Nations Development Program, and the World Bank [q.v.] provided financial and technical assistance to help Kenya contend with the AIDS epidemic. *See also* HEALTH; POPULATION.

ADAMSON, GEORGE ALEXANDER GRAHAM (1906–1989). Born in Etawah, India. Between 1916 and 1924, Adamson attended school at Dean Close in Cheltenham. In 1924, he traveled to Kenya. After a brief stint on his father's coffee [q.v.] farm, Adamson worked as a farm bailiff, sisal [q.v.] plantation worker, barman, bus driver, gold prospector, big game hunter, construction worker, goat and sheep trader, insurance agent, storekeeper, hotel manager, and locust control officer. In July 1938, he became a temporary assistant game warden and worked largely in the Northern Frontier District. Between 1940 and 1942, Adamson served in Military Intelligence there; he recruited Somali agents to spy on Italian military units along the Kenyan-Ethiopian border. During the Mau Mau Revolt [q.v.], he visited military units and reported on the capabilities of African trackers.

After both military tours of duty Adamson returned to the Game Department, where he worked until his April 1961 retirement. His work with wildlife, particularly lions, occupied the last several decades of his life. In April 1964, he accepted a position as technical adviser with the Open Road Film Company, which made the internationally acclaimed motion picture, *Born Free*. His wife, Joy Adamson [q.v.], refused to share the royalties on this film with George, ostensibly because he had refused to collaborate on the book by the same title. Contemporary biographers, however, maintain that many of the words and pictures in the *Born Free* book in fact belonged to George. He continued his work with lions, primarily in the Kora National Reserve, until his untimely death at the hands of Somali *shifta* [q.v.] on 20 August 1989. He was buried in Kora, beside his brother, Terence, and a lion called Supercub.

ADAMSON, JOY (née Friederike Viktoria Gessner) (1910–1980). Born in Troppau, Silesia (now Opava, Czech Republic). After attending boarding school for four years, she received diplomas in piano teaching (1927) and dressmaking (1928). After a brief marriage to an Austrian car dealer named Victor von Klarwill (1935–37), Joy traveled to Kenya and married a Swiss botanist named Peter Bally (1938–44). In January 1944, she divorced Bally and married George Adamson [q.v.].

During the early part of her career, Joy painted hundreds of pictures that reflected Kenya's ethnological and botanical diversity. She spent the last 30 years of her life working with wildlife in Kenya's national parks [q.v.] and game reserves. Joy became world famous after returning a lion, cheetah, and leopard to the wild. In 1961, she founded the Elsa Wild Animal Appeal, which later was known as the Elsa Conservation Trust. She earned a considerable amount of money from her many books and the motion picture *Born Free*.

Joy received several awards for her work, including the Grenfell Gold Medal from the Royal Horticultural Society for her paintings of Kenyan flowers (1947); the Award of Merit from the Czechoslovakian government (1970); the Joseph Wood Krutch Medal from the U.S. Humane Society (1971); and the Austrian Cross of Honor for Science and Arts (January 1977). She was killed at Shaba camp, Meru National Park [q.v.] on 7 January 1980. On 28 August 1981, the Nyeri High Court found Paul Nakwale Ekai guilty of murdering Adamson, apparently as a result of a pay dispute.

AFRICAN INLAND MISSION (AIM). In 1895, Peter Cameron Scott, one of the founders of AIM in the United States, arrived in Nzawi in Machakos District among the Kamba [q.v.]. In the same year, William Hotchkiss, another AIM missionary, also arrived in Kenya and began work in Ukambani. From this beginning, AIM undertook missionary work among the Kalenjin and Kikuyu [qq.v.] as well. In 1903, AIM established its headquarters in Kijabe; this became a large mission station, eventually including a hospital, schools, and the Rift Valley Academy. Additionally, AIM opened other stations at locations throughout Kenya, including Kangundo (1896), Nzaui (1896), Machakos (1902), Mukaa (1909), Rumuruti (1907), Mbooni (1908), Eldama Ravine (1909), Nyakach (1911), Mulango (1915), Siyiapei (1918), Kipkelion (1919),

Eldoret (1930), Kapsowar (1933), Lasit (1933), Kessup (1937), Liter (1955), Lokori (1959), and Kalokol (1962). In 1924, AIM temporarily withdrew from the Alliance of Protestant Missions [q.v.] because of AIM'S opposition to modernism (i.e. making Africans adopt Western ways and attitudes). In 1947, AIM members in southern Fort Hall District established the African Christian Church and Schools.

AIM work was divided into six church regions, including Machakos, Kitui, Central, Southern, Lake, and Rift Valley [q.v.]. AIM also operates a network of Bible schools; Scott Theological College, Machakos, which trains pastors of secondary education, and African Inland Press, which publishes religiously oriented items.

AFRICAN DISTRICT COUNCIL (ADC). The African District Council Ordinance, introduced in 1948 and modified in 1950, provided for the creation of ADC to replace Local Native Councils [q.v.]. ADCs had greater powers and responsibilities than the latter. An ADC could employ secretaries and other staff and could implement a much wider range of services and development initiatives than the Local Native Councils. In 1963, County Councils replaced ADCs.

AFRICAN ELECTED MEMBERS ORGANISATION (AEMO). Formed following the 1957 LEGCO elections [q.v.] at Tom Mboya's [q.v.] initiative. AEMO provided a forum for African elected members to work against the Lyttelton Constitution [q.v.]. They also opposed the Lennox-Boyd Constitution [q.v.] by refusing to accept the ministerial positions that it had created. Additionally, AEMO championed "undiluted democracy" for Kenya. In June 1958, the courts found seven AEMO members guilty of libel for statements made about Africans who had accepted office under the Lennox-Boyd Constitution. In 1959, AEMO passed out of existence, being succeeded by the Constituency Elected Members Organisation [q.v.] and, later, political parties such as the Kenya National Party [q.v.].

AFRICAN PEOPLE'S PARTY (APP). Founded by Paul Ngei [q.v.] in September 1962. Ngei had left the Kenya African National Union [q.v.] because of a dispute with Tom Mboya and Jomo Kenyatta [qq.v.] over leadership of the party's Machakos branch. Despite its nationalist stance and motto of freedom, justice, and fraternity, most of the APP's support came from Ngei's Kamba [q.v.] people. Prior to the general elections (1963) [q.v.], the APP reached a political pact with the Kenya African Democratic Union (KADU) [q.v.]. In that election, the APP won eight seats in the House of Representatives and two in the Senate. All of the successful candidates were from Machakos District or Kitui District. Following internal self-government, Ngei split from KADU, as he advocated a unitary rather than a federal independence constitution. In September 1963, the APP ceased to exist after Ngei and other party members crossed the floor to join KANU.

AFRICAN WORKERS' FEDERATION. Formed at the start of the January 1947 Mombasa General Strike to articulate workers' grievances and demands. Led by Chege Kibachia [q.v.], the federation made the case for higher wages and better working conditions before the tribunal appointed to investigate the strike. The federation opened a branch in Nairobi [q.v.] in 1947 and planned to start operations in Kisumu, Nakuru [qq.v.], and other towns. However, Kibachia's arrest and 10-year detention shortly thereafter crippled the organization. In 1949, the organization was renamed the East African Workers Federation, but by early 1950 the organization was largely dead. It was eventually replaced by the East African Trade Union Congress [q.v.].

AGRICULTURE. During the early colonial period, the colonial authorities sought to develop export agriculture to make the East Africa Protectorate [q.v.] pay for itself. Some of the first European settlers such as Lord Delamere [q.v.] sought to develop wheat and wool, both of which brought high prices on the international market. However, it took years before such experiments proved profitable. After 1905, the colonial government encouraged the production of cash crops such as coffee [q.v.], which became the colony's largest earner of foreign exchange after World War I, and sisal. Although not as strongly supported and subsidized by the colonial state, African agriculture also responded to the economic transformation engendered by colonial rule. Until the start of World War I [q.v.], the bulk of Kenya's exports came from African peasant households.

Following World War I, European agriculture held pride of place in terms of export generation and state support (land and labor). Nevertheless, in times of economic difficulty, such as during the Great Depression (1930–34), the colonial government sought to encourage African agriculture as a means of buttressing colonial finances and stabilizing European production. During the emergency, the inauguration of the Swynnerton Plan [q.v.] signaled a major change in agricultural policy as the colonial state introduced measures aimed at producing a prosperous class of African farmers.

Since independence, Kenya's agricultural sector has experienced considerable changes. During the 1963–73 period, the Kenyan government stimulated the country's agricultural growth rate (4.7 percent annually) by redistributing farms and estates previously belonging to European settlers, diffusing new crop strains, and bringing more land under cultivation. Between 1980 and 1991, the agricultural growth rate declined to less than 4 percent annually. The reasons for this reduction included bad weather, inconsistent domestic pricing policies and credit availability, and poor marketing systems.

Currently, about 75 percent of Kenyans occupy 13 percent of land classified as "high potential" while those remaining work "marginal" land. Demand for land is particularly acute in Central, Nyanza, and Western Provinces [qq.v]. In the early 1990s, the Kenyan government started liberalizing the agricultural sector by ending monopolies held by most commodity marketing boards, implementing tax reforms for coffee farmers, and introducing dollar sales at the Mombasa coffee and tea auctions [qq.v.]. For example, in December 1993 the authorities terminated all control on the movement of maize across district boundaries. Agriculture remains the most important sector of the Kenyan economy. Moreover, it is the country's major source of food, foreign exchange, and raw materials for domestic industry and employment.

AINSWORTH, JOHN DAWSON (1864–1946). Colonial administrator. Educated in Manchester. During the 1884–89 period, Ainsworth worked for a commercial firm in what is today the Congo. In 1889, he joined the service of the Imperial British East Africa Company (IBEAC) [q.v.], and following two years of work with the company's transport department at Mombasa [q.v.] became station superintendent at the company's outpost at Machakos, 432 kilometers (268 miles) from the coast. Ainsworth remained in charge of Machakos until July 1895, when the British government assumed control of IBEAC's territories. So successful had his work at Machakos been that he became subcommissioner for Ukamba Province [q.v.].

From Machakos, he gradually established control over the Kamba [q.v.] near the outpost. In 1899, he moved the provincial headquarters to Nairobi [q.v.], which recently had been made Uganda Railway [q.v.] headquarters. Until 1906, he remained in charge at Nairobi and helped to facilitate the early development of what would become Kenya's capital. Ainsworth's service at Nairobi placed him in the midst of the African land alienation controversy. According to Sir Charles Eliot [q.v.], the struggling colony would prosper if European settlers could establish farms on African land. Although he was not an advocate of white settlement in the East Africa Protectorate (EAP), Ainsworth nevertheless accepted Eliot's orders to move Africans off the land provided to settlers.

In 1907, after a brief period at Naivasha [q.v.], Ainsworth became provincial commissioner of Nyanza Province [q.v.]. For the next decade, he achieved his greatest success in stimulating African commodity production as the province became the main source of Kenya's exports by the start of World War I [q.v.]. During the 1917–18 period, he served as military commissioner for labour with the task of raising men for service in the Carrier Corps [q.v.].

From 1918 until his retirement in 1920, Ainsworth served as the governor's adviser on African affairs and then as the EAP's first chief native commissioner. He was unpopular with European settlers, given his support for African commodity production and his hostility to state recruitment of labor for settler farms. Though the Labour Circular of 1919 [q.v.] was issued over his name, Ainsworth did not support its admonition to government officials to assist in labor recruitment.

After his retirement, Ainsworth and his wife first went to Manchester, then to Guernsey, and from there to South Africa. In 1924, he carried out an administration survey of New Guinea for the Commonwealth of Australia. In 1925, he returned to Somserset West, South Africa, where in 1929 he became mayor of the town. He died on 31 March 1946.

ALLIANCE HIGH SCHOOL. First school in Kenya to offer secondary education to Africans (males). Its purpose was to train African leaders with a Christian outlook. On 1 March 1926, the Alliance of Protestant Missions [q.v.], which was the forerunner of the National Christian Council of Kenya, opened Alliance High School with 26 pupils. With financial support from various British missionary societies, the Phelps Stokes Commission, Lord Delamere [qq.v.], and other wealthy European settlers, Alliance High School quickly established a reputation of being the Eton of Kenya.

Throughout the school's history, an "Old Boys Club," made up of former students, helped to ensure that Alliance High School was adequately financed and that its graduates were well placed in the job market. By late 1996, more than 6,000 students had passed through the school, many of whom have gone on to successful careers in government, business, academia, the armed forces [q.v.], the judiciary [q.v.], and the church. *See also* EDUCATION, COLONIAL.

ALLIANCE OF PROTESTANT MISSIONS (APM). In July 1918, representatives from the Africa Inland Mission, the Church Missionary Society (CMS) [q.v.], the Church of Scotland Mission (CSM) [q.v.], and the United Methodist Mission established the APM with a senior executive body called the Representative Council. John Arthur [q.v.], a CSM missionary, was APM's first secretary. The conservative APM sought to create a united church in Kenya by using common religious services, unifying church rules, requiring all future clergy to be ordained by representatives of all member societies, and supporting common training.

Additionally, APM perceived itself as a political pressure group that would represent African interests. In 1919–20, for example, APM criticized forced labor principles contained in the Labour Circular (1919) [q.v.] on the grounds that they would benefit only the European settler community. Additionally, in 1923, APM sent Arthur to London to advise the British government about the African aspects of the Indian Question [q.v.]. In 1935, APM changed its name to the Kenya Missionary Council (1924–43), which eventually became known as the National Christian Council of Kenya [q.v.]. *See also* ALLIANCE HIGH SCHOOL; GOSPEL MISSIONARY SOCIETY.

AMBOSELI NATIONAL PARK (392 square kilometers; 151 square miles). Gazetted as a National Reserve in November 1948 and as a National Park in 1977. Located south of Nairobi [q.v.], along the Kenyan-Tanzanian border. For several decades, Amboseli has been one of Kenya's most popular tourist destinations. But in recent years, conservationists have raised concerns about the impact that tourists have on Amboseli's fragile environment. However, the Kenyan government has refused to institute a tourist quota system for the park. Amboseli is home to 56 mammal species. *See also* COWIE, MERVYN; GAME POLICY COMMITTEE; NATIONAL PARKS.

ANGAINE, JACKSON HARVESTER (1905–1999). Civil servant, businessman, farmer, and politician. Born in Meru [q.v.] and educated at Alliance High School [q.v.]. He obtained London matriculation by a correspondence course with Natal University. From 1935 to 1948, Angaine served as secretary for the Meru Local Native Council and then worked privately as a farmer and accountant.

During the 1948–52 period, he was chairman of the Kenya African Union (KAU) [q.v.] branch in Meru. He was detained by the colonial state during the Mau Mau Revolt. In 1960, Angaine joined the Kenya African National Union (KANU) [q.v.] and was elected Meru branch chairman. In the 1961 LEGCO elections [q.v.], he won one of the Meru seats on the KANU ticket. With the coalition government's formation in 1962, Angaine became parliamentary secretary to the Ministry of Tourism, Forests, and Wildlife and later moved to the ministry of education. He won a seat for KANU in the 1963 general elections [q.v.] and was appointed parliamentary secretary in the ministry of agriculture. As a result of political pressure, Angaine moved to head the newly established ministry of lands and settlement. He headed the ministry for the rest of the decade and supervised the settlement schemes that marked that era of Kenya's history.

Following his reelection in 1969, Angaine remained in charge of the ministry of lands and settlement through the 1974 general elections [q.v.] in which he was once again returned to Parliament. In 1976, he associated himself with the Change the Constitution campaign, and this may have helped to bring about his defeat in the general elections (1979) [q.v.]. In 1983, Angaine returned to Parliament. Two years later, he rejoined the cabinet as minister of state in the Office of the President and remained the dominant figure in Meru politics for the rest of the decade, thereby earning the sobriquet "King of the Meru." However, in the general elections (1992) [q.v.], Angaine failed to win the KANU nomination for the North Imenti seat, which was won by the Democratic Party [q.v.] candidate. He died on 23 February 1999. *See also* 1969 GENERAL ELECTIONS.

ANGLICAN CHURCH IN KENYA. *See* **CHURCH MISSIONARY SOCIETY.**

ANGLO-GERMAN AGREEMENT (1886). Under this agreement, Great Britain and Germany recognized the sultan of Zanzibar's control over the islands of Zanzibar [q.v.], Pemba, Lamu [q.v.], and Mafia; all coastal islands; and a continuous line of coast from the Miningani River, at the head of Tunghi Bay, on the south, to Kipini in the north. Germany pledged to adhere to the 1862 Anglo-French Declaration, which promised to maintain the integrity of the sultan's dominions. Additionally, the agreement established Germany's sphere of influence from the Rovuma to the Umba Rivers; and the British from the Umba to the Tana Rivers.

The interior was divided along a line drawn from the Umba River to Lake Victoria [q.v.], with the northern portion, except for the coastline at Witu, declared a British sphere of influence.

ANGLO-GERMAN AGREEMENT (1890). According to this agreement's terms, Germany recognized a British protectorate over Zanzibar and abandoned the protectorate of Witu and all territorial claims north of the Tana River. Additionally, Great Britain gained control of Uganda, because Germany acknowledged the extension of the boundary dividing the British and German spheres of influence to Lake Victoria [q.v.] and thence to the Congo Free State. The British ceded Heligoland Island in the North Sea to Germany and persuaded Seyyid Khalifa of Zanzibar to cede to Germany the land leased by the German East Africa Company in return for an indemnity. Also known as the Heligoland Treaty.

ANGLO-ITALIAN PROTOCOL (1891). On 24 March 1891, the British and Italian governments concluded the Anglo-Italian Protocol, which outlined their respective spheres of influence in East Africa. According to the agreement's terms, the dividing line between the two was the midchannel of the Juba River from the Indian Ocean to latitude six degrees north. The boundary then continued along the sixth parallel to longitude 35 degrees east, where it turned northward and followed the meridian to the Blue Nile. On 15 April 1891, Great Britain and Italy signed an additional protocol that demarcated the British and Italian spheres of influence from Ras Kasar on the Red Sea to the Blue Nile. Additionally, the second protocol authorized Italy to occupy Kassala, a strategic town along the Sudanese-Ethiopian border, in the event of war with Sudan.

ANYONA, GEORGE MOSETI (1945–). Civil servant, sales manager, and politician. Born in Kitutu location of the present Nyamira District. Educated at Alliance High School and Makerere University [qq.v], where he obtained a B.A. degree. Following graduation, Anyona worked as a civil servant (1968–70). After a short stint with the Red Cross, he became district sales manager for British Airways (1971–74).

In the general elections (1974) [q.v.], Anyona won the Kitutu East seat, but his criticism of government policies and ministers gained him few friends among the political establishment. In 1977, the Kenyan government detained him. After his release in 1978, the authorities barred him from standing in the general elections (1979) [q.v.]. Fears that he might join with Oginga Odinga [q.v.] to form an opposition party led to another detention for Anyona (1982–84). The authorities again barred him from standing for Parliament in the general elections (1988) [q.v.]. In July 1990, the police [q.v.] arrested Anyona and three others in a bar outside Nairobi [q.v.]. They spent a year in jail awaiting trial, and in July 1991 the four were convicted of sedition. On 15 February 1992 all of them were released. Anyona remained popular among his Gusii [q.v.] followers despite the Kenyan government's continued hostility.

With the dawn of multipartyism, he returned to politics but refused to join any of the major opposition parties. In the general elections (1992) [q.v.], Anyona ran for the presidency and Parliament under the banner of the Kenya Social Congress [q.v.]. He suffered an overwhelming defeat, obtaining only 14,200 votes out of a total poll of 5.2 million. However, Anyona won the Kitutu Masaba parliamentary seat, thus becoming the Kenya Social Congress's first and only MP. Since 1992, he has remained a strong parliamentary critic of official corruption and maladministration. In late 1997, Anyona emerged as one of the leaders of the Inter-Parties Parliamentary Group [q.v.], a reform movement in Parliament. During the general elections (1997) [q.v.] he ran for president and Parliament on the Kenya Social Congress ticket but gained only .27 percent of the vote (16,294 votes). As in 1992, he won the Kitutu Masaba seat.

ARMED FORCES. Historically, Kenya's postindependence armed forces have had the reputation of being one of Africa's best trained and most professional militaries. In recent years, however, several factors have lessened the prestige of the armed forces. The end of the cold war resulted in a diminution of foreign military assistance, which in turn has eroded the military's maintenance and training capabilities. Pay and benefits, especially among the enlisted ranks, have not kept pace with Kenya's inflation rate. Morale is also low because of President Daniel arap Moi's [q.v.] practice of favoring people of his Kalenjin [q.v.] ethnic group with promotions and choice assignments. On a more positive note, Kenya's armed forces have participated in numerous international peacekeeping operations (i.e., Angola, Bosnia, Croatia, Iraq/Kuwait, Namibia, and the Zimbabwe Western Sahara).

Additionally, the military remains largely apolitical, although there periodically are reports of activism in the junior officer corps and in the ranks. Also, unlike many other African countries, the Chiefs of the General Staff (CGS) who have commanded the Kenyan Armed Forces (Major General Joseph M. Ndolo, [1966–71]; General Jackson Kimeu Mulinge, [1971–86]; General Mohamoud Mohammed, [1986–96]; and General Daudi Tonje, [1996–]) largely have refrained from actively engaging in politics and have been loyal to the government.

On 22 January 1997, General Tonje reorganized the armed forces by creating a vice CGS and three assistant CGSs. Military analysts indicated that these changes represented a move away from the traditional British command structure toward an American-style command and control system. According to Tonje, the new arrangement will facilitate greater efficiency. Additionally, Tonje ordered the creation of a National Defence

Staff College at Karen to reduce Kenya's dependence on military training abroad.

As of 1998, Kenya's armed forces totaled about 24,200; military service is voluntary. The 20,500-man army consisted of one armored brigade, two infantry brigades, one independent infantry battalion, one artillery brigade, one air defense battalion, one engineer brigade and two engineer battalions, one independent air cavalry battalion, and one airborne battalion. The weapons inventory included tanks, armored reconnaissance vehicles, armored personnel carriers, towed artillery, antiaircraft guns, and various smaller weapons.

The air force numbers approximately 2,500, with 30 combat aircraft and 34 armed helicopters. The navy, headquartered in Mombasa [q.v.], has about 1,200 personnel and one fast patrol boat, six missile patrol craft, two amphibious craft, and one tugboat. See also ARMY MUTINY; CARRIER CORPS; COUP ATTEMPT (1982); HOME GUARDS; GENERAL SERVICES UNIT; KENYA DEFENCE FORCE; KENYA LAND AND FREEDOM ARMY; KING'S AFRICAN RIFLES; MAU MAU REVOLT; POLICE; SHIFTA WARS; GOVERNOR'S WAR COUNCIL; WORLD WAR I; WORLD WAR II.

ARMY MUTINY (1964). After independence, the British government authorized the transfer of three Kenya-based King's African Rifles [q.v.] battalions (Third, Fifth, and 11th) and their equipment to Kenya. The new 2,500-man force became known as the Kenya Rifles. From its inception, the new force faced an array of problems, the most serious of which included dissatisfaction over pay and annoyance over the retention of British officers. On 24–25 January 1964, these and other factors caused some men of the 11th Battalion, Kenya Rifles at Lanet Barracks (near Nakuru) and Langata Barracks (near Nairobi) to mutiny. Prime Minister Jomo Kenyatta [q.v.] ended the mutiny by using British troops from the Third Royal Horse Artillery and other units to recapture facilities that the mutineers had occupied. Additionally, Kenyatta announced that he would increase the size of the Kenya Rifles by 1,000 and would investigate anomalies in the pay of African soldiers.

Obviously, other Kenyan nationalists were deeply embarrassed by having to rely on the former colonial power to restore order. The Kenyan government took swift action against the mutineers. The military court-martialed or dismissed 170 troops who had participated in the mutiny; the leaders received prison sentences of up to 14 years. Kenyatta disbanded the 11th Battalion, which later was reconstituted as the First

Battalion. Additionally, the Kenyan government took steps to redress the soldiers' grievances and to increase professional training of the army.

Despite these actions, Kenyatta remained suspicious of the Kenya Rifles. He therefore started to build up the General Services Unit (GSU) [q.v.] as a counterbalance to the army. In time, the GSU gained the reputation of being the military arm of the executive branch, an allegation that continues to this day. Additionally, on 14 July 1967, Kenyatta formalized his country's military relationship with Great Britain by concluding a Status of Forces Agreement, which, among other things, authorized the presence of British troops in Kenya.

ARTHUR, JOHN WILLIAM (1881–1952). Missionary and physician. Born in Glasgow and educated at the Glasgow Academy and Glasgow University, where he qualified as a physician. After briefly being a surgeon at Glasgow's Western Infirmary, Arthur worked as a ship's doctor (1903–06). He then returned to the Western Infirmary for a short time before enrolling at the London School of Tropical Medicine and then Combe Hospital, Dublin, where he studied tropical medicine and maternity care, respectively.

On 1 January 1907, Arthur arrived at the Church of Scotland Mission's [q.v.] Kikuyu station, where he worked for the next 30 years. In 1911, he became chairman of the Kikuyu mission and shortly afterwards befriended Jomo Kenyatta [q.v.], who was one of his students. Arthur also became active in local affairs by serving as a member of the Native Labour Commission [q.v.] (1912–13) and by organizing the 1,900-man Kikuyu Missions Volunteer Corps of Porters (1917). Additionally, he was an unofficial, appointed member of the Legislative Council (LEGCO) (1924–26) [q.v.], a member of the Executive Council (1928–29) [q.v.], and of the Alliance High School's [q.v.] Board of Governors.

During the 1928–31 period, Arthur played a major role in the attempts of some Protestant mission societies to end the practice of female circumcision among the Kikuyu [q.v.]. Arthur and other European missionaries claimed this practice was incompatible with Christianity. This attitude put Arthur and many of his colleagues on a collision course with the Kikuyu Central Association [q.v.], which wanted to preserve female circumcision. He also was a strong advocate of African education and an opponent of compulsory labor for Africans.

After becoming an ordained minister of the Church of Scotland in 1936, Arthur retired from missionary work (the following year) and returned to Scotland. Throughout his retirement, he maintained an interest in Kenyan affairs and, in 1948, went back to participate in the mission's jubilee celebrations. He died on 21 November 1952.

ARWINGS-KODHEK, CHIEDO MORE GEM (1923–1969). Teacher, lawyer, politician. Born in Gem location of current Siaya District and educated at St. Mary's Yala, St. Mary's, Kisubi in Uganda, and Makerere University [q.v.], where he obtained a teaching diploma (1939). He taught in Kenya until 1946, when he gained admission to the University of Wales. Arwings-Kodhek earned a B.A. degree in 1950 and the following year was called to the bar in London. In 1953, he returned to Kenya to go into private legal practice. Arwings-Kodhek, the only African barrister at that time, took on the defense of many individuals who had been charged with criminal offenses during the Mau Mau Revolt [q.v.]. He also played a leading role in Nairobi [q.v.] politics by founding the Nairobi District National Congress [q.v.] (1956). Arwings-Kodhek stood in the LEGCO elections (1957) [q.v.], but he lost to Tom Mboya [q.v.]. Nevertheless, he remained active in the nationalist movement, joining the Kenya African National Union (KANU) [q.v.] at its inception.

For the LEGCO elections (1961) [q.v.], Arwings-Kodhek won as a KANU candidate for one of the two Central Nyanza seats. With the coalition government's formation in 1962, he was made a parliamentary secretary in the Ministry of Lands, Surveys, and Town Planning. In the general elections (1963) [q.v.], Arwings-Kodhek was returned for his home area of Gem on the KANU ticket and, until 1966, served as parliamentary secretary/assistant minister for the Ministry of Game, Fisheries, and Natural Resources; and the Ministry of Health and Housing. In 1966, he became minister of natural resources. In January 1968, Arwings-Kodhek assumed the post of minister of state for foreign affairs. On 29 January 1969, he died in an automobile accident on the Nairobi street that today bears his name (Arwings-Kodhek Road).

ASIANS. Term used to describe a Kenyan citizen or resident of Indian or Pakistani origin. Historically, Asians have enjoyed a long association with Kenya. Over the past several centuries, there have been at least four phases of Asian migration to East Africa. During the first period, between the distant past and the end of the 19th century, Asians established a trading link between India and East Africa, settling in places like Mombasa and Malindi [qq.v.], and helped to build the strategically important Fort Jesus [q.v.]. Between 1890 and 1919, Asian businessmen gained control of much of Kenya's retail trade and provided labor for the Uganda Railway [q.v.] and other public works projects. The 1919–39 migration increased Kenya's Asian population from 25,253 (1921) to 46,897 (1939). Additionally, thousands of Asians secured employment in the civil service, banking and commerce, construction and crafts, and the retail trade sector. In the 1939–62 era, the Asian community continued to grow from 46,897 (1939) to 176,613 (1962).

After independence, the Asian community, which had gained a relatively high degree of prosperity during the colonial period, came under increasing attack by the Kenyan government for a variety of shortcomings, including the refusal by some Asians to take Kenyan citizenship (the majority did not do so) and the putting of earnings and profits in foreign bank accounts. During the 1960s and 1970s, many noncitizen Asians left Kenya rather than contend with what they perceived as discrimination. Some of those who stayed lost their businesses as a result of Africanization. Many others, however, managed to be productive citizens. In 1997, there were an estimated 80,000 Asians in Kenya, slightly more than a third of whom were noncitizens. *See also* DEVONSHIRE DECLARATION; ELGIN PLEDGE; INDIAN QUESTION; ISLAM; WOOD-WINTERTON AGREEMENT.

ASKARI. Swahili name applied to African soldiers or police [q.v.] personnel. During the British colonial period, *askaris* helped to maintain security throughout the interior. During World War I [q.v.], the British and the Germans used *askaris* with great effectiveness.

AVIATION. On 1 January 1946, the colonial authorities established a Directorate of Civil Aviation for Kenya, Uganda, and Tanganyika (now Tanzania); this organization created East African Airways (EAA). In 1956, EAA initiated regular flights to Great Britain and India. By 1960, the airline had started jet services to India and elsewhere in Asia. Despite its profitability, EAA disintegrated when Kenya registered its own national airline, Kenya Airways [q.v.], on 22 January 1977. As of the mid-1990s, there was domestic commercial air service to Amboseli, Dadaalo, Eldoret [q.v.], Garissa, Kiwaiyu, Lamu [q.v.], Liboi, Lokichokio, Malindi [q.v.], Mandera, Maasai Mara, Mombasa [q.v.], Nairobi [q.v.], Nanyuki [q.v.,], Nyeri [q.v.], Samburu, Tsavo West, and Wajir. *See also* KENYA AIRWAYS; WILSON AIRWAYS.

AWORI, WYCLIFE WORK WASWA (1925–1978). Journalist, politician, farmer, and businessman. Born in what is now Western Province [q.v.] the son of prominent Anglican clergyman Canon Jeremiah Awori. Educated at Kakamega School and Mulago Hospital in Kampala, Uganda. He worked as a health inspector in Nairobi [q.v.] until 1945, when he became a journalist for several Swahili and English publications such as *Radio Posta* and *Habari za Dunia*. At the same time, Awori became active in the Kenya African Union (KAU) [q.v.] as editor of its newspaper *Sauti ya Mwafrika*, treasurer and then vice president (1946–47) and in the African Workers' Federation [q.v.]. Jomo Kenyatta [q.v.] forced him out of KAU leadership and, though he briefly served as KAU acting president prior to its proscription in 1953, he moved from Nairobi politics to success as a farmer and businessman in western Kenya.

Awori was appointed to the Legislative Council (LEGCO) [q.v.] by the colonial government from 1952 to 1956, representing the then North Nyanza District. He stood for the North Nyanza seat in the first African elections of 1957 but lost to Masinde Muliro [q.v.]. He unsuccessfully stood in the general elections (1963) [q.v.] and thereafter he left political life.

AYODO, SAMUEL ONYANGO (1931–1998). Teacher and politician. Born in Kabondo and educated at Maseno School, Makerere University [q.v.] (1950–51), and Union College (1953–55) in the United States where he obtained a B.Sc. degree in education. After returning to Kenya, Ayodo worked as a teacher and was active in the South Nyanza branch of the Kenya National Union of Teachers as well as in the district council.

In 1959, he won a by-election for the South Nyanza Legislative Council (LEGCO) seat unopposed. The following year, he founded the South Nyanza Parents' Association, and in 1960 he became one of the leaders of the Kenya African National Union (KANU) [q.v.] in the district. He won the South Nyanza seat in the LEGCO elections (1961) [q.v.] with Tom Mboya's [q.v.] backing. He won election to the House of Representatives on the KANU ticket in the general elections (1963) [q.v.]. Following the achievement of internal self-government, Ayodo was named minister of local government.

With the inauguration of a republic in December 1964, he became minister of natural resources and wildlife (later tourism and wildlife). Ayodo remained, with Tom Mboya, in KANU following the formation of the Kenya People's Union [q.v.] in 1966, but he suffered a heavy defeat in the general elections (1969) [q.v.] following the latter's death. However, Ayodo staged a comeback in 1974, when he won the Kasipul Kabondo seat he had lost five years previously. Despite this, he failed to regain a ministerial position. He lost his seat in Parliament in the general elections (1983) [q.v.]. Following that electoral setback, Ayodo concentrated on business and family affairs. He died in August 1998.

-B-

BALALA, SHEIKH KHALID SALIM AHMED (1958–). Political activist. Born in Mombasa [q.v.], where he also was educated. Balala burst on the national scene in the early 1990s as one of the leaders of the unregistered Islamic Party of Kenya (IPK) [q.v.] until 9 October 1993, when he resigned his position because of a dispute with IPK Chairman Sheikh Omar Mwinyi and joined the Forum for the Restoration of Democracy (FORD)-Asili faction.

In December 1994, the Kenyan government stripped Balala of his citizenship while he was visiting Germany. The Moi [q.v.] regime justified this action by claiming he was a Yemeni, an allegation Balala rejected. In June 1997, Balala tried to return to Kenya twice, but airport authorities refused to grant him entry into the country. On 12 July 1997, Balala finally returned to Kenya after growing domestic and international pressure forced the Kenya government to recognize him as a Kenyan citizen. *See also* ISLAM.

BANTU-SPEAKING PEOPLES. The majority of Kenya's peoples in the 20th century spoke languages belonging to the Bantu group. The earliest speakers of Bantu languages probably entered Kenya between 500 B.C.E. and the first century C.E. from the west and south. By the 20th century, people speaking Bantu languages fell into four groups. The Bantu-speakers of western Kenya form part of the Lacustrine group (the majority of whom live in present-day Uganda). These include those belonging to the Luyia, Gusii [qq.v.], and Kuria ethnic groups. Those living in east-central Kenya and in the vicinity of Mount Kenya [q.v.] belong to the Thagicu group. These include, among others, the present-day ethnic groups known as the Kamba, Kikuyu, Embu, and Meru [qq.v.]. The coastal Bantu-speakers include the Sabaki group. Among the latter are people belonging to the Mijikenda, Swahili [qq.v.], and Pokomo ethnic groups. Finally, the Taita [q.v.] of Kenya form part of the language group known as Chaga-Taita.

BARING, SIR EVELYN (1903–1973). Governor of Kenya (1952–59). Born in 1903, the younger son of the Earl of Cromer. Educated at Winchester and New College, Oxford. He entered the Indian Civil Service in 1926, retiring in 1934 to work as a merchant banker. From 1942 to 1944 he was governor of Southern Rhodesia (now Zimbabwe), and thereafter he served as British high commissioner to the Union of South Africa and for Basutoland (now Lesotho), Bechuanaland (now Botswana), and Swaziland from 1944 until 1951. In 1952, he became governor of Kenya. On 20 October 1952, shortly after the murder of Chief Waruhiu wa Kung'u, Baring declared a state of emergency, thus touching off the Mau Mau Revolt [q.v.]. However, Baring lacked a clear military strategy for ending the uprising. As a result, many influential European settlers opposed his policies and demanded more death sentences for Mau Mau personnel, forfeiture of Mau Mau land, and more stringent movement controls on Africans. To resolve these problems, Sir Winston Churchill, the British prime minister, appointed General Sir George Erskine [q.v.] as commander in chief of East Africa. With extensive British military assistance, he defeated the insurgency. Meanwhile, Baring associated himself with measures to promote African economic and social development (e.g., the Swynnerton Plan and the Lyttelton and Lennox-Boyd Constitutions [qq.v.], which sought to promote multiracialism as a blueprint for Kenya's political future). Baring completed his service as governor in late 1959. After his retirement as governor, Baring continued to be involved with Kenya as chairman of the Commonwealth Development Corporation (1960–72). He was elevated to the peerage as Baron Howick of Glendale in 1960. Baring died on 10 March 1973.

BEECHER COMMISSION (1949). This commission, headed by Archdeacon L. J. Beecher [q.v.], examined the scope, content, and methods of African education and had a significant impact on Kenya's educational history. Among the 148 recommendations, the commission's report urged the introduction of a 4-4-4 system of four-year primary, intermediate, and secondary schools. Each stage was to be a complete course with schooling beyond standard four and standard eight dependent on passing examinations. Throughout the 1950s and to independence, the Beecher Commission's report formed the basis for government policy toward African education. See also EDUCATION, COLONIAL.

BEECHER, LEONARD JAMES (1906–1987). Missionary and archbishop. Born in London and educated at St. Olaves School, Southwark; Imperial College, London; and the Institute of Education, London. In 1927, Beecher went to Kenya to become a teacher at Alliance High School [q.v.]. He was ordained and joined the Church Missionary Society (CMS) [q.v.] and married the sister of L. S. B. Leakey [q.v.] in 1930. Beecher then served as headmaster of Kahuhia Teacher Training College. Besides teaching, Beecher and his wife published a Kikuyu-English dictionary and a translation of scripture into Kikuyu [q.v.].

From 1943 to 1947, he served as member for African interests in the Legislative Council [q.v.] and as a member of the Executive Council [q.v.] (1947–52). During this time, he became archdeacon of Mombasa [q.v.] and headed the Beecher Commission [q.v.] that, in 1949, examined the African educational system in Kenya. The commission produced what has become known as the Beecher Report and its acceptance by the colonial government led to the introduction a new system of schooling. Beecher also served as CMS (Anglican) Bishop of Mombasa [q.v.] (1953–64) and as Archbishop of East Africa (1960–70), the last European to head Kenya's Anglican community. He retired to Karen, a Nairobi suburb. He died on 20 December 1987.

BELFIELD, SIR HENRY CONWAY (1855–1923). Governor of Kenya (1912–17). Educated at Rugby School and Oriel College, Oxford. In 1880, he qualified as a barrister. Four years later, Belfield joined the colonial service as a magistrate in the Malay States. He served there for the next 28 years, and at the time of his appointment as governor of Kenya, he was resident of Perak. Although many Kenyan settlers initially criticized his appointment, he became a strong advocate of European claims for greater economic and political support from the colonial government. It was as a result of his pleading that such measures as the Crown Lands Ordinance of 1915 [q.v.], the registration and *kipande* [q.v.] system for African males, elections for European representatives to the Legislative Council [q.v.], and the postwar Soldier Settlement Scheme [q.v.] came to be implemented. Nevertheless, he was seen by both the settlers and London officials as a relatively "weak" governor, incapable of providing strong leadership, particularly during World War I [q.v.]. In April 1917, he proceeded to Great Britain on home leave. His successor, General Sir Edward Northey [q.v.], did not take office until early 1919, and Sir Charles Bowring [q.v.] served as acting governor during the interim period. Belfield retired in 1918 and died on 8 January 1923.

BIWOTT, NICHOLAS KPYATOR KIPRONO ARAP (1941–). Administrator, politician, and businessman. Born in the then Elgeyo-Marakwet District and educated at the Tambach Government African School and Melbourne University in Australia, where he earned a B.A. degree. In 1966, Biwott, who calls himself the "total man," started his civil service career, working for the Ministry of Information and Broadcasting, the Provincial Administration, the Office of the President, and the Office of the Vice President. In the latter position, he began a friendship with

Daniel arap Moi [q.v.] that would become closer over the years and elevate him to a position of power and influence in the Moi regime.

In the general elections (1974) [q.v.], he stood for the Kerio South parliamentary seat but lost to Stanley Kurgat by 700 votes. In the general elections (1979) [q.v.], Kurgat stood down for Biwott. In the 1983 general elections and general elections (1988) [qq.v.], he was returned unopposed.

Biwott's electoral success thrust him into the cabinet as he became minister of state in the Office of the President (1979–82). He then served as minister of regional development, science, and technology (1982–83) and minister of energy and regional development (1983–89). Additionally, Biwott was deputy leader of government business in parliament. In 1989, he remained minister of energy as the ministry was split from regional development. In October 1991, Biwott became minister of industry.

By the early 1990s, Biwott, who had earned the reputation of being the country's "godfather," was recognized as one of the wealthiest individuals in Kenya. He owned substantial property in Nairobi [q.v.] and other Kenyan cities, extensive agricultural holdings, and numerous companies including the HZ Group, which numbered among its holdings Kenya Air Aviation, Kenya Oil Company, and Kobil Petroleum. However, it was widely believed, in Kenya and abroad, that his extensive holdings and wealth were not merely the result of financial and business acumen, but of large-scale corruption. Following the murder of Kenya's foreign minister Dr. Robert Ouko [q.v.] in February 1990, charges of Biwott's corrupt wrongdoing again became public. Although Biwott denied these allegations, the Scotland Yard detectives called in by the Kenyan government to investigate the murder identified him as a prime suspect with the alleged motive being the need to protect his corrupt dealings from exposure. On 20 November 1991, President Daniel arap Moi, clearly embarrassed by these revelations, dropped him from the cabinet without giving any reasons. Six days later, the police [q.v.] arrested Biwott as a prime suspect in the murder of Dr. Ouko. However, in December 1991, the police released him for lack of sufficient evidence.

Although Biwott's influence had seemingly suffered as a result of these events, he remained active politically and continued to be the center of controversy. A parliamentary committee identified him as one of those most responsible for instigating the ethnic clashes that marked the Rift Valley Province [q.v.] and neighboring areas during the 1991–93 period. Biwott denied this and led the way in ensuring that Parliament rejected the committee's report. In the general elections (1992) [q.v.], he won reelection to Parliament by a huge majority. After 1992, Biwott emerged as the leader of the Kenya African National Union B [q.v.], the faction of the ruling party that included Vice President George Saitoti [q.v.]. On 15 January 1997, amid much public acrimony, Moi appointed Biwott minister of state in the President's Office. Biwott easily won reelection to Parliament in the general elections (1977) [q.v.]. In January 1998, he became minister for East African and regional co-operation.

BLIXEN, BARONESS KAREN CHRISTENCE (1885–1962). Better known by her pen name Isak Dinesen. Born in Rungsted, Denmark. Educated in Denmark, England, Switzerland, Italy, and France. In 1914, she married her cousin, Baron Bror Blixen-Finecke, and went to Kenya to run a coffee [q.v.] plantation near Nairobi [q.v.]. In 1921, the couple divorced. However, Blixen continued to manage the plantation herself. During this part of her life, she maintained a relationship with big game hunter Denys Finch Hatton. In 1931, falling coffee [q.v.] prices forced her to auction off the Karen Coffee Company. Shortly thereafter, Blixen left Kenya and never returned to East Africa. She devoted the rest of her life to writing novels and memoirs. As a result of this work, she was elected to the American Academy (1957). Her *Out of Africa* remains a classic story of life in colonial Kenya. In 1985, the film version of this book won an Oscar. Blixen died on 7 September 1962.

BLUNDELL, SIR MICHAEL (1907–1993). Farmer, politician, businessman. Born in London and educated at Wellington College. Instead of attending university he went to Africa in 1925 and took a job on a European-owned farm in western Kenya. He soon obtained a position as farm manager for a settler at Solai and eventually acquired a farm of his own in the area. In January 1940, he entered the military to serve as an officer with the King's African Rifles [q.v.].

After World War II [q.v.], he bought a farm at Subukia, near Nakuru [q.v.], and entered politics, winning the Rift Valley seat in the 1948 European-only elections to the Legislative Council (LEGCO) [q.v.]. Blundell soon emerged as a leader of European unofficial LEGCO members, particularly at the start of the Mau Mau Revolt [q.v.] as he was named a member of the War Council [q.v.] set up in 1954. He then became minister for agriculture (1955–59). An advocate of a multiracial approach and the Lyttelton Constitution [q.v.], Blundell led the way in forming the United Country Party [q.v.] in 1954.

His advocacy of a multiracial approach drew strong resistance from the Federal Independence Party [q.v.] and the supporters of Group Captain Llewellyn Briggs [q.v.]. Following the dissolution of the United Country Party in early 1957, Blundell continued to advocate multiracial political cooperation; thus, in 1959 he formed the New Kenya Group, which became the New Kenya Party [q.v.] in early 1960. However, the party failed to attract significant support from Africans and Asians [q.v.] and was strongly opposed by the more numerous hard-line European settlers who opposed majority rule.

Nevertheless, Blundell played a significant role at the first Lancaster House Conference (1960) [q.v.] as he and his New Kenya Party colleagues accepted the changes imposed by the Colonial Office, which effectively ended settler political dominance. His stand drew great abuse from the European settler community, but Blundell stood in the LEGCO elections (1961) [q.v.], defeating Ferdinand Cavendish-Bentinck [q.v.] for the Rift Valley reserved seat on the strength of African votes. Following the election, he became minister for agriculture in the Kenya African Democratic Union-led [q.v.] government.

After the second Lancaster House Conference (1962) [q.v.], Blundell retired from government and politics. After independence, he remained outside politics, but he was active in farming and in numerous business ventures. He remained a member of Kenya's economic elite under the presidencies of Jomo Kenyatta and Daniel arap Moi [qq.v.]. Blundell died on 1 February 1993. He wrote two memoirs, *So Rough a Wind* (1964) and *A Love Affair with the Sun*, which was published posthumously (1994).

BOMA. Swahili word for enclosure, especially for cattle and other livestock. Also used to refer to government administrative centers.

BOMA TRADING COMPANY. In 1907, George Hutton "Jack" Riddell, a former cavalry officer and Boer War (1899–1902) veteran, founded the Boma Trading Company to foster trade between British East Africa and Abyssinia (now Ethiopia). The company maintained its headquarters next to the Norfolk Hotel in Nairobi [q.v.], and later opened trading posts at Marsabit, Moyale, and Dolo. A small, mobile force of mounted Somalis protected the company's trading routes. Norfolk Stores, operated by John Boyes [q.v.], was the Boma Trading Company's only competition. From the colonial government's viewpoint, the company was useful insofar as it established a British presence in the remote northeastern part of the country. After the colonial government created the Northern Frontier District [q.v.] in 1909, the company gradually reduced its trading activities. In 1910, the Boma Trading Company closed its trading posts and terminated its operations.

BOWRING COMMITTEE. Officially known as the Economic and Finance Committee. In April 1922, the colonial government created the committee under the chairmanship of Sir Charles Bowring [q.v.]. The Colonial Office and the Legislative Council [q.v.] wanted the committee to make recommendations for reducing government expenditure in a time of extreme revenue shortage. The committee, which had an unofficial majority including Ewart Grogan and Lord Delamere [qq.v.], examined ways of cutting expenditure and recommended increasing revenue by promoting greater exports and cutting imports. The European settler community agreed with many of the committee's recommendations, including no income tax, increased maize exports, and high protective tariffs on wheat imports.

BOWRING, SIR CHARLES CALVERT (1872–1945). Colonial administrator. Born in England and educated at Clifton College. In 1890, Bowring joined the Colonial Audit Branch of the Exchequer and saw service in the Far East until 1895, when he was appointed local auditor in the British Central Africa Protectorate (now Malawi). In 1899, he moved to Kenya as auditor for the protectorate and the Uganda Railway. In 1901, he was appointed treasurer for the protectorate, and his importance in the early colonial hierarchy was recognized in 1907 by his appointment to the Legislative Council (LEGCO) and Executive Council [qq.v]. During the 1911–24 period, he served as chief secretary. Bowring also served as acting governor on several occasions (e.g. 1912, 1919–20, 1921, 1923), his most lengthy period of service stretching from April 1917 to February 1919. During the latter period, Bowring came under strong pressure and criticism from European settlers in pursuit of their political (e.g., immediate elections to LEGCO) and economic demands (e.g. construction of a railway across the Uasin Gishu Plateau). Bowring was generally more favorably disposed to African and Asian interests in Kenya than were the governors he served under, but he invariably succumbed to settler advocacy on critical issues. In April 1922, he was appointed to head the special Economic and Finance Committee (also known as the Bowring Committee [q.v.]) established to recommend ways of cutting government expenditure and increasing production for exports. In 1924, Bowring left Kenya upon being appointed governor of Nyasaland (now Malawi). After a five-year tour of duty, Bowring retired from the colonial service. He died on 13 June 1945.

BOYES, JOHN (1874–1951). Explorer, big game hunter, and farmer. Born in Hull. Between 1880 and 1887, he lived with relatives in Engelfingen,

Germany. After returning to Hull in 1887, Boyes sought a naval career rather than an education. Over the next few years, he worked in a variety of maritime positions and eventually joined the Royal Naval Reserve. Boyes's early African experience included a stint with the Royal Niger Company, an enlistment in the Matabeleland Mounted Police and in the Africaner Corps, and a partnership in a business venture called the Colonial Fruit and Produce Stores of Bulawayo. In 1898, Boyes arrived in Mombasa [q.v.]. Two years later, he left Naivasha [q.v.] with a Maasai guide and seven porters en route to Kikuyu [q.v.] country. After reaching the first Kikuyu village, Boyes met Karuri who subsequently asked him to launch a military expedition against a rival clan which had attacked his village. After scattering Karuri's enemies, Boyes dubbed himself "King of the Wa Kikuyu." Upon learning of his exploits, the colonial authorities dispatched two officials to Kikuyu country to arrest him. After a Nairobi [q.v.] court acquitted him, Boyes resumed his trading activities among the Kikuyu. He eventually settled down as a coffee [q.v.] grower and later became a dairy farmer. Additionally, Boyes served as a commandant of the Legion of Frontiersmen. In 1911, he published his memoirs, *John Boyes: King of the Wa-Kikuyu.*

BRIGGS, LLEWELLYN ROLLS (1897–1960). Farmer and politician. Born in England, Briggs joined the Royal Air Force (RAF) at the age of 18 and was rapidly commissioned as an officer. He worked for a shipping firm in Liverpool between the wars and rejoined the RAF in World War II [q.v.]. In 1947, he moved to Kenya and bought a farm on the slopes of the Aberdare Mountains [q.v.]. Within five years, he entered politics as a member of the Legislative Council [q.v.] for the European constituency of Mount Kenya [q.v.]. Group Captain Briggs briefly held ministerial office beginning in 1956, but he resigned the following year as part of the negotiations leading to the Lennox-Boyd Constitution [q.v.]. From 1957 until mid-1960, Briggs was the acknowledged leader of the die-hard European settlers who were opposed to majority rule and decolonization. He strongly advocated the maintenance of the White Highlands [q.v.] and all-white schools. In 1959, he founded the United Party [q.v.], but despite his protests before, during, and after the first Lancaster House Conference (1960) [q.v.], the British government opened the White Highlands and moved toward putting political power in the hands of the African majority. After the Lancaster House Conference, Briggs enjoyed the support of the overwhelming majority of Kenya Europeans, but his racist advocacy for a past that could never be regained caused many settlers to turn to Sir Ferdinand Cavendish-Bentinck [q.v.]

for leadership in the hope of obtaining assistance in selling their farms at the time of Briggs's death on 15 November 1960. For a decade or more after his death, the name Briggs was synonymous, among politically aware Africans, with denigration of African abilities.

BROOKE-POPHAM, AIR CHIEF MARSHAL SIR HENRY ROBERT MOORE (1878–1953). Governor of Kenya (1937–39). Born Robert Brooke on 18 September 1878, he assumed the additional surname of Popham in 1904. After receiving an education at Haileybury and the Royal Military College, Sandhurst, he entered the army in 1898. In 1912, Brooke-Popham became a captain in the Royal Flying Corps and served in the air force during World War I [q.v.]. After the war, he held several command positions, including Iraq, the Middle East, the Chief of Air Defence of Britain, and Inspector General of the Royal Air Force. In 1937, Brooke-Popham retired from active service and took over the governorship of Kenya, a reflection of London's desire to have a military man in charge in Nairobi [q.v.] following Mussolini's takeover of Ethiopia. With the exception of his support for the creation of a national park [q.v.] system in Kenya, Brooke-Popham's tenure was undistinguished. In September 1939, he returned to active service as commander-in-chief in the Far East (1940–41). The Japanese successes in the war's early years in that region reflected negatively on Brooke-Popham's leadership. He retired in 1942 and died on 20 October 1953.

BYRNE, BRIGADIER GENERAL SIR JOSEPH ALOYSIUS (1874–1942). Governor of Kenya (1931–36). Born in England and educated at St. Georges College, Weybridge. In 1893, Byrne entered the army and saw active service in the Boer War (1899–02) and World War I [q.v.]. In 1916, Byrne was appointed deputy adjutant general for the Irish Command with a rank of brigadier general, thus beginning an association with Ireland that lasted until 1920 and culminated in his appointment as inspector general of the Royal Irish Constabulary. In 1922, he entered the colonial service as governor of the Seychelles, and, in 1927, moved to Sierra Leone.

In 1931, Byrne became governor of Kenya and served during the height of the worldwide depression. During his tenure, the colonial government, despite undertaking various economic austerity measures, implemented several initiatives to sustain European settler agriculture [q.v.]. However, it also increased official support for African peasant production. Byrne also took an interest in medical and public health matters, emphasizing his determination to upgrade the facilities at the

Nairobi and Mombasa [qq.v.] hospitals and the Nairobi jail. Additionally, Byrne's administration implemented an income tax, a measure long opposed by the European settler community. For this and his general lack of sympathy for their demands for greater political influence, Byrne was unpopular with many European settlers. He retired after leaving Kenya in 1936 and died on 13 November 1942.

-C-

CARRIER CORPS. On 13 August 1914, the colonial government established the Carrier Corps or East African Transport Corps to supply combat units. By 11 September 1914, the Carrier Corps commander, Lieutenant Colonel Oscar Ferris Watkins [q.v.], had succeeded in recruiting 5,000 Africans who were organized into five 1,000-man units, which were subdivided into 100-man companies under the command of African headmen. Initially, enlisting in the Carrier Corps was voluntary. On 21 June 1915, however, growing manpower requirements forced the colonial authorities to pass legislation that authorized the forcible recruitment of "able-bodied" men for the Carrier Corps.

In February 1916, the colonial government created the Military Labour Bureau to replace the Carrier Corps. By late March 1916, this unit reported that more than 69,000 men had been recruited for service as porters. When the East African campaign moved to southern German East Africa (now Tanzania) at the end of that year, the demand for military porters again increased. On 18 March 1917, the colonial government appointed John Ainsworth [q.v.], who had a reputation for fair dealing among the Africans, as military commissioner for labour to encourage greater enlistment. During the last two years of World War I [q.v.], his efforts helped the Military Labour Bureau to recruit more than 112,000 men.

Africans in the Carrier Corps served in extremely trying circumstances. Chronic food shortages, inadequate medical care, pay problems, and harsh field conditions plagued all who participated in the East African campaign; but Africans frequently suffered more than non-Africans. Agricultural production also declined because of labor shortages on European- and African-owned farms.

Nearly 200,000 Africans served in the Carrier Corps; about 40,000 of them never returned. Thousands received medals or other awards for the courage with which they performed their duties. On a wider level, the Carrier Corps' contribution to the war effort was crucial to the Allied victory in East Africa; indeed, without that unit's participation, the campaign never could have been fought. *See also* KING'S AFRICAN RIFLES; WORLD WAR I.

CAVENDISH-BENTINCK, SIR FERDINAND WILLIAM (1889–1980). Farmer, politician. Born in 1889. Educated at Eton College and the Royal Military College, Sandhurst. In 1925, he first went to East Africa and worked as private secretary to the governor of Uganda (1925–27). He then took up farming in Kenya. In 1930, Cavendish-Bentinck became honorary secretary of the Convention of Associations [q.v.]. From 1934 to 1960, he was a member of the Legislative Council (LEGCO) [q.v.], where he established a reputation as an ardent spokesman for the colony's European settlers. From 1938 to 1960, he was a member of the colony's Executive Council [q.v.].

During World War II [q.v.], he was one of Kenya's most influential settlers. Between 1940 and 1945, he served as chairman of the colony's Agricultural Production and Settlement Board and as a member of the East African Civil Defence and Supply Council. Cavendish-Bentinck was also timber controller for East Africa. In 1945, he became the first non-official to head, as member for agriculture, a department. In 1955, he became speaker of LEGCO. However, on 4 March 1960, he resigned from LEGCO to protest what he viewed as the too rapid pace of decolonization in Kenya as manifested in the decisions of the first Lancaster House Conference [q.v.]. On 30 March 1960, he founded the Kenya Coalition [q.v.], a political party that worked in conjunction with the Convention of Associations [q.v.], to defend the interests of the European settler community. In the LEGCO elections (1961) [q.v.], Michael Blundell [q.v.] defeated him for the Rift Valley [q.v.] seat. In 1963, the Kenya Coalition collapsed. Thereafter, Cavendish-Bentinck retired from politics but remained in Kenya. In 1977, he became the Duke of Portland. Cavendish-Bentinck died on 13 December 1980.

CENTRAL BANK OF KENYA. The Central Bank of Kenya, which officially opened on 14 September 1965, has the normal powers of a central bank. These include managing the country's money supply and foreign reserves, lending money to the government, making fiduciary issues of currency [q.v.], and marketing treasury bills and bonds to cover the government deficit. The bank governor advises the president on financial matters such as the exchange rate and exchange controls. In recent years, the bank's powers have been reduced because of the liberalization of the financial sector.

CENTRAL ORGANISATION OF TRADE UNIONS (COTU). Formed in September 1965 after the government had deregistered the rival Kenya Federation of Labour [q.v.] and the Kenya African Workers' Congress. COTU brought organized labor much more under state control. Supporters also justified COTU's existence by pointing to the need for unity and discipline to promote economic development. In 1989, COTU affiliated with the then single political party, the Kenya African National Union [q.v.]. By the 1990s, the majority of Kenyan trade unions belonged to this organization, with the exception of the Kenya Medical Practioners' Association, the Kenya National Union of Teachers, and the Union of Postal and Telecommunications Workers. *See also* AFRICAN WORKERS' FEDERATION; EAST AFRICAN TRADE UNION CONGRESS.

CENTRAL PROVINCE. In 1934, the colonial government created Central Province as an administrative unit by combining Kikuyu and Ukamba Provinces [qq.v.]. It then included Embu [q.v.], Fort Hall, Kiambu, Kitui, Machakos, Meru [q.v.], Nairobi [q.v.] (the European settled areas of Kiambu, Limuru, and Ngong), North Nyeri, and South Nyeri.

In 1953, Machakos and Kitui became part of the newly created Southern Province. In 1963, Central Province was recast as a largely Kikuyu-inhabited unit with the transfer of Embu and Meru Districts to the new Eastern Province [q.v.]. Since that time, Central Province has included Kiambu, Kirinyaga, Murang'a, Nyandarua, and Nyeri Districts (13,176 square kilometers; 5,087 square miles).

CHANGE THE CONSTITUTION CAMPAIGN (1976). This movement first surfaced in September 1976, when several prominent politicians and cabinet ministers publicly advocated changing the constitution to bar then Vice President Daniel arap Moi [q.v.] from succeeding to the presidency. Without mentioning Moi by name, the advocates of constitutional change opposed the automatic accession of the vice president to the presidency on the death or incapacity of the president for a period of up to 90 days, during which time an election for a successor would be held. The leaders in the campaign included Njoroge Mungai [q.v.], Paul Ngei [q.v.], Kihika Kimani, Jackson Angaine [q.v.], and James Gichuru [q.v.]. Following a cabinet meeting on 6 October 1976, however, Attorney General Charles Njonjo [q.v.] issued a statement warning Kenyans that it was a criminal offense, punishable by the death penalty, to "compass, imagine, devise or intend the death or deposition of the president." Njonjo's statement ended the advocacy of a change to the constitution to bar Moi from succeeding Jomo Kenyatta [q.v.].

CHOLMONDELEY, HUGH. *See* DELAMERE, LORD.

CHURCH MISSIONARY SOCIETY (CMS). The CMS was formed as part of the Anglican Church's missionary effort. In 1844, Dr. and Mrs. Johann Ludwig Krapf [q.v.] were the first CMS missionaries sent to East Africa. In 1884, religious authorities established the Diocese of Eastern Equatorial Africa, which maintained stations throughout eastern Africa. In 1898, churchmen divided this organization into the Dioceses of Uganda and Mombasa, the latter encompassing part of central German East Africa (subsequently known as Tanganyika and now Tanzania). In 1927, officials separated central Tanganyika, leaving the Diocese of Mombasa to represent Kenya.

Beginning in 1929, the female circumcision and independent schools controversies caused many Anglicans to leave the church. During the Mau Mau Revolt [q.v.], there was another exodus of Anglican Church members. In 1955, the church consecrated its first two African bishops, F. H. Olang' and O. Kariuki. In 1960, the church severed its ties with Canterbury and established the Church of the Province of East Africa, which united the Kenyan and Tanganyikan Anglican churches. In 1970, the Kenyan and Tanzanian branches separated, with the former creating the Church of the Province of Kenya (CPK), which had six dioceses. By that time, the CPK sponsored 775 primary schools and some 60 *Harambee* [q.v.] schools. In late 1996, Bishop David Gitari became the CPK's third archbishop and spiritual leader of Kenya's three million Anglicans.

Until the 1980s, the CPK was fairly supportive of government policy. However, escalating abuses of political and civil rights during Daniel arap Moi's [q.v.] presidency gradually politicized the CPK. In particular, CPK bishops Gitari, Alexander Muge, who died in 1990 in a mysterious automobile accident, Henry Okullu, and archbishop Mannasses Kuria became staunch critics of President Daniel arap Moi. In the months prior to the general elections (1997) [q.v.], relations between the CPK and the Kenyan government became particularly tense. Despite President Moi's electoral victory, the CPK pledged to continue its struggle for political reform. See also ALLIANCE OF PROTESTANT MISSIONS; CHURCH OF SCOTLAND MISSION; GOSPEL MISSIONARY SOCIETY; NATIONAL CHRISTIAN COUNCIL OF KENYA.

CHURCH OF SCOTLAND MISSION (CSM). In 1891, Sir William Mackinnon [q.v.], Thomas Fowell Buxton, and Alexander Bruce, all of whom were directors of the Imperial British East Africa Company [q.v.], established the East African Scottish Industrial Mission. In that same year, the mission built its first station at Kibwezi, some 240 kilometers (150 miles) from Mombasa [q.v.]. In 1898, unhealthy conditions at Kibwezi forced the station's transfer to Kikuyu. During these early years, the mission's activities were limited largely because of financial and personnel shortages. In 1900, however, the Church of Scotland Foreign Missions Committee assumed responsibility for the organization, which became known as the CSM. Under this new leadership, the CSM expanded its operations by opening a second station at Tumu Tumu (1909) near Mount Kenya [q.v.]; St. Andrews Church, Nairobi (1910); and Chogoria (1922). At these and other locations, the CSM sought to promote the spiritual and material development of the African through evangelical, medical, educational, and industrial training. However, by 1911, the CSM numbered only 23 baptized Christians and 42 catechumens. At the 1913 Kikuyu Conference, which addressed numerous issues pertaining to Protestant missionary activities in East Africa, the CSM unsuccessfully proposed the creation of a federation of all Protestant missions in the East Africa Protectorate [q.v.]. Despite these setbacks, the CSM played a major role in helping to define the relationship between the colonial government, the European settlers, and the colony's African population. In particular, the CSM's senior missionary, John William Arthur [q.v.], argued in favor of African education at a time when many colonial officials and European settlers remained skeptical about the wisdom of educating Africans. He also opposed compulsory labor and female circumcision.

In 1943, an autonomous Presbyterian Church of East Africa (PCEA) replaced the CSM. Until Daniel arap Moi [q.v.] became president in 1978, the PCEA maintained fairly harmonious relations with the colonial and postindependence governments. However, like the Church of the Province of Kenya, the PCEA became increasingly critical of President Moi. On 28 April 1988, for example, the PCEA rejected queue voting and argued that the secret ballot was the most appropriate voting method. In the late 1990s, PCEA Reverend Timothy Njoya became a national spokesman for political reform and democratization. *See also* ALLIANCE OF PROTESTANT MISSIONS; CHURCH MISSIONARY SOCIETY; GOSPEL MISSIONARY SOCIETY; NATIONAL CHRISTIAN COUNCIL OF KENYA.

CLOSER UNION. In 1924, Colonial Secretary Leopold S. Amery unveiled a plan to strengthen the British position in East Africa by amalgamating

Kenya, Tanganyika (now Tanzania), and Uganda into a "Closer Union." The union would have increased political powers for local European settlers. Additionally, such an organization would have created common services in areas such as railways, harbors, post, telegraphs, aviation, customs, research, and defense. In the same year, the British government appointed the Ormsby-Gore Commission [q.v.] to consider British policy throughout the region. The commission reported that, despite the common needs of the East African dependencies, there was no support for Closer Union in East Africa. However, the commission suggested that the governors of three territories meet periodically to discuss issues of mutual interest.

In 1925, Amery ignored this recommendation by appointing Sir Edward Grigg [q.v.] governor to work toward the creation of an East African Federation. Grigg gained the support of Kenya's European settlers for Closer Union, but the Hilton Young Commission [q.v.] concluded that the time was not yet ripe for such an initiative. In 1931, a Joint Select Committee of the British Parliament indicated that "Closer Union" of a political or constitutional character was out of the question.

The Closer Union idea remained dormant until the outbreak of World War II [q.v.] convinced Kenya's Governor, Sir Henry Moore [q.v.], that this concept could help to coordinate the region's war effort. In 1942–43, Secretaries of State Lord Cranborne and Oliver Stanley also supported the creation of an East African Federation [q.v.], but Moore favored a unitary approach that would have given Kenya's European settlers self-government as well as effective control of East Africa. This led the Labour Party, partners in Great Britain's wartime coalition government, to oppose any form of Closer Union that would entrench European settler political power to the disadvantage of Kenya Africans.

Governor Sir Philip Mitchell [q.v.] revived Closer Union after World War II. Under his leadership, an East African High Commission was introduced from 1 January 1948, charged with managing several common services (e.g. railways and harbors, posts and telegraphs, research, and higher education). In 1961, a new organization, the East African Common Services Organisation (EACSO) [q.v.], was created with expanded powers to administer these services. However, EACSO was far from being a political federation. In 1967, the newly established East African Community (EAC) [q.v.] superseded EACSO, but its formation marked a step toward economic rather than political integration in East Africa. The EAC collapsed in 1977.

COAST AFRICAN PEOPLE'S UNION. Political party founded in 1960 under Ronald Ngala's [q.v.] leadership. In June 1960, this party merged with similar regional/ethnic parties to form the Kenya African Democratic Union [q.v.].

COAST PEOPLE'S PARTY. During the 1961–62 period, this political party, which had been established by a group of coastal Arabs and Swahilis, advocated creation of an independent state called *Mwambao* along the Kenyan coast. This state was to be carved out of the 10-mile coastal strip, which technically remained the possession of the sultan of Zanzibar. The Kenya African National Union and the Kenyan African Democratic Union [qq.v.] rejected this demand. Instead, they announced that if the 37,000 coastal Arabs, many of whom were born in Kenya, did not want to live under a postindependence African government, they should return to Zanzibar [q.v.] or Arabia.

In September 1961, the British government appointed Sir James Robertson to recommend ways to resolve this problem. His report, entitled *The Kenya Coastal Strip: Report of the Commissioner*, rejected the notion of an independent coastal state or a state joined to or administered by Zanzibar. Instead, Robertson maintained that the coastal strip be integrated with Kenya prior to independence. To mollify the Arab population, Robertson recommended the incorporation of Muslim law, religion, and education into the Kenyan constitution [q.v.]. On 5 October 1963, then Prime Minister Jomo Kenyatta [q.v.] and Zanzibari Prime Minister M. Shamte concluded an agreement accepting Robertson's recommendations, which in turn ended the dream of the Coast People's Party to establish a separate state.

COAST PROVINCE. *See* SEYIDIYEH PROVINCE.

COFFEE. Kenya's third leading foreign exchange earner. From World War I [q.v] until the 1980s, coffee was Kenya's leading earner of foreign exchange. It was grown exclusively on European-owned estates until 1934, when the initial plantings by Africans were allowed. Only from the 1950s did the colonial government allow widespread planting by African farmers. In July 1989, the suspension of the International Coffee Agreement temporarily disrupted markets and drove coffee prices to historical lows. Since 1993–94, Kenya's coffee sector has rebounded because of higher international prices and less restrictive marketing practices. During the 1997–98 period, coffee production totaled 31,177 tonnes, and for 1998–99, production totaled 53,038 tonnes.

COLE AFFAIR. In 1911, Galbraith Cole, a prominent early European settler and substantial landholder, shot an African he suspected of stealing sheep from his estate. He failed to report the matter to the police [q.v.], who later arrested him. In May 1911, Cole went on trial. The jury of nine European men sitting at Nakuru [q.v.] took five minutes to acquit Cole. Colonial Office (CO) officials were outraged by Cole's actions and the injustice of the jury's verdict. Subsequently, the CO recommended Cole's deportation from Kenya as he was conducting himself in a manner "dangerous to peace, order, and good government." Governor Sir Percy Girouard [q.v.] initially opposed London's wishes but eventually issued the deportation order after pressure from the CO. In September 1911, Cole left the colony. However, in September 1914, the colonial government canceled the deportation order as an amnesty measure at the start of World War I [q.v.].

COLONIAL 191. This was the title of the Colonial Office document, published in December 1945, which made public the new proposals for Closer Union drawn up by Sir Philip Mitchell [qq.v.]. Upon its publication, *Colonial 191* generated much opposition from Kenya's European settlers who, while they supported *Colonial 191*'s recommendation that there should be coordination of services such as railways, research, and industrial development on a regional basis, bitterly opposed the idea of racial parity in the proposed East African assembly. African and Asian political leaders accepted *Colonial 191*, but European settler opposition forced the colonial government and Colonial Office to offer a substitute set of proposals, in what became known as *Colonial 210*, in 1947. This proved acceptable to the European settlers, but it weakened the proposed territorial union and allowed for a European majority in the assembly.

COLONY AND PROTECTORATE OF KENYA (1920–1963). On 23 July 1920, the British Crown annexed the East Africa Protectorate as a colony under the terms of the Kenya Annexation Order-in-Council. The primary reason the Colonial Office carried out the change was that far more favorable terms would be obtained for loans if the territory was a colony rather than a protectorate. Because France refused to agree to Great Britain's annexation of the 10-mile coastal strip, technically the property of the sultan of Zanzibar [q.v.], as part of the colony, the latter was made Kenya protectorate by the 1920 Kenya Protectorate Order-in-Council. Thus, until independence, the name of the territory would be the Colony and Protectorate of Kenya. Sir Edward Northey [q.v.] chose the new name, Kenya, from Mount Kenya [q.v.], which he regarded as the colony's most dominating natural feature.

COMMISSION ON CLOSER UNION OF THE DEPENDENCIES IN EAST AND CENTRAL AFRICA. *See* Hilton Young Commission.

CONSTITUENCY ELECTED MEMBERS ORGANISATION. Formed in early 1959 by the 14 African elected Legislative Council [q.v.] members who had joined with Asian [q.v.], Arab, and a single European elected members. This organization, which advocated a rapid movement toward African majority rule and independence, provided a multiracial alternative to Michael Blundell's New Kenya Party [qq.v.]. Although it dissolved itself in late 1959 because of division among African leaders and inadequate popular support, the Constituency Elected Members Organisation helped pressure the British government to accept the need for a new constitutional arrangement and the calling of the Lancaster House Conference (1960) [q.v.].

CONSTITUTION. Kenya's constitution, which was introduced on the achievement of self-government on 1 June 1963 and at independence on 12 December 1963, makes provisions for citizenship, the protection of fundamental rights and freedom of the individual, the cabinet and Parliament, the judiciary [q.v.], the Judicial and Public Service Commission, and the safeguarding of Trust Land. The independence constitution provided for a *majimbo* [q.v.]or federal system with elected regional governments. With the inauguration of a republic on 12 December 1964, Kenya became a unitary state. Other constitutional changes made at the inauguration of the republic vested executive power with the president, vice president, and cabinet. The president, initially elected by Parliament, has the right to appoint the vice president and the cabinet. A 1968 amendment provided for popular election of the president; in addition it provided that if a president dies or is removed from office, the vice president becomes interim president for up to 90 days while a successor is elected. The National Assembly [q.v.] can change the constitution when 65 percent of its members cast affirmative votes during the second and third readings of a proposed amendment. The National Assembly also can dissolve itself by a vote of "no confidence," whereupon presidential and assembly elections must be held within 90 days. The constitution stipulates that Kenya's eight provinces (including Nairobi) [q.v.] have a right to elect their representatives and obtain a equitable share of the country's national budget. *See also* NATIONAL ASSEMBLY.

CONVENTION OF ASSOCIATIONS. In November 1910, Lord Delamere's [q.v.] Colonists' Association and the Pastoralists' Association merged to form the Convention of Associations, which quickly became known as the "settler's parliament." This organization, which was the most powerful body in Kenyan politics during a portion of the colonial period, sought to keep non-Europeans out of the White Highlands [q.v.] and to increase European settler influence in the colonial government. Additionally, the Convention of Associations opposed giving the franchise to Asians [q.v.] and allowing them to have free immigration rights into the colony. The organization's attitude toward Africans was more complex. On the one hand, it opposed African political rights and, in 1921, imposed a 33 percent wage reduction on African unskilled laborers and farm workers. On the other hand, however, the Convention of Associations urged the colonial government to spend more on services such as education, hospitals, and agriculture [q.v.].

Throughout much of its existence, the Convention of Associations repeatedly clashed with colonial service personnel who advocated a diminution of European settler political power. In August 1921, the hostility between colonial government officials and influential European settlers such as Delamere and Ewart Grogan [q.v.], who was the association's first chairman, prompted the creation of a Vigilance Committee. Its purpose was to persuade the Colonial Office to reject Asian demands for a common electoral roll as expressed in the Wood-Winterton Agreement [q.v.]. Hard-liners in the Vigilance Committee, believing that sterner measures were required to preserve European settler rights, hatched a plot to seize the government by force. To accomplish this goal, the Vigilance Committee planned to kidnap the governor, take control of the Uganda Railway [q.v.] and the country's postal and telegraphic systems, and then make a unilateral declaration of independence. Although the Vigilance Committee never launched a coup attempt, the Convention of Associations remained a potent force in Kenyan politics. However, in February 1944, the European settler community formed the Electors' Union [q.v.] to coordinate their activities. During the post–World War II [q.v.] era, this organization slowly replaced the Convention of Associations as the main platform of European political activity.

CORFIELD REPORT. In 1960, F. D. Corfield published a report entitled *Historical Survey of the Origins and Growth of Mau Mau*. Although it was supposed to be the authoritative account of the origins of the rebellion, the Corfield Report was slanted and based upon a selective use of official records. Corfield, a former colonial official in the Sudan who began the task in 1957, concluded that the Kenya African Union and Jomo Kenyatta [qq.v.] had planned and led the Mau Mau Revolt [q.v.]. The governor, Sir Patrick Renison [q.v.], enthusiastically accepted the Corfield Report, but many Africans rejected its findings. Even before independence, the Corfield Report had ceased to have credibility among scholars.

CORYNDON, ROBERT THORNE (1870–1925). Governor of Kenya (1922–25). Coryndon was born in Cape Colony, South Africa and attended St Andrew's College, Grahamstown, and Cheltenham College (1884–87) in England. He worked for the British South Africa Company in its takeover of Southern Rhodesia (now Zimbabwe) and Northern Rhodesia (now Zambia). He was a protege of Cecil Rhodes, serving as the famous imperialist's private secretary (1896–97). In the latter year, he began his administrative career in Barotseland (now part of Zambia) that lasted a decade. From 1907 to 1916, Coryndon was resident commissioner for Swaziland, and during that period he chaired Southern Rhodesia's Native Reserves Commission. During the 1916–17 period, Coryndon served as the Resident Commissioner for Basutoland (now Lesotho). Between 1917 and 1922, he was governor of Uganda.

In 1922, Coryndon became governor of Kenya, replacing Sir Edward Northey [q.v.]. The Colonial Office (CO) hoped that Coryndon would resolve the Indian Question [q.v.] on the terms of the Wood–Winterton Agreement [q.v.], something that Coryndon, given his South African background and sympathies for Kenya's European settlers, failed to do. In early 1923, he convinced the CO that Kenya's settlers were planning a rebellion rather than submit to London's terms for settling the controversy. This caused the CO to impose the Devonshire Declaration [q.v.] as a settlement to the dispute later that year.

During his governorship, Coryndon advocated what he termed the Dual Policy of encouraging European settler production and African production for export. He also supported the idea of an East African Federation in which economic cooperation would precede political union. Additionally, Coryndon helped to implement a £3.5 million project to build the Uasin Gishu railway line into Uganda (1924) and supported the establishment of the Magadi-Soda Company (1924) and several tea [q.v.] factories (1925). On 10 February 1925, Coryndon died after an emergency operation. In September 1930, Sir Edward Grigg [q.v.] opened the Coryndon Memorial Museum in Nairobi.

COUP ATTEMPT (1982). On 1 August 1982, Kenya Air Force (KAF) personnel mutinied at Nanyuki, Embakasi, and Eastleigh air bases. Within a few hours, they had seized Embakasi International airport, nearby Wilson Airport, the Central Bank of Kenya and the general post office in Nairobi [qq.v.], the Voice of Kenya (VOK) studios close to the University of Nairobi [q.v.], and the VOK transmitter on Ngong Road. Shortly thereafter, a rebel spokesman announced on VOK radio that President Daniel arap Moi [q.v.] had been overthrown. The coup attempt touched off a looting spree—mainly against Asian-owned shops and homes—in Nairobi by university students and shantytown dwellers. According to the Kenyan authorities, the rioters caused about $50 million damage.

Within six hours, loyalists from the Kenyan army and the General Services Unit (GSU) [q.v.] squelched the poorly planned and executed coup. By 5 August 1982, the Kenya police [q.v.] had arrested more than 3,000 people, including the entire 2,100-man KAF, on suspicion of conspiring to overthrow the government. Those arrested included several Luo [q.v.] notables, as well as KAF commander Major General Peter N. Kariuki; police commissioner Benjamin Gethi; GSU commander Peter Ndogo Mbuthia; professor Alfred Vincent Otieno Osanya, dean of the University of Nairobi's engineering department; Otieno Mak'Onyango, former assistant managing editor of the *Sunday Standard* newspaper; and Raila Odinga [q.v.], a government engineer who was the son of the Luo leader, Oginga Odinga [q.v.]. The Kenya African National Union [q.v.] later expelled Oginga Odinga.

The Kenyan government reacted harshly to those found guilty of being implicated in the coup attempt. Two KAF personnel, Hezekiah Ochuka and Pancras Oteyo Okumu, were hanged. Additionally, the courts sentenced more than 550 low-ranking KAF personnel to prison terms of between six months and 25 years. However, on 21 February 1983, President Moi granted clemency to 473 former servicemen and students who had been awaiting trial on charges of involvement in the coup. In 1997, the Release Political Prisoners [q.v.] human rights group persuaded the Kenya government to release former serviceman James Apiny, who had been serving a life sentence in Naivasha Maximum Security Prison, for his involvement in the coup attempt. He had been the last plotter still in custody. *See also* GENERAL SERVICES UNIT.

COWIE, MERVYN (1909–1996). Founder and first director of the Royal National Parks of Kenya. Cowie was born in Kenya and educated at

Brighton College and Brasenose College, Oxford. In the 1930s, he became an ardent conservationist who succeeded in mobilizing public support for the preservation of Kenya's wildlife. As a result of his efforts, the colonial government appointed a Game Policy Committee [q.v.] to formulate a fauna protection policy for Kenya. With the initial support of governor Sir Robert Brooke-Popham [q.v.], Cowie helped to establish Nairobi National Park (1946) and Tsavo National Park (1948) [qq.v.].

In 1966, his career came to an unexpected end when the Kenyan government dismissed him because his job was being Africanized. He left the directorship of the national parks system with one month's pay and without a pension, just a letter from President Jomo Kenyatta [q.v.] expressing his thanks. In 1979, he retired to Suffolk. He died on 19 July 1996. *See also* NATIONAL PARKS.

CROWN LANDS ORDINANCE (1902). Drafted by the Foreign Office and promulgated in 1902, the ordinance set out provisions for the alienation of land to European settlers. Limits were placed on the amount that could be sold to a single applicant, leases were not to exceed 99 years with restrictions on transfer, and the commissioner was given power to confiscate land if a holder did not develop it. Sir Charles Eliot [q.v.] issued rules under the ordinance, which provided the basis for alienation of land to European settlers prior to World War I [q.v.]. European settlers complained that the ordinance was too restrictive, while the Colonial Office, from 1905, sought to tighten up Kenya's land laws rather than relax them.

CROWN LANDS ORDINANCE (1915). This ordinance, passed during wartime, marked the culmination of successful European settler resistance to directives from London to tighten up legislation with regard to land. In their demand for easier conditions, the settlers had the strong backing of governors Sir Percy Girouard and Sir Henry Belfield [qq.v.]. The 1915 ordinance allowed those holding land to convert their grants for leases of 999 years for agricultural land. Revaluation of rent every 30 years and minimum development regulations were provided for, but the ordinance was a huge victory for settlers. Moreover, the legislation defined all land occupied by Africans as crown land. Though the governor was empowered to create reserves, these were not necessarily secure as such land did not belong to the peoples concerned.

CUNINGHAME, RICHARD JOHN (1871–1925). Big game hunter; photographer; and collector of wildlife, bird, and fish trophies for various museums and other scientific institutions. He was educated at Eton and studied biology at Cambridge University, but he apparently failed to receive a degree. After abandoning plans to become a physician, Cuninghame went to Lapland to become a hunter-naturalist and later worked as an Arctic whaler. He then traveled to South Africa, where he initially worked as a transport rider for one of the Zeederberg mail coaches from Kimberley to Johannesburg. In 1898, Cuninghame hunted big game in Portuguese East Africa (now Mozambique), South Africa, Matabeleland (now Zimbabwe), and the Kalahari Desert and collected many specimens for the British Museum. Additionally, he participated in the Matabeleland campaigns. After arriving in Mombasa [q.v.] in 1899, Cuninghame joined Newland, Tarlton and Company. He also led many hunting safaris throughout British East Africa, including the Carl Akeley (1906), Percy Madeira (1907), and Theodore Roosevelt (1909) expeditions.

At the outbreak of World War I [q.v.], he was on a big game hunting expedition. He immediately went to England and tried to enlist, but a medical officer judged him unfit for duty because of his many bouts of malaria. Nevertheless, Cuninghame served as a lieutenant with the American Field Ambulance in France and subsequently became a scout (i.e., intelligence officer) in East Africa. In 1916, he was in a convalescent home in Nairobi, after completing a mission to Zanzibar [q.v.] and Mafia Island. After being released, Cuninghame joined General Sir Horace Smith-Dorien's staff as a political and intelligence officer. For this work, he received the Military Cross and was promoted to major. At the end of the war, Cuninghame returned to Scotland where he inherited an estate, married, and became wealthy. On 23 May 1925, he died of a brain tumor in Kirkcudbrightshire.

CURRENCY. Prior to the 1890s, people used several types of currency as mediums of exchange in what is now Kenya. These included cowrie shells, Maria Theresa dollars, beads and cloth, and Indian rupees. In 1888, the Imperial British East Africa Company (IBEAC) [q.v.]. introduced a rupee coin which circulated alongside the Indian rupee, when it established control over parts of East Africa. When it assumed control of the IBEAC territories in 1895, the British government made the Indian rupee the standard coin. The 1905 East Africa and Uganda (Currency) Order-in-Council, which became effective in 1906, confirmed London's decision and provided that each rupee be divided into 100 cents. This system lasted until 1920, when the governor, Sir Edward Northey [q.v.], and many European settlers pressured the Colonial Office to implement changes favorable to their interests. The Colonial Office responded, however, by replacing the Indian rupee with a currency system based on a florin worth two shillings sterling or 10 to a pound sterling. Faced with further complaints, the Colonial Office decided to introduce, before florins could actually be put in circulation, an East African shilling, which was fully convertible with the pound sterling but divided into 100 cents. The East African shilling (which was also used in Tanganyika [now Tanzania], Uganda, and Zanzibar) remained Kenya's currency until March 1966, when the Kenya shilling was introduced as the country's new currency.

CUSHITIC-SPEAKING PEOPLES. Peoples speaking languages belonging to the Cushitic family live mainly in the northern half of present-day Kenya. These include such pastoral peoples as the Oromo and Somali, who speak languages belonging to the Eastern Cushitic group, and those speaking Southern Cushitic languages. People speaking the latter were present in western and central Kenya from at least the second millennium B.C.E. However, by the end of the second millennium C.E., such languages had largely disappeared from Kenya. By contrast, though evidence exists of peoples speaking Southern Cushitic languages in several parts of Kenya during the first millennium B.C.E., most of those speaking Eastern Cushitic languages moved into northern Kenya, largely after 1500.

-D-

DECEMBER 12 MOVEMENT. Dissident opposition organization. In February 1982, this group published a pamphlet called *Pambana* (Struggle), which criticized high-level corruption in the Kenyan government. Additionally, the publication accused President Daniel arap Moi [q.v.] of allowing the country's political system and economy to be influenced by foreign interests. In November 1984, the movement distributed *Pambana* pamphlets in Nairobi [q.v.] calling on Kenyans to start a guerrilla war against the Moi regime in protest against corruption and the country's poor human rights record. The December 12 Movement eventually evolved into Mwakenya [q.v.].

DELAMERE, LORD (HUGH CHOLMONDELEY) (1870–1931). Pioneer European settler, farmer, and politician. Born at Vale Royal in Cheshire, England. Educated at Eton. At the age of 17, he succeeded his father as the third Baron Delamere of Vale Royal. In 1897, Delamere first entered Kenya on a big game hunting expedition. In 1903, he returned to Kenya, where he remained for the rest of his life. Shortly after Delamere's arrival, Sir Charles Eliot [q.v.] granted him 40,500 hectares (100,035 acres) of land on a 99-year lease in the White Highlands [q.v.]; subsequent land purchases increased the size of his estate. Delamere invested considerable capital and energy in mixed farming endeavors (e.g. sheep, wheat, dairy cattle). His farming experiments proved helpful to other European settlers.

Within a year of arriving in Kenya, Delamere established himself in the political arena by becoming president of the Colonists' Association. In 1907, he was one of the first two unofficial members appointed to the Legislative Council (LEGCO) [q.v.]. After his election to LEGCO for the Rift Valley in January 1920, Delamere became the acknowledged leader of the European settler community. Apart from helping to devise the policy that excluded African and Asian landowners from the White Highlands, reserved for the exclusive ownership of European settlers, he also led the campaign for a popularly elected unofficial majority in LEGCO (never achieved in his lifetime). Additionally, Delamere opposed Indian demands for equality, was against the imposition of an income tax, and favored the creation of a Closer Union [q.v.] between British territories in eastern Africa. His service on various committees and boards such as the Governor's War Council and the Bowring Committee [qq.v.] enabled him to further influence colonial government policy in Kenya.

Delamere's authoritarian and explosive personality cowed many government bureaucrats, all of whom he detested. However, Sir Joseph Byrne [q.v.] refused to be intimidated by Delamere and frequently clashed with him over the role of the European settler community in national politics. Nevertheless, Delamere continued to pursue his pro-settler political and economic policies until the end of his life. After a series of angina attacks, Delamere died on 13 November 1931.

DEMOCRATIC PARTY (DP). Established in 1992 following the resignation of Mwai Kibaki, Njenga Karume [qq.v.], and other prominent Kikuyu [q.v.] politicians from the government. Kibaki became party chairman and John Keen [q.v.] served as general secretary. Kibaki stood as the DP's presidential candidate in the general elections (1992) [q.v.]. He came third in the poll with 19.45 percent of the vote. The DP won 23 parliamentary seats, 19 of which were in Central and Eastern Provinces [qq.v.]. Following the election, the DP suffered a string of defections that reduced its parliamentary numbers and tarnished its image. Nevertheless, the DP received a boost by winning a victory in the Kipipiri 1995 by-election. Since 1992, those outside the party have charged that it represents a relatively narrow constituency, the wealthy and formerly politically influential Kikuyu elite.

Prior to the general elections (1997) [q.v.], DP renewed its commitment to bringing about economic recovery, liberalizing investment laws, curbing dependence on foreign aid, and achieving food self-sufficiency. Kibaki was once again the party's presidential candidate. He finished second, and DP won 39 seats in Parliament (plus two nominated MPs) to become the official opposition.

DESAI, MANILAL AMALAL (1879–1926). Born at Gotalvadi near Surat in India and educated at the Mission High School in Surat. Desai first worked with a firm of solicitors in Bombay. In October 1915, he arrived in Kenya. After a brief time in law and business, he turned to politics and journalism. After reorganizing the Nairobi Indian Association, he traveled throughout the East Africa Protectorate [q.v.] and established a network of local Indian organizations. Desai also advocated African rights and supported Harry Thuku's [q.v.] political activities. In 1921, he founded the *East African Chronicle*, which championed the cause of Asian and African rights, and became president of the Nairobi Indian Association. In 1925, Desai, who had bitterly opposed the Devonshire Declaration [q.v.], was elected to the Legislative Council [q.v.] and continued his struggles to improve the lives of the colony's non-European populations. He died on 15 July 1926, while on a political tour of East Africa. *See also* INDIAN QUESTION.

DEVONSHIRE DECLARATION (1923). Apart from being a turning point in Kenya's history, the Devonshire Declaration, issued as the white paper *Indians in Kenya*, sought to defuse and settle the controversy surrounding the Indian Question [q.v.]. It drew its name from the Duke of Devonshire, the secretary of state for the colonies, though he was in no sense the primary author of the policy. In seeking to settle a long-simmering political issue, the Colonial Office (CO) accepted Indian demands for an end to urban segregation and allowed Indian immigration into Kenya to continue, but it accepted that the White Highlands [q.v.] were to be reserved for European land ownership. The CO rejected the Indian demand for common roll elections in favor of communal voting, with 11 seats in the Legislative Council [q.v.] reserved for Europeans and five for Indians. More significantly for the future, however, London sought to defuse the crisis by declaring that future policy in Kenya would be based on African "paramountcy," which meant that African interests should override those of the European and Asian communities. As a result, London succeeded in making it impossible for the European settlers to gain control of the colonial government (as they did in Southern Rhodesia [now Zimbabwe] or South Africa). *See also* ASIANS; DESAI, MANILAL AMBALAL.

DINESEN, ISAK. *See* BLIXEN, BARONESS KAREN CHRISTENCE.

DINI YA JESU KRISTO (CHURCH/RELIGION OF JESUS CHRIST). In 1947, Ruben Kihiko, a Kikuyu [q.v.] from Kabete, founded this religious sect. Followers of the faith wore skins rather than European-style clothes and carried traditional swords (*simi*). As a result, they became known as "The Skin Men." This sect maintained that the White Highlands [q.v.] belonged to Africans and that Europeans should be driven out of Kenya. On 20 December 1947, Kihiko and 40 to 50 of his followers found Stephen Mwenja, a man who had stolen the sect's flag at an earlier demonstration, and slashed his wrist. Kihiko then started taking Mwenja to the village of Ngugi Mungai, where he intended to kill him in front of his women followers. Along the way, Kihiko's groups clashed with the Kenya police [q.v.] in Murang'a District and killed a European police officer and two African constables. By 3 January 1948, the police had rounded up Kihiko and his followers. During the ensuing trial, the court found Kihiko and three others guilty of murder. On 6 November 1948, the Nairobi prison authorities executed all four by hanging. Additionally, the colonial government banned *Dini ya Jesu Kristo*.

DINI YA MSAMBWA (DYM) (CHURCH/RELIGION OF ANCESTRAL SPIRITS). In 1943, Elijah Masinde [q.v.] founded this religion, which appealed mostly to his Bukusu subtribe of the Luyia [q.v.]. However, DYM gained adherents among other Luyia groups and some non-Luyia, most notably the Pokot. The religion was anticolonial and anti-European. DYM urged its followers to destroy their *kipande* [q.v.] identity cards and to refuse to pay taxes. Additionally, Masinde demanded "Africa for the Africans," denounced Christianity as the religion of the imperialists and urged his followers to return to the traditional Bukusu religion, attacked Asian [q.v.] businessmen for exploiting Africans, and chiefs for acting as agents of imperialism, and advocated a civil disobedience campaign against the colonial government, especially with regard to its agricultural and soil conservation policies.

In 1948, there were violent confrontations between Bukusu adherents and the colonial government, which subsequently detained Masinde and banned DYM. Nevertheless, this movement continued to attract believers, as indicated by the 24 April 1950 Kolloa Affray, when a group of

Masinde's Pokot followers clashed with government forces in the then Baringo District. This incident claimed 29 lives and wounded 50 others. A year after independence in 1963, the Kenyan government lifted the ban on DYM. However, Masinde soon ran afoul of Jomo Kenyatta's [q.v.] government and was jailed on more than one occasion. Although banned on 25 October 1968, DYM continued to agitate for an end to secular rule and a complete reorganization of Kenyan society.

DINI YA ROHO (RELIGION/CHURCH OF THE SPIRIT). There are several churches/sects in Kenya's history that go by the name "*Dini ya Roho.*" The significance of such groups lies in the fact that they were/ are separatist. They rejected European missionary leadership and reflected a merging of Christianity with traditional African beliefs. Also, at least one sect expressed some discontent with British colonial rule. In 1927, Jakobi Buluku and Daniel Sande broke away from the Quakers, founded *Dini ya Roho*, and helped to spread its beliefs throughout the area inhabited by the southern Luyia [q.v.] (present-day Kakamega and Vihiga Districts). Members believed in faith healing, participated in dancing and spirit possession ceremonies, refused to shake hands, and wore long white robes with a red cross sewn across the chest. Women wore white bandannas and men white turbans on Sunday. The church continues to be concentrated in an area inhabited by southern Luyia, although it has congregations where Luyia live and work, such as Eldoret and Nairobi [qq.v.].

Ethnic competition helped to determine the activities of another sect. In 1932–34, Reverend Alfayo Odongo Mango founded another *Dini ya Roho* sect in western Kenya. Initially, this sect was known as the Holy Ghost Church or *Dini ya Jo-Roho*, its name reflecting a mix of Swahili and Luo [qq.v.] words. Later, it became known as *Dini ya Roho*. This church drew its support from Luo in the Wanga location as a means of articulating the political demands of the Kager clan for land and political rights in the Luyia-led Wanga. From a religious perspective, it was a break from the Church Missionary Society [q.v.] church. However, ethnic factors also played an important role, as Odongo Mango and others felt that Archdeacon Owen [q.v.] favored Luyia interests, especially the language of the church, rather than the Luo of the Kager clan. In January 1934, the Wanga killed Odongo Mango and others at Masinde in retaliation for the earlier deaths of two Wanga men at the hands of some Luos. The surviving church members founded a new headquarters at Ruwe. They wore a cross with the letter *S*, which stood for the Luo word for oath. Smoking and drinking of alcohol are forbidden and Odongo

Mango is regarded as a martyr. In 1956, the colonial government recognized the sect.

DUAL POLICY. In 1922, Governor Sir Edward Northey [q.v.] proposed this economic policy, which involved limited state support to stimulate African peasant production of crops for domestic and foreign markets. Northey hoped the Dual Policy would facilitate cooperation, rather than competition, between peasant and European settler production for control of the export market. Governor Sir Robert Coryndon [q.v.] enthusiastically adopted the Dual Policy, which also gained support among Colonial Office officials who realized that in the severe post–World War I [q.v.] depression, European settler agriculture [q.v.] alone could not underwrite colonial economic solvency. Throughout the 1920s, the Dual Policy remained official policy. Nevertheless, state support for European settler agriculture far surpassed that provided to African peasants. Thus, in practice, the Dual Policy favored European settler production.

-E-

EAST AFRICA COMMISSION. *See* ORMSBY-GORE COMMISSION.

EAST AFRICA (LANDS) ORDER IN COUNCIL (1901). The order provided that African rights to land in Kenya were confined to occupation, cultivation, and grazing and did not amount to a title to the land itself. Officials drafted the Crown Lands Ordinance (1902) [q.v.] on that assumption, as all African-inhabited land was considered crown land.

EAST AFRICA PROTECTORATE. Kenya's name from 1895 until 1920. *See also* COLONY AND PROTECTORATE OF KENYA.

EAST AFRICAN AIRWAYS. *See* AVIATION; KENYA AIRWAYS.

EAST AFRICAN ASSOCIATION. In July 1921, Harry Thuku [q.v.] changed the name of the Young Kikuyu Association [q.v.] to the East African Association. The name change reflected Thuku's desire to build a pan-ethnic protest movement to provide a voice for Africans living and working in Nairobi as well as rural Kikuyu [qq.v.]. The East African Association, with help from Asian politicians, sought to articulate African demands to the colonial government and to the Colonial Office. Though its active members included the still-small educated elite, the organization gained increasing support in Nairobi [q.v.] and rural Kikuyuland by the end of 1921. The East African Association's appeal to groups other than Kikuyu and its hostility to colonial chiefs and desire to supersede the latter as intermediaries with the state, particularly among the Kikuyu, alarmed the colonial authorities. On 14 March 1922, the authorities arrested Thuku. Two days later, the police [q.v.] opened fire on the crowd that had gathered outside the central police station demanding Thuku's release. The gunfire killed at least 25 Africans. The colonial government then banned the East African Association. *See also* KIKUYU ASSOCIATION; KIKUYU CENTRAL ASSOCIATION; THUKU, HARRY; YOUNG KIKUYU ASSOCIATION.

EAST AFRICAN COMMON SERVICES ORGANISATION (EACSO). On 9 December 1961, the Colonial Office replaced the East African High Commission [q.v.] with EACSO to carry on regional cooperation in postindependence Kenya, Tanganyika (now Tanzania), and Uganda. The British intended that this action would internalize interterritorial economic and infrastructure cooperation by shifting its management from the colonial authorities to the African chief ministers of the three newly independent countries. EACSO authority included elected representatives from Kenya, Tanganyika, and Uganda, who also sat as ex-officio members in the organization's Central Legislative Assembly. A secretary-general and a legal secretary oversaw a permanent Secretariat, charged with implementing assembly measures concerning civil aviation, customs and excise revenues, income taxes, interterritorial research, university education, communications, and public service.

From its outset, EACSO experienced a basic problem that had affected its predecessor. By deliberate colonial design, Kenya's economic performance had consistently outpaced that of Tanganyika and Uganda, and the distribution of trade, tax, and investment revenues under EACSO merely reinforced this trend and threatened further to entrench an increasingly unbalanced economic relationship between Kenya and its less-favored partners, thus threatening the collapse of regional cooperation. Therefore, in 1965, the specially appointed Philip Commission examined the future of East African economic relations. The commission recommended that an East African Community (EAC) [q.v.] be created to address problems of economic imbalance while preserving and extending regional common services. The Philip Commission report led to the Treaty for East African Cooperation, concluded by the Kenyan, Tanzanian, and Ugandan governments on 1 December 1967. This treaty authorized the EAC to assume control over EACSO's economic services. An East African Common Market was also instituted to manage a common external tariff and specially permitted restraints on regional trade, termed "transfer taxes," that Tanzania and Uganda could impose on imports from Kenya. An East African Development Bank was likewise formed and mandated to make 80 percent of its investments in Tanzania and Uganda.

EAST AFRICAN COMMUNITY (EAC). Preceded by the East African High Commission and the East African Common Services Organisation [qq.v.]. On 6 June 1967, Kenya, Tanzania, and Uganda signed a treaty that established the EAC "to strengthen and regulate the industrial, commercial and other ties among [Kenya, Tanzania, and Uganda] with a view to bringing about accelerated, harmonious and balanced development." Within this context, its main objectives were to establish and maintain a common customs and excise tax, gradually to abolish trade restrictions among partner states, to coordinate economic planning and transport/communications policies, and eventually to develop a common agricultural policy. The three heads of state or their representatives comprised the East African Authority, the EAC's highest executive organ, which featured a rotating chairmanship. The EAC headquarters were located at Arusha, Tanzania, but the head offices of its various components were in major towns and cities throughout East Africa. An East African Assembly reported to the authority and presided over five councils: the Common Market Council, the Communications Council, the Finance Council, the Economic Consultation and Planning Council, and the Research and Social Council.

To manage regional economic and infrastructure cooperation, several East African corporations, administrations, and departments were brought under the jurisdiction of the authority and the assembly. The largest of these was the East African Railways Corporation; others included East African Airways, Harbours, Cargo Handling Services, Posts and Telecommunications, External Communications, Development Bank, Court of Appeal, Fishery-Marine-Freshwater, Malaria and Medical Research-TB-Leprosy-Sleeping Sickness, Customs and Excise, Meteorology, Literature Bureau, Statistics, Veterinary Research, Educational Examinations Council (localized after 1973), Inter-University Commission, and Community Training Centre for Secretariat staff.

The EAC collapsed in 1977 because of a number of factors, including Idi Amin Dada's January 1971 military coup d'etat in Uganda and its aftermath of increasing tensions between Uganda, Tanzania, and, to a lesser extent, Kenya. More basic difficulties centered on the divergent development strategies of socialist Tanzania and capitalist Kenya; the different and mutually antagonistic leadership styles of Presidents Julius

Nyerere and Jomo Kenyatta [q.v.]; and the disproportionate share of trade, investment, and other EAC benefits perennially reaching Kenya. Following a series of mutual accusations, confiscations of community assets, and repatriations of EAC employees, none of the three countries remitted its 1977–78 financial contribution to the community. Without an operating budget for the coming fiscal year, the EAC was dissolved on 1 July 1977.

Since then, Kenya, Tanzania, and Uganda periodically discussed the possibility of recreating the EAC. However, it was not until 30 November 1993 that the three nations signed the Treaty for Enhanced East African Co-operation. This agreement established a framework for regional cooperation in several areas, including trade, industry, agriculture [q.v.], energy, transport, communications, law, and security. A more significant breakthrough occurred in March 1996, when Kenya, Tanzania, and Uganda launched the East African Co-operation Secretariat, which subsequently was based in Arusha, Tanzania. By early 1997, this organization had established the East African Judicial Committee, the Lake Victoria [q.v.] Environmental Management Program, and the East African Business Council. Additionally, the East African Co-operation Secretariat has sponsored talks between the region's senior defense and security officials. *See also* EAST AFRICAN COMMON SERVICES ORGANISATION; EAST AFRICAN FEDERATION.

EAST AFRICAN FEDERATION. As Kenya neared independence, the impetus toward an East African Federation accelerated. Strongly influenced by Pan-African ideals, Kenyan nationalists championed the cause of a federation that would, unlike the Closer Union [q.v.] proposals, bring the East African nations together under African rule. Shortly after Kenya achieved internal self-government in June 1963, President Julius Nyerere of Tanganyika (now Tanzania), Prime Minister Milton Obote of Uganda, and Prime Minister Jomo Kenyatta [q.v.] met in Nairobi [q.v.] and pledged their support for a political federation of East Africa's mainland states. However, the pledge did not lead to a federation largely because of Uganda's reluctance to join such a grouping. In 1967, Kenya, Uganda, and Tanzania signed the treaty for East African Co-operation. It provided for the creation of an East African Community [q.v.] that would promote economic integration for the region rather than political federation. *See also* EAST AFRICAN COMMUNITY.

EAST AFRICAN HIGH COMMISSION (EAHC). By 1927, the British colonial authorities had joined Kenya, Tanganyika (now Tanzania),

Kenya, and Uganda into a system of common tariffs; duty-free transfers of imported goods; a single currency [q.v.]; and increasingly integrated services including railroad transportation, customs, posts and telegraphs, railways and harbors administration, civil aviation, and defense. In 1939, the colonial authorities introduced a regional income tax. On 1 January 1948, the EAHC was established to manage these and newer regional activities. As a result of the influence of British Colonial Secretary Arthur Creech Jones, the EAHC was led by a multiracial Central Legislative Assembly [q.v.] and immediately began to absorb the regional service organizations that had been created piecemeal over the preceding years. Four months after its inception, it amalgamated the East African Railways, and in 1949 the East African Posts and Telecommunications and the East African Railways and Harbours authorities were formed. The assembly's authority also extended to Makerere University [q.v.] in Uganda, then East Africa's only degree-granting higher education institution.

The EAHC likewise presided over novel attempts at regional integration. One of the best examples was the East African Literature Bureau (EALB), created in 1947. The EALB promoted African writing and advised young authors, published and disseminated literary and cultural works in and about East Africa, supported literacy campaigns in the three member territories, and managed the East African Community's [q.v.] Central Printing Section. The EALB also pioneered the public library movement in East Africa. On 9 December 1961, the East African Common Services Organisation [q.v.] replaced the EAHC.

EAST AFRICAN INDIAN NATIONAL CONGRESS (EAINC). On 7 March 1914, EAINC, which was modeled on the famous Congress in India, held its first meeting at Mombasa [q.v.]. EAINC demanded equality with Europeans and the opening of the White Highlands [q.v.] to Asian farmers. Additionally, EAINC argued that election to the Legislative Council [q.v.] should be based on a common roll of Europeans and Asians [q.v.], opposed Closer Union [q.v.], and encouraged Asian immigration to Kenya. After the Great Depression of the 1930s, EAINC became increasingly involved in humanitarian activities such as providing aid to disaster victims in India and other South Asian countries. In 1950, EAINC unsuccessfully tried to establish an alliance with the Kenya African Union [q.v.]. However, the two organizations joined ranks to oppose the Electors' Union's [q.v.] *Kenya Plan*, which called for the permanency of European settlement and the maintenance of settler leadership. In 1952, EAINC changed its name to the Kenya Indian Congress. *See also* DEVONSHIRE DECLARATION; EAST AFRICA HIGH COMMISSION; INDIAN QUESTION.

EAST AFRICAN PROFESSIONAL HUNTERS' ASSOCIATION. On 12 April 1934, a group of government officials and big game hunters held a meeting at the Norfolk Hotel and established the East African Professional Hunters' Association. Patrons included the governor, Sir Joseph Byrne [q.v.]; the Kenya game warden, A. T. A. "Archie" Ritchie; the Uganda game warden, Charles Pitman; and the Tanganyika game warden S.P. Teare. The president was Philip H. Percival, and the vice presidents were Al Klein and G. H. "Andy" Anderson. By 1950, the association had 21 full members, 15 probationary members, eight associate members, and 96 honorary members. The East African Professional Hunters' Association, which existed until the Kenyan government banned big game hunting in 1977, helped to enforce hunting regulations and to guarantee that hunting safaris for visitors met uniform standards.

EAST AFRICAN TRADE UNION CONGRESS (EATUC). On 1 May 1949, six Kenyan trade unions established EATUC, under the leadership of Fred Kubai (president) and Makhan Singh (general secretary) [qq.v.]. EATUC's goals included improving and safeguarding the welfare of Kenyan workers; securing freedom of speech, assembly, and the right to strike; establishing an eight-hour workday, a 45-hour work week, and minimum wage standards; gaining representation in the Legislative Council (LEGCO) [q.v.]; and abolishing forced labor and the employment of children. On 1 May 1950, the EATUC became the first African organization to demand independence under majority rule. The colonial government responded to this announcement by refusing to register the organization and by arresting Kubai, Singh, and several other union leaders. The police [q.v.] charged Kubai with murder and Singh with sedition but later released the two because the charges could not be substantiated. EATUC retaliated by calling a general strike, which halted all business in Nairobi [q.v.] for eight days and closed the port of Mombasa [q.v.] for two days. The police repeatedly clashed with the strikers—who numbered about 6,000 at the peak of the strike—and eventually succeeded in breaking the EATUC. With the defeat of EATUC, many union activists joined the Transport and Allied Workers' Union while others became active in secret organizations in Nairobi. Nearly all former EATUC personnel were united in their determination to end British colonial rule. *See also* AFRICAN WORKERS' FEDERATION; CENTRAL ORGANISATION OF TRADE UNIONS.

EAST AFRICAN WOMEN'S LEAGUE. On 14 March 1917, Isabel McGregor Ross founded the East African Women's League. As president, she sought to secure the right to vote in Legislative Council (LEGCO) [q.v.] elections and to improve the welfare of all women and children in the colony. To achieve the former, Ross organized public meetings and on 24 February 1919 submitted an application to LEGCO urging the granting of the franchise to all Europeans regardless of gender. On 8 April 1919, Sir Edward Northey [q.v.] cast the decisive vote giving European women the right to vote. Over the next several decades, the league devoted considerable energy to advancing the welfare of women and children.

EASTERN PROVINCE. Created in 1963 as a new administrative entity by taking districts from the former Central, Southern, and Northern Frontier Provinces. With provincial headquarters at Embu [q.v.], Eastern Province consisted of Embu, Isiolo, Kitui, Machakos, Marsabit, and Meru Districts (159,891 square kilometers; 61,734 square miles).

ECONOMIC COMMISSION (1919). In March 1917, Governor Sir Henry Belfield [q.v.] appointed the East Africa Protectorate Economic Commission to make recommendations for a postwar "commercial and industrial policy." In March 1919, the commission issued its report, which reflected the pro-settler views of members Ewart Grogan and Lord Delamere [qq.v.]. The commission criticized the colonial government for trying to foster African agricultural production and made numerous disparaging comments about the colony's African and Asian communities. As a result, the Colonial Office refused to accept the report.

ECONOMY. Kenya has the strongest economy in East Africa. However, its relations with the international donor community are becoming increasingly strained due to mismanagement, corruption, and the slow pace of democratic reforms. Nevertheless, much of the country's recent economic performance has been fairly positive. Kenya's gross domestic product (GDP) increased by 2.3 percent in 1997, compared to 4.6 percent in 1996 and 4.9 percent in 1995. Adjustment efforts fostering macroeconomic stability, currency stability, and improved investment climate, together with the liberalization of the economy, helped the GDP. The Kenyan government implemented several macroeconomic liberalization initiatives, including price decontrol, removal of import licensing and decontrol of exchange control mechanisms, freeing the movement of maize and other cereals, and the liberalization of the petroleum sector.

Agriculture [q.v.] and ranching are the mainstays of Kenya's economy, contributing approximately one-third of the GDP and about 20 percent of wage employment in the formal sector. Chief agricultural crops include tea, coffee, horticultural products, pyrethrum [qq.v.], pineapples, sisal [q.v.], tobacco, and cotton. Food crops for domestic consumption include maize, beans, cane sugar, wheat, rice, bananas, cassava, potatoes, sorghum, and millet. Livestock and dairy production are important for domestic and export markets. Industrially, Kenya is the most developed country in East Africa. However, manufacturing accounts for only about 12 percent of GDP. Kenya's main industries include food and beverages processing and the manufacture of petroleum products, textiles and fibers, garments, tobacco, processed fruits, cement, paper, pyrethrum products, engineering products, wood products, pharmaceuticals, basic chemicals, sugar, rubber, and plastics. Mining in Kenya accounts for only about 0.3 percent of GDP. Minerals production is limited largely to soda ash, fluorspar, salt, limestone products, and semi-precious stones.

In early 1996, employment outside rural small-scale agriculture and pastoralist activities increased to 3.99 million persons as a result of an additional 503,000 jobs being created. Employment in the formal sector accounted for 58.4 percent of total persons engaged in 1995, and modern sector employment expanded by 3.4 percent to 1.6 million persons. The additional jobs created in the modern sector of the economy were almost exclusively in the private sector, occasioned by the continued economic recovery in 1995. The greatest expansion in employment occurred in the informal sector, where an additional 448,100 jobs were created in 1995. As a result of the public sector reform program, public sector employment continued to decline with the downsizing of the civil service and the government's divestiture of nonstrategic parastatals.

Kenya's primary exports include coffee, horticultural products, and tea. Other important exports are beer, hides and skins, pineapples, and pyrethrum. Tanzania and Uganda represent the leading markets for Kenyan goods. Other important export markets include the nations of the European Union, with Great Britain and Germany leading the way. Kenya's chief imports include crude petroleum, industrial and electrical machinery, iron and steel, refined petroleum products, and motor vehicles and chassis. The country's main trading partners in the import sector include Germany, Great Britain, Japan, and the United Arab Emirates. Since 1990, Kenya's total external debt has been stable at about $7 billion. Among the factors that account for this situation are an increase in the concessional elements in long-term loans, donor reluctance to provide new credits, and the Kenyan government's ability to maintain a high level of debt service payments.

Kenya's eighth Development Plan (1997–2001) differs from previous plans in that its purpose is to foster an enabling environment for the private sector and to deemphasize the government's role in encouraging and sustaining growth. The country's targeted average annual economic growth rate is 5.9 percent, which entails annual investment equivalent to more than 25 percent of GDP. To achieve such growth, the Kenyan government pledged to curb corruption, enhance revenue collection, reform the civil service and the tax system, and increase market liberalization. Kenya's ability to attain these goals depends on maintaining good relations with the International Monetary Fund (IMF) and the World Bank [qq.v.].

Throughout the early 1990s, Kenya received considerable amounts of development aid. However, in the late 1990s, it has become increasingly difficult for Kenya to maintain a steady flow of such assistance because of its poor relations with the IMF. In September 1995, for example, the IMF withheld a $216 million Enhanced Structural Adjustment Facility (ESAF) pending action by the Kenyan government to reduce corruption. In April 1996, the IMF released the $216 million but postponed the second tranche of $37 million scheduled for release in November 1996 because of concerns about the slow pace of privatization and reform. In July and again in August 1997, the IMF suspended disbursement of the second and third tranches of the ESAF because of Kenya's poor performance in curbing corruption. *See also* AGRICULTURE; INTERNATIONAL MONETARY FUND; KENYA AIRWAYS; WORLD BANK.

EDUCATION, COLONIAL. Protestant and Catholic missionaries laid the foundation for modern European education in Kenya. In the mid-1800s, missionaries established a presence along the coast. Construction of the Uganda Railway [q.v.] enabled them to move inland, where by 1910 they had established a network of 35 mission schools. In 1911, the colonial government opened an education department to coordinate all education activities in the colony, provide financial aid where needed, and operate government schools in areas where there were inadequate religious and private facilities. Prior to World War I, the authorities instituted separate educational systems for African, Arab, Asian [q.v.], and European students.

In the mid-1930s the colonial government accepted the creation of the Kikuyu Karing'a (Pure) Education Association (1933) and the Kikuyu

Independent Schools Association (1934) to satisfy growing African demands for greater educational opportunities. By 1937, there were more than 7,200 students who attended some 54 independent schools. Nevertheless, until 1945, the colonial government believed that African education should be limited to vocational training and should encourage students to remain farmers. Much of the European settler community supported this policy in the belief that it would guarantee a relatively docile supply of laborers.

After World War II [q.v.], the network of independent schools gradually expanded to about 300 in the early 1950s. Many government officials and European settlers believed the independent schools were subversive because they encouraged anticolonial views among their students. As a result, the colonial government closed all independent schools after the outbreak of the Mau Mau Revolt [q.v.]. With the approach of independence, African educational institutions expanded, and many students received traditional academic training in preparation for assumption of government powers. In 1963, the separate schools for African, Arab, Asian, and European students joined to form one uniform system for all Kenyans. *See also* ALLIANCE HIGH SCHOOL; BEECHER COMMISSION; EDUCATION COMMISSION; FRAZER COMMISSION; PHELPS STOKES COMMISSION.

EDUCATION COMMISSION (1919). This commission recommended that the colonial government increase grants-in-aid to schools operated by missionary groups and other voluntary agencies on nonracial grounds. Additionally, the commission urged missionary groups and the colonial government to cooperate to achieve their common educational goals. Lastly, the commission rejected African demands for access to higher level education on the grounds that this would facilitate a rural-urban exodus by African youth in search of jobs. *See also* EDUCATION, COLONIAL.

EDUCATION, PRIMARY. After independence, primary school enrollment increased from about 890,000 in 1963 to more than 1.8 million in 1973, despite the fact that education was not compulsory and parents had to pay school fees. In 1974, the Kenyan government abolished fees for the first four standards, which further increased enrollment to more than 2.7 million. Today, primary education involves eight years of schooling, which begins at age six. In 1997, there were 17,080 primary schools. Total enrollment reached more than 5.6 million in 1997. Nevertheless, primary school gross enrollment declined from 95 percent of school age children in 1989 to 79 percent in 1995. About 47 percent of pupils who took the primary school examination gained access to secondary schools in 1995. *See also* EDUCATION, SECONDARY.

EDUCATION, SECONDARY. Since independence, Kenya has maintained a nationwide network of government-funded, *Harambee* [q.v.], and private secondary schools. The first category includes national, provincial, and district secondary schools, all of which receive funding from the Ministry of Education. National secondary schools are highly competitive and only admit the brightest students who have established their academic competence on the basis of the Kenya Certificate of Primary Education. Provincial and district secondary schools normally enroll students from the region in which they are located.

Locally established and maintained *Harambee* schools constitute another category of public educational institutions. The Ministry of Education registers these schools but has little say in their day-to-day administration. These institutions usually have a few untrained teachers and generally admit any student who can pay the school fees. Most *Harambee* secondary schools receive government funds to pay a percentage of teacher salaries, and most aim to become completely state supported. Private secondary schools usually are operated on a commercial basis by private individuals or organizations. Admission policies in private secondary schools are based on the student's ability to pay the school fees rather than an individual's academic capabilities.

According to the Kenyan government's 1989–93 development plan, there were 2,485 secondary schools (635 government maintained; 1,497 *Harambee*; and 353 private) in the country. By 1997, there were 3,028 secondary institutions, which enrolled more than 687,000 students. In 1995 27 percent of the secondary school–age population was actually enrolled in high schools. Enrollment patterns indicated a predominance of male students (52.9 percent in 1997). Most observers believe that economic and cultural factors explain this disparity. Many Kenyan parents lack the resources to educate all their children, and many send only male children to secondary school, believing this is a better investment for the future. This attitude is supported by marriage customs that require the bride to join her husband's family, which means that any benefits from her education would not accrue to her biological family.

At independence, Kenyan secondary education followed the British system in providing a four-year course of study leading to the ordinary-level school certificate examination. Those achieving the best results were able to continue to the advanced level, an additional two-year secondary course. Those most successful in the higher school certificate examination gained entrance to Kenya's public universities. With the adoption of the 8-4-4 educational system in the 1980s, officials eliminated the two-year advanced level course. From 1989, all secondary school students undertook a four-year course of study. *See also* OMINDE COMMISSION.

EDUCATION, UNIVERSITY. The history of higher education in Kenya began in 1939, with the opening of Egerton College (later renamed Egerton University [q.v.]). The next significant event occurred in 1956, when the country's Asian [q.v.] community financed the establishment of the Royal Technical College of East Africa (later renamed University of Nairobi [q.v.]). Since then, Kenya has become one of eastern Africa's more important centers of higher education. By 1998, there were five public universities, 12 private universities and colleges, 20 technical institutes, and 28 teacher training colleges. A few of the public universities, most notably the University of Nairobi, have a long tradition of postindependence antigovernment political activity. Normally, during periods of intense dissident activity, the authorities have closed the offending institution and jailed or detained troublesome students or faculty members. During the late 1980s and early 1990s, university personnel became particularly active in the pro-democracy movement. *See also* EGERTON UNIVERSITY; JOMO KENYATTA UNIVERSITY OF AGRICULTURE AND TECHNOLOGY; KENYATTA UNIVERSITY; MOI UNIVERSITY; UNIVERSITY OF NAIROBI.

EGERTON UNIVERSITY. Founded in 1939 as Egerton College. After becoming a constituent college of the University of Nairobi [q.v.], officials renamed the institution Egerton University in 1986. In the late 1990s, the university, which is located in Nakuru [q.v.], had a faculty of some 800 and a student population of about 8,000. Some of the course offerings included agriculture and food marketing, animal health, dairy technology, engineering, farm management, food science and technology, forestry [q.v.], home economics, horticulture [q.v.], range management, and wildlife conservation and management. *See also* EDUCATION, UNIVERSITY.

ELDORET. (Altitude of 2,100 meters; 6,890 feet). This town, originally known as Farm 64, is on the Uasin Gishu Plateau, where wheat, maize, and most of Kenya's wattle is grown. Following the Boer War (1899–

1902), a group of Afrikaners settled in this area. In 1912, J. C. Shaw, a settler, opened a Standard Bank of South Africa branch office, thereby establishing the town of Eldoret. The town became a center for European farmers on the Uasin Gishu Plateau, but during the colonial period, social division (e.g. separate schools) characterized the relationship between the Afrikaans- and English-speaking communities.

Under President Daniel arap Moi [q.v.], Eldoret—whose major industries include grain and dairy processing, a wattle bark extract plant, and, since independence, textile manufacturing—has prospered. Apart from Moi University [q.v.], Eldoret has a modern inland container depot and a $62 million international airport, which remained inoperative until early 1998. Many Kenyans believed that these projects reflected government favoritism toward the strong Kalenjin [q.v.] influence in Eldoret. According to the 1989 census, Eldoret had a population of 111,882; the current estimated population is more than 280,000.

ELECTORS, UNION. In February 1944, the European settler community formed the Electors' Union to replace the moribund Convention of Associations [q.v.]. This organization supported the notion that the colonial government and the European settler community should be cotrustees for the country's African population. Also, the Electors' Union opposed the proposals for Closer Union embodied in *Colonial 191* [qq.v.], which forced the colonial government and the Colonial Office to modify the plan to make it acceptable to European political opinion. In October 1949, the Electors' Union published its *Kenya Plan*, which called for the permanency of European settlement and the maintenance of settler leadership. Other Electors' Union policy statements included *Outline of Policy* (January 1946) and the *Settlers Plan for Kenya* (September 1953)—both of which argued that political power should remain in European hands and rejected the notion that Africans or Asians [q.v.] possessed the ability to elect their own representatives and govern themselves. Its uncompromising stand in favor of European domination drew strong opposition from Africans, as it advocated continued European supremacy in Kenyan politics. In the 1950s, the Electors' Union called for a strong stand against the Mau Mau Revolt [q.v.]. By the mid-1950s, the Federal Independence Party [q.v.] and the United Country Party [q.v.] had replaced the Electors' Union.

ELEMI TRIANGLE. A 3,458-square kilometer (1,335 square miles) parcel of land along the Kenyan-Ugandan-Sudanese border that supposedly is rich in gold and hydro-carbons. Since independence, Kenya has administered this region, which includes Lotikipi, Kaiemothia, Nawakaiye, Kokuro, and the Lokwanamoru range. However, in February 1989, Khartoum declared that the Elemi Triangle was Sudanese territory. As expected, Nairobi rejected this claim and refused to discuss the issue with Khartoum. This confrontation was the latest episode in a complex problem that began in 1938, when the British colonial government transferred administration of the Elemi Triangle to Kenya for geographical reasons. According to the current Sudanese government, the only legal borderline is one known as the 1914 "Uganda Line," which incorporated most of Kenya's present northwestern region. In 1926, the British transferred Uganda's then Rudolf Province to Kenya, which annexed it to Turkana District. Subsequently, the colonial authorities added a further 6,233 square kilometers (2,407 square miles), known as the Sudan Defence Force Patrol Line, or Yellow Line, to Kenya. In April 1996, MP Paul Muite [q.v.] indicated that Kenya would go to the International Court of Justice if there were another dispute over the Elemi Triangle. Some observers also claimed that the Kenya-Sudan Border Commission, which was created in 1977, might help to end this territorial dispute. However, by 1997, neither country had taken steps to resolve this problem.

ELGIN PLEDGE. In reality, two Colonial Office (CO) "pledges" during the Earl of Elgin's tenure as secretary of state (1905–08). These pledges approved the creation of the White Highlands [q.v.] as an area where land could be held by Europeans only. The 1906 pledge reserved highlands between Kiu and Fort Ternan on the Uganda Railway [q.v.] for European settlement "in view of the comparatively limited area of the Protectorate suitable for European colonisation." The March 1908 pledge stated that while the British government was not prepared to impose legal restrictions on Indian land ownership in the White Highlands, "as a matter of administrative convenience" grants in the highlands should not be made to Indians. In both cases, the policy was the work of the CO, rather than Lord Elgin personally. Thereafter, European settlers believed that these policy statements authorized them to establish exclusive control over the highlands. Initially, the British government was reluctant to admit that the Elgin pledge granted European control of the highlands. However, the growing political influence of the European settler community persuaded London to accept the fact that it had to maintain the highlands for whites only.

ELIOT, SIR CHARLES NORTON EDGECOMBE (1862–1931). Commissioner of Kenya (1900–04). Born in Oxfordshire and educated at

Cheltenham College and Balliol College, Oxford. In 1887, Eliot, a brilliant scholar, entered the diplomatic service. He held posts in Morocco, Turkey, Bulgaria, the United States, and Samoa before being named Commissioner for the East Africa Protectorate (EAP) [q.v.] in 1900. During his tenure, Eliot's accomplishments included the opening of the Uganda Railway [q.v.], extending British administration throughout much of the EAP, and incorporating Uganda's Eastern Province into the EAP. Most importantly, Eliot sought to reduce British government subsidies to the EAP by encouraging European settlement. Land grants to European settlers came at the expense of the Kikuyu and later the Maasai (qq.v.). Faced with Foreign Office criticism of his land policies and his disregard for African rights and land needs, Eliot "resigned" as commissioner in 1904. His encouragement of European settlement and alienation of African land for that purpose had a great impact on Kenya's colonial history.

After leaving the EAP, Eliot ventured into academic life, serving as vice chancellor of the Universities of Sheffield (1905–11) and Hong Kong (1912). His final post in public life was as British ambassador to Japan (1920–26). In 1905, Eliot published *The East Africa Protectorate*. He died on 16 March 1931.

EMBU. (Altitude of 1,372 meters; 4,501 feet). Originally the headquarters of Embu District, Embu became the capital of Eastern Province [q.v.] when it was created in 1963. Besides serving as an administrative center, Embu is a hub for the processing of agricultural commodities (e.g., tobacco and coffee [q.v.]) produced in the surrounding district.

EMBU. People belonging to the Thagicu group of Bantu-speakers [q.v.] who today inhabit the Mount Kenya [q.v.] region of central Kenya (1989 census: 256,623). Their language and social organization is similar to that of the Kikuyu and Meru [qq.v.] and especially to their present-day neighbors, the Mbeere [q.v.]. Starting in the 15th century, the Embu began migrating from the present-day north Meru area to the south and east around Mount Kenya; in the 17th and 18th centuries, they reached their present location along the southern and southeastern slopes of Mount Kenya. In this region, the Embu developed a way of life based on intensive cultivation of grain crops, vegetables, and bananas. The Embu were one of the last of the Thagicu-speakers to come under British rule, following a violent conquest in 1906. The Embu lost no extensive land to European settlement and soon became a part of the colonial economy as producers of commodities. From the 1930s, Embu peasants became increasingly involved in the production of cash crops, notably coffee [q.v.] and to-bacco. Despite the relative prosperity that this produced, many Embu joined with Kikuyu rebels in taking up arms against the colonial gov-ernment during the Mau Mau Revolt [q.v.]. From the 1950s, the Embu have played an important role in Kenya's agricultural economy through the production of high-value cash crops. However, Embu influence on the national political scene has not been very substantial as they histori-cally have had fewer parliamentary seats than the Gusii [q.v.] or Meru.

EMERY, JAMES BAKER (1791–1889). British naval officer and second governor of Owen's Protectorate (1824–26) [q.v.]. Born in Portsmouth. In 1808, Emery entered the British navy and subsequently served in France, Holland, the West Indies, North America, and South Africa. On 28 August 1824, he assumed command of Owen's Protectorate. During his governorship, Emery ensured that the protectorate paid its way largely through the collection of customs duties. He also maintained correct re-lations with the Omani governors of Zanzibar [q.v.], Pemba, and Lamu [q.v.]. On 25 July 1826, Emery's superior officer, Captain Charles Dyke Arland, terminated Owen's Protectorate because the small garrison could no longer protect Mombasa [q.v.] against a growing Arab threat. Four days later, Emery and his troops left Mombasa on H. M. S. *Helicon* bound for the Seychelles and Mauritius. Upon arrival on the latter island, Em-ery applied for and received extended leave on medical grounds, thus ending his East African career. He died on 16 June 1889.

ERSKINE, GENERAL SIR GEORGE (1899–1965). Commander in Chief East Africa (1953–55). Born in England and educated at Charterhouse and the Royal Military College, Sandhurst. In 1918, he was commissioned in the 60th Rifles and served for a brief time on the west-ern front. Between the two world wars, he served with his regiment, held several staff appointments in India, and attended Staff College, Camberly. During World War II [q.v.], he commanded the Seventh Armoured Di-vision, also known as the Desert Rats, in the North African campaign. From January 1949 to April 1952, he was commander of British forces in Egypt.

In June 1953, Erskine arrived in Kenya to direct operations against the Mau Mau Revolt [q.v.]. He immediately implemented an active military strategy designed to release army units from police [q.v.] duties and to use them in offensive operations in forest and mountain areas in conjunc-tion with Royal Air Force bombing campaigns. In April 1954, Erskine launched Operation Anvil to clear Nairobi [qq.v.] of Mau Mau adherents.

Under his command, the colony's security forces eventually numbered 11 battalions, more than 20,000 police, and about 25,000 Kikuyu Home Guards [q.v.]. Erskine, a blunt, plain-speaking military officer, often clashed with the governor, Sir Evelyn Baring [q.v.], and members of the European settler community. By the time he handed over his command to General Sir Gerald Lathbury [q.v.] in May 1955, Erskine had succeeded in breaking the back of the Mau Mau Revolt. After leaving Kenya, he served as commander in chief Southern Command (1955–58). He died on 29 August 1965.

EXECUTIVE COUNCIL. The Executive Council was created in 1907 at the same time as the Legislative Council [q.v.]. The body consisted of the governor, who served as its presiding officer, and a group of ex-officio members. For most of the colonial period, that included the colonial secretary, attorney general, treasurer, chief native commissioner, and principal medical officer. As a result of pressure from European settlers and the colonial government at the end of World War I [q.v.], unofficial members were appointed to the Executive Council from 1919. The council's main responsibility was to advise the governor as to policy. With the movement toward ministerial government after World War II [q.v.], the role and importance of the Executive Council was greatly reduced.

-F-

FEBRUARY 18TH RESISTANCE MOVEMENT/ARMY. In 1994, the February 18th Movement/Army, under the command of Brigadier John Odongo, emerged and announced that it wanted to launch a guerrilla war to overthrow President Daniel arap Moi's [q.v.] government. Kenyan officials blamed crimes in the Bungoma and Mount Elgon regions during the first half of 1995 on the February 18th Resistance Movement/Army. Supposedly, Odongo's followers operated from bases in eastern Uganda, which strained relations between the two countries, especially after Ugandan President Yoweri Museveni admitted that he knew Odongo. Eventually, Odongo went into exile in Ghana.

FEDERAL INDEPENDENCE PARTY. Formed in 1954 as a European political party partly as a response to the Lyttelton Constitution [q.v.] and the formation of the United Country Party [q.v.]. The party advocated European supremacy, which was to be maintained by the creation of a federal system of virtually independent provinces with full autonomy. The scheme bore considerable resemblance to South Africa's apartheid system, and the party was soon criticized for its stand. Also damaging for the provincial autonomy ideal was the fact that there was no potential European-controlled province that would not have had a majority of African inhabitants. The party put forward candidates for the September 1957 European elections, but it was overwhelmingly defeated as not a single seat was won. Hereafter, the party was largely moribund, and, in August 1959, its leaders and supporters joined the newly formed United Party [q.v.].

FIRST WORLD WAR. *See* WORLD WAR I.

FORESTRY. Kenya produces hardwoods and softwoods. The major hardwoods include camphor, muiri, mukeo, musaise, and musheragi. The chief softwoods are cedar, cypress, and podo. Wattle, which is grown by African households and on plantations, provides the base of a lucrative industry. Kenya has some 2,320,000 hectares (5,730,000 acres) in indigenous forests, mangroves, and forest plantations, representing some 4 percent of the country's total land area. In 1994, the total forest and woodland coverage was approximately 29.5 percent. In 1995, Kenyans cut about 41.7 million cubic meters of roundwood, 95 percent of which was used as fuel. *See also* GREEN BELT MOVEMENT.

FORT JESUS. Former Portuguese military installation located in Mombasa [q.v.]. For more than a century (1591–1698), Fort Jesus was Lisbon's most important military installation in East Africa, a vital link in the Portugal to India trading network. Its history began on 15 January 1591, when the king of Portugal approved construction of a fort in Mombasa. This facility was to be a bastion strong enough to dominate the East African coast and to guarantee Portugal's interests in the region in the face of long-standing hostility from Mombasa's inhabitants. In 1593, Joao Batista Cairato, chief engineer of the government of India (i.e., Portuguese India), started construction of Fort Jesus. Scores, if not hundreds, of Indian masons, quarrymen, and carpenters from Goa worked on this project. To finance the fort's construction and upkeep, the Portuguese government issued an order on 20 February 1596 that levied a six percent tax on all goods imported into Mombasa.

The strategic importance of Fort Jesus attracted the attention of the sultan of Oman, who hoped to expel the Portuguese from East Africa. To achieve this goal, he launched one of the longest sieges (33 months) in the history of warfare. On 12–13 December 1698, Omani forces finally captured Fort Jesus, ending Portuguese power between the Red Sea and the Zambezi River. Losses among the defenders from fighting and disease were about 6,500, including approximately 1,000 Portuguese and 2,500 Swahilis; the rest were noncombatants. There is no record of Omani losses.

The Omanis soon lost direct control over Fort Jesus, though an Omani Arab family, the Mazrui, gained ascendency in Mombasa affairs. Sultan Seyyid Said of Oman undertook a lengthy campaign to gain control of Fort Jesus after 1820. After several unsuccessful attempts, Said gained control of the fort in 1837. Between 1837 and 1895, Said, now ruling the East African coast from Zanzibar [q.v.], and his successors as sultan housed troops in Fort Jesus. During the 1895–1950 period, the British colonial government used the fort as a prison. In May 1958, the Gulbenkian Foundation made a £30,000 grant to restore Fort Jesus as a historical monument. On 24 October 1958, the colonial government declared the fort a national park [q.v.]. In January 1961, the authorities placed Fort Jesus under the custody of the Museum Trustees of Kenya. Since then, numerous archaeological teams have worked on Fort Jesus. The installation has also become one of the most popular tourist destinations on the Kenyan coast.

FORUM FOR THE RESTORATION OF DEMOCRACY (FORD). Opposition political party whose history began in February 1991, when Oginga Odinga [q.v.] announced the establishment of the National Democratic Party (NDEM) [q.v.]. However, the Kenyan government refused to register the NDEM. In July 1991, the Nairobi [q.v.] High Court dismissed Odinga's appeal to reverse this decision, claiming that the constitution recognized the Kenya African National Union [q.v.] as the country's sole political party. The following month, Odinga and several of his associates, including Masinde Muliro [q.v.], Martin Shikuku [q.v.], George Nthenge, Philip Gachoka, and Ahmed Bamahriz, created FORD as a pressure group rather than a political party. Nevertheless, President Moi [q.v.] denounced FORD as an illegal organization and ordered a crackdown on the group. In mid-November 1991, the Kenyan authorities arrested several senior FORD officials, including Odinga, at a pro-democracy rally. After the abolition of the one-party state in December 1991, FORD became a political party that advocated good governance, public accountability, the rule of law, and social justice.

Against a background of growing civil unrest, Kenneth Matiba [q.v.] challenged Odinga for leadership of FORD. In October 1992, after a party congress had unanimously elected Odinga as FORD's presidential candidate, Matiba broke away and established FORD-Asili [q.v.]. Odinga's faction then named their party FORD-Kenya [q.v.]. In 1997, a new faction called FORD-People [q.v.] emerged.

FORUM FOR THE RESTORATION OF DEMOCRACY—ASILI

(FORD-ASILI). Political party that emerged from the split in the Forum for the Restoration of Democracy (FORD) [q.v.] after October 1992. Led by Kenneth Matiba [q.v.] and Martin Shikuku [q.v.], FORD-Asili (original FORD) gained the most support in the 1992 general elections [q.v.] in Central and Western Provinces [qq.v.] and in Nairobi [q.v.] but lacked backing in Coast, Eastern, North Eastern, and Nyanza Provinces [qq.v.]. The party won 29 seats in Parliament, and Matiba came second in the presidential election with 26 percent of the vote.

During the 1993–94 period, FORD-Asili lost its seats in Western Province through the defection to the Kenya African National Union [q.v.] of all non-Kikuyu MPs except Shikuku. However, the party maintained its strength in Nairobi and in Central Province. From 1994, a split in FORD-Asili emerged between Shikuku and Matiba reaching irreconcilable proportions by early 1997. Matiba refused to participate in the general elections (1997) [q.v.], and most of his supporters deserted the party leaving Shikuku as the presidential candidate. Neither Shikuku nor FORD-Asili enjoyed much success in the election; the party gained only one parliamentary seat.

FORUM FOR THE RESTORATION OF DEMOCRACY—KENYA

(FORD-K). Political party that emerged from the split in the Forum for the Restoration of Democracy (FORD) [q.v.] in October 1992. Led by Oginga Odinga, Paul Muite, and Michael Wamalwa [qq.v.] FORD-K drew its strongest support from the Luo [q.v.]-inhabited areas of Nyanza Province [q.v.]. In the 1992 general elections [q.v.], FORD-K was the only party to win a parliamentary seat in each province and Nairobi [q.v.], though Odinga finished fourth in the presidential contest with only 17.48 percent of the vote. With 31 parliamentary seats, FORD-K became the official opposition in Parliament.

Unlike FORD-Asili [q.v.], the party suffered no significant loss of MPs through defections to the Kenya African National Union [q.v.] down to the end of 1996. In September 1993, Muite resigned as first vice chairman of the party, and on Oginga Odinga's death in January 1994, Wamalwa assumed the party leadership with James Orengo [q.v.] as his deputy. Soon Raila Odinga [q.v.] challenged Wamalwa, claiming that he could better lead FORD-K. By 1996, the Wamalwa-Odinga controversy split the party in two. In late 1996, Odinga, having failed to oust Wamalwa at abortive party elections in April, resigned from FORD-K, and joined the previously little-known National Development Party [q.v.]. In January 1997, Wamalwa was given a fresh term as chairman after the party elections.

Immediately prior to the general elections (1997) [q.v.], almost all the party's Luo [q.v.] MPs resigned, most of whom subsequently joined the National Development Party [q.v.]. FORD-K performed poorly during the 1997 election [q.v.] as Wamalwa won only 8.29 percent of the vote, and the party gained 17 parliamentary seats, from Eastern, Nyanza, Rift Valley, and Western Provinces, and one nominated seat. Following the election, Wamalwa embarked on a policy of cooperation with the Moi government, but this split the party once more as several MPs failed to support the initiative.

FORUM FOR THE RESTORATION OF DEMOCRACY—PEOPLE (FORD-PEOPLE). Emerged in 1997 as an offshoot of FORD-Asili [q.v.] after Martin Shikuku [q.v.], who was secretary-general of FORD-Asili, had suspended Kenneth Matiba [q.v.]. After being elected FORD-People chairman in absentia, Kenneth Matiba announced that he would have nothing to do with the new party as he still belonged to FORD-Asili. In the general elections (1997) [q.v.], Kimani wa Nyoike stood as the FORD-People's presidential candidate but won only 0.14 percent of the vote (8,564 votes). The party won three seats in Parliament.

FRANCIS, EDWARD CAREY (1897–1966). Teacher and headmaster. Educated at William Ellis School, London, and Peterhouse, Cambridge. He served in the Royal Artillery during World War I [q.v.]. After the war, Francis lectured in mathematics at Cambridge (1922–28). In 1928, he joined the Church Missionary Society [q.v.] as an educational missionary to Kenya. Francis first served as teacher and headmaster at Maseno School in western Kenya (1928–40). He then became headmaster of Alliance High School [q.v.] (1940–62) and assistant master at Pumwani Secondary School (1962–66). A brilliant teacher, Francis influenced several generations of Kenyans who became leaders in the political, academic, and business sectors. Francis, a paternalist, did not always get along with assertive African students and teachers such as James Gichuru and Oginga Odinga [qq.v.]. He died on 27 July 1966.

FRAZER COMMISSION (1909). Based on this commission's recommendations, the colonial government established a Department of Education in 1911, with Thomas Orr as its first director. On a broader level, the commission defined the nature and scope of education for the colonial era by emphasizing concepts such as the need for racially segregated schools, an industrially based curriculum, and a grants-in-aid system for African education. *See also* EDUCATION, COLONIAL.

-G-

GACHATHI COMMISSION (1976). This commission recommended that Kenya reduce regional educational inequalities and increase the primary course from seven to nine years. In 1979, the Kenyan government created a Ministry of Basic Education to start the nine-year primary course. However, the Mackay Report's [q.v.] recommendations superseded the nine-year primary course before it was implemented.

GAME POLICY COMMITTEE. There were two Game Policy Committees, both of which played a significant role in the creation and development of Kenya's national park [q.v.] system. In 1939, the colonial government established the first committee, under Cecil Hoey's chairmanship, to devise a strategy for the establishment of some national parks. In January 1945, the Legislative Council [q.v.] approved the committee's recommendations and subsequently adopted the National Parks Ordinance. Over the next five years, this legislation enabled the colonial government to establish four national parks (Tsavo, Nairobi, Mount Kenya [q.v.], and Aberdare) and six national reserves (Marsabit, the Mara, Amboseli [q.v.], Ngong, West Chyulu, and parts of Tsavo [q.v.] that were not included in the national park). In the national parks, wildlife interests supersede all other considerations. However, in the national reserves, fauna preservation was possible only if it did not interfere with the rights and needs of the human inhabitants. The National Parks' Trustees were responsible for wildlife preservation, while the colonial government protected human interests. Conflict between the two groups made the national reserve experiment unworkable. The 1956 Game Policy Committee persuaded the colonial government to abolish all national reserves. The Game Department then assumed responsibility for the administration and protection of wildlife in these areas. *See also* NATIONAL PARKS.

GEDI. Sometime in the 1200s, an unknown people established Gedi, which may also have been called Quelman, south of Malindi [q.v.] on the Kenyan coast. At its peak, the town was home to about 2,500 inhabitants. In the early 1500s, the inhabitants abandoned the town probably because of political instability along the coast. In the late 1500s, Gedi was reoccupied, most likely by Somalis. However, during the 1625–50 period, the inhabitants again fled the town, presumably as a result of renewed unrest in the area. For the next several centuries, Gedi was nearly forgotten.

In the 1920s, people started to visit the town's ruins. In 1948, the colonial government declared Gedi a national park [q.v.] and appointed James Kirkman, an archaeologist, to excavate and restore Gedi. Eventually, Kirkman determined that the town's walls enclosed approximately 18 hectares (45 acres). In this area there was a palace, several mosques, 14 large houses, three pillar tombs, a market, and many wells. Today, Gedi is a popular tourist site along the Kenyan coast.

GENERAL ELECTIONS (1963). The 1963 elections were the first common roll elections in Kenya's history and the first to be characterized by universal suffrage. They were the last to be organized in colonial Kenya. Held under the *majimbo* [q.v.] constitution, worked out after the second Lancaster House Conference (1962) [q.v.], the 1963 elections involved polls for the Regional Assemblies, the Senate, and the House of Representatives. The main political parties that participated in the election were the Kenya African National Union (KANU), the Kenya African Democratic Union (KADU), and the African People's Party (APP) [qq.v.]. In the Regional Assembly elections, KANU won control of the Central, Nyanza, and Eastern regions while KADU won the majority of seats in the Coast, Rift Valley [q.v.] and Western Regional Assemblies. Because of a Somali boycott, no elections were held in North Eastern region. In the Senate election, KANU won 19 seats, KADU 16, and APP two. In the House of Representatives, KANU took 66 seats, KADU 31, and APP eight. KANU's victory in the House and Senate elections led Governor Malcolm MacDonald to name Jomo Kenyatta [qq.v.] prime minister and ask him to form a government that would lead Kenya to internal self-government and eventual independence.

GENERAL ELECTIONS (1969). The December 1969 elections occurred after the assassination of Tom Mboya [q.v.] earlier in the year and the banning of the Kenya People's Union [q.v.] and detention of its leaders. Although the previous general election had been held more than five years earlier, the constitution [q.v.] had been amended in late 1966 to allow for the extension of the life of the Parliament; at the same time it became a single chamber. Thus, in 1969 there was a single election for parliamentary seats. More than 700 candidates stood for election, and the outcome set a trend that would continue in subsequent general elections as voters swept out incumbents. Almost half the sitting MPs lost their seats, including five cabinet ministers and 14 assistant ministers. Among the casualties were the Samuel Ayodo and Lawrence Sagini [qq.v.]. Those winning election for the first time, who would have a considerable part in national affairs in the future, included Dr. Zachary Onyonka [q.v.], who defeated Sagini; Elijah Wasike Mwangale [q.v.]; and William Omamo, who took Oginga Odinga's [q.v.] former seat. By winning the Kisumu town seat, Grace Onyango became the first woman to be elected to Parliament.

GENERAL ELECTIONS (1974). As in 1969, the October 1974 parliamentary election produced a huge turnover in MPs with 88 out of 158 defeated. Four ministers lost their seats as did 13 assistant ministers. The most prominent casualty was Dr. Njoroge Mungai [q.v.], the minister for foreign affairs. Other ministers who fell included Eluid Ngala Mwendwa and William Omamo, but former ministers Samuel Ayodo [q.v.] and J. G. Odero-Jowi regained the seats they had lost in 1969. The election also brought some newcomers to Parliament, including George Anyona [q.v.], whose stance on many issues did not endear them to the political establishment in the last years of Jomo Kenyatta's [q.v.] rule.

GENERAL ELECTIONS (1979). The 1979 general election was the first to be called by President Daniel arap Moi [q.v.]. Seventy-two MPs lost their seats, and seven ministers were retired by voters, the highest number at any election in Kenya to that point. Among the casualties were such prominent politicians as Dr. J. G. Kiano, Mbiyu Koinange, and Taaita Toweett [qq.v.], as well as non-ministers Masinde Muliro and John Marie Seroney [qq.v.] and all but one of the new slate of Kenya African National Union (KANU) [q.v.] national officers installed the previous year. Among the newcomers to be returned for the first time were Koigi wa Wamwere and Michael Wamalwa [qq.v.]. For the first time since independence, a European, Philip Leakey, and an Asian [q.v.], S. K. Gautama, won seats in Nairobi [q.v.].

GENERAL ELECTIONS (1983). In 1983, President Daniel arap Moi [q.v.] called an early general election to obtain a more productive and trusted Parliament in the wake of the coup attempt (1982) [q.v.] and the fall of Charles Njonjo [q.v.]. In what some called the Nyayo Election, voters threw out five ministers, including Munyua Waiyaki [q.v.], Joseph Kamotho, and Godfrey Kariuki [q.v.]. The electorate also rejected most politicians associated with Njonjo. Njoroge Mungai [q.v.], back in Parliament as a result of the 1979 election, also lost his seat on this occasion.

GENERAL ELECTIONS (1988). First and only election to be held under the queuing system adopted by the Kenya African National Union (KANU) [q.v.]. Any candidate obtaining 70 percent or more of the vote at the queue stage was declared elected unopposed. If a single candidate did not obtain that percentage, the top two vote-getters advanced to a secret ballot election. By most accounts, the 1988 elections were marked by massive rigging of the results. A notable winner at the first stage, after what he viewed as attempted manipulation, was Vice President Mwai Kibaki [q.v.]. Though he received 99.8 percent of the vote, he lost his high office after the election.

GENERAL ELECTIONS (1992). The December 1992 elections were the first in Kenya's history for the office of president (previously, Presidents Kenyatta and Moi [qq.v.] had been returned unopposed) and the first multiparty general election since 1963. The major parties vying for parliamentary seats were the Democratic Party (DP) [q.v.], the Forum for the Restoration of Democracy–Asili (Ford-Asili) [q.v.], FORD-Kenya (FORD-K) [q.v.], and the Kenya African National Union (KANU) [q.v.], while the contenders for the presidency included President Daniel arap Moi, Mwai Kibaki [q.v.] for the DP, Kenneth Matiba [q.v.] for FORD-Asili, and Oginga Odinga [q.v.] for FORD-K. Moi won the presidential poll with 36.4 percent of the vote (1,820,872 votes against a combined opposition total of 3,439,967) and the constitutionally mandated 25 percent in five of the eight regions. Kenneth Matiba came second in the vote (1,404,266), with Mwai Kibaki third (1,050,617) and Oginga Odinga fourth (944,197). KANU gained 93 of the 188 seats in Parliament; FORD-K won 31 seats to emerge as the official opposition in the new Parliament. The elections were not without controversy though they were monitored by numerous foreign groups. Most significant was the Commonwealth Observers Group, which found many irregularities had marred the poll and that control of the media had given KANU a huge advantage.

GENERAL ELECTIONS (1997). The December 1997 elections featured 15 presidential candidates and more than twice as many parties as the 1992 general elections [q.v.]. The Kenyan government added 22 constituencies for the parliamentary election, bringing the total number of members to 210. Some of the more powerful rivals to the incumbent, President Daniel arap Moi [q.v.], included Mwai Kibaki of the Democratic

Party (DP) [qq.v.], Raila Odinga of the National Development Party (NDP) [qq.v.], Charity Ngilu of the Social Democratic Party (SDP) [qq.v.], Martin Shikuku of the Forum for the Restoration of Democracy–Asili (FORD-Asili) [qq.v.], and Michael Wamalwa of FORD-Kenya (FORD-K) [qq.v.]. Other candidates included George Anyona of the Kenya Social Congress [qq.v], Katama Mkangi of the Kenya National Congress [q.v.], Koigi wa Wamwere [q.v.] of the Kenya National Democratic Alliance [q.v.], Kimani wa Nyoike of the FORD-People [q.v.], Wangari Maathai [q.v.] of the Liberal Party of Kenya, Munyua Waiyaki [q.v.] of the United Patriotic Party of Kenya, and Stephen Omondi Oludhe of the Economic Independence Party. SAFINA [q.v.] refrained from nominating a candidate because it maintained that there were too many opposition presidential candidates.

Voting, originally set for 29 December, was extended for a day since confusion and mismanagement, including late or non-opening polling stations and insufficient ballots, characterized the initial day's voting. Despite these and other difficulties, Kenyan electoral observers declared that the election's outcome reflected the wishes of the voters. In the presidential vote Moi outdistanced his four main rivals, gaining 40.12 percent of the vote (2,445,801 votes) and at least 25 percent of the vote in five provinces. Kibaki was the runner-up, with 31.09 percent of the vote (1,895,527 votes). He was followed by Odinga, with 10.92 percent of the vote (665,725 votes); Wamalwa, with 8.29 percent of the vote (505,542 votes); and Ngilu, with 7.71 percent of the vote (469,807 votes). In the parliamentary elections, the Kenya African National Union (KANU) [q.v.] won 107 seats with an additional six nominated. The opposition won 103 seats (DP, 39, plus two nominated; NDP, 21, plus one nominated; FORD-K, 17, plus one nominated; SDP, 15, plus one nominated; SAFINA, 5, plus one nominated; FORD-People, 3; FORD-Asili, 1; Shirikisho-1, and KSC, 1).

GENERAL SERVICES UNIT (GSU). Historically, this unit has comprised transient officers seconded from the police [q.v.] after training at the Police Training College, Kigano. These recruits received paramilitary training at the GSU school at Embakasi. Eventually, these officers are reabsorbed back into the police. The GSU has a controversial history. After the 1964 army mutiny [q.v.], Prime Minister Jomo Kenyatta [q.v.] started to build up GSU as a counter-balance to the army. After the coup attempt (1982) [q.v.], President Daniel arap Moi [q.v.] also became more dependent on the GSU, which eventually gained the reputation of being the military arm of the executive branch, an allegation that continues to this day. Some of the GSU's more controversial activities occurred in the months prior to the 1992 and 1997 general elections [qq.v.], when its personnel mobilized against pro-democracy advocates and other antigovernment elements. As of 1997, there were 5,000 personnel in the GSU. *See also* ARMED FORCES; COUP ATTEMPT.

GICHURU, JAMES SAMUEL (1914–1982). Teacher and politician. Born at Thogoto in Kiambu and educated at the Church of Scotland Mission, Alliance High School, and Makerere University (1933–34) [qq.v.]. He was master at Alliance High School (1935–40), but left after a disagreement with Edward Carey Francis [q.v.]. Gichuru then became headmaster at the Church Missionary Society [q.v.] Secondary School, Kikuyu (1940–50) and served as the secretary of the Kenya Union of Teachers throughout the 1940s.

He was among the founders of the Kenya African Study Union and the Kenya African Union (KAU) [q.v.]. From 3 February 1945 until 1 June 1947, Gichuru served as president of KAU; he was succeeded by Jomo Kenyatta [q.v.]. While active in KAU affairs, he also became vice-chairman of the Kiambu Local Native/African District Council (1948-50). Between 1950 and 1952, Gichuru was chief of Dagoretti. The colonial government restricted him during the Mau Mau Revolt [q.v.] but allowed him to continue teaching. Following the first Lancaster House Conference (1960) [q.v.], Gichuru played a leading role in the formation of the Kenya African National Union (KANU) [q.v.]. When the colonial government refused to register the party with Kenyatta as president, Gichuru became the acting president until October 1961 when, as in 1947, he stepped aside to allow Kenyatta to assume party leadership.

In the party struggles, then and later, Gichuru generally aligned with the "moderates" (e.g., Tom Mboya [q.v.] and Kenyatta). In the 1961 elections, Gichuru was returned unopposed for the Kiambu seat. He joined other KANU Legislative Council [q.v.] members in refusing to participate in government following the colonial government's refusal to release Kenyatta immediately. After the second Lancaster House Conference (1962) [q.v.], Gichuru took up the portfolio of minister of finance (1962–63) in the coalition government established to pave the way for independence elections in the following year. Gichuru won the Limuru seat unopposed in the general elections (1963) [q.v.], and he continued to represent that constituency until 1982. Following these elections, he served as minister of finance (1963–69) and then minister of defence (1969–79) under Presidents Jomo Kenyatta and Daniel arap Moi [q.v.], despite the fact that he had been associated with the Change the Constitution Campaign [q.v.] that surfaced in 1976. Gichuru then became minister of state in the Office of the President (1979–82). He died on 10 August 1982.

GIKUYU, EMBU, MERU ASSOCIATION (GEMA). Founded in 1971 as a cultural and social welfare organization. During the last decade of Jomo Kenyatta's [q.v.] presidency, GEMA became the most significant of all such ethnically based organizations. From 1973, Njenga Karume [q.v.], a businessman who had helped launch Gema Holdings Ltd, led GEMA as a holding company for varied business enterprises owned by members. GEMA's political influence reached considerable heights under Kenyatta. According to some critics, it rivaled the Kenya African National Union (KANU) [q.v.] for power and influence because it enjoyed the support and confidence of many of the Kikuyu [q.v.] elite close to the president. GEMA leaders were also associated with the Change the Constitution Campaign [q.v.]. With the advent of President Daniel arap Moi [q.v.], GEMA's influence waned. In 1980, a KANU leaders' conference called for the dissolution of all ethnic organizations and for national unity. As a result, GEMA and several other bodies terminated their activities.

GIROUARD, SIR PERCY (1867–1932). Governor of Kenya (1909–12). Born in Montreal, Canada and educated at the Royal Military College, Kingston, Ontario. In 1888, Girouard entered the British army as a royal engineer. He participated in the Dongola (1895) and Nile (1897) expeditions. From 1896 to 1898, he served as director of Sudan Railways. His skill with railway development and operation led to his appointment as president of the Egyptian Railway Board (1898–99) and during and after the Boer War, director of South African Railways (1899–1902). From 1902 to 1904, he was commissioner of railways in the Transvaal and Orange River colonies, which just had been annexed by Great Britain. Girouard's African service next took him to Northern Nigeria as high commissioner and governor (1907–09).

With a reputation as a firm administrator and follower of Sir Frederick Lugard's concept of indirect rule, Girouard moved to Nairobi in 1909 to replace Sir James Hayes Sadler [q.v.] as governor. He quickly restored order and direction to the colonial government, which had suffered because of Sadler's indecisiveness. Girouard also introduced many reforms that enabled the protectorate to achieve more efficiency in administration. Additionally, he facilitated the emergence of colonial rule in the Northern Frontier District [q.v.] by implementing a "policy of observation," which established a British presence in the region without relying on large numbers of troops to pacify the local inhabitants.

Girouard proved to be one of the most pro-settler of Kenya's governors. This was exemplified by his handling of the Maasai Treaty of 1911 [q.v.] and his attempt to move the Maasai [q.v.] to a southern reserve so as to open their Laikipia Plateau homeland to European settlement. He failed to carry out the move in 1911, however, and eventually Colonial Office officials realized that he had lied to them in denying that he had made promises of land on Laikipia to European settlers. This caused Girouard's resignation in mid-July 1912, while on leave in Great Britain. After retirement, Girouard worked as director of weapons manufacturer Armstrong-Vicker and director-general of munitions supply, Ministry of Munitions (1915). He then became a private businessman and invested in cement factories in Great Britain and also in a gold-mining venture in Columbia. Girouard died on 26 September 1932.

GITHUNGURI TEACHERS' COLLEGE. On 7 January 1939, Mbiyu Koinange [q.v.] opened this independent teacher training college. However, the college soon expanded by establishing a primary school and secondary and adult education sections. After returning from Great Britain in 1946, Jomo Kenyatta [q.v.] joined the college's staff. By 1950, the college, which relied on voluntary public donations to maintain its operations, had about 1,000 students. In 1952, the colonial government closed the college because of the outbreak of the Mau Mau Revolt [q.v.].

GOSPEL MISSIONARY SOCIETY (GMS). An evangelical/revival movement that emerged in the United States in the late 19th century. In 1899, the first GMS missionaries arrived in Kenya. At its most influential, the GMS network included large stations at Kambui, Nairobi [q.v.], Ngenda, and Thembigwa; 20 outstations; and several hospitals and schools. With the death of GMS missionary leader William Porter Knapp 1940, mission activities gradually declined. In 1946, the GMS, which had some 2,000 adherents, joined the Presbyterian Church of East Africa (PCEA) [q.v.]. *See also* ALLIANCE OF PROTESTANT MISSIONS; CHURCH MISSIONARY SOCIETY; CHURCH OF SCOTLAND MISSION; NATIONAL CHRISTIAN COUNCIL OF KENYA.

GOVERNOR'S WAR COUNCIL. In September 1915, Governor Sir Henry Belfield [q.v.] created the Governor's War Council, which was composed largely of European settlers, to advise him on how to deal with World War I's [q.v.] impact on the colony, particularly with regard to the

African population. Almost immediately, the council pressured the colonial state to introduce tighter regulation of African labor and a reduction in pay for those serving in the Carrier Corps [q.v.]. Additionally, the council facilitated the adoption of numerous measures for the benefit of the European settler community, including electoral representation in the Legislative Council [q.v.]. Because African troops fought alongside European soldiers, many council members feared that respect for the white man would be lessened after the war. To prevent this from happening, the council recommended the establishment of the Soldier Settlement Scheme [q.v.].

GREEN BELT MOVEMENT (GBM). In 1977, the National Council of Women of Kenya, led by Wangari Maathai [q.v.], launched the GBM to help resolve the problems of desertification, deforestation, soil erosion, and fuelwood scarcity. To accomplish its goals, the GBM launched a tree-planting campaign called "Save the Land Harambee" and encouraged soil and water conservation in rural areas. Additionally, the GBM sought to increase public awareness of the relationship between environmental problems and issues such as unemployment, poverty, malnutrition, and political instability. GBM also approached several other eastern and southern African countries and established what supposedly will become the All-Africa Green Belt Movement Network. By the early 1990s, the GBM had established more than 1,000 nurseries at which approximately 80,000 women grew 10 million seedlings and distributed them to farmers, schools, and churches for planting throughout Kenya. *See also* FORESTRY.

GRIGG, SIR EDWARD WILLIAM MCLEAY (1879–1955). Governor of Kenya (1925–30). Educated at Winchester College and New College, Oxford. After finishing his studies, Grigg became a journalist with, among other publications, *The Times*. In 1914, he joined the army and served as military secretary to the Prince of Wales (the future Edward VIII). After World War I [q.v.], he was active in politics as a supporter of Lloyd George, serving as the latter's private secretary (1921–22) and MP for Oldham (1922–25).

In 1925, Grigg became governor of Kenya, with a charge from Secretary of State Leopold Amery to bring about a Closer Union [q.v.] of Great Britain's East African territories. He proved incapable of accomplishing this, though he curried the favor of Kenya's settlers for the project. Grigg stayed on as governor when the Labour Party took office in 1929, but his relations with Secretary of State Lord Passfield (Sidney

Webb) were not altogether harmonious. Grigg's pro-settler policies did little for Kenya's African majority as the establishment of an East African Governors' Conference was all that could be accomplished toward regional federation. Apart from his political activities, Grigg devoted considerable energy to improving architectural standards in Nairobi [q.v.], especially with regard to government buildings. To accomplish this goal, he invited Sir Herbert Baker—who had designed several government buildings in Pretoria, South Africa— to work in Kenya. Baker agreed and designed plans for Government House (now State House) in Nairobi, Government House in Mombasa [q.v.], and the Prince of Wales School (now Nairobi School).

Following his return to Great Britain, Grigg reentered politics, this time as a Conservative Party supporter of the national government. He was MP for Altrincham (1933–45), and at the start of World War II [q.v.] he held a series of junior ministerial posts such as undersecretary of state for war (1940–42). During the 1944–45 period, Grigg was British resident minister in the Middle East. After his government service, he worked as a journalist. In 1945, he was made a peer as the first Baron Altrincham. He published *Kenya's Opportunity* in 1955. He died on 1 December 1955.

GROGAN, EWART SCOTT (1873–1967). Explorer, farmer, entrepreneur, and staunch advocate of European settler rights. Born in London and educated at Winchester and Jesus College, Cambridge. In 1896, Grogan walked from Cape Town to Cairo. In late 1903, he arrived in Kenya and quickly acquired a considerable amount of land, including the Chiromo area of Nairobi [q.v.], the Kilindini region of Mombasa [q.v.] Island, and a timber concession in the Rift Valley [q.v.]. Additionally, he was a coffee and sisal [qq.v.] farmer. He also used his skills as a writer and orator to gain influence among Kenya's European settler community as an advocate of white supremacy and a critic of Colonial Office rule. Grogan repeatedly clashed with colonial officials and the British government over what he perceived to be overly liberal policies toward the African and Asian [q.v.] communities. In his view, the European settler community represented the country's economic future. As president of the Colonists' Association and then the Convention of Associations [q.v.] and the longest serving member in the Legislative Council (LEGCO) [q.v.], Grogan advocated European political supremacy in Kenya.

One of the more controversial aspects of Grogan's life in Kenya concerned the so-called "flogging incident." On 14 March 1907, he publically whipped three Kikuyu rickshaw operators, ostensibly because they had insulted two European women, one of whom was his sister. For many Africans, this episode represented all that was evil about British colonial rule. Eventually, a court sentenced Grogan to one month in prison and fined him 500 rupees (£34). However, since there was no European prison, he served his sentence in a government bungalow. Shortly after his release, Grogan and his family returned to England for several years (1907–13). In January 1910, he unsuccessfully stood for a seat in the House of Commons.

Grogan saw military service in both world wars. During World War I [q.v.], he reported to Colonel Richard Meinertzhagen, commander of British military intelligence in East Africa. Grogan served as liaison officer to the Belgian Congo (now Democratic Republic of Congo) and organized a spy network in northern German East Africa (later Tanganyika and now Tanzania). He also was responsible for stirring up settler patriotism in 1915–16 and pressuring the colonial government to advocate measures desired by the settlers such as elective representation, registration of African males, and state assistance in labor recruitment. Additionally, Grogan was an influential member of the Governor's War Council [q.v.]. After the war, he remained politically active as a member of the Bowring Committee [q.v.], an opponent of Indian demands during the height of the Indian Question [q.v.], and an advocate of currency innovations favored by many of the larger European land owners. In World War II [q.v.], Grogan was a liaison officer to Portuguese East Africa (now Angola), French West Africa (now Mali, Côte d'Ivoire, Mauritania, Niger, Senegal, Guinea, and Benin); and the Belgian Congo. He was also commanding officer of prisoner of war camps in Nairobi [q.v.] and Gilgil.

In his later years, Grogan continued to live up to his reputation as the maverick of Kenyan politics. Among other things, he resisted granting any political rights to the Asian community, opposed the Lyttelton Constitution [q.v.], and repeatedly expressed his doubts about Africans not being ready for independence. After he retired from LEGCO in October 1956, Grogan remained active in politics, largely as a critic of British government policies in Kenya. In poor health by the start of the 1960s, Grogan remained in Kenya through independence and the creation of the republic. However, he became increasingly hostile toward an African-ruled Kenya. In early 1967, Grogan left Kenya for South Africa without informing family and friends. He died in Cape Town on 16 August 1967.

GUSII. Kenya's sixth-largest ethnic group (1989 census: 1,318,409). Currently, the Bantu-speaking [q.v.] Gusii (of the Lacustrine group that includes the Luyia [q.v.] and Kuria) occupy a highlands region in southwestern Kenya. According to their traditions, the Gusii moved to that region from Mount Elgon [q.v.] via the shores of Lake Victoria [q.v.] in present-day Siaya District, the Kano Plains, the present-day Kericho District, and the Mara River region, entering the highlands in the 19th century. As they moved, the Gusii increasingly turned away from a pastoral to an agricultural economy. They were also influenced by interaction with their neighbors, particularly the Luo [q.v.], Kipsigis (a Kalenjin [q.v.] group), and Maasai [q.v.].

By the start of the 20th century, Gusii society consisted of several clans, roughly grouped together as what were later termed subtribes. Political authority was exercised at the clan level as there were no firmly institutionalized political positions or political unity. The Gusii were one of the last peoples of southern Kenya to be conquered by the British. Indeed, because of their resistance to the imposition of colonial rule, the British deployed three major military expeditions against various Gusii groups. Until World War I [q.v.], British colonialism had little impact on the Gusii largely because of their late conquest and continued resistance, which included reluctance to embrace Christianity and Western education together with a minimal involvement in the colonial economy up to 1930. From the 1940s, the economic importance of the Gusii highlands greatly increased as the region became an important producer of coffee, tea, pyrethrum (qq.v), and bananas. However, Gusii political influence at the national level remained relatively small even after independence.

-H-

HARAMBEE. The national motto of postindependence Kenya, which is an injunction for the country's population to be self-reliant and to "let us all pull together." Porters originally used the term and Omolo Ong'iro adopted the word as a political slogan in the struggle against colonial rule. Thus, *Harambee* secondary schools are those started by local cooperative self-help groups. Jomo Kenyatta [q.v.] frequently used this term after 1963 to urge all Kenyans to contribute to the country's social and economic development by building roads, schools, medical clinics, and other facilities. Another unique aspect of this concept is the system of *Harambee* fund drives. Normally, the president, leading politicians, and influential businessmen donate large sums of money to finance Harambee projects like the construction of a road, school, or hospital. In effect, such donations have been a voluntary tax upon the wealthy, many of whom receive considerable publicity for their generosity.

HARDINGE, SIR ARTHUR (1859–1933). Commissioner of Kenya (1896–1900). Educated at Eton College and Balliol College, Oxford. In 1880, Hardinge entered the foreign service and served at the Foreign Office and such diverse postings as Petrograd, Bucharest, and Constantinople. In 1891, he went to Cairo as acting consul general, and in 1894 was posted to Zanzibar [q.v.] as agent and consul general. On 1 July 1895, he proclaimed British sovereignty over the territory that became known as the East Africa Protectorate (EAP) [q.v.]. During his tenure as commissioner, Hardinge followed a cautious approach to extending British rule over the EAP, placing greatest importance on the construction of the Uganda Railway [q.v.]. He inaugurated the colonial government on a small budget, saw the railway pass through the protectorate, and established British rule at the coast, but he left much to be done by his successor. Following his stint as Great Britain's first commissioner to the EAP, Hardinge returned to diplomatic postings, serving as British minister in Iran, Belgium, and Portugal. He retired following service as ambassador to Spain (1913–19). After retiring in 1920, Hardinge published his memoirs, *A Diplomatist in the East* in 1928. He died on 27 December 1933.

HEALTH. Despite many problems, Kenya has the best health care in eastern Africa. In 1997, Kenya had 4,078 physicians (1 for 14,100 people), 927 dentists, 1,159 pharmacists, and 8,006 registered nurses. Kenya also had 398 hospitals, 566 health centers, 3,105 health subcenters/dispensaries, and 50,909 hospital beds (1.7 hospital beds per 1,000 people). During the 1990–95 period, the country's birth rate was 44.5 per 1,000 people. In 1995, there were some 1,111,000 births, with an average life expectancy of 58.5 years; infant mortality was 58 per 1,000 live births; the general mortality rate was 11.8 per 1,000 live births; and the fertility rate was 6.3 children per Kenyan woman (during childbearing years). During the 1994–97 period, the Kenyan government allocated about five percent of its Gross Domestic Product to the health care sector.

Kenya's major health problems include tuberculosis, protein deficiency, malaria, bilharzia, sleeping sickness, polio, measles, tetanus, diphtheria, pertussis, and a variety of lesser maladies related to inadequate water supplies and poor sanitation. Over the past fifteen years, Acquired Immune Deficiency Syndrome [q.v.] has become a major health care problem.

HELIGOLAND TREATY. See ANGLO-GERMAN AGREEMENT (1890).

HILTON YOUNG COMMISSION. In 1927, Secretary of State for the Colonies Leopold Amery appointed the Commission on Closer Union of the Dependencies in Eastern and Central Africa, chaired by Sir James Hilton Young. Amery wanted the commission to recommend the establishment of a Closer Union [q.v.] or a federation between Kenya, Uganda, and Tanganyika (now Tanzania). In January 1929, the commission issued its report which rejected any Closer Union. This decision reflected the influence of one its members, J. H. Oldham, and the opposition of Asians [q.v.], the Ganda of Uganda, and Governor Sir Donald Cameron of Tanganyika. So far as Kenya was concerned, the commission reiterated the 1923 Devonshire Declaration [q.v.] in favor of African paramountcy and claimed that the most the European settlers could hope for was "partnership not control."

HOBLEY, CHARLES WILLIAM (1867–1947). Colonial administrator and anthropologist. Born at Chilvers Coton in Warwickshire. Educated at King Edward VI's School, Nuneaton; Mason Science College (1882–85); and the University of Birmingham, where he studied geology. During the 1885–90 period, Hobley worked at engineering firms in Nuneaton and in Dartford. From March 1890 to September 1893, he worked as a geologist and a transport superintendent for the Imperial British East Africa Company (IBEAC) [q.v.]. In October 1894, Hobley became a first class assistant for transport in the Uganda Protectorate administration in Kavirondo (now Nyanza). He transferred to the East Africa Protectorate (EAP) [q.v.] in 1902. Over the next several years, he served in numerous posts, including assistant deputy commissioner; acting commissioner (1904); subcommissioner, Ukamba (1906–12); and provincial commissioner, Mombasa [q.v.] (1912–21). During World War I [q.v.], Hobley served as chief political officer with the British military forces in German East Africa (later Tanganyika and now Tanzania) (1914–15). After the war, he worked for a short period as commissioner of mines and member of the Legislative Council [q.v.].

In 1921, Hobley returned to England and devoted the rest of his life to working for learned societies such as the Royal Geographical Society; Royal Anthropological Institute; Royal Colonial Institute; and the Geological, Zoological, and African Societies. Hobley also served as secretary of the Society for the Preservation of the Fauna of the Empire (1923–36). As a result of research he carried out while serving in Kenya, he published *Bantu Beliefs and Magic* in 1922. Hobley also published an account of his service in 1929 called *Kenya From Chartered Company to Crown Colony*. He died on 31 March 1947.

HÖHNEL, LUDWIG VON (1856–1942). Explorer. He graduated from the Marine Academy at Fiume (1876). He accompanied Samuel Teleki's [q.v.] 1887–88 expedition to Lake Rudolf (now Turkana) [q.v.] as geographer and recorder. In 1894, Von Höhnel published his account of the expedition in a book entitled *Discovery of Lakes Rudolf and Stefanie*. After his death in Vienna on 23 March 1942, the Nazis confiscated all Von Höhnel's private papers, which were never seen again.

HOLA CAMP AFFAIR. In March 1959, eleven hard-core Mau Mau detainees died and 22 were injured at the Hola Detention Camp. The authorities initially attributed these deaths to bad drinking water. However, it soon became clear that the men had died from violent ill-treatment meted out in trying to force them to work. The incident and the failed cover-up provoked a major political controversy in Great Britain. After the Hola affair, the colonial government abandoned its policy of trying to force detainees to give up their anticolonial stances by making confessions and began to empty the detention camps. Ian Macleod, appointed secretary of state for the colonies in October 1959, later acknowledged that the Hola Camp affair had convinced him of the need to move much more rapidly toward decolonization in Kenya. *See also* CORFIELD REPORT; MAU MAU REVOLT.

HOLLIS, SIR ALFRED CLAUD (1874–1961). Colonial administrator and anthropologist. Born at Highgate, London. After attending schools at Highgate and St. Leonards, Hollis studied privately in Switzerland and Germany. In June 1894, he arrived in East Africa. On 12 March 1897, Hollis received an appointment as assistant collector and, in 1900, became a collector (later district commissioner). In April 1900, he traveled to Dar-es-Salaam, German East Africa (GEA) (later Tanganyika and now Tanzania) to become acting British vice-consul. Over the next few years, he worked in Kenya as secretary to the administration (1901–07) and secretary for native affairs (1907–13). During his time in East Africa, Hollis also participated in numerous military expeditions, including the Uganda Mutiny (1897–98), Jubaland Expedition (1900–01), and the Nandi Expeditions (1903; 1905). Additionally, his anthropological research resulted in the publication of several academic papers and two books, *The Masai: Their Language and Folklore* (1905) and *The Nandi: Their Language and Folklore* (1909).

In 1913, Hollis left East Africa to become colonial secretary and then acting governor in Sierra Leone. In 1916, he returned to GEA as secretary to the administration. Three years later, he became chief secretary to the British colonial government in Tanganyika. His final two appointments were as resident in Zanzibar [q.v.] (1924–30) and governor of Trinidad and Tobago (1930–36). After retiring in 1936, Hollis served as the chairman of the Civil Defence Joint Committee, director of the Trinidad Petroleum Development Company, and chairman of the Imperial Communications Advisory Board. He died on 22 November 1961.

HOME GUARDS. In 1952, as part of its campaign to quell the Mau Mau Revolt [q.v.], the colonial government created the Home Guards, which were composed of African loyalists. Major General W. R. N. "Loony" Hinde, who had fought against the Afrika Korps in World War II [q.v.], organized this unit, which grew from about 8,000 in 1953 to approximately 25,000 in 1954. Initially, Home Guards personnel, nearly all of whom were Kikuyu [q.v.], carried only spears, pangas, and bows and arrows. However, after the 26 March 1953 Lari massacre, during which rebels killed 97 and wounded 32 African loyalists, burned 200 huts, and maimed more than 1,000 cattle, the colonial government started issuing rifles and shotguns to Home Guards personnel. In May 1953, the colonial government recognized the Home Guards as a branch of the armed forces [q.v.].

Their performance was mixed. Some troops were sympathetic to the rebels. Others used their power to abuse civilians, whether they supported the Mau Mau Revolt or not. Such incidents occurred primarily in Embu [q.v.] Kikuyu, and Meru [q.v.] Districts. However, from the British point of view, the Home Guards were a valuable resource insofar as they provided good intelligence, represented African opposition to Mau Mau, and helped to control the local population. As a result, the authorities often overlooked atrocities committed by Home Guards personnel. In January 1955, after the British had gained the upper hand in the struggle to end the Mau Mau Revolt, the colonial government issued a statement that it would not prosecute Home Guards personnel for past acts against the civilian population but that "strict discipline" would henceforth be required of all who wished to remain in the unit.

HORTICULTURE. Currently, horticulture is Kenya's third leading agricultural export (exports in 1996 totaled 84,824 tons) following coffee and tea [qq.v.]. This sector meets off-season demand in Europe for fresh fruit, vegetables, and flowers. Fresh produce (i.e. green beans, onions, cabbages, snow peas, avocados, mangoes, and passion fruit) constitutes 30 percent of exports.

Flowers exported include roses, carnations, astromeria, and lilies. In 1996, Kenya overtook Israel as the leading supplier of cut flowers to the Dutch auctions. *See also* AGRICULTURE.

HUMAN RIGHTS. Kenya's human rights record encompasses the pre- and postindependence eras. Each period has been characterized by varying degrees of human rights violations. To establish colonial rule, the British launched a series of wars of conquest. These included military action against many of the country's ethnic groups, including the Nandi (1895, 1897, 1900, 1903, and 1905), Kipsigis (1905), Elgeyo (1911 and 1919), Marakwet (1911), Gusii [q.v.] (1905, 1908, and 1914), and the Giriama (1914). Additionally, there were numerous punitive expeditions against the Luo, Luyia, and Kikuyu [qq.v.]. During these clashes, colonial forces often killed, wounded, or jailed noncombatants and seized moveable property, mainly livestock.

Beginning in the 1920s, the British sought to suppress African dissidents by jailing, deporting, or restricting them to isolated areas. Such actions regularly occurred without due process of law. Antigovernment demonstrations frequently degenerated into violence. In 1922, for example, the police [q.v.] opened fire on a group of unarmed people who were protesting the arrest of Harry Thuku [q.v.]. At least 25 people died in the clash. The colonial government also stifled political dissent by proscribing organizations such as the Kikuyu Central Association [q.v.] in 1940.

Some of the most egregious abuses happened during the Mau Mau Revolt [q.v.]. After the declaration of a state of emergency in 1952, the colonial government detained about 30,000 Kikuyu, Embu, and Meru [qq.v.] who were suspected of belonging to Mau Mau. The authorities confined these detainees to places like Manyani Detention Camp. Such facilities usually lacked adequate medical care, sanitation, food, and water. Suspects were regularly beaten, tortured, or kept in solitary confinement for long periods and at rations less than those authorized by regulations. *See also* HOLA CAMP AFFAIR.

The postindependence period has witnessed a steady deterioration of Kenya's human rights record. During Jomo Kenyatta's [q.v.] presidency, the government retained much of the legislation used by the British to suppress political dissent. In particular, the Outlying Districts Act and the Special District (Administration) Act allowed the authorities to wholly or partly close 19 districts, thus preventing antigovernment elements from entering areas without government permission. Kenyatta had little tolerance for political dissent. In 1969, for example, he detained Oginga Odinga [q.v.], the leader of the Kenya People's Union [q.v.], after a clash with him in Kisumu [q.v.]. In 1975, Kenyatta fired three ministers/assistant ministers who had questioned the government's report on the assassination of Josiah Kariuki [q.v.]. Additionally, the authorities jailed dissidents and periodically censored press reports that were critical of the Kenyatta regime. Many Kenyans also suspected that the Kenyatta regime was involved in the murder of several politicians, including Pio Gama Pinto (1965), Tom Mboya (1969), and Josiah Kariuki (1975) [qq.v.].

There was a significant deterioration of Kenya's human rights record after Daniel arap Moi [q.v.] became president. In November 1978, the enactment of the Preservation of Public Security Act allowed the suspension of the constitution [q.v.] or individual legal rights on the sole authority of the president. Over the next few years, opposition politicians, students, academics, lawyers, writers, and other concerned citizens became increasingly critical of the Moi regime. The president reacted by detaining or restricting numerous prominent Kenyans, including George Anyona, Oginga Odinga, Raila Odinga, and Koigi wa Wamwere [qq.v.]. In 1982, Moi amended the constitution, making Kenya a one-party state. A period of arrests and torture of suspected government opponents followed this move. In the late 1980s and early 1990s, pro-democracy advocates intensified their activities for political reforms. In 1991, Moi, under intense national and international pressure, authorized the end of one-party rule. In the 1992 general elections [q.v.] Moi was reelected president amid allegations of electoral irregularities. He continued repression of pro-democracy advocates, opposition politicians, and individuals suspected of disloyalty. By 1998, humanitarian organizations such as Africa Watch, Amnesty International, and the Kenya Human Rights Commission remained highly critical of the Moi regime's human rights record.

HUT TAX. For much of the colonial period, the hut tax was the major source of revenue collected from Africans. In 1901, the colonial authorities approved a proposal to levy a tax on all African-owned dwellings. In 1902, collection began at a rate of two rupees per dwelling (or as the colonialists termed African homes, "huts"). From the beginning the tax had the object not only of raising revenue for the colonial government but also of forcing African households into the colonial cash economy as commodity producers or wage laborers.

HUXLEY, ELSPETH JOSCELINE (1907–1997). Author, journalist, and settler. Born in London. In 1913, her family emigrated to Kenya and started a coffee [q.v.] plantation in Thika [q.v.]. Huxley studied at home and at the European School in Nairobi [q.v.]. After the outbreak of World War I [q.v.], she returned temporarily to England and attended a boarding school at Aldeburgh in Suffolk. Additionally, Huxley attended Reading University and Cornell University.

In 1921, she began her journalism career by writing an article about polo for the *East African Standard*. Three years later, Huxley won the Royal Colonial Institute's annual Empire Essay Competition. From 1929 to 1932, she was assistant press officer at the Empire Marketing Board, London. During World War II [q.v.], Huxley worked for the British Broadcasting Corporation's (BBC) war propaganda department and later became a liaison officer between the BBC and the Colonial Office. In 1948, she helped establish the East African Literature Bureau. From 1952 to 1959, Huxley was a member of the BBC's Advisory Council. In 1960, she served on the Monckton Advisory Committee on Central Africa.

Throughout her career, Huxley believed that European settlement in Kenya was an honorable undertaking that enriched the lives of all peoples in the country. Her many publications, the most important of which are *The Flame Trees of Thika* (1959) and *White Man's County: Lord Delamere and the Making of Kenya* (1935), provide revealing insights for Kenya's colonial era. She died on 10 January 1997.

-I-

IMPERIAL BRITISH EAST AFRICA COMPANY (IBEAC). Originally known as the British East African Association. In 1887, the sultan of Zanzibar [q.v.], Seyyid Barghash ibn Said, leased his possessions between the Umba River and Kipini to this association for 50 years. In exchange for full political and judicial rights, the association agreed to provide Barghash with revenues at least equal to existing customs collections. On 18 April 1888, Sir William Mackinnon [q.v.] and a group of Manchester investors reorganized the association, which henceforth was called IBEAC. On 3 September 1888, the British government granted this company a royal charter. Like its predecessor, IBEAC's purpose was to develop British economic and political interests throughout East Africa. Under Mackinnon's leadership, IBEAC acquired rights to trade and to administer a 150-mile stretch of territory along the East African coast-line, which included the port of Mombasa [q.v.]. Additionally, the company established a network of stations in the interior that enabled the British to begin to establish their influence in what became Kenya. Eventually, however, IBEAC proved to be a failure because it lacked adequate financing. Moreover, East Africa lacked easily accessible sources of wealth; company officials could not compete with Asian merchants from the coast; and agricultural development was impossible without a railway, which the company could not afford to build. As a result, IBEAC sold its concession, rights, and assets to the British government for £250,000. On 1 July 1895, the IBEAC transferred its territory to the British Crown.

INDIAN QUESTION. The so-called Indian Question directed much attention toward Kenya in the period after World War I [q.v.], but the roots of this political controversy lay in the earlier period when the colonial government prevented Indians (Asians) [q.v.] from purchasing land in the White Highlands [q.v.] and denied them political rights equal to those of European settlers despite the larger numbers of Indians in Kenya. The Indian Question revolved around four issues: the European right to exclusive ownership of land in the White Highlands, segregation in the residential and commercial areas of Kenya's towns, immigration, and political rights. Indian leaders demanded an end to segregation, access to the White Highlands, free immigration into the colony, and equality of political rights, particularly the right to elect members to the Legislative Council [q.v.]. European settlers, backed by the colonial government, opposed those demands. The government of India and the India Office in London supported Indian demands and through pressure on the Colonial Office (CO) forced the British government, by 1922, to go a considerable way toward meeting the Indian claims. When it became clear that Governor Sir Edward Northey [q.v.] was incapable of working out a settlement of the question, the CO removed him and appointed Sir Robert Coryndon [q.v.]. However, Coryndon backed the settlers in rejecting anything close to equal political rights for Indians (e.g. common roll elections) and their insistence that the White Highlands must remain for Europeans only. His report of an impending settler rebellion forced the CO to call settler and Indian representatives to London in 1923 to settle the issue. This was accomplished by the policy laid down in the white paper *Indians in Kenya* (the Devonshire Declaration [q.v.]) which left the Indians particularly disappointed because it rejected equal political rights and maintained that the White Highlands were for whites only.

INTERNATIONAL MONETARY FUND (IMF). The IMF was a product of the 1944 Bretton Woods Conference, which sought to normalize the postwar monetary regime. Since then, the IMF's mission has changed gradually and now focuses on ministering prescriptions to financially troubled Third World countries. Since 1963, the IMF, like the World Bank [q.v.], has funded numerous social and economic development projects. In the early 1980s, the IMF and the World Bank began to make aid conditional on the adoption of economic reforms. By the late 1980s, political reforms became an added prerequisite.

Oftentimes, these requirements caused clashes between the major donors and the Kenyan government. In 1997, for example, the IMF suspended a $205 million aid package because of Kenya's failure to improve governance, strengthen tax collection, end corruption at Mombasa [q.v.] port, and redefine the functions of ministries as a prelude to reducing the number of ministers and assistant ministers (after the 1997 general elections [q.v.], the number of ministers and assistant ministers increased from 22 and 36 to 25 and 42 respectively). According to IMF officials, there would be no restoration of aid until the Kenyan government resolved these problems. By early 1998, Kenya had made very little progress toward achieving that goal. *See also* ECONOMY.

INTER-PARTIES PARLIAMENTARY GROUP (IPPG). In 1997, a group of MPs from all political parties established the IPPG to institute a moderate program of constitutional, administrative, and electoral reforms. Additionally, the IPPG wanted to seize the reform initiative from the National Convention Executive Council [q.v.]. The IPPG succeeded in facilitating several reforms, including the abolition of detention without trial; the abolition of colonial-era laws that limited freedom of assembly, speech, and association; the dropping of licensing requirements for holding political rallies; and the registration of all political parties with applications that were still pending. The IPPG and President Daniel arap Moi [q.v.] also accepted a Constitutional Review Commission Bill that would examine the constitution [q.v] after the general elections (1997) [q.v.].

ISLAM. The earliest evidence of Islam in Kenya dates to the 10th and 11th centuries. The religion was carried to the Kenya coast by traders from Arabia and the Persian Gulf, some of whom settled in the coastal towns. The residence of large numbers of Muslims in the Kenya interior dates to the colonial period. About 10 percent of Kenya's population follows Islam. Most believers reside in the eastern part of Kenya, particularly along the coast and in the northeast. Arabic- and Swahili-speaking Muslims comprise the bulk of the Islamic population and are Sunni followers of the Shafi school of law. Additionally, there are some Sudanese Muslims who live in the Nairobi [q.v.] area and follow the Maliki school. There also is a group of Asians [q.v.] who adhere to the Hanafi school.

The history of Islam in Kenya has followed a pattern that some other African countries have experienced. Many Muslims were hesitant to send their children to Christian mission schools for fear they would be converted. As a result, at independence there were few educated Muslims who could participate in government. Even during the postindependence period, Muslims have exerted little political influence, and Christians have continued to dominate the government. In 1976, some Muslim leaders established the Supreme Council of Kenya Muslims, a federation of more than 100 groups. However, this group has refrained from engaging in high-profile political activities.

After the legalization of opposition political parties in December 1991, the Islamic Party of Kenya was formed. However, the Kenyan government subsequently banned religious parties from participating in the 1992 general elections [q.v.]. The Islamic Party of Kenya [q.v.], led by Sheik Khalid Salim Ahmed Balala [q.v.], responded by organizing riots in Mombasa [q.v.] and other coastal towns. In the eyes of some Muslims, this activity was incompatible with the precepts of Islam. As of 1998, the Islamic Party of Kenya has failed to shed its radical image.

ISLAMIC PARTY OF KENYA. *See* BALALA, SHEIK KHALID SALIM AHMED.

ITOTE, WARUHIU (GENERAL CHINA) (1922–1993). Trader, freedom fighter, and civil servant. Born at Kaheti in Nyeri District and educated at several Church Missionary Society [q.v.] schools in the Nyeri region while at the same time making a living as a stock trader. In 1939, he moved to Nairobi [q.v.] and in 1942 joined the King's African Rifles [q.v.]. During World War II [q.v.], Itote, who saw action in Burma, started to question his participation in the conflict. After his 1946 discharge, he worked for the railways. Itote also became involved in trade unionism and the Kenya African Union [q.v.], as he was increasingly dissatisfied with economic and political conditions in colonial Kenya. In 1952, Itote went to the forests to fight as a leader of those who wanted to forcibly overthrow the colonial government. As his reputation as a military leader grew during the Mau Mau Revolt [q.v.], he took the name General China. In January 1954, government forces wounded and captured him. At his trial, Itote received a death sentence, but this was later commuted to life imprisonment. Jomo Kenyatta [q.v.], who was a fellow inmate, taught Itote English during his imprisonment. In 1959, the colonial government commuted his life term to detention. In June 1962, Itote gained his freedom. After further military training in Kenya and Israel, Itote accepted a position with the new National Youth Service, where he worked until his retirement in 1984, serving for a time as deputy director. He published *"Mau Mau" General* in 1967. He died on 27 April 1993.

-J-

JACKSON, SIR FREDERICK JOHN (1860–1924). Early colonial administrator, big game hunter, and ornithologist. Born in Yorkshire and educated at Shrewsbury School and Jesus College, Cambridge. After arriving in East Africa in 1884, Jackson lived in Lamu [q.v.], explored the region, and hunted big game in places such as the Kilimanjaro region. On 3 October 1888, he joined the Imperial British East Africa Company (IBEAC) [q.v.]. During the 1889–90 period, Jackson led an IBEAC expedition, which, after a detour to Mount Elgon [q.v.], eventually led him to Buganda in pursuit of the German imperialist Karl Peters. On 24 September 1890, Jackson received an appointment as consular agent for Lamu. In November 1891, he agreed to serve as transport officer in an expedition led by Captain J. R. L. Macdonald to survey a route for the Uganda Railway [q.v.]. In 1892, illness forced him to return to Great Britain, but he took advantage of his African experience to gain an appointment with the new British administration in Uganda in July 1894. Jackson remained in Uganda service until the transfer of that protectorate's Eastern Province to the East Africa Protectorate (EAP) [q.v.] in 1902, when he shifted to Nairobi [q.v.] to take the new post of deputy commissioner, later lieutenant governor. In 1905 and again in 1909, Jackson took over the EAP administration pending the arrival of new governors. In 1900, Jackson served as chief political officer with the Nandi punitive expedition.

Jackson was generally not popular with superiors such as Sir Charles Eliot and Sir Percy Girouard [qq.v.] because he did not share their enthusiasm for promoting European settlement. Indeed, Jackson played a considerable part in the events that led to Eliot's resignation. In April

1911, he left Kenya to take up the post of governor of Uganda, which he held until his retirement in 1917. He died on 3 February 1924. His memoirs, *Early Days in East Africa*, were published posthumously in 1930.

JAMHURI **DAY**. National holiday celebrated on 12 December. This day commemorates independence from Great Britain on 12 December 1963 and the establishment of the republic (*Jamhuri*) on 12 December 1964.

JEEVANJEE, ALIBHAI MULLA (1856–1936). Asian [q.v.] businessman and politician. Born in Karachi, then part of British India. Jeevanjee engaged in business in Australia from 1886 to 1889. In 1890 he arrived in Mombasa [q.v.]. In 1895, Jeevanjee was hired to provide Asian laborers, oil, equipment, and provisions for the Uganda Railway [q.v.]. This contract made him a wealthy man. By the turn of the century, he was the most prominent businessman in Mombasa. In 1901, he founded the *African Standard*; in 1905, he sold this newspaper to A. G. Anderson and F. Mayer, who renamed it the *East African Standard*. In 1900, he acquired his first land in Nairobi [q.v.], and with John Ainsworth's [q.v.] support, he built much of early Nairobi as well as owning a considerable portion of the new township. During the 1909–11 period, he served as the first nominated Asian in Legislative Council [q.v.]. At this time, and for the succeeding decade and beyond, Jeevanjee was a leader in the Indian (Asian) demand for equal rights in early colonial Kenya. He was one of the founders of the East African Indian National Congress (EAINC) [q.v.] in 1914. After World War I, as president of EAINC, he took the lead in advocating equality of political rights and access to the White Highlands. He led Asian deputations to London and to India in 1920, 1921, and 1923. Like other Asian leaders, he was disappointed by the Devonshire Declaration [q.v.], and he continued to support demands for equal rights. Jeevanjee was active in Asian politics through the end of his life, though in less of a leadership role after the 1920s, while continuing to pursue his diverse business affairs and expanding his philanthropic work. He died on 2 May 1936.

JOINT SELECT COMMITTEE ON CLOSER UNION IN EAST AFRICA (1931). Despite the recommendations of the Hilton Young Commission [q.v.], the Closer Union issue, supported by European settlers in Kenya, remained alive after 1929 despite the coming to power Britain of a minority Labour government. In 1930, Secretary of State Lord Passfield issued a white paper on the subject as well as one on African policy. These provoked strong opposition from Kenya's settlers.

As a result, Passfield agreed to have these and other questions of East African policy put before a Joint Select Committee of Parliament for recommendations. The committee heard evidence, including that of three Africans from Kenya, and issued its report in 1931. The committee particularly noted African grievances over land and taxation, and further imperial enquiries into these subjects (e.g., the Kenya Land Commission [q.v.]) were made in the 1930s. The idea of Closer Union was ruled out as was the possibility of European settler political dominance in Kenya. The committee's opposition ended, for all intents and purposes, the possibility of an independent settler-governed state in Kenya. *See also* CLOSER UNION.

JOMO KENYATTA UNIVERSITY OF AGRICULTURE AND TECHNOLOGY. Opened in 1981. One of Kenya's state universities. In 1997–98, the university, which is located outside Nairobi [q.v.], had a student population of about 3,000. *See also* EDUCATION, UNIVERSITY.

JUBALAND PROVINCE. One of the original provinces of the East Africa Protectorate [q.v.]. By 1914, it consisted of four districts, largely inhabited by Somalis. As a result of an agreement with Italy during World War I [q.v.], the British government transferred the province to Italian Somaliland in 1925.

JUDICIARY. Kenyan jurisprudence is based on a combination of English common law, African customary law, legislative acts by the colonial Legislative Council, the House of Commons, and orders-in-council during the colonial era and by the National Assembly [q.v.] after independence. The judicial system consists of the Court of Appeal, which has final appellate jurisdiction, and various subordinate courts. The High Court includes a chief justice and associate judges, all of whom are appointed by the president. The High Court has jurisdiction over civil and criminal cases. Resident and district magistrates preside over Lower Courts. As of 1996, there were 300 judges and magistrates in Kenya. Military courts hear court martials of military personnel. *Qadi*s are responsible for answering questions of Islamic law.

-K-

KAGGIA, BILDAD MWANGANU (1922–). Soldier, trade unionist, and politician. Born at Dagoretti in Kiambu District and educated at Kahuhia School (1931–39). He worked as a clerk in the Murang'a (then Fort Hall)

District Commissioner's Office (1939–40). During World War II [q.v.], Kaggia joined the army and served in Egypt, Libya, Syria, and Great Britain (1940–46). After the war, he became a clerk in the National Bank of India. Kaggia also formed his own independent church, the *Dini ya Kaggia*. More importantly, he became active in trade unionism and politics by establishing and leading the Clerks and Commercial Workers' Union. He later became active in the leadership of the Labour Trade Union of East Africa. In 1947, he joined the Kenya African Union (KAU) [q.v.] and then served as the party's general secretary of the Nairobi [q.v.] branch. On 20 October 1952, the police [q.v.] arrested him along with Jomo Kenyatta, Fred Kubai [qq.v.], and four other KAU leaders for organizing Mau Mau. In 1953, he was convicted at the Kapenguria trial [q.v.] and sent to Lokitaung Prison (1953–59) and then placed under restriction at Lodwar (1959–61) for helping to organize the Mau Mau Revolt [q.v.].

After his release, Kaggia joined the Kenya African National Union (KANU) [q.v.] and became an elected member of the House of Representatives for Kandara (1963–66). Upon the achievement of self-government in 1963, Kaggia became assistant minister of education (1963–64). Within the government and KANU, he was associated with the so-called "radicals" such as Oginga Odinga [q.v.], and he became increasingly vocal in his calls for land for the landless. In June 1964, he resigned from his ministerial position, expressing concern that the Kenyatta government had forgotten the poor and those who had fought for freedom during the Mau Mau Revolt. It was thus not surprising that Kaggia left KANU after the Limuru Conference (1966) [q.v.] and joined the Kenya People's Union (KPU) [q.v.], becoming deputy leader (1966–69). At the Little General Election (1966) [q.v.], however, he lost the Kandara seat. On 19 April 1968, the authorities jailed him for 12 months for holding an unlawful meeting in South Nyanza. After his release, he rejoined KANU but lost in his bid to reenter Parliament.

Kaggia then worked as chairman of the Cotton, Lint and Seed Marketing Board (1970–71) and chairman of the Maize and Produce Board (1971). In 1978, he returned to chair the Cotton Board until the following year when Odinga replaced him. From 1979, Kaggia held no state or party positions. In 1975, he published his memoirs, *Roots of Freedom*.

KAKAMEGA. (Altitude 1,525 meters; 5,000 feet). Capital of Kenya's Western Province [q.v.]. Located 50 kilometers (31 miles) north of Kisumu [q.v.] and 115 kilometers south of Kitale. Nearby is the Kakamega Forest (45 square kilometers; 17 square miles), which was gazetted as a national reserve in 1985 and contains some of Kenya's rarest arboreal, avifaunal, faunal, and floral treasures. In 1920, the colonial government established Kakamega as a more healthy headquarters for then North Kavirondo District than Mumias. During the 1930s, the region adjacent to the township was the site of gold mining operations. The Kakamega gold rush proved to be short-lived, and mining operations ceased in 1953. In 1963, Kakamega became the capital of the newly created Western Province [q.v.]. According to the 1989 census, the municipality had a population of 63,796.

KALENJIN. The Kalenjin are Kenya's fourth-largest ethnic group (1989 census: 2,458,123). The term "Kalenjin" used to describe these people, which literally means "I say to you," only came into use in the 1950s. Rather than a single ethnic group, the Kalenjin are peoples speaking slightly different, but intelligible, dialects. These include those who speak the Keiyo, Kipsigis, Marakwet, Nandi, Pokot, Sabaot, Terik, and Tugen languages. These languages form part of the Highlands (or Central) Nilotic group, which seems to have originated in the region to the north of the present-day borders of Ethiopia, Kenya, and Sudan some 2,000 years ago. The ancestral Kalenjin gradually moved south into the Kenya highlands from the Lake Turkana [q.v.] region, finally coming to inhabit, as the subgroups noted previously rather than a unified entity, an area stretching from Mount Elgon to the edge of the Rift Valley [qq.v.]. Most Kalenjin combined stock rearing with agriculture [q.v.].

The Kalenjin governed themselves through councils of elders representing the several political sections that each subgroup was divided into. During the 19th century, many Kalenjin groups came to recognize and respect the office of *orkoiyot*, a magico-religious leader. Most Kalenjin (notably the Nandi) strongly resisted the colonial conquest; few were drawn immediately into commodity production and fewer still to wage labor. The major exception to the latter was the large number recruited for the army and police forces of the colonial government from amongst the Nandi and Kipsigis in particular. Unlike such peoples as the Kikuyu, Luyia, and Luo [qq.v], the Kalenjin responded relatively slowly to Christian missionary initiatives and Western education in the 20th century. During the period of decolonization and independence, the Kalenjin overwhelmingly supported the Kenya African Democratic Union and *majimbo* [qq.v.]. Kalenjin participation in national politics, the civil service, and the army increased markedly during Daniel arap Moi's [q.v.] presidency.

KALENJIN POLITICAL ALLIANCE (KPA). In April 1960, Daniel arap Moi [q.v.], Taaita Toweett and others formed this political group. The KPA sought to defend Kalenjin claims to ancestral lands in the Rift Valley [q.v.], particularly those held by European settlers. It was feared these lands might be taken up by Kikuyu [q.v.] at independence. Within two months of its formation, the KPA joined several other political groups to create the Kenya African Democratic Union [q.v.].

KAMBA. The Kamba are Kenya's fifth-largest ethnic group (1989 census: 2,448,302). They are Bantu-speakers [q.v.] whose language forms part of central Kenya's Thagicu group. According to their traditions, the Kamba moved north from the dry plains around Mount Kilimanjaro after 1550, and by 1650, many had settled in the Mbooni Hills. In this well-watered area, the ancestors of the Kamba turned increasingly from pastoralism to agriculture [q.v.]. In the second half of the 18th century, population pressure eventually forced many Kamba to move out of the Mbooni Hills and into what became known as Ukambani (later Machakos and Kitui Districts). During the 18th and 19th centuries, the Kamba spread across a wide geographical area encompassing different ecological zones. This required varied types of adaptation from the Kamba (e.g., from pastoralism in the drier regions to banana cultivation in the wet). The Kamba moved and settled as small groups, and as a result kinship groups became dispersed. Where they settled, the *utui* (neighborhood group) became highly significant in social and cultural life. During the 19th century, many Kamba men became involved in long-distance trade with the coast, but this did not lead to any centralization of political authority.

The Kamba were one of the first peoples of the interior to be brought under British rule as Machakos was one of the initial centers of foreign political control. Many Kamba were drawn into the colonial system as workers, particularly in the police and armed forces [qq.v.]. After losing land to European settlement, many Kamba engaged in anticolonial activity to protest the colonial government's destocking efforts in the 1930s. A few Kamba also participated in the Mau Mau Revolt [q.v.], and initially most gave strong support to the Kenya African National Union (KANU) [q.v.]. However, when Paul Ngei [q.v.] formed the African People's Party (APP) [q.v.] in 1962, Kamba voters gave the party overwhelming support. The following year, they followed Ngei back into KANU. With the advent of multipartyism in 1991–92, some Kamba turned away from KANU, and the 1992 general elections [q.v.] saw the return of some Democratic Party [q.v.] members for seats in Ukambani. In the 1997 general elections, the Social Democratic Party [q.v.] won several seats in Kamba-inhabited areas.

KAPENGURIA TRIAL. The most famous political trial in Kenya's history began at the remote government outpost of Kapenguria (in northwestern Kenya) in December 1952. Jomo Kenyatta [q.v.] and five others, Bildad Kaggia, Fred Kubai, Achieng Oneko, Paul Ngei [qq.v.], and Kungu Karumba, arrested in October 1952, were charged with organizing and managing an unlawful society called Mau Mau. The colonial government tried to use the trial to justify the declaration of a state of emergency. To ensure that Kenyatta and his associates would be found guilty, the colonial government handpicked the judge, Ransley Thacker, giving him a payment of £20,000, and coached and bribed witnesses. The most famous of the latter proved to be Rawson Macharia [q.v.], whose testimony, which he later admitted was perjured, was taken as proof of Kenyatta's guilt, in particular by Judge Thacker, over that of witnesses called to refute it by the defense lawyers, headed by D. N. Pritt. On 8 April 1953, Judge Thacker found the defendants guilty and gave them the maximum sentence of seven years hard labor. The Kapenguria trial crippled the political leadership of the Kenya African Union [q.v.], but it failed to convince the majority of Kikuyu [q.v.] and other Kenya Africans, to say nothing of world opinion, that Kenyatta was responsible for the Mau Mau Revolt [q.v.].

KARANJA, JOSEPHAT NJUGUNA (1931–1995). Diplomat and politician. Born in Githiga, Githunguri. He studied at Kagumo Government School, Alliance High School [q.v.], and at Makerere University [q.v.], where he received a diploma in education. Karanja, a Kikuyu [q.v.], then attended the University of New Delhi, Georgia State University, and Princeton University, where he received a Ph.D. in history and political science. From 1961 to 1962, he was an African studies lecturer at Fairleigh Dickinson University, New Jersey. During the 1962–63 period, he was lecturer in African and modern European history at the University of East Africa [q.v.]. Karanja then served as the Kenyan high commissioner to Great Britain (1963–70) and as vice-chancellor of the University of Nairobi [q.v.] (1970–79). He resigned the latter post in 1979, and unsuccessfully tried to enter politics by running for Central Province's [q.v.] Githunguri parliamentary seat.

However, in 1986, Karanja succeeded in winning a parliamentary seat in the Mathare constituency, Nairobi [q.v.]. In January 1987, he received an appointment as assistant minister of research, science, and technology. On 24 March 1988, Karanja became Kenya's fifth vice president and minister of home affairs and national heritage. His tenure in high office proved to be short-lived. His political enemies accused him of exceeding his authority, treating his fellow parliamentarians with contempt, and maintaining secret contacts with the Ugandan government. On 1 May 1989, Karanja resigned his ministerial post and withdrew from the Kenyan African National Union [q.v.], largely because President Daniel arap Moi [q.v.] refused to intercede on his behalf. With the advent of multipartyism, Karanja joined FORD-Asili [q.v.] and won the Githunguri parliamentary seat in the 1992 general elections [q.v.]. After early 1993, declining health limited his political activities. He died on 28 February 1995.

KARIUKI, GODFREY GITAHI (1937–). Health inspector, politician, and businessman. Born in Laikipia and educated at Kiamwamgi School and by correspondence course. Kariuki worked briefly as a health inspector and then entered politics full-time rising to Laikipia branch secretary for the Kenya African National Union (KANU) [q.v.]. In the 1963 general elections [q.v.], he easily won the then Laikipia-Nanyuki seat in the House of Representatives. Kariuki held his seat, later renamed Laikipia West, in subsequent elections through 1983.

During the 1970–79 period, he served as assistant minister for lands and settlement. Throughout these years, he also formed close political ties to Vice President Daniel arap Moi [q.v.]. After Moi assumed the presidency in 1978, Kariuki's political influence rose immensely. He became one of the new president's closest confidantes and emerged as an influential power broker in KANU elections. After the general elections (1979) [q.v.], Moi appointed Kariuki as minister of state in the Office of the President with responsibility for internal security. In 1982, Kariuki moved to the Ministry of Home Affairs as part of a major cabinet reshuffle. By this time, Kariuki was increasingly seen as an ally of Charles Njonjo [q.v.]. After the latter fell from power in 1983, so did Kariuki, losing his parliamentary seat in that year's election, though he did not accept the result as valid. In 1984, KANU expelled him, along with Njonjo and several others.

Thereafter, Kariuki maintained a low political profile. Following the general elections (1988) [q.v.], however, President Moi called for the reinstatement of Kariuki, who then rejoined KANU. In March 1992, he was elected chairman of KANU's Laikipia branch. His return to influence did not do much to help KANU prospects in the region during the general elections (1992) [q.v.] as the Democratic Party [q.v.] swept both Laikipia seats, and Kariuki himself came more than 25,000 votes short of winning Laikipia West. Nevertheless, President Moi made him a nominated MP. In the general elections (1997) [q.v.], he again failed to win a parliamentary seat.

KARIUKI, JOSIAH MWANGI (1929–1975). Freedom fighter, businessman, and politician. Born in the Rift Valley [q.v.] and educated at Karima Secondary School, Kerugoya Secondary School, and King's College in Budo, Uganda. Additionally, he took correspondence courses in economics, political science, and journalism. During the Mau Mau Revolt [q.v.], Kariuki was detained. He then worked as Jomo Kenyatta's [q.v.] private secretary (1961–63) and leader of the Kenya African National Union's [q.v.] youth movement. In 1963, he was elected to the House of Representatives for Aberdare. Kariuki eventually distanced himself from the Kenyatta government because he disagreed with the latter's approach to a free market economy and what he deemed a failure to help the poor. Also, he maintained that several government ministers had accepted bribes from foreign businesses that operated in Kenya.

As his popularity increased, especially among those Kikuyu [q.v.] who resented the power and influence of Kenyatta's inner circle, Kariuki was perceived to be a threat to the ruling elite. Also, his anticorruption campaign alienated many dishonest politicians and civil servants. Such actions doomed Kariuki. The day before Parliament opened on 4 February 1975, several witnesses saw security personnel escorting him. That was the last time he was seen alive. On 3 March 1975, a Maasai [q.v.] elder found his body at Olosho-Oibor, 19 kilometers from Ngong Township.

On 3 June 1975, a 15-man Parliamentary Select Committee, chaired by Elijah Wasike Mwangale [q.v.], issued a report that accused the police [q.v.] of a cover-up and recommended the removal of General Services Unit [q.v.] Commander Benjamin Gethi, who had been the last person to be seen with Kariuki. Many Kenyans believed that the government, and possibly even President Kenyatta, had ordered Kariuki's death. Such suspicions escalated after it became clear that the authorities never intended to file criminal charges against any suspects. The Kariuki affair marked a turning point in Kenya's postindependence history. Apart from eroding public confidence in the government, which had almost certainly engineered a cover-up of the events surrounding Kariuki's death, the affair deepened divisions in the Kikuyu community, especially between the old guard and younger politicians who wanted to institute wide-ranging reforms. Additionally, it brought Parliament into open conflict with President Kenyatta, who was unable to reassert control over the government until late 1975. Kariuki published a memoir in 1963: *"Mau Mau" Detainee.*

KARUME, JAMES NJENGA (1929–). Businessman and politician. Born in Kiambu and educated at Riara Catholic Mission School. Karume was active in several business enterprises from the 1950s, including timber (1950–53) and retail trade (1953). During the Mau Mau Revolt [q.v.], the colonial government placed him in detention (1954–55). Upon his release he opened a pub and subsequently became a distributor for East African Breweries and British American Tobacco.

Following independence, Karume's business dealings increasingly prospered. After he became the leader of the Gikuyu, Embu, Meru Association (GEMA) [q.v.] in 1973 and chairman of its associated business enterprises under Gema Holdings Ltd, his influence greatly increased. His role as a major figure in Kikuyuland, and Kiambu in particular, was recognized with his nomination to Parliament in 1974. He and GEMA supported the Change the Constitution Campaign (1976) [q.v.]. In 1979, Karume left the nominated MP seat to compete for the Kiambaa seat, and he won a dramatic victory over the formerly powerful minister, Mbiyu Koinange [q.v.]. Following this success, Karume became assistant minister of home affairs. In 1982, he moved to the Ministry of Energy and Regional Development and became chairman of the Kenya African National Union (KANU) [q.v.] Kiambu branch. In the general elections (1983) [q.v.], Karume held the Kiambaa seat with an increased majority and became an assistant minister. In the general elections (1988) [q.v.], he returned unopposed thanks to victory at the queue stage of the polls, but he later lost the chair of the KANU Kiambu branch through maneuvers he felt were illegal.

This undoubtedly began his disenchantment with those in control of the party. Thus, in late 1992, Karume resigned from KANU and joined the Democratic Party [q.v.]. In the general elections (1992) [q.v.], however, he fell victim to the Forum for the Restoration of Democracy-Asili [q.v.] sweep of Kiambu, losing Kiambaa by more than 20,000 votes. After 1992, he remained in the Democratic Party and was one of the prominent Kikuyu [q.v.] leaders who participated in the 1995 talks with Kalenjin [q.v.] leaders aimed at a rapprochement between the two communities in the wake of the 1992–94 ethnic clashes in western Kenya. In the general elections (1997) [q.v.], he stood as a Democratic Party candidate and reclaimed the Kiambaa parliamentary seat.

KAVIRONDO TAXPAYERS WELFARE ASSOCIATION. This association was formed at the initiative of the Church Missionary Society [q.v.] missionary Walter Edwin Owen [q.v.] after he assumed the leadership of the Young Kavirondo Association (YKA) [q.v.] in July 1923. Owen moved members, made up of Western-educated petty bourgeois men, to turn from demands for higher wages, the abolition of the *kipande* [q.v.], and a greater political voice for Africans within the colonial government to better education and hygiene and fair treatment for taxpayers. In line with Owen's view of improvement, members were encouraged to plant trees; kill rats; and adopt Western dress, furniture, and eating utensils. Thus, the YKA's original radicalism was diluted, and the organization became a welfare society with a limited, largely petty bourgeois, membership. By the late 1920s, the association ceased to have any political impact as a split between Luo and Luyia [qq.v.] developed and many leaders of the body were co-opted by the colonial government as chiefs, tribunal elders, or local native council [q.v.] employees.

KEEN, JOHN (1929–). Journalist and politician. Born in Laikipia and educated at Siyapei Primary School and Alliance High School [q.v.]. Keen served with the armed forces [q.v.] during World War II [q.v.], and after the conflict he worked as a journalist with Maasai- and Swahili- [qq.v.] language newspapers. At the same time, he became increasingly active in politics as a member of the Kenya African Union [q.v.] and founder and organizing secretary, in 1960, of the Masai United Front [q.v.]. Later in the same year as the Masai United Front joined other political groups to form the Kenya African Democratic Union (KADU) [q.v.], Keen became KADU's general secretary. In the LEGCO elections (1961) [q.v.], he won the Kajiado seat for the party.

However, Keen soon undertook what would be the first of many political shifts in joining the Kenya African National Union (KANU) [q.v.]. With the establishment of the coalition government in 1962, Keen became parliamentary secretary for the Ministry of Tourism, Forests and Wildlife. In the 1963 general elections [q.v.], he unsuccessfully stood against KADU leader Masinde Muliro [q.v.] in Trans Nzoia. Nevertheless, the KANU government named him a member of the East African Legislative Assembly. Outspoken criticism of a lack of progress toward federation earned Keen a brief spell in detention in 1966. In the general elections (1969) [q.v.], he returned to Parliament as member for Kajiado North, a seat he held until the general elections (1983) [q.v.], when he was ousted. During this period in Parliament, Keen served as an assistant minister of works and economic planning; and worked in the Office of the President.

Between 1983 and 1988, Keen remained politically active, though with a somewhat lower profile. He supported George Saitoti's [q.v.] bid for the Kajiado North seat in the latter year. Following the general elections (1988) [q.v.], Keen was nominated to Parliament and was appointed an assistant minister in the Office of the President. By the early 1990s, Keen had become increasingly critical of corruption in Kenya, and he spoke in favor of political reform. His stand cost him his position as assistant minister in October 1991, and in January 1992 he resigned from Parliament and KANU and joined the Democratic Party (DP) [q.v.] as its first general secretary. In the general elections (1992) [q.v.], he stood for the DP in Kajiado North but lost to Vice President Saitoti by more than 10,000 votes. In February 1995, Keen left the DP and rejoined KANU.

KEINO, KIPCHOGE HEZEKIAH (1940–). Long-distance runner, farmer, businessman, and humanitarian. Keino started running in secondary school. Within a year of becoming a physical training instructor at the National Police Academy, he captured all the Kenyan records in the one-, two-, and three-mile distance race and in the relay race. Keino also set world records in the 3,000- and 5,000-meter races and ran the second fastest mile in history. In 1962, he won the East African championship and performed well in the Commonwealth Games in Australia. He participated in the Tokyo Olympics (1964), the Mexico City Olympics (1968), and the Munich Olympics (1972), winning two gold medals. In 1973, Keino turned professional. In 1980, he retired from competition with the reputation of being one of the world's greatest all-round runners.

In more recent years, Keino has devoted much of his time to managing his tea [q.v.] estate, farm, and sporting goods store. Additionally, he has become noted for his generosity toward children. Over the years, he and his wife have given a home to hundreds of homeless children. Keino has also trained Kenyan children interested in becoming runners. In 1996, he headed the Kenyan team at the Atlanta Olympics.

KENIA PROVINCE. Created in 1902 from the western portion of Ukamba Province [q.v.]. It consisted of Embu, Fort Hall, Meru, and Nyeri Districts. In 1920, the colonial government changed the name of the province to Kikuyu [q.v.].

KENYA AFRICAN DEMOCRATIC UNION (KADU). Formed on 25 June 1960 at a meeting at Ngong outside Nairobi [q.v.]. Its formation was the work of politicians representing the so-called "minority" tribes worried about the possibility of Kikuyu/Luo [qq.v.] domination in the recently formed Kenya African National Union (KANU) [q.v.] and a fear of loss of land in the future. The main political groups involved in KADU's formation were the Kenya African People's Party [q.v.], led by Masinde Muliro [q.v.]; the Kalenjin Political Alliance, led by Daniel arap Moi [q.v.]; the Coast People's Party, led by Ronald Ngala [q.v.]; the Masai United Front [q.v.]; and the Somali National Association. Ngala became the party's president, Muliro vice president, and Moi chairman (Ngala had been earlier chosen KANU treasurer with Moi as his deputy, but they did not accept these positions). From its onset, KADU was seen as the more moderate of the two main African political parties. The party contested the LEGCO elections (1961) [q.v.] and won 11 seats to KANU's 18.

When KANU refused to participate in government upon the colonial government's refusal to release Jomo Kenyatta [q.v.], KADU agreed to do so on condition that the latter would soon be released. Ngala became the leader of government with support from Michael Blundell [q.v.] and New Kenya Party [q.v.] members, and some Asian elected members. Despite this support, the governor had to appoint nominated members to the Legislative Council [q.v.] to secure a governing majority. From this time until the second Lancaster House Conference [q.v.], KADU advocated *majimbo* [q.v.] for Kenya's constitutional future. This involved the establishment of a federal-type structure with regional governments controlling local affairs and land ownership. The party strongly advocated this position at the second Lancaster House Conference (1962) [q.v.]. The British government largely accepted KADU's position because the independence constitution [q.v.] provided for the creation of regions with elected assemblies holding specific powers. KADU participated in the coalition government of 1962–63, which paved the way for the independence elections. KADU campaigned for the general elections (1963) [q.v.] based upon this system in alliance with the recently formed APP [q.v.]. KADU won a majority in the Coast, Rift Valley, and Western Regional Assemblies, but lost to KANU in the House of Representatives elections as well as those for the Senate.

Following the achievement of internal self-government on 1 June 1963, KADU became the official opposition party, championing, in particular, the continuation of *majimbo* in the face of KANU plans to scrap those portions of the constitution providing for regionalism in favor of a unitary system. Even before independence, KADU MPs began to cross the floor to join KANU, and this trend continued through 1964. Finally, the KADU leaders decided to accept the call from the government to disband their party. In November 1964, KADU ceased to exist, and the remaining members joined the ruling party. Ngala, Muliro, and Moi, among other KADU leaders, eventually became ministers under Kenyatta.

KENYA AFRICAN NATIONAL UNION (KANU). Formed in May 1960 following the first Lancaster House Conference (1960) [q.v.]. This party, which sought to achieve rapid political independence, joined several Legislative Council [q.v.] members who had been leaders of regional parties. James Gichuru [q.v.] became president because the colonial government would not register the party if the detained Jomo Kenyatta [q.v.] was its leader. Oginga Odinga [q.v.] was vice president and Tom Mboya [q.v.] general secretary. KANU gained strong support from the then two largest ethnic groups, the Kikuyu and Luo [qq.v.], as well as backing from the Embu, Gusii, Kamba, and Meru [qq.v.]. The party won the majority of seats in the LEGCO elections (1961) [q.v.] but refused to form the government as long as Kenyatta remained in detention.

Following his release, Kenyatta assumed the leadership of KANU in October 1961 and led the party's delegation at the second Lancaster House Conference (1962) [q.v.]. During the negotiations, KANU suffered a setback in that the British government chose to implement a *majimbo* [q.v.] constitution. KANU insisted on a unitary state for Kenya's independence. Following the conference, KANU formed a coalition government (1962–63) with the Kenya African Democratic Union (KADU) [q.v.] while the details of the independence constitution [q.v.] were worked out and preparations made for elections. KANU won the 1963 general elections [q.v.], and the party formed a government at the attainment of internal self-government (1 June 1963) and led Kenya to independence on 12 December 1963.

KANU has remained Kenya's governing party ever since that time. In September 1963, the African People's Party [q.v.] joined KANU, and in November 1964, KADU dissolved itself, and its members joined KANU, bringing about the existence of the one-party state that Kenyatta and other KANU leaders had advocated. This situation did not last long: from its earliest days KANU had been marked by division based on ethnicity, ideology, personal differences, and ambition relating to the succession to Kenyatta. Thus, despite the lack of an opposition party, KANU was divided between the so-called radicals (Odinga, Bildad Kaggia [q.v.], and Achieng Oneko [q.v.]) and the moderates (Kenyatta, Mboya, Mbiyu Koinange [q.v.], and Charles Njonjo [q.v.]). Division became an open split at the party's Limuru Conference (1966) [q.v.], with Odinga founding the Kenya People's Union (KPU) [q.v.] as a rival to KANU. The 1969 banning of KPU left KANU the sole legal party once more, but division continued. In the late 1960s, the party had two camps, KANU A (the Kiambu politicians close to Kenyatta) and KANU B [q.v.] (supporters of Mboya). By the mid-1970s, division was on the basis of those opposed to, or supporting, the succession of Vice President Daniel arap Moi [q.v.] to the presidency. From the time of Mboya's death, if not before, the party played an increasingly small role in policy formulation or popular mobilization. During the 1966–79 period, there were no party elections or broad-based meetings. Rather, KANU served largely as a means of obtaining political office and patronage.

Upon becoming president in 1978, Moi sought to revitalize and strengthen the party. In 1982, he engineered a constitutional amendment to make KANU the only political party. Still, the party was rent with factionalism. In the view of critics (church leaders and lawyers particularly), the 1980s witnessed KANU adopting increasingly undemocratic procedures (e.g., queue voting for the general elections (1988) [q.v.]). As protests mounted in 1989–90, President Moi appointed the KANU Review Committee in 1990. As a result of its recommendations, queue voting was dropped. In December 1991, demands for political reform became so insistent that KANU, with a strong push from Moi, agreed to multipartyism. Nevertheless, with the full resources of the state behind it, KANU won the general elections (1992) [q.v.] in terms of gaining the most seats in Parliament and capturing the presidency, though it did not gain the majority of votes cast. Thus, since 1992, KANU has remained, as its stalwarts maintain, *chama kinachotawala* (the ruling party). Despite divisions in the party and some defections, the party was successful in the general elections (1997) [q.v.] as President Moi was reelected and KANU remained the largest single party in Parliament though with a reduced margin over all opposition parties combined.

The succession issue is the biggest problem confronting KANU. From 8 January 1998 through 3 April 1999, Moi did not have a vice president, encouraging competition among presidential hopefuls such as George Saitoti and Simeon Nyachae [qq.v.]. This rivalry helped deepen the existing party rift between the Kenya African National Union A (KANU A) and the Kenya African National Union B (KANU B) [qq.v.] factions. On 3 April 1999, Moi reappointed Saitoti vice president. Meanwhile, as long as he remains in office, Moi will be a powerful political broker, despite the fact that he is in his fifth and last term as president. *See also*

KENYA AFRICAN NATIONAL UNION A AND B; KENYA AFRICAN NATIONAL UNION REVIEW COMMITTEE.

KENYA AFRICAN NATIONAL UNION A and KENYA AFRICAN NATIONAL UNION B. Terms often used in independent Kenya to depict divisions within the ruling party, the Kenya African National Union (KANU) [q.v.]. The terms reflect different individuals and policies at various times, but their widespread use by the public and press point to on-going divisions and struggle within the party, most significantly relating to the issue of succession. For example, the terms seem to have first come into use in 1967 when KANU A was said to include close associates of President Jomo Kenyatta from Kiambu, such as Mbiyu Koinange, Njoroge Mungai and Charles Njonjo, [qq.v.], while KANU B included Tom Mboya, Ronald Ngala, and Jeremiah Nyagah [qq.v.], among others. A decade later, the faction identified as KANU A included those identified with Njoroge Mungai, who wished to block Daniel arap Moi's [q.v.] succession to the presidency, while KANU B included the latter and his supporters in the ruling party. Almost 20 years after that, KANU A and KANU B were used to depict division within the ruling party in 1995–99 over the vice presidency and succession to President Moi. KANU A included Simeon Nyachae and William Ntimama [qq.v.], among others, while KANU B grouped together Vice President George Saitoti, Nicholas Biwott [qq.v.], and their supporters.

KENYA AFRICAN NATIONAL UNION REVIEW COMMITTEE. In June 1990, President Daniel arap Moi [q.v.] appointed the Kenya African National Union (KANU) [q.v.] Review Committee, under Vice President George Saitoti's [q.v.] chairmanship. Initially, the committee was charged with making recommendations on KANU nomination rules, election rules, and a party code of discipline. When it began public hearings, the committee was faced with a huge demand for reform that went further than the matters identified by the president. Many who appeared before the commission, for example, called for an end to queue voting, the legalization of other political parties, and limitation of presidential terms of office. As a result, Saitoti widened the scope of the committee's inquiry, and despite strong opposition from KANU "hawks," the committee's report led to the party abolishing queue voting and expulsion from the party as a form of discipline.

KENYA AFRICAN PEOPLE'S PARTY. Political party that existed briefly as successor to the Kenya National Party (KNP) [q.v.] in 1960. Like the KNP, its leader was Masinde Muliro [q.v.]. It joined other parties in the foundation of the Kenya African Democratic Union (KADU) [q.v.] in June 1960.

KENYA AFRICAN STUDY UNION (KASU). *See* KENYA AFRICAN UNION.

KENYA AFRICAN UNION (KAU). On 1 October 1944, Eluid Mathu [q.v.] and other educated Africans formed this political party to support the first African member of the Legislative Council [q.v.] and articulate African political demands. Harry Thuku [q.v.] was KAU's first president. In late October 1944, the party responded to pressure from the colonial government to adopt a non-political pose by changing its name to Kenya African Study Union (KASU) [q.v.]. On 3 February 1945, James Gichuru [q.v.] replaced Thuku as president. KASU found it difficult to operate with inadequate funding and an increasingly hostile attitude from the colonial government. On 6 February 1946, the Kenya African Study Union resumed its original name, KAU. The party's existence between that date and early 1950 has been termed the moderate years. Drawing the support of the small African educated elite, members of pre-World War II local political organizations, especially the Kikuyu Central Association (KCA) [q.v.] and later the trade union movement and the African masses in Nairobi and Central Province [qq.v.], the party pressed for constitutional change aimed at expanding African political participation and economic opportunity. In June 1947, Jomo Kenyatta [q.v.] assumed the presidency of KAU. He gave the party leadership and improved its organization. However, by early 1950, little had been achieved in gaining redress for African grievances over land, a lack of political rights, and demands for more education.

The KAU's inability to fulfill these expectations led to the so-called "radical" era from early 1950 until October 1952. This period witnessed greater support and involvement with trade unions [q.v.] and the African masses in Nairobi and led to the emergence of "radical" leaders in the Nairobi branch of the party such as Fred Kubai and Bildad Kaggia [qq.v.]. Kenyatta continued to champion moderation, but with little tangible results to show for that approach in terms of land or constitutional reform. Many in the KAU became increasingly militant and supported the growing tension and violence associated with the Mau Mau Revolt [q.v.]. On 20 October 1952, the police arrested Kenyatta and other party leaders. Walter Odede then became KAU's acting president, but he also was detained in March 1953. On 8 June 1953, the colonial government proscribed the KAU as an unlawful society.

KENYA AIRWAYS. After the collapse of East African Airways (EAA), Kenya took steps to create its own national airline. On 22 January 1977, the Kenyan government authorized the incorporation of Kenya Airways; on 4 February 1977, the airline started operations with a rented Boeing 707. On 1 April 1978, the airline created a fully owned subsidiary called the Kenya Airfreight Handling Company. During the first 16 years of its existence, Kenya Airways suffered huge financial losses because of the use of foreign loans to purchase aircraft and unsound financial practices. In April 1991, the Kenyan government appointed a new board of directors, headed by former Central Bank of Kenya governor Philip Ndegwa. The authorities directed the board to commercialize the airline and prepare it for privatization. In February 1992, the board commissioned Speedwing Consulting to review the airline's performance and to make recommendations for improving its service.

Shortly afterwards, Kenya Airways became the first airline in sub-Saharan Africa to transfer ownership from government to the private sector and be managed successfully. Under the privatization scheme, the public owned 51 percent of the company; the Kenyan government held 23 percent; and KLM, the Dutch airline, owned 26 percent. Profits grew from $3.6 million in 1992/1993 to $10.1 million in 1993/1994, $16.9 million in 1994/1995, and $24.5 million in 1995/1996. As of 1998, the airline's fleet included three Airbus A310-300s, two Boeing 737-200s, three Fokker 27s, and three Boeing 737-300s. Kenya Airways operates regional services to Addis Ababa, Bujumbura, Cairo, Dar-es-Salaam, Entebbe, Harare, Johannesburg, Khartoum, Kigali, Lilongwe, and Lusaka. Internationally, Kenya Airways has flights to Amsterdam, Copenhagen, Dubai, Karachi, London, Mumbai, Paris, Rome, and Stockholm. In March 1998, Kenya Airways concluded an agreement with U.S.-based Northwest Airlines to strengthen its presence in North America. *See also* AVIATION; WILSON AIRWAYS.

KENYA COALITION. Shortly after his March 1960 resignation as speaker of the Legislative Council [q.v.] in protest against the outcome of the first Lancaster House Conference (1960) [q.v.], Sir Ferdinand Cavendish-Bentinck [q.v.] formed the Kenya Coalition. The coalition, which Cavendish-Bentinck described as a movement rather than a political party, sought to protect European settler interests, particularly economic. In September 1960, Cavendish-Bentinck announced that the Kenya Coalition would contest the seats reserved for Europeans in the LEGCO elections (1961). The coalition therefore put forward candidates for nine of the 10 seats. Despite overwhelming success in the European-only portion of the poll, the coalition won only one seat in the common roll phase of the election and a total of three overall. After the election, the Kenya Coalition disintegrated. The coalition represented a last-ditch rear guard action of the European settlers. Nevertheless, its leaders helped convince the British government of the need to provide extensive assistance to buy the farms of Europeans who wished to leave Kenya.

KENYA COASTAL STRIP CONFERENCE. This conference met in London in 1962 at the same time as the second Lancaster House Conference (1962) [q.v.]. Delegates from the British, Kenyan, and Zanzibari governments as well as representatives of the Kenya African National Union and the Kenya African Democratic Union [qq.v.] discussed the future of the 10-mile coastal strip, technically the possession of the sultan of Zanzibar [q.v.] but administered as part of Kenya since 1895. The conference was guided by the 1961 report of a special commissioner, Sir James Robertson, which rejected coastal autonomy or Zanzibari rule and recommended integration with Kenya. In 1963, an agreement between Zanzibar, Great Britain, and newly self-governing Kenya recognized that the coastal strip should continue to be administered as a part of Kenya; revoked the 1895 accord that had recognized the strip as the sultan's possession; and promised that the Kenya government would respect Muslim faith, law, and land rights in the strip.

KENYA COMMERCIAL BANK (KCB). Largest and most influential bank in Kenya. Its history began in July 1896, when the National Bank of India (NBI) opened its first office on the East African mainland at Mombasa [q.v.]. Over the next several decades, NBI established branch offices in numerous Kenyan towns, including Nairobi (1904) [q.v.], Nakuru (March 1911) [q.v.], Eldoret (1926) [q.v.], Kericho (1948), Thika (1951), Nyeri (1955) [q.v.], Embu (1957), and Kisumu (April 1958) [q.v.]. Initially, NBI concentrated on commodity trading. This involved trading gold, ivory, iron, spices, hides, and skins for foodstuffs, cotton cloth and jute from India, or ceramics from Persia (now Iran) and China. Later NBI expanded its operations by providing services to Asian businessmen and European farmers. In January 1958, NBI merged with Grindlays Bank to form the National Overseas and Grindlays Bank. The following year, the bank changed its name to the National and Grindlays Bank.

After independence, the bank continued to grow. In June 1968, it was the first bank in Kenya to computerize its operations. Two years later, the Kenyan government acquired majority shares in the bank and re-

named it the Kenya Commercial Bank (KCB). In 1971, KCB incorporated the Kenya Commercial Finance Company into its ranks. At the end
of the century, KCB had the most extensive national network, including
some 90 main branches, of all the banks operating in Kenya.

KENYA DEFENCE COUNCIL. This body, formed at the initiative of
Dedan Kimathi [q.v.] in August 1953, sought to achieve better coordination between the eight or more groups, in the forests of the Aberdare
mountains [q.v.], operating against the colonial government following the
declaration of the state of emergency during the period of the Mau Mau
Revolt [q.v.]. Not all guerrilla fighters were involved in the organization,
however; it lacked administrative and enforcement mechanisms as much
was left to individual leaders. Thus the Kenya Defence Council was a
voluntary body that proved unwieldy in the struggle against the forces
mobilized by the colonial state. By the end of the year, it was clear that
the council had not proved as effective as hoped. It was superseded by
the Kenya Parliament [q.v.] in 1954.

KENYA DEFENCE FORCE (KDF). After World War I [q.v.], the European settler community wanted to safeguard their position in Kenya by
establishing an armed force under their control. In July 1919, the Convention of Associations [q.v.] therefore appointed a three-man committee to investigate the possibility of organizing a KDF. In February 1920,
the committee recommended the creation of such an army with compulsory enlistment for all European males between the ages of 16 and 60.
However, after the *Official Gazette* published the Defence Force Bill in
July 1921, European Legislative Council [q.v.] members voiced their
opposition to the legislation because it would not be controlled by the
settler community. Instead, KDF personnel would be subject to the Army
Act, which made them subject to court martial for disobeying an order.
The Colonial Office (CO), which had to contend with threats of settler
violence during the crisis associated with the Indian Question [q.v.], also
opposed the establishment of a KDF.

  After Sir Edward Grigg [q.v.], who was sympathetic to the settlers,
became governor in 1925, there was an improvement in the political climate in Nairobi and London. Apart from his sympathetic attitude toward
the settlers, Grigg and the CO's new secretary of state, Leopold Amery,
wanted their support in creating a Closer Union [q.v.] between Great
Britain's East African territories. Both also wanted to bring the settlers
closer to the colonial government. To help achieve these goals, Grigg and
Amery supported the creation of the KDF.

On 30 November 1926, the *Official Gazette* announced the KDF's establishment. Apart from compulsory enlistment for European males between the age of 16 and 60, KDF personnel were liable for service anywhere in East Africa without time limit. Additionally, the governor received the authority to appoint all officers and to call out the KDF. In an emergency, district commissioners could order the KDF into action. Lastly, all enlistees had to take an oath of allegiance to the king and to the laws of Kenya. The KDF, which was also known as "Kenya's Damned Fools," never participated in a battle. *See also* KING'S AFRICAN RIFLES; ARMED FORCES

KENYA EDUCATION COMMISSION. *See* OMINDE COMMISSION.

KENYA FEDERATION OF LABOUR (KFL). Initially known as the Kenya Federation of Registered Trade Unions (KFRTU). On 7–8 May 1955, the KFRTU convened its first annual conference and reconstituted itself as the KFL, with Tom Mboya [q.v.] as its general secretary. Apart from representing workers' interests, Mboya used this organization as a vehicle to express anticolonial sentiments. Consequently, on 23 February 1956, the colonial government accused the KFL of engaging in political activities and raised the possibility of withdrawing its registration. In April 1956, the KFL defused this crisis by promising to refrain from engaging in politics except in matters affecting its members in their capacity as employees. During the 1959–61 period, the KFL and the International Confederation of Free Trade Unions—a largely American-financed organization that had been created in 1949—succeeded in making inroads into Kenya's rural areas by jointly establishing several agricultural unions among workers on coffee, tea, sisal [qq.v.], and sugar plantations and on European farms.

After 1960, the KFL gave strong support to the Kenya African National Union [q.v.], but the union's rank and file became increasingly militant. The 1960–63 period thus witnessed an increasing number of strikes and work stoppages that were often not supported by the union's leadership. After independence, the KFL was faced with a rival, the Kenya African Workers' Congress, for leadership in the trade union [q.v.] movement. In September 1965, rivalry between the two groups led the government to abolish both and create the Central Organisation of Trade Unions [q.v.].

KENYA FREEDOM PARTY (KFP). Established in February 1960 by Chanan Singh [q.v.] and other Asian [q.v.] radicals who believed that the Kenya Indian Congress [q.v.] had failed to be adequately supportive of the African desire for independence. The KFP advocated universal suffrage, racial integration, and immediate independence. Because of its Asian membership, the party found it difficult to gain acceptance among many African nationalists.

KENYA (HIGHLANDS) ORDER-IN-COUNCIL (1938). This order formally proclaimed the boundaries of the White Highlands [q.v.] four years after they had been proposed in the 1934 Kenya Land Commission [q.v.] report. This amounted to about 43,420 square kilometers (16,760 square miles) of land. Now, European settlers were said to have "the same measure of security" as the commission had recommended for Africans.

KENYA IMMIGRATION ACT (1967). This act abolished temporary work permits for non-African immigrants and imposed stricter conditions on the issuance of entry and work permits. Implementation of the act, along with the Trade Licensing Act [q.v.], led to the noncitizen Asian [q.v.] exodus from Kenya to Great Britain.

KENYA INDEPENDENCE MOVEMENT. In mid-1959, African elected members of the Legislative Council [q.v.] formed this organization after the emergence of the Kenya National Party [q.v.]. Led by Tom Mboya, Oginga Odinga, and Julius Gikonyo Kiano [qq.v.], this group opposed the multiracial approach being advocated by the Kenya National Party. It also called for universal suffrage on a common roll, the immediate opening of the White Highlands [q.v.] to non-Europeans, integrated schools, and Jomo Kenyatta's [q.v.] release from prison. In late 1959, the Kenya Independence Movement joined forces with the Kenya National Party to forge a united front at the first Lancaster House Conference (1960) [q.v.].

KENYA INDIAN CONGRESS. *See* EAST AFRICAN INDIAN NATIONAL CONGRESS.

KENYA LAND AND FREEDOM ARMY (KFLA). The KLFA—which had the reputation of being the last protest organization to voice the grievances of landless peasants, squatters [q.v.], and ex-freedom fighters—emerged after the suppression of the Mau Mau Revolt [q.v.] and continued to struggle for the recovery of the White Highlands [q.v.] and Kenya's independence. The KLFA, which was composed largely of hardcore ex-Mau Mau fighters and land-hungry Kikuyu [q.v.], perceived itself as *Thigari cia Bururi* (soldiers/guardians of the land). The KLFA therefore pledged to fight until the Kenya African National Union [q.v.] reached a settlement with the colonial government that would distribute land to Kikuyu squatters [q.v.].

During the 1957–65 period, but particularly in 1960–62, the KLFA conducted low-level military operations in the Central and Rift Valley Provinces [qq.v.]. In September 1962, the police and the General Services Unit [qq.v.] launched a campaign against the KLFA, which resulted in some arrests and the discovery of a few homemade guns and ammunition. The following month, the colonial government initiated a "follow-up operation" against the rebels. By March 1963, the colonial government claimed that these operations resulted in 8,762 confessions and 1,708 arrests. The authorities also captured 368 homemade guns and 767 rounds of ammunition. The crackdown against the KLFA failed to stop the growth of land agitation on European farms. The colonial and postindependence governments continued to mount operations against the KLFA until the organization disappeared around 1965.

KENYA LAND COMMISSION. The British government created the Kenya Land Commission, sometimes referred to as the Carter Commission after its Chairman Sir William Morris Carter, to investigate the land situation in Kenya specifically as a response to the recommendations of the Joint Select Parliamentary Committee of 1931 [q.v.], which had urged that African complaints about past loss of land, the definition of the White Highlands [q.v.], and the insecurity of land reserved for Africans be examined. The commission's report, published in 1934, proved a huge disappointment to Africans, particularly the Kikuyu [q.v.]. Some land would be added to African reserves, but the White Highlands would remain intact, encompassing a region of 43,420 square kilometers (16,760 square miles), as no settler land was recommended for return to African possession. Despite the collection of a great body of evidence, the commission did little to solve Kenya's land problem in the long run. *See also* KIKUYU ASSOCIATION; KIKUYU CENTRAL ASSOCIATION.

KENYA NATIONAL CONGRESS. In September 1992, a splinter group, which included former cabinet ministers Titus Mbathi, Charles Rubia [q.v.], and Maina Wanjigi formed the Kenya National Congress. In the general elections (1992) [q.v.], Chibule wa Tsuma was the party's presidential candidate, but he and the Kenya National Congress's slate of parliamentary candidates fared poorly. The party gained only one parliamentary seat (Siakago in Eastern Province [q.v.]). Most prominent party members left after 1993, joining the Kenya African National Union (KANU) or the Forum for the Restoration of Democracy-Asili (FORD-Asili) [qq.v]. In 1995, the party's only MP, Ireri Ndwiga, defected to

KANU and won reelection as a member of the ruling party. In May 1997, Katama Mkangi ousted Chibule wa Tsuma as party chairman. In the general elections (1997) [q.v.] Mkangi stood as the party's presidential candidate but won only 0.39 percent of the vote (23,484). Additionally, the party failed to gain a single parliamentary seat.

KENYA NATIONAL DEMOCRATIC ALLIANCE (KENDA). In 1992, former University of Nairobi [q.v.] history lecturer and political detainee Mukaru Ng'ang'a established KENDA. Ng'ang'a stood as the party's presidential candidate in the 1992 general elections [q.v.], but he fared poorly. Moreover, KENDA returned no members to Parliament in the election. After Mukaru Ng'ang'a died in 1997, KENDA nominated Koigi wa Wamwere [q.v.] as its presidential candidate for the 1997 general elections [q.v.]. He won little support and the party failed to win any parliamentary seats.

KENYA NATIONAL PARTY. In July 1959, African, Asian, European, and Arab Legislative Council [q.v.] members created this multiracial political party. Masinde Muliro [q.v.] served as president. It drew support from several powerful individuals, including Ronald Ngala, Daniel arap Moi, and Taaita Toweett [qq.v.]. The party opposed what it termed the dictatorial tendencies of Tom Mboya [q.v.] in the African Elected Members Organisation [q.v.]. In August 1959, Mboya and Oginga Odinga [q.v.] announced the formation of the Kenya Independence Movement [q.v.] as a rival, more radical, party. The following month, the Kenya National Party ceased to be a multiracial party and by late 1959, it had joined hands with the Kenya Independence Movement to forge a united front at the first Lancaster House Conference (1960) [q.v.]. After the Lancaster House Conference, the Kenya National Party briefly continued operations under the new name of Kenya African People's Party [q.v.]. In June 1960, the Kenya African People's Party joined other political associations to form the Kenya African Democratic Union [q.v.].

KENYA PARLIAMENT. In February 1954, Dedan Kimathi [q.v.] formed this organization to unify freedom fighters under his command and to undertake more effective military operations during the Mau Mau Revolt [q.v.] than had been possible through the Kenya Defence Council [q.v.]. Besides control of the guerrilla fighters, the Parliament, much smaller in membership than the Kenya Defence Council, claimed to be a body that could serve as a legitimate African government for Kenya. Most of the Kenya Parliament's leadership came from Nyeri District. The body was hampered by the independence of the various guerrilla leaders, some of whom, like Stanley Mathenge, refused to submit to its authority, and by the increasing scope and effectiveness of the military operations mounted against the forest fighters.

KENYA PEOPLE'S UNION (KPU). This political party was registered on 23 May 1966, following the Limuru Conference (1966) [q.v.]. After his resignation from the Kenya African National Union (KANU) [q.v.] and as vice president, on 14 April 1966, Oginga Odinga [q.v.] became KPU's leader. Eventually, 27 MPs (18 members of the House of Representatives and nine senators), including cabinet minister Achieng Oneko and assistant minister Bildad Kaggia [qq.v.], joined the KPU as did several leading trade unionists, including J. D. Akumu and O. O. Mak Anyango. The party opposed the KANU government's pro-Western stance and called for greater equalization of wealth, nationalization of industry, and an end to control of the economy by foreigners. The party was quickly faced with the need to mobilize for the Little General Election (1966) [q.v.]. The election had been forced on the KPU by the hurriedly passed constitutional amendment requiring any MP who changed his/her affiliation from the party under whose mandate he/she was elected to seek a fresh mandate from the electorate. In the electoral contest, the KPU came out the loser, capturing nine seats (seven in the House of Representatives and two in the Senate). The election showed that the party's strongest support was in Odinga's home district of Central Nyanza.

During the 1966–69 period, the KPU functioned as Kenya's official opposition party, despite government harassment and the detention of several key members. Poised to participate in the local government elections of 1968, all KPU candidates were declared ineligible on technical grounds. The party won a huge victory in the 1969 Gem by-election necessitated by the death of KANU minister C. M. G. Arwings-Kodhek [q.v.]. However, in the aftermath of Tom Mboya's [q.v.] assassination, Jomo Kenyatta [q.v.] and his government increasingly viewed the KPU with hostility and suspicion. On 25 October 1969, hostile demonstrations greeted President Kenyatta when he visited Kisumu [q.v.], and security forces opened fire, killing at least 11 people. Two days later, the government detained all KPU MPs and, on 30 October 1969, banned the KPU.

KENYA POLICE. *See* POLICE.

KENYA RAILWAYS CORPORATION. In the early 1990s, Kenya Railways employed about 20,000 personnel and operated a fleet of 218 locomotives, 6,400 wagons, and about 500 coaches. These operated to more than 150 stations along a 2,652-kilometer (1,644-mile) route that connects Mombasa [q.v.] with Malaba, Nakuru [q.v.] with Kisumu, Kisumu [q.v.] with Butere, Voi with Taveta, Konza with Magadi, Nairobi [q.v.] with Nanyuki [q.v.], Eldoret [q.v.] with Kitale, Rongai with Solai, and Gilgil with Nyahururu. Additionally, Kenya Railways operates Inland Waterways Service in Lake Victoria [q.v.] for the movement of passengers and freight in the Kenya section of the lake. There is a wagon ferry between Kisumu and Jinja, Uganda, for intercountry movement of people and goods. Kenya Railways also owns two freight tugs, nine lighters, and three passenger vessels on Lake Victoria. *See also* UGANDA RAILWAY.

KENYA SOCIAL CONGRESS (KSC). In 1992, George Anyona [q.v.] formed this political party (Anyona initially wanted to call the party the Kenya National Congress [q.v.], but other politicians had already founded a party with that name). In the general elections (1992) [q.v.], he was the party's only successful candidate, winning the Kitutu Masaba parliamentary seat. As the party's presidential candidate in 1992, Anyona gained less than 1 percent of the vote. Nevertheless, he was the Kenya Social Congress's presidential candidate in the general elections (1997) [q.v.] but again failed to gain any significant national support. As in 1992, the party won only a single parliamentary seat.

KENYATTA DAY. National holiday celebrated annually on 20 October. It marks the anniversary of the 1952 arrest of Jomo Kenyatta [q.v.] and other leaders of the Kenya African Union [q.v.] and commemorates Kenya's struggle for independence from British colonial rule.

KENYATTA, JOMO (c. 1897/1898?–1978). Civil servant, teacher, politician. Kenya's first and only prime minister and first president. A Kikuyu [q.v.] originally named Kamau wa Ngengi, baptized Johnston Kamau (August 1914), then known as Johnston Kenyatta (1921), and finally Jomo Kenyatta (1938). Born in Ngenda in then Kiambu District and educated at the Church of Scotland Mission [q.v.] at Thogoto (1909–14); Quaker College of Woodbrooke in Great Britain (1931–32); the University of the Toilers of the East, a Comintern school in Moscow (1932–33); and the University of London (1935–37). In 1914 and again in 1918, Kenyatta traveled to Nairobi [q.v.] for employment. In the interim, he worked on a sisal [q.v.] farm in Thika (1915) and for an Asian [q.v.] contractor in Narok (1917). In 1918, Kenyatta returned to Nairobi, where he became a storekeeper. Eventually, he secured a long-term position as a stores clerk and water meter reader for the Public Works Department (1922–28).

Kenyatta's political career began in 1922, when he joined the East African Association [q.v.]. In 1928, he became general secretary of the Kikuyu Central Association (KCA) [q.v.]. In May 1928, he became editor for the KCA newspaper *Muigwithania* (The Unifier [or] The Reconciler). On 17 February 1929, Kenyatta left for England as representative of the KCA. His initial stay was short, but he found time to travel in Europe, visiting Moscow among other places. In September 1930, he returned to Kenya. In 1931, the KCA sent him back to Great Britain so he could present its case before the Joint Select Committee on Closer Union in East Africa (1931) [q.v.]. Thus, he began an exile that lasted almost 17 years. During that time, Kenyatta attended various universities; traveled throughout Europe; and published numerous articles and pamphlets, and his magnum opus, *Facing Mount Kenya*, the result of his studies at the University of London. Additionally, in mid-October 1945, he attended the fifth Pan-African Conference in Manchester as an East African representative.

On 24 September 1946, Kenyatta finally returned to Kenya and in June 1947, assumed the presidency of the Kenya African Union (KAU) [q.v.]. Apart from his political activities, Kenyatta also worked as vice principal and then principal of the Githunguri Teachers' College [q.v.] (1946–47). During the 1947–49 period, he was a member of the African Land Settlement Board. Over the next three years, Kenyatta devoted an increasing amount of time to organizing KAU's efforts to win reform measures from the colonial government. He enjoyed little success in terms of specific reforms while leading resistance to colonial policies and European settler supremacy. The same period witnessed growing unrest and militancy amongst the Kikuyu in particular. The colonial government blamed the escalating violence on what it termed the Mau Mau. Kenyatta refrained from advocating violence to achieve African political goals, including self-government. In 1952, responding to colonial government pressure, he denounced the Mau Mau.

Nevertheless, on 20 October 1952, the police [q.v.] arrested Jomo Kenyatta, Bildad Kaggia, Fred Kubai, Paul Ngei, Achieng Oneko [qq.v.], and Kungu Karumba for directing the Mau Mau. In late 1952, Kenyatta and the others appeared in the Kapenguria Trial [q.v.] for managing Mau Mau. On 8 April 1953, the court convicted Kenyatta and the others. Kenyatta received a sentence of seven years hard labor at Lokitaung in northwestern Kenya. Although fear for Kenyatta's health in prison meant that he was not subjected to hard labor, he served the full sentence and then was placed under restriction by the colonial government. Despite calls from African politicians for his release from detention, it was not until August 1961 that Kenyatta gained his freedom. After trying to bring the Kenya African Democratic Union (KADU) and the Kenya African National Union (KANU) [qq.v.] together, he assumed the leadership of the latter before the end of 1961. In January 1962, Kenyatta was returned to the Legislative Council [q.v.] unopposed in a by-election. He led the KANU team at the second Lancaster House Conference (1962) [q.v.]. Following the conference's conclusion, Kenyatta served as minister of state for constitutional and economic affairs in the coalition government established to complete the constitutional arrangements leading to self-government. In the general elections (1963) [q.v.], he won the Gatundu House of Representatives seat unopposed. Upon the attainment of self-government on 1 June 1963, he became prime minister. Kenyatta led his KANU government to independence on 12 December 1963. On 12 December 1964, following the constitutional changes and dissolution of KADU, he became Kenya's first president.

In the general elections (1969, 1974) [qq.v.], Kenyatta was reelected president unopposed and won the Gatundu parliamentary seat in both elections. In his initial years as prime minister and president, he worked to establish harmonious race relations (notably his appeal to European settlers and the African majority to forget the past), a one-party state by agreement rather than legislation, a mixed economy with room for foreign investment and the safeguarding of property rights, and the increasing provision of educational and medical facilities. Kenyatta supported the self-help, or *Harambee* [q.v.], movement which gained considerable popular support and became the national credo. His support for a capitalist mixed economy, no free land, and a strongly pro-Western foreign policy did not endear him to KANU's radicals.

With Tom Mboya [q.v.] taking the lead, Kenyatta's government isolated them, forcing Oginga Odinga [q.v.] and his supporters out of the party. In countering the challenge of the Kenya People's Union [q.v.], however, Kenyatta used the state apparatus and control of the media together with appeals for ethnic solidarity to the Kikuyu people. After Mboya's death in 1969, he banned the KPU, detained Odinga and other leaders, and called for elections. For the remainder of his presidency, Kenyatta used state power (e.g., detentions), appeals to ethnic chauvinism, and patronage to maintain control over Kenya's political system. For most of his presidency, Kenya was fortunate to maintain relative economic prosperity and high economic growth, at least until the early 1970s.

After 1970, advancing age kept Kenyatta from taking an intimate part in government activities; he intervened only when necessary to settle issues of contention, as in the case of the Change the Constitution Campaign (1976) [q.v.] between his ministers and party leaders. Critics maintained that Kenyatta's relative isolation from affairs was the result of the actions of a "Kiambu clique" of leaders, such as Mbiyu Koinange [q.v.], who increasingly used their positions of influence for their own gain. In 1975, Kenyatta faced another severe crisis with the death of Josiah M. Kariuki [q.v.], but again he surmounted criticism to remain unchallenged as the head of Kenya. He published *Suffering Without Bitterness* in 1968. He died on 22 August 1978.

KENYATTA UNIVERSITY. Established in 1972 as a constituent college of the University of Nairobi [q.v.]. On 17 December 1985, this institution, which is located near Thika [q.v.], had a faculty of some 680 and a student population of about 8,700, becoming Kenya's third university. In 1997–98, the university had 9,461 students. Faculties include arts, education, commerce, environmental education, and science. *See also* EDUCATION, UNIVERSITY.

KERICHO. (Altitude of 2,010 meters; 6,694 feet). Located in Rift Valley Province [q.v.] and known as Kenya's tea [q.v.] capital. In 1906, an acting district commissioner planted Kericho's first tea [q.v.] bush; by 1932, there were more than 4,860 hectares (12,000 acres) under cultivation. According to the 1989 census, Kericho had a population of 48,511.

KERIO PROVINCE. This administrative unit was cut from Naivasha Province in 1921, and in 1923 it took the name Kerio. It consisted of districts then called Baringo, Eldama Ravine, Elgeyo, Marakwet, West Suk/Kacheliba, and (after 1926) North and South Turkana. In 1929, the colonial government dissolved Kerio Province.

KIANO, JULIUS GIKONYO (1926–). Teacher, politician, and businessman. Born in Murang'a and educated at Kagumo Government School and Alliance High School [q.v.]. After attending Makerere University [q.v.], Kiano went to the United States to further his education. He attended Antioch College; Stanford University; and the University of California, Berkeley, where he earned a Ph.D. in political science. Kiano then returned to Kenya and became a lecturer at the then Royal College (later Nairobi University) (1956–58).

He began his political career by being elected to the Legislative Council [q.v.] in 1958. In April 1960, he became minister of commerce and industry. Kiano joined the Kenya African National Union (KANU) [q.v.] and won one of the Fort Hall seats in the LEGCO elections (1961) [q.v.]. He served as a parliamentary secretary in the coalition government of 1962–63. In the general elections (1963) [q.v.], Kiano won the Kangema seat in the House of Representatives unopposed and subsequently became minister of commerce and industry. In 1966, he became minister of labour and in 1968 minister of education. In the general elections (1969) [q.v.], Kiano won the Mbiri seat and then became minister of local government. In 1973, he was appointed minister of commerce and industry again, and in 1976, he took over the ministry of water development. In the general elections (1974) [q.v.], Kiano again piled up a massive majority over his nearest rival.

However, in the general elections (1979) [q.v.], he lost at the hands of Kenneth Matiba [q.v.]. Now out of the cabinet, Kiano did not challenge for the Mbiri seat in the general elections (1983) [q.v.]. He attempted to regain the seat in the general elections (1988) [q.v.], only to be defeated again by Matiba. Even when Matiba resigned from KANU after the general elections (1988), Kiano failed to win the by-election in Mbiri. After the emergence of multipartyism, he remained in KANU which did not endear him to voters. In the general elections (1997) [q.v.], he failed to win the Kiharu parliamentary seat.

KIBACHIA, CHEGE (1920–). Trade unionist. Born in Kiambu and educated at Alliance High School [q.v.] (1939–42). In 1945, Kibachia came to national attention after he moved to Mombasa [q.v.] to work for the East African Clothing Factory. When a general strike began in Mombasa in January 1947, the African Workers' Federation [q.v.] was formed to articulate the demands of the strikers. Kibachia quickly emerged as its leader, first as executive officer and after March as president. As a result of Kibachia's leadership Mombasa workers won an increase in wages, and the appeal of trade unionism [q.v.] and industrial action spread in the colony. In August 1947, Kibachia came to Nairobi to organize a branch for the federation there, but on the 27th he was arrested. He was detained at Kabarnet for the next 10 years. After independence, he served as industrial relations officer and later senior labour officer at Mombasa. He was a member of Kenya's Industrial Court.

KIBAKI, MWAI (1931–). Economist and politician. Born in Othaya, Nyeri District. He attended the Othaya Primary School, Kirima Mission School, Nyeri Boys' School, and Mangu High School. Between 1951 and 1954, he studied at Makerere University [q.v.], where he received a first class honors degree in economics, political science, and history. Kibaki also received a B.Sc. degree from the London School of Economics (1959). He then became an economics lecturer at Makerere University (1959–60). He returned to Kenya to work for the Kenya African National Union (KANU) [q.v.] and to serve in the East African Common Services Organisation's [q.v.] legislative assembly. In May 1963, Kibaki won a parliamentary seat for Nairobi's Doornholm constituency, and at self-government received an appointment as parliamentary secretary to the treasury.

After Kenya gained independence on 12 December 1963, Kibaki served as assistant minister in the Ministry of Economic Planning and Development. For the general elections (1969) [q.v.], he contested the Othaya constituency and won the seat, being reelected again in the 1974 general elections and the general elections (1979) [qq.v.]. Following the 1966 party split that led to the formation of the Kenya People's Union [q.v.], Kibaki gained cabinet rank, becoming minister for commerce and industry (1966–69), minister of finance (1970–78), and minister of economic planning and development (1970–78).

On 14 October 1978, Kibaki became vice president but also retained the ministry of finance portfolio. Nevertheless, during the 1980–82 period, he was subjected to much criticism and attack, particularly from supporters of Charles Njonjo [q.v.]. In February 1982, he became minister of home affairs. He retained his seat in the general elections (1983) [q.v.], and in the general elections (1988) [q.v.], Kibaki scored an impressive electoral victory (99.8 percent of the vote) by again winning the parliamentary seat for Othaya. His political influence had begun to wane, however, largely because of numerous personal differences with President Daniel arap Moi [q.v.]. Consequently, on 24 March 1988, Moi dropped Kibaki as vice president and minister of home Affairs. By appointing him as minister of health, Moi succeeded in eliminating a potential rival. However, Moi's tactics further alienated many of the Kikuyu [q.v.] people, most of whom believed that Kibaki had been treated unfairly.

On 26 December 1991, Kibaki resigned from the government and KANU and subsequently became leader of the Democratic Party (DP) [q.v.]. In the general elections (1992) [q.v.], he stood for the presidency on the DP ticket but gained only 19.45 percent (1,050,617) of the vote; however, he won the Othaya parliamentary seat. In the general elections (1997) [q.v.], Kibaki again stood for president as the DP candidate, coming in second with 31.09 percent (1,895,527) of the vote. He also retained his parliamentary seat. As the DP emerged from the election as the second-largest party in the new parliament, Kibaki became leader of the opposition. However, Kibaki claimed the election was rigged and promised to fight President Moi's electoral victory in court and Parliament.

KIKUYU (Also known as GIKUYU). The Kikuyu are Kenya's largest ethnic group (1989 census: 4,455,865). They form part of the Thagicu group of Bantu-speaking [q.v.] peoples. During the first half of the second millennium C.E., those speaking the Kikuyu language probably differentiated from other Thagicu speakers north of Mount Kenya [q.v.]. Beginning in the 17th and 18th centuries, the agricultural Kikuyu ancestors moved south and then east, entering what became known as the White Highlands [q.v.] stretching from Mount Kenya's southern slopes and along the Nyandarua range. Small groups of people, driven by expanding population and the needs of shifting cultivation, thus gradually settled present-day Central Province [q.v.]. By the late 19th century, such settlements had reached the outskirts of present-day Nairobi and the edge of the Rift Valley [qq.v.]. In the process of this settlement, the Kikuyu ancestors came into contact with peoples such as the Gumba agriculturalists, Okiek hunter/gatherers, and Maasai [q.v.] pastoralists. The descendants of those who settled Kikuyuland soon developed localized lineages that came to be organized into territorial councils of elders. This political system gave greatest influence to age and wealth, as was the case with most of Kenya's agricultural peoples.

The onset of British colonial rule had a huge impact on the Kikuyu as they were among the first to feel the impact of the arrival of Christian missionaries and loss of land to European settlement. The latter led many Kikuyu to move to European farms in the Rift Valley [q.v.] as squatters [q.v.], while others became involved in commodity production and/or wage labor. A sense of grievance at the land loss was perhaps the most powerful of many factors that propelled Western-educated Kikuyu into political action through such organizations as the East African Association, the Kikuyu Central Association, the Kenya African Union, and the Kenya African National Union [qq.v.]. Many Kikuyu played leading roles in the nationalist movement, and the people were deeply involved, and divided, by the Mau Mau Revolt [q.v.].

KIKUYU ASSOCIATION (KA). In 1919, a group of Kiambu chiefs, headed by Koinange wa Mbiyu (president) [q.v.] and Philip Karanja (secretary), formed the KA to protect their land from further alienation. Some of the KA's early activities included requesting a survey of Kiambu farms and the issuance of title deeds to landholders. Additionally, the Kiambu chiefs protested such practices as forced labor, land alienation, lack of public services, taxes, and the *kipande* [q.v.] registration system. The colonial government cooperated with the KA because it was less radical than the Kikuyu Central Association (KCA) [q.v.], which had been created in 1924. As a result, some Kenyans perceived the conservative Koinange wa Mbiyu and his followers as instruments of European control. Nevertheless, the KA facilitated reforms such as the improvement and expansion of the educational and agricultural sectors.

Harry Thuku's East African Association [qq.v.] provided a strong challenge to the KA during the 1921–22 period as the chiefs, allied to the colonial government, seemed unable to mount a strong campaign on behalf of discontented Kikuyu [q.v.]. The leaders of the KA were angered by Thuku's attacks, and most were not unhappy to witness his detention and the end of the EAA. During the 1929 female circumcision dispute, the KA supported European missionaries who wanted the practice abolished. This policy alienated many Kikuyu, especially those who belonged to the KCA, which opposed the missionaries' position on female circumcision. Thus, by 1929, its popular backing had shrunk in comparison to that of the KCA. Faced with increasing hostility from the colonial government in 1930, the leaders changed the KA's name to Kikuyu Loyal Patriots [q.v.]. The new organization had little success and by 1938, Koinange and others having joined the KCA, it faded from the political scene of central Kenya.

KIKUYU CENTRAL ASSOCIATION (KCA). This political association was launched in 1924 at Kahuhia in Murang'a and also gained support in Kiambu and Nyeri. The KCA's membership was from the first petty bourgeois, individuals with Western education, often employed as clerks or teachers; active as traders; or involved in commercial agriculture [q.v.]. The KCA was particularly concerned with the issue of land: the fact that the Kikuyu [q.v.] had lost land to European settlement and were faced with land shortage and the insecurity of tenure that characterized the land cultivated by Kikuyu and other Africans. During the 1920s, the KCA not only championed land issues but called for the release of Harry Thuku [q.v.], the appointment of a paramount chief for the Kikuyu, the construction of more schools, and permission to grow coffee [q.v.]. KCA members in the Kikuyu-inhabited districts initially participated in the Local Native Councils [q.v.] set up after 1925, but these were dominated by the colonial government and such members soon recognized that relatively little could be accomplished there.

In 1928, Jomo Kenyatta [q.v.] became general secretary. He used the party newspaper (*Muigwithania*), which he edited, to broaden the organization, spread news of its activities and promote cultural pride. It continued to call for safeguards for African land, the abolition of the *kipande* [q.v.] system, and greater improvement and government services in the rural areas. Kenyatta was sent to Great Britain in 1929 to present KCA's grievances directly to the metropolitan government. At the end of the decade, the KCA became involved in cultural nationalism in defense of Kikuyu traditional customs, particularly female circumcision, under attack by Christian missionaries. Although its representative (Kenyatta) was not allowed to present evidence to the 1931 Joint Select Committee [q.v.] in London, most KCA members were pleased with the announcement that the imperial government had appointed the Kenya Land Commission [q.v.] to thoroughly investigate that issue. The commission's report, released in 1934, disappointed the KCA. During the decade, the KCA thus continued to put forward Kikuyu claims over land, and, despite the setback it suffered when Thuku broke away to form the rival Kikuyu Provincial Association [q.v.], members were involved in the independent schools and churches movement that grew out of the missionaries' attempts to force church members to accept their edicts against female circumcision. The KCA also gained influence among Kikuyu living as squatters [q.v.] in the Rift Valley. Under the pretext of wartime necessity, the colonial government proscribed the KCA in 1940. In 1945, the KCA, which remained intact during World War II [q.v.], was reactivated as part of the Kenya African Union [q.v.].

KIKUYU LOYAL PATRIOTS (KLP). In 1931, the Kikuyu Association [q.v.] changed its name to Kikuyu Loyal Patriots to emphasize the organization's loyalty to the colonial government in the face of hostility from government officials and rivalry with the Kikuyu Central Association [q.v.]. The KLP soon experienced criticism and animosity from European missionaries as well. The appointment of the Kenya Land Commission [q.v.] gave the organization reason for action and hope that land grievances might be redressed. The 1934 publication of the commission's report, which disappointed all Kikuyu, discredited the KLP's approach to politics. Leaders like Chief Koinange [q.v.] joined the KCA, and by 1938, the KLP ceased to exist.

KIKUYU PROVINCE. In 1920, the colonial government created Kikuyu Province by renaming Kenia Province [q.v.]. It consisted of Embu,

Kiambu, Fort Hall, Meru, North Nyeri (European-settled area), South Nyeri and (after 1929) Nairobi [q.v.] Districts. In 1934, the colonial government merged Kikuyu Province with Ukamba Province to form Central Province [q.v.].

KIKUYU PROVINCIAL ASSOCIATION (KPA). In April 1935, Harry Thuku [q.v.] formed the KPA following his break with the Kikuyu Central Association (KCA) [q.v.]. Although the KPA—which emphasized self-help, local reform, and support for most colonial policies—enrolled several KCA members, it never gained a large following. By World War II [q.v.], the KPA had ceased to exist as an effective protest organization.

KIMATHI, DEDAN (1920–1957). Leader of the forest freedom fighters in the Mau Mau Revolt [q.v.]. Born in Tetu division of Nyeri [q.v.]. After elementary schooling, he attended the Church of Scotland Mission School at Tumu Tumu without completing his course of study. In 1941, Kimathi joined the King's African Rifles [q.v.]; however, a month later, he was dismissed for misconduct. Kimathi returned to school but in 1944, was expelled for failure to pay his school fees. He then worked as a dairy clerk in Nyeri [q.v.], a timber clerk near the Aberdare [q.v.] forest, and a clerk in a Shell Company oil depot in the Thomson's Falls area. In 1949, Kimathi joined the "Forty Group," the Kikuyu Central Association's [q.v.] militant wing, and became a youth winger and a political organizer. In mid-1952, he became the Kenya Africa Union's [q.v.] branch secretary in the Ol Kalou and Thomson's Falls area.

During the Mau Mau Revolt [q.v.] Kimathi took up arms against the colonial state and commanded fighters in the Aberdare and Nyandarua forests. He was an influential leader of the Kenya Defence Council and the Kenya Parliament [qq.v.]. On 22 October 1956, Ndirangu Mau, a police constable, shot and wounded Kimathi near Kahiga-ini, Tetu. On 19 November 1956, the Nyeri Supreme Court opened his trial. After seven days, the court found him guilty of being in unlawful possession of a firearm and six rounds of ammunition and sentenced him to death (the authorities had dropped an earlier murder charge). The Court of Appeal of Eastern Africa and the Judicial Committee of the Privy Council rejected his appeals. On 18 February 1957, the colonial authorities hanged him at Kamiti Maximum Security Prison, Nairobi.

Kimathi remains an enigmatic figure. To some, he is the greatest of Kenyan freedom fighters and a nationalist whose contributions to the struggle for independence have not been properly recognized by the Kenyan government. To others, he was merely the leader of a sectional revolt whose personality made him difficult to work with and uncooperative with others.

KING'S AFRICAN RIFLES (KAR). The history of the KAR in the East Africa Protectorate began in 1895, when Commissioner Sir Arthur Hardinge [q.v.] petitioned London to establish a 1,000-man force to garrison the territory. The British government approved this request, resulting in the creation of the East Africa Rifles. This force garrisoned its troops in three military districts, including Seyidieh and Tanaland Provinces [qq.v.], Ukamba Province [q.v.], and Jubaland Province [q.v.]. During its existence, the East Africa Rifles provided internal security, suppressed the Mazrui Rebellion (1895–96) and launched numerous punitive expeditions against Somali elements in Jubaland (1895–1901).

In 1901, the British government announced its intention to consolidate its military forces in East and Central Africa. On 1 January 1902, the KAR came into being, with an authorized strength of six battalions manned by 104 European officers and 4,579 African noncommissioned officers and men. During the 1902–14 period, the KAR's activities were limited largely to maintaining internal security and crushing African opposition to British colonial rule throughout the colony. The latter involved launching punitive expeditions against numerous indigenous groups, some of which included the Embu, Gusii [qq.v.], Kipsigis, Marakwet, Nandi, and Turkana.

The outbreak of World War I [q.v.] forced the British government to expand the KAR's size to 22 battalions. During World War I , 22 KAR battalions participated in the East African campaign. It was reorganized into a northern and southern brigade, the latter of which maintained its headquarters in Dar-es-Salaam. In 1939, the War Office assumed control of the KAR. At the beginning of World War II [q.v.], there were two infantry brigades stationed in Kenya. The First (E.A.) Infantry Brigade, headquartered in Nairobi [q.v.], was responsible for the defense of Kenya's coast. This unit included the Second KAR (Mbagathi; less one company in Zomba), Third KAR (Nairobi), and Fourth KAR (Malindi [q.v.]; less one company in Nairobi and Garissa). The Second (E.A.) Infantry Brigade, headquartered in Nanyuki [q.v.], was responsible for defending the country's interior. This unit included the First KAR (Isiolo; less one company in Wajir), Fifth KAR (Nanyuki; less one company in Moyale), and the Sixth KAR (Nanyuki). As the war progressed, the number of Kenyan KAR units expanded. Many took part in various campaigns in East Africa and Southeast Asia. The 31st KAR also performed garrison duty in Mauritius. After the war, several Kenyan KAR units, supported by the police [q.v.] and British military forces, fought in the Mau Mau Revolt [q.v.]. At independence, the three Kenya-based battalions (the Third, Fifth, and 11th) became known as the Kenya Rifles. *See also* KENYA DEFENCE FORCE; MAU MAU REVOLT.

KIPANDE. The registration card that all African males were required to carry under the 1915 Registration Ordinance. Ostensibly, the *kipande* (which means "piece" in Swahili—in this case a piece of paper) provided a means of identification of the African population. However, its primary purpose, as advocated by Kenya's European settlers, was to enhance labor recruitment and control. The Colonial Office deferred implementation of the *kipande* registration system until the end of World War I [q.v.]. During the 1919–20 period, the colonial government put the *kipande* into general use. The *kipande* came to be a most hated symbol of African subserviency, partly because of the initial requirement that it was to be carried by African males at all times in a metal container tied by string around the neck. The *kipande* would long be a source of great unhappiness that generated political protest for many years. In December 1947, the colonial government sought to mollify the Africans by the adoption of a Registration of Persons Ordinance, which applied to all races. Moreover, the new identity cards contained no employment information.

KISUMU. (Altitude of 1,145 meters; 3,757 feet). Local name is *Winam* (the head of the lake). Established in 1900 by District Commissioner C.W. Hobley [q.v.] who surveyed and laid out the town. Also, capital of western Kenya, administrative and commercial center of Nyanza Province [q.v.], and home of the Luo [q.v.] community. Kisumu, which is Kenya's third-largest town and the country's chief lake port, is located on Lake Victoria's [q.v.] eastern shore. The city is linked by road to Nairobi via Kericho [qq.v].

In 1901, the Uganda Railway [q.v.] reached Kisumu (then called Port Florence). The railway's completion had an important impact on western Kenya's development. Apart from stimulating the local economy, the railway enabled the British colonial authorities to consolidate their control over the peoples of western Kenya by deploying troops and other personnel to Kisumu, which served as the main base for the pacification of the region. Additionally, the railway affected Kenyan-Ugandan relations. To keep the Uganda Railway under a single administration, the

Foreign Office transferred Uganda's Eastern Province to Kenya, which assumed responsibility for governing the eastern shore of Lake Victoria and most of the Rift Valley [q.v.] highlands. By the 1930s, Kisumu had become one of East Africa's leading ports, with shipping to and from Mwanza and Musoma in Tanzania and Kampala, Uganda. Additionally, the city was the main administrative, military, and economic hub for the entire region. Many Asians [q.v.] settled in the town and opened small businesses.

After independence on 12 December 1963, Kisumu underwent several changes. The 1977 collapse of the East African Community (EAC) [q.v.] ended the town's prosperity, which was based on the fact that it was an important transshipment point for trade between Kenya, Uganda, and Tanzania. In the political arena, the Luo community became increasingly disenchanted with what it perceived as the discriminatory policies of the Kikuyu [q.v.]-dominated government of Jomo Kenyatta [q.v.]. Tensions between the Luos and Nairobi continued after Daniel arap Moi [q.v.] became president in 1978, and especially after the 1990 murder of Minister of Foreign Affairs Robert Ouko [q.v.], who also was an influential Luo politician and represented Kisumu Town in Parliament.

By the late 1990s, Kisumu had yet to regain its former prominence despite the fact that the city had a thriving fishing industry, a sugar refinery, marine workshops, and flour mills. Also, cross-border trade between Kenya and Uganda, both legal and illegal, accounted for a significant portion of the city's economic activity. However, many local businessmen believed that the city's future prosperity depended upon the extent to which the East African Co-operation Secretariat, which was established in March 1996 to replace the defunct EAC, would revive trade between Kenya, Uganda, and Tanzania. On a more practical level, Kisumu suffers from a lack of adequate garbage collection and from poor road maintenance. Additionally, unclean drinking water is responsible for numerous waterborne diseases. Efforts by local leaders to correct these problems have made little progress. According to the 1989 census, Kisumu had a population of 255,381.

KITALE. (Altitude of 1,890 meters; 6,200 feet). Originally known as Quitale, a station along the old slave route between Uganda and Tanzania. In 1920, the colonial government made Kitale the capital of Trans Nzoia District. After World War I, the first European settlers arrived and established the modern town. In 1925, the railway started service to Kitale, which enabled European farmers to export coffee, tea [qq.v.], maize, wheat, pyrethrum [q.v.], and dairy products. According to the 1989 census, Kitale had a population of 56,218.

KIVULI, DAVID ZAKAYO (1896?–1974). Religious leader who founded the African Israel Church Nineveh (AICN), one of East Africa's largest independent churches. Kivuli's religious career began in 1925, when he became a preacher and school supervisor for the Pentecostal Assemblies of Canada mission. After returning to Kenya, he gained many followers, especially among western Kenya's Luo and Luyia [qq.v.] peoples. In 1942, Kivuli broke away from the Pentecostal Assemblies of Canada mission and established the AICN. In 1957, the National Christian Council of Kenya [q.v.] rejected the AICN's application for membership. However, in 1970, Kivuli succeeded in gaining probationary membership for his movement. In 1975, the AICN became affiliated with the World Council of Churches.

KOINANGE, MBIYU (1907–1981). Educator and politician. Son of Koinange wa Mbiyu [q.v.], one of the most influential chiefs in southern Kiambu during the interwar period. Born in Njunu in Kiambu District. Educated at Church Missionary Society (CMS) [q.v.] school Kiambaa; Kabete Primary School; Buxton High School; Alliance High School [q.v.] (1926–27); Hampton Institute, Virginia (1927–31); Ohio Wesleyan University (1931–35); Columbia University (1935–36); St. John's College, Cambridge (1936–37); and the University of London (1937–38). During the 1939–48 period, he served as the principal of the Githunguri Teachers' College [q.v.], which opened on 7 January 1939.

Koinange began his political career in 1944, when he helped establish the Kenya African Union [q.v.]; subsequently, he served as that organization's European representative and worked with the London Cooperative Society (1951–59). Koinange then headed the Bureau of African Affairs in Ghana (1959–60) and was secretary-general of the Pan African Freedom Movement for East, Central, and South Africa in Tanzania (1961–62). After returning to Kenya, Koinange joined the Kenya African National Union (KANU) [q.v.] and served as MP for Kiambaa (1963–79). He also held several senior government positions, including minister for pan-African affairs (1963–64); minister of education (1964–66); minister of state, Office of the President (1966–78); and minister for water development (1978–79). During the Jomo Kenyatta [q.v.] era, Koinange was one of the president's closest advisers, and he was widely viewed as one of Kenya's most powerful individuals. Following Kenyatta's death, Koinange's influence rapidly declined. In the 1979 general election [q.v.], he lost his seat to Njenga Karume [q.v.]. He died on 2 September 1981.

KOINANGE WA MBIYU (c. 1878/1881–1960). Colonial chief. Koinange was born into *mbari ya Njunu* (lineage/clan of Njunu), which held extensive lands in southern Kiambu. His father, Mbiyu, was friendly toward the first British administrators and was made a chief. In 1905, he made Koinange a headman, and in 1908 the son succeeded the father as government-appointed chief. During the first decade of the 20th century, he and his people experienced first-hand the impact of European settlement in loss of land and demands for labor. In 1914, he left home and obtained land in Kiambaa, away from the European settlers, but for the rest of his life Koinange championed Kikuyu [q.v.] demands for a return of land they felt had been stolen. As a chief, Koinange established a reputation for efficiency and as a champion of "improvement."

After World War I [q.v.], Koinange entered local politics as a principal mover behind the formation of the Kikuyu Association [q.v.], the rival of Harry Thuku's [q.v.] East African Association [q.v.] in the postwar period. Throughout the 1920s, land was a major concern in sparking his political activity, though as the leading member of the Kiambu Local Native Council, he also advocated agricultural development and the opening of more schools. During the 1920s, he remained a moderate and generally worked against the Kikuyu Central Association (KCA) [q.v.]. He sided with those Protestant missionaries who sought to suppress female circumcision among the Kikuyu. This and his reputation as a pro-government chief caused him to be selected as one of three Kenya Africans to testify before the 1931 Joint Select Committee on Closer Union [q.v.] in London, but he proved a strong critic of colonial rule, attacking loss of land, high taxation, the *kipande* [q.v.] system, and a lack of development in the African reserves. He supported the appointment of the Kenya Land Commission [q.v.], but its 1934 report disappointed him. Thereafter, he became increasingly militant in his activities and he joined the KCA. In 1938, he became senior chief of Kiambu. When his son, Mbiyu [q.v.], returned from study abroad in 1938, the chief started to promote the idea of establishing a Githunguri Teachers' College [q.v.].

After World War II [q.v.], Chief Koinange became involved with the Kenya African Union [q.v.], especially after Jomo Kenyatta [q.v.] took up the leadership. The two became close allies because Kenyatta married the chief's daughter. As a result, the colonial government looked upon Koinange with increasing suspicion. After the 1952 assassination of Chief Waruhiu, the police arrested Koinange. Although he was acquitted of any crime, the authorities detained him for the remainder of the Mau Mau Revolt [q.v.]. In late June 1960, the colonial government finally released him as he was near death. He died on 28 July 1960.

KOLLOA AFFRAY (1950). According to the colonial government, the Kolloa Affray, which occurred on 24 April 1950, was a confrontation between the police [q.v.] and Pokot supporters of *Dini ya Msambwa* [q.v.] that occurred at Kolloa in Baringo District. Lucas Pkiech (Kipkoech), who was killed in the clash, led the Pokot. According to the official inquiry into the affray, the Pokot *Dini ya Msambwa* adherents had 28 dead and 50 wounded while the police lost four dead. The colonial government blamed the confrontation on the sect's anti-European fanaticism and took stern action. Seven men were hanged for causing the deaths of the police, and more than 100 were prosecuted for being members of a proscribed organization. In addition, the authorities confiscated 5,000 cattle and imposed compulsory labor on those Pokot who supported the sect.

KRAPF, JOHANN LUDWIG (1810–1881). Missionary and explorer. Born in Derendingen, Germany, and educated at the Basle Mission College (1827–29) and in Tubingen, where he completed his theological studies (1834). Initially, Krapf worked in Ethiopia (1837–42) as a member of the Church Missionary Society (CMS) [q.v.] However, because of unsettled conditions throughout much of Ethiopia, Krapf moved his area of operations further south. On 13 March 1844, Krapf and his wife and daughter arrived in Mombasa [q.v.]. Despite the loss of his wife and daughter to malaria, Krapf continued his work and he established East Africa's first European mission station, at Rabai near Mombasa. During the 1847–49 period, he and Johann Rebmann, another German missionary-explorer who had arrived in East Africa on 10 June 1846, made six trips to the East African interior. Apart from establishing contact with local peoples and preaching Christianity, the two acquired important geographical information. On 11 May 1848, for example, Rebmann sighted Mount Kilimanjaro, and, on 3 December 1849, Krapf saw Mount Kenya [q.v.].

In late 1849, Krapf returned to Europe. Two years later, he was back in Africa after receiving CMS approval to establish a string of mission stations in the East African interior. Due to a lack of resources and differences with other missionaries, Krapf never achieved this ambitious goal. In mid-1853, he returned to Germany, where he eventually regained his health. He died on 26 November 1881.

KUBAI, FREDERICK POLWARTH KIBUTHU (1915–1996). Trade unionist, nationalist, and politician. Born in Kiambu District and educated at the Church Missionary Society (CMS) [q.v.] School, Nairobi [q.v.], and Buxton High School, Mombasa [q.v.]. Kubai began his career by working as a telegraphist in the East African Posts and Telegraphs Department (1930–46). In 1946, he became active in Kenya's labor movement by organizing the African Workers' Federation [q.v.]. Kubai then served as the organizing secretary of the Kenya African Road Transport and Mechanics' Union (later known as the Transport and Allied Workers' Union) (1947) before becoming that group's acting general secretary (1948). In 1949, he and Makhan Singh [q.v.] founded the East African Trade Union Congress [q.v.]. Two years later, Kubai became chairman of the Kenya African Union [q.v.], Nairobi branch, and editor of *Sauti ya Mwafrika*.

On 20 October 1952, the colonial authorities arrested Kubai, Jomo Kenyatta [q.v.], and four other nationalist leaders for directing the Mau Mau Revolt [q.v.]. He was convicted along with Kenyatta at the 1953 Kapenguria Trial [q.v.]. Upon gaining his freedom in 1961, Kubai unsuccessfully tried to defeat Tom Mboya [q.v.] for control of Kenya's trade union [q.v.] movement. Kubai won election to Parliament and was MP for Nakuru East (1963–69, 1973–74, and 1983–88). Between 1963 and 1974, Kubai served as assistant minister of labour and social services. In July 1985, he became assistant minister of state, Office of the President. In 1988, Kubai retired from politics and moved to his Mai Mahiu farm, which was about 70 kilometers from Nairobi. He died on 1 June 1996.

-L-

LABOUR CIRCULAR (1919). Sometimes known as the Northey or Ainsworth Circular. In October 1919, this circular was issued to all administrative officers in the East Africa Protectorate [q.v.] over then Chief Native Commissioner John Ainsworth's [q.v.] name. Actually drafted by Governor Sir Edward Northey [q.v.], the circular made clear his desire that administrators at all levels should insist that Africans, including women and children, leave their homes to work for European settlers. It thus put the colonial government in the business of labor recruitment for private enterprise. Publication of the circular stirred up protest from missionaries and humanitarian groups in East Africa and in Great Britain. This forced the Colonial Office to insist on the issuance of a revised circular in July 1920. However, the new circular failed to quiet the critics in Great Britain. In mid-1921, following consultation with Ainsworth, who indicated that the circular was unnecessary and not supported by most administrators, the Colonial Office decided to revise Northey's labor policy. In September 1921, London adopted a new policy that directed government officials to refrain from recruiting labor for private enterprise. Compulsory labor for government undertakings was still possible, but only with prior approval from the secretary of state for the colonies.

LABOUR TRADE UNION OF EAST AFRICA. Formed in March 1935, the Labour Trade Union of East Africa at first had largely Asian [q.v.] membership and enjoyed support from workers in building trades and the railways. Makhan Singh [q.v.] was the union's secretary. By 1939, he had forged ties with African workers and the Kikuyu Central Association (KCA) [q.v.]. Singh's internment in India during World War II [q.v.] crippled the union's activities. Nevertheless, it remained in existence and in February 1949, it joined with other trade unions to form the East Africa Trade Union Congress [q.v.].

LAKE BARINGO. (168 square kilometers; 65 square miles). Located on the Rift Valley's [q.v.] floor. Three ethnic groups live around the lake. Pokot cattle herders live in the north and east; Njemps cattle herders and fishermen inhabit the south; and the Tugen reside on the lake's west side in the hills that bear their name. The lake is noted for its bird life; more than 460 species have been reported.

LAKE BORGORIA. (107 square kilometers; 41 square miles). Called Lake Hannington during the colonial era. Located south of Lake Baringo and north of Lake Nakuru [qq.v.] in a cleft below a sheer fault scarp on the east that leads to the Laikipia Plateau. The shallow lake is extremely alkaline so it supports no fish. However, flamingos rely on the lake's blue-green algae as a food source. In 1973, the Kenyan government made the lake a national reserve.

LAKE ELMENTEITA. 1,786 meters (5,860 feet) above sea level, this shallow soda lake, which is similar to Lake Nakuru [q.v.] but does not attract large numbers of flamingos, is about 14.5 kilometers (9 miles) long by 7.2 kilometers (4.5 miles) wide.

LAKE MAGADI. (100 square kilometers; 40 square miles). The world's second-largest source of trona, a monoclinic mineral that consists of sodium carbonate. In 1901, Thomas Deacon and John R. Walsh, two mining prospectors, staked a claim around the lake. Shortly thereafter, they transferred their interest in Lake Magadi to the East Africa Syndicate Ltd. in exchange for 20 percent of the profits that might be derived from the sale of soda ash. Deacon and Walsh subsequently sold their interest for modest compensation in 1902 and 1903, respectively. On 12 April 1911, the newly created Magadi Soda Company unveiled a project to build a 150-kilometer (93-mile) railway from Konza to Magadi. Since then, soda ash gradually grew in commercial importance. Currently, the lake is a major foreign currency earner producing 200,000 to 250,000 tonnes of soda ash annually for export markets in the Far East and Southeast Asia.

LAKE NAIVASHA. (160 square kilometers; 62 square miles). The lake's name is derived from the Maa word *en-aiposha* (the lake). It is located in the Rift Valley [q.v.]. Apart from its natural beauty, this freshwater lake, which is 1,870 meters (6,135 feet) above sea level, is also a bird sanctuary where more than 400 species have been recorded. Since 1980, a small but growing wine industry has been active in the Lake Naivasha area.

LAKE NAKURU. (188 square kilometers; 73 square miles). Located about 150 kilometers (93 miles) northwest of Nairobi [q.v.]. Established as a bird sanctuary in 1960 and gazetted as a national park [q.v.] in 1967. Historically, Lake Nakuru, which is 1,782 meters (5,846 feet) above sea level, has been considered one of the world's great flamingo sanctuaries. However, in the late 1970s increased rainfall and decreased evaporation lowered Lake Nakuru's salinity, which in turn caused a flamingo exodus to other lakes in the region. Additionally, numerous ecologists maintained that a Japanese-built sewage and rehabilitation facility in the area precipitated the drying up of the lake and another flight of flamingos. On 20 March 1997, the Kenyan government denied these charges and claimed that such migrations were natural phenomena as had previously occurred in 1933, 1937, 1939, 1947, and 1967 and that these are a normal part of Lake Nakuru's existence. Nevertheless, many environmentalists continued to worry about Lake Nakuru's future well-being.

LAKE TURKANA. Originally called Lake Rudolf; renamed in 1975 in honor of the people who inhabit the area. Also known as the Jade Sea. This lake, which is the largest freshwater body of water in northern Kenya, measures 250 kilometers (155 miles) long and 16–48 kilometers (10–30 miles) wide. The lake has existed for at least three million years and, prior to the last Ice Age, was a major tributary of the Nile River. The Omo River, which carries water from the Ethiopian highlands, empties into the northern part of Lake Turkana. This inflow helps to keep the lake's water fresh. However, the southern portion of Lake Turkana, in which there is no inflowing river, suffers from high salinity.

In recent years, a fishing industry has been developing on Lake Turkana. Sibiloi National Park [q.v.] is located on the lake's northeastern shore. Thanks to the work of Richard Leakey [q.v.] and several other archaeologists, some of the earliest examples of man have been found in the area. As a result, Lake Turkana and its surrounding territory have gained notoriety as the "cradle of mankind."

LAKE VICTORIA. Formerly known as Lake Nyanza. Lake Victoria, which is the source of the Nile River, is the largest freshwater lake in Africa, having an area of about 69,930 square kilometers (27,000 square miles) and a coastline of more than 3,200 kilometers (1,900 miles). This lake, which is 3,717 feet above sea level and about 352 kilometers (218 miles) in diameter, is quite shallow, with a maximum depth of about 91 meters (300 feet). The inflow from rainfall is an estimated 98 billion cubic meters (384 billion cubic feet) and from tributaries about 16 billion cubic meters (63 billion cubic feet). The outflow due to evaporation is approximately 93 billion cubic meters (365 billion cubic feet) and into the Nile River is about 21 billion cubic meters. The soils of the Lake Victoria basin and its islands are suitable for intensive cultivation. As a result, this region has a dense population, which is supported by a variety of rail, road, and shipping services.

In recent years, several problems have brought Lake Victoria to the verge of an ecological disaster. Many scientists maintain that the 1962 introduction of the Nile perch (*Lates niloticus*), which experts believed would be a high-yielding source of protein for Tanzania, Uganda, and Kenya, was a mistake. The proliferation of this fish, a voracious predator that can weigh more than 200 pounds, now poses the greatest threat to Lake Victoria's delicate ecological balance. This species feeds on smaller fish, including haplochromines, which, along with other species such as catfish, eat algae at the bottom of the lake. As the Nile perch reduced the population of algae-eating fish by at least one-half, the lake's self-cleaning system collapsed and oxygen levels dropped to almost zero, thereby choking the life out of Lake Victoria. Another threat to the lake is the South American water hyacinth (*Eichhornia crassipes*), a large, free-floating aquatic weed that forms a mat on still or slow-flowing water. Since first appearing in the 1980s, this weed multiplied rapidly and covered many vast parts of Lake Victoria with a dense mat that deprives fish and plankton of the oxygen essential for their survival.

Pollution from sewage and runoff of fertilizers, pesticides, and industrial wastes caused massive algae blooms. As the algae died and fell to the lake's bottom, bacteria decomposed them. This process required increasing amounts of oxygen, which left the deeper waters too poor in oxygen for fish. As a result, fish went into the shallow inshore waters where they were eaten by Nile perch and caught by fishermen. By the 1990s, oxygen levels in shallow waters had also started to drop because of the introduction of the water hyacinth.

The gradual degradation of Lake Victoria poses a threat to the 30 million people who depend on the lake for their livelihood. This situation is unlikely to change anytime soon as the rivers flowing in and out of Lake Victoria are so languid that it takes up to 100 years for the lake to clean itself. On 8 July 1994, Tanzania, Kenya, and Uganda responded to this ecological catastrophe by signing an agreement which established the Lake Victoria Fisheries Organization. This organization, which commenced operations in 1995, will implement a five-year US$20 million program to ensure the rational exploitation of Lake Victoria's resources. Despite this action, however, many scientists and ecologists remain concerned about Lake Victoria's long-term well-being.

LAMU. Altitude is at sea level. Lamu, which is Kenya's oldest existing town, was an important island city-state with a thriving port by the early 1500s. In 1813, Lamu defeated Paté, another island city-state, at the battle of Shela. Shortly thereafter, Lamu became subject to the sultanate of Zanzibar [q.v.]. Until the beginning of the 20th century, Lamu had a slave-based economy that enabled the island to grow rich. After the British outlawed slavery in 1907, Lamu's economy all but collapsed. During the post-World War II period, the island slowly recovered as tourism [q.v.] became the mainstay of its economy. According to the 1989 census, there were 8,959 people in Lamu town. The current estimated population is 15,000; this figure is expected to increase to about 30,000 by the end of the century.

LANCASTER HOUSE CONFERENCE (1960). Usually known in Kenya history as the first Lancaster House Constitutional Conference, this conclave was held at Lancaster House in London during January and February 1960. Chaired by Secretary of State for the Colonies Ian Macleod, the conference included all Kenya Legislative Council [q.v.] members plus senior colonial government officials. In trying to work out a future constitution for Kenya that would move the colony toward self-government, the British government found little common ground between the demands of European settlers for continued colonial rule, segregation, and protection of their economic interests (i.e., land in the White Highlands [q.v.]) and the call from African elected members for one man, one vote; an end to white privilege; and rapid *uhuru* [q.v.]. Without agreement among the legislators, Macleod had to impose a settlement that effectively ended European political influence in Kenya while at the same time closing the door on the multiracialism that had been the basis of the Lyttelton and Lennox-Boyd Constitutions [qq.v.].

LANCASTER HOUSE CONFERENCE (1962). Known as the second Lancaster House Conference, this meeting of Kenya Legislative Council [q.v.] members and the British government produced a blueprint for Kenya's postindependence constitution [q.v.]. Chaired by Secretary of State Reginald Maudling, the conference, which met from mid-February to early April, was divided between the views of the Kenya African Democratic Union (KADU), led by Ronald Ngala, and the Kenya African National Union (KANU), led by Jomo Kenyatta [qq.v.]. KADU advocated a *majimbo* [q.v.] constitution as the best way of protecting the position and rights, particularly land, of what it termed the "minority" tribes. Thus, the party insisted on the establishment of strong regional governments rather than the unitary state advocated by KANU. Ultimately, Maudling supported KADU and imposed a federal system on independent Kenya. While details remained to be worked out, the British decision called for the creation of six regions (later seven with the decision to create a North Eastern Region in the Somali-inhabited portion of Kenya) with elected assemblies responsible for land, primary and intermediate education, local government, and public health. It also called for a bicameral legislature, a House of Representatives, and a Senate (one member for each existing district). KANU reluctantly accepted the conference's outcome so as not to further delay progress toward independence. Also, KANU realized that the constitution could be altered toward the unitary state it desired following independence. At the conference's conclusion, KANU and KADU agreed to form a coalition government to work out the constitutional details. In April 1963, the parties published the constitution and subsequently held the general elections (1963) [q.v.].

LANCASTER HOUSE CONFERENCE (1963). The last in the series of Lancaster House conferences. On 25 September 1963, Prime Minister Jomo Kenyatta [q.v.] and several members of his Kenya African National

Union (KANU) [q.v.] cabinet started discussions with the British government. Kenyatta demanded constitutional changes to give more power to the central government. Opposition leader Ronald Ngala [q.v.] opposed any changes. After lengthy discussions and a threat by KANU to abandon the talks, Secretary of State Duncan Sandys announced changes in the independence constitution [q.v.] that would provide for a single public service commission and greater central control over the police [q.v.]. The powers of regional governments could now be changed by a two-thirds majority in a nationwide referendum. On 19 October 1963, the conference closed with agreement between the British and Kenyan governments. Both sides also fixed Kenya's independence day (12 December 1963).

LAND AND AGRICULTURAL BANK OF KENYA. The Land Bank Ordinance (1930) established this bank, which commenced operations on 3 March 1931. This institution invested public funds and provided credit to European farmers for crops and stocks. In 1968, the bank was amalgamated with the Agricultural Finance Corporation.

LATHBURY, GENERAL SIR GERALD (1906–1978). Born in England and educated at Wellington College and the Royal Military College, Sandhurst. In 1926, Lathbury received a commission into the Oxfordshire and Buckinghamshire Light Infantry. Two years later, he was seconded to the Royal West African Frontier Force. Between 1928 and 1933, Lathbury served in the Gold Coast Regiment. After attending Staff College (1937–38), he saw service during World War II [q.v.] in North Africa, Sicily, Italy, and northern Europe. After the war, Lathbury attended the Imperial Defence College (1948), commanded the 16th Airborne Division, and served as commandant of the Staff College (1951–53). In 1954, he received an appointment as vice adjutant general. In 1955, Lathbury went to Kenya as commander in chief, East Africa to end the Mau Mau Revolt [q.v.]. After leaving Kenya, he served as commander in chief, Eastern Command (1960) and quarter master general (1961). In August 1965, he became governor of Gibraltar. After retiring in 1969, Lathbury devoted his time to wildlife conservation and ornithology. He died on 16 May 1978.

LEAKEY, LOUIS SEYMOUR BAZETT (1903–1972). First paleontologist to prove that East Africa was the "cradle of mankind." Born at Kabete to Church Missionary Society [q.v.] parents and educated by a series of governesses; Weymouth College; and St. John's College, Cambridge. Upon graduation, he received support for the first of four archaeological expeditions to East Africa (1926–27, 1928–29, 1931–32, and 1934–35). In 1929, Leakey made his first major find, a 200,000-year-old settlement in the Great Rift Valley [q.v.]. On 14 October 1930, Leakey received a Ph.D. largely because of his archaeological work near Elmenteita. In addition to his archeological work, which focused largely on Stone Age cultures, Leakey also undertook extensive anthropological work on the Kikuyu [q.v.], among whom he had grown up. During World War II [q.v.], Leakey worked for the Criminal Investigation Department special branch in Nairobi [q.v.]. He then developed a reputation as a handwriting expert and an authority on Kikuyu political activity.

In January 1941, Leakey received an appointment as honorary curator of the Coryndon Memorial Museum (at independence, the name was changed to the National Museum of Kenya). In 1945, he became the museum's full-time curator, a post he held until 1 June 1961, when he relinquished the position to Robert Carcasson. After World War II, Leakey continued archaeological research, working with his wife Mary Leakey [q.v.]. In 1947, he organized the first Pan African Congress on Prehistory in Nairobi [q.v.]. With the upsurge of Kikuyu militancy that led to the Mau Mau Revolt [q.v.], Leakey supported the colonial government's efforts to defeat what he viewed as a dangerous and evil resistance movement. He served as government interpreter at the Kapenguria Trial of Jomo Kenyatta [qq.v.]. From the late 1950s, Leakey took advantage of grants from the National Geographic Society in the United States to undertake excavations at Olduvai Gorge in Tanganyika (now Tanzania). The discoveries Leakey and his wife made at this site made major contributions to the knowledge of human evolution and prehistory. Additionally, Leakey took considerable interest in East Africa wildlife. During the 1962–72 period, he served as director of the Centre for Prehistory and Paleontology in Nairobi. Leakey also mentored Jane Goodall and Dian Fossey, both of whom established international reputations for their work among East Africa's primates. On 26 March 1968, several wealthy Americans financed the establishment of the Leakey Foundation, an organization that continues to provide grants to anthropologists and primatologists for research into human origins and primate studies.

In recognition of his numerous achievements, Leakey received honorary doctorate degrees from prestigious universities such as Oxford, Witwatersrand, Guelph, Utah, California, and East Africa. Additionally, he was given the Haile Selassie I Award for African Research (1968), the Royal African Society's Wellcome Medal (1968), Senegal's Commander of the National Order of the Republic award, and the National Geographic Society's Franklin L. Burr Prize and the Hubbard Medal (1962). Leakey died on 1 October 1972.

LEAKEY, MARY DOUGLAS (1913–1996). Born in London, Leakey had an erratic education. After being expelled from several Catholic convents for untoward behavior, she briefly studied under private tutors. In 1930, she audited archaeology and geology courses at University College, London and at the British Museum. In 1930, 1931, 1932, and 1934 she also worked as a summer assistant for the Devon Archaeological Exploration Society, which had undertaken a study of Neolithic sites in southern England. On 24 December 1936, Mary married Louis Leakey [q.v.], and three weeks later the couple sailed for Kenya.

For more than three decades, Mary and Louis worked on several archaeological sites throughout East Africa. During this time, Mary established a reputation as one of the world's foremost archaeological researchers. Among her achievements are discoveries of *Proconsul africanus* (now termed *Proconsul beseloni*) on Rusinga Island (1948) and a *Zinjanthropus* skull at Olduvai Gorge, Tanzania (1959). Between 1968 and 1972, Mary spent an increasing amount of time at Olduvai Gorge, in part because her marriage to Louis had deteriorated. Following her husband's death in 1972, Mary continued her work at Olduvai Gorge until 1975, when she moved her operations to nearby Laetoli. This decision proved to be fortuitous. In January 1978, she announced that her expedition had discovered a series of early hominid footprints that were approximately 3.6 million years old.

In late 1983, Mary retired from fieldwork and moved to Langata, a Nairobi [q.v.] suburb. In recognition of her many accomplishments, Leakey received honorary doctorate degrees from prestigious institutions such as Oxford, Cambridge, Chicago, Witwatersrand, and Yale. In 1962, Mary and Louis Leakey received the Hubbard Medal, the first time this honor had been bestowed jointly on a couple. She also was the first woman to win the Royal Swedish Science Academy's Golden Linnaean Medal (1978) for her research on the evolution of man. Additionally, the Society of Women Geographers conferred a Gold Medal on Mary. She was a fellow of the British Academy and an honorary foreign member of the American Academy of Arts and Sciences. She died on 9 December 1996.

LEAKEY, RICHARD ERSKINE FRERE (1944–). Born in Nairobi [q.v.] and educated at the Lenana School (1956–59). During his early years, Leakey worked as a tour guide and a trapper and led photographic safaris throughout East Africa. He also undertook important scientific expeditions, including Lake Natron (1963 and 1964), Lake Baringo (1966), the Omo River (1967), Lake Rudolf (1968), Koobi Fora (1972), Buluk (1981), and West Turkana (1983 and 1985). Leakey was also active in the museum sector. In early 1967, for example, he established Kenya Museum Associates. Additionally, he served as administrative director (1968–74) and director (1974–81) of the National Museums of Kenya.

From 1989 to 1990, he was director of the Kenya Wildlife Conservation and Management Department. On 20 April 1989, President Daniel arap Moi [q.v.] appointed Leakey as the chairman of the Board of Trustees, Kenya Wildlife Service. Over the next few years, Leakey worked tirelessly to end the destruction of Kenya's fauna. He increasingly found his work subjected to criticism from powerful figures in the Kenya African National Union (KANU) [q.v.] establishment. In March 1994, Leakey resigned his post because of this opposition and his inability to stamp out corruption in the wildlife sector. President Moi refused to accept the resignation, but within weeks, Leakey was out for good. In April 1994, he was dropped from the board of the National Museums of Kenya.

In 1995, Leakey burst into the political limelight with the announcement that he had joined the SAFINA [q.v.] party and had become its general secretary. His entry into Kenyan politics drew heavy criticism from KANU figures, especially President Moi. Nevertheless, Leakey continued his pro-democracy activities and worked to end official corruption. In the 1997 general elections, SAFINA won five parliamentary seats which entitled the party to appoint one candidate for nomination by the president. Leakey received the appointment and promised to continue the struggle for political reform and democratization. To the surprise of many, Leakey accepted President Moi's call to head Kenya Wildlife Service once more in mid-1998, resigning his seat in Parliament as a result. Leakey has received numerous awards for his work, including the National Geographic Society's Franklin L. Burr Prize (1973) and Hubbard Medal (1993).

LEGISLATIVE COUNCIL (LEGCO). In 1907, the colonial government created LEGCO as the East Africa Protectorate's [q.v.] legislative branch. From its initial meeting in August 1907 until the end of its existence in 1963, LEGCO had an official (civil servant/government appointee) majority, though unofficial members (European and then Asian) could be appointed by the governor, who was the presiding officer for the council until the governorship of Sir Philip Mitchell [q.v.] when a speaker was chosen from among the members. The first African unofficial LEGCO member was appointed in 1944, though Europeans had been appointed from the 1920s to represent African interests. LEGCO had the power to enact ordinances and approve the revenue measures of the colonial government (e.g., taxation and expenditure), but these became law only with the assent of the British government. LEGCO ceased to exist following the 1963 general elections [q.v.] when a self-governing parliament first came into existence. *See also* LEGCO ELECTIONS; LEGCO ELECTIONS (1957); LEGCO ELECTIONS (1958); LEGCO ELECTIONS (1961).

LEGCO ELECTIONS. In 1916, the Colonial Office (CO) finally conceded the principle of electoral representation to the Legislative Council (LEGCO) [q.v.], long a demand of Kenya's European settlers, but implementation awaited the end of World War I [q.v.]. After 1918, the colonial government introduced a system of European-only (women were allowed the franchise) elections for 11 constituencies, heavily weighted in favor of the rural areas. The right to vote was not accorded to Asians [q.v.], Arabs, or Africans. In 1920, the first European LEGCO elections occurred. By law, LEGCO elections were held every three years (unless unusual circumstances such as World War II [q.v.] forced postponement). Asians gained the right to elect five members to LEGCO as a result of the 1923 Devonshire Declaration [q.v.]. However, for most of the 1920s, Asians boycotted these polls. Only the crucial LEGCO elections of 1957, 1958, and 1961 are described below.

LEGCO ELECTIONS (1957). This was one of the last LEGCO elections to be held on a completely communal franchise. The March 1957 elections were the first held for Africans. Eight representatives were elected on a qualified franchise that gave up to three votes to an individual based on education, income, and government service. Only a small portion of the African population qualified to vote in the elections. These elections proved a victory for African nationalism as the majority of the nominated members failed to gain election, most notably the longest-serving representative, Eluid Mathu [q.v.]. Moreover, the voters rejected those candidates who advocated gradual progress toward self-government. Instead, a new group of African political leaders, wedded to the rapid achievement of independence, emerged. Among these were several who played major roles in the nationalist movement, including Tom Mboya, Masinde Muliro, Ronald Ngala, and Oginga Odinga [qq.v.]. Of the LEGCO incumbents, the most influential victor in the election was Daniel arap Moi [q.v.].

LEGCO ELECTIONS (1958). Held in March 1958 to choose an additional six African Legislative Council members pursuant to the terms of the Lennox-Boyd Constitution [q.v.]. Among those elected who would have long and influential political careers were Julius Kiano, Jeremiah Nyagah, Justus ole Tipis, and Taaita Toweett (unopposed) [qq.v.].

LEGCO ELECTIONS (1961). The last election for a colonial Legislative Council [q.v.] was held following the new constitution [q.v.] introduced as a result of the first Lancaster House Conference [q.v.]. Usually termed the Kenyatta Election, since the position of the still-detained leader and his release were major issues. Though far from universal suffrage, the franchise for this poll was much wider than for the (1957 and 1958) LEGCO elections [qq.v.] with the majority of voters African. Thirty-three seats were designated as open with twenty seats reserved for the minority communities: 10 for Europeans, eight for Asians [q.v.], and two for Arabs. For the reserved seats primary elections were held on a communal basis. Candidates had to achieve at least 25 percent of the votes cast to advance to the common roll where the majority of the voters would be African. For the European elections, the major competitors were the Kenya Coalition and the New Kenya Party [qq.v.]. Candidates from the latter party won none of the primary contests, but they captured four seats in all to three for the Kenya Coalition, with independent candidates taking the other three. For the open seat contests, the main protagonists were the Kenya African National Union (KANU) and the Kenya African Democratic Union (KADU) [qq.v.]. KANU won nineteen seats and 67.4 percent of all votes, while KADU gained eleven seats but only 16.4 percent of the vote (three candidates were elected unopposed). Despite the victory, KANU refused to take part in government because the colonial government refused to release Jomo Kenyatta [q.v.].

LENNOX-BOYD CONSTITUTION (1957). Following consultations in Nairobi, Secretary of State for the Colonies Alan Lennox-Boyd announced new constitutional arrangements that continued to be characterized by the concept of multiracialism that had marked the Lyttelton Constitution (1954) [q.v.]. In the course of negotiations, Lennox-Boyd obtained the resignation of the European and Asian ministers, thereby freeing him to work toward a new constitution on the pretext that the Lyttelton Constitution had broken down. On 8 November 1957, he announced the new arrangements, which included provisions for Africans to receive six additional elective Legislative Council (LEGCO) [q.v.] seats, thus giving them parity with the European elected members. No more communal seats would be added, and the racial proportion (14 Africans/14 Europeans) would remain fixed for 10 years. As a new innovation, there would be 12 specially elected seats (four Asians [q.v.], four Africans, four Europeans) chosen by LEGCO sitting as an electoral college. Lennox-Boyd's constitution also provided for a multiracial Council of State to protect against discriminatory legislation. Largely as a result of opposition from African elected members, the Lennox-Boyd Constitution had a much shorter life than had been anticipated. By mid-1959, the secretary of state had accepted the need for a conference to work out a new constitution for Kenya. This led to the first Lancaster House Conference (1960) [q.v.].

LIMURU CONFERENCE (1966). The Kenya African National Union's (KANU) [q.v.] March 1966 delegates' conference held at Limuru outside Nairobi [q.v.] marked the culmination of a struggle within the party between the moderates and radicals. At the conference, the moderates, led by Tom Mboya [q.v.], outmaneuvered the radicals. The party constitution was altered to do away with a single vice president, and in its place there were eight vice presidents, one for each province and Nairobi. KANU's then vice president Oginga Odinga [q.v.] not only lost his post, but he failed to be elected vice president for Nyanza. Bildad Kaggia [q.v.], one of the radicals, was initially declared vice president for Central Province [q.v.], but this was quickly reversed on orders from President Jomo Kenyatta [q.v.]. Shortly after the conference's conclusion, Odinga resigned from the government and KANU and launched the Kenya People's Union [q.v.] as an opposition party.

LITTLE GENERAL ELECTION (1966). The so-called Little General Election was actually several by-elections for House of Representatives and Senate seats. These were necessitated by an amendment to the constitution [q.v.], following the resignation of Oginga Odinga [q.v.] and other MPs from the Kenya African National Union (KANU) [q.v.] and the formation of the Kenya People's Union (KPU) [q.v.], which required all MPs leaving the party they were elected under to seek a fresh mandate from the electorate. The polling for the House of Representatives and Senate seats took place on separate days in June. KPU complained of government harassment and lack of access to state-owned media during the campaign. KANU won 20 seats (12 in the House and eight in the Senate) to KPU's nine (seven in the House and two in the Senate). Odinga and fellow KPU members swept the board in his home district of Central Nyanza, but the party won only three seats elsewhere in the country. Notable losers in the poll were Bildad Kaggia and Achieng Oneko [qq.v.].

LOCAL NATIVE COUNCIL. In 1924, the colonial government passed legislation providing for the creation of Local Native Councils. The following year, officials established councils in Kenya's African-inhabited districts to allow African involvement in local affairs. Initially, the district commissioner appointed council members but later members were selected by queue voting. Local Native Councils levied rates and made expenditures for local development (e.g. education, health, roads, markets). With the governor's approval, the councils could enact by-laws applicable to the district. However, district commissioners exerted considerable administrative control over Local Native Councils as they served as chairs and controlled expenditures. All districts had a single council except South Nyanza which initially had two (one for Luo [q.v.] inhabitants of the district and the other for the Gusii [q.v.] and Kuria). In 1948, the colonial government created African District Councils [q.v.], which superseded Local Native Councils.

LUO. The Luo are Kenya's third-largest ethnic group (1989 census: 2,653,932). They speak a language belonging to the River-Lake (Western) Nilotic group. The Luo represent the southernmost extension of the Lwoo-speaking peoples whose original homeland was in southern Sudan. The first Luo migrants entered what is today Kenya sometime after 1490 with the arrival of the Joka-Jok group. Following their arrival, the incoming Luo pushed some Bantu-speaking [q.v.] groups away from the lake shore (the ancestors of the Luyia and Gusii [qq.v.]) and intermarried with others. Around 1625, a second group of Luo migrants to the Nyanza Region, known as the Joka-Owiny, started arriving in Kenya. Somewhat later, the Joka-Omolo moved to western Kenya from northern Uganda. These three migrant groups spread across the areas now inhabited by Luo people during the course of several generations, in the process interacting with each other and with peoples speaking Bantu languages in the region. From about 1730, for example, Luo began to move across Nyanza Gulf to what became known as South Nyanza. Over time, several Luo clans came to be joined together in a rough political grouping known as an *oganda*, which was headed by a *ruoth* (chief) advised by a council of elders representing the major clans in the unit.

Throughout the colonial and independence periods, the majority of Luo lived in Nyanza Province [q.v.]. During the 1895–1905 period, the Luo were brought under colonial control by the Uganda and East Africa Protectorate [q.v.] colonial states. Many Luo, particularly those near to Kisumu [q.v.], responded quickly to colonial pressures to engage in commodity production and migrant labor. Many also joined the Christian missions established in western Kenya from the earliest days of colonial rule. Many Luo were thus residents in urban areas and involved in protest organizations and nationalist politics. Together with the Kikuyu [q.v.], the Luo made up the core of support for the Kenya African National Union (KANU) [q.v.] from its founding in 1960 until 1966. Following Oginga Odinga's [q.v.] resignation from KANU, the majority of Luo expressed little support for the Jomo Kenyatta [q.v.] government. This anti-Nairobi stance continued to characterize the regime of President Daniel arap Moi [q.v.] as well.

LUYIA (LUHYA). The Luyia are Kenya's second-largest ethnic group (1989 census: 3,083,273). Rather than a single, unified group, those calling themselves Luyia actually constitute some 17 "subtribes," each speaking slightly different, though mutually intelligible, languages. Historically, the Luyia represent a "hybrid" community. Their languages are Bantu [q.v.], of the Lacustrine group, most closely related to those spoken in what is today eastern Uganda. Historians believe that, beginning in the mid-15th century, ancestors of the Luyia moved from that region to western Kenya. In their new homeland, these migrants met and interacted with peoples speaking Bantu, Kalenjin, Luo, and Maasai [qq.v.] languages and practicing a variety of customs. By at least the 18th century, one of the Luyia "subtribes," the Wanga, had developed a monarchy ruled by a *nabongo* (king). However, such government institutions did not characterize the other Luyia peoples who were governed by clan leaders and councils of elders.

Between 1895 and 1905, the Luyia were subjected to colonial conquest by the Uganda and East Africa Protectorate [q.v.] administrations following a policy of divide and conquer. The Luyia quickly responded to the colonial government's pressures to enter into commodity production and migrant labor. Many also became Christians. Most Luyia lived in the North and Central Nyanza districts of Kenya during the colonial period, and the majority of inhabitants of Western Province [q.v.] after 1963 were Luyia. At the end of the 1980s, they constituted Kenya's third-largest group of urban residents.

LYTTLETON CONSTITUTION (1954). In March 1954, Secretary of State for the Colonies Oliver Lyttelton visited Nairobi [q.v.] and proposed new constitutional arrangements for the colony. Announced in the midst of the colonial and British governments' campaign to defeat the Mau Mau Revolt [q.v.], Lyttelton's constitutional proposals attempted to enshrine multiracialism as the basis for Kenya's future political system. To involve all Kenya's racial groups in government, Lyttelton provided for a council of ministers that would include two Asians [q.v.] and one African, all of whom would be unofficial members of Legislative Council. Lyttelton also promised that the colonial government would introduce an electoral system for African members to the LEGCO. The Lyttelton Constitution never enjoyed strong support from European settlers or Africans. In particular, the African elections produced not the hoped-for moderates, but politicians who advocated rapid progress toward majority rule. Thus in 1957, Lyttelton's successor, Alan Lennox-Boyd, scrapped the constitution and imposed the Lennox-Boyd Constitution [q.v.].

-M-

MAASAI. Although numerically one of the smallest of Kenya's ethnic groups (1989 census: 377,089), the Maasai have attracted considerable attention from Europeans for much of the 19th and 20th centuries. They form part of the Plains (or Eastern) Nilotic-speaking peoples who inhabit Kenya. The Maasai are descended from Maa-speaking peoples who took up residence, largely in the Rift Valley [q.v.] and adjacent regions, after 1000 C.E. The ancestors of the Kenya Maasai took control of grazing lands in the Rift Valley in the 17th and 18th centuries, displacing earlier Kalenjin [q.v.] and Southern Cushitic-speaking groups [q.v.].

By 1800, Maa-speaking groups lived in an area that stretched from Lake Turkana in the north to central Tanzania. Until the end of the 19th century, the Maasai were divided into a number of autonomous social and political sections that were essentially territorial units, each occupying recognized areas. The Maasai were pastoralists, subsisting on their livestock (principally cattle), though at times economic and ecological pressures forced some Maa-speakers to adopt cultivation or hunting as a mode of subsistence. Decentralization also characterized the political structure of the Maasai, as there existed no recognized ruling families or chiefs wielding extensive political authority. *Olaiboni* (*laibons*) (prophets/ritual experts) exercised influence at particular times, but this was not continuous political authority. By the mid-19th century, Maasai pastoral groups had spread across the Rift Valley south into what is today central Tanzania.

From the 1830s, these communities were split by strife, often referred to as Maasai civil wars. These pit the so-called Il Maasai, the pastoralists, against groups referred to as Iloikop, ex-pastoralists, engaged, temporarily they felt, in cultivation. Lasting until the 1880s, these conflicts witnessed the defeat of Iloikop groups and the dispersal of those such as the Liakipiak and Uas Nkishu from the regions that today bear their names. The civil wars were followed in the 1880s and 1890s by stock disease, smallpox, and drought, all of which had a negative impact on the Maasai. Thus, at the start of the British conquest of Kenya, the Maasai were willing to assist the colonial authorities by lending their numbers to the colonial forces in exchange for livestock captured by the early "punitive expeditions." This alliance between the Maasai and the British proved short-lived as the latter soon ceased to need indigenous military help.

Subsequently, the Maasai lost access to extensive grazing lands as a result of the Maasai Treaties of 1904 and 1911 [qq.v.]. For most of the colonial period, moreover, the authorities encouraged Maasai isolation from the impact of colonial capitalism and Western education. Thus by the end of that era, Maasailand, as it came to be known, was underdeveloped in comparison to most of the rest of southern Kenya. (In some early studies about Kenya, Maasai is spelled Masai.)

MAASAI TREATY (1904). This treaty moved the Maasai [q.v.] into two reserves (Northern and Southern). Commissioner Sir Donald Stewart [q.v.] finalized the treaty on the advice of his senior officials who believed that the Maasai should be moved away from the Uganda Railway [q.v.] line through the Rift Valley [q.v.], thereby leaving the land open to European settlers. Stewart believed that this would minimize the potential for conflict between the Maasai and the European settlers and that the Maasai wanted to move to the Laikipia Plateau, which became the Northern Reserve for the pastoralists. The treaty stated that the Maasai agreed that the settlement should endure as long as they "as a race shall exist" and that European settlers would not be allowed to take up any land in either the Northern or Southern Reserve. The move of the Maasai into the two reserves was completed in 1905.

MAASAI TREATY (1911). The Maasai Treaty of 1904 [q.v.], despite its wording, had a relatively short life. In 1910, Governor Sir Percy Girouard [q.v.] began to plan a move to open the Laikipia Plateau to European settlers by moving the Maasai [q.v.] from this area to an expanded reserve south of the Uganda Railway [q.v.]. The Colonial Office (CO) warned the colonial government to make no promises of Laikipia land to European settlers and to undertake no move without Maasai consent. Girouard therefore pressured some Maasai leaders to agree to a treaty in which they expressed a desire to move to the south in 1911. When the Maasai move actually began, it broke down as the Maasai sent south refused to complete the journey. Consequently, Girouard reluctantly sent them back to Laikipia. Thus began a correspondence between London and Nairobi that revealed that the governor had misled the secretary of state for the colonies. The episode culminated with Girouard's resignation in 1912.

Despite proof that Girouard actually had promised Laikipia land to European settlers in opposition to London's directives, the CO eventually allowed the move to the southern reserve to be carried out in 1912 and allocated farms in Laikipia to European settlers. In response to this, Maasai elders hired a European lawyer and filed a court suit claiming they had a right to return to Laikipia under the terms of the 1904 Maasai Treaty. When the case came before the protectorate's High Court in 1913, the suit was thrown out on the technical ground that the Maasai were not "subjects of the Crown" and as the 1904 agreement was a treaty between the East Africa Protectorate [q.v.] and "a foreign tribe," the court had no jurisdiction over the matter. The Maasai treaties epitomized the lack of security for African land that characterized the history of early colonial Kenya.

MAATHAI, WANGARI (1940–). Born in Nyeri [q.v.] and raised on a farm in the White Highlands [q.v.]. She attended Loreto Girls High School. Maathai then received a B.A. in biology (1964) from Mount Saint Scholastica College, in Atchinson, Kansas; an M.S. degree from the University of Pittsburgh (1965); and a Ph.D. from the University of Nairobi (1971) [q.v.]. Maathai then held several teaching positions at the University of Nairobi, where she became the first African woman professor. During the 1973–77 period, she was a director of the Kenya Red Cross. In 1977, Maathai persuaded the National Council of Women of Kenya to support her efforts to establish the Green Belt Movement [q.v.]. Additionally, she served as president of Environment Liaison Centre International (1974–84) and belonged to the National Council of Women of Kenya (1977–87).

Maathai also compiled an impressive record as a political dissident. In 1989, for example, she led a successful campaign to stop construction of the proposed Kenya Times Media Trust building in Nairobi's Uhuru Park on environmental grounds. This action earned Maathai the enmity of several powerful Kenyan African National Union [q.v.] members who had invested in the project and put her on a collision course with the Kenyan authorities. In March 1990, the police [q.v.] arrested her in connection with rumors sweeping through Kenya about the death (under mysterious circumstances) of Robert Ouko [q.v.]. In January 1992, police again arrested Maathai after she claimed she had evidence that the government intended to hand over power to the armed forces [q.v.].

After her release, she formed the Tribal Clashes Resettlement Volunteer Service in February 1993 to assist victims of political violence in Burnt Forest and elsewhere. The authorities retaliated by accusing her of being responsible for the ongoing ethnic clashes in western Kenya and by preventing her from holding three conferences on reducing ethnic violence. Nevertheless, Maathai's organization initiated a resettlement program and published and distributed pamphlets that urged Kenyans to stop fighting one another. In recent years, she has been active in the human rights group Release Political Prisoners [q.v.]. In the general elections (1997) [q.v.], Maathai became Kenya's second female presidential candidate and stood for office for the Liberal Party of Kenya. However, she performed poorly, receiving only 0.07 percent of the vote (4,133 votes) and less than 1,000 votes in her parliamentary bid.

Maathai has won numerous awards, including the Sasakawa Environment Prize (1990), Green Century Environmental Award for Courage (1990), Goldman Environmental Prize (1991), and Jane Addams International Leadership Award (1993). She has also received an honorary LL.D. degree from Williams College.

MACDONALD, MALCOLM JOHN (1901–1981). Kenya's last governor and first and only governor-general. Born in Lossiemouth, Scotland and educated at the City of London School; Bedales School, Petersfield; and Queen's College, Oxford. MacDonald was the son of British Prime Minister Ramsay MacDonald, and this led him into politics. He first served on the London County Council and in 1929, was elected to Parliament. MacDonald served as an MP until 1945 and followed his father into the National Government in 1931, serving first as parliamentary undersecretary in the Dominions Office and as secretary of state in the same office 1935–38 after a short stint as secretary of state for the colonies. During the 1938–39 period, he headed the Colonial and Dominions Offices, continuing to lead the former until 1940. During that time, MacDonald was forced to take notice of affairs in Kenya as he had to defend the Kamba [q.v.] destocking policies that provoked the rise of the Ukamba Members Association [q.v.]. From 1940 until the fall of the

Chamberlain government in 1941, MacDonald served as minister of health. From 1941 until 1946, he was high commissioner to Canada. Following that appointment, MacDonald spent most of the next decade in the Far East as governor-general of Malaya, Singapore, and Borneo (1946–48), special representative to Indonesia (1949), and British representative on the Southeast Asia Defence Council (1948–55). From 1955 to 1960, he was British high commissioner to India. Following the sacking of Sir Patrick Renison [q.v.] in late 1962, MacDonald became Kenya's governor faced with the tasks of finalizing the independence constitution [q.v.] and moving the colony to self-government as rapidly as possible. That this was accomplished by December 1963 owed much to his skill as diplomat as well to the fact that, unlike his predecessor, he developed warm relations with African nationalist leaders, particularly Jomo Kenyatta [q.v.]. MacDonald served as governor-general until Kenya became a republic in December 1964. Subsequently, he served as British high commissioner to Kenya (1965). In 1966–67, MacDonald returned to Nairobi as British special representative to East and Central Africa. He then served as special representative of the British government in Africa (1967–69). As governor, governor-general, and diplomat, Malcolm MacDonald played a most significant role in solidifying the close political and economic ties between Kenya and Great Britain that marked the period since 1963.

After retiring in 1969, MacDonald wrote several books, served as chancellor of Durham University, and was president of the Royal Commonwealth Society and the Voluntary Service Overseas. He devoted his last months to finishing an autobiography that never was published. MacDonald died on 11 January 1981.

MACHARIA, RAWSON (1911–). Teacher, clerk, trader, and chief witness against Jomo Kenyatta at the Kapenguria Trial [qq.v.]. Born in Kiambu and educated at Kambui Mission School. Macharia, who grew up among Kikuyu squatters [qq.v.] in the Rift Valley [q.v.], qualified for admission to Alliance High School [q.v.] but could not afford to pay the fees. He instead attended medical training school but was expelled. Macharia then worked as a teacher, clerk, and trader. After World War II [q.v.], he became interested in politics and joined the Kenya African Union (KAU) [q.v.]. By 1950, Macharia had ceased active participation in the KAU and returned to Kiambu where he became known to the colonial authorities as a "bush lawyer." In August 1952, he wrote a letter, which he later admitted was a fabrication, to the local district commissioner giving an account of the Mau Mau movement. This letter caused the colonial government to use him as a witness at the Kapenguria Trial [q.v.], where he gave false testimony, particularly relating to Jomo Kenyatta [q.v.], in exchange for money and an educational course in Great Britain. During the 1952–56 period, he lived in Britain but never finished his education. After returning to Kenya, the colonial government treated him as a loyalist and gave him a job as a rehabilitation officer. In December 1958, Macharia, who was increasingly dissatisfied with his treatment by colonial officials, announced that his testimony at Kapenguria had been false. In January 1959, the police [q.v.] arrested him, and the courts eventually convicted him of perjury. Macharia was imprisoned until October 1960, when he returned to Kiambu District, where he remained free throughout the Kenyatta era. In 1991, Macharia published his version of the Kapenguria Trial and his conviction for perjury, *The Truth about the Trial of Jomo Kenyatta.*

MACKAY REPORT (1981). This report recommended the creation of a second university in 1985. The Kenyan government therefore opened Moi University [q.v.]. Additionally, this report led to the restructuring of the country's educational system from 7-4-2-3 to 8-4-4. The new system extended the primary course to eight years, introduced a four-year terminal secondary course, abolished the 'A' level cycle of the secondary course, and expanded university education to four years. In January 1986, the Kenyan government implemented the 8-4-4 system. *See also* EDUCATION, PRIMARY; EDUCATION, SECONDARY.

MCKENZIE, BRUCE ROY (1919–1978). Farmer, politician, and businessman. Born in Richmond, Natal, South Africa, and educated at Hilton College, South Africa, and at an agricultural college. After the outbreak of World War II [q.v.], McKenzie joined the South African Air Force (SAAF) only to be seconded to the Royal Air Force (RAF) for the duration of the conflict. He saw action in North Africa, the Mediterranean, and Europe. As a result of his many wartime accomplishments, McKenzie became a colonel at the age of 24—the youngest SAAF officer of that rank.

In 1946, he moved to Kenya and started farming near Nakuru [q.v.]. McKenzie soon ventured into politics as a member of the New Kenya Party (NKP) [q.v.]. During the 1957–63 period, he served as a nominated member in the Legislative Council (LEGCO) [q.v.]. In 1959, McKenzie succeeded Michael Blundell [q.v.] as minister for agriculture, animal husbandry, and water resources. Two years later, he resigned this position and left the NKP to join the Kenya African National Union (KANU) [q.v.]. Although he did not stand in the LEGCO elections (1961) [q.v.], McKenzie was elected a national LEGCO [q.v.] member with KANU support following the vote. After the second Lancaster House Conference (1962) [q.v.], he became minister of land settlement and water development in the coalition government formed to work out an independence constitution. With KANU'S victory in the general elections (1963) [q.v.], McKenzie once again became a special member of Parliament. In June 1963, Jomo Kenyatta [q.v.] appointed McKenzie minister for agriculture to facilitate the departure of European settlers from the White Highlands [q.v.] and the resettlement of Africans on their farms. After the general elections (1969) [q.v.], Kenyatta nominated him to Parliament. In 1970, McKenzie retired from the cabinet and concentrated on a number of business ventures. He died when an airplane en route from Kampala to Nairobi [q.v.] crashed 6.4 kilometers (four miles) from Ngong township on 24 May 1978.

MACKINNON, SIR WILLIAM (1823–1893). Businessman and imperialist. Born in the village of Campbeltown, Argyllshire, Scotland. Mackinnon left elementary school to become a grocery clerk and subsequently moved to Glasgow, where he worked for a merchant who traded with India and the Far East. In 1847, he went to India and joined forces with a former schoolmate named Robert MacKenzie who owned a general store. Together, they established the firm of Mackinnon, MacKenzie, and Company, which became one of the leading mercantile companies in the Indian Ocean region. On 29 September 1856, Mackinnon founded the Calcutta and Burmah Steam Navigation Company (later known as the British India Steam Navigation Company). Mackinnon's relationship with East Africa began in 1873, when he started a mail service between Aden and Zanzibar [q.v.]. He also persuaded the British government to grant a royal charter to his Imperial British East Africa Company [q.v.] in 1887. Apart from his commercial activities, Mackinnon founded the East African Scottish Industrial Mission (1891). After ceasing his connection with East Africa, he worked as a director of the City of Glasgow Bank. Mackinnon died on 22 June 1893.

MADARAKA DAY. Annual national holiday on 1 June, which commemorates the achievement of internal self-government on 1 June 1963.

MAJIMBO. A Swahili word that means "provinces" or "regions"; in a political context, it has been loosely interpreted as "federalism" or "regionalism." By early 1962, the Kenya African Democratic Union

(KADU) [q.v.] adopted the concept as a major demand for Kenya's future constitutional framework. The second Lancaster House Conference (1962) [q.v.] accepted *majimbo* as the basis for the independence constitution. After independence, the Kenyan government significantly altered the *majimbo* constitution, especially after KADU's dissolution, by the abolition of regional assemblies and the creation of a unicameral parliament. Since 1991, however, there have been periodic calls, especially heated in 1994, until President Daniel arap Moi [q.v.] ordered an end to public discussion for a renewal of *majimbo*. Nevertheless such calls continued, both before and after the general elections (1997) [q.v.], largely from Kalenjin and Maasai [qq.v.] political leaders, who largely stood alone in seeing *majimbo* as appropriate for Kenya's future.

MAKERERE UNIVERSITY. One of Africa's oldest educational institutions, which began in 1921 as a technical school in Kampala, Uganda. In 1922, Makerere became the first college in East Africa. Its status as an institution of higher learning attracted students from throughout Africa. Many notable Kenyans, including Josephat Karanja and Mwai Kibaki [qq.v.], also studied at Makerere, which became a university college associated with the University of London in 1949. During the late 1970s and early 1980s, warfare and instability throughout Uganda all but destroyed the institution. After a new government, headed by Yoweri Museveni, seized power in January 1986, Makerere University began the long, slow process of rebuilding and rehabilitation. As of 1999, however, the university had yet to regain its earlier stature.

MALINDI. Altitude is at sea level. As early as the ninth century, Chinese geographers wrote about this town. Arab historians called Malindi the "capital of the Land of the Zinj." On 13 April 1498, the Portuguese explorer Vasco da Gama landed at Malindi. The sultan allied himself with the Portuguese as a deterrent against Mombasa [q.v.], the town's larger and more powerful neighbor. Lisbon, which had poor a relationship with Mombasa, welcomed the alliance, as Malindi was an important port in a trading network that extended from Europe to India and the Far East. Gradually, however, relations between Portugal and Mombasa improved. Consequently, in 1593, the Portuguese moved their headquarters to Mombasa, which caused the political and economic decline of Malindi.

MASAI PROVINCE. In 1924, the colonial government turned what had been known since the first days of colonial rule as the Masai reserve (the land inhabited by Maasai [q.v.]) into a province. In 1934, the colonial government reduced the province, which consisted of Kajiado and Narok, to the status of an extraterritorial district. In 1953, it became part of the newly created Southern Province [q.v.].

MASAI UNITED FRONT. In April 1960, John Keen [q.v.] and David Lemomo founded this political party to defend Maasai [q.v.] claims to land in the White Highlands [q.v.] (especially that taken from the Maasai as a result of the 1904 and 1911 Maasai Treaties [qq.v.]). The Masai United Front stated that it was not against democracy but felt that "one man, one vote" was unsuitable for Kenya. Later in 1960, this party joined other political groups to form the Kenya African Democratic Union [q.v.].

MASINDE, ELIJAH (1910–1987). Born in Maeni village in Kimilili, Bungoma District. Educated at several mission schools, including the Church of God Mission School at Kima, in western Kenya. In 1928, he began an association with the Quaker Mission in then North Kavirondo district, where he excelled as one of the district's greatest soccer players. In the 1930s, Masinde broke with the Quakers as he could see no need for the guidance of European missionaries in religious or family matters. He increasingly developed his own religious ideas and was contemptuous of the colonial government's authority. During the 1937–42 period, he worked as a Native Tribunal Court process server.

In April 1943, Masinde concluded that God had visited him and had charged him to be the leader of *Dini ya Msambwa* (Church/Religion of Ancestral Spirits) [q.v.], a politico-religious sect active in western Kenya. His followers regarded him as a prophet. He therefore easily spread the sect among his Bukusu people as well as other Luyia [q.v.] sub-tribes and neighboring peoples, but the popularity of *Dini ya Msambwa* and its message of nonrecognition of secular authority brought him into collision with the colonial government. On 26 April 1945, the colonial authorities committed him to Mathari Mental Hospital for about two years. After gaining his release in 1947, Masinde resumed his preaching and opposition to government authority and European supremacy. He also called for the expulsion of all Europeans from Kenya and championed opposition to soil conservation measures forced on the Bukusu by the colonial government. These activities led to a violent confrontation with the police [q.v.] at Malakisi on 16 February 1948, which resulted in 11 dead and 16 wounded. The police then arrested Masinde and deported him to Lamu [q.v.] (later, he was moved to Marsabit). In May 1961, he finally gained his freedom and started religious and political agitation as an advocate of African independence.

In April 1964, the Kenyan government lifted the ban on *Dini ya Msambwa*; however, Masinde soon found himself in trouble with the authorities. The police jailed him several times for defying authority and calling for an end to secular rule and a complete reorganization of Kenyan society. In October 1968, the Kenyan government banned *Dini ya Msambwa* and jailed Masinde for two years. Following his release from prison in November 1970, Masinde was quickly back in court again, and in June 1972, he was sentenced to six years of imprisonment. Upon his release, Masinde continued to preach his antiauthoritarian message. He died on 8 June 1987.

MATHU, ELUID WAMBU (1910–). Teacher, politician, and civil servant. Educated at Alliance High School [q.v.], Fort Hare University in South Africa, Exeter University, and Oxford University. Mathu was one of the first Kenyan Africans to obtain a university degree. He then taught at Alliance High School (1940–43) and served as headmaster of Dagoretti High School (1943). The colonial government nominated Mathu as the first African Legislative Council [q.v.] member (1944–57). In 1952, he was nominated to the Executive Council. Mathu helped to found the Kenya African Union [q.v.] but played no significant role in the party after Jomo Kenyatta's [q.v.] return. Until 1957, Mathu was a well-known figure in Kenya politics because he sought to defend African interests and give voice to grievances. Nevertheless, an increasing number of Kenyan Africans viewed him as too moderate and closely tied to the colonial government. Thus, he lost the Central Province [q.v.] seat in the first African elections of 1957. In the March 1958 elections, Mathu again failed to win a seat. He left politics, though he remained a member of the East African Central Legislative Assembly until 1960. Mathu then worked with the Economic Commission for Africa (1960–64). Independence brought him back into public affairs. During the 1963–69 period, he was chairman of the Council of the University of East Africa [q.v.]. More significantly, he held the position of controller of State House and private secretary to the president (1964–77).

MATIBA, KENNETH STANLEY NJINDO (1932–). Educator, politician, businessman, and dissident. Born in Kahuhia and educated at Kahuhia Primary School, Mariira Primary School, Alliance High School (1951–54) [q.v.] and Makerere University (1955–60) [q.v.]. In 1960, Matiba, a Kikuyu [q.v.], joined Kangaru High School as a teacher and then moved to the Ministry of Education (1960–61). His early positions included senior education officer for secondary education and teacher training colleges (1963); permanent secretary, Ministry of Education (1963–64); permanent secretary, Ministry of Home Affairs (1964–65); and permanent secretary, Ministry of Commerce, Industry and Cooperatives (1965–68).

Matiba then started a business career with Kenya Breweries (1969–73). Four years later, he became chairman of Kenya Breweries and East African Breweries. Matiba was also influential in several other organizations, including the Civil Aviation Board, Kenya Safari Lodges and Hotels, and Wangu Investments. Additionally, he served as director of the Central Bank of Kenya [q.v.] and the Kenya Tourist Development Corporation and chairman of the Kenya Football Federation (1974–78). Additionally, Matiba was a member of the Horticultural Crops Development Authority and operated the Alliance Group of Hotels.

In the general elections (1979) [q.v.], Matiba began his political career by defeating former cabinet minister Julius Gikonyo Kiano [q.v.] for the parliamentary seat of then Mbiri constituency. Re-elected in the 1983 general elections [q.v.], he held several portfolios, including transport and communications.

At the time of the general elections (1988) [q.v.], Matiba reacted strongly against what he perceived to be attempts by powerful forces in the Kenya African National Union (KANU) [q.v.] to force him out of Parliament. He nevertheless defeated Kiano and retained his parliamentary seat. In the KANU elections later that year, Matiba accused his political opponents of using the provincial administration to bring about his defeat. He thereupon resigned his position as minister of transport and communications. KANU then expelled him from the party, and he consequently lost his seat in Parliament.

In 1990, Matiba began his campaign for the introduction of a multiparty political system in Kenya in tandem with Charles Rubia [q.v.]. In June 1990, the police [q.v.] detained both of them because of their prodemocracy activities. During his time in detention, Matiba suffered a stroke, and after his release he spent a lengthy period in Great Britain undergoing medical treatment. From Great Britain, he stated his backing for the Forum for the Restoration of Democracy (FORD) [q.v.]. In May 1992, Matiba returned to Kenya, though not fully recovered from the effects of the stroke, and launched a strong campaign to be FORD's presidential candidate.

This put him at odds with Oginga Odinga [q.v.]. By September-October 1992, disagreements between the two had split FORD into two parties. Matiba became chairman of FORD-Asili [q.v.] and was its presidential candidate in the general elections (1992) [q.v.]. With 1.35 million votes, he took second place to President Daniel arap Moi [q.v.]. However, Matiba maintained that he had actually won the presidential race. He won a parliamentary seat in the 1992 poll, but his time as leader of the opposition in Parliament proved short as FORD-Asili suffered when a number of its MPs defected to KANU. From 1993, Matiba made only token appearances in Parliament. By 1995, his leadership had been challenged by some of the party's MPs led by General Secretary Martin Shikuku [q.v.]. Ultimately, the struggle between the two factions caused a split in FORD-Asili. In the build-up to the general elections (1997) [q.v.], Matiba became highly controversial by promising to expel the country's Asians [q.v.]. Additionally, he continued to articulate a strong anti-Moi stance, but he refused to register as a voter for the 1997 general elections and thus could not stand for any elective office.

MAU MAU REVOLT. The Mau Mau Revolt began after the October 1952 declaration of a state of emergency by the colonial government. Although the latter had declared Mau Mau an unlawful organization in 1950, there is little historical evidence that an organization by that name existed then or later. The name "Mau Mau" has no meaning in any Kenyan language. Nevertheless, the colonial government's use of the term for the rebellion has made that name an important part of Kenya's history.

The armed rebellion that began in the forests of Mount Kenya and Central Province [qq.v.] had its roots in long-standing African grievances and discontent, particularly among the Kikuyu [q.v.]. Some, including such Kenya African Union [q.v.] leaders as Bildad Kaggia and Fred Kubai [qq.v.], helped plan the armed insurgency. After fighting began, increasing numbers of Embu, Kikuyu, and Meru [qq.v.] joined the anticolonial struggle as forest fighters. Not all people belonging to these ethnic groups participated in the conflict, however, as the Mau Mau Revolt caused deep divisions within those societies. On the whole, those who joined the armed struggle against colonialism and European supremacy were the poor and landless, while those who were more wealthy, called loyalists, supported the colonial government.

For the most part, the revolt was confined to Nairobi and the Rift Valley [qq.v.] and Central Provinces. Led by such figures as Dedan Kimathi and Waruhiu Itote [qq.v.], the forest freedom fighters held the initiative in the struggle against the colonial and British security forces through at least the first half of 1953. Perhaps the rebels' most significant successes occurred on the same night, 26 March 1953, with the successful raid on the Naivasha [q.v.] police station and the attack on loyalists at Lari. With the arrival of growing numbers of British troops and the British government's takeover of military operations, however, the rebels were increasingly on the defensive. Besides direct military action against the rebels, the British, through initiatives such as Operation Anvil [q.v.], arrested, interrogated, placed in detention camps, and imprisoned thousands of Embu, Kikuyu, and Meru. The authorities moved rural Kikuyu into fortified camps. By mid-1955, the colonial authorities had gained the upper hand, and the October 1956 capture of Kimathi is usually taken as the end of the military phase of suppressing the rebellion, though the emergency was not officially ended until January 1960. At the end of military operations, official estimates listed more than 10,500 rebels killed, while colonial and British forces lost some 600. Additionally, more than 1,800 loyalists had been killed, and 32 European civilians died during the fighting. *See also* ARMED FORCES; ERSKINE, GENERAL SIR GEORGE; HOLA CAMP AFFAIR; HOME GUARDS; ITOTE, WARUHIU (GENERAL CHINA); KENYA LAND AND FREEDOM ARMY; KING'S AFRICAN RIFLES; LATHBURY, GENERAL SIR GERALD.

MBEERE. People who belong to the Thagicu group of Bantu-speakers resident in central Kenya (1989 census: 101,007). The Mbeere are closely related to the Embu [q.v.] as they share linguistic and cultural similarities. Beginning in the 15th century, the Mbeere migrated to the southern and eastern slopes of Mount Kenya [q.v.] with the Embu. However, the Mbeere occupied a lower and drier savanna region, and thus they came to develop a different kind of economy than the Embu (grain crops and cattle rearing). The economies of the two peoples complemented one another with extensive economic and cultural exchanges marking their relations. Like the Embu, the Mbeere were brought under colonial rule in 1906, and the colonial government administered them as part of Embu District. Increasing differentiation between the two groups marked the colonial era as Embu access to commodity production and high-value cash crops was not shared by the Mbeere. By independence, the differential development of the two portions of Embu District had become a source of political contention, a situation that continued to mark politics to the end of the century.

MBOYA, THOMAS JOSEPH ODHIAMBO (1930–1969). Born on a sisal estate at Kilima Mboga, near Nairobi [q.v.]. Between 1942 and 1945, he attended St. Mary's Catholic mission school at Yala. Mboya then studied at the Holy Ghost College in Mangu, Central Province [q.v.] (1946–48); the Royal Sanitary Institute's Medical Training School, where he graduated in January 1951; and Ruskin College, Oxford (1955–56).

During the 1951–52 period, he worked as a sanitary inspector for the Nairobi City Council. In 1952, Mboya joined the Kenya African Union [q.v.] while also serving as the general secretary of the Kenya Local Government Workers' Union. He quickly assumed a leadership position in the labor movement, becoming general secretary of the Kenya Federation of Labour (KFL) [q.v.] (1953–62). His action in organizing workers, articulating their demands, and settling strikes soon made Mboya an important figure during the Mau Mau Revolt [q.v.]. He used his trade union influence to political advantage in Nairobi as well.

In 1957, Mboya founded the Nairobi People's Convention Party [q.v.] and stood for the Nairobi seat in the first African LEGCO Elections (1957) [q.v.], defeating C. M. G. Arwings-Kodhek [q.v.]. The victory thrust Mboya into a leadership position among the newly elected African Legislative Council [q.v.] members. Additionally, he led the African Elected Members Organisation [q.v.] and assumed a major role in opposing the Lyttelton and Lennox-Boyd Constitutions [qq.v.]. But Mboya's political activities also brought hostility and opposition from other African politicians, among them Oginga Odinga and Masinde Muliro [qq.v.].

Mobya attended the Lancaster House Conference (1960) [q.v.], and upon his return joined the Kenya African National Union (KANU) [q.v.] as general secretary. He won the Nairobi seat in the LEGCO Elections (1961) [q.v.] and helped organize KANU's victory in that poll. Like other KANU leaders, Mboya refused to participate in government unless Jomo Kenyatta [q.v.] was released from detention. After Kenyatta gained freedom in 1961, Mboya accepted Kenyatta's leadership of the party and worked to ensure the success of KANU's drive for rapid independence and a unitary state. After the second Lancaster House Conference (1962) [q.v.], Mboya became minister of labour in the coalition government. In the general elections (1963) [q.v.], he once again gained a seat in Nairobi and then received an appointment as minister of justice and constitutional affairs at the time of internal self-government. In this position, he brought about the constitutional changes desired by KANU, which included the scrapping of the *majimbo* [q.v.] constitution. After Kenya became a republic in December 1964, Mboya became minister of economic planning and development.

For the rest of the decade, Mboya played a leading part in laying the foundations of Kenya's economic policies and development strategies.

These supported a capitalist-oriented mixed economy with ties to the Western bloc in the Cold War. Mboya was also one of the leading moderates in Kenyatta's government advocating these policies against the radicals led by Odinga. At the KANU Limuru Conference (1966) [q.v.], Mboya masterminded Odinga's isolation, which led to the latter's resignation as vice president. Following the formation of the Kenya People's Union [q.v.] in 1966, Mboya ensured KANU's supremacy in the Little General Election (1966) [q.v.]. Nevertheless, he still faced opposition within KANU as the party continued to be riven by factionalism, with subgroups known then as KANU A and KANU B [q.v.].

On 5 July 1969, he was assassinated while shopping at Chani's Pharmacy in Nairobi. On 21 July 1969, the Kenyan authorities announced that Nahashon Isaac Njenga Njoroge had been charged with the crime. After a trial, the suspect, supposedly a Kikuyu [q.v.], was found guilty, sentenced to death, and executed on 8 November 1969. To this day, many Kenyans remain convinced that there was a wider conspiracy associated with the Mboya assassination.

MERU. The people (1989 census: Meru, 1,087,778; Tharaka 92,528) known collectively as the Meru inhabit the region northeast of Mount Kenya [q.v.]. These Meru-speaking peoples, including the Igembe, Tigania, Imenti, Miutini, Igoji, Mwimbi, Mutambi, and Tharaka, form part of the Thagicu group of Bantu-speakers [q.v.] of central Kenya, along with the Embu and the Kikuyu [qq.v.]. Meru traditions claim that they moved to their highland home from the Kenya coast, but this is not in accord with other pieces of historical evidence relating to early Meru history. Nevertheless, by the 18th century, the Meru occupied the north and northeastern slopes of Mount Kenya and the plains to the north and northeast of the mountain. Those living on the mountain slopes developed intensive agriculture [q.v.], while those Meru-speakers resident in the plains cultivated grains and raised cattle. During the colonial period the Meru were not as deeply involved in anticolonial activity as the Kikuyu, but they became increasingly involved in the colonial economy through commodity production and wage labor. The Meru were one of the first African peoples to be allowed to plant arabica coffee [q.v.].

MERU NATIONAL PARK. (870 square kilometers; 336 square miles). Gazetted in 1960 as a national reserve and in 1966 as a national park. Meru [q.v.], which is located northeast of Mount Kenya [q.v.], contains many large mammals, including black rhinoceros, cheetah, elephant, giraffe, Grant's gazelle, hartebeest, hippopotamus, leopard, lesser kudu, lion, oryx, and zebra. There also are 277 recorded bird species. *See also* NATIONAL PARKS.

MIJIKENDA (Literally, Nine Towns). Name applied collectively to several ethnic groups resident at the southern Kenya coast. These include the Kauma, Giriama, Chonyi, Jibana, Kambe, Ribe, Rabai, Duruma, and Digo. Together they made up the eighth-largest ethnic group at the time of the 1989 census (1,007,371). The Mijikenda are Bantu-speakers [q.v.] whose languages are closely related to Swahili [q.v.]. They migrated south from the Tana River Valley in the late 16th century as a result of pressure from the Oromo [q.v.] peoples and first settled in six villages or *kaya*. Three others were established later. These were the original areas of settlement where the Mijikenda developed distinctive cultures in the 17th and 18th centuries and from which the people spread out over the coastal hinterland. The Mijikenda mixed agriculture (e.g., grain crops and coconuts) [q.v.] with stock rearing. They were rapidly drawn into trade with the towns of the Kenya coast, and by the 19th century this had reached substantial proportions with Mombasa [q.v.]. Many were also involved with the expansion of caravan trade in the interior as well. In the 1890s, the Mijikenda came under colonial control as British authorities began to assert authority from Mombasa to the surrounding coastal areas. Subjected to demands for labor and competition for land from European-owned plantations established at the coast prior to World War I, the Giriama rebelled against colonial rule in 1914. Overall, the impact of the colonial economy on the Mijikenda peoples was often negative as peoples of the interior came to dominate commodity production and to rival Mijikenda for work in colonial Mombasa.

MILLION ACRE SCHEME. One of the most famous land settlement programs launched at the time of independence (1962–70). *See also* SETTLEMENT SCHEMES.

MITCHELL, SIR PHILIP EUEN (1890–1964). Governor of Kenya (1944–52). Born in Spain and educated at St. Paul's School and Trinity College, Oxford. After university, he joined the Colonial Service and became assistant resident in Nyasaland (now Malawi) (1912–15). During World War I [q.v.] Mitchell served in the King's African Rifles [q.v.] as a lieutenant (1915–18). After the war, he returned to Malawi but in 1919 was transferred to Tanganyika (now Tanzania), where Great Britain had assumed control from the Germans.

In 1926, Governor Sir Donald Cameron appointed him assistant secretary for native affairs. Following a brief stint as a provincial commissioner, Cameron then appointed him secretary for native affairs (1928). Mitchell held that post until 1934, when he became chief secretary, the second-highest position in the colonial government. He then became governor of Uganda (1935–40). During his tenure in Uganda, Mitchell solidified his reputation as one of Great Britain's most outstanding pro-consuls in Africa and established a record of progressive administration, especially in education. Upon completion of his term, he declined an offer to become governor of Kenya. Instead, he served as deputy chairman of the East African Governors' Conference until 1941, when he was attached to the command of the British forces involved in the conquest of Ethiopia and Italian Somaliland. In 1942, Mitchell became governor of Fiji and high commissioner in the Western Pacific, working to coordinate British and American war efforts in the Pacific.

In 1944, Mitchell became governor of Kenya. Of all of Kenya's colonial governors, he was by far the best qualified for the position. Though he served longer than any of Kenya's colonial governors, Mitchell's performance was mixed. He inaugurated the linking of Great Britain's East African colonies through common control over such services as railways, harbors, and post offices. However, Mitchell failed to reassert metropolitan authority over the European settlers. Moreover, he was unwilling to make any concessions to African nationalism. Indeed, as time passed, Mitchell believed that decolonization in British Africa could not possibly be accomplished until well into the 21st century. Most serious of all, Mitchell turned a blind eye to the growth of African discontent and resistance that finally erupted in the Mau Mau Revolt [q.v.]. After his retirement from office, Mitchell took up residence on a farm in Subukia until 1963. Faced with the prospect of living in a Kenya led by Jomo Kenyatta [q.v.], Mitchell sold his farm and moved to Gibraltar. He died there on 11 October 1964. Mitchell published *African Afterthoughts* in 1954.

MOI, DANIEL TOROITICH ARAP (1924–). Second president of Kenya. Born in Baringo District in Rift Valley Province [q.v.]. Moi is a Tugen, an ethnic group that forms part of the Kalenjin [q.v.]. He received his early education at the Africa Inland Mission School, Kabartonjo, and then at the Africa Inland Mission School, Kapsabet and Government African School, Kapsabet. Moi then chose to undertake a teacher's course at Kapsabet Teacher Training College and at Tambach Teachers College. He started his academic career at Tambach Government African School (1945–47) and as headmaster at Kabarnet Government African School (1948). Other academic appointments included assistant principal,

Tambach Teacher Training College (1950–55) and headmaster at Kabarnet (1955–57).

Moi's political career began in 1955, when he was nominated to the Legislative Council (LEGCO) [q.v.] to replace the African member for the Rift Valley [q.v.]. In October 1955, Moi took the oath of office and remained a member of Kenya's legislative body through early 1999. Unlike most of the then African LEGCO members, Moi won a seat in the 1957 LEGCO elections [q.v.] held for Africans. He belonged to the African Elected Members Organisation and the Constituency Elected Members Organisation [qq.v.].

During the late 1950s, he was overshadowed in terms of leadership by figures such as Tom Mboya, Oginga Odinga, Ronald Ngala, and Masinde Muliro [qq.v.]. Moi joined the latter in the Kenya National Party [q.v.], so it was not surprising that he would join them in forming the Kenya African Democratic Union (KADU) [q.v.] in 1960 despite the fact that he had been elected assistant treasurer of the Kenya African National Union (KANU) [q.v.] in absentia. By the time of KADU's formation, Moi had emerged as leader and spokesman of the Kalenjin Political Alliance [q.v.] in articulating Kalenjin land claims in the White Highlands [q.v.]. Additionally, he became KADU's chairman and won the Baringo seat in the LEGCO elections (1961) [q.v.]. When KADU agreed to form the government, Moi accepted office as parliamentary secretary in the Ministry of Education. In December 1961, he became minister of education. He held this post until after the second Lancaster House Conference (1962) [q.v.], when he became minister of local government in the coalition government formed after the conference.

Moi campaigned vigorously for KADU and *majimbo* [q.v.] in the 1963 general elections [q.v.]. He was returned unopposed and was also elected to head the Rift Valley Regional Assembly where KADU had a large majority. In the 1963–64 constitutional changes, KANU eliminated the latter position. After KADU's dissolution in 1964, Moi joined KANU and associated himself with the party's moderates. With the establishment of a republic in December 1964, Moi returned to the cabinet as minister for home affairs, the only former KADU leader to gain a ministerial position at that time. At the Limuru Conference (1966) [q.v.], he became KANU's vice president for Rift Valley Province [q.v.]. In January 1967, Moi became Kenya's third vice president after the incumbent, Joseph Murumbi, resigned. Thus, until President Jomo Kenyatta's [q.v.] death in August 1978, Moi served as vice president and minister for home affairs. In 1969 and 1974, he was reelected to Parliament unopposed.

Loyalty to the president marked Moi's tenure as vice president. He carried out many leadership tasks, such as representing Kenya at international conferences and meetings that the aging Kenyatta [q.v.] could not undertake. Additionally, he served as leader of government business in Parliament, where he loyally advocated and defended the policies of the Kenyatta era, from pro-Western foreign policy and the rejection of socialism to the banning of the Kenya People's Union [q.v.] and the detention of those deemed dissidents. However, Moi's years as vice president were not without controversy as he was often attacked over the issue of succession to the presidency. This reached a peak in 1976 with the Change the Constitution campaign [q.v.], which was orchestrated largely by Kikuyu [q.v.] politicians and the Gikuyu, Embu, Meru Association (GEMA) [q.v.], which did not want the presidency to fall into the hands of another ethnic group. Under the terms of Kenya's constitution [q.v.], Moi became acting president on Kenyatta's death in August 1978. KANU then nominated Moi as the sole candidate for president. He was elected unopposed and was sworn into office as Kenya's second president in October 1978.

Moi began his presidency by adopting the Swahili word *nyayo* (footsteps) [q.v.] as his administration's watchword. By using *nyayo*, he sought to reassure Kenyans that he was following in Kenyatta's footsteps. However, in time *nyayo* came to denote the policies associated with Moi's presidency. He sought from the first to make himself a populist president. Unlike Kenyatta, Moi maintained an active profile, traversing the nation and addressing public meetings several times a week. As president, he used patronage and the huge powers of the executive branch to keep his enemies divided and off balance. By the late 1980s, Moi had solidified his power, which had become increasingly personal and authoritarian. The use of state power to enhance political and personal fortunes became one of the characteristics of the *nyayo* era.

In 1991, President Moi reluctantly accepted multipartyism. However, thanks to a divided opposition and his use of state resources and control of broadcast media, he won the general elections (1992) [q.v.], despite receiving less than 35 percent of the vote. Following the election, President Moi refrained from altering his political tactics, which combined populist initiatives with patronage and state power to maintain his dominant position in KANU while opposition political parties remained divided. In the general elections (1997) [q.v.], Moi was reelected to his fifth and last term as president, receiving 40.12 percent of the vote (2,445,801 votes). Some Kenyans expected him to appoint a more ethnically representative ministerial cabinet. However, Moi gave only a single ministerial portfolio to a Kikuyu and none to Luos [q.v.]. Additionally, he failed to appoint a vice president from 8 January 1998 through 3 April 1999, thus raising speculation about his possible successor.

MOI DAY. First celebrated as a national holiday on 10 October 1989. The holiday celebrates the achievements of the *nyayo* [q.v.] era and marks Daniel arap Moi's [q.v.] taking office as president in that month in 1978.

MOI UNIVERSITY. Opened in 1984 on land donated by the British multinational corporation LONHRO. In 1997–98, the university, which is located in Eldoret [q.v.], had a student population of about 7,600 (including 2,800 in its constituent institution, Maseno University College). Some of the courses offered include forest resources and wildlife management, education, information sciences, health sciences, agriculture, and technology. *See also* EDUCATION, UNIVERSITY.

MOMBASA. Kenya's second-largest city and the country's major seaport, located on Mombasa Island. Altitude is at sea level. Over the past several centuries, the city had a number of foreign rulers, including the Portuguese (1498–1698), the Omanis (1698–1724), the Mazruis (1726–1837), the al-Busaidis based in Zanzibar (1837–95), and the British (1895–1963).

Mombasa was probably founded in the 10th century as a commercial center inhabited by Swahili [q.v.]-speaking people [q.v.]. By the 14th century, if not earlier, Mombasa had become the most important commercial town on the coast of what is today Kenya. The arrival of Portuguese ships at the end of the 15th century had a negative impact on Mombasa as the Portuguese burned and looted the town on several occasions. At the end of the 16th century, the Portuguese made Mombasa their center of influence on the northern portion of the East African coast by constructing Fort Jesus [q.v.]. Portuguese dominance in Mombasa lasted scarcely a century with the Omani Arabs ending the European presence in the city.

Under the leadership of the Mazrui Arabs from Oman, the 12 Swahili [q.v.] tribes of Mombasa successfully repelled Omani attempts to take control until the third decade of the 19th century, when the city fell under the control of the sultan of Zanzibar. When it gained the approval of the sultan and the British government for its takeover of the British sphere of influence in East Africa, the Imperial British East Africa Company [q.v.] made Mombasa its headquarters in 1888. After the British government assumed control of the

East Africa Protectorate [q.v.] in 1895, Mombasa became the new colony's capital. In 1907, the colonial government moved the capital to Nairobi [q.v.]. Mombasa retained its commercial importance, however, as the major port for Kenya and Uganda and the Indian Ocean terminus of the Uganda Railway [q.v.], which had been begun from Mombasa in 1896. Mombasa's significance as a shipping and commercial center attracted workers to the port city from the Mijikenda [q.v.] and from such up-country peoples as the Kamba, Luo, and Kikuyu [qq.v.]. After World War II [q.v.], businessmen inaugurated several manufacturing endeavors, but these were less extensive than those in Nairobi [q.v.]. According to the 1989 census, Mombasa had a population of 461,753; the current estimated population is one million.

MOORE, SIR HENRY MONCK-MASON (1887–1964). Governor of Kenya (1940–44). Known affectionately to his friends as "Monkey" Moore. Born in England and educated at King's College School and Jesus College, Cambridge. In November 1910, he joined the colonial service and became a cadet in the Ceylon (now Sri Lanka) civil service. After holding a variety of positions in Ceylon, Greece, Bermuda, and Nigeria, Moore became the colonial secretary in Kenya (1929–34). He also served as acting governor (1930) before becoming governor of Sierra Leone (1934–37). After a tour of duty in the Colonial Office (1937–40), Moore accepted the governorship of Kenya (1940–44). He was the first of Kenya's governors to have spent his entire career in the colonial service. During his tenure, he allowed European settlers to make considerable political and economic gains. Additionally, Moore unsuccessfully sought to persuade the British government to unify its East African territories under the rule of the European settlers. After leaving Kenya, he served as governor of Ceylon (1944–48) and governor-general of Ceylon (1948–49). In 1949, he retired to Cape Town, South Africa. He died on 26 March 1964.

MOUNT ELGON (Altitude of 4,321 meters; 14,176 feet). Also called Mount Masaba. Known to the Maasai [q.v.] as *Ol Doinyo Igoon* (mountain shaped like breasts), this extinct volcano is more than 15 million years old. Mount Elgon, whose western flank is bisected by the Kenyan-Ugandan border, covers 169 square kilometers (65 square miles). The four highest peaks are Wagagai (4,321 meters; 14,176 feet), Lower Elgon (4,300 meters; 14,110 feet), Sudek (4,310 meters; 14,140 feet), and Koitobos (4,231 meters; 13,881 feet). Mount Elgon derives most of its rainfall from Lake Victoria [q.v.].

MOUNT ELGON NATIONAL PARK (169 square kilometers; 65 square miles). Gazetted in 1968. Located on the western border with Uganda. Park fauna includes buffalo, bushbuck, colobus monkey, duiker, eland, elephant, giant forest hog, and leopard. There is also a basalt column called Koitobos (Table Rock) and the "lava-tube" caves, which elephants visit in search of salt. *See also* NATIONAL PARKS.

MOUNT KENYA (Altitude of 5,199 meters; 17,057 feet). Located 193 kilometers (120 miles) northeast of Nairobi [q.v.]. Nanyuki [q.v.] lies at the northwestern part of the mountain. The Kikuyu [q.v.] often refer to Mount Kenya, which is a long-extinct volcano, as *Kirinyaga* or *Kere-Nyaga* (mountain of whiteness). The three highest peaks are Batian (5,199 meters; 17,058 feet), Nelion (5,188 meters; 17,021 feet), and Lenana (4,985 meters; 16,355 feet). Johann Ludwig Krapf [q.v.] was the first European to see Mount Kenya (1849), while Halford John Mackinder was the first to reach the summit (1899).

　　Mount Kenya is crucial to Kenya's ecosystem as the country's most important watershed and its largest forest reserve. The mountain also has a diverse environment. Apart from a variety of alpine and subalpine flora (there are 13 plant species that are endemic to the mountain), Mount Kenya contains montane and bamboo forests, moorlands, and tundra. Cedar, yellowwood, and bamboo are also found on the mountain. The Embu, Kikuyu, and Meru [qq.v.] peoples cultivate the lower slopes.

MOUNT KENYA NATIONAL PARK. (588 square kilometers; 227 square miles). Gazetted in December 1949. Located along the equator, 193 kilometers (120 miles) from Nairobi [q.v.] and 480 kilometers (about 300 miles) from the Kenyan coast. Fauna includes black rhinoceros, duiker, elephant, giant forest hog, leopard, suni, and tree hyrax. *See also* NATIONAL PARKS.

MUITE, PAUL (1946–). Lawyer and politician. Born in Kikuyu in Kiambu District. In the late 1970s and early 1980s, Muite came to public notice as a pro-establishment lawyer noted for his close ties to Charles Njonjo [q.v.]. This relationship probably caused the Law Society of Kenya to reject his 1982 bid to become chairman. After this setback, however, Muite moved even more into the limelight with his defense of the Kenya Air Force commander on trial for the 1982 abortive coup attempt [q.v.]. He also served as a member of Njonjo's legal team during the long public inquiry into the latter's affairs.

　　By the late 1980s, Muite had established relations with other Law Society of Kenya members who opposed queue voting, executive domination of the judiciary [q.v.], and human rights abuses. In 1989, he stood for the chairmanship of the Law Society but lost amidst charges that the exercise had been rigged with the government's connivance. After 1990, Muite came to even greater prominence as he was finally elected chairman. Additionally, he served as advocate for several high-profile clients (e.g., Kenneth Matiba [q.v.]), and as defense attorney in criminal cases where he alleged the defendants were actually being prosecuted on trumped-up charges for their political beliefs (e.g., George Anyona and Koigi wa Wamwere [qq.v.]).

Muite also became an articulate advocate for political reform, joining Matiba, Charles Rubia, and Oginga Odinga [qq.v.] in the demand for multipartyism. In 1992, Muite joined the Forum for the Restoration of Democracy (FORD) [q.v.] as an ally of Odinga. Unlike other prominent Kikuyu [q.v.] opposition activists, he stayed with Odinga in the Forum for the Restoration of Democracy-Kenya (FORD-K) [q.v.] and became first vice-chairman of the party. In the general elections (1992) [q.v.], Muite won the Kikuyu seat. When FORD-K became the official opposition in Parliament, he became deputy leader of the opposition. In September 1993, however, Muite resigned from this post and his position of first vice chairman in protest against the sacking of Gitobu Imanyara as the party's general secretary. Muite did not resign his parliamentary seat even after May 1995, when he announced his intention to launch a new political party, later to be known as SAFINA [q.v.]. President Daniel arap Moi [q.v.] reacted with hostility to the new party, which finally gained official registration in November 1997. In the general elections (1997) [q.v.], Muite was reelected to Parliament on a SAFINA ticket.

MULIRO, MASINDE (1920–1992). Teacher, politician, farmer, and businessman. Born at Matili in Bungoma District and educated at Matili and Misikhu Roman Catholic primary schools. During the 1940–43 period, he attended Busoga College in Uganda. After studying at St. Mary's, Yala, he went to St. Peters College in Tororo, Uganda, and the University of Cape Town, where he received a B.A. in history, philosophy, and education (1954). Upon his return to Kenya in 1954, Muliro taught at Alliance Girls High School and Siriba Teachers College. In the LEGCO elections (1957) [q.v.], he won a seat for North Nyanza. In July 1959, he formed the multiracial Kenya National Party [q.v.], which proved short-lived because of opposition by the Kenya Independence Movement [q.v.]. Muliro participated in the first Lancaster House Conference [q.v.], and afterwards he joined with Ronald Ngala, Daniel arap Moi [qq.v.], and others to form the Kenya African Democratic Union (KADU) [q.v.]. He served as KADU's deputy leader and won the Elgon Nyanza seat in the LEGCO elections (1961) [q.v.] unopposed. Muliro campaigned for KADU's *majimbo* [q.v.] policy, advocating in particular the creation of a new Western Region with the addition of Kitale and Trans Nzoia District. He was obviously disappointed when Kitale and Trans Nzoia were not included in the new Western Province [q.v.]. Still, Muliro successfully ran for a seat in Trans Nzoia for KADU in the general elections (1963) [q.v.].

After KADU dissolved itself in late 1964, Muliro joined KANU but he had to wait longer than Moi or Ngala to attain ministerial office. In 1969, he became minister of co-operatives and social services, and after success in the general elections (1969) [q.v.], he became minister of works. In 1975, President Jomo Kenyatta [q.v.] fired him from the latter position after he voted against the government front bench on the report of the select committee investigating the murder of J. M. Kariuki [q.v.]. The dismissal made Muliro a political outcast. Without government support, he lost his seat in the general elections (1997) [q.v.]. After losing again in the 1983 general elections [q.v.], Muliro successfully petitioned that the election had been fraudulent. He then won the seat in a by-election, claiming that he had never lost a fair election in his political career. In the general elections (1988) [q.v.], he retained his seat by the slim margin of seven votes. Officials nullified the election after his opponent filed an election petition. Muliro refused to take part in the 1989 by-election for his seat, labeling it a "farce." As a result, he had to relinquish his parliamentary seat. In 1990 and 1991, he added his voice to those favoring multipartyism, and he was one of the founders of the Forum for the Restoration of Democracy [q.v.]. He became interim vice chairman of the party and supported Oginga Odinga [q.v.], who eventually broke away from the party to form the Forum for the Restoration of Democracy-Kenya [q.v.]. Muliro died on 14 August 1992.

MUMBO. In 1913, the cult of Mumbo, or Mumboism, first emerged among the Luo [q.v.] of Central Nyanza. The cult rejected European ways and advocated a return to the traditional way of life. Belief involved acceptance of a millennial vision of renewal in which the Europeans would leave Kenya. Mumboism quickly spread to South Nyanza, and toward the end of World War I [q.v.], it gained increasing support among the Gusii [q.v.], who found the cult's political appeal more attractive than its religious message. Those who believed in Mumbo had only to wait and be true to the faith, and the colonialists would be swept out of Kenya along with the chiefs and others who supported colonial rule. The appeal of Mumboism was strongest in those areas of western Kenya in the post-World War I depression, a time of increasing government pressure in the form of higher taxes, forced labor, and the *kipande* [q.v.]. The cult gained additional members during the Great Depression. On both occasions, the colonial government sought to check the cult's influence by arresting its leaders and exiling them to the coast.

MUMIA WA SHIUNDU (1849?–1949). *Nabongo* (king) of the Wanga (the Wanga are a Luyia [q.v.] subethnic group) state, colonial chief of Wanga, and paramount chief of then North Kavirondo District. In the late 1870s, Mumia succeeded his father Shiundu as *nabongo*. As ruler, Mumia welcomed the first European adventurers; indeed, he was so hospitable that his capital, later known as Mumias, became a regular stopping point for those visiting western Kenya or going on to Uganda. When the scramble for East Africa placed Mumia's kingdom in the Uganda Protectorate in 1894, he cooperated with the British in the conquest of the Luyia-inhabited areas of Uganda's Eastern Province. Mumias thus became the capital of Eastern Province [q.v.] until 1899, and thereafter it was the headquarters of Elgon, later North Kavirondo, District. With the colonial conquest of the Luyia largely complete by the time of the transfer of Uganda's Eastern Province to the East Africa Protectorate [q.v.] in 1902, the British expected Mumia to fill the role of collaborator as a colonial chief. He did so as part of a process of Wanga subimperialism that saw several of his brothers and relatives installed as chiefs over other Luyia peoples, causing much resentment and opposition to Mumia and Wanga domination. Nevertheless, in 1909, Mumia became paramount chief over all North Kavirondo chiefs.

This appointment, which represented the height of Mumia's collaboration with colonial authorities, did not last long. By the end of World War I [q.v.], his reputation as a friendly and cooperative chief had been tarnished, and most of his powers and influence had been stripped from him. In 1926, he stepped down as chief of Wanga, and the colonial government, using anti-Wanga sentiment in the district as justification, abolished the position of paramount chief, though Mumia was allowed to keep the title as long as he lived. Mumia spent the rest of his active political life trying to regain the power and privileges associated with the paramountcy, without success. Neither his brothers nor his sons were successful in seeking to convince the colonial government to name a successor to Mumia as paramount chief of the district. Mumia died on 24 April 1949, reportedly embittered against the colonial system he had helped to install in western Kenya.

MUNGAI, NJOROGE (1926–). Physician, politician, and businessman. Born at Dagoretti and educated at Alliance High School [q.v.]; Fort Hare University, South Africa; and Stanford University where he obtained an M.D. In 1959, Mungai returned to Kenya and opened several clinics. After the founding of the Kenya African National Union (KANU) [q.v.] in 1960, he became involved in politics full-time though he served for a time as Jomo Kenyatta's [q.v.] personal physician. In the general elections (1963) [q.v.], he was elected for Nairobi [q.v.] West and was appointed minister of health upon the achievement of self-government. In 1965, Mungai became minister of internal security and defence (later Defence). Four years later, he won the Dagoretti parliamentary seat and became minister for foreign affairs. At the peak of his influence, Mungai was seen by many as a possible successor to President Jomo Kenyatta [q.v.]. However, in 1974, he suffered one of independent Kenya's greatest electoral upsets when he lost to Dr. Johnstone Muthiora, thus losing his ministerial portfolio.

In June 1975, he was nominated to Parliament. Despite his involvement in the Change the Constitution Campaign (1976) [q.v.], he won the Dagoretti parliamentary seat in 1979. Mungai did not return to the cabinet, however, and in the general elections (1983) [q.v.] he failed to hold the Dagoretti parliamentary seat. In the general elections (1988) [q.v.], he switched his interest to the Westlands parliamentary seat which he won narrowly. With the dawn of multipartyism, Mungai, unlike many other Kikuyu [q.v.] politicians, stuck with KANU after flirting with the Forum for the Restoration of Democracy (FORD) [q.v.], but he failed to win a parliamentary seat in the general elections (1992) [q.v.]. He remained active in Nairobi KANU politics, but he again failed to return to Parliament in 1997.

MWAKENYA. One of several clandestine dissident organizations that emerged in the early 1980s to overthrow President Daniel arap Moi's [q.v.] government. Mwakenya, which is an acronym for *Muungano wa Wazalendo Kukomboa Kenya* (Union of Nationalists to Liberate Kenya), gained an international reputation largely because its ranks included several leading dissidents, including Ngugi wa Thiong'o [q.v.]. Also, the group attracted attention because of its supposed links to Libya. During a 1986–88 crackdown, the police [q.v.] arrested scores of people who supposedly belonged to Mwakenya. Since then, apart from periodically releasing anti-Moi pamphlets, the organization has been relatively inactive. *See also* DECEMBER 12 MOVEMENT; UKENYA.

MWAMBAO UNITED FRONT. Political organization that emerged in early 1962 to campaign for *mwambao* (autonomy) for Kenya's coastal strip. The front, largely supported by coastal Arabs, demanded union with Zanzibar [q.v.] or, failing that, the creation of a self-governing coastal state. However, this organization had little support from coastal Africans, other Kenyans, or the British government. As the latter accepted the recommendation of the special commissioner that there could be no autonomy for the coastal strip, the Mwambao United Front was unsuccessful. This was made clear by the 1962 Kenya Coastal Strip Conference [q.v.], and the Mwambao United Front soon went out of existence.

MWANGALE, ELIJAH WASIKE (1939–). Teacher, politician, and businessman. Born in Kimilili, Bungoma district. He attended Egerton College (1961–63), where he received a diploma in agriculture. Mwangale then studied at West Virginia University, where he gained a B.Sc. degree in agriculture and a master's degree in soil science (agronomy). He briefly taught chemistry at Egerton College. In 1969, Mwangale won a parliamentary seat for Bungoma East; in 1974, he retained his seat with a majority of 20,000 votes over his rival. In 1975, Mwangale served as chairman of the Parliamentary Select Committee that investigated the assassination of Josiah Kariuki [q.v.]. In 1977, he was elected Bungoma branch chairman of the Kenya African National Union (KANU) [q.v.]. On 28 November 1979, following success in the general election, he became minister of labour. Mwangale then served as minister of tourism (1980–83), minister of foreign affairs (1983–88), minister of agriculture (1988–89), and minister of livestock development (1989–92). Because of his staunch support of President Daniel arap Moi [q.v.], Mwangale wielded considerable power in the 1980s, as witnessed by the fact that he accused Charles Njonjo [q.v.] of being a traitor at a time when no other government official would challenge this formidable politician.

Mwangale lost the general elections (1992) [q.v.] to Dr. Mukhisa Kituyi, the Forum for the Restoration of Democracy (FORD)-Kenya [q.v.] candidate. Mwangale then returned to his farm in Bungoma and remained outside the political arena for a time. Finally, in December 1995, he succeeded in being elected KANU sub-branch chairman for Kimilili. On 28 August 1996, Mwangale was elected KANU branch chairman for Bungoma District, thanks to Moi's support. After his political rehabilitation, Mwangale failed to regain a place in Parliament.

MWENDWA, KITILI (1929–1985). Lawyer, civil servant, judge, politician, and businessman. Born in Matinyani location of Kitui District to a former colonial senior chief and educated at Alliance High School and Makerere University [qq.v.]. After completing his studies at Makerere in 1950, Mwendwa first worked as a teacher. In 1952, he enrolled at the University of London, earning a law degree in 1955. He then undertook further studies in Great Britain. In 1962, Mwendwa returned to Kenya and joined the civil service. In 1963, he became one of the first African permanent secretaries. The following year, he became Kenya's first African solicitor general. In 1967, President Jomo Kenyatta [q.v.] named Mwendwa as the first African chief justice of Kenya. However, in 1971, he resigned this office because he had been implicated in a coup plot. For more than a decade, he remained out of the political limelight. However, in the general elections (1983) [q.v.], he reentered politics but narrowly lost the Kitui West seat. Subsequently, the courts overturned the result and, in a 1984 by-election, Mwendwa was returned to Parliament. His political career was cut short by his death in an automobile accident on 27 September 1985.

-N-

NAIROBI. (Altitude of 1,675 meters; 5,495 feet). Nairobi, which is a Maasai [q.v.] word meaning "place of cool waters," is the largest city in eastern and central Africa. Its initial importance stemmed from the fact that the British chose it for the Uganda Railway's [q.v.] headquarters (1899). On 16 April 1900, Sir Arthur Hardinge [q.v.] gave Nairobi township status. In 1907, Nairobi became the East Africa Protectorate's [q.v.] capital. To the end of World War II [q.v.], Nairobi served as Kenya's administrative, commercial, and financial center. After the war, it also became the country's most important industrial city thanks to the development of secondary, import-substitution industries.

Since 1963, the city has continued to grow as multinational firms have located there and tourism [q.v.] has become increasingly important. Additionally, Nairobi became the major transportation, communications, and diplomatic center for eastern Africa. The city's popularity also attracted hundreds of thousands of rural Kenyans who sought employment and a new life. The government's inability to cope with this influx of people facilitated the spread of ghettos in and around Nairobi. Social services (i.e., housing, sanitation, medical facilities, schools, adequate police [q.v.] protection, etc.) in these areas are nonexistent to minimal. The high growth rate of the city's population has also caused crime rates to escalate and has given rise to serious pollution problems.

At independence, the city's population was approximately a half million people. According to the 1989 census, Nairobi's population was 1,324,570; by the mid-1990s, the city had an estimated population of some two million. Nairobi is ranked as Province for administrative purposes (684 square kilometers; 264 square miles). *See also* NAIROBI DISTRICT NATIONAL CONGRESS; NAIROBI NATIONAL PARK; NAIROBI STOCK EXCHANGE.

NAIROBI DISTRICT NATIONAL CONGRESS (NDNC). In 1956, C. M. G. Arwings-Kodhek [q.v.] formed the NDNC following the colonial government's refusal to register his Kenya African National Congress. The NDNC was the first of the district parties to emerge during the period when colony-wide African political parties were banned. Arwings-Kodhek ran for the Nairobi [q.v.] seat on the party's ticket in the LEGCO elections (1957) [q.v.] but lost to Tom Mboya [q.v.]. In 1960, most NDNC supporters, including Arwings-Kodhek, joined the Kenya African National Union [q.v.].

NAIROBI NATIONAL PARK. (117 square kilometers; 45 square miles). Gazetted in December 1946 as Kenya's first national park [q.v.]. Carved out of what was once a Somali reserve, Nairobi Common; a World War I [q.v.] training area; and a World War II [q.v.] firing range. The park, which is located about eight kilometers (five miles) south of Nairobi [q.v.], contains most larger mammals found in Kenya except for elephant. There are also approximately 500 bird species. In 1963, conservationists founded the Nairobi Animal Orphanage in the park. The David Sheldrick Conservation Foundation, which cares for orphaned elephants and rhinoceroses, is also located in the park. *See also* NATIONAL PARKS.

NAIROBI PEOPLES CONVENTION PARTY (NPCP). A Nairobi political party formed in 1957 as an alternative to the Nairobi District National Congress [q.v.] in 1957. In 1958 Tom Mboya [q.v.] assumed the presidency of NPCP. The party campaigned against the Lennox-Boyd Constitution [q.v.] and for the rapid achievement of African majority rule. In early 1959, the NPCP adopted increasingly militant tactics, and the colonial state arrested several of the party's leaders and banned its newspaper in March as a result. These actions failed to break the party or

Mboya's support in Nairobi. Mboya dissolved the party in 1960 with the formation of the Kenya African National Union (KANU) [q.v.].

NAIROBI PROVINCE. *See* NAIROBI.

NAIROBI STOCK EXCHANGE. The Nairobi Stock Exchange, which was established in 1965 with six members, is currently the fourth-largest stock market in sub-Saharan Africa, behind South Africa, Nigeria, and Zimbabwe. As of the end of 1995, the exchange had a market capitalization of $1.9 billion and 56 listed companies. In January 1995, the market received a boost as the Kenyan government, for the first time in 30 years, allowed direct foreign investment in the country.

NAIVASHA. (Altitude of 1,890 meters; 6,201 feet). Naivasha, which is 86 kilometers (57 miles) from Nairobi, has a Maasai [qq.v.] name meaning "rippling waters." Shortly after its establishment, the town became a government center, and much land nearby was alienated to European settlers. In the early 1920s, three brothers, James, Andrew, and Robert Macrae planted about 12,150 hectares (30,000 acres) of sisal [q.v.] in an area that stretched from Lake Naivasha [q.v.] to Mount Longonot. During the 1927–28 period, Lord Delamere [q.v.] and Thomas Chillingworth financed the construction of the Co-operative Creamery in Naivasha. According to the 1989 census, Naivasha's population was 34,519; the current estimated population is about 100,000.

NAIVASHA PROVINCE. Created in 1902 from the territory transferred from Uganda to the East Africa Protectorate [q.v.]. In 1929, the colonial government divided the province into Nzoia [q.v.], Rift Valley, and Turkana Provinces, leaving a much smaller Naivasha. By 1935, Naivasha, Nzoia, and Rift Valley Provinces merged to form a new Rift Valley Province [q.v.].

NAKURU. (Altitude of 1,830 meters; 6,004 feet). Nakuru was started as a small town adjacent to the Uganda Railway [q.v.] in 1900. Nakuru, which is located on an arid, windswept plain that the Maasai [q.v.] called "the place where the cows won't eat grass," became the "capital" of the White Highlands [q.v.]. On 28 January 1904, the British colonial government proclaimed Nakuru a township. In addition to serving European farmers as a site for processing grain and dairy products, Nakuru served as Rift Valley Province [q.v.] headquarters. Since independence, Nakuru has remained an administrative and farming center. Additionally, textile and light consumer goods industries have developed in the city. Nakuru is also the headquarters of the Kenya Farmer's Association, which was formally known as the Kenya Grain Growers Co-operative Union, and the Pyrethrum [q.v.] Board of Kenya. Egerton University [q.v.] is located within about 19 kilometers (12 miles) of Nakuru.

During much of the colonial and early postindependence periods, Nakuru had the reputation of being East Africa's cleanest town. Over the past two decades, however, there has been a significant deterioration in services such as solid waste collection and road and street maintenance. Additionally, there is a housing shortage, and Nakuru's drainage system is in poor condition. By 1997, efforts by local leaders to restore the town's former glory had made little progress. According to the 1989 census, Nakuru's population was 849,096, making it Kenya's fourth-largest city.

NANYUKI. (Altitude of 1,850 meters; 6,070 feet). In 1899, Sir Halford Mackinder camped at the place where Nanyuki now lies prior to his ascent of nearby Mount Kenya [q.v.]. Eleven years later, Arnold Paice became the first European farmer to settle in Nanyuki. After World War I [q.v.], more European settlers arrived in the area under the aegis of the Soldier Settlement Scheme [q.v.]. In 1920, the colonial government established Nanyuki Township; 10 years later, the railway reached the town. Throughout the colonial period, Nanyuki remained a small farming town, but with the departure of most European settlers after independence, its economic importance declined. In more recent years, the town has become the home of a Kenyan Air Force base, a British military training facility, and the world-famous Mount Kenya Safari Club. According to the 1989 census, Nanyuki's population was 24,070.

NATIONAL ASSEMBLY. Kenya's Parliament. The assembly, which has 210 elected members and 12 members nominated by the president, has a maximum life of five years from the date of its first meeting. The assembly can also dissolve itself by a vote of "no confidence," whereupon presidential and assembly elections must be held within 90 days. A MP must be a Kenyan citizen, more than 18 years of age, and registered as a voter. Candidates for the National Assembly are selected by political parties. Since independence, general elections have been held on 6 December 1969, 4 October 1974, 8 November 1979, 27 September 1983, 21 April 1988, 29 December 1992, and 29–30 December 1997. *See also* CONSTITUTION.

NATIONAL CHRISTIAN COUNCIL OF KENYA (NCCK). The NCCK evolved from the Alliance of Protestant Missions [q.v.] (1918–35); the Kenya Missionary Council (1924–43); and its successor organization, the Christian Council of Kenya (1943–66). Currently, the NCCK represents some 35 Protestant churches and six million members. The NCCK sponsors numerous national and local projects, including rural training centers, village polytechnics, irrigation schemes, urban improvement, and youth and social work. For more than a decade, the NCCK has also been politically active. On 21 August 1986, for example, the NCCK announced that it would not participate in any future Kenya African National Union [q.v.] preliminary elections that required voters to queue up behind candidates. In December 1986, the NCCK expressed "deep concern" over a series of recently enacted constitutional amendments that enhanced President Daniel arap Moi's [q.v.] powers. In the months before and after the general elections (1997) [q.v.], the NCCK continued its struggle for political reform and democratization. *See also* ALLIANCE OF PROTESTANT MISSIONS; CHURCH MISSIONARY SOCIETY; CHURCH OF SCOTLAND MISSION; GOSPEL MISSIONARY SOCIETY.

NATIONAL CONVENTION EXECUTIVE COUNCIL (NCEC). The NCEC emerged in 1997 as a coalition comprised of religious leaders, opposition politicians, lawyers, and human rights activists. On 26 August 1997, the NCEC declared that the Kenya African National Union [q.v.] was incapable of making meaningful, peaceful reforms. Consequently, the NCEC promised to step up its campaign for free and fair elections. Also, the NCEC supported and helped organize demonstrations in support of the repeal of colonial laws and substantial constitutional change before the 1997 general elections [q.v.] could be held during the May-August period. During the Saba Saba Riots (1997) [q.v.], security forces violently dispersed demonstrators, many of whom were killed or injured. Afterwards, the NCEC called for a further demonstration combined with a general strike to facilitate immediate reform on *nane nane* (8 August). These actions were only partially successful, but the NCEC continued to press its demands for reform before the general elections (1997).

Temporarily, it seemed that the NCEC might push the reform movement to radical goals such as the establishment of a Constituent Assembly and government of national unity. However, politicians representing KANU and the parliamentary opposition seized the reform initiative by establishing the Inter-Parties Parliamentary Group (IPPG) [q.v.], that spearheaded a reforms package which the government approved during the September-October period. The NCEC responded by calling for more comprehensive constitutional changes prior to the elections. Most

Kenyans refused to support the NCEC on this issue as the elections followed shortly after the approval of the IPPG reform package. Following the general elections (1997), the NCEC continued to advocate the comprehensive reform of the constitution [q.v.] and a national Constituent Assembly.

NATIONAL DEMOCRATIC PARTY (NDEM). As part of the campaign for multipartyism and political reform, Oginga Odinga [q.v.] sought to register the NDEM, which had been launched in February 1991, as an opposition political party. When the registrar of societies refused to register the NDEM, Odinga took the matter to court. Although James Orengo [q.v.] presented a good case for registering the NDEM, the court ruled against Odinga. Thereafter, Odinga joined the Forum for the Restoration of Democracy [q.v.] to bring about political reform.

NATIONAL DEVELOPMENT PARTY (NDP). In 1992, the Kenyan government registered this party. However, it made little impact in the general elections (1992) [q.v.]. The NDP was relatively unknown to Kenyans until late 1996, when Raila Odinga [q.v.] left the Forum for the Restoration of Democracy (FORD)-Kenya [q.v.], joined the NDP, and won a by-election. The NDP then endorsed him as its presidential candidate for the general elections (1997) [q.v.]. During the election, he won 10.92 percent of the vote (665,725 votes), coming in third after President Daniel arap Moi and Mwai Kibaki [qq.v.]. The NDP also gained 21 parliamentary seats (plus one nominated). From early 1998, the NDP pursued a policy of cooperation with KANU.

NATIONAL LIBRARY SERVICE. Established in 1965 by an Act of Parliament to establish and maintain a nationwide library network in Kenya. Its headquarters are in Nairobi [q.v.]. Branch libraries are located in several towns, including Embu, Kakamega, Kisumu, and Nyeri [qq.v.]. Mobile services operate from Nairobi to locations without a permanent library.

NATIONAL PARKS. The history of Kenya's national parks system began in 1933, when an international convention, meeting in London, devised guidelines for the creation of national parks and national reserves. In the former, the interests of wildlife take precedent over all other considerations; in the latter the fauna preservation occurs only if it does not conflict with human activities such as farming or cattle raising. In 1935, the British government, acting for all its colonies and overseas territories, ratified the 1933 convention. In 1939, Kenya's colonial government appointed a Game Policy Committee [q.v.], which suggested a course of action for the establishment of a national parks system. However, the outbreak of World War II prevented the colony from acting on the committee's recommendations. In 1946, the colonial government finally created Kenya's first national park on the outskirts of Nairobi [q.v.]. By the 1990s, there were 16 national parks and 25 national reserves located throughout Kenya.

During the immediate postindependence era, Kenya's national park system was a model for the rest of Africa. However, in the mid-1970s, poaching became a serious threat to the well-being of several of the parks. In particular, the growing international demand for ivory and rhinoceros horn for markets in Hong Kong, Taiwan, Oman, Kuwait, and Yemen caused a significant increase in poaching in places like Tsavo National Park [q.v.]. By the end of the 1970s, poachers, armed with modern automatic weapons, had slaughtered an estimated 104,000 elephants (62 percent of the total) and nearly the entire rhinoceros population. There was little improvement during the early 1980s, as poachers continued to operate with near impunity and corrupt government officials profited from illegal trafficking in wildlife trophies.

In 1989, President Daniel arap Moi [q.v.] showed his determination to protect Kenya's fauna by appointing Richard Leakey [q.v.] head of the ministry of wildlife. He also burned 12 tons of ivory at Nairobi National Park [q.v.] as an indication of his commitment to eliminating poaching. Along with scores of other nations, Kenya signed a five-year moratorium on ivory trade advocated by the Convention on International Trade in Endangered Species of Wild Fauna and Flora (CITES). In 1990, Moi authorized the creation of the Kenya Wildlife Service, which sought to enhance community participation in the management of wildlife. Additionally, he ordered the deployment of about 200 American-trained paramilitary personnel to some of the country's national parks with orders to "shoot to kill" all poachers. According to many wildlife conservationists, these efforts saved Kenya's elephant population from certain destruction. Also, there has been progress in restoring the country's rhinoceros population and in providing adequate protection to other wildlife species.

However, this progress, while encouraging, has not resolved all of Kenya's wildlife preservation problems. Indeed, as the turn of the century approaches, it will be increasingly difficult to strike a balance between the demands of conservation and the needs of Kenya's growing human population. Additionally, the environmental impact of hundreds of thousands of foreign tourists on many of the country's national parks has persuaded some experts to predict that Kenya may eventually be forced to restrict the number of visitors entering the parks. Such a policy could have an negative impact on the Kenyan economy which earns more than $400 million annually from the tourist trade. *See also* AMBOSELI NATIONAL PARK; COWIE, MERVYN; GAME POLICY COMMITTEE; MERU NATIONAL PARK; MOUNT ELGON NATIONAL PARK; MOUNT KENYA NATIONAL PARK; NAIROBI NATIONAL PARK; SIBILOI NATIONAL PARK; TSAVO NATIONAL PARK.

NATIVE LABOUR COMMISSION (1912–1913). J. W. (later Sir) Barth, one of the colony's most capable judges, headed the commission, which sought to resolve a chronic shortage of African farm laborers. After hearing evidence from more than 200 Europeans and 60 Africans, the commission issued an almost unanimous report. Major recommendations included instructions to district officers to "encourage" the maximum number of Africans to work for European farmers, the reorganization of the administration so as to separate the European settled areas from African reserves, and the creation of a chief native commissioner who would supervise administration in the African reserves. The commission also felt that the African population was capable of paying a higher rate of taxation, which could particularly be justified to pay for an identification system to deal with worker desertions. Additionally, the commission urged the government to improve the conditions of African laborers who traveled by train and to establish transit camps for African workers who went by road.

However, Governor Sir Henry Belfield [q.v.] did not send his recommendations relating to the commission's report to London until March 1914. The Colonial Office was not quick to react to the proposals, and the start of World War I [q.v.] further deferred action. The new administrative design worked out in detail by Belfield was thus never implemented though certain committee recommendations were put into effect during and after the war (e.g., increased taxation, the registration or *kipande* [q.v.] system, and the creation of the post of chief native commissioner).

NATIVE LANDS TRUST ORDINANCE (1930). First introduced to the Legislative Council (LEGCO) [q.v.] in 1928, the ordinance was the result of African fears over the insecurity of land in the reserves that had been made clear by the Ormsby-Gore and Hilton Young Commissions [qq.v.]. Besides reserving land for the use of African tribes "for ever,"

Labour Secretary of State Lord Passfield insisted, against the advice of Governor Sir Edward Grigg [q.v.], that the legislation include provision that if any land was taken from a reserve for public purposes, then land equal in amount and value must be added to the reserve. Also, the bill provided that Local Native Councils [q.v.] would have to be consulted in any such alienation. Because of opposition in LEGCO from European settlers, Governor Grigg was forced to use the official majority to pass the ordinance in 1930. In 1932, the discovery of gold in Kakamega [q.v.] led the colonial government to amend the measure to supply monetary compensation, rather than land of equal size and value, and to eliminate the need to consult Africans in the area concerned. The measure drew great criticism in Kenya and Great Britain and increased African feelings of insecurity over land.

NEUMANN, ARTHUR HENRY (1850–1907). Big game hunter. Born in Bedfordshire. Nothing is known about his education. In early 1869, he went to South Africa. Over the next two decades, Neumann was a coffee [q.v.] plantation worker, farmer, gold prospector, soldier, magistrate, and big game hunter. On 19 May 1890, he joined the Imperial British East Africa Company [q.v.] and worked with the survey team that was laying the Uganda Railway [q.v.]. He returned to South Africa to participate in the Boer War (1899–1902). After arriving back in Kenya, Neumann devoted most of energies to hunting elephants, which he recounted in his autobiography, *Elephant Hunting in East Equatorial Africa* (1898). In September 1906, he returned to England, where he subsequently developed a severe case of influenza. Neumann, who always had been subject to black moods, became increasingly despondent after a woman rejected his offer of marriage. On 29 May 1907, he shot himself.

NEW KENYA PARTY (NKP). Kenya's first political party to be open to members of all races. On 2 April 1959, Michael Blundell [q.v.] established the New Kenya Group to replace the United Country Party, which had been formed in 1954 to support the Lyttelton Constitution [q.v.]. The New Kenya Group sought to rally popular support for a multiracial political party that would oppose the radicalism of African nationalists and the extreme conservatism of some European settlers. In January 1960, the New Kenya Group transformed itself into the New Kenya Party. The party's political platform promised eventual independence under a multiracial government. Additionally, the New Kenya Party supported the creation of an East African federation, the retention of British military bases in Kenya, and called for protection from the British government against unjust expropriation of property. In the LEGCO elections (1961) [q.v.], the party won four seats, mainly on African votes. Following the election, Blundell and other members agreed to support the government formed by the Kenya African Democratic Union (KADU) [q.v.] with the backing of the colonial state. By the time of the second Lancaster House Conference [q.v.], the party had ceased to exist. Most of its members lined up with KADU during the final days of colonial rule.

NGALA, RONALD GIDEON (1922–1972). Teacher and politician. Born in Mombasa [q.v.] and educated at Kaloleni School, Alliance High School, and Makerere University [qq.v], qualifying as a teacher. In 1946, he was posted to Kaloleni School and later transferred to Maynard School as headmaster. During the 1952–55 period, Ngala worked as headmaster at Buxton School in Mombasa. After attending an education course at Redland College in Great Britain, he returned to Kenya and became the supervisor of African Anglican Schools in Mombasa.

In 1953, Ngala entered coast politics when he was appointed to the Mombasa African Advisory Council. The following year, he was named to the Mombasa Municipal Board. Ngala ran in the initial African LEGCO Elections (1957) [q.v.] for the coast constituency, and he defeated more moderate rivals. He quickly became a leading figure in the African Elected Members Organisation [q.v.] as the African Legislative Council (LEGCO) [q.v.] members, dissatisfied with the Lennox-Boyd Constitution [q.v.], pushed for new constitutional arrangements and majority rule. Ngala was a member of the Constituency Elected Members Organisation [q.v.] and in 1959, joined the Kenya National Party [q.v.] rather than the Kenya Independence Movement. Such were his abilities that he became leader of the African LEGCO members who joined together to make common cause at the Lancaster House Conference (1960) [q.v.].

Upon his return to Kenya, Ngala formed the Coast African People's Union [q.v.]. He was elected treasurer of the newly formed Kenya African National Union [q.v.] in absentia but failed to take up the post. In May 1960, he was appointed minister for labour, social security, and education in a caretaker government. In June 1960, he joined with others to form the Kenya African Democratic Union (KADU) [q.v.], becoming its first and only president. In the LEGCO elections (1961) [q.v.], he led KADU and won a huge victory in his home area of Kilifi, but the party came second overall to Kenya African National Union (KANU) [q.v.] in the election. Afterward, Ngala resigned his ministerial post and called for the release of Jomo Kenyatta [q.v.] but later agreed to take KADU into government. He became leader of government business and minister of education. After the election, Ngala became an articulate spokesman in favor of KADU's *majimbo* [q.v.] constitutional philosophy. His advocacy met with some success: at the second Lancaster House Conference (1962) [q.v.], the British government agreed that Kenya should have a federal constitution. Following the conference, he became co-leader of the coalition government formed with KANU as minister of constitutional affairs and administration. In the general elections (1963) [q.v.], Ngala led the KADU fight for *majimbo*, but KADU failed to gain a majority in the House of Representatives or the Senate. He became leader of the parliamentary opposition and unsuccessfully opposed the 1963–64 constitutional changes that scrapped *majimbo*. As many of his KADU colleagues crossed the floor, Ngala eventually bowed to the inevitable, dissolving KADU in November 1963 and joining KANU.

With KADU's demise, Ngala, who became identified with KANU's moderate wing, first served as a backbencher and chairman of the Maize Marketing Board. At the Limuru Conference (1966) [q.v.], he was chosen KANU vice president for the Coast Province [q.v.]. He then became minister of co-operatives and social services. After 1967, Ngala was associated with the party faction led by Tom Mboya [q.v.], then called KANU B [q.v.]. Despite several attempts by party adversaries to remove him as KANU leader at the coast, his political standing among the coast's people remained strong enough for Ngala to overcome these machinations. In the general elections (1969) [q.v.], he won an overwhelming victory for his Kilifi South seat and subsequently became minister of power and communications. Ngala died in an automobile accident on 25 December 1972.

NGEI, PAUL JOSEPH (1923–). Politician, farmer, and businessman. Born at Kangundo in Machakos and educated at Alliance High School [q.v.], Makerere University [q.v.] (1948–50), and the University of London (correspondence). During World War II [q.v.], Ngei served in the military as a warrant officer. During the 1950–51 period, he worked as a journalist for the *East African Standard* and subsequently founded and edited *Uhuru wa Mwafrika*, one of the African nationalist newspapers. Between 1951 and 1952, he served as the national deputy general secretary of the Kenya African Union (KAU) [q.v.]. On 20 October 1952, the colonial authorities arrested Ngei, Jomo Kenyatta [q.v.], and four others for directing the Mau Mau Revolt [q.v.]. The British kept Ngei in prison or under restriction until 25 May 1961, when he became president of the Kenya Farmers and Traders Union.

After joining the Kenya African National Union (KANU) [q.v.] in 1962, he repeatedly clashed with Tom Mboya [q.v.] over political tactics. A few months later, Ngei resigned from KANU and created the African People's Party (APP) [q.v.]. In May 1963, he won a parliamentary seat as an APP member for Machakos North, and until September 1963, he served as deputy leader of the opposition in the House of Representatives. At that time, he returned to KANU and soon achieved cabinet office as minister for co-operatives and marketing (1964–65) and then minister for housing and social services (1965–66). Jomo Kenyatta [q.v.] also appointed him as chairman of the Maize Marketing Board (1963–65). However, Kenyatta temporarily suspended Ngei because of a government inquiry into a maize shortage scandal. A few months later, Ngei was reappointed to his post as minister for housing and social services, a position he held until 1974, when he received an appointment as local government minister (1974–75). In late 1975, Ngei was convicted of an election offense which resulted in his removal from Parliament and the cabinet. President Kenyatta had a constitutional amendment rushed through Parliament in December empowering the president to pardon anyone convicted of an electoral offense. Kenyatta subsequently pardoned Ngei, and on 24 March 1976, Ngei became minister for co-operative development.

After becoming Kenya's president, Daniel arap Moi [q.v.] selected Ngei as minister for works (1979–82). Ngei then served as minister of livestock and development (1982), minister of lands and settlement (1983–84), minister of environment and natural resources (1984–86), minister for water development (1986–87), minister of livestock and development (1987–88), and minister of culture and social services (1988–89). On 1 May 1989, Ngei became minister of manpower development. At approximately the same time, he received a six-month prison sentence for contempt of court for refusing to comply with a court ruling over a land deal. On 22 November 1990, Ngei declared bankruptcy with debts of more than £400,000. After losing his parliamentary seat and his ministry, he retired from politics and returned to farming.

However, Ngei remained politically active despite the fact that Kenya's constitution [q.v.] forbids any person declared bankrupt from holding public office. On 27 December 1991, he resigned from KANU because of the government's failure to apprehend the killers of Robert Ouko [q.v.]

and formed his own opposition party. Nevertheless, on 14 July 1992, he said he wanted to campaign for the presidency on the KANU ticket; however, party members endorsed President Moi as the sole candidate. On 26 October 1992, Ngei then joined the opposition Democratic Party [q.v.] but later rejoined KANU on 3 June 1993, claiming that the latter was the only political party capable of uniting all Kenyans. In January 1997, the High Court discharged Ngei from bankruptcy. He then expressed an interest in running for office in the general elections (1997) [q.v.] but KANU failed to select him as a parliamentary candidate.

NGILU, CHARITY KALUKI (1952–). Businesswoman and opposition politician. Born in Machakos. Ngilu, who is a Kamba, began her business career by working as a secretary for the Central Bank of Kenya [q.v.]. After receiving Kenya Institute of Administration diplomas as a public certified secretary and in business management, she became a manager with Chase Manhattan Overseas Corporation in Nairobi [q.v.] (1978–82). Ngilu then started several of her own businesses, including a bakery, restaurant, and a plastic sheeting company called Ani-Plastics Ltd., which is located in the Athi River Export Processing Zone. In 1992, she launched her political career by being elected MP for Kitui Central under the Democratic Party (DP) [q.v.] banner. In early 1997, she quit the DP and joined the Social Democratic Party [q.v.]. On 9 July 1997, she announced that she would stand for the presidency.

Her political platform included promises to end what she termed "politics of the belly." More specifically, Ngilu pledged to institute further constitutional reforms and to generate the country's wealth without relying on foreign aid. Additionally, she promised to remain in office for only one term and swore to stop using political and tribal patronage as the basis for making political appointments and awarding government business contracts. However, in the general elections (1997) [q.v.] Ngilu came in fifth, behind President Daniel arap Moi, Mwai Kibaki, Raila Odinga, and Michael Wamalwa [qq.v.], with 7.71 percent (469,807) of the vote.

NGUGI WA THIONG'O (1936–). Novelist and dissident. Born in Limuru and educated at Makerere University [q.v.] and the University of Leeds. Throughout the 1960s and most of the 1970s, the government tolerated his views and criticisms of the ruling elite. However, on 31 December 1977, the authorities detained him without charges under the Public Security Act. The following year, he gained his freedom in a general amnesty granted by President Daniel arap Moi [q.v.] but was not allowed to return to his university post.

NILOTIC-SPEAKING PEOPLES. Those speaking Nilotic languages constitute the second-largest population group in 20th-century Kenya. The first Nilotic speakers moved into Kenya from the north, probably at the start of the first millennium C.E. Most languages that constitute this group came to Kenya during the second millennium, however. The Nilotic speakers are categorized on linguistic grounds as belonging to three groups: River-Lake (or western), Highlands (or central), and Plains (or eastern). The western group consists of the Kenya Luo [q.v.]; this language was brought to western Kenya by migrants from Uganda, probably at the end of the 15th century. The Highlands Nilotic-speaking group that came to reside in Kenya is known as the Kalenjin [q.v.], while the Plains Nilotic-speaking group that was most significant in Kenya was the Teso-Maasai. This came to include peoples belonging to the present-day ethnic groups known as Maasai [q.v.], Teso, Turkana, Samburu, and Njemps.

NJONJO, CHARLES (1920–). Lawyer, civil servant, politician. Born in Kiambu District, Njonjo attended Alliance High School [q.v.]. In 1946, he received a postgraduate degree in public administration from Exeter University College. After attending the London School of Economics, Njonjo studied law in London (1950–54), eventually becoming barrister-at-law at Gray's Inn in London in 1954. During the 1955–60 period, he worked in the Registrar General's department in Nairobi [q.v.]. From 1961–62, Njonjo was crown counsel and senior crown counsel. He then held the post of deputy public prosecutor (1962–63).

At self-government in June 1963, Njonjo was appointed attorney general with a seat in Parliament. He held that office under the republican constitution, serving Presidents Jomo Kenyatta and Daniel arap Moi (qq.v) until 1980. In his nonelected position, Njonjo became one of Kenya's most powerful political figures as evidenced by his success in stopping the Change the Constitution Campaign (1976) [q.v.]. In 1980, he resigned as attorney general, was elected unopposed at a by-election for the Kikuyu constituency, and subsequently appointed minister of home and constitutional affairs. During the 1980–82 period, Njonjo repeatedly clashed with Vice President Mwai Kibaki [q.v.] over a variety of policy issues. In February 1982 President Moi moved Kibaki to the home affairs ministry, leaving Njonjo responsible for constitutional affairs.

In 1982–83, Njonjo's career began to disintegrate as he was singled out as a government enemy who was being groomed for the presidency in the place of Moi. In 1983, he resigned from Parliament and the cabinet amid accusations of corruption and abuse of power. Shortly thereafter, Moi appointed a judicial tribunal to examine Njonjo's affairs. Completing its work in 1984, the tribunal found Njonjo guilty of corruption, involvement in the illegal import of firearms into Kenya, and an attempt to overthrow the government of the Seychelles. Although he eventually received a presidential pardon, Njonjo was prevented from rejoining the Kenya African National Union [q.v.]. After 1983, he made no effort to reenter political life until 1998 when President Moi appointed him chairman of the Kenya Wildlife Service.

NORTH EASTERN PROVINCE. (126,902 square kilometers; 48,997 square miles). This administrative unit was created in 1963 as the mainly Somali-inhabited districts of Garissa, Mandera, and Wajir were placed in a separate province. Although sparsely populated, the province was created to counter Somali demands for union with the Somali Republic. *See also* NORTHERN FRONTIER DISTRICT/PROVINCE; *SHIFTA*; *SHIFTA* WARS.

NORTH KAVIRONDO CENTRAL ASSOCIATION (NKCA). This protest organization was formed in 1934 by young, Western-educated Luyia [q.v.] (such as Andrea Jumba and John Adala), most of whom had a connection with the Quaker mission in the district then known as North Kavirondo (later North Nyanza). It was never a "mass" organization, representing a small number of petty bourgeoisie.

Initially, the NKCA's major concern was security for African land in the face of gold-mining operations in the vicinity of Kakamega [q.v.], which had led to the alienation of land for foreign-owned mining companies. The NKCA also advocated the appointment of a Luyia paramount chief, Chief Joseph Mulama, brother of Mumia [q.v.]. During the late 1930s, it opposed the colonial government's use of forced labor for soil conservation work in South Maragoli and Bunyore locations. In 1940, the NKCA voluntarily dissolved itself, though colonial administrators continued to see the NKCA as the force behind opposition to soil conservation work during World War II.

NORTHERN FRONTIER DISTRICT/PROVINCE (NFD). In 1909, the colonial government inaugurated this administrative unit. Unlike Kenya's southern regions, the NFD only came gradually under British rule and was never closely administered down to the end of colonial rule. From 1921 to 1925, the area was under military administration. By 1929, civil administration of Northern Frontier Province included the districts of Isiolo, Marsabit, Moyale, Telemugger, and Wajir. In 1934, the colonial government withdrew the region's provincial status. In 1947, the authorities added Turkana District, creating a province that covered the whole north of the colony. This area included Garissa, Isiolo, Mandera, Marsabit, Moyale, Turkana, and Wajir Districts. In 1963, the districts were moved into three new administrative units (Eastern, North Eastern, and Rift Valley Provinces [qq.v.]), and the NFD/P ceased to exist. *See also* BOMA TRADING COMPANY; *SHIFTA*; *SHIFTA* WARS; SOMALI.

NORTHERN FRONTIER DISTRICT COMMISSION. In 1962, the British government appointed this commission to ascertain and report on public opinion in the then Northern Frontier District (NFD) [q.v.] regarding arrangements for its future in light of Kenya's impending independence. The commission, which issued its report in December 1962, stated that the Somali-inhabited portions of the NFD unanimously favored succession from Kenya at independence with the ultimate aim of joining the Somali Republic. The Oromo [q.v.] and Tana River peoples, on the other hand, expressed a wish to remain in Kenya. The British government decided that the NFD would remain part of Kenya at independence and in March 1963, announced that the Somali-inhabited portions of the district would become the North Eastern Region. The Somali Republic thereupon broke diplomatic relations with Great Britain. *See also* NORTHERN FRONTIER DISTRICT/PROVINCE; NORTHERN FRONTIER DISTRICT LIBERATION FRONT; *SHIFTA*; *SHIFTA* WARS; SOMALI.

NORTHERN FRONTIER DISTRICT LIBERATION FRONT (NFDLF). In 1962, radical Kenyan Somalis [q.v.] broke away from the Northern Province People's Progressive Party [q.v.] and established this organization, which maintained headquarters in Mogadishu. The NFDLF pledged itself to carry out violent campaigns against Kenya until the government allowed North Eastern Province [q.v.] to secede and join Somalia. For several decades, the NFDLF carried out small-scale military operations in northeast Kenya. In December 1983, the Kenyan government offered an amnesty to these rebels. In mid-September 1984, 331 NFDLF personnel returned to Kenya, surrendered, and announced that their Mogadishu headquarters had been closed. *See also SHIFTA*; *SHIFTA* WARS; SOMALI.

NORTHERN PROVINCE PEOPLE'S PROGRESSIVE PARTY (NPPPP). Founded in 1960 as the largest and most active of the Somali [q.v.] secessionist parties. The NPPPP had the support of almost all the

Somali chiefs and elders in northeast Kenya and other breakaway Somali groups such as the Northern Democratic Party, the People's National, and the National Political Movements. The NPPPP supported the secession of the Northern Frontier District [q.v.] prior to independence, a period under British administration, and eventual union with Somalia. *See also* NORTHERN FRONTIER DISTRICT LIBERATION FRONT; *SHIFTA*; *SHIFTA* WARS.

NORTHEY, MAJOR GENERAL SIR EDWARD (1868–1953). Governor of Kenya (1919–22). Educated at Eton College and the Royal Military Academy, Sandhurst. During his early military career, he participated in the North West Frontier operations (1891) and the Boer War (1899–1902). In 1914, Northey became a brigade commander and served in France and Belgium. Two years later, he served as commander of the Nyasaland/Rhodesia Field Force. In 1919, he became one of the more controversial governors of Kenya because of his policies to consolidate the political and economic dominance of the European settler community. Within two months of his arrival, Northey revised Sir Henry Belfield's [q.v.] plan to settle ex-soldiers on Kenyan farms. Northey hastily implemented the Soldier Settlement Scheme [q.v.]. With regard to the Indian Question [q.v.] he responded to Asian [q.v.] demands for greater equality by informing the Indian Association [q.v.] that "though Indian interests should not be lost sight of, European interests must be paramount throughout the Protectorate." He thus failed to implement the Wood-Winterton Agreement [q.v.] as a basis of settling the Indian Question. As the settlers' champion, Northey implemented electoral representation for Europeans, made Kenya a colony, and was primarily responsible for its new name in 1920.

Northey's view of Africans was that they should work for European settler farmers rather than produce commodities on their own land. In October 1919, he issued the Labour Circular (1919) [q.v.], which called upon administrative officials and African chiefs to take an active role in labor recruitment for European settlers. During the 1920–22 period, Northey also pushed for currency [q.v.] changes that would have benefitted large European land holders at the expense of Africans. His policies raised considerable criticism in Great Britain and in India. For a time, the Colonial Office (CO) stood behind Northey, but his inability to solve the Indian Question, coupled with his even greater failure to deal with the colony's serious financial position that resulted from the postwar depression finally led to his removal.

On 29 June 1922, Secretary of State for the Colonies Winston Churchill removed Northey shortly after the latter, paradoxically, had become a convert to the proposition later to be known as the Dual Policy [q.v.]. The CO then appointed Sir Robert Coryndon [q.v.] as governor. After returning to England, Northey commanded the 43rd (Wessex) Division, Territorial Army and South Western Area (1924–26). He retired in 1926 and died on 25 December 1953.

NTIMAMA, WILLIAM OLE (1930–). Teacher, civil servant, politician, farmer, and businessman. Born in Melili in Narok and educated at Narok Government School and Kahuhia Teacher Training College. One of a small number of educated Maasai [q.v.] of his generation, Ntimama worked as a teacher (1947–58) while entering politics as a member of the Narok African District Council. He failed to win a seat in the LEGCO elections (1958) [q.v.] but became a nominated member the following year. In 1960, Ntimama left the Legislative Council (LEGCO) [q.v.] to become a district officer with the provincial administration. Four years later, he resigned from administration to concentrate on farming and business. In 1974, he won election as chair of the Narok County Council. He used this base to oust Justis ole Tipis [q.v.] from the chair of the Narok Kenyan African National Union [q.v.] branch (1976).

Ntimama planned to challenge Tipis in the general elections (1979) [q.v.], but he was prevailed upon, according to some by President Daniel arap Moi [q.v.], to withdraw from the election, leaving Tipis to be elected unopposed. Again in 1983, Ntimama withdrew in favor of Tipis. However, the latter's national clout gradually waned over the following years, enabling Ntimama to defeat Tipis in the general elections (1988) [q.v.] for the Narok North parliamentary seat. He then became minister of local government.

He quickly emerged as a strong *nyayo* [q.v.] supporter, a vigorous opponent of political reform, and above all, an outspoken defender of what he perceived to be Maasai interests. He used often violent language in attacking advocates of political pluralism and in calling for the expulsion of non-Maasai peoples from what he termed Maasai lands. From 1991, Ntimama stood out as one of the main proponents of a *majimbo* [q.v.] constitution for Kenya's future. He won his seat in the general elections (1992) [q.v.] and was reappointed to the cabinet. By 1995–96, Ntimama was associated with the party faction known as the Kenya African National Union A (KANU A) [q.v.], thus an opponent of Vice President George Saitoti and Nicholas Biwott [qq.v.]. In January 1997, however, he experienced a political reversal, along with others identified with

KANU A as he was demoted to take charge of the Ministry of Home Affairs and National Heritage. Nevertheless, Ntimama won reelection to Parliament in the general elections (1997) [q.v.] and returned to the cabinet as minister for transport and communications.

NYACHAE, SIMEON (1932–). Administrator, businessman, and politician. Born in then South Kavirondo District, the son of prominent Gusii [q.v.] colonial chief Musa Nyandusi. Educated at Kisii Secondary School, Torquay College (1957–58), where he received a diploma in public administration, and the Kenya Institute of Administration (1962–63). Nyachae joined Kenya's provincial administration shortly before independence after a brief period working for Kenya Breweries. He rose rapidly under President Jomo Kenyatta [q.v.], serving as a provincial commissioner in the Central and Rift Valley Provinces [qq.v.]. In 1979, President Daniel arap Moi [q.v.] appointed him permanent secretary in the Office of the President. In July 1984, he became chief secretary and head of the civil service. Nyachae was the second, and last, person to hold this powerful position created by a constitutional amendment in 1982. The Kenyan government abolished this office after Nyachae's retirement in December 1986.

Upon his retirement from government service in February 1987, Nyachae pursued several business ventures. Despite strong support in his home area of Nyaribari and among the Gusii generally, his attempt to move into politics by running for Parliament was blocked in 1988, largely because he had made some very powerful enemies during his government service, notably Nicholas Biwott [q.v.]. Though he espoused the need for political reform after 1988, Nyachae resisted calls to join the opposition political parties that emerged in 1991–92.

In February 1992, he bought advertising space in the major newspapers to state that he would remain a member of the ruling Kenya African National Union [q.v.]. Some of his critics believed his decision resulted from the promise of high office by President Moi. In the 1992 general elections [q.v.], Nyachae won the Nyaribari Chache parliamentary seat and became minister of agriculture. Since then, Nyachae has emerged as the leader of the Kenya African National Union A [q.v.] faction, presumably in hopes of using this position to push for the vice presidency held by Kenya African National Union B [q.v.] leader George Saitoti [q.v.] until the 1997 election. In January 1997, President Moi demoted Nyachae to the Ministry of Land Reclamation, Water, and Regional Development. In the general elections (1997) [q.v.], he retained his parliamentary seat and afterwards received a promotion to minister for finance. In the latter post, Nyachae attempted to implement reforms demanded by the IMF and World Bank [qq.v.] aimed at reducing budget deficits and corruption, but in February 1999 President Moi demoted him from the treasury to the ministry of industrial development. Rather than accept this, Nyachae resigned from the cabinet.

NYAGAH, JEREMIAH JOSEPH MWANIKI (1921–). Born in Embu [q.v.] District and educated at Alliance High School and Makerere University [qq.v.]. Nyagah worked as a teacher and education officer before winning a seat in the LEGCO elections (1958) [q.v.]. In 1960, he was chosen deputy speaker. In 1960, he helped found the Kenya African National Union [q.v.] and won the Embu seat in the LEGCO elections (1961) [q.v.]. In the general elections (1963) [q.v.], Nyagah was returned unopposed for Embu South. He won a seat in Parliament at every election until his retirement in 1992; throughout his years in politics he remained one of dominant figures in Embu.

At the Limuru Conference (1966) [q.v.], he was chosen vice president for Eastern Province [q.v.]. His ministerial service included assistant minister of works, communications and power (1963); minister of home affairs (1964); minister of education (1966); minister of natural resources (1968); minister of information, (1969); minister of agriculture (1974); minister for livestock development (1979); minister of culture and social services (1980); minister of water development (1983); and minister of environment and natural resources (1986). Prior to the general elections (1992) [q.v.], Nyagah announced his retirement from Parliament and the cabinet. However, he remained, despite some local opposition, KANU leader in Embu [q.v.].

NYANZA PROVINCE. First known as Kisumu Province, Nyanza included part of the land transferred from Uganda in 1902. Initially, it consisted of what came to be known as the Central, North, and South Nyanza (prior to 1948, Kavirondo) Districts as well as Kericho (then Lumbwa) and Nandi Districts. In 1929, Nandi District was transferred to Nzoia Province [q.v.]. By that time, Kisumu-Londiani District had been created for the administration of the areas of the province settled by European and Asian farmers. It was abolished in 1948.

In 1963, Nyanza Province was reduced in size by making what had been prior to 1955 North Nyanza District Western Province [q.v.], while Kericho district moved to the Rift Valley Province [q.v.]. Until 1989, Nyanza Province consisted of Kisii, Kisumu, Siaya, and South Nyanza

Districts (16,162 square kilometers; 6,240 square miles). Since then several new districts, including Gucha, Migori, and Nyamira, have been created by subdividing the existing units.

NYAYO. Swahili [q.v.] word meaning "footprints" or "footsteps." After becoming president in 1978, Daniel arap Moi [q.v.] adopted this word as a slogan to underscore his commitment to follow in the "footsteps" of former President Jomo Kenyatta [q.v.]. Theoretically, *nyayo* espouses political stability, good government, being mindful of the welfare of others, and economic development. In practical terms, however, Moi used *nyayo* to justify his own, often highly controversial, political and economic policies. Additionally, Moi has repeatedly justified harsh treatment of government critics by claiming they had been engaged in anti-*nyayo* activities. Later in the Moi presidency, the term developed the connotation of personal loyalty to Moi and his policies.

NYERI. (Altitude of 1,770 meters; 5,807 feet). Known as the capital of Kikuyuland. This town, which is administrative headquarters of Central Province [q.v.] and gateway to Aberdare National Park, is located beneath the eastern slopes of the Aberdare Mountains [q.v.].

NYIKA. Swahili [q.v.] word meaning "desolate wilderness." In Kenya, *nyika* refers to the dry hinterland that separates the East African coast from the interior plateau.

NZOIA PROVINCE. Created in 1929. During its short history, this province included the districts of Elgeyo-Marakwet, Nandi, Trans Nzoia, and Uasin Gishu. In 1934, the colonial government ended its existence and made its districts part of the Rift Valley Province [q.v.].

-O-

ODEDE, WALTER FANUEL (1912–1974). Civil servant, politician, businessman. Born at Uyoma, Central Nyanza District (then Central Kavirondo District). Educated at Maseno School; Alliance High School [q.v.]; the Veterinary Training Centre, Maseno; and Makerere University [q.v.]. In 1941, Odede became assistant veterinary officer, Maseno. He first served in the Legislative Council [q.v.] in 1945, but his sympathies were with the Kenya African Union (KAU) [q.v.]. In October 1952, he became acting KAU president, after the colonial government arrested Jomo Kenyatta [q.v.]. During the March 1953–October 1960 period,

Odede was in detention. After his release, he returned to Central Nyanza District, where he headed a Kenya African National Union [q.v.] faction that opposed Oginga Odinga [q.v.].

Although he ran for the LEGCO elections (1961) [q.v.], he failed to win in the face of the rivalry of the powerful Odinga and C. M. G. Arwings-Kodhek. Odede tried to win the Kisumu [q.v.] town seat in 1963 as an independent, but he failed to defeat the Odinga-sponsored KANU candidate. By this time, his rivalry with Odinga intensified because he was Tom Mboya's [q.v.] father-in-law. In the Little General Election (1966) [q.v.], Odede stood for Bondo, but lost overwhelmingly to Odinga. During the 1969–74 period, he served as chairman of KANU's Siaya District branch. On 31 October 1974, Odede was nominated to Parliament. However, his tenure was brief as he died on 24 December 1974.

ODINGA, JARAMOGI AJUMA OGINGA (1911–1994). Teacher, businessman, politician. Kenya's first vice president. Born in Sakwa location in what was then Central Nyanza District. Educated at Maranda Primary School; Maseno School; Alliance High School; and Makerere University (qq.v), where he received a diploma in education (1939). Odinga then returned to Maseno as a teacher, but he left in 1942 after disagreements over school policies with, among others, Edward Carey Francis [q.v.]. He then took a position at the Maseno Veterinary School, but he resigned in 1946 to go into business. Odinga helped found the Bondo Thrift Association, which, in 1947, changed its name to the Luo Thrift and Trading Corporation. The latter involved itself not only in commerce but also operated a press, restaurants, and hotels. Odinga's success in business soon gave him a base to move into politics.

By the late 1940s, he had joined the Kenya African Union [q.v.] and gained election to the Central Nyanza African District Council. During the Mau Mau Revolt [q.v.], Odinga emerged as a leading political figure among the Luo [q.v.] of western Kenya. He championed Luo traditions, but he also took an increasingly nationalist line. This was apparent in the first African LEGCO elections (1957) [q.v.] as Odinga won the Central Nyanza constituency and soon established himself as one of the most anticolonial of the new legislators. He wore traditional attire, criticized colonial rule, rejected the Lennox-Boyd Constitution [q.v.], and called for the release of Jomo Kenyatta [q.v.].

In the splits that developed among the African elected members after 1959, Odinga invariably stood with the "radicals" in advocating an end to European supremacy, rapid independence, and what he termed a "socialist" approach to Kenya's economic problems. He attended the first

Lancaster House Conference [q.v.], helped found the Kenya African National Union (KANU) [q.v.] and became KANU's vice president. In this party, as in previous groupings of African LEGCO members, Odinga allied himself with Tom Mboya [q.v.]. However, the two were already fierce personal and ideological rivals, a fact that had a major impact on Odinga's career up to the time of Mboya's 1969 death.

In the LEGCO elections (1961) [q.v.], Odinga won an overwhelming victory in Central Nyanza. With Kenyatta's release and assumption of KANU leadership in 1961, Odinga continued to hold the vice presidency. Odinga attended the 1962 Lancaster House Conference [q.v.], but the British government objected to his inclusion in the coalition government formed at its conclusion for what were perceived to be his pro-Soviet views. Nevertheless, Odinga continued to be a major player in Kenyan politics as he cemented the Luo-Kikuyu [qq.v.] political alliance that formed the core of KANU. In the general elections (1963) [q.v.], he won the Bondo seat in the House of Representatives for KANU. With the advent of self-government on 1 June 1963, Odinga became minister of home affairs. He held this position until December 1964 when, at the inauguration of a republican constitution, he became vice president and minister without portfolio.

Over the next 15 months, Odinga became increasingly dissatisfied with the government's economic and social policies. As leader of the "radical" group within KANU, he opposed what he saw as the capitalist orientation of development policies and pro-Western trend of Kenya's foreign policy. However, Mboya and his "moderate" supporters outmaneuvered Odinga, which culminated in the latter's removal from the party vice presidency at the Limuru Conference (1966) [q.v.]. Odinga then resigned from KANU and as Kenya's vice president, and founded the Kenya People's Union (KPU) [q.v.].

For the rest of his life Odinga would be associated with opposition to the Kenya government. Following his reelection to Parliament in the Little General Election (1966) [q.v.], he served as official opposition leader for the next three years. Relations between Odinga and Kenyatta also became increasingly tense. On 25 October 1969, for example, President Kenyatta, who had gone to Kisumu [q.v.] to open a Soviet-built hospital, clashed with Odinga and his followers. The incident culminated in riots that left numerous people dead. Kenyatta banned the KPU and placed Odinga and other party leaders in detention without trial. In 1971, Odinga gained his freedom. Although his popularity among the Luo was undiminished, he was unable to return to political life for the rest of the

Kenyatta era. Allowed to rejoin KANU, the party barred him from standing for the general elections (1974 and 1979) [qq.v.].

Nevertheless, in the years after President Kenyatta's death in 1978, Odinga began to be rehabilitated. He received a life membership in KANU and became chairman of the Cotton Lint and Seed Marketing Board. Odinga also lavished praise on President Daniel arap Moi's [q.v.] leadership. The stage seemed set for Odinga's return to Parliament when, in early 1981, the MP for Bondo, Odinga's old constituency, resigned to make way for the veteran politician. However, this opportunity evaporated after an April 1981 speech in Mombasa [q.v.] in which Odinga called former President Kenyatta a land-grabber. This incident provoked a public outcry and a rebuke from Moi. As a result, KANU barred Odinga from standing for the by-election. He also lost his position at the Cotton Lint and Seed Marketing Board.

Odinga reacted to these setbacks by abandoning his attempts to return to Parliament and rehabilitate himself in KANU. He repeatedly spoke out against the Moi government and its policies. After rumors surfaced in 1982 that Odinga and George Anyona [q.v.] planned to form a new opposition party, Moi expelled Odinga from KANU and rushed a constitutional amendment through Parliament to make Kenya a one-party state. After the abortive coup attempt [q.v.] later in 1982, Moi placed Odinga under house arrest. In 1983, he gained his freedom but remained an outcast as far as the political establishment was concerned.

However, Odinga refused to keep quiet. Beginning in 1987, he made a series of critical observations relating to the country's political system and policies in the form of open letters to the president and interviews with journalists. Additionally, Odinga advocated democratic reform and political pluralism. In 1990, opposition elements launched a multi-partyism campaign with support from clergymen and lawyers. Odinga, along with politicians like Kenneth Matiba and Charles Rubia [qq.v.], became leaders of this movement. In mid-1990, the police [q.v.] detained Matiba, Rubia, and Odinga's son Raila Odinga [q.v.] but allowed the elder politician to remain free. In February 1991, Odinga announced the formation of the National Democratic Party (NDEM) [q.v.]. However, the government refused to register the NDEM. Odinga then linked up with other reform campaigners to found the Forum for the Restoration of Democracy (FORD) [q.v.]. He became interim FORD chairman.

In December 1991, Kenya ceased to be a one-party state, enabling Odinga to attempt to use FORD as a vehicle for removing President Moi from power. During 1992, however, splits in FORD developed over, among other things, who should be the FORD presidential candidate. By October 1992, FORD had split with Odinga chairing FORD-Kenya (FORD-K) [q.v.] and standing as its presidential candidate. In the 1992 general elections, Odinga came in fourth in the presidential election, winning only 17.48 percent of the vote. However, he finally returned to Parliament as he won the Bondo seat. As FORD-K came to occupy the position of official opposition party, Odinga became leader of the opposition for a second time in Kenya's history. Despite unhappiness with the way the 1992 general elections [q.v.] had been carried out and infirmity brought on by old age, Odinga remained politically active. He committed FORD-K to working within the system as a loyal opposition party and cooperating with the Moi government when it was in the nation's best interests. He died on 20 January 1994. He published a memoir, *Not Yet Uhuru* in 1967.

ODINGA, RAILA AMOLO (1944–). Engineer, businessman, civil servant, and politician. Born in Maseno, son of Jaramogi Oginga Odinga [q.v.]. Educated at Kisumu and Maranda primary schools, Raila then studied at the Herder Institute and the Magdeburg College of Advanced Technology (in the former East Germany), graduating from the latter with an M.A. degree (1970). Additionally, Raila was an engineering student in Kenya and in the former Soviet Union. Upon his return to Kenya, he lectured at the University of Nairobi [q.v.] until 1974, when he joined the East African Spectre company. The following year, Raila took a position with the Kenya Bureau of Standards, rising to the position of deputy director in 1978. During the 1982–88 period, he was detained on suspicion of participating in the coup attempt (1982) [q.v.]. After his release in February 1988, Raila worked for East African Spectre as managing director. However, within seven months, the police [q.v.] again detained him after linking him to anti-government activities.

After his release on Madaraka Day [q.v.] 1989, he threw himself into the campaign for political reform spearheaded by his father, Kenneth Matiba, and Charles Rubia [qq.v.]. This led to his detention, for a third time, in June 1990. Released with Matiba and Rubia in 1991, Raila helped establish the Forum for the Restoration of Democracy (FORD) [q.v.]. When this party split prior to the 1992 general elections [q.v.], he stayed with his father in the Forum for the Restoration of Democracy-KENYA (FORD-K) [q.v.], filling the post of director of elections. During the election, he won the Langata parliamentary seat in Nairobi [q.v.].

Following his father's death on 20 January 1994, Raila found himself left out of the top leadership positions in FORD-K. For the next three years, he unsuccessfully tried to wrest the party leadership from Michael Wamalwa and James Orengo [qq.v.]. Having failed to dislodge Wamalwa as FORD-K chairman by late 1996, Raila left the party and joined the little-known National Development Party (NDP) [q.v.]. In March 1997, he won the by-election for his Langata parliamentary seat and the NDP named him as its presidential candidate for the general elections (1997) [q.v.]. However, Odinga came in third, behind President Daniel arap Moi and Mwai Kibaki [qq.v.], with 10.92 percent (655,725) of the vote. Also, he retained his parliamentary seat. Following the election, he surprised many Kenyans by taking the NDP into close collaboration with the Moi government.

OKULLU, JOHN HENRY (1929–1999). Church leader, journalist, and political activist. Born in Rambo, Nyanza and educated at Ramba Primary School (1940–43); Kisumu Primary School (1944–45); Kima Central School (1946–48); Bishop Tucker Theological College, Uganda (1956–58); and Virginia Theological Seminary (1963–65). During the early part of his career, Okullu worked as a clerk for the Military Construction Unit (1948–51) and a clerk for the East African Railways and Harbours in Kampala, Uganda (1952–56). In 1958, he was ordained and served as the publicity director of the Church of Uganda. Okullu was the first African editor of the Church of Uganda's *New Day* (1966–67). Okullu was also the executive officer for the joint Protestant-Catholic Council of Uganda.

In 1967, he returned to Kenya, and in 1968 became editor of *Target* and *Lengo*, both of which were National Christian Council of Kenya [q.v.] publications. In 1971, Okullu became provost of All Saints Cathedral in Nairobi [q.v.]. Three years later, he became bishop of the Diocese of Maseno South, where he worked to improve the social and economic welfare of his flock. From that position, he became a major voice criticizing the policies of the Moi era government along with such other church leaders as Bishop Alexander Muge. From 1990, he was a strong advocate of political pluralism and constitutional reform. After retiring from the church in 1994, Okullu remained active in opposition politics. On 12 March 1996, he formed a group called the Friends of Democracy, which advocated a united opposition that would select a single candidate for the general elections (1997) [q.v.]. Okullu also continued to criticize the Kenyan government for ethnic discrimination, corruption, and land-grabbing. He died on 13 March 1999.

OLENGURUONE. Site of a 1941 settlement scheme for Kikuyu squatters [qq.v.]. It was an important reason for Colonial Office approval of the implementation of the Resident Native Labour Ordinance of 1937 [q.v.], but the Olenguruone scheme was a failure from the start. The site, high up the Mau escarpment in the Rift Valley [q.v.], was unsuitable, climatically and in soil fertility, for peasant agriculture [q.v.]. The some 4,000 people moved to the site in 1941 were not Kikuyu squatters evicted from European settler farms in the White Highlands [q.v.], but families who had settled in Maasailand during the previous two decades.

Conflict soon developed between the Kikuyu settlers at Olenguruone and the colonial government over land ownership and land use; neither side was prepared to back down. The Kikuyu settlers at Olenguruone developed a new oath of unity as a source of strength in this struggle, and, according to many authorities, this was the first Mau Mau oath, as the Olenguruone residents made contacts with Kikuyu squatters in neighboring areas of the White Highlands. From 1946, the colonial government sought to break the unconditional resistance of the settlers and evict them; in 1950, despite legal challenges, the authorities finally achieved this goal. Olenguruone was only the beginning of Kikuyu opposition to British rule in the 1950s. It served as an inspiration before and during the Mau Mau Revolt [q.v.].

OLOITIPTIP, STANLEY SHAPSHINA (1927–1985). Hospital worker, politician, and businessman. Born at Loitokitok and educated at Loitokitok Government School and Narok Government School. During the 1945–46 period, Oloitiptip worked as a nurse's orderly in the East African Medical Corps and served in India, Burma, and Ceylon (now Sri Lanka). He rose to the rank of sergeant. After being discharged, he worked as a hospital dresser with the Tanganyika (now Tanzania) Medical Service in Maasailand (1948–50). Oloitiptip held a similar position in Kajiado District (1951–60). He then entered politics as a member of the Kenya African Democratic Union (KADU) [q.v.] (1960–62); as that organization's national organizing secretary, he pressed Maasai [q.v.] land claims. In 1963, he was elected to the House of Representatives as member for Kajiado District, but he defected to the Kenya African National Union (KANU) [q.v.] the following year, prior to KADU's dissolution.

In the general elections (1969) [q.v.], Oloitiptip took the Kajiado South seat and subsequently received an appointment as assistant minister for commerce and industry and then for health. In 1974, he was reelected to Parliament and served as minister for natural resources. Oloitiptip gradually emerged as one of Daniel arap Moi's [q.v.] strongest supporters during the Change the Constitution Campaign (1976) [q.v.]. When Moi became president in 1978, Oloitiptip's star rose as he was made minister of home affairs. When Charles Njonjo [q.v.] was made minister of home affairs (1980), Oloitiptip moved to the Ministry of Local Government. In the early 1980s, he abandoned Moi and moved into Charles Njonjo's camp. As a result, Moi dropped him from the cabinet despite his victory in the general elections (1983) [q.v.]. In September 1984, KANU expelled him, which in turn brought about the loss of his parliamentary seat. By this time, the former minister was in poor health. He died on 22 January 1985.

OMINDE COMMISSION (1964). Within a week of independence, the government appointed the Kenya Education Commission, better known as the Ominde Commission after its chairman, Professor S. H. Ominde. The commission surveyed existing educational resources and made recommendations for future policy. The commission's report, published in December 1964, had a significant impact on government policy. It called for racial and religious integration in education with a single curriculum, but it accepted the existence of the so called "high fee" schools, those previously reserved for Europeans and Asians [q.v.]. The commission endorsed free primary education as an ultimate aim, but universal primary education was its initial goal. Because of Kenya's needs for high-level manpower, however, the commission recommended that greatest emphasis be given to expanding secondary and higher education. After 1964, Kenya's educational system was restructured along the lines advocated by the commission.

ONEKO, RAMOGI ACHIENG (1921–). Born in Kobudho village, Uyoma location in then Central Nyanza and educated at Maseno High School, where he was taught by Oginga Odinga [q.v.]. In 1941, he received an appointment as a clerk in the Meteorological Department. Four years later, Oneko resigned this position and became manager of Ramogi Press and secretary of the Luo Thrift and Trading Corporation. In 1951, he started a Kenya African Union (KAU) [q.v.] branch at Kisumu [q.v.]. On 20 October 1952, the police [q.v.] arrested him along with Jomo Kenyatta [q.v.] and four other KAU leaders. The 1953 Kapenguria Trial [q.v.]. convicted all of them for managing the Mau Mau Revolt [q.v.] On 15 January 1954, Kenya's Supreme Court acquitted Oneko on appeal, but the colonial authorities detained him without trial.

After being released in 1961, he served as Kenyatta's personal secretary (1961–63). He also joined the Kenya African National Union (KANU) [q.v.], and won the Nakuru [q.v.] town seat in the general elections (1963) [q.v.]. During the 1963–66 period, Oneko served as minister of information and broadcasting. In 1966, Oneko resigned from Kenyatta's government and joined the Kenya People's Union (KPU) [q.v.]. In the Little General Election (1966) [q.v.], he lost his seat, but he remained active in the KPU's affairs. In 1969, the authorities banned the party and detained Oneko for a longer period than any other KPU member. On 10 October 1975, he finally gained his freedom. Unlike Oginga Odinga [q.v.], Oneko was allowed to reenter politics under Presidents Jomo Kenyatta and Daniel arap Moi [q.v.]. However, he failed in attempts to win the Langata seat in Nairobi [q.v.] in the 1983 general elections [q.v.] and the Rarieda seat in Nyanza in the 1988 general elections [q.v.].

In the 1990–91 campaign for multipartyism, Oneko joined other veteran politicians and created the Forum for the Restoration of Democracy (FORD) [q.v.]. In the general elections (1992) [q.v.], he won the Rarieda seat for FORD-Kenya (FORD-K) [q.v.]. In the 1996–97 struggle for control of FORD-K, Oneko remained in the party rather than follow Raila Odinga to the National Development Party [qq.v.]. In the general elections (1997) [q.v.], he suffered an overwhelming defeat at Rarieda.

ONYONKA, DR. ZACHARY THEODORE (1941–1996). Teacher, politician, businessman, longest-serving MP from the Gusii [q.v.]. Born in Kisii [q.v.] and educated at Mosocho Primary School (1947–51); Nyabururu Intermediate School (1952–54); St. Mary's High School, Yala (1955–58); the Inter-American University in Puerto Rico, where he received a B.A. in economics and business administration; and Syracuse University (1965–68), where he earned a Ph.D. degree. He was a research fellow at the University of Nairobi's [q.v.] Institute for Development Studies (1967), and worked as Lecturer in Economics (1967–69).

In 1969, Onyonko won the Kitutu West seat and became minister for planning and economic development (1969–72). He then served as minister for information and broadcasting (1973–74) and minister of health (1975). Reelected to Parliament in 1974 by defeating Lawrence Sagini [q.v.] as in 1969, Onyonka became minister for education (1976–79), and then minister for housing and social services (1979). Returned to Parliament in the general elections (1979) [q.v.], Onyonka served as minister of planning and economic development (1979–83). In July 1983, he won reelection, but violence at one of his last campaign rallies led to a murder charge against him. In 1984, the courts acquitted him but he lost his ministerial position. In June 1987, President Daniel arap Moi [q.v.] appointed Onyonka minister for foreign affairs. He was returned to Parliament unopposed at the general elections (1988) [q.v.] by winning more than 70 percent of the votes at the queue stage. Onyonko then moved to the Ministry of Planning and National Development. After reelection in the general elections (1992) [q.v.], he became minister for research, technical training, and applied technology, a position he held until his death on 22 October 1996 in London.

OPERATION ANVIL. An operation launched in April 1954 against the rebel forces during the Mau Mau Revolt [q.v.]. Planned by General Sir George Erskine [q.v.] and carried out by colonial and British military forces, Operation Anvil involved the round-up of virtually the entire African population of Nairobi [q.v.], including some 70,000 Kikuyu [q.v.]. Aimed at crippling the rebels' supply network from the capital, the operation led to the detention, following interrogation, of some 27,000 people.

ORENGO, JAMES (1951–). Lawyer and politician. Born in Ugenya and educated at Alliance High School and the University of Nairobi [qq.v.]. In 1980, Orengo entered politics by winning the Ugenya by-election and quickly established a reputation as a fiery radical. This not only put him at odds with the politically powerful but also brought him under the scrutiny of the security services. In 1982, the authorities charged him with making false mileage claims, but Orengo jumped bail and fled to Tanzania. As a result, he lost his parliamentary seat. In 1983, the Tanzanian government returned him to Kenya's custody. The following year, the courts dropped the charges against him and Orengo resumed work as a lawyer.

With the advent of multipartyism, Orengo took up the cause, through the courts, on behalf of Oginga Odinga's [q.v.] National Democratic Party (NDEM) [q.v.]. The party was not registered, but Orengo soon emerged as one of the most prominent of the younger lawyers backing the Forum for the Restoration of Democracy (FORD) [q.v.]. His actions caused him to be arrested in 1991 and 1992, but charges were eventually dropped. Orengo stayed with Odinga and joined FORD-Kenya (FORD-K) [q.v.] in 1992; he also won the Ugenya seat in the general elections (1992) [q.v.] with a huge majority. Orengo quickly became one of the most articulate and outspoken opposition members of Parliament. Following Odinga's death on 20 January 1994, Orengo rose to second in command of FORD-K behind Michael Wamalwa [q.v.]. He remained loyal to Wamalwa and opposed to Raila Odinga [q.v.] in the party split of 1995–96. However, in 1997, Orengo split with Wamalwa as he supported the National Convention Executive Committee [q.v.] reforms initiative. In the general elections (1997) [q.v.], he won reelection to Parliament on a FORD-K ticket though he did not support Wamalwa's leadership. Following the election, Orengo remained one of the most adamantly anti-government of all opposition legislators. In 1998, he moved only the second parliamentary motion of no-confidence in Kenya's history.

ORMSBY-GORE COMMISSION (1924). This imperial commission, officially known as the East Africa Commission, visited East Africa in 1924 under the chairmanship of Conservative MP Sir William Ormsby-Gore to examine the region's problems and prospects. The commission supported the Dual Policy [q.v.] concept but reported that little had been done to promote African agriculture [q.v.] or to provide educational or medical services for the African population. It particularly called attention to African fears for their land, leading to the promulgation of additional African reserves and to the introduction of the Native Lands Trust Ordinance [q.v.]. Significantly, the commission reported that there was no support for an East African Federation [q.v.].

OROMO. Oromo-speaking peoples (1989 census: 161,448) inhabit the northern and north-central parts of Kenya. Also known as Galla, pastoralists speaking Oromo languages belonging to the Eastern Cushitic [q.v.] family began a rapid expansion early in the 16th century from southern Ethiopia to the north, east, and south. The latter made their way into Kenya, rapidly settling a large area of what is today the northern half of the nation and even down to Malindi [q.v.] at the coast. The Oromo migration appears to have been one of the few (involving Kenyan people) that was characterized by mass movement of peoples over a relatively brief period of time. Only in the 19th century was this expansion checked and reversed. The main Oromo groups that came to inhabit northern Kenya are the Boran, Gabra, and Orma. These groups were among the last to be brought under control in colonial Kenya, administered within the Northern Frontier District/Province [q.v.]. Little was done during the colonial period to develop economically the regions they inhabit (e.g., Marsabit and Moyale), nor was Christian missionary work encouraged. Since independence, the Oromo-speaking pastoralists have contributed marginally to the national economy and to national politics.

OUKO, DR. ROBERT JOHN (1939–1990). Civil servant, politician, and farmer. Born in Kisumu [q.v.]. He attended Ogada Primary School and then studied at Siriba Teachers College, University of Addis Ababa, and Makerere College [q.v.], where he received degrees in public administration, political science, and economics. In 1962–63, he joined the civil service and first worked in the Office of the Prime Minister. At independence, Ouko was permanent secretary in charge of foreign affairs. He also served as permanent secretary of the Ministry of Power and Communications and the Ministry of Works. In 1969, Ouko received an appointment as minister for finance and administration in the East African Community (EAC) [q.v.]; in 1970, he became that organization's minister for common market and economic affairs. After the EAC collapsed in 1977, he was nominated to Parliament and appointed minister for community affairs. The following year, he became minister for economic planning and community Affairs. Until 1979, Ouko was a nominated member of Parliament. In the general elections (1979) [q.v.], he won the Kisumu Rural seat. In the general elections (1983) [q.v.], he was reelected and switched to the Ministry of Labour, and, in 1985, he shifted to the new Ministry of Planning and National Development. For the general elections (1988) [q.v.], he switched to the Kisumu town seat, which he won narrowly. In 1988, he returned as minister of foreign affairs and international co-operation. On 13 February 1990, unknown assailants killed Ouko. The murder has not been solved, and the linking of the names of other influential political figures such as Nicholas Biwott [q.v.] to Ouko's death caused continuing controversy after 1990. Shortly after the killing, President Daniel arap Moi [q.v.] asked Scotland Yard to conduct an investigation of Ouko's death. On 28 August 1990, John Troon, who headed the group of British detectives, submitted a report of his findings to Moi, but the report was only released to the general public at the end of March 1999. On 2 October 1990, President Moi established a judicial commission of inquiry to probe into Ouko's death. After the commission implicated Nicholas Biwott [q.v.] in the assassination, Moi dropped him from his cabinet. The authorities eventually charged Jonah Anguka with the Ouko murder, but he was acquitted. Only in November 1998 did the Kenyan government issue an official statement on matters surrounding the death of Dr. Ouko.

OWEN, ARCHDEACON WALTER EDWIN (1879–1945). Anglican clergyman and missionary. Born in Great Britain and educated at St. Enoch's, Belfast and Islington Theological College. In 1901, Owen joined the Church Missionary Society (CMS) [q.v.] and was ordained three years later. After a period in Reading, he was posted to Uganda by the CMS. During World War I [q.v.], Owen served as a chaplain to British forces fighting in German East Africa (now Tanzania). He then became archdeacon of Kavirondo (1918–45).

Owen worked tirelessly to improve the social and political welfare of Africans throughout the colony. He also dabbled in archaeological and paleontology work throughout the region. However, Owen is best known for establishing the Kavirondo Taxpayers Welfare Association [q.v.] in 1923 and serving as its president. He used this organization to defend and improve African rights with regard to issues such as local taxation, allocation of public funds, improved housing, child welfare, and health matters. Yet Owen's main achievement was to turn the association away from political activism and toward acceptance of the colonial system. In 1929, he complained to the Colonial Office and to the British press about the use of forced labor by colonial government officials. Additionally, he criticized the colonial authorities for failing to address his many complaints about taxation and maladministration.

After 1935, a growing number of Africans looked upon Owen and other European missionaries with increasing suspicion. Nevertheless, he continued to agitate for improvements in the welfare of Kenya's Africans. Throughout the 1938–39 period, he worked against the newly enacted Employment of Servants Ordinance, which authorized children as young as 10 to work as laborers, by speaking to various clerical groups in Great Britain, writing letters to the *Manchester Guardian* newspaper, and publishing a pamphlet entitled *Child Labour in Kenya Colony*. During World War II [q.v.], Owen opposed the British government's decision to conscript African labor for use on European farms. He died on 18 September 1945.

OWEN'S PROTECTORATE (1824–1826). On 9 February 1824, Captain William Fitzwilliam Wentworth Owen, R.N., of H.M.S. *Leven*, proclaimed a protectorate over Mombasa [q.v.] without the knowledge or approval of the British government. He acted because the local Mazrui leaders repeatedly had asked for British protection against a reimposition of Omani rule. According to the agreement concluded with the leaders, the British would ensure the survival of Mazrui leadership in Mombasa in exchange for abolishing the slave trade, an equal division of customs revenues, and permission to explore the interior. Eventually, the British government refused to recognize Owen's Protectorate. During the 1824–26 period, however, the small British force at Mombasa not only sought to accomplish the goals set forth in the treaty that had been concluded with the city's Mazrui leadership but also helped to facilitate Great Britain's slowly growing interest in East Africa.

-P-

PARTY OF INDEPENDENT CANDIDATES OF KENYA (PICK). Political party formed in 1992 by businessman and Olympic sharpshooter John Harun Mwau, who failed to win a parliamentary seat in the general elections (1992) [q.v.]. Additionally, his presidential bid drew the least support of all the candidates sponsored by opposition parties. However, his party gained one seat in Parliament, winning Mandera East in the North Eastern Province [q.v.]. It made no impact on the general elections (1997) as Mwau joined government service a few months before the poll.

PERIODICALS. The press has had a lively history in Kenya. During the colonial era, the *East African Standard* (initially called the *African Standard*) largely represented the views of the European settler community. Regional newspapers such as the *Kenya Weekly Review* also reported from a European settler point of view. As early as the 1920s, radical African newspapers such as *Muigwithania*, which was edited by Jomo Kenyatta [q.v.], attracted a following among the Kikuyu [q.v.]. By independence, the Kenyan press dominated eastern Africa with such newspapers as the *Daily Nation*, *Kenya Times*, *Kenya Leo*, and the *Standard*.

There also is a considerable amount of periodical literature in Kenya. The *Weekly Review*, which first appeared in 1975, was the most authoritative newsmagazine in the country but it ceased publication in May 1999. Other publications like the *Economic Review*, *Nairobi Law Monthly*, and *Patriot* normally contained political articles that are critical of the government.

Scholarly journals encompass an array of academic and professional sectors. Some of the more important journals include the *East African Journal of Rural Development*, *East African Medical Journal*, *Kenya Journal of Education*, and the *Transafrican Journal of History*, all of which have a sizeable domestic, regional, and international readership. See below for a more detailed list of Kenyan publications.

Advertiser of British East Africa (1907–1908)
The Advocate: The Official Law Society of Kenya Magazine (1984–present)
Agricultural Journal of British East Africa (1908–1913)
Azania (1966–present)
The Baobob: Newsletter for Churches' Involvement in Grassroots Development (1985–present)
Baraza (1939–1979)

Business Chronicle (1995–present. Until 1997, known as *The East African Chronicle*)

Coastweek (1978–present)

Colonial Times (1933–1963)

Daily Chronicle (1947–1954)

Daily Nation (1961–present)

East Africa Journal (1964–present)

East Africa Natural History Society (1910–1966)

East Africa Quarterly (1904–1906)

The East African (1995–present)

East African Agricultural and Forestry Journal (1935–present)

East African Chronicle (?–present)

East African Economic Review (1954–present; suspended publication 1977–1985)

East African Journal of Rural Development (1968–present)

East African Medical Journal (1923–present)

Eastern Africa Law Review (1967–present)

The Economic Review (1992–1998)

Economic Review of Agriculture (1968–present)

Education in Eastern Africa (1970–present)

Egerton Journal (1995–present)

Electors News (1944)

Executive (1980–present)

Finance (1984–present)

Habari (1922–1931)

The Independent (1949–1959)

The Kenya Adult Educator: Journal of the Kenya Adult Education Association (1993–present)

Kenya and Uganda Critic: Without Malice (1922–1923)

Kenya Church Review (1943–1958)

Kenya Daily Mail (1927–1963)

Kenya Education Journal (1958–present)

Kenya Export News

Kenya Farmer (1954–present)

Kenya Gazette (1898–present)

Kenya Journal of Education (1984–present)

Kenya Leo (1983–present)

The Kenya Observer

Kenya Past and Present (1971–present)

Kenya Police Review (1927–present)

Kenya Times (1983–present)
The Kenya Weekly News (1928–1969)
Kenya Yetu (1965–present)
Leader of British East Africa (1908–1922)
Maseno Journal of Education, Arts, and Science (1992–present)
Medicus: Magazine of the Kenya Medical Association (1981–present)
Mombasa Times (1910–?)
Monthly News (1992-present)
Muigwithania (1928–1940)
Mumenyereri
Mwalimu
Nairobi Law Monthly (1987–present)
Nyanza Times (1960–1964)
The Option (1995–present)
Patriot (1994–present)
The People (1993–present)
Quarterly Index to Periodical Literature, Eastern and Southern Africa (1991–present)
Ramogi
Sauti ya Mwafrika (1945–1954)
Society (1988–present)
East African Standard (1902–present; originally called the *African Standard* and then *The Standard*)
The Star (1998-present)
Sunday Nation (1967–present)
Taifa Jumapili (1987–present)
Taifa Leo (1960–present)
Tangazo
Target (1964–present)
Taveta Chronicle (1895–1901)
Thika Star (1994–present)
The Thika Times
Transafrican Journal of History (1971–present)
The Trumpet
Weekly Mail (1994–present)
Weekly Review (1975–1999)

PHELPS STOKES COMMISSION. In 1920–21 and again in 1924, a group of British and American educators and missionaries and one African studied ways to devise an appropriate educational policy for colonial Africa that would facilitate the emergence of an African elite and educate the general population through pragmatic courses related to life on the land. According to commission chairman Jesse Jones, formerly of the Hampton Institute, Virginia, these goals could be achieved by adopting educational practices associated with American rural black communities. In particular, Jones and his colleagues believed that, apart from training in the three Rs, African schools should provide courses on medicine, health, and hygiene; agriculture [q.v.]; theology; home economics; teaching; and industrial training. The commission also recommended that qualified African students should have access to higher education in their own countries rather than having to study at European or North American institutions.

The British government and the colonial authorities in Kenya welcomed these suggestions. However, many Africans opposed the commission's findings, because in their view any schooling that failed to conform to the European model was inferior. Numerous European missionaries who supported this criticism eventually persuaded the authorities to improve the quality of teaching in mission schools by enlarging government grants. The increased funding enabled the Church Missionary Society [q.v.] and several other religious societies, known collectively as the Alliance of Protestant Missions [q.v.], to establish Alliance High School [q.v.], which opened its doors on 1 March 1926.

In the long term, the Phelps Stokes Commission marked a turning point in the development of African educational practices in Kenya insofar as it generated sufficient criticism to convince the colonial government to abandon its policy of supporting African technical and practical training. Instead, African students studied the same subjects as their European and Asian [q.v.] counterparts. This in turn eventually enabled African graduates to compete for jobs in the civil service, academia, and in the business sector. *See also* EDUCATION, COLONIAL.

PINTO, PIO GAMA (1927–1965). Trade unionist, journalist, and nationalist. Born in Nairobi [q.v.] and educated at Bangalore and Dharwar College, Bombay, but never received a degree. Pinto spent 18 months in the Indian Air Force and helped to found the Goan National Congress, which fought against Portuguese imperialism. In 1949, he returned to Kenya to avoid being arrested by the Portuguese authorities. After working as a secretary to the director of a commercial firm, Pinto became assistant secretary of the Kenya Indian Congress (1950) [q.v.]. In 1953, he became editor of the *Daily Chronicle*, a radical Indian newspaper; worked for All India Radio; and became a member of the Indian National Congress.

In June 1954, the colonial authorities arrested Pinto for supporting the Mau Mau Revolt [q.v.]. According to the Advisory Committee on Detainees, several factors led to his arrest, including hiding a Mau Mau terrorist and possessing knowledge of illegal arms shipments to the rebels. He was one of two Asians [q.v.] detained, and, after his release in August 1959, Pinto rejoined the struggle against British colonial rule and helped found the Kenya Freedom Party [q.v.]. In 1960, he joined the Kenya African National Union (KANU) [q.v.] and established its newspaper, *Sauti ya Kanu*. With money received from Jawaharlal Nehru, Pinto started the Pan African Press, which published *Sauti ya Mwafrika*, *Nyanza Times*, and *Pan Africa*. In 1964, he helped to establish the Lumumba Institute, a Nairobi-based organization that trained KANU party officials. During the same year, he was elected to Parliament. His views on trade unionism [q.v.] made him unpopular with many senior Kenyan government officials. On 24 February 1965, a gunman shot and killed Pinto outside his Nairobi home. His murder, which many claim was Kenya's first political assassination, was never solved.

POLICE. The modern-day Kenya police is descended from the first armed guards hired by the Imperial British East Africa Company [q.v.] to protect the Mombasa [q.v.]-Uganda caravan route by establishing fortified posts at several trading stations, including Mazeras, Machakos, Ngong, Fort Smith, Eldama Ravine, and Mumias. In early 1896, Sir Arthur Hardinge [q.v.] established a police force at Mombasa; by 1901, this unit included a European assistant superintendent, three European inspectors, three Indian or Somali deputy inspectors, and 150 other ranks. Apart from its headquarters in Mombasa, this force stationed small detachments at Vanga, Rabai, Malindi [q.v.], Lamu [q.v.], and Kismayu. In 1897, another independent force, the Uganda Railway Police, emerged to safeguard those who worked on the railroad. Other early police units operated at Nairobi and Kisumu [qq.v.]. In February 1902, the colonial government consolidated these organizations by forming the British East Africa Police with C. G. D. Farquhar as its first inspector general. In July 1920, the force changed its name to the Kenya police. By 1925, there were 31 police stations and 57 police outposts located throughout the country. During the Mau Mau Revolt [q.v.], the Kenya police more than doubled in size to 13,000 in addition to about 9,000 men in the Kenya police reserve. At independence, the British transferred the Kenya police intact to the Kenyan government. During the postindependence period, the Kenya police continued to grow and by the mid-1980s, there were some 19,000 men and women in the police force, not including administrative and reserve police personnel. The organizational structure included the general duty police, the General Services Unit [q.v.], and the Railways and Harbours Police. Specialized units included the Criminal Investigation Directorate, the Intelligence Directorate, a stock theft unit, the Police Air Wing, and a dog unit. By the early 1990s, there was considerable domestic and international criticism of the Kenya police because of corruption and human rights violations. After police killed one student at Egerton University [q.v.] on 17 December 1996 and two more at the University of Nairobi [q.v.] the next day, President Daniel arap Moi [q.v.] appointed a new police commissioner, Duncan Wachira, and instructed him to improve the image and efficiency of the police. However, despite the appointment of a new commissioner in February 1999, little progress has been made and many Kenyans remained fearful of the police. *See also* PRISONS.

POLL TAX. The colonial government introduced this method of taxation largely in response to protests from European settlers in 1907 and 1908 over the shortage of African labor. The tax's primary purpose was to force young, unmarried men out to work rather than to raise additional revenue. Only those who did not pay the hut tax [q.v.] would be liable to pay, and those men who worked for wages at least one month of a year would not be required to pay.

POOLE CASE. In October 1959, Peter Harold Richard Poole shot and killed an African in the Kilimani area of Nairobi [q.v.] for throwing stones at his dogs which had attacked the man riding on his bicycle. Although he claimed to have acted in self-defense, Poole was put on trial for murder. In December 1959, he was convicted and sentenced to death. Poole's appeals against the verdict and the sentence failed, and on 18 August 1960, he became the first European in Kenya's history to be executed for killing an African.

POPULATION. The earliest effort to determine Kenya's population occurred in 1897, when Sir Arthur Hardinge [q.v.] conducted the East Africa Protectorate's [q.v.] first official census, which estimated an African population of 2.5 million. By 1914, officials estimated the country's population to be about 3.4 million. During the interwar period, estimates of the African population ranged from 2,549,300 in 1925 to 3,413,371 in 1939. In 1948, the colonial government conducted a more systematic census that revealed a total population of 5,407,599, of whom 5,252,753 (97 percent) were Africans and 154,846 were non-Africans. The next census occurred in August 1962, when officials determined that the country's population was 8,636,263, of whom 8,365,942 (97 percent) were Africans and 270,321 were non-Africans. After independence, Kenya conducted decennial censuses as required by the United Nations. The 1969, 1979, and 1989 censuses put the country's population at 10.9 million, 15.3 million, and 21.4 million, respectively. The next census is scheduled to be carried out in 1999. These figures represented a growth rate that was about two percent annually during the 1940s; approximately four percent annually during the 1970s; and 2.6 percent annually during the 1980s. As of early 1997, the Kenyan government estimated that the country had an annual 2.88 percent growth rate, which is lower than that of Uganda (3.5 percent) and Tanzania (3.0 percent). Demographers predict that Kenya's population will increase by at least 50 percent by 2020. *See also* ACQUIRED IMMUNE DEFICIENCY SYNDROME; HEALTH.

PRESBYTERIAN CHURCH OF EAST AFRICA (PCEA). *See* CHURCH OF SCOTLAND MISSION.

PRISONS. Prison conditions in Kenya are harsh. In September 1995, a Kenyan High Court judge described them to Amnesty International as "death chambers" because of the high mortality rate. He noted that "going to prison these days has become a sure way for a death certificate." In October 1995, the minister for home affairs, Francis Lotodo, announced that more than 800 prisoners had died since the beginning of the year. Prisoners suffer from severe overcrowding; insanitary conditions; and a lack of adequate food, clothing, and blankets. In these conditions infectious diseases spread easily, and there are few medical facilities.

PYRETHRUM. Introduced in Kenya in 1928. Pyrethrum flowers contain pyrethrins, which are used in the manufacture of insecticides. Pyrethrum, which is an important cash crop that currently employs about 200,000 farmers, is popular because it is practically nonpoisonous to mammals, rapidly breaks down without leaving a residue, and poses little threat other than to insect populations. The primary growing areas are the highlands districts of Kiambu, Kisii, Nyamira, Gucha, Nakuru, and Nyandarua, where high altitude and adequate rainfall favor production. Processing is done at the Nakuru [q.v.] pyrethrum plant, which currently has a processing capacity of about 8,000 tons. Kenya produces about 70 to 80 percent of the world's pyrethrum (Australia, Papua New Guinea, Rwanda, and Tanzania are the other producers).

As of the late 1990s, world demand for pyrethrum was about 20,000 tons of dried flower annually, of which Kenya provided approximately 9,000 tons. Despite repeated attempts, Kenya has failed to increase pyrethrum production. In fact, production has fallen for much of the mid-1990s largely because of poor rainfall and the failure of the government-controlled marketing system to pay growers promptly. Nevertheless, Kenya remains the world's largest producer and exporter of pyrethrum. In 1996 and 1997, the Pyrethrum Board of Kenya distributed seedlings (three million and five million, respectively) to farmers to boost pyrethrum production.

-R-

REGIONAL BOUNDARIES COMMISSION (1962). The British government appointed this commission after the second Lancaster House Conference (1962) [q.v.] to draw up regions and adjust boundaries in line with the decision to implement a *majimbo* [q.v.] constitution for Kenya. In November 1962, the commission issued its report, which recommended the creation of six regions in addition to Nairobi [q.v.] as an extraprovincial area, including the new Western and Eastern Regions, as well as a number of land transfers to meet popular desires. The commission's report has remained the basis of Kenya's administrative structure since independence, with one exception. That was the March 1963 creation of North Eastern region, which included most of the Somali [q.v.]-inhabited areas in northeast Kenya. With the scrapping of the *majimbo* constitution after 1964, the regions became known, as in colonial times, as provinces.

REITZ, JOHN (1801–1824). British naval officer and first governor of Owen's Protectorate [q.v.] (1824). Born in Cape Town. Reitz was an excellent linguist, speaking French, Portuguese, Spanish, and Arabic. On 11 March 1824, he became governor and commandant of Mombasa [q.v.], which was also known as Owen's Protectorate. Reitz's duties included abolishing the slave trade in Mombasa, supervising the collection of customs revenue, issuing passes to ships leaving Mombasa, and exploring the protectorate. On 4 May 1824, he led a 70-man column to explore the Pangani River. On the return journey to Mombasa, Reitz fell ill, presumably with malaria, and died on 29 May 1824. For the next three months, midshipman George Phillips served as acting governor and commandant. On 28 August 1824, James Barker Emery [q.v.] replaced Phillips.

RELEASE POLITICAL PRISONERS (RPP). Nonviolent anti-Moi dissident group. Established in 1992, this organization supports political prisoners and campaigns for their release. On 24 March 1996, an unidentified person(s) killed the RPP's general secretary, Karimi Ndutu, at his home. According to eyewitnesses, the police [q.v.] who investigated the murder seized Nduthu's books, papers, computer and computer files, and typewriter. The human rights organization Amnesty International sent a pathologist to witness Nduthu's postmortem examination. The doctor later informed Amnesty International that the autopsy failed to meet adequate medical standards. Since Nduthu's death, RPP members and other human rights activists have expressed concern at the lack of progress of the police investigation.

Another incident occurred on 19 July 1996, when police arrested 21 RPP members, all of whom had been trying to attend a three-day cultural meeting they had organized in Nduthu's memory. Three days later, the authorities charged them with sedition and holding an illegal meeting. On 23 July 1996, a Nairobi [q.v.] court denied them bail and remanded them to prison until a 19 August 1996 hearing. Female prisoners were held in Lang'ata Women's Prison and the men in Industrial Area Remand Prison; conditions in both facilities are extremely bad. The defendants then went on a hunger strike to protest their arrest and detention. As of 1997, charges still were pending. *See also* PRISONS.

RENISON, SIR PATRICK MUIR (1911–1965). Governor of Kenya (1959–62). Born in England and educated at Uppingham School and Corpus Christi College, Cambridge. In 1932, Renison entered the colonial service. During the 1935–44 period, he served in the Ceylon (now Sri Lanka) civil service. From 1944 until 1948, he worked in the Colonial Office (CO). He impressed his superiors, and in 1948 he was appointed colonial secretary of Trinidad and Tobago, thus beginning more than a decade of service in the Caribbean. In 1952, he became governor of British Honduras, and from 1955 to 1959, he was Governor of British Guiana (now Guyana).

In 1959, Renison arrived in Kenya, without any African experience, at the end of the Mau Mau Revolt [q.v.]. Although the British government and African nationalists wanted to accelerate the pace of decolonization, Renison failed to accomplish this goal. He proved particularly unable to deal with Jomo Kenyatta [q.v.], labeling him a leader to darkness and death in 1960 and resisting his release from detention. In November 1962, he "resigned" his office, the last of four chief executives to be removed by London in Kenya's colonial history. He died on 11 November 1965.

RESIDENT NATIVE LABOURERS ORDINANCE (1937). The Legislative Council [q.v.] passed this legislation at the behest of European farmers, particularly in the Rift Valley [q.v.], as a means to control and remove African (mainly Kikuyu [q.v.]) squatters [q.v.]. Under this ordinance, European settler-farmers had the power to eliminate squatter stock, limit the number of acres under squatter cultivation, and raise the number of working days required of squatters from 180 to 240 and then to 270 per year. The legislation made it clear that squatters were not tenant farmers and that they could remain on the land only as long as they worked for the European settler. Most significantly, the ordinance passed control of the squatters from the colonial government to European settler-controlled district councils. The implementation of the ordinance was delayed until 1940, as the Colonial Office (CO) insisted that land should be found for those who would be evicted. Wartime conditions further delayed the full implementation of the act. After 1945, the conditions of squatters in the Rift Valley deteriorated badly. This produced massive discontent among the squatters, which culminated in the outbreak of the Mau Mau Revolt [q.v.].

RIFT VALLEY. A great depression in the earth's surface that extends from the Middle Eastern country of Jordan to Mozambique. The valley, which is more than 8,700 kilometers (5,394 miles) long, contains a series of geological faults that resulted from ancient volcanic activity. The Kenyan portion—which runs through the middle of the country from north to south—includes the former White Highlands [q.v.], numerous volcanoes, and a chain of seven lakes (Baringo, Borgoria, Elmenteita, Magadi, Naivasha, Nakuru, and Turkana). Since none of them has an obvious outflow, these lakes rely on rainfall. They have a high evaporation rate, which causes an accumulation of salts and minerals. As a result, with the exception of Lakes Naivasha and Turkana [qq.v.], all are highly saline. The alkaline soils around the lakes helps bones turn into fossils. This has made the Rift Valley a rich source of information about human evolution and ancient history.

RIFT VALLEY PROVINCE. Created in 1929, with Baringo, Eldama Ravine, and Nakuru as its districts. Naivasha [q.v.] (1930) and Nzoia [q.v.] (1934) Provinces were incorporated with the Rift Valley Province. In 1935, Samburu District was added and in 1941, West Suk (later West Pokot) District was added. In 1963, the province was restructured as Kericho, Kajiado, Narok, and Turkana Districts were added, making it the largest of Kenya's provinces (173,868 square kilometers; 67,130 square miles).

RUBIA, CHARLES WANYOIKE (1923–). Businessman and politician. Born in Muriaini, in present-day Murang'a District, and educated at Alliance High School [q.v.]. After completing his studies, Rubia joined the post office, and in 1946, he took a job in Nairobi [q.v.]. Thereafter, the capital was his political and economic base. By the late 1950s, he was one of Nairobi's most successful African businessmen. In 1955, he entered politics when he was nominated to Nairobi's African General Ward Council. Two years later, Rubia was nominated to the city council and in 1958, he was nominated to the Legislative Council [q.v.]. Rubia held that position until late 1960, when was elected an alderman in the then government of Nairobi. From that post, he became Nairobi's first African mayor (1962–69).

In the general elections (1969) [q.v.], Rubia won a Nairobi seat (Starehe) in Parliament. He then became assistant minister for education and later local government, but Jomo Kenyatta [q.v.] dropped him from office after the 1974 general elections [q.v.]. Never close to those wielding power during the Kenyatta era, Rubia earned a reputation as an independent and outspoken backbencher. In 1977–78, he chaired Parliament's public accounts committee. Initially, Rubia gained considerable influence under President Daniel arap Moi [q.v.]. After his success in the general election (1979) [q.v.], Moi appointed him minister for local government and urban development. He later served as minister of works and physical planning. By 1983, Rubia was an ally of the now-discredited Charles Njonjo [q.v.]. Additionally, he had been far from enthusiastic for the move to make Kenya legally a one-party state. Thus, Rubia lost his cabinet status despite holding on to his parliamentary seat in the general election (1983) [q.v.].

Thereafter, he was one of the few backbench critics in Parliament, opposing queue voting and the rapidly passed constitutional amendments of the 1980s. His stance won him many enemies in the Kenya African National Union (KANU) [q.v.], which resulted in his expulsion from the party and missing the general elections (1988) [q.v.]. In 1990, he joined with former minister Kenneth Matiba [q.v.] to launch a campaign for political reform and multipartyism. Shortly afterward, the police [q.v.]

detained the two without trial. When released from detention on 12 April 1991, he continued his support for political pluralism, eventually gravitating to the Forum for the Restoration of Democracy-Asili (FORD-Asili) [q.v.]. However, in September 1992, he and others left FORD-Asili to join the Kenya National Congress [q.v.]. He sought the Starehe seat on the Kenya National Congress ticket in the general elections (1992) [q.v.], but he was decisively defeated by the FORD-Asili candidate. In February 1994, Rubia left the Kenya National Congress for FORD-Asili.

-S-

SABA SABA RIOTS (1990). On 7 July 1990, thousands of people attended a pro-democracy rally at Kamukunji, an area adjacent to Nairobi's [q.v.] poorer suburbs and shantytowns. Kenneth Matiba and Charles Rubia [qq.v.], two former cabinet ministers, organized the event to press their demands for the establishment of a multiparty political system in Kenya. The crowd unexpectedly turned violent and stoned two police [q.v.] cars. General Services Unit [q.v.] personnel responded by firing tear gas and beating many of the demonstrators. For the next three days, protestors battled police throughout parts of Nairobi and demanded the release of Matiba and Rubia, both of whom had been detained on 4 July 1990. Violence also spread to numerous other towns, including Kiambu, Kisumu [q.v.], Limuru, Muranga, Naivasha [q.v.], Nakuru [q.v.], and Nyeri [q.v.]. President Daniel arap Moi [q.v.] ordered security units to use "all necessary force" to restore order throughout the country. According to the Kenyan government, the Saba Saba riots resulted in the death of 20 people; however, various human rights organizations claimed the number of fatalities was higher. In the aftermath of these disturbances, police charged 1,056 people with riot-related offenses. On 10 July 1990, 511 defendants appeared before a Nairobi chief magistrate; at least 122 others were tried in other courts. The sentences of those found guilty ranged from fines (Shs 1,000–2,000; $38–$78) to jail terms of three months to two years.

SABA SABA RIOTS (1997). On 7 July 1997, riots rocked Nairobi [q.v.] and several other Kenya towns, including Thika [q.v.]. These were caused by violent police [q.v.] suppression of planned demonstrations for constitutional reform. The police killed at least 14 people, beat women and clubbed and tear-gassed students at the University of Nairobi [q.v.]. Additionally, the Presidential Security Guard entered Nairobi's Anglican All

Saints Cathedral and attacked pro-democracy clergy at prayer. In the aftermath of this incident, which attracted widespread domestic and international condemnation, the Kenyan government implemented a three-pronged strategy. The Kenya African National Union (KANU) [q.v.] approved the establishment of a constitutional review commission. Next, President Daniel arap Moi [q.v.] invited opposition politicians such as Michael Wamalwa [q.v.] to State House to discuss the country's future. Lastly, KANU launched a domestic and international diplomatic offensive to deflect criticism away from President Moi. Although these actions undoubtedly placated some Kenyans and non-Kenyans, many people in and out of Kenya remained highly skeptical of the government's sincerity. The Inter-Parties Parliamentary Group [q.v.] introduced reforms which sought to reduce the ferment for reform that had sparked the demonstrations.

SADLER, SIR JAMES HAYES (1851–1922). Commissioner of the East Africa Protectorate (EAP) [q.v.] (1905–06) and governor (1906–09). In 1870, Sadler joined the army and served in India. In 1877, he joined the Indian political service and in 1892, moved to the diplomatic service as British consul at Muscat. In 1898, Sadler took up the post of consul general in British Somaliland (now comprises much of the so-called Republic of Somaliland), and in 1901, the Foreign Office sent him to Uganda as commissioner. In 1905, he became commissioner of the EAP after Sir Donald Stewart [q.v.] suddenly died. He was the first chief executive of the colonial government to hold the title of governor.

On the whole, Sadler's tenure in the EAP was distinguished by weakness and an inability to deal with the demands of European settler politicians. Known as "Old Flannelfoot" because he repeatedly changed his mind to please whatever party was representing its case to him, Sadler acceded to settlers' demands to institute a poll tax [q.v.] to force young African men out to work. By 1909, most of southern Kenya was under British control, but he had failed to devise policies for its effective administration. Following his service in the EAP, the Colonial Office demoted Sadler by appointing him to the far less prestigious post of governor of the Windward Islands (1909–14). He died on 21 April 1922.

SAFINA. On 7 May 1995, Paul Muite [q.v.] and other opposition MPs formed this political party with human rights lawyer Muturu Kigano as chairman. Richard Leakey [q.v.], who recently had left government service, also joined the party. On 20 June 1995, SAFINA, which is the Swahili name for Noah's ark, applied for registration. However, the government rejected its application because it did not want "foreigners" participating in the country's political leadership. The party leaders unsuccessfully sought registration for the new organization but claimed that they had no intention of nominating a presidential candidate for the 1997 general elections [q.v.]. Instead, they indicated that SAFINA's aim was to work for constitutional and legal reform to advance the cause of democratization. The party and its organizers drew strong hostility from President Daniel arap Moi [q.v.], who repeatedly claimed he would never recognize SAFINA. However, on 26 November 1997, the Kenyan government gave in to domestic and international pressure and registered SAFINA. The following day, the party announced that it would field a limited number of candidates for parliamentary and civic elections but that it would refrain from nominating a presidential candidate. In the general elections (1997), SAFINA won five parliamentary seats, plus one nominated seat.

SAGINI, LAWRENCE GEORGE (1926–1995). Teacher, politician, and businessman. Born in Ikruma in present-day Kisii district and educated at Kisii School; Mangu High School; Holy Ghost College; and Kagumo Teacher Training College. He taught in several schools in western Kenya prior to attending Allegheny College in Pennsylvania, United States, where he earned a B.A. degree in 1959. Upon returning to Kenya, he served briefly as an assistant education officer. In 1960, he joined the Kenyan African National Union (KANU) [q.v.]. In the LEGCO elections (1961) [q.v.], he won the Kisii seat as an independent. Upon election, he quickly aligned himself with KANU. In 1962, Sagini became minister of education after the coalition government's formation. The following year, he won the Kitutu West parliamentary seat and received an appointment as minister for natural resources in Kenya's independence cabinet; Sagini later served as minister of local government. He was elected as KANU vice president for Nyanza Region at the Limuru Conference (1966) [q.v.]. In the general elections (1969) [q.v.], however, Sagini lost his parliamentary seat to Zachary Onyonka [q.v.]. After failing to recapture the seat in 1974, he left elective politics, though he remained an influential party member at local and national levels. Sagini worked for Firestone, was a long-serving director of the Kenya Power and Lighting Company, and served on the University of Nairobi's [q.v.] council. Following the general elections (1992) [q.v.], President Daniel arap Moi [q.v.] nominated Sagini to Parliament. He died on 4 August 1995.

SAITOTI, PROFESSOR GEORGE (1944–). Teacher, politician, businessman, and farmer. Born in Kiambu District. When he was a child, his family moved to Kajiado in Maasailand. Saitoti attended Ollolua Primary School; the Catholic Primary School; and Mangu High School (1959–62). From 1962 until 1967, he studied at Brandeis University in Waltham, Massachusetts, where he received a B.A. in mathematics. Saitoti then received an M.S. from Sussex University and a Ph.D. from Warwick University, both of which are in Great Britain. In 1971, he returned to Kenya and accepted a position as mathematics lecturer at the University of Nairobi [q.v.]; by 1978, he had become senior lecturer and head of the mathematics department. Saitoti then went into business as chairman of Mumias Sugar Company and a director (later, executive chairman) of Kenya Commercial Bank.

Saitoti's political career began on 1 October 1983, when President Daniel arap Moi [q.v.] nominated him to Parliament and appointed him minister of finance. In March 1988, he won a parliamentary seat for Kajiado North. At about the same time, he was elected chairman of the Kenya African National Union [q.v.] branch for Kajiado District. On 1 May 1989, Saitoti replaced Josephat Karanja [q.v.] as vice president; interestingly, Saitoti had worked under him at the University of Nairobi.

Controversy marred his tenure as vice president. Apart from corruption charges that emerged from submissions to the commission investigating Robert Ouko's [q.v.] death in 1990, many Kenyans believed he was one of the beneficiaries of the Goldenburg Scandal and one of the prime architects of the government-supported ethnic fighting that swept throughout the Rift Valley [q.v.] and elsewhere during the early 1990s. At this time and later, Saitoti's political fate was closely linked to that of Nicholas Biwott [q.v.].

Despite these and other allegations of wrongdoing, Saitoti remained the vice president after winning his seat in the 1992 general elections [q.v.]. He then moved from the Ministry of Finance to that of Planning and National Development. By 1996, Saitoti was acknowledged as a leader of the Kenya African National Union B (KANU B) [q.v.] faction. During the general elections (1997) [q.v.], he won a parliamentary seat for the Maasai [q.v.]-dominated constituency of Kajiado North and retained his portfolio in the Ministry of Planning and National Development. However, President Moi failed to reappoint him as vice president when naming a new cabinet in January 1998. After some 14 months without a vice president, President Moi announced Saitoti's return to the post on 3 April 1999.

SCOTT, LORD FRANCIS MONTAGU-DOUGLAS (1879–1952). Farmer and politician. Scott was the sixth son of the Duke of Buccleuch. After receiving an education at Eton College and Oxford, he served in the army (1899–1919). In 1919, he came to Kenya under the Soldier Settlement Scheme [q.v.] and took up a farm at Rongai. Scott soon became involved in politics and was first appointed and then elected to the Legislative Council [q.v.] in 1925 for the Rift Valley [q.v.]. He was also appointed to the Executive Council [q.v.]. Following Lord Delamere's [q.v.] death in 1931, Scott emerged as the leader of the European settlers. He clashed with the colonial government on several issues during Sir Joseph Byrne's [q.v.] governorship. In 1941, Scott rejoined the army and participated in the Ethiopian campaign. During the 1940s, his political influence waned as he was defeated by Michael Blundell [q.v.] in the 1948 LEGCO election, and Sir Ferdinand Cavendish-Bentinck [q.v.] came to occupy a more important political position in the European settler community. Lord Francis died in London on 26 July 1952.

SECOND WORLD WAR. *See* WORLD WAR II.

SERONEY, JOHN MARIE (1928–1982). Lawyer and politician. Born in Kapsabet, Nandi District and educated at the Government African School, Kapsabet; Alliance High School (1941–44); Makerere University (1945–46) [qq.v.]; University of Allahabad (1947–51) in India; and London's Inner Temple (1952–55), where he qualified as a barrister. Following his return to Kenya, he served as public prosecutor (1956–58) and then went into private legal practice (1959–61) in Nairobi [q.v.]. He entered politics in the LEGCO elections (1961) [q.v.], winning the Nandi seat as a Kenya African Democratic Union (KADU) [q.v.] independent candidate.

Seroney served as a parliamentary secretary (1961–62) and in the coalition government (1962–63). He won the Nandi North seat for KADU in the general elections (1963) [q.v.]. In November 1963, a year before KADU's dissolution, Seroney joined the Kenya African National Union (KANU) [q.v.]. In the 1969 and 1974 general elections [qq.v.], Seroney easily won the Tinderet seat. Following the latter election, he became deputy speaker in the Parliament. His ruling that Martin Shikuku's [q.v.] statement that "KANU is dead" did not require substantiation in October 1975 led to his detention without trial (1975–78). Following his release, Seroney failed to capture the Tinderet seat in the 1979 general elections [q.v.]. He then left politics. Seroney was chairman of the Industrial Development Bank at the time of his death on 6 December 1982.

SESSIONAL PAPER NO. 10, AFRICAN SOCIALISM AND ITS APPLICATION TO PLANNING IN KENYA (1965).

The sessional paper, written mainly by Kenya's minister for economic planning, Tom Mboya, and his assistant minister, Mwai Kibaki [qq.v.], set out guiding principles for Kenya's development strategies when it was made public on 27 April 1965. The paper emphasized the government's commitment to the Africanization of the economy and called for equal opportunity; progressive taxation to ensure equitable distribution of wealth; the right of private ownership of property; freedom from want, disease, and exploitation; and the encouragement of foreign investment, public and private. A mixed economy was the ideal. Nationalization would be used only where assets in private hands threatened national security or integrity or when productive resources were being wasted. The definition of African Socialism was thus a far cry from Marxist ideals. The paper's general procapitalist tenor guided Kenya's economic strategy for the succeeding decades, but it provoked hostility over economic goals and policies that was partially responsible for the split in the Kenya African National Union [q.v.] that occurred after the Limuru Conference (1966) [q.v.] and for the formation of the Kenya People's Union (KPU) [q.v.].

SETTLEMENT SCHEMES. Land settlement schemes formed an important part of Kenya's decolonization experience. Starting in 1962, the Kenya government, with financial support from the British government and the World Bank [q.v.], began an ambitious program of land settlement that was largely complete by the early 1980s. The target of these schemes was the former White Highlands [q.v.]. More than a million hectares were transferred from white to African ownership. The most famous of the settlement initiatives was the 1962–70 million-acre scheme [q.v.], which involved the subdivision of European settler mixed farms for African smallholders. The 1969 Harambee scheme and the Haraka scheme dating from the mid-1960s both sought to do the same thing. Neither proved satisfactory to the government, and they were supplanted by the 1971 Shirika scheme which sought to settle landless Africans on former European settler farms by keeping the farms intact and running them cooperatively. This did not meet the wishes of the newly settled farmers, and most Shirika farms were thus subdivided into smaller farms.

In addition to these government-financed and -run settlement schemes, some 600,000 hectares were transferred to African ownership intact.

Those rendered landless or short of land by Kenya's colonial experience benefited little from this process. This settlement process did not include most ranches and estates, and that guaranteed that large farms, now owned by wealthy Africans, would continue to play a role in Kenya's agriculture [q.v.].

SEYIDIYE(H) PROVINCE. One of the original provinces of the East Africa Protectorate [q.v.], which initially consisted of Malindi, Mombasa, and Vanga Districts. After World War I [q.v.], Kilifi District became a part of the province. In 1920, it was renamed Coast Province, and Lamu and Tana River Districts were added. Taita District became part of the province in 1934. From 1963, Coast Province consisted of Kilifi, Kwale, Lamu, Mombasa, Taita Tana River, and Taveta Districts (83,603 square kilometers; 32,279 square miles).

SHIFTA. In the 1960s, the Kenyan government initially used this term, which means "bandit" and had long been in common use in the Northern Frontier District/Province [q.v.] to describe Somali [q.v.] dissidents who sought to break away from Kenya and join a Greater Somalia, which supposedly included North Eastern Province [q.v.]. The 1963–67 *Shifta* Wars [q.v.] affected much of North Eastern Province. In more recent years, the term has been applied to Somali criminal elements, cattle raiders, nomads, arms dealers, and poachers who are active in the province. Some Somalis resent the use of this term, which they feel is derogatory. *See also SHIFTA* WARS.

SHIFTA **WARS (1963–1967).** Instability has plagued the Kenyan-Somali border region for decades as cattle raiders, nomads, arms dealers, and poachers crossed freely from Somalia to northeastern Kenya. During the 1948–60 period, the colonial government unsuccessfully tried to resolve this problem by designating the Northern Frontier District (NFD) [q.v.] a closed area. This meant that travelers needed entry and exit permits to go from Kenya proper into the NFD, and vice versa. Between 1960 and 1963, the newly independent Somali government repeatedly tried to persuade the British to allow the NFD to join Greater Somalia, an entity that supposedly would include the Somali [q.v.] -inhabited regions of Djibouti, Ethiopia, and Kenya. The British compromised by recognizing Somali influence in the Northern Frontier District and by arranging to pass control of the area, which eventually was to be renamed North Eastern Province [q.v.], to an independent Kenyan government. On 12 March 1963, Somalia rejected this arrangement and broke diplomatic relations with Great Britain. Two days later, Jomo Kenyatta [q.v.] announced that he would oppose handing over North Eastern Province to Somalia once Kenya had gained its independence.

On 25 December 1963, the Kenyan government, which had abandoned any hope of reaching a diplomatic settlement of the problem, declared a state of emergency in North Eastern Province, broke diplomatic relations with Mogadishu, and subsequently imposed a trade ban against Somalia. Over the next several years, low-level clashes between Kenyan security forces and Somali *shifta*s [q.v.] regularly occurred throughout North Eastern Province. According to the Kenyan government, the first three years of the *Shifta* Wars resulted in the deaths of approximately 1,650 Somalis, 69 Kenyan military and police [q.v.] personnel, and at least 500 Kenyan civilians.

The Organisation of African Unity (OAU), which advocated the recognition of colonial borders, initially failed to resolve the crisis as Somalia refused to recognize the existing border. However, at the 1967 annual OAU summit, Zambian President Kenneth Kaunda agreed to act as a mediator in the dispute. In October 1967, Kaunda finally persuaded Kenya and Somalia to end their hostilities. This agreement resulted in a restoration of diplomatic relations and a lifting of the state of emergency and the trade ban. Nevertheless, North Eastern Province remained an area of tension between the two countries. During the 1977–78 Somali-Ethiopian Ogaden War, for example, Kenya increased its military presence in the region to deter Somali border incursions. There were also minor security incidents in 1980 and again in 1984 that resulted in a limited number of deaths and injuries.

In September 1981, relations between Nairobi [q.v.] and Mogadishu improved after Somali President Siad Barre indicated that his country no longer laid claim to North Eastern Province. In December 1984, the two nations concluded a border security agreement. Despite these actions, Somali border incursions have continued to plague North Eastern Province. *See also* NORTHERN FRONTIER DISTRICT/PROVINCE; NORTHERN FRONTIER DISTRICT LIBERATION FRONT; NORTHERN PROVINCE PEOPLE'S PROGRESSIVE PARTY; *SHIFTA*; SOMALI.

SHIKUKU, MARTIN JOSEPH (1932–). Politician. Born at Magadi and educated at Lake Magadi Primary School; Mumias Primary School (1941–46); and St. Peter's Seminary, Kakamega (1947–52). Shikuku worked for the Magadi Soda Company, East African Railways (1952–

56), and the Caltex Oil Company (1956–58) prior to entering politics in Nairobi [q.v.], initially as a supporter of Tom Mboya [q.v.] In 1959, he became general secretary for the Nairobi People's Convention Party [q.v.]. In 1960, he joined the Kenya African Democratic Union (KADU) [q.v.], serving first as leader of the party's youth wing and later as secretary-general (1961–64). He failed to defeat Tom Mboya for the Nairobi East seat in the LEGCO elections (1961) [q.v.]. For the general elections (1983) [q.v.], Shikuku won the Butere seat in Kakamega District. He held the seat at subsequent polls down to 1988, with the exception of his time in detention (1975–78). In 1964, Shikuku joined the Kenya African National Union (KANU) [q.v.] after KADU's 1964 dissolution, but he was proud to have been the last KADU member to cross the floor.

In KANU, Shikuku gained a reputation as an outspoken backbencher, critical of corruption and abuses of power, and a defender of parliamentary privileges. During the 1969–74 period, he was assistant minister in the Office of the Vice President and minister of home affairs. In 1975, the police [q.v.] detained him and John Marie Seroney [q.v.] following his statement in Parliament that "KANU is dead." In December 1978, President Daniel arap Moi [q.v.] released him. Shikuku regained his seat in Parliament in the general elections (1979) [q.v.]. Following this success, he was appointed assistant minister for economic planning and development and later took the same post in the Office of the President. Shikuku successfully defended the seat in the General Elections (1983) [q.v.] and then received an appointment as assistant minister for the environment and natural resources (1983–85), but government office did not dampen his criticism of the wealthy and corruption. In 1985, he was dropped from office and in the general elections (1988) [q.v.], he lost in circumstances that led him to allege that he was "rigged" out of Parliament by those who disliked his criticism.

During the 1991–92 period, Shikuku served as interim secretary-general of the Forum for the Restoration of Democracy (FORD). After FORD collapsed into competing factions in 1992, Shikuku joined forces with Kenneth Matiba in FORD-Asili [qq.v.], holding the position of secretary-general. In the general elections (1992) [q.v.], he won Butere for FORD-Asili. By 1995, Shikuku had split with Matiba and had assumed the leadership of a group of FORD-Asili's MPs who refused to recognize the latter's authority. In the general elections (1997) [q.v.], he stood for the presidency as the FORD-Asili candidate. However, Shikuku came in sixth, behind President Daniel arap Moi, Mwai Kibaki, Raila Odinga, Michael Wamalwa, and Charity Ngilu [qq.v.], with 0.60 percent (36,302) of the vote. Additionally, he lost his parliamentary seat for Butere constituency to Frederick Amangwe Amukowa.

SIBILOI NATIONAL PARK. (1,570 square kilometers; 606 square miles). Gazetted in 1973. Located on Lake Turkana's [q.v.] eastern shore, about 720 kilometers (446 miles) from Nairobi [q.v.]. Fauna includes cheetah, gazelle, hartebeest, lion, oryx, topi, and zebra. There are also about 12,000 crocodiles on Central Island. Additionally, Sibiloi is the home of Koobi Fora, one of East Africa's richest paleontological sites. *See also* NATIONAL PARKS.

SINGH, CHANAN (1908–1977). Lawyer, journalist, politician, judge. Born in Iholaha, Punjab, India. Educated locally but left school two years before matriculation. In 1923, Singh went to Kenya and worked as a fitter on the Uganda Railway [q.v.] and then as a rate clerk with the Kenya and Uganda Railways and Harbours. Additionally, he studied as a University of London external student and in 1940 received a B.Sc. (Economics). In 1944, he qualified by correspondence as a lawyer at Lincoln's Inn. The following year, Singh resigned from the railway and started a private practice in Nairobi [q.v.]. For a short time in 1946, Singh published the *Forward* newspaper, which promoted Asian [q.v.] and African interests, condemned the *kipande* [q.v.] system, and demanded elected representation and employment equality. He also became active in Indian politics, serving as a president and secretary of the Nairobi Indian Association, Executive Committee member of the Kenya Indian Congress [q.v.], and president of the Indian Youth League. Additionally, Singh sought to facilitate the growth of nationalism by contributing scores of articles and editorials to the *Colonial Times* of Nairobi. He was elected to the Legislative Council (LEGCO) [q.v.] and served as the member for Central Area, Nairobi (1952–56). However, in 1956 and again in 1958, Singh failed to win reelection to LEGCO. In February 1960, he helped to establish the Kenya Freedom Party [q.v.]. After winning the Nairobi South seat in the LEGCO elections (1961) [q.v.], Singh received appointments as parliamentary secretary, minister of state for constitutional affairs (1962–63) and parliamentary secretary, Prime Minister's Office (1963). In 1964, he became a judge and served with distinction until the end of his career. Singh died on 2 July 1977, while on vacation in Canada.

SINGH, MAKHAN (1913–1976). Communist agitator and labor leader. Born in India. In 1927, Singh came to Kenya with his parents and was educated at Government Indian High School, Nairobi [q.v.]. In 1934, he formed the Labour Trade Union of Kenya (subsequently known as the Labour Trade Union of East Africa). During World War II [q.v.], Singh was interned in India. On 22 August 1947, he returned to Kenya and worked for the East African Indian National Congress (1947–49). With Fred Kubai's [q.v.] help, Singh organized the East African Trade Union Congress (1949) [q.v.]. On 15 May 1950, the police [q.v.] arrested him at the start of the Nairobi general strike and kept him in detention until October 1961, because he was a communist and belonged to the Indian Communist Party. After his release, Singh failed to reenter the trade union [q.v.] movement, but he was a strong supporter of the Kenya African National Union and Jomo Kenyatta [qq.v.]. In his later years, Singh became interested in historical research, and he published *History of Kenya's Trade Union Movement to 1952* (1969) and posthumously *History of Kenya's Trade Union Movement, 1952–1956* (1980). He died in 1976.

SISAL. Sisal, which is used to make sacking and ropes, normally is produced on large estates by wage laborers. Large capital investments are needed to operate such estates as sisal requires a six-year growing period before it can be harvested. During World War II [q.v.], the United States depended on Kenya's sisal. As a result, the colonial government established controls on sisal prices, enabling many farmers to become wealthy during the war. As the petroleum industry increased production of nylon, which made excellent ropes, world demand for sisal fell. However, sisal remains of local importance as artisans produce items such as baskets, bags, and place mats that are popular purchases for foreign tourists who visit Kenya.

SOCIAL DEMOCRATIC PARTY (SDP). In 1992, Johnstone Makau established this party. After he rejoined the Kenya African National Union [q.v.] prior to the general elections (1992) [q.v.], the SDP was left without a presidential candidate and had no successful parliamentary candidates. Prior to the general elections (1997) [q.v.], Charity Ngilu [q.v.] joined the SDP and became its presidential candidate. She came fifth in the presidential contest, and the party won 15 seats, plus one nominated, in Parliament.

SOLDIER SETTLEMENT SCHEME. There were two Soldier Settlement Schemes. The first had it roots in World War I, when Sir Henry Belfield [qq.v.] convened a Governor's War Council [q.v.], composed of European settlers, to advise him about how to lessen the conflict's impact on the colony's political, economic, and social systems. To strengthen the European community and to reward ex-military personnel for their sacrifices during the conflict, the Governor's War Council recommended the creation of the Soldier Settlement Scheme. The British government eventually approved, and in 1919, the colonial government prepared a plan to provide more than one million hectares (2.47 million acres) to war veterans.

Under the program, 257 farms of about 65 hectares (160 acres) would be given free of charge to applicants who lacked the money to buy farms. Additionally, there were 1,053 farms available for purchase on easy terms. Selection boards in London and Nairobi [q.v.] conducted lotteries to determine the successful applicants. Eventually, some 2,200 war veterans made application to the Soldier Settlement Scheme, which resulted in an influx of European settlers into Nanyuki, Thomson's Falls, and Trans Nzoia Districts. The new settlers also augmented the number of European settlers in the colony's older districts. The scheme created economic difficulties by stimulating a demand for African labor and improved transportation infrastructure at a time of severe depression. Though many of the farms granted to the ex-soldiers were in areas already set aside for European settlement, the scheme also led to further loss of African land (e.g., by the Nandi) and heightened African feelings of insecurity.

The second Soldier Settlement Scheme occurred in 1946, when the colonial government established the European Agricultural Settlement Board to administer the settlement scheme. To acquire land for new farms, the board bought the leases of European farms whose owners had neglected them or subdivided large estates. All the new farms were much smaller than those disbursed after World War I. Also, newcomers had to undertake mixed farming rather than developing the monoculture farms that had been popular under the earlier scheme. The board operated two programs. One enabled men under the age of 35 to buy their farms outright, while the other made them tenant farmers. By late 1956, the board had helped 406 veterans to settle in Kenya (57 bought their farms, 40 were assisted owners, and 309 were tenants). The board invested just under £2.5 million in the scheme and parceled out a total of about 208,000 hectares (513,760 acres).

SOMALI. Eastern Cushitic-speaking [q.v.] pastoral peoples (1989 census: 419,259) who make up the majority of the inhabitants of North Eastern Province [q.v.]. Somali-speakers constitute several distinct groups or clans that moved south into Kenya from the region of the present-day Somali Republic and Ethiopia over a period of time. The earliest migration dates possibly to the 14th century. Further movements took place in the 17th century. In the 19th century, several Somali clans from the Ogaden Region, which is in eastern Ethiopia along the Somali border, made their way to Kenya (e.g., the Hawiyya and Darod). In the last decades of the 19th century, they displaced the Orma from the Juba River region and the Boran from Kenya's northeastern corner to become the dominant pastoralists in this region of Kenya.

From the establishment of colonial rule, the Somalis proved difficult for the British to conquer and control. Not until after World War I [q.v.] was even rudimentary administration established among them. Despite the 1925 transfer of Jubaland Province [q.v.] to Italian Somaliland, many Somalis remained in Kenya. The colonial government experienced little success with economic development initiatives directed toward the Somalis and refrained from encouraging the development of Christianity and Western education among Somalis who were Muslim. After the Somali Republic gained independence in 1960, political awareness among Kenya Somalis heightened.

In 1961, the Somali government and Somalis in the Northern Frontier District [q.v.] began to demand secession from Kenya and union with the Somali Republic. The Kenya African National Union and the Kenya African Democratic Union [qq.v.] strongly opposed secession. As a result, most Somalis boycotted the general elections (1963) [q.v.]. Many also participated in or supported the *Shifta* Wars 1964–67 [q.v.]. By the late 1990s, the Kenyan government had done little to normalize relations with the country's Somali community. Consequently, the Somali-inhabited region of northeast Kenya remains unstable, underdeveloped, and hostile. *See also SHIFTA; SHIFTA* WARS.

SQUATTER. A term used during the colonial period to describe a labor tenant. Squatters provided part-time labor to the landowner in exchange for the right to cultivate a piece of land and to graze livestock. Most squatters worked on European settlers' farms, especially in the Rift Valley Province [q.v.].

STEWART, SIR DONALD (1860–1905). Commissioner of the East Africa Protectorate (EAP) [q.v.] (1904–05). Educated at the Royal Military College, Sandhurst, Stewart joined the army in 1879. He saw active service in the Afghan War (1878–97) and in the Transvaal (1881). He then served in the Sudan (1884–85), and in 1896 he was political officer with the expedition against the Asante in the Gold Coast (now Ghana). From 1897, he served in the Gold Coast.

In 1904, Stewart arrived in the EAP as the first commissioner to have had any significant experience in African administration. He was also the first commissioner to have his duties confined to the EAP as he was not made responsible for the administration of Zanzibar [q.v.]. Relying upon his senior officials, he finalized the Maasai Treaty of 1904 [q.v.] that provided for their administration in northern and southern reserves. In line with his belief that no new colony could be properly administered until "The natives had been knocked into shape," he sent punitive expeditions against the Gusii and Kipsigis [qq.v.] in western Kenya, and he prepared the 1905 expedition against the Nandi. During Stewart's administration the Colonial Office assumed responsibility for the EAP on 1 April 1905. He died on 1 October 1905.

STONE BOWL CULTURE. Archaeological evidence indicates that beginning in the second millennium B.C.E. a considerable portion of the western Kenya highlands was occupied by agriculturalists who used stone tools. Their use of stone "bowls" led this culture to be termed Stone Bowl. This culture flourished in the first millennium B.C.E., and in addition to stone tools, distinctive forms of pottery, baskets, and beads were produced and utilized. The people kept livestock and probably had domesticated crops such as sorghum, millet, and vegetables. It is generally accepted that the peoples associated with the Stone Bowl culture originated in the Ethiopian highlands and spoke Southern Cushitic [q.v.] languages. Most of those associated with the Stone Bowl culture seem to have been absorbed by peoples speaking Highlands and Plains Nilotic languages in the first and second millennia C.E.

SWAHILI. The Swahili (1989 census: 13,920) are Bantu-speaking [q.v.] peoples who have long been resident in Kenya's coastal towns and cities. They belong to the Sabaki-speaking group of Bantu and are thus related to the Mijikenda [q.v.], from whom they had differentiated by the end of the first millennium C.E. By the end of the ninth-century, Swahili-speakers had founded settlements on Manda, Pate, and Shanga in the Lamu archipelago. Around 1000 C.E., the Swahili-speakers established themselves at Mombasa [q.v.].

In the coastal towns, the Swahili became involved in Indian Ocean trade, and interaction with traders from Arabia and the Persian Gulf had an impact on Swahili culture. Besides trade, the Swahili-inhabited coastal towns were involved in fishing and farming from the 10th century. Until the 19th century, Arab influence on the Swahili was small, and even from that time far from overwhelming, despite the long, popularly held (and false) view in the West that the Swahili people, culture, and language represent a "mixture" of Arabic and Bantu. Unlike other Kenya peoples prior to the 20th century, the Swahili were an urban people who resided in towns like Lamu, Malindi [q.v.], and Mombasa. By the 14th century, each urban settlement had formed a city-state with its own government, often an oligarchy. Of these, the most important was Mombasa, which by the 17th century was inhabited by 12 Swahili tribes.

After 1500, the coming of the Portuguese to the coast disrupted the Swahili society and economy. After 1700, the coastal cities and people came under periodic Omani dominance, culminating in Sayyid Said's takeover of these towns in the first half of the 19th century. While they increasingly lost their political and economic independence as a result of these external factors, many Swahili participated in the 19th-century expansion of trade with the East African interior as caravan leaders, porters, and traders. The Imperial British East Africa Company [q.v.] and then the colonial government employed many of them as porters and soldiers, but in general the colonial period witnessed the marginalization of Kenya's Swahili. Even at the coast, their influence was small, nor did the support of some for the *Mwambao* [q.v.] movement aiming at the succession of the coastal strip from Kenya at the time of independence alter this situation. *See also* SWAHILI LANGUAGE.

SWAHILI LANGUAGE (*KISWAHILI*). Swahili is a Bantu language that has been much influenced by contact with other languages, notably Arabic. There are seven dialects and three subdialects spoken in Kenya. As early as the 13th century, Swahili was fast becoming the *lingua franca* for much of the East African coast, especially among the region's businessmen. By the 18th century, written Swahili had appeared in many coastal towns, largely in the form of theological tracts and official records and documents. In 1865, Johann Krapf of the Church Missionary Society [qq.v.] published the first Swahili dictionary. Traders facilitated the language's spread to the East African interior, and it became the language of colonial administration. As a result, Swahili is used by all levels of society in Kenya. In 1964, the Kenyan government made Swahili one of the country's official languages, the other being English. In recent years, Swahili-language novels, plays, essays, and historical studies have appeared with increasing frequency. *See also* SWAHILI.

SWYNNERTON PLAN (1954). Roger Swynnerton, later director of agriculture, provided a blueprint for changing African agriculture in Kenya by drafting a scheme officially titled *A Plan to Intensify the Development of African Agriculture in Kenya*. Published at the height of the Mau Mau Revolt [q.v.], the £10.5 million plan sought to create a group of middle-class African farmers by introducing individual land tenure, consolidation of holdings, and improved access to credit and marketing and processing services. The scheme also called for abolishing restrictions on African farmers growing high-value cash crops such as coffee, tea, and pyrethrum [qq.v.], previously the almost exclusive preserve of European settlers. While opening new opportunities for African farmers, the plan failed to relax government control over production and marketing. During the succeeding decades, the scheme had a huge impact on many parts of rural Kenya by widening peasant access to commodity production.

-T-

TAITA. Bantu-speaking [q.v.] people who have lived for some time in the Taita hills near the East African coast west of Mombasa [q.v.]. The Taita speak languages quite distinct from the Mijikenda [q.v.] peoples who, in recent centuries, have lived in the coastal hinterland. Some Taita speak languages more closely related to the Chagga of Tanzania, while others speak Saghala, which belongs to the coastal Bantu group. The former language group probably began its development in the early first millennium C.E. in the Mount Kilimanjaro area. These ancestors of the Taita moved north over succeeding centuries and interacted with peoples speaking other Bantu languages, such as the Saghala-speakers from the north as well as Cushitic and Khoisan as the Taita hills seem to have long been a "melting pot" for peoples speaking different languages. The Taita eventually occupied valleys and slopes in the Taita hills that stand out in the midst of the Taru Desert. They practiced a mixed economy, exploiting the differing environments in the region. Most studies of colonial Kenya give little attention to the Taita experience.

TANALAND PROVINCE. One of the early administrative divisions of the East Africa Protectorate [q.v.], Tanaland Province included most of the Tana River valley and adjacent regions. For most of its existence, Tanaland included the districts of Lamu, Tana River, and Witu. In 1920, the colonial government abolished Tanaland Province, with most of the territory becoming part of Coast Province [q.v.] and a small portion being added to the Northern Frontier District [q.v.]

TEA. Introduced in Kenya in 1903. Tea is Kenya's major foreign exchange earner. In 1996, the country produced 257,000 tons, worth $350 million in exports. Some 260,000 farmers grow tea on small farms or large estates. Tea is grown at altitudes between 1,800 and 2,100 meters (5,905–6,890 feet) in various parts of the highlands, including districts in Central, Eastern, Nyanza, Rift Valley, and Western Provinces [qq.v.].

In 1964, the Kenya Tea Development Authority, which also markets tea, increased smallholder (viz. African) tea planting from some 4,400 hectares (10,868 acres) in 1965 to 54,689 hectares (135,082 acres) in 1982. The plantation area under tea cultivation also expanded from 17,969 hectares (44,383 acres) in 1963 to more than 27,000 hectares (66,690 acres) in 1980. By the late 1990s, the Kenya Tea Development Authority controlled 260,000 smallholder farmers. The tea estates, which consisted of 60–75 private companies, operated on their own. On 8 December 1997, the Kenya Tea Authority announced the implementation of a liberalization program to encourage production by allowing farmers to participate in all important financial and operational decisions. Currently, Kenya is Africa's leading tea producer and is third in the world behind India and China.

TELEKI, SAMUEL (1845–1916). Explorer. Teleki, an independently wealthy Hungarian count of the Austro-Hungarian Empire, decided to undertake an expedition to the little-known lands north of Lake Baringo [q.v.] after learning of Joseph Thomson's [q.v.] exploits in East Africa. Crown Prince Rudolf, son of the Austrian Emperor Franz-Josef I, persuaded Teleki to include Ludwig von Höhnel [q.v.], a naval officer, in his plans. On 23 January 1887, Teleki's expedition—which included 668 porters, guides, and bodyguards—set off from Zanzibar [q.v.]. After traveling for seven months, he reached Lake Baringo, where the expedition rested for several months. Finally, on 5 March 1888, Teleki reached Lake Rudolf (now Lake Turkana [q.v.]). On 20 April 1888, he also sighted Lake Stefanie named in honor of her Imperial Highness Archduchess Stefanie, who was the widow of Crown Prince Rudolf. On 26 October 1888, the expedition ended at Zanzibar. Teleki died in Budapest on 10 March 1916.

TESO. One of the ethnic groups resident in western Kenya (1989 census: 178,455). A larger number of Teso reside in Uganda. The Teso are part of the plains (or eastern) Nilotic-speaking peoples [q.v.]. Their language and culture is similar to that of the Karamojong of Uganda and is part of the larger Teso-Maasai group. The ancestors of the Teso living in western Kenya made their way from eastern Uganda just before and during the 19th century. They moved into areas that had been inhabited by Luyia-speakers. The Teso thus dispersed some of the Luyia [q.v.] groups. Originally pastoralists, the Teso turned to agriculture [q.v.] as well in western Kenya. Like their neighbors, the Teso were conquered prior to 1905, and under colonial rule they were administered as parts of units where they were greatly outnumbered by the Luyia. The Teso waited until the 1990s to have their own administrative district.

THAGICU. Language group that includes the Bantu-speaking peoples of Kenya's central highlands. Thagicu-speakers include the Embu, Kikuyu, Kamba, and Meru [qq.v.]. Linguists place the origin of this group between the upper reaches of the Athi and Tana Rivers. Differentiation into the various languages noted above occurred in the first half of the second millennium C.E.

THIKA (Altitude of 1,495 meters; 4,905 feet). In 1906, Jamal Hirji opened a shop that was the first business in the town. On 15 March 1924, Thika became a township, and on 5 July 1963, it became a municipality. By 1967, there were nine industries in the town employing more than 5,000 people. According to the 1989 census, the municipality's population was 57,603.

THOMSON, JOSEPH (1858–1895). Explorer. Born in Penpont, Scotland, and educated at Penpont village school, Morton School (1869–72) and the University of Edinburgh (1875–78). Thomson's connection with Kenya began on 13 December 1882, when the Royal Geographical Society sent him to explore the "snowy range of Eastern Equatorial Africa" and to establish a direct route from the Indian Ocean to Lake Victoria [q.v.]. During the 1883–84 period, he traveled through Maasailand, a journey that helped lay the groundwork for the future British penetration of Kenya. Additionally, Thomson explored Mount Kenya, Lakes Baringo and Naivasha, and the Rift Valley [qq.v.]. On a broader level, this 3,000-mile journey proved that the route from Mombasa [q.v.] to Buganda was passable. As a result of these exploits, he became the youngest man to receive the Royal Geographical Society's Gold Founder's Medal (1885). In future years, Thomson explored the Niger River (1885), the Atlas Mountains (1888), and Southern Africa (1890–91). Chronic medical problems ended his career as an African explorer. Thomson died on 2 August 1895 of tuberculosis and pneumonia. His most famous published work is *Through Masai Land* (1885).

THUKU, HARRY (1895–1970). Civil servant, politician, farmer. Educated at the Gospel Missionary School, Kambui, Thuku first worked in Nairobi [q.v.] for the *Leader of British East Africa*, a settler newspaper (1911–17). He then worked as a telephone operator at the Treasury (1917–21). After World War I, Thuku became active in politics to protest the Kikuyu [q.v.] loss of land, raises in African taxation, the introduction of the *kipande* [q.v.], and the political gains made by European settlers. In 1921, he formed the Young Kikuyu Association [q.v.] but, several months later, changed its name to the East African Association [q.v.] to broaden its appeal to other African ethnic groups. Thuku's association received assistance from Indian politicians during this time and was strongly opposed to the Kikuyu Association [q.v.] led by Kiambu chiefs and backed by Protestant missionaries.

Thuku's increasing popularity in Nairobi and among the rural Kikuyu and the hostility of the chiefs and missionaries led Sir Edward Northey's [q.v.] government to order his arrest in March 1922. The police [q.v.] opened fire on demonstrators demanding Thuku's release on 22 March 1922; he was subsequently detained until December 1930. In August 1932, Thuku became president of the Kikuyu Central Association [q.v.] but eventually left the organization as a result of disagreements with other leaders. In 1935, he formed the Kikuyu Provincial Association [q.v.], which many Kenyans perceived as instrument of colonial rule, and briefly served as president of the Kenya African Union [q.v.] (1944–45). However, Thuku was too conservative for that body as he had been coopted by the colonial government. He was a strong loyalist during the Mau Mau Revolt [q.v.]. He published *Harry Thuku: An Autobiography* (1970). On 14 June 1970, Thuku died after a short illness.

TIPIS, JUSTUS KANDET OLE (1924–1995). Born in Narok and educated at the Narok Government African School (1931–34) and the Veterinary School at Ngong (1934–38). He then worked in the Veterinary Department (1938–41) and served in World War II [q.v.] with the East African Army Service Corps (1942–46). In the LEGCO elections (1957) [q.v.], Tipis lost his bid for the Rift Valley [q.v.] to Daniel arap Moi [q.v.]. However, in the LEGCO elections (1958) [q.v.], he was elected to represent the central Rift Valley. In 1960, together with others in the Masai United Front [q.v.], he joined the Kenya African Democratic Union (KADU) [q.v.]. In the LEGCO elections (1961) [q.v.], Tipis, who served as treasurer for KADU throughout most of its existence, won the Narok seat unopposed. He was parliamentary secretary for agriculture in the government formed by KADU after that election. Following the coalition government's formation in 1962, Tipis became parliamentary secretary for defence. The following year, he won Narok East for KADU.

In 1964, Tipis joined the Kenya African National Union (KANU) when KADU MPs crossed the floor. He then served as KANU's national treasurer (1966–88). In the general elections (1969) [q.v.], Tipis lost his parliamentary seat, but he came back to Parliament in 1974. As a supporter of Daniel arap Moi throughout the 1970s, Tipis moved into a much more powerful position with Moi's ascension to the presidency in 1978. Despite the presence of a strong rival in Narok in the person of William Ntimama [q.v.], Tipis was elected unopposed in 1979 and 1983. He was elevated to the cabinet and served as minister of state in the Office of the President, dealing with internal security from 1979 until early 1988, when he moved to the Ministry of Works. In the general elections (1988) [q.v.], Tipis lost to Ntimama who now assumed the mantle of chief spokesman for the Narok Maasai [q.v.]. Shortly thereafter, he lost his post as KANU's national treasurer. Tipis left politics after those defeats. In 1990, he was appointed chairman of the Transport Licensing Board. He died on 3 July 1995.

TOURISM. In 1996, about 820,000 foreign tourists visited Kenya, and tourism earned some $427 million. Photo safaris to the country's various national parks [q.v.] and game reserves are a major attraction. An increasing number of foreign tourists have also been taking beach vacations along Kenya's coast. Other major tourist attractions include oldtown Mombasa and the Great Rift Valley [q.v.]. In recent years, the number of foreign tourists visiting Kenya has declined periodically as a result of instability in the game parks. With alarming frequency, criminal elements and poachers have attacked and robbed tour buses and campers. Political and criminal violence in Nairobi [q.v.] and elsewhere has also frequently dissuaded foreign tourists from visiting Kenya. Although the Kenyan government has promised to resolve these problems, a gradually growing number of international tour operators are becoming increasingly skeptical about Kenya as a tourist destination. In 1997 a decline in the number of tourist visits reduced earnings from tourism to some $377 million.

TOWEETT, TAAITA (1925–). Civil servant, politician, and publisher. Born in Kericho District and educated at the Africa Inland Mission School, Litein (1938); Government African School, Kabianga (1939–42); Alliance High School [q.v.] (1943–47); and Makerere University [q.v.] (1948–49). He also obtained a diploma from Great Britain's South Devon Technical College (1955). Toweett also studied privately at the University of South Africa and eventually received a B.A. degree (1956). He earned an M.A. and Ph.D. degree from the University of Nairobi [q.v.]. Toweett worked first as a welfare and community development officer for local councils. In the LEGCO elections (1957) [q.v.], he failed to win the South Nyanza seat (South Nyanza and Kericho Districts). The following year, he was appointed to the Legislative Council [q.v.]. In 1960, he became assistant minister of agriculture. While holding this post, Toweett helped found the Kenya African Democratic Union (KADU) [q.v.] and served as its political advisor. In the LEGCO elections (1961) [q.v.], he won the Kipsigis seat, with one of the largest majorities in a contested election in Kenya's history. Following KADU's 1961 decision to form a government, Toweett served as minister for labour and housing, and in the coalition government formed in 1962, he held the post of minister of land, surveys, and town planning.

In the general elections (1963) [q.v.], Toweett won a parliamentary seat, but in November, he left KADU to sit as an independent member before eventually joining the Kenya African National Union [q.v.]. Following the general elections (1969) [q.v.], Toweett returned to the cabinet as minister for education. In 1974, he moved to the Ministry of Housing and Social Services. During the 1976–79 period, he was minister for education. During Daniel arap Moi's [q.v.] presidency, Toweett's political fortunes took a downturn. He lost his seat in the general elections (1979), and he did not stand in 1983. Following this election, President Moi nominated Toweett to Parliament. After the general elections (1992) [q.v.], the president again named Toweett to Parliament. He sought election to Parliament in the general elections (1997) [q.v.], but failed in his bid.

TRADE LICENSING ACT (1968). Passed in 1967, the act gave the Kenya government means to speed up the Africanization of trade when it came into effect in 1968. It limited the areas where noncitizens (viz. Europeans and Asians [q.v.]) could trade and specified certain goods and types of businesses that were reserved for citizens. Noncitizens were given until the end of 1968 to leave the affected retail and wholesale businesses. This law, together with the Immigration Act of 1967 [q.v.], caused a rush among noncitizen Asians to obtain entry into Great Britain in late 1967 and early 1968.

TRADE UNIONS. *See* AFRICAN WORKERS' FEDERATION; CENTRAL ORGANISATION OF TRADE UNIONS; EAST AFRICAN TRADE UNION CONGRESS; KENYA FEDERATION OF LABOUR.

TSAVO NATIONAL PARK. (21,283 square kilometers; 8,217 square miles). Gazetted in April 1948. Tsavo, which is Kenya's largest national park [q.v.], is located halfway between Nairobi and Mombasa [qq.v.] at an altitude between 229 to 2,000 meters (751–6,562 feet). This region is comprised of Chyulu Hills National Park and Tsavo West and East National Parks. In the early 1990s, nearly 500,000 tourists visited Tsavo annually. More than 60 mammal species and more than 1,000 plant species are found in the park. Bird life is also prolific.

During the 1970s and 1980s, poachers and drought devastated the park's elephant and rhinoceros populations, but both species are now recovering. In 1991, an aerial survey of Tsavo's elephant population revealed nearly 7,000 elephants, the largest population in any Kenyan park. During the same year, there were no elephants poached in Tsavo and only 18 in the whole of Kenya. This figure compares with an average of 5,000 elephants killed annually by poachers in the so-called ivory wars during the 1973–89 period. *See also* GAME POLICY COMMITTEE; NATIONAL PARKS.

-U-

UGANDA RAILWAY. Since the early 1890s, the British government had been interested in building a railway in East Africa. Apart from its economic benefits, such a railway would be of strategic value insofar as it would open Uganda and other parts of the East African interior to greater British penetration. Also, a railway was the only means of quickly deploying large numbers of troops should British supremacy on the Upper Nile be challenged. Lastly, the prospects of a railway had an emotional appeal to those who believed that a stronger British presence in East Africa would end the slave trade.

Thus, on 5 August 1896, construction of the Uganda Railway started in Mombasa [q.v.]. Upon completion on 20 December 1901, the line was 936 kilometers (582 miles) long with 43 stations, 21 bridges, 35 viaducts, and 1,280 smaller bridges and culverts. The capital cost was £5,502,592, while the human cost in lives was 2,493 Asians [q.v.] and five Europeans. Altogether, the railway had imported 31,983 coolies from India to work on the line, 6,454 of whom were invalided back to India. The railway repatriated or dismissed another 16,321 Asians. Some 6,724 remained in Kenya and formed part of the country's present Asian population. Thousands of African laborers also helped to build the railway.

In February 1926, an order-in-council changed the name of the railway to the Kenya and Uganda Railway. After World War II [q.v.], the Uganda Railway underwent several organizational changes. In 1948, it was part of the East African Railways and Harbours Administration, and in 1967, it operated under the East African Railways Corporation. After the collapse of the East African Community (EAC) [q.v.] in 1977, the Kenyan government established the Kenya Railways Corporation as a parastatal responsible to the Ministry of Transportation and Communications. *See also* KENYA RAILWAYS.

UHURU. Swahili [q.v.] word for freedom. Nationalist politicians used *uhuru* as a slogan during the struggle to end British colonial rule in Kenya.

UKAMBA MEMBERS ASSOCIATION (UMA). The UMA emerged as a protest movement against the compulsory destocking campaign launched by the colonial government in 1938 among the Kamba [q.v.]. This particularly involved cattle sales in Machakos, partly as a means of reducing pressure on overgrazed pastures but also to provide livestock for the meat packing plant started at Athi River by the Liebigs Company. Thus, beginning in 1937, the forcible sale of cattle to the factory was imposed by the colonial authorities. Between April and August 1938, some 22,500 cattle were sold at prices well below the market price (of these, 9,000 went to European settlers for building their herds). The UMA was formed to protest the destocking. The UMA, led by Samuel Muindi, sent a protest petition to the Colonial Office, and in late July 1938, some 3,000 Kamba marched from Machakos to Nairobi [q.v.] to see the governor. Most camped out in the open for four weeks waiting to see Governor Sir Robert Brooke-Popham [q.v.]. Finally, at a *baraza* in Machakos on 25 August 1938, the governor announced that compulsory sales of livestock would be replaced by voluntary sales. Those were stopped in December 1938. While the UMA thus won something of a victory, its leader, Muindi, was detained in September. In 1940, the colonial government proscribed the UMA.

UKAMBA PROVINCE. Ukamba was one of the original provinces of the East Africa Protectorate [q.v.]. With headquarters at Machakos, it included districts known as Kitui, Kikuyu, Taita, and Ulu (later Machakos). In 1899, the colonial authorities shifted provincial headquarters to Nairobi [q.v.], and in 1902, Ukamba lost the territories that became Kenia Province [q.v.] and Taita. In 1934, the colonial government merged Kikuyu Province [q.v.] with Ukamba to form Central Province [q.v.].

UKENYA. Dissident opposition group. On 18 February 1987, Yusuf Hassan established the Movement for Unity and Democracy in Kenya (*Umoja wa Kupigania Demokrasia Kenya*—Ukenya) in London. According to Hassan, Ukenya differed from Mwakenya [q.v.] in that it was an overt organization, while the latter was a covert group. This organization has never been very active in Kenya.

UNITED COUNTRY PARTY. This short-lived party was formed in July 1954 with the intention of mobilizing people for the multiracial principle of the Lyttelton Constitution [q.v.]. It drew its support from Michael Blundell [q.v.] and other like-minded Europeans. Despite its backing for multiracialism, the party was open to whites only. It stood for the sanctity of the White Highlands [q.v.] and against common-roll elections, but it did not have a large following among the European settlers. After the European elections of September 1956, the party largely ceased to exist as Blundell and his supporters had stood as independents. In 1957, the party was dissolved.

UNITED PARTY. In August 1959, Group Captain Llwellyn Briggs [q.v.], spokesman for the European settler "die-hards" in Kenya, formed this political party. It drew together Briggs's Legislative Council (LEGCO) [q.v.] supporters who had gained eight of the 14 European seats in the election (1957), with those who had been in the largely defunct Federal Independence Party [q.v.]. It was formed mainly in response to, and to counter, the New Kenya Party [q.v.]. The United Party stood against independence for Kenya, common-roll elections, the opening up of the White Highlands [q.v.] to other races, and integrated education. It called for an ending of LEGCO and its replacement by an advisory council of all races while settler control of local affairs in the highlands would increase. Briggs and other LEGCO members attended the first Lancaster House Conference (1960) [q.v.]. However, they exercised little influence on proceedings and criticized the outcome as "a victory for Mau Mau," according to Briggs. With the Kenya Coalition's [q.v.] formation, the United Party threw its support behind the new grouping, and, by the time of Briggs's death in November 1960, the former had ceased to exist.

UNIVERSITY OF EAST AFRICA (UEA). On 28 June 1963, Tanzanian President Julius Nyerere inaugurated the University of East Africa and became its first chancellor. The UEA amalgamated the Royal College, Nairobi; Makerere University College [q.v.], Kampala; and the University College of Tanganyika (now Tanzania). During its seven-year existence, the UEA enjoyed considerable international support. In 1963 and 1967, two donor conferences resulted in substantial financial grants to the university. In 1965, the authorities, amid some controversy, lowered entrance requirements to allow more students to enter the UEA. The 1967 treaty for East African Cooperation established a committee to review higher education in East Africa. As part of that process, the committee agreed to the abolishment of the UEA in 1970, after which three or more separate universities would emerge in the member countries. *See also* EAST AFRICAN COMMUNITY; UNIVERSITY OF NAIROBI.

UNIVERSITY OF NAIROBI. Kenya's premier university. In 1956, the Asian [q.v.] community funded the creation of the Royal Technical College of East Africa as a memorial to Mahatma Gandhi. Initially, this institution offered degree courses in five faculties, including arts, science, engineering, art and architecture, and special professional studies. The college quickly established a reputation for offering the most advanced technical courses in East Africa. By September 1963, the British government had given the college £600,000 in grants and had helped to recruit a large proportion of its staff. On 28 June 1963, the institution became part of the University of East Africa [q.v.]. In May 1964, the Royal Technical College of East Africa changed its name to University College, Nairobi. In 1970, the name changed to the University of Nairobi. For the 1997–98 academic year, the university had a student population of about 15,400. The university offered a variety a courses similar to those found in major European or North American institutions. *See also* EDUCATION, UNIVERSITY.

-V-

VASEY, SIR ERNEST ALBERT (1901–1984). Businessman, politician, civil servant. Born in Great Britain, Vasey left Bromley school at age 12. In 1937, after a brief career in British politics, he migrated to Kenya and quickly became involved in European settler politics, serving on Nairobi [q.v.] Municipal Council (1938–50) and as the town's mayor (1941–42 and 1944–46). In 1945, Vasey succeeded Ferdinand Cavendish-Bentinck [q.v.] as legislative councillor for Nairobi North, a post he held until he was member for education, health, and local government (1950–52) and minister for finance and development (1952–59). During the 1950s, Vasey was the most effective spokesman for a multiracial Kenyan society among all European politicians. This reputation did not endear him to most European settlers. In late 1959, he moved to Tanganyika (now Tanzania) to serve as minister of finance (1959–62). After leaving East Africa, he was an economic advisor to the World Bank [q.v.] (1962–66) and resident representative of the World Bank in Pakistan (1963–66). After he retired, he returned to Nairobi, where he died on 10 January 1984.

-W-

WAIYAKI, FREDERICK LAWRENCE MUNYUA (1932–). Physician and politician. Born in Kiambu and educated at Alliance High School [q.v.], Adams College and Fort Hare University in South Africa, and the University of St. Andrews in Scotland. Waiyaki qualified as a physician in Great Britain and returned to Kenya to work for the Medical Department (1957–58). He then went into private practice (1958–59). In 1961, he joined the Kenya African National Union (KANU) [q.v.] and ran in the LEGCO elections (1961) [q.v.] as an independent candidate but failed to defeat Tom Mboya [q.v.] for the Nairobi East seat. In the general elections (1963) [q.v.], Waiyaki won the Nairobi Northeast seat in the House of Representatives election on the KANU ticket.

Following self-government, Waiyaki served as assistant minister in the Ministries of Health and Housing, Internal Security and Defence, and in the Vice President's Office. In 1966, he followed Oginga Odinga's [q.v.] lead in resigning from office. Waiyaki rejoined KANU and won Nairobi's Mathare seat in the general elections (1969) [q.v.], and he held the seat at the general elections (1974 and 1979) [qq.v.]. Following his 1969 election, Waiyaki became deputy speaker of Parliament. After the 1974 election, President Jomo Kenyatta [q.v.] appointed him minister for foreign affairs, a post he held until 1979 when he was reassigned as minister for energy by President Daniel arap Moi [q.v.]. He also served as minister for industry (1980–82) and agriculture (1982–83). Waiyaki's ministerial career ended after he lost in the general elections (1983) [q.v.].

In 1991, Waiyaki reentered politics as he joined other veteran politicians in launching the Forum for the Restoration of Democracy (FORD) [q.v.]. After this party split into factions in 1992, he became secretary-general of the Forum for the Restoration of Democracy-Kenya (FORD-K) [q.v.]. In the general elections (1992) [q.v.], he lost his bid to return to Parliament on the FORD-K ticket. In 1995, Waiyaki resigned from

FORD-K and formed the United Patriotic Party of Kenya, which was eventually registered by the government in 1997. During the general elections (1997) [q.v.] he was the party's presidential candidate but gained only 0.01 percent of the vote (6,103 votes). Waiyaki also failed to win a parliamentary seat.

WAMALWA, MICHAEL KIJANA (1944–). Lawyer, teacher, farmer, businessman, and politician. Born in Trans Nzoia, the son of politician William Wamalwa. Educated at Chewoyet Secondary School, Strathmore College, and the University of London, where he obtained a B.A. and LL.B. In 1969, he qualified as a barrister in London and also earned an aviation law diploma from the Hague Academy of International Law. After returning to Kenya, Wamalwa, a Luyia [q.v.], accepted a position at the University of Nairobi [q.v.] teaching international law (1970–74). After failing to be elected to Parliament in 1974, he became general manager of Kenyastone Mining Company and chief executive officer of the Kenya-Japan Association. In the general elections (1979) [q.v.], he won the Trans Nzoia parliamentary seat as a political ally and protégé of Masinde Muliro [q.v.] and subsequently served as secretary of the Kenya African National Union (KANU) [q.v.] parliamentary group. His association with Muliro and his criticism of those wielding political power brought him business and financial difficulties. A court nullified his general elections (1988) [q.v.] victory because of voting irregularities. Wamalwa refused to stand in the 1989 by-election.

Afterwards, Wamalwa, like Muliro and many other Kenyan politicians, became associated with the campaign to establish a multiparty political system. In 1991–92, he became increasingly active in the Forum for the Restoration of Democracy (FORD) [q.v.]. Following the 1992 FORD split, Wamalwa became second vice chairman of FORD-Kenya (FORD-K) [q.v.]. In the general elections (1992) [q.v.], Wamalwa won the Saboti parliamentary seat in Rift Valley Province [q.v.]. The following year, he became first vice chairman of FORD-K after the resignation of Paul Muite [q.v.]. With the death of party chairman Oginga Odinga [q.v.] on 20 January 1994, Wamalwa became chairman of FORD-K and leader of the opposition.

Wamalwa's repeated disagreements with Raila Odinga [q.v.] eventually caused the latter to resign from FORD-K and to join the National Development Party [q.v.]. As a result, FORD-K lost most of its Luo [q.v.] supporters and the party became dominated mainly by Wamalwa's Luyia followers. Nevertheless, on 26 January 1997, a FORD-Kenya Congress elected him party chairman and subsequently nominated him as the party's presidential candidate in the general elections (1997) [q.v.]. However, Walmalwa came in fourth, behind President Daniel arap Moi, Mwai Kibaki, and Raila Odinga [qq.v.], with 8.29 percent (505,542) of the vote, though he retained his Saboti parliamentary seat.

WAMWERE, KOIGI WA (1949–). Activist and politician. Born to a squatter [q.v.] family in then Nakuru District [q.v.]. Educated at Mother of Apostles Seminary, Nyeri High School, and Cornell University. After his return from the United States, Wamwere threw himself into the politics of rural Nakuru District, championing the cause of the poor and landless. In 1974, he stood for the Nakuru North seat, but lost to Kihika Kimani. In September 1975, the police [q.v.] detained him, largely because his activism had irritated many powerful Kenyan officials. In December 1978, Wamwere gained his freedom as part of a nationwide amnesty. The following year, he won a huge electoral victory, more than doubling the vote of his 10 competitors for the constituency. In Parliament, Wamwere worked to improve the welfare of the poor and advocated wide-ranging political reforms. Such activities put him on a collision course with the Kenyan government.

In August 1982, the police again detained him for possible complicity in the coup attempt (1982) [q.v.] against President Daniel arap Moi [q.v.]. In December 1984, the police released him but he failed to regain his parliamentary seat. In 1986, he therefore went into exile in Norway, though he continued to be a strong critic of President Moi's government. He maintained that independence had not given Kenyans the political and economic freedom that colonialism had denied them. In October 1990, after he had returned to Kenya, the police arrested Wamwere and charged him with treason. Shortly thereafter, Amnesty International adopted him as a prisoner of conscience. Additionally, several other legal and human rights associations continued to publicize his case, claiming that the Kenyan government fabricated the case to rid itself of an internationally known critic of the Moi regime. Although the Kenyan government eventually dropped the charges against him, Wamwere was unable to stand in the general elections (1992) [q.v.] because of his time in jail.

In January 1993, Wamwere finally gained his freedom and then established the National Democratic and Human Rights Organization. In September 1993, the police again arrested him and several others, including the well-known lawyer Mirugi Kariuki. The authorities charged them with possessing seditious publications, administering an unlawful oath, and traveling in a restricted zone that had been declared as a result of ethnic violence in western Kenya. However, on 19 October 1993, the police released Wamwere and fellow prisoner Mirugi Kariuki on bail. On 5 November 1993, the authorities accused Wamwere and 14 others with attempting to rob the Bahati police station in Nakuru [q.v.]. On 2 October 1995, he was convicted and sentenced to four years imprisonment and six strokes with a cane for simple robbery (not the original charge). While in custody during the trial, Wamwere announced that he was a cofounder of SAFINA [q.v.].

On 13 December 1996, the Kenyan authorities, under growing domestic and international pressure, finally released Wamwere on bail while he appealed his conviction. Shortly thereafter, he went back to Norway but returned to Kenya to continue pro-democracy activities. On 2 December 1997, the Kenyan government rescinded his four-year jail term to enable him to stand as the presidential candidate of the Kenya National Democratic Alliance (KENDA) [q.v.] in the general elections (1997) [q.v.]. He not only performed poorly in the presidential election, winning only .12 percent of the vote (7,463 votes), but also failed to win a parliamentary seat in his Subukia constituency in the Rift Valley Province [q.v.]. His views about the problems confronting Kenya are contained in his memoirs, *the People's Representative and the Tyrants of Kenya: Independence without Freedom* (1992).

WAR COUNCIL. The War Council was set up in March 1954 at the time the Lyttleton Constitution [q.v.] was finalized, largely as a response to demands by European settlers for a more effective prosecution of the military operations against the Mau Mau Revolt [q.v.]. The small council initially consisted of the governor, Sir Evelyn Baring; General Sir George Erskine [qq.v.], commander of military forces in Kenya; the deputy governor, and Michael Blundell [q.v.] as minister without portfolio. The council, normally meeting twice weekly, discussed military operations, Kikuyu [q.v.] "rehabilitation," manpower utilization, and the economic restructuring of Kikuyuland. The council met until 1956. Unlike the Governor's War Council [q.v.] of World War I [q.v.], this council did not produce any long-term gains for the European settlers.

WATKINS, OSCAR FERRIS (1877–1943). Colonial administrator. Born in India and educated at Marlborough and Oxford. Watkins served in the Boer War (1899–1901) and later with the South African Mounted Constabulary (1902–04). He then held several civil service positions in South Africa. On 8 January 1908, he arrived in Mombasa [q.v.] to join the colonial service in Kenya. Until 1911, he served as a district officer in Coast Province [q.v.]. After a brief stint in Kiambu, Watkins was posted to Mumias, where he served under John Ainsworth [q.v.]. In 1913, he returned to the coast. When World War I [q.v.] started, he helped inaugurate the Carrier Corps [q.v.]. As Carrier Corps commander, he worked to ensure maximum recruitment and effective use of the porters. After the conflict, Watkins became deputy to Chief Native Commissioner John Ainsworth. Both were unpopular with European settlers for what was perceived to be their pro-African viewpoints and their determination to resist further alienation of African land.

When Ainsworth retired in 1920, Watkins served as acting chief native commissioner. However, he was not promoted to the position; rather, he remained as deputy to G. V. Maxwell, who was brought in from Fiji. Watkins did not get along with Maxwell, who was determined to maintain good relations with Governor Sir Edward Grigg [q.v.], who supported European settler views on African land alienation and the need for compulsory labor. Watkins repeatedly clashed with Grigg over these issues. His commitment to African rights had a negative impact on his career. On 1 January 1927, Grigg retaliated against what he perceived as a disloyal official by demoting Watkins to provincial commissioner at Mombasa and subsequently posting him to the mainly European settler district of Eldoret (Nzoia Province [q.v.]). Despite these actions, Watkins never wavered in his determination to protect African rights. In 1932, Watkins retired from the colonial service. After a few years in Great Britain, he returned to Kenya and before World War II [q.v.] helped to resettle Jewish refugees there. With the start of the war, he worked as editor of a Swahili [q.v.]- language newspaper called *Baraza*. He died of stomach cancer on 27 December 1943.

WESTERN PROVINCE. This administrative unit was created in 1963 out of Nyanza Province [q.v.]. Until 1990, it consisted of Bungoma (formerly Elgon Nyanza), Busia, and Kakamega (formerly North Nyanza) Districts. After 1990, the province, with headquarters at Kakamega [q.v.], experienced subdivision through the creation of new districts such as Mount Elgon, Teso, and Vihiga. (8,360 square kilometers; 3,228 square miles).

WHITE HIGHLANDS. The central highland area begins around Limuru, northwest of Nairobi [q.v.], and continues to Maralal. Also located in this region are the Aberdares and Mount Kenya [qq.v.]. Historically, the Kikuyu [q.v.] cultivated this fertile area, and the Maasai [q.v.] grazed their livestock in the drier plains. However, European settlers began to arrive in the highlands shortly after the completion of the Uganda Railway [q.v.]. After 1902, the colonial government reserved the highlands for European settlement and land ownership. Originally, the area for white settlement was recognized as falling roughly between the Kiu and Fort Ternan stations on the Uganda Railway, but over time it came to include the Uasin Gishu and Laikipia Plateaus, the vicinity of Mount Kenya, and the Trans Nzoia Region as well as smaller blocks of land.

The exclusive rights for Europeans (excluding those of Africans and Asians [q.v.]) in the region was long a primary demand of Kenya's settlers. This was first recognized by the imperial government through the 1908 Elgin Pledge [q.v.] and reemphasized by the 1923 Devonshire Declaration [q.v.], but it was only given statutory standing through the Kenya (Highlands) Order-in-Council, 1938 [q.v.], following the recommendation of the Kenya Land Commission [q.v.]. Growing African animosity over European domination of this region contributed to the Mau Mau Revolt [q.v.]. In 1960, the imperial government finally abolished European control of the highlands by allowing other races to settle in that area.

As a result of independence negotiations, the British government agreed to provide loans to Africans who wanted to buy land in the highlands. After 1963, Kenyan authorities therefore devised several Settlement Schemes [q.v.], including the Million-Acre Scheme and the Haraka Program to make European-owned land available to wealthy, low-income, and poor African farmers. By 1970, the former resettled some 35,000 households on about 486,000 hectares (1.2 million acres), while the latter resettled about 13,000 households on four-hectare (10-acre) plots. After 1970, an increasing number of farms were subdivided as a result of land being parceled out to an owner's sons. Consequently, in recent years, ecologists have become concerned about the long-term environmental impact of the growing human population in the highlands.

WILSON AIRWAYS. Wilson Airways played a significant role in the development of Kenya's commercial aviation industry. On 31 July 1929, Tom Campbell Black, financed by Florence Kerr Wilson, established Wilson Airways with a capital of £50,000 and one Gipsy Moth aircraft. Initially, the airline operated from a grass strip known as Dagoretti Airfield. However, in 1930, Wilson Airways moved to Nairobi West Airfield, which in 1962 became known as Wilson Airport. By 1931, Wilson and Black had convinced the colonial government to establish landing strips at nearly all principal towns along the coast and in the White Highlands [q.v.].

During its first year of operations, the airline flew more than 150,000 passenger miles. By 1931, Wilson Airways had a fleet of two Avro Fives, two DH Puss Moths, and three Gipsy Moths; there were three pilots. Black was the first person to fly nonstop from Nairobi to Zanzibar [qq.v.] and roundtrip from Nairobi to Mombasa [q.v.] in a day. Wilson Airways also operated service to England, via the Congo (now Democratic Republic of Congo), Nigeria, and Senegal. During World War II [q.v.], the airline's pilots and engineers joined the Kenya Auxiliary Air Unit. Eventually, Wilson Airways merged into East African Airways [q.v.].

WOMEN FOR PROGRESS (*Maendeleo ya Wanawake*). Founded in 1956 with assistance from British and Canadian charities. Initially, Women for Progress taught women domestic science and encouraged them not to support the Mau Mau Revolt [q.v.]. Much of the organization's early activities occurred in Kikuyu [q.v.] communities near Nairobi [q.v.] but later spread to Embu and Meru [qq.v.]. During Daniel arap Moi's [q.v.] presidency, Women for Progress became a Kenya African National Union [q.v.] affiliate; although these ties eventually severed, the organization remains close to the ruling party. In recent years, Women for Progress has received funding from a variety of donors, including the World Bank [q.v.], United Nations Development Program, Ford Foundation, and Rockefeller Foundation, and several Scandinavian governments. During the 1990s, some of the organization's major projects included legal reform, voter education, rural credit, girls' education, and programs to oppose rape and genital mutilation.

Women for Progress is a member of the National Council of Women in Kenya, an umbrella organization of all voluntary women's groups. As of mid-1999, Zipporah Kittony was chairperson for Women for Progress.

WOOD–WINTERTON AGREEMENT. Concluded by officials from the Colonial and India Offices, led respectively by E. F. L. Wood and Lord Winterton, to resolve the Indian Question [q.v.]. This agreement provided for common-roll elections in which both Asian [q.v.] and European voters would participate with the likely outcome of Asians [q.v.] holding four seats in the Legislative Council [q.v.]. The plan called for no segregation in commercial or residential areas in Kenya's towns, no change in immigration regulations, and the maintenance of the White Highlands [q.v.] for Europeans only. In September 1922, Kenya's new governor, Sir Robert Coryndon [q.v.], received a draft of the Wood-Winterton Agreement, which he, with support from the European settler community, opposed. However, in late November 1922, the newly appointed Secretary of State, the Duke of Devonshire, insisted that the agreement should be implemented. In February 1923, the Colonial Office (CO) finally dropped its support for the plan after Coryndon warned London that Kenya's European settlers were planning an armed rebellion rather than accept the Wood-Winterton Agreement as a basis for Kenya's political future. Later in 1923, the CO unveiled another initiative, known as the Devonshire Declaration [q.v.], to resolve the Indian Question.

WORLD BANK. The World Bank, known officially as the International Bank for Reconstruction and Development, was a product of the 1944 Bretton Woods Conference, which sought to normalize the postwar monetary regime. Since 1963, the World Bank has played an increasingly important role in the Kenyan economy. During the 1960s and 1970s, the World Bank financed the development of Kenya's ports, highways, water supplies, agriculture, and transport capabilities. After Kenya developed economic problems in the early 1980s, the World Bank made aid contingent on economic reforms. In July 1982, the World Bank approved a $131 million Structural Adjustment Programme. However, in 1983, the World Bank suspended the disbursement of the second tranche because Kenya had failed to meet its requirements for decontrolling maize marketing. With the emergence of Kenya's pro-democracy movement in the late 1980s, the World Bank, often operating in concert with the International Monetary Fund (IMF) [q.v.], became increasingly active in efforts to encourage political reforms and end official corruption. On 26 November 1991, the World Bank responded to complaints of human rights violations by informing Kenya that it would get no new aid for at least six months.

The World Bank's dissatisfaction with Kenya's failure to improve its human rights record and to make other political and economic reforms resulted in an extension of the ban on assistance. Finally, on 21 April 1993, the World Bank announced that it would resume aid to Kenya. As of 1998, the World Bank, despite its ongoing concern about political and economic problems in Kenya, continued to fund projects in the country's agriculture [q.v.], industry and finance, education and health, energy, infrastructure, and population sectors. *See also* ECONOMY; INTERNATIONAL MONETARY FUND.

WORLD WAR I (1914–1918). The East African campaign was one of the most remarkable military adventures in history. Initially, the colonial government in German East Africa (GEA; later Tanganyika and now Tanzania) had no intention of getting involved in a conflict with the British (contingents from South Africa, Southern Rhodesia [now Zimbabwe], and India also served under British command) and Allied forces, which included Belgian and Portuguese units. The German governor, Heinrich Schnee, wanted to remain neutral. However, the German military commander, General Paul von Lettow-Vorbeck [q.v.], believed that by launching a guerrilla war against the British, he could pin down a large number of troops and force the British to divert soldiers destined for the western front to East Africa. Therefore, after the Royal Navy shelled a wireless station near Dar-es-Salaam [q.v.] on 8 August 1914, Lettow-Vorbeck defied Schnee and captured Taveta, a small settlement just inside the border of what today is Kenya. At the beginning of the campaign, the *Schütztruppe* numbered only 218 Germans and 2,542 *askaris* [q.v.] organized into 14 companies; eventually, this force totaled 3,007 German troops and 12,100 *askaris*.

With his army, Lettow-Vorbeck battled an allied force, which numbered about 70,000 soldiers for four years. Several hundred thousand African carriers supported these troops throughout the war. Relying largely on raids, hit-and run-tactics, and the skillful use of internal lines of communication, Lettow-Vorbeck wrecked havoc upon the British by destroying bridges, blowing up trains along the Uganda Railway [q.v.], ambushing convoys, and capturing military equipment and other supplies. The fighting encompassed three phases. In the first two years of the campaign, Lettow-Vorbeck largely succeeded in eluding British forces. During the 1916–17 period, Jan Smuts fought the *Schütztruppe* to a stalemate. In late 1917, General J. L. van Deventer assumed command of British forces in East Africa and eventually forced the Germans to retreat into Portuguese East Africa (now Mozambique). On 28 September 1918, Lettow-Vorbeck crossed back into GEA, but before he could launch a new offensive, the war ended.

In more than four years of fighting, the Germans had 439 killed in action and 874 wounded, while British forces had 3,443 combat deaths and 7,777 wounded in action. Disease claimed 256 German soldiers and 6,558 British troops. African losses on the German side included 1,290 *askaris* killed in action and about 7,000 carriers dead from disease; 3,669 Africans sustained wounds. British forces lost 376 African carriers in combat and 1,645 wounded; 44,911 died of disease. The Belgians and their Congolese troops had approximately 3,000 killed or wounded. Portugal and its African soldiers had 1,734 killed and several hundred wounded. See also *ASKARI*; CARRIER CORPS; GOVERNOR'S WAR

COUNCIL; KING'S AFRICAN RIFLES; SOLDIER SETTLEMENT SCHEME; WATKINS, OSCAR FERRIS.

WORLD WAR II (1939–1945). Kenya played a significant role during the fighting in East Africa. After Allied forces evacuated British Somaliland on 17 August 1940, military authorities in Kenya escalated planning for the conquest of Italian East Africa. To achieve this goal, British generals assembled the 11th African Division of the 21st, 25th, and 26th East African Brigades, and the 12th African Division, which included the 22nd East African Brigade, the 24th Gold Coast Brigade, and the First South African Brigade. Both divisions had artillery, engineers, and reserve forces. The East African Pioneers also supported the divisions.

On 4 February 1941, the offensive started when the 25th East African Brigade invaded Ethiopia and the 22nd East African Brigade captured Gugnani oasis in Italian Somaliland. Also, the 24th Gold Coast Brigade and the First South African Brigade scored several victories along the Juba River in Italian Somaliland. By March 1941, allied forces had occupied Italian Somaliland and had recaptured British Somaliland. During the fighting, these units captured 10,350 Italian and 11,732 African troops. Some 30,000 African soldiers had deserted. Total casualties included 445 killed and wounded. Allied forces then invaded Ethiopia as the 11th Division advanced toward Jijiga and the 12th Division moved toward Neghelli. Clashes occurred at several places, including Soddu, Jimma, Demli Gimbi, Chilga, Wolchefit Pass, Kulkaber, and Gondar. On 27 September 1941, the Italians surrendered and the British established a military administration over Ethiopia. Approximately 80,000 Italians became prisoners of war in Kenya, 3,000 of whom lived at a camp in Londiani.

Kenyans, both European and African, also fought in other theaters. On 11 September 1941, the 22nd East African Brigade deployed to Madagascar to support Great Britain's campaign against Vichy, France. In 56 days of fighting, the 22nd East African brigade had 33 killed and 96 hospitalized because of wounds or sickness. In North Africa, some 30,000 East African Pioneers supported the Eighth Army by fighting fires, participating in demining campaigns, and manning flak guns. Approximately 45,000 East Africans, many of whom were from Kenya, served in Ceylon, Burma, and India. Altogether, 1,924 East Africans lost their lives during these campaigns. Apart from creating economic hardships for Africans throughout Kenya, World War II helped to lay the groundwork for the emergence of the post-1945 nationalist movement, which eventually

brought about the country's independence. See also KING'S AFRICAN
RIFLES; SOLDIER SETTLEMENT SCHEME.

-Y-

YOUNG KAVIRONDO ASSOCIATION (YKA) (*Piny Owacho*). A protest organization founded at a 23 December 1921 meeting in Lundha in
then Central Kavirondo district. The organizers were young, Church
Missionary Society (CMS) [q.v.]–educated men, both Luo and Luyia
[qq.v.], who were concerned about high taxes, forced labor, the *kipande*
[q.v.], low wages, and the 1920 annexation of Kenya as a colony. At the
Lundha meeting, the YKA called for the establishment of a separate legislature for Nyanza, abolition of the *kipande* and of forced labor, reduction of taxation, and the return of Kenya to the status of protectorate. The
YKA also advocated measures for general improvement, such as the
construction of a government school, and it called for the appointment
of paramount chiefs in Central and South Nyanza.

In 1922, the YKA placed its demands before the colonial government
at the same time that the East African Association [q.v.] was advocating
similar measures in Nairobi [q.v.] and Kikuyuland. Following the suppression of the East African Association [q.v.], the colonial government
offered concessions; following a visit from Governor Sir Edward Northey
[q.v.] in July 1922 taxes were lowered, forced labor relaxed, and labor
camps closed. More significantly, the state subverted the organization and
turned its aims toward improvement on the local level rather than activist politics. This was accomplished with the aid of the senior CMS missionary in western Kenya, Walter Edwin Owen [q.v.], who became president of the Young Kavirondo Association in 1923. He immediately
convinced members to change its name to the Kavirondo Taxpayers
Welfare Association [q.v.] and to concern themselves with welfare and
modernization rather than politics.

YOUNG KIKUYU ASSOCIATION (YKA). Formed in June 1921 by
Harry Thuku [q.v.] and other young, educated Kikuyus [q.v.] living in
Nairobi [q.v.]. It sought to articulate African complaints, particularly the
kipande [q.v.], forced labor, high taxation, and the Soldier Settlement
Scheme [q.v.]. YKA leaders visited African reserves and other places in
the Kikuyu, Machakos, and Nyanza areas to voice these grievances. After solidifying his support among the Luo and Kamba [qq.v.] peoples,

Thuku changed the YKA's name to the East African Association [q.v.].
See also EAST AFRICAN ASSOCIATION; KIKUYU ASSOCIATION.

-Z-

ZANZIBAR. A 1,660-square-kilometer (640-square-mile) coral island that
is less than 132 meters (400 feet) above sea level, and 37 kilometers (23
miles) from the East African mainland. Zanzibar has played a critical role
in the historical development of the Kenyan coast. During the precolonial
and early colonial periods, the island was the gateway to the mainland
for European traders, missionaries, soldiers, and administrators. Many
caravans bound for Uganda passed through Kenya, following the routes
that had been first traveled by the explorer Joseph Thomson [q.v.] and
stopping at the stations that he had established. In May 1887, the sultan
of Zanzibar, Barghash ibn Said, granted a 50-year lease to the Imperial
British East Africa Company (IBEAC) [q.v.] for a coastal strip of territory along the East African coast. Working primarily from Mombasa
[q.v.], IBEAC slowly penetrated the interior and laid the groundwork for
the eventual establishment of British colonial rule in Kenya. Following
the establishment of colonial rule, the initial commissioners of the East
Africa Protectorate [q.v.] also headed the colonial administration of Zanzibar.

Appendix A
British Commissioners and Governors of the East Africa Protectorate/Kenya Colony (1895–1963)

Commissioners:

Hardinge, Sir Arthur (also, Consul General in Zanzibar until 1896). 1 July 1895–7 October 1900.*

Craufurd, C. H. Acting. 7 October–30 December 1900.

Eliot, Sir Charles. 30 December 1900–20 May 1904.*

Jackson, Frederick. Acting. 20 May–1 August 1904.*

Stewart, Sir Donald. 1 August 1904–1 October 1905.*

Jackson, Frederick. Acting. 1 October 1905–12 December 1905.

Sadler, Sir James Hayes. 12 December 1905–1906.*

Governors:

Sadler, Sir James Hayes. 1906–12 April 1909.*

Bowring, Charles. Acting 12 April–16 September 1909.*

Girouard, Sir Percy. 16 September 1909–17 July 1912.*

Bowring, Charles. Acting. 17 July–4 October 1912.*

Belfield, Sir Henry. 4 October 1912–14 April 1917.*

Bowring, Charles. Acting. 14 April 1917–1 February 1919.*

Northey, Major General Sir Edward. 1 February 1919–28 August 1922.*

Coryndon, Sir Robert. 31 August 1922–10 February 1925.*

Denham, Edward. Acting. 10 February–3 October 1925.

Grigg, Sir Edward (later Lord Altrincham). 3 October 1925–27 September 1930.*

Moore, Sir Henry Monck-Mason. Acting. 27 September 1930–13 February 1931.*

Byrne, Sir Joseph. 13 February 1931–22 December 1936.*

Wade, Sir Armigel de Vins. Acting. 22 December 1936–6 April 1937.

Brooke-Popham, Air Chief Marshal Sir Robert. 6 April 1937–30 September 1939.*

Harragin, Sir Walter. Acting. 30 September 1939–9 January 1940.

Moore, Sir Henry Monck-Mason. 9 January 1940–25 October 1944.*

Rennie, Gilbert M. Acting. 25 October 1944–12 December 1944.

Mitchell, Sir Philip. 12 December 1944–21 June 1952.*
Potter, Henry S. Acting. 21 June 1952–29 September 1952.
Baring, Sir Evelyn. 29 September 1952–14 October 1959.*
Coutts, Walter Fleming. Acting. 14 October 1959–23 October 1959.
Renison, Sir Patrick Muir. 23 October 1959–17 November 1962.*
Griffith-Jones, Eric. Acting. 17 November 1962–4 January 1963.
MacDonald, Malcolm John. 4 January 1963–12 December 1963.*

*Entry in Dictionary

Appendix B
Prime Minister and Presidents of Kenya

Prime Minister:
Kenyatta, Jomo. 1 June 1963–11 December 1964

Presidents:
Kenyatta, Jomo. 12 December 1964–22 August 1978
Moi, Daniel arap. Acting. 22 August 1978–13 October 1978
Moi, Daniel arap. 14 October 1978-present.

Appendix C
Economic Data

Gross Domestic Product: $8.5 billion (1997)

Annual Gross Domestic Product Growth Rate: 2.3 percent (1997)

Gross Domestic Product per Capita: $296 (1997)

General Inflation Rate: 11.2 percent (1997)

Labor Force by Occupation: Agricultural—75/80 percent; Non-Agricultural—20/25 percent (1997)

Wage Employment: Private Sector, 57 percent; Public sector, 43 percent (1997)

Imports: $3.2 billion (1997)

Exports: $2.1 billion (1997)

External Debt: $6.9 billion (1997)

Fiscal Year: 1 July–30 June

Bibliography

A. Kenya Bibliography, Library Science, and Reference Materials
B. History: Precolonial
C. History: Colonial Period
D. History: Independence Period
E. Military and Security Affairs
F. Economic Affairs
G. General Studies
H. Regional Studies
I. Religion, Missions, and Missionaries
J. Ethnology, Sociology, and Folklore
K. Agriculture, Land Tenure, and Local Administration
L. Foreign Affairs
M. Women's Affairs
N. Arts, Architecture, and Music
O. Education
P. Environment and Geography
Q. Legal Affairs
R. Mau Mau
S. Medicine, Health, and Social Services
T. Literature and Language
U. Communications, Media, and Transport
V. Urban Centers and Urbanization Studies
W. Travel and Exploration
X. Asians

ABBREVIATIONS

AA   African Affairs
ACTS   African Centre for Technology Studies
ACOP   African Curriculum Organisation Project
AHS   African Historical Studies

271

AI	Amnesty International
AQ	Africa Quarterly
AR	Africa Report
AS	African Studies
ASR	African Studies Review
AT	Africa Today
CH	Current History
CJAS	Canadian Journal of African Studies
CUP	Cambridge University Press
EAAJ	East African Agricultural Journal
EAEP	East African Education Publishers
EAER	Eastern Africa Economic Review
EAJ	East Africa Journal
EAJRD	East African Journal of Rural Development
EALB	East African Literature Bureau
EALR	Eastern Africa Law Review
EAMJ	East African Medical Journal
EAPH	East African Publishing House
EAR	East Africa and Rhodesia
EEA	Education in Eastern Africa
FAO	Food and Agriculture Organisation
GJ	Geographical Journal
GP	Government Printer
HIA	History in Africa: A Journal of Method
HMSO	Her/His Majesty's Stationery Office
IAI	International African Institute
IDA	International Development Association
IDS	Institute for Development Studies
IFO	Ifo Institut für Wirtschaftsforschung
IJAHS	International Journal of African Historical Studies
IRM	International Review of Missions
JAA	Journal of African Administration
JAE	Journal of African Economics
JAH	Journal of African History
JAL	Journal of African Law
JAS	Journal of African Studies
JDA	Journal of Developing Areas
JEARD	Journal of Eastern African Research and Development
JEAUNHS	Journal of the East African and Ugandan Natural History Society
JHE	Journal of Human Evolution
JICH	Journal of Imperial and Commonwealth History

JMAS	Journal of Modern African Studies
JRA	Journal of Religion in Africa
JRAI	Journal of the Royal Anthropological Institute
JRAS	Journal of the African Society
KHR	Kenya Historical Review
KLB	Kenya Literature Bureau
NGM	National Geographic Magazine
NLM	Nairobi Law Monthly
ODI	Overseas Development Institute
OUP	Oxford University Press
RA	Rural Africana
ROAPE	Review of African Political Economy
SIAS	Scandinavian Institute of African Studies
SIDA	Swedish International Development Authority
SOAS	School of Oriental and African Studies, University of London
SSM	Social Science and Medicine
TAR	The African Review
TJH	Transafrican Journal of History
UJ	Uganda Journal
UNESCO	United Nations Educational, Scientific and Cultural Organization
UNEP	United Nations Environment Program
USGPO	United States Government Printing Office
WD	World Development
WP	Westview Press
WT	World Today
YUP	Yale University Press

INTRODUCTION

The following bibliography provides readers with a general introduction to the field of Kenyan studies. Most of the available literature is in English, although useful material appears in other languages such as French, German, Italian, and Swahili. Scholars who desire more comprehensive surveys of writings should refer to the Kenya Bibliography, Library Science, and Reference Materials section of this bibliography, which contains references to the more significant compilations of sources on Kenya.

Over the past few decades, there has been an impressive array of scholarly publications on most aspects of Kenya's history. However, additional work still is needed on Kenyan military affairs, especially during the postindependence period; the careers of some colonial governors and officials and many of Kenya's African political leaders; opposition movements; environmental problems; transportation infrastructure; the judiciary; and the political, economic, social, and medical impact of Acquired Immune Deficiency Syndrome (AIDS).

Concerning the British colonial period, books and articles normally fall into two categories. Those written before independence usually extoll the virtues of British colonial rule, while those produced after independence are often highly critical of British colonialism. Future, more balanced, assessments of the political, military, economic, and social implications of the colonial experience undoubtedly will result in greater understanding of Kenya's historical development.

Apart from books and articles, archival data is essential to Kenya scholars. Most available archival material is limited to the colonial and immediate postcolonial periods and is located on three continents. The Kenya National Archives in Nairobi, the University of Nairobi Library, and the Macmillan Library house a variety of documents from the British colonial period. In the United Kingdom, there are several repositories that are indispensable. This includes the Public Record Office, Kew; the Royal Commonwealth Society Collection, Cambridge University; Foreign and Commonwealth Office Library, London; House of Lords Record Office, London; Hydrographic Department, Taunton; Royal Botanic Gardens Library, Kew; Imperial War Museum, London; National Army Museum, London; British Library: Oriental and India Office Collections, London; Royal Geographical Society, London; and Rhodes House, Oxford. In North America, archival materials are housed at the Consortium for Africa Microfilm Project (CAMP) in Chicago, Illinois. Microfilm copies of full or partial archival files are also located in many major universities, including Indiana University, Michigan State University, Syracuse University, University of Wisconsin-Madison, and West Virginia University. Before visiting any of these archival locations, researchers should inquire as to the use of specific collections of official documents and other materials.

Apart from the items contained in this bibliography, readers interested in recent Kenyan affairs should consult contemporary periodicals such as *Africa Analysis, Africa Confidential, Africa Research Bulletin, Focus on Africa,* and *New African*; as well as leading scholarly journals including *African Affairs, African Studies Review, Canadian Journal of African Studies,* and *Journal of Modern African Studies.* The Economist Intelligence Unit's quarterly and annual country reports on Kenya are also useful, especially with regard to economic matters. Lastly, annuals such as *Africa Contemporary Record* and *Africa South of the Sahara* provide valuable sources of information.

A. KENYA BIBLIOGRAPHY, LIBRARY SCIENCE, AND REFERENCE MATERIALS

Abstracts of Social Science Theses and Dissertations Submitted to Eastern African Universities. 2 vols. Addis Ababa, Ethiopia: Organization for Social Science Research in Eastern Africa, 1989–1990.

African Bibliographic Center. *The Scene Is Kenya and the Personage Is Jomo Kenyatta: A Selected Current Reading List from 1953 to 1962.* Washington, D.C.: African Bibliographic Center, 1963.

Library of Congress. African Section. *Africa South of the Sahara: Index to Periodical Literature, 1900–1970.* 4 vols. Boston: G.K. Hall, 1971–, supplements.

Alem, Seged Hailu. *Rural Development in African Countries: A Selected Bibliography with Special Reference to Mali and Kenya.* Monticello, IL: Vance Bibliographies, 1982.

Araya, R. *Library and Information Services in East Africa: Kenya, Tanzania, Uganda.* Warsaw: University, Institute of Oriental Languages and Cultures, 1986.

Bell, Simon. *Women in Rural Development in Kenya, Tanzania, and Zimbabwe: A Partially Annotated Bibliography.* Norwich, UK: School of Development Studies, University of East Anglia, 1985.

Birdsall, S. S. "Urban Geographic Studies in East Africa: A Selected List of Published Literature." *Bulletin of the Special Libraries Association Geography and Map Division* (1972): 16–22.

Blackhurst, Hector, ed. *Africa Bibliography.* Manchester: Manchester University Press, 1984–annual.

———. *East and Northeast Africa Bibliography.* Lanham, MD: Scarecrow Press, 1996.

Boalt, Carin, Suzanne Grant Lewis, and Dorothy Myers. *Bibliography on Human Settlements with Emphasis on Households and Residential Environment: Kenya.* Stockholm: Swedish Council for Building Research, 1982.

Burt, Eugene C. *Annotated Bibliography of the Visual Arts of East Africa.* Bloomington: Indiana University Press, 1980.

Camerapix. *Spectrum Guide to Kenya.* Edison, NJ: Hunter Publishing, 1992.

Casada, James Allen. "British Exploration in East Africa: A Bibliography with Commentary." *Africana Journal* (1974): 195–239.

———. *Sir Harry Hamilton Johnston: A Bio-Bibliographical Study.* Basel, Switzerland: Basler Afrika Bibliographien, 1977.

———. *Sir Richard F. Burton: A Bio-Bibliographical Study.* Boston: G. K. Hall, 1990.

CDR Library Holdings of Publications (Governmental, Parastatal, Institutional, and Periodicals) Published in Kenya. Copenhagen: Centre for Development Research, 1989.

Chandler, Dale, and R. Thairu. *Women of Kenya: An Annotated Bibliography.* Nairobi: Women's Bureau of the Ministry of Housing and Social Services, and United Nations, 1978.

Clough, Marshall S., and Kennell A. Jackson. *Bibliography on Mau Mau*. 2 Vols. Stanford, CA: Stanford University, 1975.

Coger, Davan. *Kenya*. Oxford: Clio Press, 1996.

Collison, Robert L. *Kenya*. Oxford: Clio Press, 1982.

Conover, Helen F., and Audrey Walker. *Official Publications of British East Africa. Pt. 1: The East Africa High Commission and Other Regional Documents*. Washington, D.C.: Library of Congress, 1960.

Curutchet, Mirina. *Bibliography on Human Settlements in Developing Countries. References with Relevance to Eastern Africa*. Lund, Sweden: University of Lund School of Architecture, 1982.

Daniels, Robert E., Mari H. Clark, and Timothy J. McMillan, eds. *Bibliography of the Kalenjin Peoples of East Africa*. Madison: University of Wisconsin Press, 1987.

Darch, Colin, ed. *Africa Index to Current Periodical Literature*. Munich: K. G. Saur Verlag (Hans Zell), annual, 1977–.

Department of Resources Surveys and Remote Sensing. *Kenya from Space: An Aerial Atlas*. Nairobi: EAEP, 1992.

Doro, Marion E. "Bibliographic Essay on Kenya Colony: Political Themes and Research Sources." *Current Bibliography on African Affairs* 5 (2) (1972): 480–96.

Downing, Laura J. J. *A Bibliography of East African Languages and Linguistics 1880–1980*. Urbana, IL: Author, 1989.

Downing, T. E. A. *Bibliography on Drought in Kenya*. Nairobi: National Environment Secretariat, 1989.

DuPré, Carole E. *Luo of Kenya: An Annotated Bibliography*. Washington, D.C.: Institute for Cross-Cultural Research, 1968.

East African Annual. Nairobi: East African Standard, various years.

East, John. *Campaign in East Africa 1914–1918: A Select Annotated Bibliography*. London: Privately Printed, 1987.

Easterbrook, David L., et al. *Microfilms Relating to Eastern Africa, Pt 3: Kenya and Miscellaneous. A Guide to Recent Acquisitions of Syracuse University*. Syracuse, NY: Syracuse University, Maxwell School of Citizenship and Public Affairs, Program of Eastern African Studies, 1975.

Fedha, Nathan W., and John B. Webster. *A Catalogue of the Kenya National Archive Collection on Microfilm at Syracuse University*. Syracuse, NY: Syracuse University, 1967.

Finucane, Brendan, Lawrence Rupley, and Tony Killick. "Economic Literature for Kenya, Tanzania, Uganda, 1974–1980: An Analysis." *African Research and Documentation* (33) (1983): 12–22.

Ford, Michael, and Frank Holmquist. "Review Essay: The State and Economy in Kenya." *African Economic History* (1988): 153–63.

Gakobo, J. K. *History of Christianity in Kenya, 1844–1977: A Select Bibliography*. Nairobi: Kenyatta University College Library, 1979.

Garver, R. A., ed. *Research Priorities for East Africa*. Nairobi: EAPH, 1966.

Gertzel, Cherry. *Bibliography: East and Central Africa for the Period 1940–1975.* Bedford Park, AU: Flinders University, Politics Discipline, 1978.

Getahun, A., et al. *Agroforestry for Development in Kenya: An Annotated Bibliography.* Nairobi: International Council for Research in Agroforestry, 1991.

Gillett, Mary. *Tribute to Pioneers: Mary Gillett's Index of Many of the Pioneers of East Africa.* Oxford: Parchment (Oxford), 1986.

Gregory, Robert G., and Richard E. Lewis. *A Guide to Daily Correspondence of the Coast, Rift Valley, Central, and Northern Frontier Provinces.* Syracuse, NY: Syracuse University, 1984.

———. *Guide to the Kenya National Archives: To the Microfilms of the Provincial and District Annual Reports, Record Books, and Handing-Over Reports, Miscellaneous Correspondence, and Intelligence Reports.* Syracuse, NY: Syracuse University, 1968.

———. *Guide to Secretariat Circulars: Kenya National Archives Microfilm.* Syracuse, NY: Syracuse University, Maxwell School of Citizenship and Public Affairs, 1984.

Gregory, Robert G., Robert M. Maxon, and Leon P. Spencer. *Guide to the Kenya National Archives.* Syracuse, NY: Syracuse University, Program of Eastern African Studies, 1968.

Hailu, Alem Seged. *Rural Development in African Countries: A Selected Bibliography with Special Reference to Mali and Kenya.* Monticello, IN: Vance Publications, 1982.

Hakes, Jay E. *Study Guide for Kenya.* Boston: Boston University, 1969.

Hendriks, Melvin K., Theophilus R. Brainerd, and Thomas Omara-Alwala. *Working Bibliography on East African Fisheries.* Kingston, RI: International Center for Marine Resource Development, University of Rhode Island, 1984.

Hess, Robert L., and Dalvan M. Coger. *Bibliography of Primary Sources for Nineteenth-Century Tropical Africa.* Stanford, CA: Hoover Institution Press, 1972.

Higher Degree Theses and Dissertations of the University of Nairobi, 1970–1979. Nairobi: University of Nairobi Libraries, 1980.

Hino, S. "Bibliography on Swahili Studies in Japan." *African Urban Studies* 2 (1992): 139–58.

Holland, Killian. *A Selected Bibliography of the Maasai of Kenya and Tanzania.* Montreal: McGill University, Department of Anthropology, 1989.

Holmquist, Frank W. "Select Bibliography [on Politics and Public Policy in Kenya and Tanzania]." In *Politics and Public Policy in Kenya and Tanzania,* edited by Joel D. Barkan, 337–59. New York: Praeger, 1984.

———, and Joel D. Barkan. *Comprehensive Bibliography: Politics and Public Policy in Kenya and Tanzania.* Iowa City: University of Iowa, Center for International and Comparative Studies, 1984.

Howell, John Bruce. *East African Community: Subject Guide to Official Publications.* Washington, D.C.: Library of Congress, 1976.

———. *Kenya: Subject Guide to Official Publications.* Washington, D.C.: Library of Congress, 1978.

————. *Rural Health in Kenya: A Guide to the Literature.* Iowa City: University of Iowa Libraries, 1989.

Jacobs, Alan H. "Bibliography of the Masai." *African Studies Bulletin* 8 (3) (1965): 40–60.

Karanja, Gichuki, and Fissiha Tefera. *Soil and Water Conservation in Kenya: Bibliography with Annotations.* Nairobi: University of Nairobi, 1990.

Kemoni, Henry. "Preservation and Conservation of Archive Materials: The Case of Kenya." *African Journal of Library, Archives and Information Science* 6 (1) (1996): 46–51.

Kenya Books in Print. Nairobi: Kenya Publishers Association, 1997.

Kenya National Archives. *Guide to Agriculture in Kenya: Selected Documents Held by the Kenya National Archives.* Nairobi: Kenya National Archives, 1985.

————. *Guide to Education in Kenya: Selected Documents Held by the Kenya National Archives.* Nairobi: Kenya National Archives, 1985.

————. *Guide to Government Monographs, Reports, and Research Works.* Nairobi: Kenya National Archives, 1984.

————. *Guide to Records Retrieved from U.K. and U.S.A.* Nairobi: Kenya National Archives, 1989.

————. *Guide to the Private (Local) Archives.* Nairobi: Kenya National Archives, 1987.

————. *Guide to Selected Documents on Political Organizations in Kenya.* Nairobi: Kenya National Archives, 1984.

————. *Nyanza Province Microfilm Collection, 1899–1963.* Nairobi: Kenya National Archives, 1964.

————. *Preserving the Images and Sounds of Kenya's Past: Planning for an Audiovisual Archive.* Nairobi: Kenya National Archives, 1978.

————. *Provincial and District Annual Reports.* Nairobi: Kenya National Archives, 1984.

————. *Records in the Kenya National Archives Relating to Land Tenure in Kenya.* Nairobi: Kenya National Archives, n.d.

————. *Records in the Kenya National Archives Relating to Religions.* Nairobi: Kenya National Archives, n.d.

Kenya National Bibliography. Nairobi: Kenya National Library Service, National Reference and Bibliographic Department, 1980.

Kenya National Library Service. *Kenya Population: Annotated Bibliography 1975–85.* Addis Ababa, Ethiopia: Coordinating Unit, Population Information Network for Africa, 1986.

Kenya Rural Enterprise Programme. *Jua Kali Literature: An Annotated Bibliography.* Nairobi: Kenya Rural Enterprise Programme, 1993.

Khamadi, S. I. D. "Moi University Library's Bibliographic Instruction Programme: A Proposal for Change." *Library Review* 45 (3) (1996): 44–49.

Killick, Tony. *Economies of East Africa, a Bibliography: 1974–1980.* Boston: G. K. Hall, 1984.

Kirk Greene, Anthony H.M. *Biographical Dictionary of the British Colonial Governor*. Vol. I: *Africa*. Brighton, UK: Harvester Press, 1981.

————. *Biographical Dictionary of the British Colonial Service, 1939–1966*. London: Hans Zell, 1991.

Kirkpatrick, B. J. A. *Catalogue of the Library of Sir Richard Burton, K. C. M. G., Held by the Royal Anthropological Institute*. London: Royal Anthropological Institute, 1979.

Krummes, Daniel C. *Transportation in East Africa: A Bibliography*. Monticello, IL: Vance Bibliographies, 1980.

Langlands, Bryan W. *Bibliography on the Distribution of Disease in East Africa*. Kampala, Uganda: Makerere University College, 1965.

Legum, Colin, ed. *Africa Contemporary Record: Annual Survey and Documents*. New York and London: Africana Publishing Company, annual—1968/69–.

Leigh, David, and R. F. Morton. *Microfilms Relating to Eastern Africa, Pt 2: Kenya, Asian and Miscellaneous. A Guide to Recent Acquisitions of Syracuse University*. Syracuse, NY: Syracuse University, Maxwell School of Citizenship and Public Affairs, Program of Eastern African Studies, 1973.

Lekyo, Christopher M., and Agnetta Mirikau, eds. *Directory of Non-Government (Voluntary) Organizations in Kenya*. Nairobi: Kenya National Council of Social Service, 1988.

Library of Congress. *Accessions List for East Africa*. Nairobi: Library of Congress Office, 1968–.

————. *Quarterly Index to Periodical Literature, Eastern and Southern Africa*. Nairobi: Library of Congress Office, 1991–.

Liyai, H. A. *Co-operative Development in Kenya: A Bibliography*. Nairobi: Kenyan Economic Association, 1986.

Macdonald, R. "A Local Collection of Historical Photographs at Fort Jesus Museum, Mombasa, Kenya." In *Photographs as Sources of African History: Papers Presented at a Workshop Held at SOAS, 12–13 May, 1988*, edited by A. D. Roberts, 149–58. London: SOAS, 1988.

McIntosh, B. G. "Archival Resources of the University College, Nairobi, Relative to Missionary Work and Independent Churches in Kenya." *Bulletin of the Society for African Church History* 4 (1968): 350–51.

McKay, Vernon. "Research Climate in Eastern Africa (Report on a Mission for the Research Liaison Committee of the African Studies Association, July-September, 1967)." *ASR* 11 (1) (1968): 1–17.

McKinley, Juanita E. *Education in Kenya: A Selected List of Sources*. Stanford, CA: Stanford University Libraries, 1981.

Mahadevan, Vijitha. *Contemporary African Politics and Development: A Comprehensive Bibliography, 1981–1990*. Boulder, CO: Lynne Rienner Publishers, 1994.

Mahlmann, Peter. "Sport as a Weapon of Colonialism in Kenya: A Review of the Literature." *TJH* 17 (1988): 152–71.

Maina, Patrick M. "Kenya Librarianship Index, 1969–1980." *Nairobi University Library Magazine* 3 (1980): 69–96.

Martin, L. A. *Education in Kenya before Independence.* Syracuse, NY: Syracuse University, 1969.

Matogo, B. W. K. "Public Library Trends in East Africa, 1945–65." *International Library Review* 9 (1) (1977): 67–82.

Matson, A. T., and Thomas P. Ofcansky. "A Bio-Bibliography of C. W. Hobley." *HIA* 8 (1981): 253–60.

———, and Donald H. Simpson. "A Bibliography of the Published and Unpublished Writings of A. T. Matson." *African Research Documentation* 42 (1986): 20–31.

Mazingira Institute. *Guide to Women's Organizations and Agencies Serving in Kenya.* Nairobi: Mazingira Institute, 1985.

Merrick, H. V. "Annotated Bibliography of Kenyan Prehistoric Archaeology, 1896–1981." *African Archaeological Review* 1 (1983): 143–77.

Mezger, D., and E. Littich. *Recent English Economic Research in East Africa—A Selected Bibliography.* Munich: IFO, 1967.

Miller, E. Willard, and Ruby M. Miller, eds. *Tropical, Eastern and Southern Africa: A Bibliography of the Third World.* Monticello, IL: Vance Bibliographies, 1981.

Molnos, Angela. *Development in Africa: Planning and Implementation: A Bibliography (1946–1969) and Outline with Some Emphasis on Kenya, Tanzania, and Uganda.* Nairobi: East African Academy Research Information Centre, 1970.

———. *Language Problems in Africa: A Bibliography (1946–1967) and Summary of the Present Situation with Special Reference to Kenya, Tanzania, and Uganda.* Nairobi: East African Research Information Centre, 1969.

———. *Sources for the Study of East African Cultures and Development: A Bibliography of Social Scientific Bibliographies, Abstracts, Reference Works, Catalogues, Directories, Writings on Archives, Bibliographies, Book Production, Libraries, and Museums with Special Reference to Kenya, Tanzania, and Uganda, 1946–1966 (1967–1968).* Nairobi: East African Research Information Centre, 1968.

———. *Die Sozialwissenschftliche Erforschung Ostafrika, 1954–1963 (Kenya, Tanganyika, Sansibar, Uganda).* Berlin: Ifo Institute für Wirtschaftsforschung Afrika-Studienstelle Springer, 1965.

Morton, Rodger F., and Harvey Soff. *Microfilms Relating to Eastern Africa. Pt. 1: Kenya Miscellaneous. A Guide to Recent Acquisitions of Syracuse University.* Syracuse, NY: Syracuse University, Maxwell School of Citizenship and Public Affairs, Program of Eastern African Studies, 1971.

Moses, Larry. *Kenya, Uganda, Tanganyika, 1960–1964: A Bibliography.* Washington, D.C.: Department of State, External Research Staff, n.d.

Muller, A. S., et al. *Bibliography of Health and Disease in East Africa.* Amsterdam: Elsevier Science Publishing Company, 1988.

Murray, Jocelyn. "Bibliography of the East African Revival Movement." *JRA* 8 (2) (1976): 144–47.

Musisi, J. S. "The Development of Libraries in Kenya." *International Federation of Library Associations and Institutions Journal* 10 (2) (1984): 125–38.

———, and J. L. Abukutsa. "Evolution of Library Associations in Kenya." *International Library Review* 10 (4) (1978): 345–54.

Mutibwa, O. M. N. *Education in East Africa, 1970: A Selected Bibliography.* Kampala, Uganda: Makerere University Library, 1971.

Mwasha, A. Z. *Librarianship in East Africa: A Selected Bibliography.* Dar-es-Salaam: National Central Library, n.d.

Nadanasabapathy, V. "Medical Literature of East Africa: Sources." *Africana Library Journal* 1 (1973): 14–15.

National Archives Library. *Annual Reports from Government Ministries and Departments, Parastatal Organizations, Local and International Organizations and Institutions Which Are in the National Archives Library.* Nairobi: The Library, 1983–.

National Archives Library (Kenya). *List of Kenya Government Monographs in the National Archives Library.* Nairobi: National Archives Library, 1983.

———. *Theses, Dissertations* [sic]*, and Other Research Findings in the National Archives Library.* Nairobi: National Archives Library, 1982.

Ndegwa, R. N. *Mau Mau: A Select Bibliography.* Nairobi: Kenyatta University College, 1977.

Ndei, J. "A Bibliography of Children's Literature in Kenya." *Maktaba* 6 (1) (1979): 81–114.

Ng'ang'a, James Mwangi. "Development of Kenyatta University College Library 1972–1984." *Maktaba* 9 (1) (1982): 29–36.

———. *Education in Kenya Since Independence: A Bibliography, 1963–1983.* Nairobi: Kenyatta University College Library, 1983.

———, ed. *Kenya: A Subject Index, 1967–1976.* Nairobi: Africa Book Services, 1983.

———. *Theses and Dissertations on Kenya: An International Bibliography.* Nairobi: African Book Services, 1983.

Njau, P. W., and W. M. Lema. *A Review of Research in Adolescent Fertility in Kenya.* Nairobi: The Centre for the Study of Adolescence, 1988.

Norgaard, Ole. *Kenya in the Social Sciences: An Annotated Bibliography 1967–1979.* Nairobi: KLB, 1980.

North, Stephen J. *Europeans in British Administered East Africa: A Provisional List 1889 to 1903.* Oxford: Privately Printed, 1995.

Nyambok, Isaac D. *Bibliography of Kenya: Geosciences.* Uppsala: SIAS, 1977.

Nzioki, M. "Bibliography of Kenya Agriculture 1979–80." *Egerton College Agricultural Bulletin* 4 (2) (1980): 71–79.

Nzioki, Mutuku, and M. B. Dar, eds. *Who Is Who in Kenya, 1982–1983.* Nairobi: Africa Book Services, 1982.

Obudho, Robert A. *Demography, Urbanization, and Spatial Planning in Kenya: A Bibliographical Survey.* Westport, CT: Greenwood Press, 1985.

————. *Nairobi, Kenya: A Bibliographic Survey.* Monticello, IL: Vance Bibliographies, 1984.

Ocholla, D. N., and J. B. Ojiambo. *Issues in Library and Information Studies.* Nairobi: Jomo Kenyatta Foundation, 1993.

Ofcansky, Thomas Paul. "Bibliography of the East African Campaign, 1914–1918." *Africana Journal* 4 (1981): 338–51.

————. "Bio-Bibliography of E. S. Grogan." *HIA* 10 (1983): 239–45.

————. "A Bio-Bibliography of F. D. Lugard." *HIA* 9 (1982): 209–19.

————. *British East Africa, 1856–1963: An Annotated Bibliography.* New York and London: Garland Publishing, Inc., 1985.

————. "L. S. B. Leakey: A Bio-Bibliographical Study." *HIA* 12 (1985): 211–24.

————. "Margery Perham: A Bibliography of Published Work." *HIA* 15 (1988): 339–50.

————. "Mau Mau Revolt in Kenya: A Preliminary Bibliography." *Africana Journal* 15 (1990): 97–126.

————. "Tom Mboya: A Bibliography." *Africana Journal* 1 (1982): 72–83.

Ogot, Bethwell A. *Historical Dictionary of Kenya.* Metuchen, NJ: Scarecrow Press, 1981.

Olsen, Maria M., with Karel J. Lenselink. *Annotated Bibliography on Irrigation and Drainage in Kenya.* Nairobi: Department of Agricultural Engineering, University of Nairobi, 1988.

Ombati, Koo. "Arrangement and Description of Archives at the Kenya National Archives: The Deposit System." *Escarbica Journal* 6 (1983): 53–59.

————. "Review of the Kenya National Archives and Documentation Service 1980–1990." *Escarbica Journal* 12 (1990): 35–44.

Ong'any, M. J. *Bibliography on Turkana.* Nairobi: Institute for Development Studies, University of Nairobi, 1981.

Otike, J. N. "Library Cooperation in Kenya." *Journal of Librarianship* 21 (1) (1989): 36–48.

————. "Special Libraries in Kenya." *International Library Review* 3 (1987): 271–85.

Owen, D. F., ed. *Research and Development in East Africa.* Nairobi: EAPH, 1966.

Pearson, James Douglas. *Guide to Manuscripts and Documents in the British Isles Relating to Africa.* 2 vols. London: Mansell, 1993, 1994.

Penzer, Norman M. *Annotated Bibliography of Sir Richard Burton, K.C.M.G.* London: A. M. Philpot, Ltd., 1923.

Pugliese, Cristiana. "The Life-Story in Kenya: A Bibliography (1920–1984)." *Africa* 41 (3) (1986): 440–46.

Rheker, J. R., et al. *Bibliography of East African Mountains, Compiled on the Occasion of the 'Workshop on Economy and Socio-Economy of Mount Kenya Area' in Nanyuki, Kenya, March 5–12th 1989.* Berne, Switzerland: University of Berne, Institute of Geography, 1989.

Robins, Kate, and Akinyi R. Mulaha, eds. *Subject Guide to Information Sources in Kenya*. Nairobi: Kenya Library Association, National Council for Science and Technology, 1984.

Roe, Emery M. "Lantern on the Stern: Policy Analysis, Historical Research, and Pax Britannica in Africa." *ASR* 30 (1) (1987): 45–62.

Rosenberg, Diana B. *Nairobi Hebrew Congregation Archives: A Descriptive*. Nairobi: Nairobi Hebrew Congregation, 1977.

Schatzberg, Michael G. "Two Faces of Kenya: The Researcher and the State." *ASR* 29 (4) (1986): 1–15.

Scheven, Y. *Bibliographies for African Studies 1979–1986*. Oxford: Hans Zell, 1988.

Selected and Brief Guide to Kenya Politics and Government, 1965–1967. Washington, D.C.: African Bibliographic Center, 1968.

Shields, James A. *Selected Bibliography on Education in East Africa 1941–1961*. Kampala, Uganda: Makerere University College, 1962.

Sicherman, Carol. *Ngugi wa Thiong'o: A Bibliography of Primary and Secondary Sources 1957–87*. Oxford: Hans Zell, 1989.

————. *Ngugi wa Thiong'o: The Making of a Rebel: A Source Book in Kenyan Literature and Resistance*. London: Hans Zell, 1990.

Sircelj, Martina. *Handicapping Conditions in Kenya with Special Emphasis on Children: An Annotated Bibliography*. Nairobi: University of Nairobi, Bureau of Educational Research, 1978.

Slattery, Alice. *Agricultural and Rural Development in Kenya: A Select Annotated Bibliography, 1960–1981*. Nairobi: USAID/Kenya, 1982.

Soff, Harvey G. *Guide to the Coast Province Microfilm Collection, Kenya National Archives*. Syracuse, NY: Syracuse University, 1971.

Srinivasan, Padma. "Contemporary Kenya: A Select Classified Bibliography." *AQ* 18 (2/3) (1979): 67–70.

Survey of Kenya. *Atlas of Kenya: A Comprehensive Series of New and Authentic Maps*. Nairobi: Survey of Kenya, 1962.

————. *National Atlas of Kenya*. Nairobi: Survey of Kenya, 1970.

Tanno, Yasuko. *Kenia no Kyoiku: Bunken Kara no Apurolhi (Education in Kenya: A Bibliographical Approach)*. Tokyo: Ajia Keizai Kenkyujo, 1990.

Thairu, R. W. "Cataloguing Policies and Problems in Kenyan Libraries." *African Research and Documentation* 40 (1986): 8–15.

————. "Women of Kenya: A Bibliographical Guide." *Maktaba* 2 (2) (1975): 8–16.

Thomas, Ruth A., ed. *Weekly Review Index 1975–1989*. Nairobi: Stellagraphics Ltd., 1993.

Thurston, Anne. *Guide to Archives and Manuscripts Relating to Kenya and East Africa in the United Kingdom*. 2 vols. London: Hans Zell, 1991.

————. "Kenya Copying Project." *African Research and Documentation* 27 (1981): 15–21.

Tirmizi, Sayyid Akbarali Ibrahimali. *Indian Sources for African History: Guide to the Sources of the History of Africa and of the Indian Diaspora in the Basin of the Indian Ocean in the National Archives of India.* 2 vols. Delhi: International Writers' Emporium [with UNESCO], 1988–1989.

Umbima, W. E. *Research in Education on East Africa (Kenya, Tanzania, Uganda): Periodical Articles, Theses, and Research Papers, 1900–1976.* Nairobi: University of Nairobi, Library, 1977.

University of Nairobi. Libraries. *Higher Degree Theses and Dissertations of the University of Nairobi 1970–1979.* Nairobi: University of Nairobi, 1980.

Vaghela, B. G., and J. M. Patel, eds. *East Africa To-Day (1958–1959): Comprehensive Directory of British East Africa with Who's Who.* Bombay: Overseas Information Publishers, 1959.

Von Pischke, J. D. *Bibliography of Agricultural Credit in Kenya.* Nairobi: IDS, 1973.

Wachtel, A., et al. *Bibliography of Urbanisation in Kenya.* Nairobi: IDS, 1974.

Wadsworth, Gail M. *Women in Development: A Bibliography of Materials Available in the Library and Documentation Centre, Eastern and Southern African Management Institute.* Arusha, Tanzania: Eastern and Southern African Management Institute, 1982.

Walford, John. "Colonial Archives and the Kenya National Archives." *African Research and Documentation* (32) (1983): 13–21.

Walker, Audrey A. *Official Publications of British East Africa: Part 3, Kenya and Zanzibar.* Washington, D.C.: Library of Congress, 1963.

Wallenius, Anna-Britta, ed. *Libraries in East Africa.* Uppsala, Sweden: SIAS, 1971.

Webster, John, et al. *Bibliography on Kenya.* Syracuse, NY: Eastern African Studies Program, Syracuse University, 1967.

Who Is Who in Kenyan Politics Today. Nairobi: Kenya Periodicals, 1993.

Who's Who in East Africa, 1963–1964. Nairobi: Marco, 1964.

Who's Who in East Africa, 1965–1966. Nairobi: Marco, 1966.

Who's Who in East Africa, 1967–1968. Nairobi: Marco, 1968.

Wilding, Richard. *Swahili Bibliography of the East African Coast.* Nairobi: Lamu Society, 1990.

———. *Swahili Culture: A Bibliography of the History and People of the Swahili-Speaking World.* Nairobi: Lamu Society, 1976.

Wise, Michael. *Libraries and Information in East and Southern Africa: A Bibliography.* [Birmingham]: International and Comparative Librarianship Group Library Association, 1989.

B. HISTORY: PRECOLONIAL

Allen, James de Vere. "Swahili Culture Reconsidered: Some Historical Implications of the Material Culture of the Northern Kenya Coast in the Eighteenth and Nineteenth Centuries." *Azania* (1974): 105–38.

———— and Thomas H. Wilson, eds. *From Zinj to Zanzibar: Studies in History, Trade and Society on the Eastern Coast of Africa.* London: Variorum Reprints, 1988.

Ambrose, Stanley H. "Excavations at Deloraine, Rongai, 1978." *Azania* 19 (1984): 79–104.

————. "Excavations at Masai Gorge Rockshelter, Naivasha." *Azania* 20 (1985): 29–67.

Amin, Mohamed. *Cradle of Mankind.* London: Chatto and Windus, 1981.

Barbour, Jane, and Simiyu Wandibba. *Kenyan Pots and Potters.* Nairobi: OUP, 1989.

Barut, Sibel. "Later Stone Age Lithic Raw Material Use at Lukenya Hill, Kenya." Ph.D. diss., University of Illinois, 1997.

Batibo, H. M., and M. Bolling. "Outline of Pre-Colonial Pokot History." *Afrikanistische Arbeitspapiere* (1990): 73–93.

Benefit, B. R., and M. L. McCrosson. "New Primate Fossils from the Middle Miocene of Makobo Island, Kenya." *JHE* 18 (5) (1989): 493–97.

Bower, John R. F. "Early Pottery and Other Finds from Kisii District, Western Kenya." *Azania* 13 (1973): 131–40.

————. "Notes on and Archaeological Reconnaissance of Mt. Elgon, Kenya." *Azania* 14 (1974): 223–25.

Boxer, Charles Ralph, and Carlos de Azevedo. *Fort Jesus and the Portuguese in Mombasa, 1593–1729.* London: Hollis and Carter, 1960.

Brantley, Cynthia. "Gerontocratic Government: Age Sets in Pre-Colonial Giriama." *Africa* 48 (3) (1978): 248–64.

Brown, E. Jean. "Excavation of a Group of Burial Mounds at Ilkek Near Gilgil, Kenya." *Azania* 1 (1966): 59–77.

Brown, F. H., and C. S. Feibel. "Revision of Lithostratigraphic Nomenclature in the Koobi Fora region, Kenya." *Journal of the Geological Society* 143 (2) (1986): 297–310.

Bye, Bethany A. "Increased Age Estimate for the Lower Palaeolithic Hominid Site at Olorgesailie, Kenya." *Nature* 6136 (17 September 1987): 237–39.

Chittick, Neville. *Manda: Excavations at an Island Port on the Kenya Coast.* Nairobi: British Institute in Eastern Africa, 1984.

Clark, Carolyn M. "Louis Leakey as Ethnographer: On the Southern Kikuyu before 1903." *CJAS* 23 (3) (1989): 380–98.

Cohen, Mark. "Reassessment of the Stone Bowl Cultures of the Rift Valley Kenya." *Azania* 5 (1970): 27–38.

Cole, Sonia. *Early Man in East Africa.* London: Macmillan, 1958.

————. *Leakey's Luck: The Life of Louis Seymour Bazett Leakey, 1903–1972.* London: Collins, 1975.

————. *Prehistory of East Africa.* London: Weidenfeld and Nicolson, 1964.

Coppens, Yves, et al., eds. *Earliest Man and Environments in the Lake Rudolf Basin: Stratigraphy, Paleoecology and Evolution.* Chicago: University of Chicago Press, 1976.

Davison, S. "Early Pottery on the Tiwi Coast, South of Mombasa." *Azania* 28 (1993): 127–30.

Dugas, Daniel P., and Gregory J. Retallack. "Middle Miocene Fossil Grasses from Fort Ternan, Kenya." *Journal of Paleontology* 1 (1993): 113–28.

Ehret, Christopher, and M. Posnansky, eds. *Archaeological and Linguistic Reconstruction of East African History*. Berkeley: University of California Press, 1982.

Fadiman, Jeffrey A. *Mountain Warriors: The Pre-Colonial Meru of Mt. Kenya*. Athens, OH: Ohio University Center for International Studies, 1976.

Feddes, Andrew, and Cynthia Salvadori. *Turkana: Pastoral Craftmen*. Nairobi: Transafrica, 1977.

Foley, Robert. *Off-Site Archaeology and Human Adaption in Eastern Africa*. Oxford: British Archaeological Reports, 1981.

Freeman-Grenville, G. S. P., ed. and trans. *Mombasa Rising Against the Portuguese, 1631: From Sworn Evidence*. London: OUP, 1980.

Frontera, Ann. "Taveta Economy in the Pre-Colonial Period." *KHR* 5 (1) (1977): 107–14.

Gallagher, Joesph T., ed. *East African Culture History*. Syracuse, NY: Syracuse University, Maxwell School of Citizenship and Public Affairs, 1976.

Galloway, A. "Stone Structures on the Uasin Gishu Plateau, Kenya Colony." *South African Journal of Science* 32 (1935): 656–68.

Gifford-Gonzalez, D. P. "Faunal Assemblages from Masai Gorge Rockshelter and Marula Rockshelter." *Azania* 20 (1985): 69–88.

Hakansson, Thomas N. "Grain, Cattle, and Power: Social Processes of Intensive Cultivation and Exchange in Precolonial Western Kenya." *Journal of Anthropological Research* (1994): 249–76.

Harris, J. M., et al. "Pliocene and Pleistocene Hominid-Bearing Sites from West of Lake Turkana, Kenya." *Science* 4835 (1 January 1988): 27–33.

Harrison, T. "New Postcranial Remains of *Victoriapithecus* from the Middle Miocene of Kenya." *JHE* 18 (1) (1989): 3–54

Hartwig, Gerald W. "Demographic Considerations in East Africa During the Nineteenth Century." *IJAHS* 12 (4) (1979): 653–72.

Herlehy, Thomas J. *Ties That Bind: Palm Wine and Blood-Brotherhood at the Kenya Coast During the Nineteenth Century*. Boston: Boston University, 1983.

Hopwood, A. Tindell. "Miocene Primates from Kenya." *Journal of the Linnaean Society of London (Zoology)* (1933): 437–64.

Huntingford, G. W. B. "Azanian Civilization of Kenya." *Antiquity* 7 (26) (1933): 153–65.

———. "Local Archaeology in Kenya Colony." *JEAUNHS* 7 (1926): 5–26.

Isaac, Glynn Llywelyn. *Olorgesailie: Archaeological Studies of a Middle Pleistocene Lake Basin in Kenya*. Chicago: University of Chicago Press, 1977.

———, Richard E. F. Leakey, and A. K. Behrensmeyer. "Archaeological Traces of Early Hominid Activities, East of Lake Rudolf, Kenya." *Science* (17 September 1971): 1129–34.

———— and E. R. McCown. *Human Origins: Louis Leakey and the East African Evidence.* New York and London: W.A. Benjamin, 1976.

Kaufulu, Zefe M. "Formation and Preservation of Some Earlier Stone Age Sites at Koobi Fora, Northern Kenya." *South African Archaeology Bulletin* 42 (1987): 12–22.

Kimbel, W. H. "Identification of a Partial Cranium of *Australopithecus Afarensis* from the Koobi Fora Formation, Kenya." *JHE* 17 (7) (1988): 647–56.

Kirkman, James S. *Arab City of Gedi: Excavations at the Great Mosque: Architecture and Finds.* London: OUP, 1954.

————. "Culture of the Kenya Coast in the Later Middle Ages." *South African Archaeological Bulletin* 11 (44) (1956): 88–99.

————. "Excavations at Kilepwa: An Introduction to the Medieval Archaeology of the Kenya Coast." *Antiquaries Journal* 32 (3/4) (1952): 168–84.

————. *Gedi: The Palace.* The Hague: Mouton, 1963.

————. "Great Pillars of Malindi and Mambrui." *Oriental Art* 4 (2) (1958): 55–67.

————. "Historical Archaeology in Kenya 1948–1956." *Antiquaries Journal* 37 (1/2) (1957): 16–28.

————. "Potters' Marks from Medieval Arab Sites in Kenya." *South African Archaeological Bulletin* 13 (52) (1958): 156–59.

Koch, Christopher P. "Vertebrate Taphonomy and Palaeoecology of the Olorgesailie Formation (Middle Pleistocene, Kenya)." Ph.D. diss., University of Toronto, 1986.

Lamphear, John. "Kamba and Northern Mrima Coast." In *Pre-Colonial African Trade: Essays on Trade in Central and Eastern Africa Before 1900*, edited by Richard Gray and David Birmingham, 75–101. London: OUP, 1970.

Leakey, Louis Seymour Bazett. *By the Evidence.* London: Collins, 1974.

————. "Outline of the Stone Age in Kenya." *South Africa Journal of Science* 26 (1929): 749–57.

————. "Stone-Age Archaeology of Kenya Colony." Ph.D. diss., Cambridge: Cambridge University, 1930.

————. *Stone Age Cultures of Kenya Colony.* Cambridge: The University Press, 1931.

————. *Stone Age Races of Kenya.* Oxford: OUP, 1935.

————. *White African: An Early Autobiography.* London: Hodder and Stoughton, 1937.

Leakey, Maeve G., et al. "New Four-Million-Year-Old Hominid Species from Kanapoi and Allia Bay, Kenya." *Nature* 376 (17 August 1995): 565–71.

Leakey, Mary Douglas. *Disclosing the Past: An Autobiography.* Garden City, NY: Doubleday and Company, 1984.

————. "Report on the Excavation at Hyrax Hill, Nakuru, Kenya Colony, 1937–38." *Transactions of the Royal Society of South Africa* 30 (1945/1946): 271–409.

————, and Louis Seymour Bazett Leakey. *Excavations at the Njoro River Cave: Stone Age Cremated Burials in Kenya Colony.* London: OUP, 1950.

Leakey, Richard, and Roger Lewin. *Origins.* New York: E. P. Dutton, 1977.
————. *Origins Reconsidered: In Search of What Makes Us Human.* Boston: Doubleday, 1993.
————. *People of the Lake: Mankind and Its Beginnings.* Garden City, NY: Anchor Press/Doubleday, 1978.
————, and B. A. Wood. "New Evidence of the Genus Homo from East Rudolf, Kenya." *American Journal of Physical Anthropology* 41 (2) (1974): 237–43.
Le Gros Clark, Wilfrid E. "Fossil Hominoids from Kenya." *Proceedings of the Zoological Society of London* (1952): 273–86.
Lofgren, Laurel. "Stone Structures of South Nyanza, Kenya." *Azania* 2 (1967): 75–88.
McCrossin, Monte L., and Brenda R. Benefit. "Recently Discovered Kenyapithecus Mandible and Its Implications for Great Ape and Human Origins." *Proceedings of the National Academy of Sciences of the United States of America* 5 (1 March 1993): 1962–66.
McKay, W. F. "A Pre-colonial History of the Southern Kenya Coast." Ph.D. diss., Boston University, 1975.
Marsden, Michael. "Origin and Evolution of the Pleistocene Olorgesailie Lake Series: Kenya Rift Valley." Ph.D. diss., McGill University, 1979.
Merrick, H. V., and M. C. Monaghan. "Date of the Cremated Burials in Njoro River Cave." *Azania* 19 (1984): 7–11.
Mgomezulu, Gadi G. Y. "Recent Archaeological Research and Radiocarbon Dates from Eastern Africa." *JAH* 22 (4) (1981): 435–56.
Morley, C. K., et al. "Tectonic Evolution of the Northern Kenyan Rift." *Journal of the Geological Society* (1992): 333–48.
Morrell, Virginia. *Ancestral Passions: The Leakey Family and the Quest for Humankind's Beginnings.* New York: Simon and Schuster, 1995.
Munro, J. Forbes. "Migrations of the Bantu-Speaking Peoples of the Eastern Kenya Highlands: A Reappraisal." *JAH* 8 (1) (1967): 25–8.
Mutoro, Henry. "An Archaeological Study of the Mijikenda Kay Settlements on the Hinterland Kenya Coast." Ph.D. diss., University of California, Los Angeles, 1987.
Mwaniki, Henry S. "Precolonial History of the Chuka of Mount Kenya c. 1400–1908." Ph.D. diss., Dalhousie University, 1982.
Nelson, C. "Comparative Analysis of Thirteen Later Stone Age Sites in East Africa." Ph.D. diss., University of California, Berkeley, 1973.
Ng'ang'a, Patrick. "Ostracode Typology and Oxygen Isotopes in Carbonates: A Comparison of Methods in Paleoclimate Reconstruction, Lake Turkana, Kenya." Ph.D. diss., Duke University, 1996.
Ochieng', William Robert. *An Outline History of the Rift Valley of Kenya up to AD 1900.* Nairobi: EALB, 1975.
————. *Pre-Colonial History of the Gusii of Western Kenya from c. 1500 to 1914.* Kampala, Uganda: EALB, 1974.

Odner, Knut. "Excavations at Narosura, A Stone Bowl Site in the Southern Kenya Highlands." *Azania* 7 (1972): 25–92.

Ogot, Bethwell A., ed. *Kenya Before 1900: Eight Regional Studies*. Nairobi: EAPH, 1976.

———. *Kenya in the Nineteenth Century*. Nairobi: Bookwise, 1985.

Olago, D. D. "Late Quaternary Lake Sediments of Mount Kenya, Kenya." D.Phil. diss., Oxford University, 1995.

Oliver, Roland. "Problem of Bantu Expansion." *JAH* 7 (1966): 361–76.

Onyango-Abuje, J. C. "A Contribution to the Study of the Neolithic in East Africa with Particular Reference to Nakuru-Naivasha Basins." Ph.D. diss., University of California, Berkeley, 1977.

———. "L. S. B. Leakey: The Man and His Contribution to the Understanding of the Evolution of Man in Africa." *JEARD* 5 (2) (1975): 121–36.

Parkinson, John. *The Dinosaur in East Africa*. London: H. F. and G. Witherby, 1930.

Phillipson, D.W. *Later Prehistory of Eastern and Southern Africa*. New York: Africana, 1977.

Plummer, Thomas W., and Richard Potts. "Excavations and New Findings at Kanjera, Kenya." *JHE* 18 (3) (1989): 269–76.

———. "Hominid Fossil Sample from Kanjera, Kenya: Description, Provenance, and Implications of New and Earlier Discoveries." *American Journal of Anthropology* (1995): 7–23.

Posnansky, Merrick, ed. "Cairns in the Southern Part of the Kenya Rift Valley." *Azania* 3 (1968): 181–87.

———. "Excavations at Lanet, Kenya." *Azania* 2 (1967): 89–114.

———. *Prelude to East African History*. London: OUP, 1966.

———, and B. Grinrod. "Iron Smelting Furnaces at North Kinangop." *Azania* 3 (1968): 191–95.

Potts, R. "Olorgesailie: New Excavations and Findings in Early and Middle Pleistocene Contexts, Southern Kenya Rift Valley." *JHE* 18 (5) (1989): 477–84.

Ricketts, Richard Douglas. "Paleoclimate Interpretation of Stable Isotope Records from Inorganic Carbonates, Lakes Malawi and Turkana, East Africa." Ph.D. diss., Duke University, 1996.

Robbins, Lawrence H. "Archaeology in the Turkana District, Kenya." *Science* (28 April 1972): 359–66.

———. *Lopoy—A Late Stone Age Fishing and Pastoralist Settlement in the Lake Turkana Basin, Kenya*. East Lansing: Michigan State University Press, 1980.

Robertshaw, Peter. *Early Pastoralists of South-Western Kenya*. Nairobi: British Institute in Eastern Africa, 1990.

Ruff, C. B., et al. "Body Mass, Sexual Dimorphism and Femoral Proportions of *Proconsul* from Rusinga and Mfangano Islands, Kenya." *JHE* 18 (6) (1989): 515–36.

Sassoon, Caroline. *Chinese Porcelain Marks from Coastal Sites in Kenya: Aspects* of Trade in the Indian Ocean, XIV-XIX Centuries. Oxford: British Archaeological Reports, 1978.

Schmidt, Peter R. Iron Technology in East Africa: Symbolism, Science and Archaeology. Oxford: James Currey, 1997.

Scholfield, John Frank. "City of Gedi, Kenya." South African Archaeological Bulletin 10 (38) (1955): 35–42.

Shipman, Pat. Reconstructing the Paleoecology and Taphonomic History of Ramapithecus Wickeri at Fort Ternan, Kenya. Columbia, MO: Museum of Anthropology, University of Missouri-Columbia, 1982.

Siiriainen, Ari. "Iron Age Site at Gatung'ang'a, Central Kenya: Contributions to the Gumba Problem." Azania 1 (1971): 219–39.

Sikes, Nancy E. "Early Hominid Habitat Preferences in East Africa: Stable Isotopic Evidence from Paleosols." Ph.D. diss., University of Illinois, 1995.

Soper, Robert. "Archaeological Sites in the Chyulu Hills, Kenya." Azania 11 (1976): 83–116.

———. "Kwale: An Early Iron Age Site in South-Eastern Kenya." Azania 2 (1967): 1–17.

———. "Petroglyphs in Northern Kenya." Azania 3 (1968): 189–91.

———. "Radiocarbon Dating of 'Dimple-Based Ware' in Western Kenya." Azania 4 (1969): 148–53.

Spear, Thomas Turner. Kaya Complex: A History of the Mijikenda Peoples of the Kenya Coast to 1900. Nairobi: KLB, 1978.

———. Kenya's Past: An Introduction to Historical Method in Africa. London: Longman, 1981.

Stern, Nicola, et al. "Structure of the Lower Pleistocene Archaeological Record: A Case Study from the Koobi Fora Formation." Current Anthropology 3 (1993): 201–26.

Stiles, Daniel. "Azanian Civilization and Megalithic Cushites Revisited." Kenya Past and Present 16 (1983): 20–27.

Sutton, John Edward Giles. Archaeology of the Western Highlands of Kenya. Nairobi: British Institute in Eastern Africa, 1973.

———. "Deloraine: Further Excavations and the Iron Age Sequence of the Central Rift." Azania 28 (1993): 103–25.

———. "Later Prehistory of the Western Highlands of Kenya." Ph.D. diss., Makerere University, 1964.

———. "Review of Pottery from the Kenya Highlands." South African Archaeological Bulletin 19 (74) (1964): 27–35.

———. "Some Reflections on the Early History of Western Kenya." In Hadith 2: Proceedings of the 1968 Conference of the Historical Association of Kenya, 1967, edited by Bethwell A. Ogot, 17–29. Nairobi: EAPH, 1970.

Toth, N. "Olduwan Reassessed: A Close Look at Early Stone Artifacts." Journal of Archaeology Science 12 (2) (1985): 101–20.

Walker, Alan, and Richard Leakey, eds. Nariokotome Homo Erectus Skeleton. Cambridge, MA: Harvard University Press, 1993.

Were, Gideon S. "Ethnic Interaction in Western Kenya: The Emergence of the Abaluyia up to 1850." *KHR* 2 (1) (1974): 39–44.

West, Jolee Ann. "Taphonomic Investigation of Aquatic Reptiles (Crocodylus, Trionyx, and Pelusios) at Lake Turkana, Kenya: Significance for Early Hominid Ecology at Olduvai Gorge, Tanzania." Ph.D. diss., University of Illinois, 1995.

Wilding, Richard. "Ancient Buildings of the North Kenyan Coast." *Plan East Africa* 3 (2) (1972): 41–46.

Wilson, T. H. *Monumental Architecture and Archaeology North of the Tana River.* Nairobi: National Museums of Kenya, 1978.

———. *Monumental Architecture and Archaeology of the Central and Southern Kenya Coast.* Nairobi: National Museums of Kenya, 1980.

———. "Swahili Funerary Architecture of the North Kenya Coast." *Art and Archaeology Research Papers* (1979): 33–46.

Wright, R. "Painted Rock Shelter on Mt. Elgon, Kenya." *Proceedings of the Prehistoric Society* 2 (1961): 28–34.

Ylvisaker, M. "Ivory Trade in the Lamu Area, 1600–1870." *Paideuma* (1982): 221–31.

———. *Lamu in the Nineteenth Century: Land, Trade, Politics.* Boston: African Studies Center, Boston University, 1979.

C. HISTORY: COLONIAL PERIOD

Aaronovitch, Samuel, and K. Aaronovitch. *Crisis in Kenya.* London: Lawrence and Wishart, 1947.

Abour, C. Ojwando. *White Highlands No More.* Nairobi: Pan African Researchers, 1971.

Adewoye, O. "Nationalism in Kenya, 1920–63." *Tarikh* 4 (1) (1971): 28–40.

Ainsworth, John. "British East Africa Protectorate: Early History and Development. The Native Tribes and Their Progress." *The Journal of the Manchester Geographical Society* 29 (1913): 10–22.

———. "Commercial Possibilities of Kenya Colony." *The Journal of the Manchester Geographical Society* 37/38 (1921/1922): 53–63.

———. "Description of the Ukamba Province East Africa Protectorate and Its Progress Under British Administration." *The Journal of the Manchester Geographical Society* 26 (1900): 178–96.

———. "East Africa Protectorate and Development." *East Africa Quarterly* (1906): 840–47.

Ambler, Charles H. *Kenyan Communities in the Age of Imperialism: The Central Region in the Late Nineteenth Century.* New Haven, CT: YUP, 1988.

———. "Renovation of Custom in Colonial Kenya: The 1932 Generation Succession Ceremonies in Embu." *JAH* 30 (1) (1989): 139–56.

Anderson, David M. "Black Mischief: Crime, Protest and Resistance in Colonial Kenya." *Historical Journal* 36 (4) (1993): 851–77.

————. "Stock Theft and Moral Economy in Colonial Kenya." *Africa* 56 (4) (1986): 399–416.

Archer, Sir Geoffrey. *Personal and Historical Memoirs of an East African Administrator.* London: Oliver and Boyd, 1963.

Aschan, Ulf. *The Man Who Women Loved: The Life of Bror Blixen.* New York: St. Martin's Press, 1987.

Askwith, Tom. *From Mau Mau to Harambee,* edited by Joanna Lewis. Cambridge: African Studies Centre Publications, 1995.

Atieno-Odhiambo, E. S. "Colonial Government, the Settlers, and the 'Trust' Principle in Kenya to 1939." *TJH* 2 (2) (1972): 94–113.

————. "History of the Kenya Executive Council, 1907–1939." Ph.D. diss., University of Nairobi, 1973.

————. *SIASA: Politics and Nationalism in E.A. 1905–1939.* Nairobi: KLB, 1981.

————. "Some Reflections on African Initiative in Early Colonial Kenya." *EAJ* 8 (1) (1971): 30–36.

Barber, James. *Imperial Frontier.* Nairobi: EAPH, 1968.

Beard, Peter. *Longing for Darkness: Kamante's Tales from Out of Africa.* New York and London: Harcourt Brace Jovanovich, 1975.

Bennett, George. "Development of Political Organizations in Kenya." *Political Studies* 5 (2) (1957): 113–30.

————. "Early Parliamentary Developments in the Kenya Legislative Council." *Parliamentary Affairs* 10 (3) (1957): 296–307; 10 (4) (1957): 469–79.

————. "Imperial Paternalism: The Representation of African Interests in the Kenya Legislative Council." In *Essays in Imperial Government,* edited by Kenneth Robinson and F. Madden, 142–62. Oxford: Basil Blackwell, 1963.

————. *Kenya, A Political History: The Colonial Period.* Oxford: OUP, 1963.

————. "Kenya's Frustrated Election." *WT* 17 (6) (1961): 254–61.

————. "Kenyatta and the Kikuyu." *International Affairs* 37 (4) (1961): 356–61.

————. "Paramountcy to Partnership: J. H. Oldham and Africa." *Africa* 30 (4) (1960): 356–61.

————. "Political Realities in Kenya." *WT* 19 (7) (1963): 294–301.

————, and Carl G. Rosberg. *Kenyatta Election: Kenya 1960–61.* Oxford: OUP, 1961.

Berman, Bruce J. "Administration and Politics in Colonial Kenya." Ph.D. diss., Yale University, 1974.

————. *Control and Crisis in Colonial Kenya: The Dialectic of Domination.* Athens, OH: Ohio University Press, 1990.

————, and John M. Lonsdale. *Unhappy Valley: Conflict and Africa.* 2 vols. London: James Currey, 1992.

Best, Nicholas. *Happy Valley: The Story of the English in Kenya.* London: Secker and Warburg, 1979.

Binks, Herbet K. *African Rainbow.* London: Sidgwick and Jackson, 1959.

Blixen, Karen [Isak Dinesen]. *Out of Africa*. New York: Random House, 1938.
————. *Shadows on the Grass*. New York: Random House, 1960.
Blixen-Finecke, Bror. *African Hunter*. New York: St. Martin's Press, 1986.
————. *Bror Blixen: The Africa Letters*. New York: St. Martin's Press, 1988.
Blundell, Michael. *Love Affair with the Sun: A Memoir of Seventy Years in Kenya*. Nairobi: Kenway Publications, 1994.
————. "Making a Nation in Kenya." *AA* 58 (232) (1959): 221–28.
————. "Present Situation in Kenya." *AA* 54 (215) (1955): 99–108.
————. *So Rough a Wind*. London: Weidenfeld and Nicolson, 1964.
Bogonko, Sorobea Nyachieo. *Kenya 1945–1963: A Study in African National Movements*. Nairobi: KLB, 1980.
Bollig, Michael. "The Imposition of Colonial Rule in North West Kenya: Interethnic Conflicts and Anti-Colonial Resistance." *Afrikaanse Arbeitspap* 11 (1987): 5–39.
Boyes, John. *Company of Adventurers*. London: East Africa, 1927.
————. *John Boyes, King of the Wa-Kikuyu*. London: Methuen, 1911.
Brantley, Cynthia. *Giriama and Colonial Resistance in Kenya, 1800–1920*. Berkeley: University of California Press, 1981.
Breen, Rita M. "Politics of Land: The Kenya Land Commission (1932–33) and Its Effects on Land, Policy in Kenya." Ph.D. diss., Michigan State University, 1976.
Brockway, Fenner. *Outside the Right*. London: George Allen and Unwin, 1963.
Brown, Monty. *Where Giants Trod: The Saga of Kenya's Desert Lake*. London: Quiller Press, 1989.
Bunche, Ralph J. "The Land Equation in Kenya Colony As Seen by a Kikuyu Chief." *Journal of Negro History* 24 (1) (1939): 33–43.
Buxton, Clarence. *The Kenya Question*. London: Longman, 1947.
Buxton, M. A. *Kenya Days*. London: Edward Arnold, 1927.
Cameron, Roderick. *Equator Farm*. London: Heinemann, 1955.
Carey-Jones, N. S. "Decolonisation of the White Highlands of Kenya." *GJ* 131 (2) (1965): 186–201.
Carnegie, V. M. *A Kenyan Farm Diary*. Edinburgh: William Blackwood and Sons, 1930.
Caruso, Joseph Samuel. "Politics in Colonial Kenya, 1929–1963: A History of Kilifi District." Ph.D. diss., Columbia University, 1993.
Cashmore, T.H.R. "Random Factor in British Imperialism: District Administration in Colonial Kenya." In *Imperialism, The State and the Third World*, edited by Michael Twaddle, 124–35. London: British Academic Press, 1992.
————. "Studies in District Administration in the East Africa Protectorate, 1895–1918." Ph.D. diss., Cambridge University, 1965.
Cavendish-Bentinck, Ferdinand W. *Urgent Problems in Kenya*. London: Parliamentary Association, 1946.
Cell, John W., ed. *By Kenya Possessed*. Chicago: University of Chicago Press, 1976.
Church, Archibald George. *Our Newest Colony*. Nairobi: East African Standard Press, 1910.

Churchill, Winston S. *My African Journey.* London: Hodder and Stoughton, 1908.

Clayton, Anthony, and Donald Savage. *Government and Labour in Kenya.* London: Frank Cass, 1974.

Clough, Marshall S. *Fighting Two Sides: Kenyan Chiefs and Politicians, 1918–1940.* Boulder: University Press of Colorado, 1990.

Cobbold, Evelyn. *Kenya: The Land of Illusion.* London: John Murray, 1935.

Cole, Eleanor. *Random Recollections of a Pioneer Kenya Settler.* Woodbridge, UK: Baron, 1975.

Cooper, Frederick. *From Slaves to Squatters: Plantation Labor and Agriculture in Zanzibar and Coastal Kenya, 1890–1925.* New Haven, CT: YUP, 1980.

Coray, Michael S. "Kenya Land Commission and the Kikuyu of Kiambu." *Agricultural History* 52 (1) (1978): 179–95.

Cranworth, Lord. *Colony in the Making or Sport and Profit in British East Africa.* London: Macmillan and Company Ltd., 1912.

———. *Kenya Chronicles.* London: Macmillan and Company Ltd., 1939.

———. "Kenya Colony—Her Present Progress and Future Possibilities." *United Empire* 17 (5) (1926): 260–69.

———. *Profit and Sport in British East Africa.* London: Macmillan and Company Ltd., 1919.

Curtin, Patricia W. Romero. "Lamu and Suppression of the Slave Trade." *Slavery Abolition: A Journal of Comparative Politics* 7 (2) (1986): 148–59.

———. "'Where Have All the Slaves Gone?' Emancipation and Post-Emancipation in Lamu, Kenya." *JAH* 27 (3) (1986): 481–512.

Curtis, Arnold., ed. *Memories of Kenya: Stories from the Pioneers.* London: Evans Brothers, 1986.

Davis, Alexander. *Microcosm of Empire (British East Africa).* Nairobi: Caxton Printing and Publishing Company, 1917.

———, and H. J. Robertson. *Chronicles of Kenya.* London: C. Palmer, 1928.

De Kiewiet, Marie. "History of the Imperial British East Africa Company, 1876 to 1895." Ph.D. diss., University of London, 1955.

Dilley, Marjorie Ruth. *British Policy in Kenya Colony.* New York: Barnes and Noble, 1966.

Donelson, Linda G. *Out of Isak Dinesen in Africa: The Untold Story.* Iowa City, IA: Coulsong List, 1995.

Douglas-Home, Charles. *Evelyn Baring: The Last Proconsul.* London: Collins, 1984.

Duder, C. J. D., and G. L. Simpson. "Land and Murder in Colonial Kenya: The Leroghi Land Dispute and the Powys 'Murder' Case." *JICH* 25 (1997): 440–65.

Duder, C. J. D., and Christopher P. Youé. "Paice's Place: Race and Politics in Nanyuki District, Kenya, in the 1920s." *AA* 93 (371) (1994): 253–78.

Duignan, Peter. "Sir Robert Coryndon: A Model Governor (1870–1925)." In *African Proconsuls: European Governors in Africa,* edited by Lewis H. Gann and Peter Duignan, 313–52. New York: The Free Press, 1978.

Dutton, E. A. T. *Lillibullero or the Golden Road*. Zanzibar: Printed Privately by Hamish Craigie, 1946.

Dwarkadas, Jamnadas. "Kenya Question." *Asiatic Review* (1923): 378–85.

Eliot, Sir Charles. *East Africa Protectorate*. London: Edward Arnold, 1905.

————. "East Africa Protectorate." In *Empire and the Century*, edited by C. S. Goldman, 861–76. London: John Murray, 1905.

————. "East African Protectorate As a European Colony." *Nineteenth Century and After* 56 (331) (1904): 370–85.

————. "Native Races of the British East Africa Protectorate." *Journal of the Royal Anthropological Institute* 18 (1905): 105–21.

————. "Progress and Problems of the East Africa Protectorate." *Proceedings of the Royal Colonial Institute* 37 (1905/1906): 81–111.

Ellis, Diana. "Nandi Protest of 1923 in the Context of African Resistance to Colonial Rule in Kenya." *JAH* 17 (4) (1976): 555–75.

Engholm, G. F. "African Elections in Kenya, March 1957." In *Five Elections in Africa*, edited by W. J. M. Mackenzie and K. E. Robinson, 391–461. Oxford: Clarendon Press, 1960.

————. "Kenya's First Direct Elections for Africans, March 1957." *Parliamentary Affairs* 10 (4) (1957): 424–33.

Fabian Society. Colonial Bureau. *Kenya Controversy*. London: Fabian Publications and Victor Gollancz, 1947.

————. *Opportunity in Kenya*. London: Fabian Publications, 1953.

————. *White Man's Country*. London: Fabian Publications, 1944.

————. *Opportunity in Kenya: A Report to the Fabian Colonial Bureau*. London: Fabian Colonial Bureau, 1953.

Fadiman, Jeffrey A. *Moment of Conquest: Meru, Kenya, 1907*. Athens, OH: Ohio University Press, 1979.

Fane, Rebecca. "Nationalism in Kenya." *AA* 55 (221) (1956): 294–96.

Farrant, Leda. *Legendary Grogan*. London: Hamish Hamilton, 1981.

Farson, Negley. *Behind God's Back*. London: Victor Gollancz, 1940.

————. *Last Chance in Africa*. New York: Harcourt, Brace, 1950.

Flint, John E. "Frederick Lugard: The Making of an Autocrat (1858–1943)." In *African Proconsuls: European Governors in Africa*, edited by Lewis H. Gann and Peter Duignan, 290–312. New York: The Free Press, 1978.

Fox, James. *White Mischief: The Murder of Lord Erroll*. London: Jonathan Cape, 1982.

Frost, Richard A. *Enigmatic Proconsul: Sir Philip Mitchell and the Twilight of Empire*. London and New York: Radcliffe Press, 1992.

————. *Race Against Time*. London: Rex Collings, 1978.

————. "Sir Philip Mitchell, Governor of Kenya." *AA* 78 (313) (1979): 535–53.

————. "Trusteeship, Discrimination and Attempts to Promote Interracial Cooperation in Kenya, 1945–1963." D.Phil. diss., Oxford University, 1972.

Gilbert, A. J. "Closer Union in British East Africa: The Controversy, 1923–31." Ph.D. diss., University of Bristol, 1979.

Githumo, Mwangi wa. "Controversy over Jewish Ante-Chamber in Kenya: British Settlers' Reaction to the Proposed Jewish Settlement Project in Kenya, 1902–1905." *TJH* 22 (1993): 87–99.

————. *Land and Nationalism: The Impact of Land Expropriation and Land Grievances upon the Rise and Development of Nationalist Movements in Kenya, 1885–1939.* Lanham, MD: University Press of America, 1981.

Gold, Alice E. "Nandi in Transition: Background to the Nandi Resistance to the British 1896–1906." *KHR* 6 (1/2) (1978): 84–104.

Goldsmith, F. H., ed. *John Ainsworth: Pioneer Kenya Administrator, 1864–1946.* London: Macmillan, 1955.

Gordon, David F. "Colonial Crisis and Administrative Response: Kenya 1945–60." *JAS* 6 (2) (1979): 98–111.

————. *Decolonization and the State in Kenya.* Boulder, CO: WP, 1986.

Grant, Nellie. *Nellie's Story.* New York: William Morrow, 1981.

Gray, Sir John Milner. *British in Mombasa, 1824–1826.* London: Macmillan, 1957.

Great Britain. *East Africa Royal Commission 1953–1955 Report.* London: HMSO, 1955.

————. *Report of the Kenya Constitutional Conference.* London: HMSO, 1962.

————. Colonial Office. *Kenya Constitution: Summary of the Proposed Constitution for Internal Self-Government.* London: HMSO, 1963.

Gregory, John Walter. *Foundation of British East Africa.* London: Horace Marshall and Son, 1901.

Gregory, Robert G. *Sydney Webb and East Africa Labour's Experiment with the Doctrine of Native Paramountcy.* Berkeley: University of California Press, 1962.

Grigg, Sir Edward. "British Policy in Kenya." *JRAS* 26 (103) (1927): 193–208.

————. "Closer Union in East Africa." *National Review* 97 (1931): 351–56.

————. *The Constitutional Problem in Kenya.* Nottingham: University College, 1933.

———— (Lord Altrincham). *Kenya's Opportunity.* London: Faber and Faber, 1955.

————. "Land Policy and Economic Development in Kenya." *JRAS* 31 (122) (1932): 1–14.

————. "The Problems of Governments in East Africa." *United Empire* 22 (3) (1931): 127–36.

Grogan, Ewart S. *From the Cape to Cairo.* London: Hurst and Blackett, 1900.

Hall, D. "The Native Question in Kenya." *Nineteenth Century and After* 107 (1930): 70–80.

Handbook of British East Africa. Nairobi: Ward and Milligan, 1912.

Hardinge, Sir Arthur H. *A Diplomatist in the East.* London: Jonathan Cape, 1928.

Harris, Joseph E. *Repatriates and Refugees in a Colonial Society: The Case of Kenya.* Washington, D.C.: Howard University Press, 1987.

Hennings, R. O. *African Morning.* London: Chatto and Windus, 1951.

Hickey, Dennis C. "Frontier Banditry and 'Legitimate' Trade: The Moyale Cattle Market, 1913–1923." *Northeast African Studies* 8 (2/3) (1986): 169–79.

Hill, Mervyn F. *Cream Country: The Story of Kenya Co-operative Creameries Limited*. Nairobi: Co-operative Creameries 1956.

————. *Dual Policy in Kenya*. Nakuru: Kenya Weekly News, 1944.

————. "White Settler's Role in Kenya." *Foreign Affairs* 38 (4) (1960): 638–45.

Hindlip, Lord. *British East Africa: Past, Present, and Future*. London: T. Fisher Unwin, 1905.

Hislop, Francis Daniel. *Story of Kenya*. London: OUP, 1961.

Hobley, Charles William. *Kenya: From Chartered Company to Crown Colony*. London: H. F. and G. Witherby, 1929.

Hotchkiss, Willis R. *Then and Now in Kenya Colony: Forty Adventurous Years in East Africa*. London and New York: Fleming H. Revell, 1937.

Hoyt, Alta Howard. *We Were Pioneers*. Wichita, KS: Friends University, 1971.

Hunter, J. A. *Hunter's Tracks*. London: Hamish Hamilton, 1957.

————, and Daniel P. Mannix. *African Bush Adventures*. London: Hamish Hamilton, 1954.

————. *Tales of the African Frontier*. New York: Harper and Brothers, 1954.

Huxley, Elspeth. *Flame Trees of Thika: Memories of an African Childhood*. New York: Morrow, 1959.

————. *Mottled Lizard*. London: Chatto and Windus, 1962.

————. *Nellie: Letters from Kenya*. London: Weidenfeld and Nicholson, 1980.

————. *New Earth: An Experiment in Colonialism*. London: Chatto and Windus, 1960.

————. *Nine Faces of Kenya: Portrait of a Nation*. London: Collins Harvill, 1990.

————. *No Easy Way: A History of the Kenya Farmers' Association and Unga Limited*. Nairobi: East African Standard Ltd., 1957.

————. *Out in the Midday Sun: My Kenya*. New York: Viking, 1987.

————. *Red Strangers*. London: Chatto and Windus, 1939.

————. *Settlers of Kenya*. Westport, CT: Greenwood Press, 1975.

————. *Sorcerer's Apprentice*. London: Chatto and Windus, 1948.

————. *White Man's Country: Lord Delamere and the Making of Kenya*. 2 vols. London: Chatto and Windus, 1935.

————, and Arnold Curtis, eds. *Pioneers' Scrapbook: Reminiscences of Kenya 1890 to 1968*. London: Evans Brothers, 1980.

————, and Margery Perham. *Race and Politics in Kenya: A Correspondence between Elspeth Huxley and Margery Perham*. London: Faber and Faber Ltd., 1944.

Ingham, Kenneth. "Uganda's Old Eastern Province: The Transfer to the East Africa Protectorate in 1902." *Uganda Journal* 21 (1) (1957): 41–46.

Izuakor, Levi I. "Colonial Challenges and Administrative Response: Sir Charles Eliot and 'Native' Trusteeship in Kenya, 1901–1904." *TJH* 17 (1988): 34–49.

————. "Environment of Unreality: Nurturing a European Settlement in Kenya." *Journal of Asian and African Studies* 13 (3/4) (1988): 317–24.

————. "Kenya: Demographic Constraints on the Growth of European Settlement, 1900–1956." *Africa* 42 (3) (1987): 400–16.

Jackson, Sir Frederick. *Early Days in East Africa*. London: Edward Arnold, 1930.

Johnston, Harry H. "British East Africa." In *Oxford Survey of the British Empire: Africa*, edited by A. J. Herbertson and O. J. R. Howairth, 261–80. Oxford: Clarendon Press, 1914.

Kabourou, Aman W. "Maasai Land Case of 1912: A Reappraisal." *TJH* 17 (1988): 1–20.

Kamoche, Jidlaph G. "African Responses to Imposition of British Rule in Central Province, Kenya, 1895–1930." *Umoja* 5 (2) (1981): 1–14.

———. *Imperial Trusteeship and Political Evolution in Kenya 1923–1963: A Study of Official Views and the Road to Decolonization*. Lanham, MD: University Press of America, 1981.

Kennedy, Dane. *Islands of White: Settler Society and Culture in Kenya and Southern Rhodesia, 1890–1939*. Durham, NC: Duke University Press, 1987.

"Kenya: The Settler's Case." *Round Table* 101 (1935): 82–97.

Kenyatta, Jomo. *Kenya: The Land of Conflict*. London: African International Service Bureau, 1945.

King, Kenneth J. "Nationalism of Harry Thuku: A Study in the Beginnings of African Politics in Kenya." *TJH* 1 (1) (1971): 39–59.

Kinyatti, M. *Kenya's Freedom Struggle: The Dedan Kimathi Papers*. London: Zed Books, 1987.

Kipkorir, B.E., ed. *Biographical Essays on Imperialism and Collaboration in Colonial Kenya*. Nairobi: KLB, 1980.

Kirk-Greene, Anthony H. M. "Canada in Africa: Sir Percy Girouard, A Neglected Colonial Governor." *AA* 83 (331) (1984): 207–39.

Kitching, Gavin. *Class and Economic Change in Kenya*. New Haven, CT: YUP, 1980.

Knauss, Peter. "From Devil to Father Figure: The Transformation of Jomo Kenyatta by Kenya Whites." *JMAS* 9 (1) (1971): 131–37.

Komma, Toru. "Language As a Ultra-Human Power and the Authority of Leaders as Marginal Men: Rethinking Kipsigis Administrative Chiefs in the Colonial Period." *Senri Ethnological Studies* 31 (1992): 105–57.

Korir, Kipkoech Motonik arap. "Outline Biography of Simeon Kiplang'at arap Baliach: A 'Colonial African Chief' from Kipsigis." *KHR* 2 (2) (1974): 163–73.

Kyle, K. "Gandhi, Harry Thuku and Early Kenya Nationalism." *Transition* 27 (4) (1966): 16–22.

Lamphear, John. "Aspects of Turkana Leadership during the Era of Primary Resistance." *JAH* 17 (2) (1976): 225–43.

———. *Scattering Time: Turkana Responses to Colonial Rule*. Oxford: Clarendon Press, 1992.

Leakey, Louis Seymour Bazett. *Kenya: Contrasts and Problems*. London: Methuen, 1936.

Leo, Christopher. "Who Benefited from the Million-Acre Scheme? Toward a Class Analysis of Kenya's Transition to Independence." *CJAS* 15 (2) (1981): 201–22.

Leys, Norman Maclean. *Kenya*. London: Hogarth Press, 1924.

————. *Last Chance in Kenya*. London: Hogarth Press, 1931.

Lipscomb, John Francis. *We Built a Country*. London: Faber and Faber, 1956.

————. *White Africans*. London: Faber and Faber, 1955.

Lonsdale, John M. "European Penetration into the Nyanza Province of Kenya, 1890–1914." Ph.D. diss. Cambridge University, 1964.

————. "Political Associations in Western Kenya." In *Protest and Power in Black Africa*, edited by Robert I. Rotberg and Ali Mazrui, 589–638. New York: OUP, 1970.

————. "Crises of Accumulation, Coercion and the Colonial State: The Development of the Labor Control System in Kenya, 1919–1929." *CJAS* 14 (1) (1980): 37–54.

————, and Bruce Berman J. "Coping with the Contradictions: The Development of the Colonial State in Kenya, 1895–1914." *JAH* 20 (4) (1979): 487–505.

Lovell, Mary. *Straight on Until Morning: The Biography of Beryl Markham*. New York: St. Martin's Press, 1987.

Loveridge, Arthur. *Many Happy Days I've Squandered*. New York: Harper and Brothers, 1944.

Lugard, Frederick D. *Dual Mandate in British Tropical Africa*. 1st ed. 1922. Hamden, CT: Archon Books, 1965.

————. *Rise of Our East African Empire*. 2 Vols. Edinburgh and London: Blackwood and Sons, 1893.

McDermott, P. L. *British East Africa or IBEA: A History of the Formation and Work of the Imperial British East Africa Company*. London: Chapman and Hall, 1893.

MacDonald, J. R. L. *British East Africa 1891–1894*. London: Dawsons, 1973.

MacRae, D.S. "Import-Licensing System in Kenya." *JMAS* 17 (1) (1979): 29–46.

Mambo, Robert M. "Nascent Political Activities Among the Mijikenda of Kenya's Coast during the Colonial Era." *TJH* 16 (1987): 92–120.

Markham, Beryl. *West with the Night*. London: Penguin, 1942.

Matson, A. T. *Nandi Resistance to British Rule*. Nairobi: EAPH, 1972.

Maxon, Robert M. "Absence of Political Associations among the Gusii Prior to 1940." *TJH* 10 (1/2) (1981): 112–24.

————. "The Colonial Roots." In *Politics and Administration in East Africa*, edited by Walter O. Oyugi, 33–67. Nairobi: EAEP, 1994.

————. *Conflict and Accommodation in Western Kenya: The Gusii and the British, 1907–1963*. Rutherford, NJ: Farleigh Dickinson University Press, 1989.

————. *John Ainsworth and the Making of Kenya*. Lanham, MD: University Press of America, 1980.

————. "Judgement on a Colonial Governor: Sir Percy Girouard in Kenya." *TJH* 18 (1989): 90–100.

————. "Kenya Currency Crisis, 1919–21 and the Imperial Dilemma." *JICH* 17 (3) (1989): 323–48.

————. "A Kenya Petite Bourgeoisie Enters Local Politics: The Kisii Union, 1945–1949." *IJAHS* 22 (3) (1986): 451–62.

————. *Struggle for Kenya: The Loss and Reassertion of Imperial Initiative, 1912–1923.* Rutherford, NJ: Farleigh Dickinson University Press, 1993.

————, and David Javersak. "Kedong Massacre and the Dick Affair: A Problem in the Early Colonial Historiography of East Africa." *HIA* 8 (1981): 261–69.

Mitchell, Sir Phillip. *African Afterthoughts.* London: Hutchinson, 1954.

Morgan, W. T. W. "The 'White Highlands' of Kenya." *GJ* 129 (2) (1963): 140–55.

Morton, Fred. *Children of Ham: Freed Slaves and Fugitive Slaves on the Kenya Coast, 1873–1907.* Boulder, CO: WP, 1990.

Mungeam, Gordon Hudson. *British Rule in Kenya 1895–1912: The Establishment of Administration in the East Africa Protectorate.* New York: OUP, 1966.

————. "Masai and Kikuyu Responses to the Establishment of British Administration in the East Africa Protectorate." *JAH* 11 (1) (1970): 127–43.

Munro, J. Forbes. *Colonial Rule and the Kamba: Social Change in the Kenya Highlands, 1889–1939.* Oxford: OUP, 1975.

Muriuki, Godfrey. "Kikuyu Reaction to Traders and British Administration, 1850–1904." In *Hadith 1: Proceedings of the Conference of the Historical Association of Kenya, 1967*, edited by Bethwell A. Ogot, 101–18. Nairobi: EAPH, 1968.

Murphy, John F. "Legitimation and Paternalism: The Colonial State in Kenya." *ASR* 29 (3) (1986): 55–65.

Newman, John R. *Ukamba Members Association.* Nairobi: Transafrica, 1974.

Ochieng', William Robert. "Colonial Famines in Luoland, Kenya, 1905–1945." *TJH* 17 (1988): 21–33.

————. "Moralism and Expropriation in a British Colony: The Search for a White Dominion in Kenya, 1895–1923." *Présence Africaine* 133/134 (1985): 214–32.

————, ed. *A Modern History of Kenya, 1895–1980.* London: Evans Brothers, 1989.

Oculi, Okello. "Imperialism, Settlers and Capitalism in Kenya." *Mawazo* 4 (3) (1975): 113–28.

Ogot, Bethwell A. "British Administration in the Central Nyanza District of Kenya, 1900–1960." *JAH* 4 (2) (1963): 249–74.

————, ed. *Politics and Nationalism in Colonial Kenya.* Nairobi: EAPH for Historical Association of Kenya, 1972.

Ogula, Paul H. A. "Political Chief: A Biography of Ex-Senior Chief Mukudi of Samia and Bunyala: c. 1881–1969." *KHR* 2 (2) (1974): 175–87.

Overton, John. "Colonial State and Spatial Differentiation: Kenya, 1895–1920." *Journal of Historical Geography* 13 (3) (1987): 267–82.

————. "Origins of the Kikuyu Land Problem: Land Alienation and Land Use in Kiambu, Kenya, 1895–1920." *ASR* 31 (2) (1988): 109–26.

Parker, Mary. "Race Relations and Political Development in Kenya." *AA* 50 (198) (1951): 41–52.

Patterson, J. H. *In the Grip of the Nyika.* London: Macmillan, 1909.

————. *Man-Eaters of Tsavo and Other East African Adventures*. London: Macmillan, 1907.

————. *Man-Eating Lions of Tsavo*. Chicago: Field Museum of Natural History, 1925.

Percival, Philip H. *Hunting, Settling and Remembering*. Agoura, CA: Trophy Room Books, 1997.

Perham, Margery. *Lugard*. 2 vols. Hamden, CT: Archon Books, 1968.

————, and Mary Bull, eds. *Diaries of Lord Lugard*. 3 vols. London: Faber and Faber, 1959.

————, and Elspeth Huxley. *Race and Politics in Kenya*. London: Faber and Faber, 1956.

Playne, S., ed. *East Africa (British): Its History, People, Commerce, Industries and Resources*. Woking, U.K.: Foreign and Colonial Compiling and Publishing Company, 1908–09.

Preston, R. O. *Descending the Great Rift Valley*. Nairobi: Colonial Printing Works, n.d.

————. *Early Days in East Africa*. Nairobi: Colonial Printing Works, n.d.

————. *Genesis of Kenya Colony*. Nairobi: Colonial Printing Works, 1947.

Rawcliffe, D. H. *Struggle for Kenya*. London: Gollancz, 1954.

Redley, M. G. "Politics of a Predicament: The White Community in Kenya, 1918–1932." Ph.D. diss., Cambridge University, 1977.

Remole, Robert A. "White Settlers, or the Foundation of European Agricultural Settlement in Kenya." Ph.D. diss., Harvard University, 1959.

Renison, Sir Patrick. "The Challenge in Kenya." *Optima* 13 (1) (1963): 8–16.

————. "Kenya in Transition." *AA* 62 (249) (1963): 341–55.

Riddell, Jack. "The Boma Trading Company." *Blackwood's Magazine* 23 (1943): 258–68.

Rogers, P. "British and the Kikuyu, 1890–1905: A Re-Assessment." *JAH* 20 (2) (1979): 255–69.

Ross, W. McGregor. *Kenya from Within: A Short Political History*. London: Frank Cass, 1968.

Russell, John. *Kenya, Beyond the Marich Pass: A District Officer's Story*. London and New York: Radcliffe Press, 1994.

Saberwal, Satish. "Political Change among the Embu of Central Kenya (1900–1964)." *Political Science Review* 12 (1/2) (1973): 35–96.

Salvadori, Max. *La Colonisation Europeene au Kenya*. Paris: Larose Éditeurs, 1938.

Sandford, G. R. *Administrative and Political History of the Masai Reserve*. London: Waterlow and Sons Ltd., 1919.

Sanger, Clyde. *Malcolm Macdonald: Bringing an End to Empire*. Liverpool: Liverpool University Press, 1996.

————, and John Nottingham. "Kenya General Election of 1963." *JMAS* 2 (1) (1964): 1–40.

Scott, H. S. "European Settlement and Native Development in Kenya." *JRAS* 35 (1936): 178–90.

Seitz, Jacob R. "A History of Samia Location in Western Kenya, 1890–1930."
Ph.D. diss., West Virginia University, 1978.

Shimanyula, James Bandi. *Elijah Masinde and the Dini ya Musambwa*. Nairobi:
Transafrica, 1978.

Simpson, Alyse. *Land That Never Was*. Lincoln: University of Nebraska Press,
1937.

Simpson, George L. "Frontier Banditry and the Colonial Decision-Making Process:
The East Africa Protectorate's Northern Borderland Prior to the First World
War." *IJAHS* 29 (2) (1996): 279–308.

———. "On the Frontiers of Empire: British Administration in Kenya's Northern Frontier District, 1905–1935." Ph.D. diss., West Virginia University, 1994.

Smith, Alison. "'Dear Mr. Mboya': Correspondence with a Kenya Nationalist."
JICH 19 (3) (1991): 159–84.

Smith, Mackenzie and Company Limited. *History of Smith, Mackenzie and Company, Limited*. London: East Africa, 1938.

Sorrenson, M. P. K. *Origins of European Settlement in Kenya*. London: OUP, 1968.

Spencer, John. *Kenya African Union*. London: Kegan Paul International, 1985.

———. "Kikuyu Central Association and the Genesis of Kenya Africa Union."
KHR 2 (1) (1974): 67–80.

Spencer, Leon P. "Notes on the Kamba Destocking Controversy of 1938." *IJAHS*
5 (4) (1972): 629–36.

T[ate], H. R. "Opening of British East Africa." *JRAS* 4 (1904): 44–55.

Thomas, T. S. *Jubaland and the Northern Frontier District*. Nairobi: Uganda Railway Press, 1917.

Thomason, M. A. "Little Tin Gods: The District Officer in British East Africa."
Albion 7 (2) (1975): 145–60.

Thurman, J. *Isak Dinesen: The Life of Karen Blixen*. London: Weidenfeld and
Nicolson, 1982.

Tidrick, Kathryn. "Masai and Their Masters: A Psychological Study of District
Administration." *ASR* 23 (1) (1980): 15–31.

Tignor, Robert L. *Colonial Transformation of Kenya: The Kamba, Kikuyu and
Maasai from 1900 to 1939*. Princeton, NJ: Princeton University Press, 1976.

———. "Kamba Political Protest: The Destocking Controversy of 1938." *AHS*
4 (2) (1971): 237–51.

———. "Maasai Warriors: Pattern Maintenance and Violence in Colonial Kenya."
JAH 13 (2) (1972): 271–90.

———. "Race, Nationality, and Industrialization in Decolonizing Kenya, 1945–
1963." *IJAHS* 26 (1) (1993): 31–64.

Trench, Charles Chenevix. *Desert's Dusty Face*. Edinburgh: William Blackwood
and Sons, 1964.

———. *Men Who Ruled Kenya: The Kenya Administration, 1892–1963*. New
York: St. Martin's Press, 1993.

———. "Why a Greek? An East African Frontier in 1905." *History Today* 15 (1)
(1965): 48–56.

Trzebinski, Errol. *Kenya Pioneers*. London: Heinemann, 1985.

————. *The Lives of Beryl Markham: Out of Africa's Hidden Free Spirit and Denys Finch Hatton's Last Great Love*. New York: W. W. Norton, 1993.

————. *Silence Will Speak*. London: Heinemann, 1977.

Turton, Edmond Romilly. "Impact of Mohammad Abdille Hassan in the East Africa Protectorate." *JAH* 10 (4) (1969): 641–57.

————. "Somali Resistance to Colonial Rule and the Development of Somali Political Activity in Kenya 1893–1960." *JAH* 13 (1) (1972): 119–43.

Vere-Hodge, E. R. *Imperial British East Africa Company*. London: Macmillan, 1960.

Waller, Richard. "Maasai and the British 1895–1905: The Origins of an Alliance." *JAH* 17 (4) (1976): 529–53.

Wasserman, Gary. "European Settlers and Kenya Colony: Thoughts on a Conflicted Affair." *ASR* 17 (2) (1974): 425–34.

Watkins, Elizabeth. *Oscar from Africa: The Biography of O. F. Watkins*. London and New York: Radcliffe Press, 1995.

Weisbord, Robert. *African Zion*. Philadelphia: Jewish Publication Society of America, 1968.

Weller, Henry Owen. *Kenya Without Prejudice*. London: East Africa, 1931.

————. *Short History of Kenya Colony*. Nairobi: CMS, 1942.

Whyte, Michael A., and Susan Reynolds Whyte. "Peasants and Workers: The Legacy of Partition among the Luyia-Speaking Nyole and Marachi." *Journal of the Historical Society of Nigeria* 3/4 (1984/1985): 139–58.

Wilson, Christopher J. *One African Colony*. London: McCorquodale, 1945.

Wood, Susan. *Kenya: The Tensions of Progress*. London: OUP, 1962.

Wray, J. Alfred. *Kenya Our New Colony (1882–1912)*. London: Marshall Brothers, 1913.

Wylie, Diana. "Confrontation over Kenya: The Colonial Office and Its Critics, 1918–1940." *JAH* 18 (3) (1977): 427–47.

————. "Norman Leys and McGregor Ross: A Case Study in the Conscience of African Empire, 1900–1939." *JICH* 6 (3) (1977): 294–309.

Wymer, Norman. *Man from the Cape*. London: Evans Brothers Ltd., 1959.

Youé. Christopher P. *Robert Thorne Coryndon: Proconsular Imperialism in Southern and Eastern Africa, 1897–1925*. Waterloo, Canada: Wilfrid Laurier University Press, 1986.

————. "Settler Capital and the Assault on the Squatter Peasantry in Kenya's Uasin Gishu District, 1942–1963." *AA* 87 (348) (1988): 393–418.

Zwanenberg, Roger van. "Background to White Racialism in Kenya." *KHR* 2 (1) (1974): 5–11.

D. HISTORY: INDEPENDENCE PERIOD

Acworth, William. "Interview with Ngugi wa Thiong'o." *Ufahamu* 18 (2) (1990): 41–46.

Ahluwalia, D. Pal. "Democratic Transition in African Politics: The Case of Kenya." *Australian Journal of Political Science*, 23 (3) (1993): 499–514.

————. "Political Succession in Kenya: The Transition from Kenyatta to Moi." *TAR* 12 (2) (1985): 1–12.

————. *Post-Colonialism and the Politics of Kenya*. New York: Nova Science Publishers, 1996.

————. "The 1983 Nyayo Elections: A Quest for Legitimacy." *TAR* 13 (1) (1986): 89–105.

————, and Jeffrey S. Steeves. "Political Power, Political Opposition and State Coercion: The Kenya Case." In *The Political Economy of Crime*, edited by Brian D. Maclean, 93–105. Scarborough, MA: Prentice-Hall, 1986.

Ajulu, Rok. "Kenya: The Road to Democracy." *ROAPE* 53 (1992): 79–87.

————. "The Left and the Question of Democratic Transition in Kenya: A Reply to Mwakenya." *ROAPE* 64 (1995): 229–35.

————. "The 1992 Kenya General Elections: A Preliminary Assessment." *ROAPE* 56 (1993): 98–102.

Amsden, Alice H. "Review of Kenya's Political Economy since Independence." *JAS* 1 (4) (1974): 417–40.

Archer, Jules. *African Firebrand: Kenyatta of Kenya*. New York: Messner, 1969.

Astrow, Andre. "Maina wa Kinyatti: A History of Resistance." *AR* 34 (4) (1989): 55–58.

Barkan, Joel D. "Electoral Process and Peasant-State Relations in Kenya." In *Elections in Independent Africa*, edited by Fred M. Hayward, 213–37. Boulder and London: WP, 1987.

————. "Kenya: Lessons from a Flawed Election." *Journal of Democracy* 4 (3) (1993): 85–99.

————. "Rise and Fall of a Governance Realm in Kenya." In *Governance and Politics in Africa*, edited by Goran Hyden and Michael Bratton, 167–92. Boulder and London: Lynne Rienner, 1991.

————, and Michael Chege. "Decentralising the State: District Focus and the Politics of Reallocation in Kenya." *JMAS* 25 (3) (1989): 431–53.

————, and Njuguna Ng'ethe. "Kenya Tries Again." *Journal of Democracy* 9 (2) (1998): 32–48.

————, and John J. Okumu, eds. *Politics and Public Policy in Kenya and Tanzania*. New York: Praeger, 1984.

Bates, Robert. *Beyond the Miracle of the Market: The Political Economy of Agrarian Development in Kenya*. Cambridge: CUP, 1989.

Bennett, George. "Succession in Kenya." *WT* 24 (8) (1968): 333–38.

Berg-Schlosser, Dirk. "Consociationalism in Kenya." *European Journal of Political Research* 13 (1) (1985): 95–110.

————. "Democracy and the One-Party State in Kenya." In *Democracy and the One-Party State in Africa*, edited by Peter Meyns and Dan Wadada Nabudere, 111–24. Hamburg: Institut für Afrika-Kunde, 1989.

————. "Ethnicity, Social Classes & the Political Process in Kenya." In *Politics and Administration in East Africa*, edited by Walter O. Oyugi, 244–96. Nairobi: EAEP, 1994.

———. "Modes and Meaning of Political Participation in Kenya." *Comparative Politics* 14 (4) (1982): 397–416.

———. *Tradition and Change in Kenya.* Paderborn, Germany: Ferdinand Schoningh, 1984.

Berkeley, Bill. "An Encore for Chaos." *Atlantic Monthly* 277 (2) (1996): 30–36.

Bienen, Henry. *Kenya: The Politics of Participation and Control.* Princeton, NJ: Princeton University Press, 1974.

Biles, Peter. "Rifts in the Opposition." *AR* 37 (4) (1992): 20–23.

———. "Yearning for Democracy." *AR* 36 (6) (1991): 32–34.

Blommaert, J. M. E. "Nation-Building, Democracy and Pragmatic Leadership in Kenya." *Communication and Cognition* 24 (2) (1991): 181–94.

Bourmaud, D. "Élections et Autoritarisme: La Crise de la Régulation Politique au Kenya." *Revue Française de Science Politique* 35 (2) (1985): 106–35.

Brass, W., and C. L. Jolly, eds. *Population Dynamics of Kenya.* Washington: National Academy Press, 1993.

Buijtenhuijs, Robert. "L'Évolution du Kenya Après l'Indépendance." *Revue Française d'Études Politiques Africaines* 87 (1973): 39–65.

———. "Kenya African National Union." *International Journal of Politics* 4 (4) (1974/75): 58–76.

Cable, Vincent. *Whither Kenyan Emigrants?* London: Young Fabian Society, 1969.

Campbell, Horace. "The So-Called National Bourgeoisie in Kenya." *Ufahamu* 7 (2) (1979): 86–118.

Carey-Jones, N. S. *Anatomy of Uhuru.* Manchester, UK: Manchester University Press, 1966.

Cohen, John M. "Importance of Public Service Reform: The Case of Kenya." *JMAS* 31 (3) (1993): 449–76.

Commonwealth Secretariat. Observer Group. *Presidential, Parliamentary and Civic Elections in Kenya: The Report of the Commonwealth Observer Group.* London: Commonwealth Secretariat, 1993.

Court, David, and Kenneth C. Prewitt. "Nation As Region in Kenya: A Note on Political Learning." *British Journal of Political Science* 4 (1) (1974): 109–14.

Cox, R. *Kenyatta's Country.* London: Hutchinson, 1967.

Cross, Sholto. *L'Etat C'est Moi: Political Transition and the Kenya General Election of 1979.* Norwich, UK: School of Development Studies, University of East Anglia, 1983.

Currie, Kate, and Larry Ray. "State and Class in Kenya—Notes on the Cohesion of the Ruling Class." *JMAS* 22 (3) (1984): 559–93.

Cursed Arrow: Contemporary Report on the Politicized Land Clashes in Rift Valley, Nyanza and Western Provinces. Nairobi: National Christian Council of Kenya, 1992.

Dauch, Gene, and Denis Martin. *L'Héritage de Kenyatta: La Transition Politique au Kenya, 1975–1982.* Paris: L'Harmattan, 1985.

Doro, Marion E. "'Human Souvenirs of Another Era': Europeans in Post-Kenyatta Kenya." *AT* 26 (3) (1979): 43–54.

Dubell, F. *Kenya: Från Enpartistat till Demokrati?* Uppsala, Sweden: SIAS, 1994.

Enahoro, Peter. "Kenya: The Kariuki Affair." *Africa* 46 (1975): 12–19.

Fowler, Alan Frederick. "Nongovernmental Organisations and the Promotion of Democracy in Kenya." D.Phil. diss., University of Sussex, 1994.

Fox, Roddy. "Bleak Future for Multi-Party Elections in Kenya." *JMAS* 34 (4) (1996): 597–607.

Gatabaki, Njehu. *Twenty Great Years of Independence 1963–1983.* Nairobi: Productions and Communications, 1983.

Gertzel, Cherry J. "Constitutional Position of the Opposition in Kenya: The Appeal for Efficiency." *EAJ* 4 (6) (1967): 9–11.

———. "Development in the Dependent State: The Kenya Case." *Australian Outlook* 32 (1) (1978): 84–100.

———. "Kenya's Constitutional Changes." *EAJ* 3 (9) (1966): 19–31.

———. "Parliament in Independent Kenya." *Parliamentary Affairs* 19 (4) (1966): 486–504.

———. *Politics of Independent Kenya 1963–1968.* Nairobi: EAPH, 1970.

———. "The Provincial Administration in Kenya." *Journal of Commonwealth Political Studies* 4 (3) (1966): 201–15.

Gibbon, Peter, ed. *Markets, Civil Society and Democracy in Kenya.* Uppsala, Sweden: SIAS, 1995.

Gimode, Edwin. *Tom Mboya: A Biography.* Nairobi: EAEP, 1996.

Godia, George. *Understanding Nyayo: Principles and Policies in Contemporary Kenya.* Nairobi: Transafrica, 1984.

Goldsworthy, David. "Ethnicity and Leadership in Africa: The 'Untypical' Case of Tom Mboya." *JMAS* 20 (1) (1982): 107–26.

———. "Kenyan Politics since Kenyatta." *Australian Outlook* 36 (1) (1982): 27–32.

———. *Tom Mboya: The Man Kenya Wanted to Forget.* Nairobi: Heinemann, 1982.

Good, Kenneth. "Kenyatta and the Organization of KANU." *CJAS* 2 (1968): 115–36.

Gordon, David F. *Decolonization and the State in Kenya.* Boulder, CO: WP, 1986.

Grignon, François. *Understanding Multi-Partyism in Kenya: The 1990–1992 Years.* Nairobi: French Institute for Research in Africa, 1994.

Gupta, Desh Bandhu. "Regional Imbalance and Migration in Kenya." *JAS* 6 (1) (1979): 36–46.

Gupta, Vijay. *Kenya: Politics of (In)dependence.* New Delhi: People's Publishing House, 1981.

Gupta, Vijaya. "Emergence and Decline of Multi-Racialism in Kenya." *United Asia* (1968): 234–42.

Harbeson, John W. *Nation-Building in Kenya: The Role of Land Reform.* Evanston, IL: Northwestern University Press, 1973.

Harris, C. "Persistence and Fragility of Civilian Rule on Kenya." In *Civilian Rule in the Developing World,* edited by C. P. Danopoulos, 125–40. Boulder, CO and London: WP, 1992.

Haugerud, Angelique. *Culture of Politics in Modern Kenya*. Cambridge: CUP, 1995.

Hempstone, Smith. "Kenya: A Tarnished Jewel." *The National Interest* 42 (1995/1996): 50–57.

Hilsum, Lindsey. "Kenya: The Dynamics of Discontent." *AR* 33 (1) (1988): 22–26.

Historical Association of Kenya. *Politics and Nationalism in Kenya*. Nairobi: EAPH, 1972.

Hodder-Williams, Richard. "Kenya after Kenyatta." *WT* 36 (12) (1980): 476–83.

Holmquist, Frank, and Michael D. Ford. "Slouching toward Democracy." *AT* 39 (3) (1992): 97–111.

———. "Stalling Political Change: Moi's Way in Kenya." *CH* 94 (591) (1995): 177–81.

———, and Frederick S. Weaver. "Structural Development of Kenya's Political Economy." *ASR* 37 (1) (1994): 69–105.

Hopkins, Raymond F. "Kenyan Legislature: Political Functions and Citizen Perceptions." In *Legislative Systems in Developing Countries*, edited by G. R. Boynton and Chong Lim Kim, 207–31. Durham, NC: Duke University Press, 1975.

Hornsby, Charles P. W. "Member of Parliament in Kenya, 1969–1983: Election, Background, and Position of the Representative and Its Implications for His Role in the One-Party State." D.Phil. diss., Oxford University, 1985.

———. "Social Structure of the National Assembly in Kenya, 1963–83." *JMAS* 27 (2) (1989): 275–96.

———, and David W. Throup. "Elections and Political Change in Kenya." *Journal of Commonwealth and Comparative Studies* 30 (2) (1992): 172–99.

———. *Triumph of the System: The Rise and Fall of Multiparty Politics in Kenya*. London: James Currey, 1995.

Hyden, Goran, Robert Jackson, and John Okumu, eds. *Development Administration: The Kenyan Experience*. Nairobi: OUP, 1970.

Independent Kenya. London: Zed Press, 1982.

International Republican Institute. *Kenya: The December 29, 1992, Elections*. Washington, D.C.: International Republican Institute, 1993.

———. *Kenya: Pre-Election Assessment Report*. Washington, D.C.: International Republican Institute, 1992.

Jones, Norman Stewart Carey. *Anatomy of Uhuru: Dynamics and Problems of African Independence in an Age of Conflict*. Manchester, UK: Manchester University Press, 1966.

Kamundia, C. A. "Primaries in Kenya." *EAJ* 6 (5) (1969): 9–14.

Karimi, Joseph, and Philip Ochieng. *The Kenyatta Succession*. Nairobi: Transafrica, 1980.

Katz, Stephen. "Succession to Power and the Power of Succession: Nyayoism in Kenya." *JAS* 12 (3) (1985): 155–61.

Kenya. Institute of Administration. *Guide to the Constitutional Development of Kenya*. Nairobi: GP, 1970.

"Kenya's Watershed Elections." *African Business* (1997): 18–21.

Kenyatta, Jomo. *Challenge of Uhuru: The Progress of Kenya, 1968 to 1970.* Nairobi: EAPH, 1971.

————. *Harambee!: The Prime Minister of Kenya's Speeches, 1963–1964.* Nairobi: OUP, 1964.

————. *Suffering without Bitterness: The Founding of the Kenya Nation.* Nairobi: EAPH, 1968.

Khadiagala, Gilbert M. "Kenya: Intractable Authoritarianism." *SAIS Review* 15 (2) (1995): 53–73.

Khapoya, Vincent B. "Kenya under Moi: Continuity or Change?" *AT* 27 (1) (1980): 17–32.

————. "Moi and Beyond: Towards Peaceful Succession in Kenya." *Third World Quarterly* 10 (1) (1988): 54–66.

————. "Politics of Succession in Africa: Kenya After Kenyatta." *AT* 26 (3) (1979): 7–20.

Knauss, Peter. "From Devil to Father Figure: The Transformation of Jomo Kenyatta by Kenyan Whites." *JMAS* 9 (1) (1971): 131–36.

Koff, David. "Kenya's Little General Election." *AR* 11 (7) (1966): 57–60.

Kuria, Gibson Kamau. "Confronting Dictatorship in Kenya." *Journal of Democracy* 2 (4) (1991): 115–26.

Lamb, G. B. "Political Crisis in Kenya." *WT* 17 (12) (1969): 537–44.

"Leakey Factor." *Finance* (30 September 1995): 20–33, 26–27, 30–32, 40.

Leakey, Richard E. F. *One Life: An Autobiography.* London: Michael Joseph, 1983.

Leo, Christopher. *Land and Class in Kenya.* Toronto: University of Toronto Press, 1984.

Leys, Colin. "Capital Accumulation, Class Formation and Dependency: The Significance of the Kenyan Case." In *Socialist Register, 1978*, edited by Ralph Miliband and John Saville, 241–66. London: Merlin Press, 1978.

————. "Kenya: What Does 'Dependency' Explain?" *ROAPE* 27 (1980): 83–105.

————. "Learning from the Kenya Debate." In *Political Development and the New Realism in Sub-Saharan Africa*, edited by David E. Apter and Carl G. Rosberg, 220–43. Charlottesville, VA and London: University Press of Virginia, 1994.

————. "Politics in Kenya: The Development of a Peasant Society." *British Journal of Political Science* 1 (3) (1971): 307–37.

————. *Politics in Kenya: The Political Economy of Neo-Colonialism, 1964–1971.* Berkeley: University of California Press, 1974.

————. *Underdevelopment in Kenya: The Political Economy of Neo-Colonialism.* London: Heinemann, 1975.

Likimani, Muthoni G. *10 Years of Nyayo Era, 1878–1988: Kenya Silver Jubilee, 25 Years of Development, 1963–1988.* Nairobi: Noni's Publicity, 1988.

Maillu, David G. *Pragmatic Leadership: Evaluation of Kenya's Cultural and Political Development, Featuring Daniel arap Moi, President of Republic of Kenya.* Nairobi: Maillu, 1988.

Maina, Kaniaru wa. "Future of Democracy in Kenya." *AT* 39 (1/2) (1992): 122–27.

Maina, Kiongo, and Kaaea wa Macharia. *Matiba: Let the People Decide.* Nairobi: Berisco, 1992.

Makinda, Samuel M. "Kenya: The End of an Illusion." *Race and Class* 24 (3) (1983): 221–44.

———. "Kenya: Out of the Straightjacket, Slowly." *WT* 48 (10) (1992): 188–92.

Mans, Rowland. *Kenyatta's Middle Road in a Changing Africa: A Model for the Future?* London: Institute for the Study of Conflict, 1977.

Maren, Michael Paul. "Hear No Evil." *AR* 31 (6) (1986): 67–71.

———. "Kenya: The Dissolution of Democracy." *CH* 86 (520) (1987): 209–12, 228–29.

Matiba, Kenneth. *Kenya: Return to Reason.* Nairobi: Kalamka, 1993.

Mbithi, P. M., and Carolyn Barnes. *Spontaneous Settlement Problem in Kenya.* Kampala, Uganda: EALB, 1975.

———, and R. Rasmusson. *Self-Reliance in Kenya: The Case of Harambee.* Uppsala, Sweden: SIAS, 1977.

Mboya, Tom. *The Challenge of Nationhood.* New York: Heinemann, 1970.

———. *Freedom and After.* London: Andre Deutsch, 1963.

———. *Kenya Faces the Future.* New York: American Committee on Africa, 1959.

———. *The Kenya Question: An African Answer.* London: Fabian Colonial Bureau, 1956.

Meisler, Stanley. "Changing Kenya." *Mankind* 4 (2) (1973): 24–31.

———. "Tribal Politics Harass Kenya." *Foreign Affairs* 49 (1) (1970): 111–22.

Miller, Norman N. *Assassination and Political Unity: Kenya.* Hanover, NH: American Universities Field Staff Reports, 1969.

M'Inoti, K. "Beyond the 'Emergency' in Northeastern Province." *NLM* (41) (1992): 37–43.

Moi, Daniel T. arap. *Continuity and Consolidation in Kenya: Select Speeches, August 1978–October 1979.* Nairobi: EAPH, 1982.

———. *Kenyan African Nationalism: Nyayo Philosophy and Principles.* London: Macmillan, 1986.

———. *Transition and Continuity in Kenya: Select Speeches, August 1978–October 1979.* Nairobi: EAPH, 1979.

Mueller, Susanne. "Government and Opposition in Kenya, 1966–1969." *JMAS* 22 (3) (1984): 399–427.

Muigai, Githu. "Ethnicity and the Renewal of Competitive Politics in Kenya." In *Ethnic Conflict and Democratization in Africa,* edited by Harvey Glickman, 161–96. Atlanta, GA: African Studies Association Press, 1995.

———. "Kenya's Opposition and the Crisis of Governance." *Issue: A Journal of Opinion* 21 (1/2) (1993): 26–34.

Mulaa, John. "Politics of a Changing Society: Mumias." *ROAPE* (20) (1981): 89–107.

Muriuki, Godfrey. "Central Kenya in the Nyayo Era." *AT* 26 (3) (1979): 39–42.

Murray, John. "Succession Prospects in Kenya." *AR* 13 (11) (1968): 44–48.

Murungi, Kiraitu. *Ethnicity and Multi-Partyism in Kenya.* Nairobi: Kenya Human Rights Commission, 1995.

———. "President Moi and the Decline of Democracy in Kenya." *TransAfrica Forum* 8 (1991/1992): 3–17.

Mutiso, G. C. M. *Kenya: Politics, Policy and Society.* Nairobi: EALB, 1975.

Mutua, Makau wa. "Break with the Past?" *AR* 37 (1) (1992): 21–24.

———. "Changing of the Guard." *AR* 37 (6) (1992): 56–58.

———. "Politics of Doom." *AR* 37 (3) (1992): 13–16.

———. "Troubled Transition." *AR* 37 (5) (1992): 34–38.

Mwakenya. "Democratisation in Kenya: Should the Left Participate or Not?" *ROAPE* 1 (1994): 475–78.

National Election Monitoring Unit. *Courting Disaster: Report on the Continuing Terror, Violence, and Destruction in the Rift Valley, Nyanza, and Western Provinces of Kenya.* Nairobi: NEMU, 1993.

———. *Multi-Party General Election in Kenya.* Nairobi: NEMU, 1993.

Ndegwa, Stephen N. "Civil Society and Political Change in Africa: The Case of Non-Governmental Organizations in Kenya." *International Journal of Comparative Sociology* 35 (1/2) (1994): 19–36.

———. *NGOs as Pluralizing Agents in Civil Society in Kenya.* Nairobi: IDS, 1993.

Ndeti, Kivuto. *Cultural Values and Population Policy in Kenya.* Nairobi: KLB, 1980.

Ndumbu, Abel. "Seven Years of Nyayo." *AR* 30 (6) (1985): 51–53.

Nellis, John R. "Expatriates in the Government of Kenya." *Journal of Commonwealth Political Studies* 11 (3) (1973): 251–64.

———. "Three Aspects of the Kenyan Administrative System." *Culture et Développement* 3 (1973): 541–70.

Ngau, Peter N. "Tensions in Empowerment: The Experience of the Harambee (Self-Help) Movement in Kenya." *Economic Development and Cultural Change* 35 (3) (1987): 523–38.

Njiro, Stephen. *Daniel arap Moi: Man of Peace, Love and Unity.* Nairobi: Transafrica, 1980.

Njonjo, Apollo. "The Africanization of the 'White Highlands': A Study in Agrarian Class Struggles in Kenya, 1950–1974." Ph.D. diss., Princeton University, 1977.

Nyang'oro, Julius E. "Quest for Pluralist Democracy in Kenya." *Transafrican Forum* 7 (3) (1990): 73–83.

Nyong'o, Peter Anyang'. *Challenge of National Leadership and Democratic Changes in Kenya.* Nairobi: Shirikon Publishers, 1993.

———. "Class Struggles in Kenya." *Mawazo* 5 (2) (1983): 25–42.

———. "Decline of Democracy and the Rise of Authoritarian and Factionalist Politics in Kenya." *Horn of Africa* 6 (3) (1983/84): 25–34.

———. "State and Society in Kenya: The Disintegration of the Nationalist Coalitions and the Rise of Presidential Authoritarianism 1963–78." *AA* 88 (351) (1989): 229–51.

Ochieng', William Robert. "Tribalism and National Unity: The Kenyan Case." In *Politics and Leadership in Africa*, edited by Aloo Ojuka and William Robert Ochieng', 254–71. Nairobi: EALB, 1975.

Odinga, Oginga. *Not Yet Uhuru: An Autobiography*. New York: Hill and Wang, 1967.

Ofcansky, Thomas P. "Future Stability of Kenya." *Journal of Defence and Diplomacy* 6 (9) (1988): 57–60, 62.

Ogot, B. A. and W. R. Ochieng', eds. *Decolonization and Independence in Kenya, 1940–93*. Nairobi: EAEP, 1995.

Ogutu, Gilbert Edwin Meshack. *Ker Jaramogi is Dead: Who Shall Lead My People?* Kisumu: Palwa Research Service, 1995.

Ojwang, J. B., and J. N. K. Mugambi. *The S. M. Otieno Case: Death and Burial in Modern Kenya*. Nairobi: Nairobi University Press, 1989.

Okoth-Ogendo, H. W. O. "Politics of Constitutional Change in Kenya Since Independence, 1963–1969." *AA* 71 (282) (1972): 9–34.

Oruka, H. O. *Oginga Odinga: His Philosophy and Beliefs*. Nairobi: Initiatives Publishers, 1992.

Owuor, G. "Scaring Moi." *Society* 2 (13) (1992): 32–35.

Pio Gama Pinto: Independent Kenya's First Martyr. Nairobi: Pan African Press, 1966.

Pio Gama Pinto, Independent Kenya's First Martyr: Socialist and Freedom Fighter. Nairobi: Pan African Press, 1968.

Proctor, J. H. "The Role of the Senate in the Kenyan Political System." *Parliamentary Affairs* 18 (4) (1965): 389–415.

Rake, Alan. *Tom Mboya: Young Man of New Africa*. New York: Doubleday, 1962.

Report of the Parliamentary Select Committee to Investigate Ethnic Clashes in Western and Other Parts of Kenya. Nairobi: GP, 1992.

Repression Intensifies in Kenya since the August 1st Coup Attempt. London: Committee for the Release of Political Prisoners in Kenya, 1983.

"Repression Intensifies in Kenya: The Need for Solidarity." *ROAPE* 25 (1982): 112–17.

Roberts, John S. *Land Full of People: Life in Kenya Today*. New York: Praeger, 1967.

Rosberg, Carl G. "Independent Kenya: Problems and Prospects." *AR* 8 (11) (1963): 3–7.

Rothchild, Donald S. "Ethnic Inequalities in Kenya." *JMAS* 7 (4) (1969): 689–711.

———. "Kenya's Africanization Program: Priorities of Development and Equity." *The American Political Science Review* 64 (3) (1970): 737–53.

———. *Racial Bargaining in Independent Kenya: A Study of Minorities and Decolonization*. London: OUP, 1976.

Sanger, Clyde, and John Nottingham. "The Kenya General Election of 1963." *JMAS* 11 (1) (1964): 1–40.

Savage, Donald C. "Kenyatta and the Development of African Nationalism in Kenya." *International Journal* 25 (3) (1970): 518–37.

Schaar, Stuart H. *Note on Kenya*. Hanover, NH: American Universities Field Staff Reports, 1968.

Schatzberg, Michael, ed. *The Political Economy of Kenya*. New York: Praeger, 1987.

Segal, Aaron. "Kenya: Africa's Odd Man in." *CH* 80 (464) (1981): 106–10, 130.

Shields, Todd. "Kenya: The Queuing Controversy." *AR* 33 (3) (1988): 47–49.

Solomon, Joel A. *Failing the Democratic Challenge: Freedom of Expression in Multi-Party Kenya—1993*. Washington, D.C.: Robert F. Kennedy Memorial Center for Human Rights, 1994.

Southall, Roger, and Geoffrey Wood. "Local Government and the Return to Multi-Partyism in Kenya." *AA* 95 (381) (1996): 501–27.

Srinivasan, Padma. "Kenyatta Era: A Critical Study." *AQ* 18 (2/3) (1979): 52–66.

Stamp, Patricia. "Kenya: The Echoing Footsteps." *CH* 81 (473) (1982): 115–18, 130, 137–38.

———. "Kenya's Year of Dissent." *CH* 82 (482) (1983): 102–5.

———. "Politics of Dissent in Kenya." *CH* 90 (556) (1991): 205–8, 27–29.

Steeves, Jeffrey S. "Re-Democratisation in Kenya: 'Unbounded Politics' and the Political Trajectory towards National Elections." *Journal of Commonwealth and Comparative Politics* 35 (3) (1997): 27–52.

Swainson, Nicola. "Rise of a National Bourgeoisie in Kenya." *ROAPE* 8 (1977): 339–60.

Tamarkin, Mordechai. "From Kenyatta to Moi—The Anatomy of a Peaceful Transition of Power." *AT* 26 (3) (1979): 21–37.

———. "Recent Developments in Kenyan Politics: The Fall of Charles Njonjo." *Journal of Contemporary African Studies* 3 (1/2) (1983/84): 59–77.

———. "Roots of Political Stability in Kenya." *AA* 77 (308) (1978): 297–320.

Teubert-Seiwert, Bäbel. *Parteipolitik in Kenya, 1960–1969*. Frankfurt am Main: Peter Lang, 1987.

Thiong'o, Ngugi wa. *Barrel of a Pen: Resistance to Repression in Neo-Colonial Kenya*. London: New Beacon Books, 1983.

Thomas-Slayter, Barbara P. "Class, Community, and the Kenyan State: Community Mobilization in the Context of Global Politics." *International Journal of Politics, Culture and Society* 3 (1991): 301–21.

Throup, David. "Elections and Political Legitimacy in Kenya." *Africa* 63 (3) (1993): 371–96.

United Movement for Democracy in Kenya. *Moi's Reign of Terror: A Decade of Nyayo Crimes Against the People of Kenya*. London: United Movement for Democracy in Kenya, 1989.

———. *Struggle for Democracy in Kenya: Special Report on the 1988 General Elections in Kenya*. London: United Movement for Democracy in Kenya, 1988.

Wanjohi, Nick Gatheru. *Challenges of Democratic Governance: Parliament, Executive, and the Citizen in Kenya.* Nairobi: National Council of Churches of Kenya, 1993.

Waruhi, S. N. *From Autocracy to Democracy in Kenya: Past Systems of Government and Reforms for the Future.* Nairobi: the author, 1994.

Wasserman, Gary. "Continuity and Counter-Insurgency: The Role of Land Reform in Decolonizing Kenya, 1962–1970." *CJAS* 7 (1) (1973): 99–120.

————. "Independence Bargain: Kenya Europeans and the Land Issue, 1960–1962." *Journal of Commonwealth Political Studies* 9 (2) (1973): 99–120.

————. *Politics of Decolonization: Kenya Europeans and the Land Issue, 1960–1965.* Cambridge: CUP, 1976.

Wells, R. "What Mandate for Moi?" *AR* 28 (6) (1983): 10–13.

Widner, Jennifer A. "Interest Group Structure and Organisation in Kenya's Informal Sector: Cultural Despair or a Politics of Multiple Alliances?" *Comparative Political Studies* 24 (1) (1991): 31–56.

————. "Kenya's Slow Progress toward Multiparty Politics." *CH* 91 (565) (1992): 214–18.

————. *Rise of a Party-State in Kenya: From Harambee! to Nyayo!* Berkeley: University of California Press, 1992.

Wilson, L. S. "Kenyanisation and African Capacity 'Shuffling.'" *Public Administration and Development* 13 (5) (1993): 489–99.

World Bank. *Growth and Structural Change in Kenya.* Washington, D.C.: World Bank, 1982.

E. MILITARY AND SECURITY AFFAIRS

Anderson, David M. "Policing, Prosecution and the Law on Colonial Kenya c.1905–1939." In *Policing the Empire: Government, Authority and Control, 1830–1940,* edited by David M. Anderson and David Killingray, 183–200. Manchester, UK: Manchester University Press, 1991.

Atambo, Peter G. *National Security Implications of 1984 Drought in Kenya.* Maxwell Air Force Base, AL: Air War College, 1987.

Battle of Bukoba. Nairobi: East African Standard, [1915].

Baynham, Mark. "East African Mutinies of 1964." *Journal of Contemporary African Studies* 8/9 (1/2) (1989/1990): 153–80.

Beachey, R. W. "The Arms Trade in East Africa in the Late Nineteenth Century." *JAH* 3 (3) (1962): 451–67.

Bellegarde, Carlo de. *African Escape.* London: William Kimber, 1957.

Benuzzi, Felice. *No Picnic on Mount Kenya.* London: William Kimber, 1952.

Bienen, Henry. "Military and Society in East Africa: Thinking about Praetorianism." *Comparative Politics* 6 (4) (1974): 489–518.

————. "Public Order and the Military in Africa: Mutinies in Kenya, Uganda, and Tanganyika." In *The Military Intervenes: Case Studies in Political Development*, edited by Henry Beenen, 35–69. New York: Russell Sage Foundation.

Bollig, Michael. "Imposition of Colonial Rule in North West Kenya: Interethnic Conflicts and Anti-Colonial Resistance." *Afrikaanse Arbeitspap* 11 (1987): 5–39.

———. "Intra and Interethnic Conflict in Northwest Kenya." *Anthropos* 88 (1/2) (1993): 176–84.

Buchanan, Angus. *Three Years of War in East Africa*. London: John Murray, 1919. Reprint, New York: Negro Universities Press, 1969.

Campbell, Guy. *Charging Buffalo: A History of the Kenya Regiment, 1937–1963*. London: Leo Cooper in Association with Secker and Warburg, 1986.

Capstick, Peter Hathaway. *Warrior: The Legend of Colonel Richard Meinertzhagen*. New York: St Martin's Press, 1998.

Cheserem, Salina J. "African Responses to Colonial Military Recruitment: The Role of Askari and Carriers in the First World War in the British East Africa Protectorate (Kenya)." M.A. thesis, McGill University, 1987.

Christie, W. D. M. "The Mackinnon Road Depot." *Royal Engineers Journal* 66 (1) (1952): 71–84.

Clifford, Sir Hugh. *Gold Coast Regiment in the East African Campaign*. London: John Murray, 1920.

Crowe, J. H. V. *General Smuts' Campaign in East Africa*. London: John Murray, 1918.

Currie, Kate, and Larry Ray. "The Pambana of August 1: Kenya's Abortive Coup." *Political Quarterly* 57 (1) (1986): 47–59.

Dodd, Norman L. "Armed Forces of Nigeria, Ghana and Kenya." *Asian Defence Journal* 4 (1984): 78–79, 81–84, 86–88.

Draffan, W. D., and J. W. Howard. *5 KAR 1939–1945*. Nairobi: East African Standard, n.d..

———, and T. C. C. Lewin. *War Journal of the 5th (Kenya) Battalion, The King's African Rifles*. Nairobi: n.p., c. 1946.

Duder, C. J. D. "Army of One's Own: The Politics of the Kenya Defence Force." *CJAS* 25 (2) (1991): 207–25.

———. "'Men of the Officer Class': The Participants in the 1919 Soldier Settlement Scheme in Kenya." *AA* 92 (366) (1993): 69–87.

———. "The Soldier Settlement Scheme of 1919 in Kenya." Ph.D. diss., University of Aberdeen, 1978.

Easterbrook, David L. "Kenyan Askari in World War II and Their Demobilization, with Special Reference to Machakos District." In *Three Aspects of Crisis in Colonial Kenya*, B. Myrick, David L. Easterbrook, and J. R. Roelker. Syracuse: Syracuse University, 1975: 27–58.

Edwards, G. D. H. "The Settlement of Ex-Soldiers in the British Empire, 1915–23, With Particular Reference to East and Central Africa." M.A. thesis, University of Leeds, 1983.

Fadiman, Jeffery A. *An Oral History of Tribal Warfare: The Meru of Mt. Kenya*. Athens, OH: Ohio University Press, 1982.

Fendall, Charles Pears. *The East African Force, 1915–1919*. London: H. F. and G. Witherby, 1921.

Foran, William Robert. *A Cuckoo in Kenya: The Reminiscences of a Pioneer Police Officer in British East Africa*. London: Hutchinson and Company, 1936.

——. *Kenya Police 1887–1960*. London: Robert Hale, 1962.

Forster, Kent. "The Quest for East African Neutrality in 1915." *ASR* 22 (1) (1979): 73–82.

Fukui, Katsuyoshi, and David Turton, eds. *Warfare Among East African Herders*. Osaka: National Museum of Ethnology, 1979.

Gadsden, Fay. "Wartime Propaganda in Kenya: The Kenya Information Office, 1939–1945." *IJAHS* 19 (3) (1986): 401–20.

Gardner, Brian. *German East: The Story of the First World War in East Africa*. London: Cassell and Company, 1963.

Gogarty, H. A. *In the Land of the Kikuyu*. Dublin: M. H. Gill and Sons, 1920.

Grahame, Ian. *Jambo Effendi: Seven Years with the King's African Rifles*. London: J. A. Allen, 1968.

Great Britain. *Correspondence Respecting the Recent Rebellion in British East Africa*. London: HMSO, 1896.

Great Britain. Admiralty. Naval Intelligence Division. *East Africa Protectorate*. London: Naval Staff. Intelligence Department, 1919.

——. *Handbook of Kenya Colony (British East Africa) and the Kenya Protectorate (Protectorate of Zanzibar)*. London: HMSO, 1920.

Great Britain. Admiralty. Naval Staff. Intelligence Department. *East African Protectorate, March 1919*. London: HMSO, 1919.

Great Britain. Army. East Africa Command. *Infantry of East Africa Command, 1890–1944*. Nairobi: East African Standard, 1944.

Great Britain. Army. King's African Rifles. *Regulations for the King's African Rifles*. London: Waterlow, 1908.

Great Britain. Colonial Office. *Papers Relating to Native Disturbances in Kenya (March 1922)*. London: HMSO, 1922.

Great Britain. Foreign Office. *Correspondence Respecting Abyssinian Raids and Incursions into British Territory and the Anglo-Egyptian Sudan*. London: HMSO, 1928.

Great Britain. War Office. General Staff. *Kenya: Military Report*. London: HMSO, 1939.

——. *Military Report on the East Africa Protectorate and Zanzibar*. London: HMSO, 1910.

Great Britain. War Office. Intelligence Division. *Précis of Information Concerning the East Africa Protectorate and Zanzibar*. London: HMSO, 1901.

Greenstein, Lewis J. "Africans in a European War: The First World War in East Africa with Special Reference to the Nandi of Kenya." Ph.D. diss., Indiana University, 1975.

——. "The Impact of Military Service in World War I on Africans: The Nandi of Kenya." *JMAS* 16 (3) (1978): 495–507.

————. "The Nandi Experience in the First World War." In *Africa and the First World War*, edited by Melvin E. Page, 81–94. London: Macmilan, 1987.

————. "Nandi 'Uprising' of 1923." *Pan-African Journal* 9 (4) (1976): 397–406.

Hanley, Gerald. *Monsoon Victory*. London: Collins, 1946.

Harris, Cobie. "Kenya." In *The Political Role of the Military*, edited by Constantine P. Danopoulos and Cynthia Watson, 256–70. Westport, CT: Greenwood Press, 1996.

Hodges, Geoffrey W. T. "African Manpower Statistics for the British Forces in East Africa, 1914–1918." *JAH* 19 (1) (1978): 101–16.

————. *The Carrier Corps: Military Labor in the East African Campaign, 1914–1918*. New York: Greenwood Press, 1986.

————. "Military Labour in East Africa and Its Impact on Kenya." In *Africa and the First World War*, edited by Melvin Page, 137–51. New York: St. Martin's Press, 1987.

Hordern, Charles. *Military Operations, East Africa*. London: HMSO, 1941.

Hoyt, Edwin P. *The Germans Who Never Lost: The Story of the Königsberg*. New York: Funk and Wagnalls, 1968.

————. *Guerrilla: Colonel von Lettow-Vorbeck and Germany's East African Empire*. New York: Macmillan Publishing Company, 1981.

Jones, Robert F. "Kipkororor Chronicles." *MHQ: The Quarterly Journal of Military History* 3 (3) (1991): 38–47.

Kakembo, R. H. *An African Soldier Speaks*. London: Livingstone Press, 1946.

Keane, G. J. "African Native Medical Corps." *JRAS* 19 (86) (1920): 295–304.

————, and D. G. Tomblings. *The African Native Medical Corps in the East African Campaign*. London: Richard Clay and Sons, 1920.

"Kenya." In *World Encyclopedia of Police Forces and Penal Systems*, edited by George Thomas Kurian, 109–12. New York and Oxford: Facts on File, 1989.

"Kenya." In *World Police and Paramilitary Forces*, edited by John Andrade, 79. New York: Stockton Press, 1985.

"The Kenya Police, before Uhuru." *Kenya Police Review* (June 1992): 17–21.

Kenyatta, Jomo. "Security of the State." In *Harambee: The Prime Minister of Kenya's Speeches 1963–1964*, Jomo Kenyatta, 96–104. Nairobi: OUP, 1964.

Kibwana, J. R. "Military Balance in East Africa: A Kenyan View." *Naval War College Review* 30 (2) (1977): 97–101.

Kipkoria, B. E. "Kolloa Affray, Kenya 1950." *TJH* 2 (2) (1972): 114–29.

Lambie, I. C. "Lanet Mutiny." *Journal of the Royal Artillery* 92 (1) (1965): 59–66.

Lane, Hugh Shannon. "The East African Campaign, 1914–1918." M.A. thesis, California State University, Fresno, 1994.

Lettow-Vorbeck, Paul von. "Die Ost-Afrikaner im Weltkrieg." In *Im Felde Unbesiegt* edited by Gustaf Dickhuth-Harrach, 315–26. München: J.F. Lehmanns Verlag, 1921.

————. *East African Campaigns*. New York: Robert Speller and Sons, 1957.

————. *Heia Safari, Deutschlands Kampf in Ostafrika*. Leipzig: Hafe und Kohler, 1920.

————. *Mein Leben*. Miberach an der Riss: Koehlers, 1957.

————. *My Reminiscences of East Africa*. London: Hurst and Blackett, 1920.

————. *Um Vaterland und Kolonie*. Berlin: H. Bermüher, 1919.

————. *Was Mir die Engländer über Ostafrika Erzählten: Zwanglose Unterhaltungen mit Ehemaligen Gegnern*. Leipzig: Koehler, 1932.

Lloyd, A. *"Jambo," or With Jannie in the Jungle*. Johannesburg: South African Central News Agency, 1917.

Lloyd Jones, W. *Havash!* London: Arrowsmith, 1925.

————. *K.A.R.: Being an Unofficial Account of the Origins and Activities of the King's African Rifles*. London: Arrowsmith, 1926.

Lonsdale, John M. "Depression and the Second World War in the Transformation of Kenya." In *Africa and the Second World War*, edited by David Killingray and Richard Rathbone, 97–142. New York: St. Martin's Press, 1986.

————. "Politics of Conquest: The British in Western Kenya 1894–1908." *Historical Journal* 20 (4) (1977): 841–70.

Lord, John. *Duty, Honor, Empire: The Life and Times of Colonel Richard Meinertzhagen*. New York: Random House, 1970.

Macdonald, J. R. L. *Soldiering and Surveying in British East Africa*. London: Edward Arnold, 1897.

Macharia, Paul Wanjohi. "Toward a Nation-Building Role for the Armed Forces in Kenya." Thesis, US Army Command and General Staff College, 1991.

McMillan, Timothy John. "Colonial Resistance in Kenya: The Kipsigis Orgoiik." Ph.D. diss., NC: University of North Carolina, 1989.

Matthews, L. L. "Kenya." In John Keegan (ed.). *World Armies*. New York: Facts on File, 1979: 402–3.

Maxon, Robert M. "Gusii Resistance to British Rule and Its Suppression, 1908." *TJH* 2 (1) (1972): 65–82.

————. "Thorny Road from Primary to Secondary Source: The Cult of Mumbo and the 1914 Sack of Kissi." *HIA* 13 (1986): 261–68.

Mazrui, Ali A. "Language in Military History: Command and Communication in East Africa." *Mawazo* 4 (2) (1974): 19–36.

————, and Donald Rothchild. "The Soldier and State in East Africa." *Western Political Quarterly* 20 (1) (1967): 82–96.

Meinertzhagen, Richard. *Army Diary, 1899–1926*. Edinburgh: Oliver and Boyd, 1960.

————. *Kenya Diary 1902–1906*. Edinburgh: Oliver and Boyd, 1957.

Miller, Charles. *Battle for the Bundu: The First World War in East Africa*. New York: Macmillan, 1974.

M'Inoti, K. "Beyond the 'Emergency' in the North Eastern Province." *NLM* (41) (1992): 37–43.

Mkungusi, Oliver C. *Defence Policy of Kenya: Policy Implications for the United States*. Carlisle Barracks, PA: Army War College, 1987.

Mosley, Leonard. *Duel for Kilimanjaro*. London: Weidenfeld and Nilcolson, 1963.

Moyse-Bartlett, H. "King's African Rifles." *Army Quarterly* 71 (1) (1955): 66–73.

————. *The King's African Rifles.* Nairobi: The Regal Press, c.1952.

————. *The King's African Rifles: A Study in the Military History of East and Central Africa, 1890–1945.* Aldershot, UK: Gale and Polden, 1956.

Nyamora, P., et al. "Police Raid Society." *Society* 11 (1992): 35–46.

Ogutu, M. A. "Forts and Fortifications in Western Kenya (Marachi and Ugenya) in the 19th Century." *TJH* (1991): 77–96.

Okete, James Ellysham Shiroya. *African Politics in Colonial Kenya: Contribution of World War II Veterans, 1945–1960.* Nairobi: Educational Research and Publications, 1992.

————. "Impact of World War II on Kenya: The Role of Ex-Servicemen in Kenya Nationalism." Ph.D. diss., Michigan State University, 1969.

————. *Kenya and World War II: African Soldiers in the European War.* Nairobi: KLB, 1985.

Orr, G. M. "Indian Army in East Africa, 1914–1917." *Journal of the United Service Institution of India* 48 (215) (1919): 244–61.

————. "1914–1915 in East Africa." *Journal of the United Service Institution of India* 56 (245) (1926): 58–86.

————. "Random Recollections of East Africa, 1914–1918." *Army Quarterly* 11 (2) (1926): 282–93.

————. "Smuts v. Lettow: A Critical Phase in East Africa: August to September, 1916." *Army Quarterly* 9 (2) (1925): 287–99.

————. "Some Afterthoughts of the War in East Africa, 1914–1918." *Journal of the Royal Service Institution* 69 (476) (1924): 692–702.

Overton, John. "War and Economic Development: Settlers in Kenya, 1914–1918." *JAH* 27 (1) (1986): 79–104.

————. "War and Economic Underdevelopment? State Exploitation and African Response in Kenya 1914–1918." *IJAHS* 22 (2) (1989): 201–21.

Page, Malcolm. *A History of the King's African Rifles and East African Forces.* London: Leo Cooper, 1998.

Page, Melvin E. "With Jannie in the Jungle: European Humor in an East African Campaign, 1914–1918." *IJAHS* 14 (3) (1981): 466–81.

Parsons, Timothy Hamilton. "East African Soldiers in Britain's Colonial Army: A Social History, 1902–1964." Ph.D. diss., Johns Hopkins University, 1997.

Patterson, K. David. "Giriama Risings of 1913–1914." *AHS* 3 (1) (1970): 89–99.

Pennycuick, K. *The War in East Africa (1914–18).* London: White Crescent Press, 1968.

Pentzel, Otto. *Buschkampf in Ostafrika.* Stuttgart: R. Thienemann, 1942.

Pesenti, G. *Fronte Kenya (La Guerre in A.O.I., 1940–41).* Bargo S. Damlazzo: Bertello, 1952.

Pradhan, S. D. *Indian Army in East Africa.* New Delhi: National Book Organisation, 1991.

Sampson, Philip J. *Conquest of German East Africa.* Cape Town: Argus Printing and Publishing Company, 1917.

Scully, R. T. K. "Two Accounts of the Chetambe War of 1895." *IJAHS* 6 (3) (1973): 480–92.

Shiroya, Okete James Ellysham. *See* Okete, James Ellysham Shiroya.

Smallwood, R. E. R. "Developing the K.A.R." *Army Quarterly* 49 (2) (1945): 214–18.

Spencer, Ian G. "The First World War and the Origins of the Dual Policy of Development in Kenya, 1914–1922." *WD* 9 (8) (1981): 735–48.

———. "Settler Domination, Agricultural Production and the Second World War in Kenya." *JAH* 21 (4) (1980): 497–514.

Story of the Kenya Regiment, TF, 1937–1959. Nairobi: The English Press, c. 1959.

Terrell, W. E. W. *With the Motor Transport in British East Africa, February, 1916–November, 1918*. London: Privately Printed, 1923.

Throup, David. "Crime, Politics and the Police in Colonial Kenya, 1939–1963." In *Policing and Decolonisation*, edited by David M. Anderson and David Killingray, 127–57. Manchester, UK: Manchester University Press, 1992.

Versi, Anver. "Kenya: The Anatomy of a Failed Coup." *New African* 181 (1982): 25–27.

Vowles, P. F. *Eleventh (Kenya) Battalion, King's African Rifles, 1941–1945*. Bihar, India: Catholic Press, c. 1946.

Walmsley, Leo. "An Airman's Experiences in East Africa." *Blackwood's Magazine* 1249 (1919): 633–52; 1250 (1919): 788–810; 1251 (1920): 53–69; and 1252 (1920): 189–209.

———. *Flying and Sport in East Africa*. Edinburgh: Blackwood, 1920.

Wandibba, B. J. Simiyu. "The Bukusu Forts." B.A. thesis, University of Nairobi, 1972.

Ward, Rebecca. "Kenya Women in Wartime." *East Africa Annual* (1941/1942): 102–9.

———. "Kenya's War Effort: Women on the Land." *East Africa Annual* (1945/1946): 63–70.

Watkins, Oscar Ferris. *Report on Military Labour*. Nairobi: Government Printer, 1920.

Waweru, Peter M. "Anti-Poaching Campaign: Role of the Kenya Armed Forces." Carlisle Barracks, PA: Army War College (US) Study Project, 1991.

Whipper, Audrey. "The Gusii Rebels." In *Protest and Power in Black Africa*, edited by Robert I. Rotberg and Ali Mazrui, 377–426. New York: OUP, 1970.

———. *Rural Rebels: A Study of Two Protest Movements in Kenya*. Nairobi: OUP, 1977.

Wild, Percy Turner. *Bwana Polisi (Under Three Flags)*. Braunton, UK: Merlin Books, 1993.

Wilson, Christopher James. "Reminiscences of the Last East African Campaign." *EAMJ* 16 (8) (1939): 282–87.

———. *Story of the East African Mounted Rifles*. Nairobi: East African Standard, 1938.

Wilson, H. A. *A British Borderland: Service and Sport in Equatoria.* London: John Murray, 1913.

Wolf, James B. "Asian and African Recruitment in the Kenya Police, 1920–1950." *IJAHS* 6 (3) (1973): 401–12.

Yardley, John. *Parergon or Eddies in Equatoria.* London: J. M. Dent and Sons, 1931.

Zeleza, Tiyambe. "Kenya and the Second World War, 1939–1950." In *A Modern History of Kenya 1895–1980,* edited by William Robert Ochieng', 144–72. London: Evans Brothers Ltd., 1989.

F. ECONOMIC AFFAIRS

Ackello-Ogutu, Christopher, and John J. Waelti. *Basic Concepts of Microeconomics with Special Reference to Kenya.* Nairobi: University of Nairobi Press, 1990.

Adam, C. "On the Dynamic Specification of Money Demand in Kenya." *JAE* 1 (2) (1992): 233–70.

Ahmed, O. S., and A. J. Field. "Potential Effects of Income-Redistribution Policies on the Final Pattern of Income Distribution: The Case of Kenya." *JDA* 20 (1) (1985): 1–22.

Allen, C., and K. J. King, eds. *Developmental Trends in Kenya.* Edinburgh: Centre of African Studies, Edinburgh University, 1972.

Anderson, David M. "The 'Crisis of Capitalism' and Kenya's Social History: A Comment." *AA* 92 (367) (1993): 285–90.

Bakuli, D. Luvisia. "Pitfalls in Technology Transfer: Kenya's Construction Industry." *WD* 22 (10) (1994): 1609–12.

Bigsten, Arne. *Regional Inequalities and Development: A Case Study of Kenya.* Farnborough, UK: Gower, 1980.

———. "Race and Inequality in Kenya, 1914–1976." *EAER* 4 (1) (1988): 1–11.

———. "Welfare and Economic Growth in Kenya, 1914–76." *WD* 14 (1986): 1151–60.

Bradshaw, York W. "Reassessing Economic Dependency and Uneven Development: The Kenyan Experience." *American Sociological Review* (5) (1988): 693–708.

Bruce, Colin A., and David Ndii. *Framework for Macroeconomic Analysis: Applied to Kenya.* Washington, D.C.: World Bank, 1991.

Burbank, K. *Survey of NGOs As Small Business Development Agencies in Kenya.* Nairobi: IDS, 1994.

Butt, S. A. *Business Finance in Kenya.* Nairobi: Book Sales Kenya, 1979.

Chakrabarti, S. K., and J. A. Ali. *Prices in Kenya: An Empirical Investigation.* Cambridge, MA: Harvard Institute for International Development, 1992.

Chege, Michael. "Introducing Race as a Variable into the Political Economy of Kenya Debate: An Incendiary Idea." *AA* 97 (1998):

Cohen, J. M., and R. M. Hook. "Decentalised Planning in Kenya." *Public Administration and Development* 2 (1) (1987): 77–93.

Collier, Paul, and Deepak Lal. *Labour and Poverty in Kenya 1900–1980*. Oxford: Clarendon Press, 1986.

Coughlin, Peter. "Development Policy and Inappropriate Product Technology: The Kenyan Case." *EAER* 4 (1) (1988): 18–35.

————, and Gerrishon K. Ikiara. *Industrialization in Kenya: In Search of a Strategy*. Nairobi: Heinemann Kenya, 1989.

————. *Kenya's Industrialization Dilemma*. Nairobi: EAEP, 1991.

Curtin, Philip D. "African Enterprise in the Mangrove Trade: The Case of Lamu." *African Economic History* 10 (1981): 23–33.

Diejomaoh, Victor. "Taxation and Government Savings in Kenya." *EAER* 17 (1970): 15–30.

Ensminger, Jean. "Co-opting the Elders: The Political Economy of State Intervention in Africa." *American Anthropologist* 92 (3) (1990): 662–75.

————. *Making a Market: The Institutional Transformation of an African Society*. Cambridge: CUP, 1992.

Faaland, J., and H. E. Dahl. *Economy of Kenya*. 2 vols. Bergen: Christian Michelsen Institute, 1967.

Fearn, Hugh. *African Economy: A Study of the Economic Development of the Nyanza Province of Kenya 1903–1953*. London: OUP, 1961.

Forrester, Marion W. *Kenya Today: The Social Prerequisites for Economic Development*. New York: Humanities Press, 1962.

Geheb, Kim, and Tony Binns. "'Fishing Farmers' or 'Farming Fisherman'? The Quest for Household Income and Nutritional Security on the Kenyan Shores of Lake Victoria." *African Affairs* 96 (382) (1997): 73–93.

Ghai, D., and M. Godfrey, eds. *Essays on Employment in Kenya*. Nairobi: KLB, 1979.

Ghazanfar, S. M., and C. A. Bailey. "Kenya: Promoting Employment Through Small-Scale Enterprises Development." *Scandinavian Journal of Development Alternatives* 4 (1991): 47–61.

Godfrey, Martin E. *Kenya: Economic Prospects to 1985*. London: Economist Intelligence Unit, 1981.

Groot, A. W. de. "Adjustment Policies and the Real Exchange Rate in Kenya Since 1975." *WD* 19 (10) (1991): 1399–1408.

Grosh, Barbara. *Public Enterprise in Kenya: What Works, What Doesn't and Why*. Boulder, CO: Lynne Rienner Publishers, 1991.

Haji, S. H. H. A. "Dynamic Model of Industrial Energy Demand in Kenya." *Energy Journal* 15 (4) (1994): 203–24.

Harbeson, John W. *Structural Adjustment and Development Reform in Kenya: The Missing Dimension*. Hanover, NH: Universities Field Staff International, 1984.

Hazlewood, Arthur. *Economy of Kenya: The Kenyatta Era*. Oxford: OUP, 1979.

————. "Kenya: Income Distribution and Poverty—An Unfashionable View." *JMAS* 16 (1) (1978): 81–95.

Heald, Suzette. "Tobacco, Time, and the Household Economy in Two Kenyan Societies: The Teso and the Kuria." *Comparative Studies in Society and History* 33 (1) (1991): 130–57.

Hecox, Walter E. "World Recession and Structural Adjustment in Africa: The Case of Kenya." *African Studies Association Papers* 28 (54) (1984): 1–23.

Heller, Peter S. "Public Investment in LDC's with Recurrent Cost Constraint: The Kenyan Case." *Quarterly Journal of Economics* (1974): 251–76.

Helmschrott, H. *Development and Development Policy in East Africa: Kenya.* Munich: IFO, 1965.

Henley, John S. "Employment Relationships and Economic Development: The Kenyan Experience." *JMAS* 6 (4) (1973): 559–89.

———. "On the Lack of Trade Union Power in Kenya." *Industrial Relations* 4 (1976): 655–67.

Hetherington, Penelope. "Explaining the Crisis of Capitalism in Kenya." *AA* 92 (366) (1993): 89–103.

Himbara, David. "Failed Africanization of Commerce and Industry in Kenya." *WD* 22 (3) (1994): 469–82.

———. *Kenyan Capitalists: The State and Development.* Boulder, CO: Lynne Rienner, 1993.

———. "Myths and Realities of Kenyan Capitalism." *JMAS* 31 (1) (1993): 93–107.

Hodd, Michael. "Income Distribution in Kenya (1963–1972)." *Journal of Development Studies* 12 (3) (1976): 221–28.

Hosier, Richard N. "Informal Sector in Kenya: Spatial Variation and Development Alternatives." *JDA* 21 (4) (1987): 383–402.

House, William J. "Earning-per-Worker Differentials in the Provinces of Kenya, 1963–1970." *JDA* 9 (3) (1975): 359–76.

———. "Market Structure and Industry Performance: The Case of Kenya." *Oxford Economic Papers* 25 (3) (1973): 405–19.

Howe, Charles W., and Hiram Karani. "Projection Model for the Kenya Economy: A Study in Development Planning and Comparative Economic Structure." *EAER* 12 (1965): 21–31.

Hyden, Goran, Robert Jackson, and John Okumu, eds. *Development Administration: The Kenyan Experience.* Nairobi: OUP, 1970.

Institute of Economic Affairs. *Agenda 94: People, Economic Affairs and Politics.* Nairobi: The Institute, 1994.

International Bank for Reconstruction and Development. *Economic Development of Kenya.* Baltimore, MD: Johns Hopkins University Press, 1963.

———. *Kenya: Into the Second Decade.* Baltimore, MD: Johns Hopkins University Press, 1975.

International Labour Office. *Employment, Incomes and Equality: A Strategy for Increasing Productive Employment in Kenya.* Geneva: International Labour Office, 1972.

International Monetary Fund Institute. *Financial Policy Workshops: Case of Kenya.* Washington, D.C.: International Monetary Fund, 1981.

Kaplinsky, Raphael, ed. *Readings on the Multinational Corporations in Kenya.* Nairobi: OUP, 1978

Karani, H. "Projection Model for the Kenya Economy: Implications of the Kenya Development Plan, 1966–1970." *EAER* 14 (1967): 45–54.

Kariuki, P. W. "Effects of Liberalization on Access to Bank Credit in Kenya." *Small Enterprise Development* 1 (1995): 15–23.

Kenya: Land of Opportunity. Nairobi: Central Bank of Kenya, 1991.

Kesterton, A. "Finance for Microenterprise: Innovations in Kenya." *Small Enterprise Development* 2 (1993): 16–23.

Killick, Tony. "The Influence of Balance of Payments Management on Employment and Basic Needs in Kenya." *EAER* 1 (1) (1985): 57–69.

————. *IMF and Economic Management in Kenya.* London: ODI, 1981.

————, ed. *Papers on the Kenyan Economy: Performance, Problems and Policies.* Nairobi: Heineman Educational Books, 1981.

————, and J. K. Kinyua. "On Implementing Development Plans: A Case Study." *ODI Review* 1 (1980): 30–47.

Kimambo, Isaria N. "Economic History of the Kamba, 1850–1950." In *Hadith*, edited by Bethwell A. Ogot, Vol. 2, 79–103. Nairobi: KLB, 1970.

Kimuyu, P. K. "The Disintegration of the International Oil Industry and After: Implications for Kenya." *Eastern Africa Social Science Research Review* 3 (2) (1987): 62–70.

King, J. R. *Stabilization Policy in an African Setting: Kenya 1963–1973.* London: Heinemann Educational Books, 1979.

Kinyanjui, Mary Njeri. "Finance, Availability of Capital and New Firm Formation in Central Kenya." *JEARD* 23 (1993): 63–87.

Kliest, T. *Regional and Seasonal Food Problems in Kenya.* Leiden, Netherlands: Institute of African Studies, 1985.

Langdon, Steven W. *Multinational Corporations in the Political Economy of Kenya.* New York: St. Martin's Press, 1981.

————. "Multinational Corporations, Taste Transfer and Underdevelopment: A Case Study from Kenya." *ROAPE* 2 (1975): 12–35.

————. "State and Capitalism in Kenya." *ROAPE* 8 (1977): 90–98.

Levin, J. *Kenya 1991–1993: Two Steps Backwards and One Step Forward.* Stockholm, Sweden: SIDA, 1994.

Lewis, Blane D., and Erik Thorbecke. "District-Level Economic Linkages in Kenya: Evidence Based on a Small Regional Social Accounting Matrix." *WD* 20 (6) (1992): 881–97.

Leys, Colin. "Interpreting African Underdevelopment: Reflections on the ILO Report on Employment, Incomes and Equality in Kenya." *AA* 52 (1973): 419–29.

————. "Learning from the Kenya Debate." In *Political Development and the New Realism in Sub-Saharan Africa*, edited by David E. Apter and Carl G. Rosberg, 220–43. Charlottesville, VA and London: University Press of Virginia, 1994.

Lofchie, Michael F. "Kenya: Still an Economic Miracle?" *CH* 87 (547) (1990): 209–12, 222–24.

Low, Patrick. "Export Subsidies and Trade Policy: The Experience of Kenya." *WD* 10 (4) (1982): 293–304.

Lumbembe, Clement K. *Inside of the Labour Movement in Kenya.* Nairobi: Equatorial Publishers, 1968.

McCormack, Robert L. "Imperialism, Air Transport and Colonial Development: Kenya, 1920–46." *JICH* 17 (3) (1989): 374–95.

Makhan, Singh. *History of Kenya's Trade Union Movement to 1952.* Nairobi: EAPH, 1969.

———. *History of Kenya's Trade Union Movement, 1952–56.* Nairobi: Uzima Press, 1980.

Manley, Mary L. *Marketing in Kenya.* Washington, D.C.: U.S. Domestic and International Business Administration, 1977.

Marris, Peter, and Anthony Somerset. *African Businessmen: A Study of Entrepreneurship and Development in Kenya.* London: Routledge and Kegan Paul, 1971.

Matthews, Ron. "Appraising Efficiency in Kenya's Machinery Manufacturing Sector." *AA* 90 (358) (1991): 65–88.

Maxon, Robert M. "Up in Smoke: Peasants, Capital and the Colonial State in the Tobacco Industry in Western Kenya, 1930–1939." *African Economic History* 22 (1994): 111–39.

Metts, Robert Lyle. "Institutional Aspects of International Trade: The Case of Kenya Colony and Protectorate (1895–1963)." Ph.D. diss., University of California, Berkeley 1985.

———, and T. Oleson. "Assisting Disabled Entrepreneurs in Kenya: Implications for Developed Countries." *Small Enterprise Development* 4 (1995): 23–33.

Mikkelsen, Britha. *Formation of an Industrial Labour Force in Kenya: Experiences of Labour Training in the Metal Manufacturing Industries.* Copenhagen: Centre for Development Research, 1986.

Mosley, Paul. "How to Confront the World Bank and Get Away with It: A Case Study of Kenya, 1980–87." In *Policy Adjustment in Africa*, edited by C. Milner and A. J. Rayner, 99–131. London: Macmillan, 1992.

———. "Politics of Economic Liberalization: USAID and the World Bank in Kenya, 1980–84." *AA* 85 (338) (1986): 107–19.

———. *Settler Economies: Studies in the Economic History of Kenya and Southern Rhodesia, 1900–1963.* Cambridge: CUP, 1983.

Muir, J. Douglas, and John L. Brown. "Trade Union Power and the Process of Economic Development: The Kenyan Example." *Industrial Relations* 29 (3) (1974): 474–94.

Mukonoweshuro, E. "Authoritarian Reaction to Economic Crises in Kenya." *Race and Class* 31 (4) (1990): 39–59.

Mukui, J. T. "Politics and Economics of the 1979 Tripartite Agreement in Kenya: A Note." *AA* 82 (329) (1983): 559–63.

Mullei, A. K. "Determining the International Competitive Value of the Kenya Shilling." *EAER* 7 (2) (1991): 17–25.

————, and J. M. Ng'elu. "Evolution, Structure and Performance of Kenya's Financial System." *Savings and Development* 14 (3) (1990): 265–84.

Mutunga, Willy. "Finance Capital and the So-Called National Bourgeoisie in Kenya." *Ufahamu* 12 (1) (1982): 51–80.

Mwau, Geoffrey, and Jagdish Handa. *Rational Economic Decisions and the Current Account in Kenya.* Aldershot, UK: Avebury Press, 1995.

Mwega, F. M. "Import Demand Elasticities and Stability During Trade Liberalisation: A Case Study of Kenya." *JAE* 2 (3) (1993): 381–416.

————. "Trade and Macroeconomic Policies and the Industrialisation Experience in Kenya in the 1970s and 1980s." In *Trade Policy and Industrialisation in a Turbulent Time*, edited by G. K. Helleiner, 487–514. London: Routledge, 1994.

National Christian Council of Kenya. *Who Controls Industry in Kenya? Report of a Working Party.* Nairobi: EAPH, 1968.

Ndege, Peter O. "Struggles for the Market: The Political Economy of Commodity Production and Trade in Western Kenya, 1929–1939: Ph.D. diss., West Virginia University, 1993.

Nellis, John R. "Who Pays Tax in Kenya?" *TAR* 2 (1972): 345–63.

Nyamu, H. J. *Aspects of Kenya's Development: A Participant's View.* Nairobi: EAPH, 1980.

Nyamwange, M. "Population Growth and Development: The Kenyan Experience." *Scandinavian Journal of Development Alternatives* 1/2 (1995): 149–60.

Nyoike, P.M. and B.A. Olech. "Case of Kenya." In *Energy Management in Africa*, edited by M. R. Bhagavan and S. Karekezi, 87–123. London: Zed Press, 1992.

Nzomo, N. D. "Entrepreneurship Development Policy in National Development Planning: The Kenya Case." *EAER* 2 (1) (1986): 99–105.

Ochieng', William Robert, and Robert M. Maxon, eds. *Economic History of Kenya.* Nairobi: EAEP, 1992.

O'Keefe, Phil, Paul Raskin, and Steve Bernow, eds. *Energy and Development in Kenya.* Uppsala, Sweden: SIAS, 1984.

Omide, S. H., ed. *Population and Development in Kenya.* London: Heinemann, 1984.

Oser, Jacob. *Promoting Economic Development: With Illustrations from Kenya.* Evanston, IL: Northwestern University Press, 1967.

Oshikoya, T. W. "Interest Rate Liberalization, Savings Investment and Growth: The Case of Kenya." *Savings and Development* 3 (1992): 305–20.

Pack, Howard. "Unemployment and Income Distribution in Kenya." *Economic Development and Cultural Change* 26 (1) (1977): 157–68.

Parkinson, John M. "The Nairobi Stock Exchange in the Context of Development in Kenya." *Savings and Development* 8 (4) (1984): 363–72.

Paulson, Jo Ann. "Structure and Development of Financial Markets in Kenya." Ph.D. diss., Stanford University, 1984.

Pokhariyal, G. P., and P. V. Joshi. "Analysis of Present State of the Kenyan Economy." *Africa Quarterly* 34 (4) (1994): 85–94.

Reichelt, Hans. *Chemical and Allied Industries in Kenya*. Munich: Weltforum Verlag, 1967.

Rempel, Henry, and William J. House. *Kenya Employment Problem*. Nairobi: OUP, 1978.

Republic of Kenya. *African Socialism and its Application to Planning in Kenya*. Nairobi: GP, 1965.

———. *Development Plan*. Nairobi: GP, various years.

———. *Economic Management for Renewed Growth*. Nairobi: GP, 1986.

———. *Economic Survey*. Nairobi: GP, various years.

———. *Sessional Paper No. 1 of 1986 on Economic Management for Renewed Growth*. Nairobi: GP, 1986.

———. *Statistical Abstract*. Nairobi: GP, various years.

Republic of Kenya. Ministry of Economic Planning and Development. *Economic Survey, 1969*. Nairobi: GP, 1969.

———. *High Level Manpower Requirements and Resources in Kenya 1964–70*. Nairobi: GP, 1965.

———. *Kenya Development Plan 1965–70*. Nairobi: GP, 1966.

———. *Three Years of Independence: Building for a Better Future*. Nairobi: GP, 1966.

———. *Towards a Better Future for Our People*. Nairobi: GP, 1966.

Richardson, Julie A. *Structural Adjustment and Environmental Linkages: A Case Study of Kenya*. London: Overseas Development Institute, 1996.

Rwegasira, Delphin G. "Balance-of-Payments Adjustment in Low-Income Developing Countries: The Experiences of Kenya and Tanzania in the 1970s." *WD* 15 (10/11) (1987): 1321–35.

Ryan, T. C. I., and W. J. Milne. "Analysing Inflation in Developing Countries: An Econometric Study with Application to Kenya." *Journal of Development Studies* 31 (1) (1994): 134–56.

Sandbrook, Richard. "Patrons, Clients, and Unions: The Labour Movement and Political Conflict in Kenya." *Journal of Commonwealth Political Studies* 10 (1) (1972): 3–27.

———. *Proletarians and African Capitalism: The Kenyan Case, 1960–1972*. London: CUP, 1975.

Schapiro, M. O., and S. Wainaina. "Kenya's Export of Horticultural Commodities." *Public Administration and Development* 11 (3) (1991): 257–61.

Semboja, Haji Hatibu Haji. "Effects of an Increase in Energy Efficiency on the Kenyan Economy." *Energy Policy* 22 (3) (1994): 217–25.

———. "Effects of Energy Taxes on the Kenyan Economy: A CGE Analysis." *Energy Economics* 16 (3) (1994): 205–15.

Smith, Lawrence D. "Aspects of the Employment Problem: A Case Study of Kenya." *Round Table* 249 (1973): 105–14.

Spencer, Ian R. "Development of Production and Trade in the Reserve Area of Kenya, 1895–1929." Ph.D. diss., Simon Fraser University, 1974.

Steele, David. "Theory of the Dual Economy and African Entrepreneurship in Kenya." *Journal of Development Studies* 12 (1) (1975): 18–38.

Stichter, Sharon. *Migrant Labour in Kenya: Capitalism and African Response, 1895–1975.* London: Longman, 1982.

Swainson, Nicola. *Development of Corporate Capitalism in Kenya, 1918–1977.* London: Heinemann, 1980.

———. "State and Economy in Post-Colonial Kenya, 1963–1978." *CJAS* 12 (2) (1978): 357–81.

Swamy, G. *Kenya: Structural Adjustment in the 1980s.* Washington, D.C.: World Bank, 1994.

Taylor, D. R. F. "Internal Trade of Fort Hall District, Kenya." *CJAS* 1 (2) (1967): 111–22.

Thomas, Barbara P. *Politics, Participation and Poverty: Development through Self-Help in Kenya.* Boulder, CO and London: WP, 1985.

———. "State Formation, Development, and the Politics of Self-Help in Kenya." *Studies in Comparative International Development* 23 (3) (1988): 3–27.

Tiffen, Mary. "Population Density, Economic Growth and Societies in Transition: Boserup Reconsidered in a Kenyan Case-Study." *Development and Change* 26 (1) (1995): 31–65.

———, and Michael Mortimore. "Environment, Population Growth and Productivity in Kenya: A Case Study of Machakos District." *Development Policy Review* 14 (4) (1992): 359–87.

———. "Malthus Controverted: The Role of Capital and Technology in Growth and Environment Recovery in Kenya." *WD* 22 (7) (1994): 997–1010.

Tomecko, J. "Mainstreaming Small Enterprises in Kenya." *Small Enterprise Development* 1 (3) (1990): 17–26.

Vandemoortele, J. "Causes of Economic Instability in Kenya: Theory and Evidence." *EAER* 1 (1) (1985): 87–96.

Wakhungu, J. W. "Underdevelopment and Dependency: The Case of Kenya's Energy Sector." *Bulletin of Science, Technology and Society* 13 (6) (1993): 332–40.

Wa'weru, Murathi. *Management of Human Resources in Kenya.* Nairobi: KLB, 1984.

Werlin, H. H. "Informal Sector: The Implications of the ILO's Study of Kenya." *ASR* 17 (1) (1974): 205–12.

West, R. L. "An Estimated Balance of Payments for Kenya, 1923–1939." *EAER* 3 (1) (1956): 181–90.

Wilson, L. S. "Harambee Movement and Efficient Public Good Provision in Kenya." *Journal of Public Economics* 48 (1) (1992): 1–19.

———. "Kenyanization and African Capacity 'Shuffling.'" *Public Administration and Development* 13 (5) (1993): 489–99.

Wolff, Richard D. *Economics of Colonialism: Britain and Kenya, 1895–1930.* New Haven, CT and London: YUP, 1977.

World Bank. *Kenya: Growth and Structural Change.* 2 vols. Washington, D.C.: World Bank, 1983.

————. *Kenya Local Government Finance Study.* Washington, D.C.: World Bank, 1992.

————. *Kenya: Reinvesting in Stabilization and Growth Through Public Sector Adjustment.* Washington, D.C.: World Bank, 1992.

Zeleza, Paul Tiyambe. "Dependent Capitalism and the Making of the Kenyan Working Class During the Colonial Period." Ph.D. diss., Dalhousie University, 1982.

————. "Economic Policy and Performance in Kenya since Independence." *TJH* (1991): 35–76.

————. "Strike Movement in Colonial Kenya: Era of the General Strikes." *TJH* (1993): 1–23.

Zwanenberg, Roger van. "Aspects of Kenya's Industrial History." *KHR* 1 (1) (1973): 45–61.

————. *Colonial Capitalism and Labour in Kenya, 1919–39.* Nairobi: EALB, 1972.

————. "Kenya's Primitive Colonial Capitalism: The Economic Weakness of Kenya's Settlers up to 1940." *CJAS* 9 (2) (1975): 277–92.

G. GENERAL STUDIES

Amin, Mohamed, and Peter Moll. *Mzee Jomo Kenyatta: A Photobiography.* Nairobi: Marketing and Publishing, 1978.

Archer, Jules. *African Firebrand: Kenyatta of Kenya.* New York: Julian Messner, 1970.

Arnold, Guy. *Kenyatta and the Politics of Kenya.* London: J. M. Dent and Sons, 1974.

————. *Modern Kenya.* London: Longman, 1981.

Aseka, E. *Makers of History, 1: Jomo Kenyatta.* Nairobi: EAEP, 1993.

————. *Makers of History, 2: Ronald Ngala.* Nairobi: EAEP, 1993.

Bailey, Jim. *Kenya: The National Epic.* Nairobi: Kenway Publications, 1993.

Berghe, M. V. D. *Le Kenya.* Paris: Harmattan, 1991.

Bolton, Kenneth. *Harambee Country: A Guide to Kenya.* London: Geoffrey Bles, 1970.

————, ed. *The Lion and the Lilly: A Guide to Kenya.* London: 1962.

Daystar Communications. *Baseline Country Profiles for Open Doors: Country Report, Kenya.* Nairobi: Daystar Communications, 1984.

Dealing, James Ralph. "Politics in Wanga, Kenya, c. 1650–1914." Ph.D. diss., Northwestern University, 1974.

Delf, George. *Jomo Kenyatta: Towards Truth about "The Light of Africa."* London: Gollancz, 1961.

Friedmann, J. *Jomo Kenyatta.* London: Wayland Publishers, 1975.

Great Britain. War Office. Intelligence Division. *Handbook of British East Africa.* London: HMSO, 1893.

Groen, Gerrit D. "Afrikaners in Kenya, 1903–1969." Ph.D. diss., Michigan State University, 1974.

Halkin, John. *Kenya.* New York: Beaufort Books, 1983.

Horrobin, David F. *A Guide to Kenya and Northern Tanzania.* New York: Charles Scribner's Sons, 1971.

Howarth, A. *Kenyatta: A Photographic Biography.* Nairobi: EAPH, 1967.

Kaggia, Bildad. *The Roots of Freedom 1921–1963: The Autobiography of Bildad Kaggia.* Nairobi: EAPH, 1975.

Kaplan, I. et al. *Area Handbook for Kenya.* Washington, D.C.: USGPO, 1976.

Kenya: An Official Handbook. Nairobi: EAPH, 1973.

Kenya: Official Handbook. Nairobi: Government of the Republic of Kenya, 1983.

King, Kenneth, and Ahmed Salim, eds. *Kenya Historical Biographies.* Nairobi: EAPH, 1971.

MacPhee, A. Marshall. *Kenya.* New York: Praeger, 1968.

Magary, Alan, and Kerstin Fraser Magary. *East Africa: A Travel Guide.* New York: Harper and Row, 1975.

Maren, Michael. *The Land and the People of Kenya.* New York: Lippincott, 1989.

Middleton, John. *World of the Swahili: An African Mercantile Civilization.* New Haven, CT: YUP, 1992.

Miller, Norman N. *Kenya: The Quest for Prosperity.* Boulder, CO: WP, 1984.

Mueller, Susanne. "Political Parties in Kenya: The Politics of Opposition and Dissent, 1919–1969." Ph.D. diss., Princeton University Press, 1972.

Murray-Brown, Jeremy. *Kenyatta.* Boston: George Allen and Unwin, 1979.

Nazareth, John Maximian. *Brown Man, Black Country: A Peep into Kenya's Freedom Struggle.* New Delhi: Tidings Publications, 1981.

Nelson, Harold D., ed. *Kenya: A Country Study.* 3rd Edition. Washington, D.C.: USGPO, 1984.

Ochieng', William Robert. *Eastern Kenya and Its Invaders.* Nairobi: EALB, 1975.

———. *The First Word: Essays on Kenya History.* Nairobi: EALB, 1975.

———. *The Second Word: More Essays on Kenya History.* Nairobi: EALB, 1977.

———. *The Third Word: Essays on Kenyan History and Society.* Nairobi: KLB, 1984.

———, ed. *Themes in Kenyan History.* Nairobi: Heinemann, 1990.

Ogot, Bethwell A., ed. *Hadith 1: Proceedings of the Conference of the Historical Association of Kenya, 1967.* Nairobi: EAPH, 1968.

———. *Hadith 2: Proceedings of the 1968 Conference of the Historical Association of Kenya, 1967.* Nairobi: EAPH, 1970.

———. *Hadith 3: Proceedings of the Conference of the Historical Association of Kenya, 1969/70.* Nairobi: EAPH, 1971.

————. *Hadith 4: Politics and Nationalism in Colonial Kenya*. Nairobi: EAPH, 1973.

————. *Hadith 5: Economic and Social History of East Africa*. Nairobi: EALB, 1975.

————. *Hadith 6: History and Social Change in East Africa*. Nairobi: EALB, 1976.

————. *Hadith 7: Ecology and History in East Africa*. Nairobi: KLB, 1980.

————. "Towards a History of Kenya." *KHR* 4 (1) (1976): 1–9.

Ogot, Bethwell A., and Tiyambe Zeleza. "Kenya: The Road to Independence and After." In *Decolonization and African Independence*, edited by Prosser Gifford and Wm. Roger Louis, 401–26. New Haven, CT: YUP.

Pateman, Robert. *Kenya*. New York: Marshall Cavendish, 1993.

Perham, Margery. *East African Journey. Kenya and Tanganyika 1929–30*. London: Faber and Faber, 1976.

Roelker, Jack R. *Mathu of Kenya: A Political Study*. Stanford, CA: Hoover Institution Press, 1976.

Salim, A. *Swahili-Speaking Communities of the Kenya Coast 1895–1965*. Nairobi: EAPH, 1972.

Stamp, Patricia. "Government in Kenya: Ideology and Political Practice, 1895–1974." *ASR* 29 (4) (1986): 17–42.

Thuku, Harry. *Harry Thuku: An Autobiography*. Nairobi: OUP, 1970.

Wepman, Dennis. *Jomo Kenyatta*. London: Burke Publishing Company, 1988.

Were, Gideon S. *History of the Abaluyia of Western Kenya, c. 1500–1930*. Nairobi: EAPH, 1967.

H. REGIONAL STUDIES

Acland, J. D. *East African Crops: An Introduction to the Production of Field and Plantation Crops in Kenya, Tanzania, and Uganda*. London: Longman for FAO, 1971.

Akiwumi, A. M. "The East African Community." *Journal of World Trade Law* 6 (2) (1972): 203–26.

Alabaster, John S. *Review of the State of Aquatic Pollution of East African Inland Waters*. Rome: FAO, 1981.

Alpers, Edward A. *East African Slave Trade*. Nairobi: EAPH, 1967.

————. "French Slave Trade in East Africa (1721–1810)." *Cahiers d'Études Africaines* 37 (1970): 80–124.

————. *Ivory and Slaves: Changing Pattern of International Trade in East Central Africa to the Later Nineteenth Century*. Berkeley and Los Angeles: University of California Press, 1975.

————, and Christopher Ehret. "Eastern Africa." In *Cambridge History of Africa*. Vol. 4, edited by Richard Gray, 469–576. Cambridge: CUP, 1975.

Amann, Hans. *Energy Supply and Economic Development in East Africa*. Munich Weltforum-Verlag, c. 1969.

Anderson, David M. "Depression, Dust Bowl, Demography and Drought: The Colonial State and Soil Conservation in East Africa During the 1930s." *AA* 83 (332) (1984): 321–41.

————, and Douglas H. Johnson, eds. *Revealing Prophets: Prophecy in Eastern African History*. London: James Currey, 1995.

Apthorpe, Raymond, ed. *Land Settlement and Rural Development in East Africa*. Kampala, Uganda: Transition Books, 1968.

Arens, William, ed. *Century of Change in Eastern Africa*. The Hague: Mouton, 1976.

Atieno Odhiambo. E. S. *History of East Africa*. London: Longmans, 1977.

Austen, Ralph A. "Nineteenth Century Islamic Slave Trade from East Africa (Swahili and Red Sea Coasts): A Tentative Census." *Slavery and Abolition* (1988): 21–44.

————. "Patterns of Development in Nineteenth-Century East Africa." *AHS* (1971): 645–57.

Ayot, Henry Okello. *Historical Texts of the Lake Region of East Africa*. Nairobi: KLB, 1977.

————. *Topics in East African History, 1000–1976*. Kampala, Uganda: EALB, 1976.

Baker, S. J. K. "Population Geography of East Africa." *East African Geographical Review* (1963): 1–6.

Barkan, Joel D., and David F. Gordon, eds. *Beyond Capitalism and Socialism in Kenya and Tanzania*. Boulder, CO: Lynne Rienner, 1993.

Beachey, R. W. *Documents: Slave Trade of Eastern Africa*. London: Rex Collings, 1971.

————. "East African Ivory Trade in the Nineteenth Century." *JAH* 8 (2) (1967): 269–90.

————. *History of East Africa, 1592–1902*. London: Tauris, 1995.

————. *Slave Trade of Eastern Africa*. London: Rex Collings, 1976.

Beck, Ann. "East African Community and Regional Research in Science and Medicine." *AA* 72 (288) (1973): 300–308.

Bennet, Norman R. *Studies in East African History*. Boston: Boston University Press, 1963.

Berg-Schlosser, Dirk, and Rainer Siegler. *Political Stability and Development: A Comparative Analysis of Kenya, Tanzania, and Uganda*. Boulder, CO: Lynne Rienner, 1990.

Bogonko, Sorobea Nyachieo. *Reflections on Education in East Africa*. Nairobi: OUP, 1992.

Bohnet, M., and H. Reichelt. *Applied Research and Its Impact on Economic Development: The East African Case*. Munich: IFO, 1972.

Brett, E. A. *Colonialism and Underdevelopment in East Africa: The Politics of Economic Change 1919–39*. London: Heinemann, 1973.

Brode, H. *British and German East Africa.* London: Edward Arnold, 1911.

————. *Tippo Tib.* London: Edward Arnold, 1907.

Brokensha, David W., and Peter D. Little, eds. *Anthropology of Development and Change in East Africa.* Boulder, CO: WP, 1988.

Brown, B. B. *Women and the Law in East Africa.* New York: Council for Inter-Cultural Studies and Programs, 1982.

Brown, Leslie. *East African Coasts and Reefs.* Nairobi: EAPH, 1975.

"Brushfire in East Africa." *AR* 2 (1964): 21–24.

Chambers, Robert. *Managing Rural Development: Ideas and Experience from East Africa.* Uppsala, Sweden: Scandinavian Institute of African Studies, 1974.

Chittick, H. Neville. "East Coast, Madagascar and the Indian Ocean." In *Cambridge History of Africa.* Vol. 3, edited by Roland Oliver, 183–231. Cambridge: CUP, 1977.

————. "'Shirazi' Colonization of East Africa." *JAH* 6 (3) (1965): 275–94.

————, and Robert I. Rotberg, eds. *East Africa and the Orient: Cultural Synthesis in Pre-Colonial Times.* New York: Africana Publishing, 1975.

Church, Archibald. *East Africa: A New Dominion.* London: H. F. and G. Witherby, 1927.

Clark, Paul G. *Development Planning in East Africa.* Nairobi: EAPH, 1966.

————. "Towards a More Comprehensive Planning in East Africa." *EAER* 10 (2) (1963): 65–74.

Cliffe, Lionel. "Reflections on Agricultural Development in East Africa." *EAJ* 7 (November 1965): 26–35.

————, J. S. Coleman, and M. R. Doornbos, eds. *Government and Rural Development in East Africa: Essays on Political Penetration.* The Hague: Martinus Nijhoff, 1977.

Cohen, Sir Andrew. *British Policy in Changing Africa.* London: Routledge and Kegan Paul, 1959.

Collinson, Michael. *Farming Systems Research in East Africa: The Experience of CIMMYT and Some National Agricultural Research Services.* East Lansing: Michigan State University, 1982.

Columbia University School of Law. *Public International Development Financing in East Africa.* New York: Columbia University Press, 1962.

Cotran, Eugene. "Unification of Laws in East Africa." *JMAS* 1 (2) (1963): 209–20.

Coupland, Sir Reginald. *East Africa and Its Invaders, from the Earliest Times to the Death of Seyyid Said in 1856.* Oxford: Clarendon Press, 1938.

————. *Exploitation of East Africa: The Slave Trade and the Scramble 1856–1890.* London: Faber and Faber, 1939.

Davey, K. J. *Programme Budgeting for East Africa.* Nairobi: East African Staff College, 1972.

————. *Taxing a Peasant Society: The Example of Graduated Taxes in East Africa.* London: Charles Knight, 1974.

Davidson, Basil. *East and Central Africa to the Late Nineteenth Century.* Nairobi: Longman, 1967.

Diamond, Stanley, and Fred G. Burke. *Transformation of East Africa.* New York: Basic Books, 1966.

Di Delupis, Ingrid Doimi. *East African Community and Common Market.* London: Longman, 1970.

Due, John F. "Reform of East African Taxation (Tanganyika, Kenya and Uganda)." *EAER* 11 (1) (1964): 57–68.

Durand, P. P. *Index to East African Cases Referred to, 1868–1968.* Nairobi: Legal Publications, 1969.

East African Institute of Social and Cultural Affairs. *Problems of Economic Development in East Africa.* Nairobi: EAPH, 1965.

East African Poll on Federation. Nairobi: Marco Publishers, 1962.

Ehret, Christopher. "The East African Interior." In *Africa from the Seventh to the Eleventh Century,* edited by M. El Fasi, 616–42. London: Heinemann, 1988.

Elkan, Walter. "Some Social and Political Implications on Industrial Development in East Africa." *International Social Science Journal* 3 (1964): 390–400.

Engberg, H. L. "Commercial Banking in East Africa, 1950–1963." *JMAS* 3 (2) (1965): 175–200.

Franck, Thomas M. *East African Unity through Law.* New Haven, CT: YUP, 1964.

Frank, C.S. *The Sugar Industry of East Africa.* Nairobi: EAPH, 1965.

Freeman-Grenville, G. S. P. *The East African Coast: Select Documents.* Oxford: Clarendon Press, 1962.

Friedland, William H. "Some Urban Myths in East Africa." *Rhodes-Livingston Conference Proceedings* 14 (1960): 83–97.

———, et al. *Public International Development Financing in East Africa: Kenya, Tanganyika, Uganda.* New York: Columbia University Press, 1962.

Galbraith, John S. *Mackinnon and East Africa, 1878–1895: A Study in the "New Imperialism."* Cambridge: CUP, 1972.

Garver, R. A., ed. *Research Priorities for East Africa.* Nairobi: EAPH, 1966.

Georgulas, Nikos. "Approach to Urban Analysis for East African Towns." *Ekistics* 109 (1964): 436–40.

———. *Taxation for Development in East Africa.* Nairobi: EAPH, 1967.

Githige, R. M. "Issue of Slavery: Relations Between the CMS and the State on the East African Coast Prior to 1895." *Journal of Religion in Africa* 3 (1986): 209–25.

Goldthorpe, J. E. *Outlines of East African Society.* Kampala: Makerere University College, 1959.

———, and F. B. Wilson. *Tribal Maps of East Africa and Zanzibar.* Kampala, Uganda: East African Institute of Social Research, 1960.

Goodman, Stephen H. "Eastern and Western Markets for the Primary Products of East Africa." *EAER* 14 (1967): 77–83.

Gray, C. S. "Development Planning in East Africa: A Review Article." *EAER* 13 (2) (1966): 1–18.

Gray, Richard, and David Birmingham, eds. *Pre-Colonial African Trade: Essays on Trade in Central and Eastern Africa Before 1900.* London: OUP, 1970.

Gulhati, Ravi, and Gautam Datta. *Capital Accumulation in Eastern and Southern Africa: A Decade of Setbacks.* Washington, D.C.: World Bank, 1983.

Gulliver, Philip Hugh, ed. *Tradition and Transition in East Africa.* Berkeley: University of California Press, 1969.

Hailey, Lord. *An African Survey.* London: OUP, 1957.

———. *Native Administration and Political Development in British Tropical Africa.* London: HMSO, 1940.

———. *Native Administration in British African Territories.* Part 1. London: HMSO, 1950.

Hall, Susan. *Preferential Trade Area (PTA) for Eastern and Southern African States: Strategy, Progress, and Problems.* Nairobi: Institute for Development Studies, University of Nairobi, 1987.

Hamilton, A. C. *Environmental History of East Africa: A Study of the Quaternary.* London and New York: Academic Press, 1982.

Hamilton, G. *In the Wake of Da Gama: The Story of Portuguese Pioneers in East Africa, 1497–1729.* London: Skeffington, 1951.

Harlow, Vincent, and E. M. Chilver, eds. *History of East Africa.* Vol. II. Oxford: Clarendon Press, 1965.

Hazlewood, Arthur. "East African Common Market: Importance and Effects." *Bulletin of the Oxford University Institute of Economics and Statistics* 28 (1) (1966): 1–18.

———. *Economic Integration: The East African Experience.* London: Heinemann, 1975.

———. "End of the East African Community: What Are the Lessons for Regional Integration Schemes?" *Journal of Common Market Studies* 18 (1) (1979): 40–58.

———. *Rail and Road in East Africa: Transport Coordination in Underdeveloped Countries.* Oxford: Basil Blackwell, 1964.

———. "The 'Shiftability' of Industry and the Measurement of Gains and Losses in the East African Common Market." *Bulletin of the Oxford University Institute of Economics and Statistics* 28 (2) (1966): 63–72.

Helleiner, G. K. "The Measurement of Aggregative Economic Performance in East Africa." *EAER* 15 (1) (1968): 87–93.

Hollingsworth, Lawrence William. *Short History of the East Coast of Africa.* London: Macmillan, 1960.

Hosier, Richard H. "Economics of Deforestation in Eastern Africa." *Economic Geography* 64 (2) (1988): 121–36.

Hourani, George. *Arab Seafaring in the Indian Ocean in Ancient and Early Medieval Times.* Princeton, NJ: Princeton University Press, 1995.

Hughes, Anthony J. *East Africa: The Search for Unity.* Baltimore, MD: Penguin, 1963.

Hutchinson, E. *Slave Trade of East Africa.* London: Low, Marston, Low, and Searle, 1874.

Ingham, Kenneth. *History of East Africa*. London: Longman, 1962.

Ireri, D. "Proposed Model to Analyse Economic Interdependence among the Member Countries of the East African Community." *EAER* 16 (2) (1969): 75–87.

Joelson, Ferdinand Stephen. *Eastern Africa Today*. London: East Africa, 1928.

Kanyinga, Karuti, Andrew S.Z. Kiondo, and Per Tidemand. *New Local Level Politics in East Africa: Studies on Uganda, Tanzania and Kenya*. Uppsala, Sweden: SIAS, 1994.

Khapoya, Vincent B., and Baffour Agyeman-Duah. "Cold War and Regional Politics in East Africa." *Conflict Quarterly* (1985): 18–32.

Kieran, J. "Origins of Commercial Arabica Coffee Production in East Africa." *AHS* (1969): 51–67.

Kilbride, Philip Leroy, and Janet Capriotti Kilbride. *Changing Life in East Africa: Women and Children at Risk*. University Park, PA: Penn State University Press, 1990.

Kirkman, James S. *Men and Monuments on the East African Coast*. New York: Praeger, 1966.

Kjerkshus, Helge. *Ecology Control and Economic Development in East African History*. London: James Currey, 1996.

Knight, John B., and Richard H. Sabot. *Education, Productivity, and Inequality: The East African Natural Experiment*. Oxford: OUP, 1990.

Labour Research Department. *British Imperialism in East Africa*. London: Labour Research Department, 1926.

Leys, Colin, and Peter Robson, eds. *Federation in East Africa: Opportunities and Problems*. Nairobi: OUP, 1965.

Leys, Norman. *Colour Bar in East Africa*. London: Hogarth Press, 1941.

Lonsdale, John M. "Some Origins of Nationalism in East Africa." *JAH* 9 (1) (1968): 119–46.

Low, D.A., and Alison Smith, eds. *History of East Africa*. Vol. III. Oxford: Clarendon Press, 1976.

Lugard, Sir Frederick D. *Rise of Our East African Empire*. 2 Vols. London: Blackwood, 1893.

Lundahl, Mats. *Incentives and Agriculture in East Africa*. London: Routledge, 1990.

McCall, D. F., et al., eds. *Eastern African History*. London: Pall Mall, 1969.

McEwen, A. C. *International Boundaries of East Africa*. London: OUP, 1971.

McIntosh, Brian G., ed. *Ngono: Studies in Traditional and Modern East African History*. Nairobi: EAPH, 1969.

McLoughlin, Peter F. M. *Research on Agricultural Development in East Africa*. New York: Agricultural Development Council, 1967.

Macmillan, Mona. *Introducing East Africa*. London: Faber and Faber, 1952.

Malecela, John S. "What Next for the East African Community?—The Case for Integration." *TAR* 2 (1) (1972): 211–17.

Marlin, Peter, ed. *Financial Aspects of Development in East Africa*. Munich: Weltforum Verlag, 1970.

Marsh, Zoë. *East Africa through Contemporary Records*. London: CUP, 1961.

————, and G. W. Kingsnorth. *Introduction to the History of East Africa*. Cambridge: CUP, 1957.

Martin, B. G. "Arab Migration to East Africa in Medieval Times." *IJAHS* 7 (3) (1975): 367–90.

Masao, F. T., and H. W. Mutoro. "East African Coast and the Comoros Islands." In *Africa from the Seventh to the Eleventh Century*, edited by M. El Fasi, 596–615. London: Heinemann, 1988.

Massell, Benton F. *Distribution of Economic Gains within the Common Market Formed by Kenya, Uganda and Tanganyika*. Santa Monica, CA: The Rand Corporation, 1964.

————. *East African Economic Union: An Evaluation and Some Implications for Policy*. Santa Monica, CA: The Rand Corporation, 1963.

————. *Economic Union in East Africa: An Evaluation of Gains*. Santa Monica, CA: The Rand Corporation, 1964.

————. "Industrialization and Economic Union in Greater East Africa." *EAER* 9 (2) (1962): 108–23.

Maxon, Robert M. *East Africa: An Introductory History*. 2nd ed. Morgantown: West Virginia University Press, 1994.

Mazrui, Ali A. "Language and Politics in East Africa." *AR* 12 (6) (1967): 59–61.

————. "Tanzania Versus East Africa: A Case of Unwitting Federal Sabotage." *Journal of Commonwealth Political Studies* 3 (3) (1965): 209–25.

Mazzeo, Domenico. *Foreign Assistance and the East Africa Common Services, 1960–1970, with Special References to Multilateral Contributions*. Munich: Weltforum, 1975.

Mbilinyi, S. M. "East African Export Commodities and the Enlarged European Economic Community." *TAR* 3 (1) (1973): 85–110.

Mead, D. C. "Economic Cooperation in East Africa." *JMAS* 7 (2) (1969): 277–87.

Meeker, Michael E. *Pastoral Son and the Spirit of Patriarchy: Religion, Society and Person among East African Stock Keepers*. Madison and London: University of Wisconsin Press, 1989.

Meister, Albert. *East Africa: The Past in Chains, The Future in Pawn*. New York: Walker and Company, 1966.

Merritt, Herbert Paul. "Bismarck and the First Partition of East Africa." *English Historical Review* 360 (1976): 585–97.

————. "Bismarck and the German Interest in East Africa, 1884–1885." *Historical Journal* 21 (1) (1978): 97–116.

Middleton, John. *World of the Swahili: An African Mercantile Civilization*. New Haven, CT and London: YUP, 1992.

Mmuya, Max. *The Functional Dimension of the Democratization Process: Tanzania and Kenya: With Some Experiences from Former Eastern Europe*. Dar-es-Salaam, Tanzania: Dar-es-Salaam University Press, 1994.

Morgan, D. J. *British Private Investment in East Africa: Report of a Survey and a Conference*. London: ODI, 1965.

Morgan, W. T. W. *East Africa*. London: Longman, 1973.

————, ed. *East Africa: Its Peoples and Resources*. Nairobi: OUP, 1969.

Mugomba, A. T. "Regional Organisations and African Underdevelopment: The Collapse of the East African Community." *JMAS* 16 (2) (1978): 261–72.

Müller, Fritz Ferdinand. *Deutschland-Zanzibar-Ostafrika*. Berlin: Rütten u. Loening, 1959.

Munro, J. Forbes. "British Rubber Companies in East Africa before the First World War." *JAH* 24 (3) (1983): 369–79.

Mwase, N. R. L. "Last Days of the East African Community." *Tanzania Notes and Records* (88/89) (1982): 63–66.

Ndegwa, Philip. *Common Market and Development in East Africa*. Nairobi: EAPH, 1965.

Newlyn, W. T. "Gains and Losses in the East African Common Market." *Yorkshire Bulletin of Economic and Social Research* 2 (1965): 130–38.

Nicholls, C. S. *The Swahili Coast: Politics, Diplomacy and Trade on the East African Littoral, 1798–1856*. London: Allen and Unwin, 1971.

North, Stephen J. *British India's Steam Navigation Company's Mail Packets to East Africa 1890–1905*. London: East Africa Study Circle, 1990.

Nthamburi, Zabion, ed. *From Mission to Church: A Handbook of Christianity in East Africa*. Nairobi: Uzima Press, 1991.

Nye, Joseph S. "East African Economic Integration." *JMAS* 1 (4) (1963): 475–502.

————. *Functionalism and Federalism in East Africa*. Geneva: International Political Science Association, 1964.

————. *Pan-Africanism and East African Integration*. Cambridge, MA: Harvard University Press, 1965.

Nyerere Doctrine of State Secession and the New States of East Africa. Arusha, Tanzania: EAPH, 1984.

O'Connor, Anthony M. *Economic Geography of East Africa*. London: Bell, 1966.

Odingo, R. S. "Geopolitical Problems of East Africa." *EAJ* 2 (9) (1966): 17–24.

Ogot, Bethwell A. *Economic Adaption and Change Among the Jii-Speaking Peoples of Eastern Africa*. Nairobi: Anyange Press, 1996.

————, and J.A. Kieran, eds. *Zamani: A Survey of East African History*. Nairobi: EAPH, 1968.

Okoth, P. Godfrey. "Preferential Trade Area for Eastern and Southern African Studies and its East African Community Heritage." *JEARD* 20 (1990): 162–85.

Oliver, Roland. "East African Interior." In *Cambridge History of Africa*. Vol. III, edited by Roland Oliver, 621–69. Cambridge: CUP, 1977.

Oliver, Roland, and Gervase Mathew, eds. *History of East Africa*. Vol. I. Oxford: Clarendon Press, 1976.

Oloya, J. J. *Coffee, Cotton, Sisal and Tea in East African Economies*. Nairobi: EALB, 1969.

————. *Some Aspects of Economic Development, With Special Reference to East Africa*. Nairobi: EALB, 1968.

Ouma, Joseph P. B. M. *Evolution of Tourism in East Africa (1900–2000)*. Nairobi: EALB, 1970.

Owen, D. F., ed. *Research and Development in East Africa*. Nairobi: EAPH, 1966.

Oyugi, Walter O., ed. *Politics and Administration in East Africa*. Nairobi: EAEP, 1994.

Pauw, E. J. *Banking in East Africa*. Munich: IFO, 1969.

Potholm, Christian P. "Who Killed Cock Robin? Perceptions Concerning the Break-up of the East African Community." *World Affairs* 142 (1) (1979): 45–56.

Pouwels, Randall L. *Horn and Cresent: Cultural Change and Traditional Islam on the East African Coast, 800–1900*. Cambridge: CUP, 1987.

Problems of Economic Development in East Africa. Nairobi: The East African Institute of Social and Cultural Affairs, 1965.

Proctor, J. C. "Effort to Federate East Africa: A Post Mortem." *Political Quarterly* 27 (1) (1966): 46–69.

Pruen, C. M. "Slavery in East Africa." *CMIR* New Series, (1888): 661–65.

Puffer, Frank. *Informal Markets: Smuggling in East Africa: A Preliminary Discussion*. Worcester, MA: International Development Program, Clark University, 1982.

Ravenhill, John. "Regional Integration and Development in Africa: Lessons from the East African Community." *Journal of Commonwealth and Comparative Politics* 17 (3) (1979): 227–46.

Reusch, Richard. *History of East Africa*. Stuttgart: Evangelischer Missionsverlag, 1954.

Richards, Audrey I., ed. *East African Chiefs*. New York: Praeger, 1960.

Ricks, Thomas M. "Persian Gulf Seafaring and East Africa: Ninth–Twelfth Centuries." *AHS* (1970): 339–57.

Roberts, A. D. "East Africa." In *Cambridge History of Africa*. Vol. VII, edited by A. D. Roberts, 649–701. Cambridge: CUP, 1986.

Ross, D. H. *Educating Handicapped Young People in Eastern and Southern Africa in 1981–83*. Paris: UNESCO, 1988.

Rotberg, Robert I. "Federation Movement in British East and Central Africa, 1889–1953." *Journal of Commonwealth Political Studies* 2 (2) (1964): 141–60.

Rothchild, Donald, ed. *Politics of Integration: An East African Documentary*. Nairobi: EAPH, 1968.

Russell, E. W., ed. *Natural Resources of East Africa*. Nairobi: EALB, 1962.

Saberwal, Satish. "Oral Tradition, Periodization, and Political Systems: Some East African Comparisons." *CJAS* 1 (2) (1967): 155–62.

Saeed, M., and G. P. Setia, eds. *India and East Africa: Trade Ties*. Delhi: Triveni, 1986.

Safier, M. "Towards the Definition of Economic Development Over East Africa." *East African Geographical Review* (1969): 1–13.

Salim, A. I. "East African Coast and Hinterland, 1800–45." In *Africa in the Nineteenth Century Until the 1880s*, edited by J. F. Ade Ajayi, 211–33. Berkeley: University of California Press, 1989.

Sarone, O. S. *Development and Education for Pastoralists: Maasai Responses in East Africa*. Montreal: Centre for Developing-Area Studies, McGill University, 1984.

Saul, John S. *State and Revolution in Eastern Africa*. London and Nairobi: Heinemann, 1979.

Schoff, W. H. *Periplus of the Erythraean Sea: Travel and Trade in the Indian Ocean by a Merchant of the First Century*. London: Longman, Green, 1912.

Seavoy, Ronald E. *Famine in East Africa: Food Production and Food Policies*. New York: Greenwood Press, 1989.

Segal, Aaron. *East Africa: Strategy for Economic Co-operation*. Nairobi: The East African Institute of Social and Cultural Affairs, 1965.

————. "Politics of Land in East Africa." *AR* 12 (4) (1967): 46–50.

————. "Postscript to East African Federation." *AR* 8 (10) (1963): 12–13.

Segal, Mark D. "East African Common Market: Historic, Structural and Incidental Dysfunctions." *TAR* 7 (1/2) (1978): 77–123.

Seidman, Ann. *Comparative Development Strategies in East Africa*. Nairobi: EAPH, 1972.

Semboja, Joseph, and Ole Therkildsen, eds. *Service Provision in East Africa: The State and Voluntary Organizations in Kenya, Tanzania and Uganda*. London: James Currey, 1995.

Sharkansky, Ira, and Dennis L. Dresang. "International Assistance: Its Variety, Coordination, and Impact among Public Corporations in Kenya and the East African Community." *International Organization* 28 (2) (1974): 207–31.

Strandes, Justus. *Portuguese Period in East Africa*. Nairobi: EALB, 1968.

Sutton, John E. G. *Early Trade in Eastern Africa*. Nairobi: EAPH, 1973.

————. *East African Coast: An Historical and Archaeological Review*. Nairobi: EAPH, 1966.

————. *A Thousand Years of East Africa*. Nairobi: British Institute in Eastern Africa, 1990.

Tandon, Yashpal, ed. *Technical Assistance Administration in East Africa*. Uppsala, Sweden: Almqvist and Wiksell, 1973.

Thomas, P. A. *Private Enterprise and the Corporate Form in East Africa*. Nairobi: EAPH, 1968.

————, ed. *Private Enterprise and the East African Company*. Dar-es-Salaam: Tanzania Publishing House, 1969.

Twining, William. *Place of Customary Law in the National Legal Systems of East Africa*. Chicago: University of Chicago Law School, 1964.

Unomah A. C., and J. B. Webster. "East Africa: The Expansion of Commerce." In *Cambridge History of Africa*. Vol. V, edited by John E. Flint, 270–318. Cambridge: CUP, 1976.

Vente, Rolf E. *Planning Processes: The East African Case*. Munich: Weltforum Verlag, 1970.

Waller, Richard. "Ecology, Migration and Expansion in East Africa." *AA* 84 (336) (1985): 347–70.

Ward, W. E. F., and L. W. White. *East Africa: A Century of Change 1870–1970*. New York: Africana Publishing Corporation, 1971.

Westcott, Nicholas J. "Closer Union and the Future of East Africa, 1939–48: A Case Study in the Official Mind of Imperialism." *JICH* 10 (1) (1981): 67–88.

———. "East African Sisal Industry, 1929–1949: The Marketing of a Colonial Commodity during Depression and War." *JAH* 25 (4) (1984): 445–61.

Whitaker, Philip. *Political Theory and East African Problems.* London: OUP, 1964.

Who Wants an East African Federation. Nairobi: Marco Publishers, 1965.

Wood, L. J., and Christopher Ehret. "Origins and Diffusion of the Market Institution in East Africa." *JAS* 4 (1) (1978): 1–17.

Wraith, Ronald E. *East African Citizen.* New York: OUP, 1959.

Wright, Marcia. "East Africa, 1870–1905." In *Cambridge History of Africa.* Vol. VI, edited by J. D. Fage and Roland Oliver, 539–91. Cambridge: CUP, 1985.

Yoshida, Masao. *Agricultural Marketing Intervention in East Africa: A Study in the Colonial Origins of Marketing Policies 1900–1965.* Tokyo: Institute of Developing Economies, 1984.

Zajadacs, Paul, ed. *Studies in Production and Trade in East Africa.* Munich: Weltforum Verlag, 1970.

Zwanenberg, Roger van, with Anne King. *Economic History of Kenya and Uganda, 1800–1970.* Atlantic Highlands, NJ: Humanities Press, 1975.

I. RELIGION, MISSIONS, AND MISSIONARIES

Abungu, G. H. O. "Islam on the Kenyan Coast: An Overview of Kenyan Coastal Sites." In *Sacred Sites, Sacred Places*, edited by D. Carmichael, et al., 152–62. London: Routledge, 1994.

Adelphoi. *His Kingdom in Kenya.* London: Hodder and Stoughton, 1953.

American Friends Board of Missions. *Twenty-Five Years in East Africa.* Richmond, IN: American Friends Board of Missions, 1928.

Anderson, Dick. *Team for Turkana.* London: Africa Inland Mission, 1969.

Anderson, W. B. *The Church in East Africa 1840–1974.* Nairobi: Uzima, 1977.

———. "Experience and Meaning of Conversion for Early Christian Converts in Kenya." In *Theory and Practice in Church Life and Growth: 56 Studies in Eastern, Central and Southern Africa Over the Last Hundred Years*, edited by David B. Barnett, 157–67. Nairobi: Workshop in Religious Research, 1968.

Atieno Odhiambo, E. S. "Portrait of the Missionaries in Kenya Before 1939." *KHR* 1 (1) (1973): 1–14.

Barnett, Anne. "Christian Home and Family Life in Kenya Today." *IRM* 49 (1960): 420–26.

Barrett, David B., et al. *Kenya Churches Handbook: The Development of Christianity, 1498–1973.* Kisumu: Evangel Publishing House, 1973.

Beckerleg, Susan. "'Brown Sugar' or Friday Prayers: Youth Choices and Community Building in Coastal Kenya." *AA* 94 (374) (1995): 23–38.

Beecher, L. J. "African Separatist Churches in Kenya." *World Dominion* 31 (1) (1953): 5–12.

Bennett, Norman R. "Church Missionary Society at Mombasa, 1873–1894." *Boston University Papers in African History* 1 (1964): 159–95.

Berger, I. *Religion and Resistance: East African Kingdom in the Pre-Colonial Period*. Tervuren, Belgium: Musée Royal de l'Afrique Centrale, 1981.

Bernardi, B. *The Mugwe, A Failing Prophet: A Study of a Religious and Public Dignitary of the Meru of Kenya*. Oxford: OUP, 1959.

Bewes, T. C. F. "Christian Revival in Kenya." *World Dominion* 34 (2) (1956): 110–14.

————. "Kikuyu Religion Old and New." *AA* 52 (207) (1953): 202–10.

————. "The Work of the Christian Church among the Kikuyu." *International Affairs* 29 (3) (1952): 316–25.

Blakeslee, Helen V. *Beyond the Kikuyu Curtain*. Chicago: Moody Press, 1956.

Bogonko, Sorobea Nyachieo. "Catholicism and Protestantism in the Socio-Economic and Political Progress of Kenya, 1920–1963." *JEARD* 12 (1982): 83–123.

Booth, Karen M., and Newell S. Booth. "Islam and Political Development in Kenya." *African Studies Association Papers* 28 (12) (1985): 1–18.

Bottignole, S. *Kikuyu Traditional Culture and Christianity*. Nairobi: Heinemann Educational Books, 1984.

Bridges, Roy C. "Krapf and the Strategy of the Mission to East Africa." *Makerere Journal* 5 (1961): 37–51.

Britton, J. "The Missionary Task in Kenya." *IRM* 12 (1923): 412–20.

Brown, Evelyn M. *Edel Quinn: Beneath the Southern Cross*. London: Burns and Oates, 1967.

Bunger, R. L. *Islamization Among the Upper Pokomo of Kenya*. Syracuse, NY: Syracuse University Press, 1973.

Burgman, H. *The Way the Catholic Church Started in Western Kenya*. London: Mission Book Service, 1990.

Capon, Martin. *Towards Christian Unity in Kenya*. Nairobi: CCK, 1962.

Carlebach, J. *Jews of Nairobi, 1903–1962*. Nairobi: Nairobi Hebrew Congregation, c. 1962.

Cathedral of the Highlands, 1917–1950. Nairobi: East African Standard, 1950.

Chepkwony, Agnes. *The Role of Non-Governmental Organizations in Development: A Study of the National Christian Council of Kenya, 1963–1978*. Uppsala, Sweden: University of Uppsala, 1987.

"Church and the Churches: Kikuyu." *Candid Quarterly* (1914): 513–26.

Church of Scotland. Foreign Mission Committee. *Kenya: 1898–1948. The Jubilee Book of the Church of Scotland Mission, Kenya Colony*. Edinburgh: Church of Scotland Foreign Mission Committee, 1948.

The Churches' Role in Kenya: A Report of the Conference on the Role of Churches in Independent Kenya, January 1964. Nairobi: CCK, 1964.

Ciekawy, Diane. "Policing Religious Practice in Contemporary Coastal Kenya." *Political and Legal Anthropology Review* 20 (1) (1997): 62–72.

Cole, E. K. *Cross over Mount Kenya*. Nairobi: Church Missionary Historical Publications, 1970.

————. *History of Church Co-operation in Kenya*. Limuru: St. Paul's College Press, 1957.

Connolly, Yolanda Evans. "Roots of Diversity: American Protestant Missions in Kenya, 1923–1946." Ph.D. diss., University of Illinois, 1975.

Conquest for Christ in Africa, 1902–52: A History of the Consolata Fathers in Kenya. Nyeri, Kenya: Catholic Printing School, 1952.

Cooper, Frederick. "Islam and Cultural Hegemony: The Ideology of Slaveowners on the East African Coast." *The Ideology of Slavery in Africa*, edited by P. E. Lovejoy, 271–307. Beverly Hills: Sage, 1981.

Crawford, E. May. *By the Equator's Snowy Peak*. London: Church Missionary Society, 1913.

Dawson, E. C. *James Hannington: First Bishop of Eastern Equatorial Africa*. London: Seeley and Company, 1886.

Dougall, J. W. C. *Building Kenya's Future*. Edinburgh: Church of Scotland Foreign Missions Committee, 1955.

Eastern Equatorial Africa Mission of the Church Missionary Society. London: CMS, 1891.

Eglin, Lorna. *Child of Two Worlds*. Cape Town: Africa Inland Mission, 1971.

Elolia, Samuel K. "Christianity and Culture in Kenya: An Encounter between the African Inland Mission and the Marakwet Belief System and Culture." Ph.D. diss., University of St. Michael's College, 1992.

Esmail, A. "Towards a History of Islam in East Africa." *KHR* 3 (1) (1975): 147–58.

Falda, B. *Ricordi Personali*. 3 vols. Turin: Edizioni Missioni Consolate, 1969.

Feldman, D. M. "Christians and Politics: The Origins of the Kikuyu Central Association in Northern Murang'a, 1890–1930." Ph.D. diss., Cambridge University, 1979.

Forbes-Watson, R. *Charles New*. London: Nelson, 1950.

Freeman-Grenville, G. S. P. "Martyrs of Mombasa, 1631." *African Ecclesiastical Review* 4 (1967): 353–64.

Frere, Sir Bartle. *East Africa As a Field for Missionary Labour*. London: John Murray, 1874.

Fueter, P. S. "A Christian Council in Action: The Christian Council of Kenya." *IRM* 49 (1960): 291–300.

Gilpin, Clifford Wesley. "The Church and the Community: Quakers in Western Kenya, 1902–1963." Ph.D. diss., Columbia University, 1976.

Githige, Renison Muchiri. "The Issue of Slavery: Relations between the CMS and the State on the East African Coast Prior to 1895." *JRA* 16 (3) (1986): 209–25.

————. "Mission-State Relationship in Colonial Kenya: A Summary." *JRA* 13 (2) (1982): 110–25.

————. "Mission-State Relationship in Kenya, 1888–1935." Ph.D. diss.. University of Aberdeen, 1982.

Gratian, John Alexander. "Relationship of the Africa Inland Mission and Its National Church in Kenya Between 1895 and 1971." Ph.D. diss., New York University, 1974.

Gray, Sir John. *Early Portuguese Missionaries in East Africa.* London: Macmillan, 1958.

Greaves, L. B. *Carey Francis of Kenya.* London: Rex Collings, 1969.

Hake, A. "An Urban Mission Course in Kenya." *IRM* 52 (1963): 173–81.

Harries, L. P. *Islam in East Africa.* London: Longman, 1952.

Harris, Grace Gredys. *Casting out Anger: Religion among the Taita of Kenya.* Cambridge: CUP, 1978.

Holway, James D. "C.M.S. Contact with Islam in East Africa Before 1914." *JRA* 4 (3) (1972): 200–12.

————. "Religious Composition of the Population of the Coast Province of Kenya." *JRA* 3 (3) (1970): 228–39.

Hooton, W. S., and J. Stafford Wright. *The First Twenty-Five Years of the Bible Churchman's Society (1922–47).* London: Bible Churchman's Society, 1947.

Horner, Norman A. "An East African Orthodox Church." *Journal of Ecumenical Studies* 12 (2) (1975): 221–33.

Hoskins, Irene. *Friends in Africa.* Richmond, IN: American Friends Board of Foreign Missions, 1944.

Hoyt, Alta Howard. *We Were Pioneers.* Wichita, KS: Privately Printed, 1971.

Hurd, A. E. S. *Serving the Church in Kenya.* London: Bible Churchman's Society, 1963.

Kangethe, Kamuyu wa. "African Response to Christianity: A Case Study of the Agikuyu of Central Kenya." *Missiology* 16 (1988): 23–44.

Kariuki, Obadiah. *A Bishop Facing Mount Kenya: An Autobiography, 1902–1978.* Nairobi: Uzima Press, 1985.

Keller, Marion. *Twenty Years in East Africa.* Toronto: Full Gospel Publishing Company, n.d.

Kenya, 1898–1948: The Jubilee Book of the Church of Scotland Mission, Kenya Colony. Kikuyu: Church of Scotland Foreign Mission Committee, 1948.

Kenya Present and Future: A Statement of Christian Principles. Nairobi: CCK, c. 1961.

Kieran, J. A. "Christian Church in East Africa in Modern Times." *Neue Zeitschrift für Missionswissenschaft* 4 (1969): 273–87.

————. "Holy Ghost Fathers in East Africa, 1863 to 1914." Ph.D. diss., University of London, 1966.

Kikuyu: 1898–1923. Semi-Jubilee Book of the Church of Scotland Mission. London: William Blackwood and Sons, 1923.

Kikuyu 1918. Report of the United Conference of Missionary Societies in British East Africa. London: CMS Bookshop, 1918.

Kimilu, D. N. "Separatist Churches." *Dini na Mila* 2/3 (1967): 11–61.

King, Kenneth J. "Kenya Maasai and the Protest Phenomenon, 1900–1960." *JAH* 12 (1) (1971): 117–37.

Krapf, Johann Lewis. *Travels, Researches and Missionary Labours During an Eighteen Years' Residence in Eastern Africa.* London: Trubner and Company, 1860.

Kubai, A. N. "The Muslim Presence and Representations of Islam Among the Meru of Kenya." Ph.D. diss., University of London, 1995.

Langford-Smith, N. "Revival in East Africa." *IRM* 43 (1954): 77–81.

Langley, Myrtle, and T. Kiggins. *A Serving People: The Church in East Africa.* Nairobi: OUP, 1973.

Livingstone, David. *On Tana River: A Story of Kenya's Tana Church.* London: Cargate Press, n.d.

Lloyd, T. E. *African Harvest.* London: Lutterworth, 1953.

Lonsdale, John M. "Archdeacon Owen and the Kavirondo Taxpayers Association." *East African Institute of Social Research* (1963): 1–16.

———. "European Attitudes and African Pressures: Missions and Government in Kenya Between the Wars." *Race* 10 (2) (1968): 141–52.

———, and S. Booth Clibbon. "The Emerging Pattern of Church and State Cooperation in Kenya." In *Christianity in Independent Africa*, edited by E. Fashole-Luke et al, 267–82. London: Rex Collings, 1978.

McIntosh, Brian G. "Kenya 1923: The Political Crisis and the Missionary Dilemma." *TJH* 1 (1) (1971): 103–29.

———. "Scottish Mission in Kenya 1891–1923." Ph.D. diss., University of Edinburgh, 1969.

Macpherson, Robert. *Presbyterian Church in Kenya: An Account of the Origins and Growth of the PCEA.* Nairobi: PCEA, 1970.

Matson, A. T. "Holy Ghost Mission at Kosi on the Tana River." *Bulletin of the Society for African Church History*, 2 (1966): 174–79.

Mbotela, James Juma. *Recollections of James Juma Mbotela.* Nairobi: EAPH, 1977.

Murray, Jocelyn Margaret. "The Church Missionary Society and the 'Female Circumcision' Issue in Kenya 1929–1932." *JRA* 8 (2) (1976): 92–104.

———. "Kikuyu Female Circumcision Controversy, With Special Reference to the Church Missionary Society's 'Sphere of Influence.'" Ph.D. diss., University of California, 1974.

———. "Kikuyu Spirit Churches." *JRA* 5 (3) (1973): 198–234.

Murray, Nancy Uhlar. "Archdeacon W. E. Owen: Missionary as Propagandist." *IJAHS* 15 (4) (1982): 653–70.

———. "Need to Get There First: Staking a Missionary Claim in Colonial Kenya." *JAS* 12 (4) (1986): 181–93.

New, Charles. *Life, Wanderings and Labours in Eastern Africa.* London: Hodder and Stoughton, 1873.

Njoroge, Lawrence. "Catholic Missions in Kenya: The Case of the Spiritans and the Consolata, 1870–1970." Ph.D. diss., University of Notre Dame, 1991.

Nthamburi, Zabion John. *History of the Methodist Church in Kenya.* Nairobi: Uzima Press, 1982.

Okullu, John Henry. *Church and Marriage in East Africa*. Nairobi: Uzima Press, 1976.

————. *Church and Politics in East Africa*. Nairobi: Uzima Press, 1975.

Oliver, Roland. *Missionary Factor in East Africa*. London: Longman, 1965.

Omulokoli, Watson A. O. "The Historical Development of the Anglican Church Among Abaluyia, 1905–1955." Ph.D. diss., University of Aberdeen, 1981.

Painter, L. K. *Hill of Vision: The Story of the Quaker Movement in East Africa, 1902–1965*. Nairobi: East Africa Yearly Meeting of Friends, 1966.

Parsons, R. *Towards One People*. Nairobi: Department of Biblical Study and Research, NCCK, 1970.

Perlo, F. *Karoli, il Constantino Magno del Kenya*. Torino, Italy: Institute Missioni Conzolata, c. 1925.

Phillips, Kenneth Norman. *Tom Collins of Kenya: Son of Valour*. London: Africa Inland Mission, n.d.

Philp, Horace R.A. *God and the African in Kenya*. London: Marshall, Morgan and Scott, n.d.

————. *New Day in Kenya*. London: World Dominion Press, 1936.

Price, P. *God in the Valley*. London: Patmos Press, 1970.

Priest, D. "Do the Maasai Know God? An Exercise in Cultural Exegesis." *Africa Theological Journal* 20 (2) (1991): 81–88.

Rabai to Mumias: Short History of the Church of the Province of Kenya 1884 to 1994. Nairobi: Uzima Press, 1994.

Rasmussen, Ane Marie Bak. *Modern African Spirituality: The Independent Holy Spirit Churches in East Africa, 1902–1976*. London and New York: British Academic Press, 1996.

Richards, Charles G. *Archdeacon Owen of Kavirondo: A Memoir*. Nairobi: EALB, 1947.

————. *Krapf: Missionary and Explorer*. London: Nelson, 1950.

Richards, Elizabeth. *Fifty Years in Nyanza, 1906–1956: The History of the CMS and the Anglican Church in Nyanza Province, Kenya*. Maseno, Kenya: Nyanza Jubilee Committee, 1956.

Rickman, Mary. *Seven Whole Days: A Week of Life on a Country Mission Station in Kenya, East Africa*. London: Highway Press, 1950.

Sabar-Friedman, Galia. "Church, State and Society in East Africa: The Anglican Church in Kenya 1957–1978." Ph.D. diss., Hebrew University, 1993.

————. "Church and State in Kenya, 1986–1992: The Churches' Involvement in the 'Game of Change.'" *AA* 96 (382) (1997): 25–52.

————. "Power of the Familiar: Everyday Practices in the Anglican Church of Kenya (CPK)." *Journal of Church and State* 38 (2) (1996): 377–95.

Sandgren, David P. *Christianity and the Kikuyu: Religious Divisions and Social Conflict*. New York: Peter Lang, 1989.

————. "Twentieth-Century Religious and Political Divisions Among the Kikuyu of Kenya." *ASR* 25 (2/3) (1982): 195–207.

Scott, H. E. *Saint in Kenya*. London: Hodder and Stoughton, 1933.

Smith-Akubue, Dorothy Ann Robinson. "Evangelism and Western Education in Western Kenya: Church of God (Anderson, Indiana), 1905–1949." Ph.D. diss., West Virginia University, 1995.

Spencer, Leon Pharr. "Christian Missions and African Interests in Kenya, 1905–1924." Ph.D. diss., Syracuse University, 1975.

————. "Christianity and Colonial Protest: Perceptions of W. E. Owen, Archdeacon of Kavirondo." *JRA* 13 (1) (1982): 47–60.

————. "Church and State in Colonial Africa: Influences Governing the Political Activity of Christian Missions in Kenya." *Journal of Church and State* 31 (1) (1989): 115–32.

————. "Defence and Protection of Converts: Kenya Missions and the Inheritance of Christian Widows, 1912–1931." *JRA* 5 (2) (1973): 107–27.

Sperling, David. "The Growth of Islam Among the Mijikenda of the Kenya Coast 1826–1933." Ph.D. diss., University of London, 1988.

Stock, Eugene. *History of the Church Missionary Society*. 4 Vols. London: CMS, 1899, 1916.

Stovold, K. E. *C.M.S. in Kenya: The Coast, 1844–1944*. Nairobi: EALB, 1946.

Strayer, Robert William. "Church Missionary Society in Eastern and Central Kenya, 1875–1935: A Mission Community in a Colonial Society." Ph.D. diss., University of Wisconsin, 1971.

————. "Dynamics of Mission Expansion: A Case Study from Kenya, 1875–1914." *IJAHS* 6 (2) (1973): 229–48.

————. *Making of Mission Communities in East Africa: Anglicans and Africans in Colonial Kenya, 1875–1935*. London: Heinemann, 1979.

Suenens, L. J. *Edel Quinn: Envoy of the Legion of Mary to Africa*. Dublin: C. L. Fallon, 1953.

Sulumeti, P. "Church Missionary in Kenya in Light of Vatican II." Ph.D. diss., Rome: Pontifical Urban University, 1970.

Tablino, Paolo. *African Traditional Religion: Time and Religion Among the Gabra Pastoralists of Northern Kenya*. Marsabit, Kenya: Marsabit Catholic Parish, 1989.

————. *Diocese of Marsabit: Some Historical Notes*. Marsabit: Catholic Diocese of Marsabit, 1989.

Temu, Arnold J. "British Protestant Missions on the Kenya Coast and Highlands, 1873–1929." Ph.D. diss., University of Alberta, 1967.

Thomas, J. Y. "The Role of the Medical Missionary in British East Africa, 1874–1904." D.Phil. diss., University of Oxford, 1982.

Trevisiol, A. "I Primi Missionari della Consolata nel Kenya: 1902–1905." Ph.D. diss., Pontificia Universitas Gregoriana, 1979.

Trimingham, J. S. *Islam in East Africa*. New York: OUP, 1964.

Tucker, A. R. *Eighteen Years in Uganda and East Africa*. 2 Vols. London: Edward Arnold, 1908.

Twenty-Five Years in East Africa. Richmond, IN: American Friends Board of Foreign Missions, 1927.

Wakefield, E. S. *Thomas Wakefield: Missionary and Geographical Pioneer in East Equatorial Africa*. London: Religious Tract Society, 1904.

Wanyoike, E. N. *An African Pastor*. Nairobi: EAPH, 1974.

Ward, Kevin. "Development of Protestant Christianity in Kenya, 1910–40." Ph.D. diss., Cambridge University, 1976.

————. "Evangelism or Education? Mission Priorities and Educational Policy in the African Inland Mission 1900–1950." *KHR* 3 (2) (1975): 243–60.

Warren, E. R. *Revival: An Inquiry*. London: SCM Press, 1954.

Watt, Rachel Stuart. *In the Heart of Savagedom: Reminiscences of Life and Adventure During a Quarter of a Century of Pioneering and Missionary Labours in the Wilds of East Equatorial Africa*. London and Glasgow: Pickering and Inglis, 1913.

Welbourn, F. B. *East African Christian*. London: OUP, 1965.

————. *East African Rebels: A Study of Some Independent Churches*. London: SCM, 1961.

————, and Bethwell A. Ogot. *A Place to Feel at Home: A Study of Two Independent Churches in Western Kenya*. London: OUP, 1966.

Welch, F. G. *Towards an African Church*. Nairobi: CCK, 1962.

Wentink, D. E. "Orthodox Church in East Africa." *Ecumenical Review* 1 (1968): 33–43.

Were, Gideon S. *Essays on African Religion in Western Kenya*. Nairobi: KLB, 1979.

Westervelt, Josephine Hope. *On Safari for God: An Account of the Life and Labors of John Stauffacher, A Pioneer Missionary of the Africa Inland Mission*. Brooklyn, NY: African Inland Mission, 1954.

Weston, Frank. *The Case against Kikuyu*. London: Longman, 1915.

White, Gavin. "Kikuyu, 1913: An Ecumenical Controversy." Ph.D. diss., University of London, 1970.

Willis, John Jamieson. *Kikuyu Conference: A Study in Christian Unity*. London: Longman, 1913.

————. *Towards a United Church, 1913–1947*. London: Edinburgh House Press, 1947.

————. "Presentation of Christianity to Primitive Peoples; A Statement by Christian Converts in Kavirondo Addressed to Their Heathen Friends." *IRM* 4 (1915): 382–95.

Wilson, Bryan R. "Jehovah's Witnesses in Kenya." *JRA* 5 (2) (1973): 128–49.

Wiseman, Edith M. *Kenya—Then and Now*. London: CMS, 1950.

————. *Kikuyu Martyrs*. London: Highway Press, 1958.

————. *Story of the Church Missionary Society in Kenya*. London: CMS, 1954.

Wolf, Jan J. de. *Differentiation and Integration in Western Kenya: A Study of Religious Innovation and Social Change among the Bukusu*. The Hague and Paris: Mouton, 1977.

Wouters, A. *Mission and Development in Kisumu*. Tilburg, Netherlands: Stichting Band Kisumu-Tilburg, 1968.
Yannoulatos, A. "Brief Diary of a Tour Among the Orthodox of West Kenya." *Porefthendes* 2 (1965): 24–8; and 3/4 (1965): 48–52.

J. ETHNOLOGY, SOCIOLOGY, AND FOLKLORE

Adams, B. N., and E. Mburugu. "Kikuyu Bridewealth and Polygyny Today." *Journal of Comparative Family Studies* 25 (2) (1994): 159–66.
Adamson, Joy. *Peoples of Kenya*. London: Collins and Hartville, 1967.
Ambler, Charles H. "Renovation of Custom in Colonial Kenya: The 1932 Generation Succession Ceremonies in Embu." *JAH* 30 (1) (1989): 139–56.
Baker, Richard St. Barbe. *Kabongo: The Story of a Kikuyu Chief*. Oxford: George Ronald, 1955.
Barnet, Guy. *By the Lake*. London: CUP, 1965.
Barrett, W. E. H. "Notes on the Customs and Beliefs of the Wa-Giriama, etc., British East Africa." *JRAI* 41 (1911): 20–39.
Barton, Juxon. "Notes of the Kipsigis or Lumbwa Tribe of Kenya Colony." *JRAI* 53 (1923): 42–78.
———. "Notes on the Turkana Tribe of British East Africa." *JRAS* 20 (78) (1921) 107–15; and 20 (79) (1921): 204–11.
Baxter, P. T. W. "Social Organization of the Boran of Northern Kenya." D.Phil. diss. Oxford University, 1954.
Beech, Mervyn W. H. *The Suk: Their Language and Folklore*. Oxford: Clarendon Press, 1911.
Berman, Bruce. "Ethnography As Politics, Politics As Ethnography: Kenyatta, Malinowski, and the Making of *Facing Mount Kenya*." *CJAS* 30 (3) (1996): 313–44.
Bernardi, B. *The Mugwe, A Failing Prophet: A Study of a Religious and Public Dignitary of the Meru of Kenya*. New York: OUP, 1959.
———. "Old Kikuyu Religion *Igongona* and *Mambura*: Sacrifice and Sex. Rereading Kenyatta's Ethnography." *Africa* 48 (2) (1993): 167–83.
Berntsen, John L. "Maasai Age-Sets and Prophetic Leadership: 1850–1910." *Africa* 49 (2) (1979): 134–46.
———. "The Maasai and Their Neighbours: Variables of Interaction." *African Economic History* 2 (2) (1976): 1–11.
———. "Pastoralism, Raiding and Prophets: Maasailand in the Nineteenth Century." Ph.D. diss., University of Wisconsin, 1979.
Bostock, P. G. *Taita*. London: Macmillan, 1950.
Brantley, Cynthia. "An Historical Perspective of the Giriama and Witchcraft Control." *Africa* 49 (2) (1979): 112–33.
Cagnolo, C. *The Akikuyu: Their Customs, Traditions and Folklore*. Nyeri, Kenya: Mission Printing School, 1933.

Carson, J. B., ed. *Life Story of a Kenya Chief*. London: Evans Brothers, 1958.

Champion, Arthur M. *The Agiryama of Kenya*. Edited by John Middleton. London: Royal Anthropological Institute, 1967.

————. "Atharaka." *JRAI* 42 (1912): 68–90.

Cronk, L. "Wealth, Status, and Reproductive Success Among the Mukogodo of Kenya." *American Anthropologist* 93 (2) (1991): 533–38.

Donley, Linda. "Turkana Material Culture." *Kenya Past and Present* (7) (1976): 36–42.

Dundas, C. C. F. "History of Kitui." *JRAI* 43 (1913): 480–549.

Dundas, K. R. "Notes on the Tribes Inhabiting the Baringo District, East African Protectorate." *JRAI* 40 (1910): 49–72.

————. "Wawanga and Other Tribes of the Elgon District, British East Africa." *JRAI* 43 (1913): 19–75.

Emley, E. D. "Turkana of the Kalosia District." *JRAI* 57 (1927): 157–202.

Evans-Pritchard, Edward Evans. "Marriage Customs of the Luo of Kenya." *Africa* 20 (2) (1950): 132–42.

Fadiman, Jeffrey A. "Mountain Witchcraft: Supernatural Practices and Practitioners among the Meru of Mount Kenya." 20 (1) (1977): 87–101.

————. *When We Began There Were Witchmen: An Oral History from Mount Kenya*. Berkeley: University of California Press, 1994.

Fish, Burnette C., and Gerald W. Fish. *Kalenjin Heritage: Traditional Religious and Social Practices*. Marion, IN: World Gospel Mission, 1995.

Fisher, J. *Anatomy of Kikuyu Domesticity and Husbandry*. London: D.T.C., 1962.

Fox, D. Storrs. "Further Notes on the Masai of Kenya Colony." *JRAI* 60 (1930): 447–65.

Fratkin, Elliot. "Loibon As Sorcerer: A Samburu Loibon among the Ariaal Rendille." *Africa* 61 (3) (1991): 318–33.

————. "Stability and Resilience in East African Pastoralism: The Rendille and the Ariaal of Northern Kenya." *Human Ecology* 14 (1986): 269–86.

Gecaga, B. Mareka. *Home Life in Kikuyu-Land: Or Kariuki and Muthoni*. Nairobi: Eagle Press, 1949.

Gilette, Cynthia. "Test of the Concept of Backwardness: A Case Study of Digo Society in Kenya." Ph.D. diss., Cornell University, 1978.

Glazier, Jack. "Conflict and Conciliation Among the Mbeere of Kenya." Ph.D. diss., University of California, Berkeley, 1972.

————. "Generation Classes among the Mbeere of Central Kenya." *Africa* 46 (4) (1976): 313–26.

Griffiths, J. B. "Glimpses of a Nyika Tribe (Wanduruma)." *JRAI* 65 (1935): 267–96.

Gulliver, Philip H. *Family Herds: A Study of Two Pastoral Tribes in East Africa: The Jie and Turkana*. New York: Humanities Press, 1955.

Harris, Alfred. "Social Organization of the Wataita." Ph.D. diss. Cambridge University, 1958.

————, and Grace Harris. "Property and the Cycle of Domestic Groups in Taita."

In *Family Estate in East Africa*, edited by Robert F. Gray and P. H. Gulliver, 117–53. London: Routledge and Kegan Paul, 1964.

Harris, Grace. "Ritual Systems of the Waitaita." Ph.D. diss., Cambridge University, 1965.

————. "Taita Bridewealth and Affinal Relations." In *Marriage in Tribal Societies*, edited by Meyer New York: CUP, 1962: 55–87.

Heald, Suzette. *Controlling Anger: The Sociology of Gisu Violence*. Manchester, U.K.: Manchester University Press, 1989.

————. "Witches and Thieves: Deviant Motivations in Gisu Society." *Man* 21 (1) (1986): 65–78.

Hillman, E. "Pauperisation of the Maasai in Kenya." *AT* 41 (4) (1994): 57–65.

Hinde, Sidney Langford, and Hildegard Hinde. *Last of the Masai*. London: Heinemann, 1901.

Hobley, Charles William. "Anthropological Studies in Kavirondo and Nandi." *JRAI* 33 (1903): 325–59.

————. *Bantu Beliefs and Magic: With Particular Reference to the Kikuyu and Kamba Tribes of Kenya Colony*. London: H.F. and G. Witherby, 1922.

————. *Eastern Uganda: An Ethnological Survey*. London: Anthropological Institute, 1902.

————. *Ethnology of the Akamba and Other East African Tribes*. Cambridge: CUP, 1910.

————. "Further Researches into Kikuyu and Kamba Religious Beliefs and Customs." *JRAI* 41 (1911): 406–57.

————. "Kikuyu Customs and Beliefs: Thahu and Its Connection with Circumcision Rites." *JRAI* 40 (1910): 428–52.

Hollis, Alfred Claude. *The Masai: Their Language and Folklore*. Oxford: Clarendon Press, 1905.

————. *The Nandi: Their Language and Folklore*. Oxford: Clarendon Press, 1909.

————. "Notes on the History and Customs of the People of Taveta, East Africa." *JRAS* 1 (1) (1901): 98–125.

————. "Nyika Enigmas." *JRAS* 16 (62) (1917): 135–42.

————. "Nyika Proverbs." *JRAS* 16 (61) (1916): 62–70.

————. "Taveta Enigmas." *JRAS* 10 (38) (1911): 200–12.

————. "Taveta Sayings and Proverbs." *JRAS* 9 (35) (1910): 255–66.

Huntingford, G. W. B. "Azanian Civilization of Kenya." *Antiquity* 7 (26) (1933): 153–65.

————. *Eastern Tribes of the Bantu Kavirondo*. Nairobi: W. Boyd, 1944.

————. "Economic Life of the Dorobo." *Anthropos* 50 (4/6) (1955): 602–34.

————. *Nandi of Kenya: Tribal Control in a Pastoral Society*. London: Routledge and Kegan Paul, 1953.

————. *Nandi Work and Culture*. London: HMSO, 1950.

————. "Political Organization of the Dorobo." *Anthropos* 49 (1954): 123–48.

————. "Social Institutions of the Dorobo." *Anthropos* 46 (1951): 1–48.

————. "Social Organization of the Dorobo." *African Studies* 1 (3) (1942): 183–200.

Johnstone, H. B. "Notes on Customs of Tribes Inhabiting Mombasa Sub-District, British East Africa." *JRAI* 32 (1902): 263–72.

Kamoche, K. "Rhetoric, Ritualism, and Totemism in Human Resource Management." *Human Relations* 4 (1995): 367–85.

Karp, Ivan. *Fields of Change Among the Iteso of Kenya.* London: Routledge and Kegan Paul, 1978.

Kassam, A. "The Fertile Past: The Gabra Concept of Oral Tradition." *Africa* 56 (2) (1986): 193–209.

Kenyatta, Jomo. *Facing Mount Kenya: The Tribal Life of the Gikuyu.* London: Secker and Warburg, 1953.

————. "Kikuyu Religion: Ancestor Worship and Practices." *Africa* 10 (3) (1937): 308–28.

————. *My People of Kikuyu and the Life of Chief Wangombe.* Oxford: Lutterworth Press, 1942.

Kershaw, Greet. "The Land Is the People: A Study of Kikuyu Social Organization in Historical Perspective." Ph.D. diss., University of Chicago, 1972.

Kilson, Martin L. "Land and the Kikuyu: A Study of the Relationship Between Land and Kikuyu Political Movements." *Journal of Negro History* 40 (2) (1955): 103–53.

————. "Land and Politics in Kenya: An Analysis of African Politics in a Plural Society." *Western Political Quarterly* 10 (3) (1957): 559–81.

Kipkorir, Benjamin E., with F. B. Welbourn. *The Marakwet of Kenya.* Nairobi: EALB, 1973.

Kituyi, Mukhisa. *Becoming Kenyans: Socio-Economic Transformation of the Pastoral Maasai.* Nairobi: ACTS, 1990.

Kratz, Corinne A. "Genres of Power: A Comparative Analysis of Okiek Blessings, Curses and Oaths." *Man* 24 (4) (1989): 636–56.

Lado, C. "Perceptions of Pastoralism and Rural Change in Maasailand, Kenya." *Journal of Third World Studies* 10 (1) (1993): 148–83.

La Fontaine, S. H. "Taveta Customs and Beliefs in Connection with Religion, Burial, and Disease." *JRAS* 13 (62) (1914): 385–94.

Lambert, H. E. *Kikuyu Social and Political Institutions.* London: OUP. 1956.

Langley, Myrtle S. *The Nandi of Kenya: Life Crisis Rituals in a Period of Change.* New York: St. Martin's Press, 1979.

Larby, Norman. *Kamba.* Nairobi: Highway Press, 1944.

Lauren, W. L. "Masai and Kikuyu: An Historical Analysis of Culture Transmission." *JAH* 9 (4) (1968): 571–83.

Leakey, Louis Seymour Bazett. "The Economics of Kikuyu Tribal Life." *EAER* 3 (1) (1956): 165–80.

————. *Southern Kikuyu Before 1903.* 3 Vols. London: Academic Press, 1978.

Le Guennec-Coppens, Françoise. "Social and Cultural Integration: A Case Study of East African Hadramis." *Africa* 59 (2) (1989): 185–95.

————. *Wedding Customs in Lamu.* [Nairobi]: Lamu Society, 1980.

Levine, Robert A. "Wealth and Power in Gusiiland." In *Markets in Africa*, edited by Paul Bohannan and George Dalton, 520–36. New York: Doubleday-Anchor Books, 1965.

————. "Witchcraft and Co-Wife Proximity in Southwestern Kenya." *Ethnology* 1 (1) (1962): 39–45.

————, and Barbara B. Levine. *Nyansongo: A Gusii Community in Kenya.* New York: John Wiley, 1966.

Lewis, I. M. "The Problem of the Northern Frontier District of Kenya." *Race* 5 (1) (1963/1964): 48–60.

Lewis, Kepler. "Pastoral Peoples of Northwestern Kenya." *New York Academy of Sciences Transactions* 10 (7) (1948): 245–50.

Lindblom, K. Gerhard. *Akamba in British East Africa: An Ethnological Monograph.* Uppsala, Sweden: Appelbergs Boktryckeri Aktiebolog, 1920.

————. *Carved Initiation Sticks and Bows from Taveta, Kenya Colony.* Stockholm: Ethnographical Museum, 1950.

————. *Kamba Tales of Supernatural Beings and Adventures.* Uppsala, Sweden: Appelbergs, 1935.

Little, M. A. "Growth of Young Nomadic and Settled Turkana Children." *Medical Anthropology Quarterly* 4 (3) (1990): 296–314.

————, et al. "Growth of Nomadic and Settled Turkana Infants of Northwest Kenya." *American Journal of Physical Anthropology* 92 (3) (1993): 273–89.

Malusu, Joseph. *Luyia Way of Death: Based on the Isukha People of Kakamega District.* Nairobi: OUP, 1978.

Massama, J. A. *Cliff Dwellers of Kenya.* London: Frank Cass and Company Ltd., 1968.

Matheson, A. *African Peoples of Kenya: A Brief Guide to the Various African Peoples of Kenya.* Nairobi: Ministry of Information, Broadcasting and Tourism, 1964.

Matson, A. T. *Kipsigis.* Kampala: EALB, 1961.

Maxon, Robert M. "Gusii Oral Texts and the Gusii Experience Under British Rule." *IJAHS* 9 (1) (1976): 74–82.

Mayer, Iona. *Nature of Kinship Relations: The Significance of the Use of Kinship Terms Among the Gusii.* Manchester: Manchester University Press, 1965.

Mayer, Philip. *Gusii Bridewealth Law and Custom.* Cape Town: OUP for Rhodes-Livingston Institute, 1950.

Middleton, John, and Greet Kershaw. *Central Tribes of the North-Eastern Bantu: The Kikuyu and Kamba of Kenya.* London: IAI, 1953.

Middleton, John, and E. H. Winter. *Witchcraft and Sorcery in East Africa.* London: Routledge and Kegan Paul, 1963.

Muriuki, Godfrey. *History of the Kikuyu, 1500–1900.* Nairobi and New York: OUP, 1974.

Muthiani, Joseph. *Akamba from Within: Egalitarianism in Social Relations.* New York: Exposition Press, 1973.

Mwaniki, H. S. K. *Categories and Substance of Embu Traditional Folksongs and Dances.* Nairobi: KLB, 1986.

———. *Embu Historical Texts.* Nairobi: EALB, 1974.

———. *Living History of Embu and Mbeere to 1906.* Nairobi: EALB, 1973.

Ndeti, Kivuti. *Elements of Akamba Life.* Nairobi: EAPH, 1972.

Nida, Eugene A. "Akamba Initiation Rights and Culture Themes." *Practical Anthropology* 9 (4) (1962): 145–55.

Northcote, G. A. S. "Nilotic Kavirondo." *JRAI* 37 (1907): 58–66.

Nottingham, J. C. "Sorcery Among the Akamba in Kenya." *JAA* 11 (1) (1959): 2–14.

Nurse, Derek, and Thomas T. Spear. *The Swahili: Reconstructing the History and Language of an African Society, 800–1500.* Philadelphia: University of Pennsylvania Press, 1985.

"Nyangweso: The Cult of Mumbo in Central and South Kavirondo." *JEAUNHS* (38/39) (1930): 13–17.

Odegi-Awuondo, C. *Life in the Balance: Ecological Sociology of Turkana Nomads.* Nairobi: African Centre for Technology Studies, 1990.

Ogot, Bethwell A. *Ethnicity, Nationalism and Democracy in Africa.* Maseno, Kenya: Institute of Research and Postgraduate Studies, Maseno University College, 1997.

———. *History of the Southern Luo: Migration and Settlement 1500–1900.* Nairobi: EAPH, 1967.

———. "Kingship and Statelessness among the Nilotes." In *Historians in Tropical Africa,* edited by Jan Vansina, 284–305. London: OUP, 1964.

Ole Sankan, S.S. *Maasai.* Nairobi: EALB, n.d.

Omosule, M. "Kalenjin: The Emergence of a Corporate Name for the 'Nandi-Speaking Tribes' of East Africa." *Genève Afrique* 27 (1) (1989): 73–88.

Orchardson, Ian Q. "Notes on the Marriage Customs of the Kipsigis." *JEAUNHS* 10 (40/41) (1930–31): 99–112.

Orde-Brown, G. St. J. "Mount Kenya and Its People: Some Notes on the Chuka Tribe." *JRAS* 15 (59) (1916): 225–31.

———. *Vanishing Tribes of Kenya.* London: Seeley, Service, 1925.

Osogo, John N.B. *History of the Baluyia.* Nairobi: OUP, 1966.

———. *Life in Kenya in the Olden Days: The Baluyia.* Nairobi: OUP, 1965.

Owen, Walter E. "Bantu of Kavirondo." *JEAUNHS* 45/46 (1932): 67–77.

———. "Good Production and Kindred Matters among the Luo." *JEAUNHS* (49/50) (1933): 235–49.

Parkin, D. J. "Medicines and Men of Influence." *Man* 3 (3) (1968): 424–39.

Parkin, David. *Sacred Void: Spatial Images of Work and Ritual Among the Giriama of Kenya.* Cambridge: CUP, 1991.

Penley, E. W. "Superstition Among the Turkana: A Southern Turkana Heaven." *Man* 30 (113) (1930): 139–40.

Penwill, D. J. *Kamba Customary Law: Notes Taken in the Machakos District of Kenya Colony.* London: Macmillan, 1951.

Peristiany, Jean G. *Social Institutions of the Kipsigis.* London: George Routledge, 1939.

Prins, Adriaans Hendrick Johan. *Coastal Tribes of the North-Eastern Bantu.* London: IAI, 1952.

————. *East African Age-Class Systems: An Inquiry into the Social Orders of Galla, Kipsigis and Kikuyu.* Groningen: J. B. Wolters, 1953.

Rayne, H. "Turkana." *JRAS* 18 (71) (1919): 182–89; and 18 (72) (1919): 254–65.

Robinson, P. W. "Gabbra Nomadic Pastoralism in Nineteenth and Twentieth Century Northern Kenya." Ph.D. diss., Northwestern University, 1985.

Roth, Eric Abella. "Education, Tradition, and Household Labor among the Rendille Pastoralists of Northern Kenya." *Human Organization* 50 (2) (1991): 136–41.

————. "Reexamination of Rendille Population Regulation." *American Anthropologist* 95 (3) (1993): 597–611.

————. "Traditional Pastoral Strategies in a Modern World: An Example from Northern Kenya." *Human Organization* 55 (2) (1996): 219–24.

Routledge, W. Scoresby, and Katherine Routledge. *With a Prehistoric People: The Akikuyu of British East Africa.* London: Edward Arnold, 1910.

Ruel, M. J. "Religion and Society among the Kuria of East Africa." *Africa* 35 (3) (1965): 295–306.

Saberwal, Satish. "Historical Notes on the Embu of Central Kenya." *JAH* 8 (1967): 29–38.

————. *Traditional Political System of the Embu of Central Kenya.* Nairobi: EAPH, 1970.

Sangree, Walter H. *Age, Prayer and Politics in Tiriki, Kenya.* London: OUP, 1966.

Sato, S. "Camel Trust System in the Rendille Population Society of Northern Kenya." *African Study Monographs* 13 (2) (1993): 69–89.

Schapera, Isaac. *Some Problems of Anthropological Research in Kenya Colony.* London: IAI, 1949.

Schlee, Gunther. *Identities on the Move: Clanship and Pastoralism in Northern Kenya.* Manchester, UK: Manchester University Press, 1989.

————. "Interethnic Clan Identities among Cushitic-Speaking Pastoralists." *Africa* 55 (1) (1985): 17–38.

Shaw, K. C. "Some Preliminary Notes on Luo Marriage Customs." *JEAUNHS* 45/46 (1932): 39–50.

Shipton, Parker. "Luo Entrustment: Foreign Finance and the Soil of the Spirits in Kenya." *Africa* 65 (2) (1995): 165–96.

Snell, G. S. *Nandi Customary Law.* New York: St. Martin's Press, 1954.

Sobania, N. W. "Historical Tradition of the Peoples of the Eastern Lake Turkana Basin c. 1840–1925." D.Phil. diss., University of London, 1980.

Somjee, S. *Material Culture of Kenya.* Nairobi: EAEP, 1993.

Southall, Aiden W. "From Segmentary Lineage to Ethnic Association: Luo, Luyha,

Ibo. and Others." In *Colonialism and Change*, edited by Maxwell Owusu, 203–29. The Hague: Mouton, 1975.

———. *Lineage Formation among the Luo*. London: OUP, 1952.

Spear, Thomas. *Traditions of Origin and Their Interpretation: The Mijikenda of Kenya*. Athens, OH: Center for International Studies, Ohio University, 1981.

———, and Richard Waller, eds. *Being Maasai: Ethnicity and Identity in East Africa*. London: James Currey, 1993.

Spencer, Paul. *Samburu: A Study of Gerontocracy in a Nomadic Tribe*. Berkeley: University of California Press, 1965.

Storrs-Fox, D. "Notes on Marriage Customs Among the Masai." *JEA UNHS* 42/43 (1931): 183–92.

Tate, H. R. "Further Notes on the Kikuyu Tribe of British East Africa." *JRAI* 34 (1904): 255–65.

———. "Further Notes on the Southern Gikuyu of British East Africa." *JRAS* 10 (39) (1911): 285–97.

———. "Kikuyu and Kamba Tribes of British East Africa." *JRAI* 34 (1904): 130–48.

———. "Native Law of the Southern Gikuyu of British East Africa." *JRAS* 9 (35) (1910): 233–54.

Totty, L. H., and G. H. Chaundy. *People and District of West Suk*. Nairobi: W. Boyd, 1944.

Turton, Edmond Romilly. "Pastoral Tribes of Northern Kenya 1800–1916." Ph.D. diss., London University, 1970.

Wagner, Günter. "Abaluyia of Kavirondo (Kenya)." In *African Worlds*, edited by Daryll Forde, 41–79. New York: OUP, 1966.

———. *Bantu of North Kavirondo*. 2 vols. New York: OUP, 1949, 1956.

———. *Bantu of Western Kenya*. London: OUP, 1970.

———. "Political Organizations of the Bantu of Kavirondo." In *African Political Systems*, edited by Meyer Fortes and E. E. Evans-Pritchard, 197–237. New York: OUP, 1940.

Weatherby, John M. "The Secret Spirit Cult of the Sor in Karamoja." *Africa* 58 (2) (1988): 210–29.

Webster, E. J. *Boran, Rendille, and Samburu: Nomadic Tribes of the Northern Frontier Districts*. Nairobi: W. Boyd, 1944.

Were, Gideon S. *History of the Abuluyia of Western Kenya: c. 1500–1930*. Nairobi: EAPH, 1967.

———. *Western Kenya Historical Texts: Abaluyia, Teso, and Elgon Kalenjin*. Nairobi: EAPH, 1967.

Werner, Alice. "Bantu Coast Tribes of the East Africa Protectorate." *JRAI* 45 (1915): 326–54.

———. "Galla of the East Africa Protectorate." *JRAS* 13 (50) (1914): 121–42; 13 (51) (1914): 262–87.

356 • BIBLIOGRAPHY

————. "Some Notes on the Wapokomo of the Tana Valley." *JRAS* 12 (48) (1913): 359–84.

Whisson, M. G. *Change and Challenge: A Study of the Social and Economic Changes Among the Kenya Luo*. Nairobi: CCK, 1964.

————, and John M. Lonsdale. "The Case of Jason Gor and Fourteen Others: A Luo Succession Dispute in Historical Perspective." *Africa* 45 (2) (1974): 50–66.

White, R. F. "Notes on the Turkana Tribe." *Sudan Notes and Records* 3 (3) (1920): 216–22.

Whitehouse, L. E. "Masai Social Customs." *JEAUNHS* 47/48 (1933): 146–53.

Wienpahi, Jan. "Turkana Herds under Environmental Stress." *Nomadic Peoples* 17 (1985): 59–87.

Willis, Justin, and Suzanne Miers. "Becoming a Child of the House: Incorporation, Authority and Resistance in Giryama Society." *JAH* 38 (3) (1997): 479–95.

Wilson, Gordon M. "Homicide and Suicide Among the Luo of Kenya." In *African Homicide and Suicide*, edited by Paul Bohannan, 179–213. Princeton, NJ: Princeton University Press, 1960.

————. *Luo Customary Law and Marriage Laws*. Nairobi: GP, 1961.

Wingfield, Alys. "Tribespeople of Kenya's Northern Frontier District." *Geographical Magazine* 9 (1948): 351–62.

Wolf, Jan J. de. "Diffusion of Age-Group Organization in East Africa: A Reconsideration." *Africa* 50 (3) (1980): 305–10.

Yokoo, S. "Death among the Abaluyia." Ph.D. diss., Makerere University, 1966.

K. AGRICULTURE, LAND TENURE, AND LOCAL ADMINISTRATION

Abrams, P. D. *Kenya's Land Resettlement Story*. Nairobi: Challenge Publishers and Distributors, 1979.

Abwunza, Judith M. "Nyayo: Cultural Contradictions in Kenya Rural Capitalism." *Anthropologica* (1990): 183–203.

Ackello-Ogutu, A. C., ed. *Kenya's Rural Research Priorities*. Nairobi: Institute of Development Studies, 1989.

Adams, M. "Slow Progress with Integrated Rural Development Programmes in Kenya's Arid and Semi-Arid Lands." *Land Degradation and Rehabilitation* 2 (2) (1990): 285–99.

Ainsworth, John. "East Africa and Agriculture." *East Africa Quarterly* (1904): 14–16.

————. "Staple Products for East Africa." *East Africa Quarterly* (1906): 685–89.

Akabwai, D. M. *Extension and Livestock Development: Experience from Among the Turkana Pastoralists of Kenya*. London: ODI, 1992.

Akinboade, O. A. "Technical Efficiency Change in Kenyan Agriculture and the

Poor: A Computable General Equilibrium Analysis." *Canadian Journal of Development Studies* 15 (1) (1993): 55–74.

Akivaga, S. Kichamu, Martin W. Opi, and Wanyama Kulundu-Bitonye. *Local Authorities in Kenya*. Nairobi: Heinemann, 1985.

Anderson, David, and David Throup W. "Africans and Agricultural Production in Colonial Kenya: The Myth of the War as a Watershed." *JAH* 26 (4) (1985): 327–45.

Arwings-Kodhek, G., et al. "Impact of Maize Market Liberalisation in Kenya." *Food Research Institute Studies* 22 (3) (1993): 331–48.

Asmerom, H. K. "Development Administration and Rural Development Strategy in Kenya: A Review of Its Special Rural Development Programmes (SRDP)." *Indian Journal of Public Administration* (1984): 954–75.

Barger, Torben. *Marketing Cooperatives and Peasants in Kenya*. Uppsala: SIAS, 1980.

Barasa, T. N., et al. "Economic Analysis of Small-Holder Cotton Production in Kenya: A Linear Programming Case Study of Funyula Division, Busia District." *EAER* 8 (2) (1992): 142–58.

Barkan, Joel, and Frank Holmquist. "Peasant-State Relations and the Social Base of Self-Help in Kenya." *World Politics* 41 (3) (1989): 359–80.

Barnes, Carolyn. "Experiment with African Coffee Growing in Kenya: The Gusii, 1933–1950." Ph.D. diss., Michigan State University, 1976.

———. "Experiment with Coffee Production by Kenyans, 1933–48." *African Economic History* (8) (1979): 198–209.

Bates, Robert A. *Beyond the Miracle of the Market: The Political Economy of Development in Kenya*. Cambridge: CUP, 1989.

Beech, Mervyn H. "Kikuyu System of Land Tenure." *JRAS* 7 (65) (1917): 46–59.

Bekure, S., et al. *Maasai Herding: An Analysis of the Livestock Production Systems of Maasai Pastoralists in Eastern Kajiado District, Kenya*. Addis Ababa, Ethiopia: International Livestock Centre for Africa, 1991.

Bernard, Frank E. *East of Mount Kenya: Meru Agriculture in Transition*. Munich: IFO, 1975.

———, and Derrick J. Thom. "Population Pressure and Human Carrying Capacity in Selected Locations of Machakos and Kitui Districts." *JDA* 15 (3) (1981): 381–406.

Bevan, D. *Agriculture and the Policy Environment: Tanzania and Kenya*. Paris: OECD Development Centre, 1993.

———, et al. "Anatomy of a Temporary Trade Shock: The Kenyan Coffee Boom of 1976–79." *JAE* 1 (2) (1992): 271–305.

———, et al. "Government Policies and Agricultural Performance: Tanzania and Kenya." In *Economic Reform, Trade and Agricultural Development*, edited by I. Goldin, 19–47. Basingstoke, UK: Macmillan, 1993.

Bilsborrow, Richard E., et al. "Economic and Ethnic Factors in Kenya Migration Movements." *EAER* 2 (1) (1986): 31–50.

Bradford, E. L. "African Mixed Farming Economics as Applied to Bukura, Nyanza Province, Kenya." *EAAJ* 12 (1946): 74–83.

Bradshaw, York W. "Perpetuating Underdevelopment in Kenya: The Link Between Agriculture, Class, and State." *ASR* 33 (1) (1990): 1–28.

Brokensha, David, and Jack Glazier. "Land Reform Among the Mbeere of Central Kenya." *Africa* 43 (3) (1973): 182–206.

Brokensha, David, and John Nellis. "Administration in Kenya: A Study of the Rural Division of Mbere." *Journal of Administration Overseas* 3 (1974): 510–23.

Brokensha, David, and Bernard W. Riley. "Introduction of Cash Crops in a Marginal Area of Kenya." In *Agricultural Development in Africa: Issues of Public Policy*, edited by R. H. Bates and Michael F. Lofchie, 244–74. New York: Praeger, 1980.

Brown, Brack. "Political Administration and Rural Development in Kenya: Lessons from Settlement and Other Rural Programs." Ph.D. diss., Syracuse University, 1977.

Brown, L. H. "Agricultural Change in Kenya, 1945–1960." *Food Research Institute Studies* 8 (1) (1968): 33–90.

————. "Agriculture and Land Tenure in Kenya Colony." In *Natural Resources of East Africa*, 103–16. Nairobi: EALB, 1962.

————. "Development and Farm Planning in the African Areas of Kenya." *EAAJ* 23 (1957): 67–73.

————. *National Cash Crops Policy for Kenya*. Nairobi: GP, 1963.

Buch-Hansen, M., and J. Kieler. "Development of Capitalism and the Transformation of the Peasantry in Kenya." *RA* 15/16 (1983): 13–40.

Bullock, Ronald A. "Subsistence to Cash: Economic Change in Rural Kiambu." *Cahiers d'Études Africaines* 4 (1974): 699–714.

Campbell, David J. *Pastoralism in Kenya*. Hanover, NH: American Universities Field Staff, 1980.

————. "The Prospect for Desertification in Kijiado District, Kenya." *GJ* 152 (1986): 44–55.

————. "Response to Drought Among Small Farmers and Herders in Southern Kajiado District, Kenya." *Human Ecology* 12 (1) (1984): 35–64.

Cardenas, M. "Stabilisation and Redistribution of Coffee Revenues: A Political Economy Model of Commodity Marketing Boards." *Journal of Development Economics* 44 (2) (1994): 352–80.

Carlsen, John. *Economic and Social Transformation in Rural Kenya*. Uppsala, Sweden: SIAS, 1980.

Carter, M. R., et al. "Tenure Security for Whom? Differential Effects of Land Policy in Kenya." In *Searching for Land Tenure Security in Africa*, edited by J. W. Bruce and S. E. Migot-Adholla, 141–68. Dubuque, IA: Kendall/Hunt, 1994.

Chambers, R., and Jon R. Moris, eds. *Mwea: An Irrigated Rice Settlement in Kenya*. Munich: Weltforum-Verlag, 1973.

Cheatle, R. J., and S. N. J. Njoroge. "Smallholder Adaption of Some Land Husbandry Practices in Kenya." In *Working With Farmers*, edited by N. Hudson and R. J. Cheatle, 130–41. London: Intermediate Technology Publications, 1993.

Chessa, Samuel R. "Use and Spread of Agricultural Innovations Among Small-Holding Farming Communities in Busia District, Kenya: Issues in Agricultural Extension." Ph.D. diss., University of New Brunswick, 1992.

Chitere, P., and J. Monya. "Decentralisation of Rural Development: The Case of the Kenya District Focus Approach." *African Administrative Studies* 32 (1989): 31–52.

————, and B. A. Omolo. "Farmer's Indigenous Knowledge of Crop Pests and Their Damage in Western Kenya." *International Journal of Pest Management* 39 (2) (1993): 126–32.

Clayton, Eric S. *Agrarian Development in Peasant Economies: Some Lessons from Kenya*. New York: Pergamon Press, 1964.

Collier, Paul. "Contractual Constraints on Labor Exchange in Rural Kenya." *International Labour Review* 128 (6) (1989): 745–68.

Colony and Protectorate of Kenya. *African Land Development in Kenya, 1946–1962*. Nairobi: Ministry of Agriculture, 1962.

————. *Decade of Agricultural Progress in Kenya*. Nairobi: Department of Agriculture, 1931.

Cone, L. Winston, and J. F. Lipscomb. *History of Kenya Agriculture*. New York: International Publications Service, 1972.

Conelly, W. Thomas. "Population Pressure, Labor Availability, and Agricultural Disintensification: The Decline of Farming on Rusinga Island, Kenya." *Human Ecology* 22 (2) (1994): 145–70.

Cowen, M. P. "Capital and Household Production: The Case of Wattle in Kenya's Central Province, 1903–64." Ph.D. diss., University of Cambridge, 1978.

————. "Change in State Power, International Conditions and Peasant Producers: The Case of Kenya." *Journal of Development Studies* 22 (2) (1986): 585–95.

Cox, Pamela. "Implementing Agricultural Development Policy in Kenya." *Food Research Institute Studies* 16 (2) (1984): 153–76.

Deacon, Patricia J., and Michael B. K. Darkoh. "Policies and Practices Behind the Degradation of Kenya's Land Resources: A Preliminary Review." *JEARD* 17 (1987): 34–52.

Dietz, Tom. *Pastoralists in Dire Straits: Survival Strategies and External Interventions in a Semi-Arid Region at the Kenya/Uganda Border*. Amsterdam: Koninklijk Nederlands Aardrijkskundig Genootschap, 1987.

Doherty, Deborah A. "Maasai Pastoral Potential: A Study of Ranching in Narok District, Kenya." Ph.D. diss., McGill University, 1987.

Dow, Thomas E., et al. "Wealth Flow and Fertility Decline in Rural Kenya, 1981–92." *Population and Development Review* 20 (2) (1994): 343–64.

Dowker, B. D., and V. G. Mathews. *Report on the Kenya Maize Industry*. Nairobi: GP, 1963.

Due, John M. "'They Said It Couldn't Be Done' Two Agricultural Development Projects in Kenya." *CJAS* 4 (3) (1970): 595–613.

Ergas, Zaki R. "Kenya's Special Rural Development Program (SRDP): Was It Really a Failure." *JDA* 17 (1) (1982): 51–66.

Etherington, Dan M. *Smallholder Tea Production in Kenya: A Econometric Study.* Nairobi: EALB, 1973.

Evans, H. E. " Virtuous Circle Model of Rural-Urban Development: Evidence from a Kenyan Small Town and its Hinterland." *Journal of Development Studies* 28 (4) (1992): 640–47.

————, and P. Ngau. "Rural-Urban Relations, Household Income Diversification and Agricultural Productivity." *Development and Change* 22 (3) (1991): 519–45.

Fearn, Hugh. "Cotton Production in the Nyanza Province of Kenya Colony, 1908–1954." *The Empire Cotton Growing Review* 33 (92) (1956): 1–14.

Fliedner, H. *Land Tenure Reform in Kenya.* Berlin: Springer-Verlag, 1965.

Foeken, Dick, and Nina Tellegen. *Tied to the Land: Living Conditions of Labourers on Large Farms in Trans-Nzoia District, Kenya.* Aldershot, UK: Avebury Press, 1995.

Fordham, Paul. *Rural Development in the Kenya Highlands.* Nottingham, UK: University of Nottingham, 1973.

Francis, E., and J. Hoddinott. "Migration and Differentiation in Western Kenya: A Tale of Two Sub-Locations." *Journal of Development Studies* 30 (1) (1993): 115–45.

Franke, Richard W. "Land Reform Versus Inequality in Nadur Village, Kerala." *Journal of Anthropological Research* 2 (1992): 81–116.

Freeman, Donald B., and G. B. Norcliffe. "National and Regional Patterns of Rural Nonfarm Employment in Kenya." *Geography* 69 (3) (1984): 221–33.

Fumagalli, Carl T. "Evaluation of Development Projects Among East African Pastoralists." *ASR* 21 (3) (1978): 49–63.

Gacheru, E. N., et al. "Effects of Land Preparation and Weeding on Maize (Zea Mays) Grain Yields in the Coastal Region of Kenya." *International Journal of Pest Management* 39 (1) (1993): 57–60.

Gadsen, Fay. "Further Notes on the Kamba Destocking Controversy of 1938." *IJAHS* 7 (4) (1974): 681–87.

Gaston, Jessie Ruth. "Land Issue in Kenya Politics: Pre- and Post-Independence Development." *Ufahamu* 9 (2) (1979): 30–58.

Geheb, Kim, and Tony Binns. "'Fishing Farmers' or 'Farming Fisherman'? The Quest for Household Income and Nutritional Security on the Kenyan Shores of Lake Victoria." *AA* 96 (382) (1997): 73–93.

Gerhart, John D. "Rural Development in Kenya." *RA* (13) (1971): 60–66.

Goldman, Abe. "Agricultural Innovation in Three Areas of Kenya: Neo-Boserupian Theories and Regional Characterization." *Economic Geography* 69 (1) (1993): 44–71.

Golkowsky, R. *Irrigated Agriculture in Kenya: A Presentation of the Basic Relations Exemplified by the Mwea Irrigation Settlement.* Munich: IFO, 1969.

Greer, Joel, and Eric Thorbecke. *Food Poverty and Consumption Patterns in Kenya.* Geneva: International Labour Organization, 1986.

――――. "Food Poverty Profile Applied to Kenyan Smallholders." *Economic Development and Cultural Change* 35 (1) (1986): 115–41.

――――. "Methodology for Measuring Food Poverty Applied to Kenya." *Journal of Development Economics* 24 (1) (1986): 59–74.

Grosh, Barbara. "Performance of Agricultural Public Enterprises in Kenya: Lessons from the First Two Decades of Independence." *EAER* 3 (1) (1987): 51–64.

Gwyer, G. D. "Trends in Kenyan Agriculture in Relation to Employment." *JMAS* 11 (3) (1973): 393–403.

Gyllström, Björn. *State-Administered Rural Change: Agricultural Cooperatives in Kenya.* London: Routledge, 1991.

Harbeson, John W. "Land Reforms and Politics in Kenya, 1954–1970." *JMAS* 9 (2) (1971): 231–51.

――――. *Nation-Building in Kenya: The Role of Land Reform.* Evanston, IL: Northwestern University Press, 1973.

Harper, Malcolm, ed. *Kenyan Smallholders: Their Attitudes and Problems.* Rome: FAO, 1973.

Haugerud, Angelique. "Consequences of Land Tenure Reform Among Smallholders in the Kenya Highlands." *RA* 15/16 (1983): 65–89.

――――. "Food Surplus Production, Wealth and Farmers' Strategies in Kenya." In *Satisfying Africa's Food Needs: Food Production and Commercialization in African Agriculture,* edited by Ronald Cohen, 153–89. Boulder, CO: Lynne Rienner Publishers, 1988.

――――. "Household Dynamics and Rural Political Economy Among Embu Farmers in the Kenya Highlands." Ph.D. diss., Northwestern University, 1984.

――――. "Land Tenure and Agrarian Change in Kenya." *Africa* 59 (1) (1989): 61–90.

――――, and K. Njogu. *State Voices in the Countryside: Politics and the Kenyan Baraza.* Boston: African Studies Center, Boston University, 1991.

Hay, Margaret Jean. "Economic Change in Luoland: Kowe 1890–1945." Ph.D. diss., University of Wisconsin, 1972.

Heald, S. "Tobacco, Time, and Household Economy in Two Kenyan Societies: The Teso and Kuria." *Comparative Studies in Society and History* 33 (1) (1991): 130–57.

Hedlund, Hans G. B. *Coffee, Co-operatives, and Culture: An Anthropological Study of a Coffee Co-operative in Kenya.* Nairobi: OUP, 1992.

Helleiner, G. K. "Agricultural Development Plans in Kenya and Tanzania." *RA* (13) (1971): 36–42.

Hennings, R. O. "Grazing Management in the Pastoral Areas of Kenya." *JAA* 13 (4) (1961): 191–203.

————. "Some Trends and Problems of African Land Tenure." *JAA* 4 (4) (1952): 122–34

Heyer, Judith. "Kenya's Agricultural Development Policy." *EAER* 2 (1966): 35–47.

————. "Origins of Regional Inequalities in Smallholder Agriculture in Kenya." *EAJRD* 8 (1/2) (1975): 142–81.

————, J. K. Maitha, and W. M. Senga. *Agricultural Development in Kenya: An Economic Assessment.* Nairobi: OUP, 1976.

Hoddinott, John. "Model of Migration and Remittances Applied to Western Kenya." *Oxford Economic Papers* 46 (3) (1994): 459–76.

————. "Modelling Remittance Flows in Kenya." *JAE* 1 (2) (1992): 206–32.

Hogg, Richard. "Irrigation Agriculture and Pastoral Development: A Lesson from Kenya." *Development and Change* 14 (4) (1983): 577–91.

————. "New Pastoralism: Poverty and Dependency in Northern Kenya." *Africa* 56 (3) (1986): 319–33.

————. "Pastoralism and Impoverishment: The Case of the Isiolo Boran of Northern Kenya." *Disasters* 4 (3) (1980): 299–310.

————. "Small Is Also Complex: A Study of Rural Development from Kenya." *Manchester Papers of Development* 1 (1) (1985): 91–100.

Holmes, R. S. "Land Tenure and Agricultural Productivity in the Trans-Nzoia, Kenya." *Geography* 60 (267) (1975): 137–39.

Holmquist, Frank. "Peasant Organization, Clientelism and Dependency: A Case Study of an Agricultural Producer's Cooperative in Kenya." Ph.D. diss., Indiana University, 1975.

————. "Self-Help: The State and Peasant Leverage in Kenya." *Africa* 54 (3) (1984): 72–91.

Hughes, R. "Examining the Roots of Educational Demand: The Case Supporting Rural Agrarian Development." *WD* 19 (2/3) (1991): 213–23.

Hunt, Diana. "Chayanov's Model of Peasant Household Resource Allocation and Its Relevance to Mbere Division, Eastern Kenya." *Journal of Development Studies* 15 (1) (1978): 59–86.

————. *Impending Crisis in Kenya: The Case for Land Reform.* Aldershot, UK: Gower, 1984.

Hyden, Goran. "Local Government Reform in Kenya." *EAJ* 4 (1970): 19–24.

Jabara, Cathy L. "Agricultural Pricing Policy in Kenya." *WD* 13 (5) (1985): 611–26.

Jama, M. A. "Smallholder Farmers Credit Repayment Performance in Lugari Division, Kakamega District, Kenya." *EAER* 8 (2) (1992): 85–91.

Jamieson, Barbara M. "Resource Allocation to Agricultural Research in Kenya from 1963 to 1978." Ph.D. diss., University of Toronto, 1981.

Jones, Eugene, and J. Mutuura. "Supply Responsiveness of Small Kenyan Cotton Farmers." *JDA* 23 (4) (1989): 535–44.

Jones, William I. "Small Farmers and the Green Revolution in Kenya." *African Economic History* 4 (1977): 182–85.

Kakili, J. "NGO Involvement in Agricultural Activities in Machakos District." In *Non-Governmental Organisations and the State in Africa: Rethinking Roles in Sustainable Agricultural Development*, edited by K. Wellard and J. C. Copestake, 111–17. London: Routledge, 1993.

Kiamba, Makau. "Introduction and Evolution of Private Landed Property in Kenya." *Development and Change* 20 (1) (1989): 121–47.

Kibera, Francis N. "Communication and Modernisation in Central Kenya: An Experiment." *Business Management* 2 (2) (1991): 71–84.

———. "Effects of Selected Communications Variable on the Adoption of New Agricultural Practices by Smallholders in Central Kiambu, Kenya." Ph.D. diss., University of Toronto, 1979.

Kisovi, Leonard M. "Changing Land-Use and Population Problems in Kitui District, Kenya." *JEARD* 22 (1992): 92–104.

Kitching, G. N. *Land, Livestock, and Leadership: The Rise of an African Petiti-Bourgeoise [sic] in Kenya, 1905–1918*. Nairobi: KLB, 1981.

Knowles, O. S. "Agricultural Marketing in Kenya." D.Phil. diss., Oxford University, 1955.

———. "Development of Agricultural Marketing in Kenya." *EAER* 3 (1) (1956): 191–97.

Kongstad, Per. *Family, Labour, and Trade in Western Kenya*. Uppsala: SIAS, 1980.

La Fontaine, S. H., and J. H. Mower. *Local Government in Kenya: Its Origins and Development*. Nairobi: Eagle Press, 1955.

Lelei, Vincent K. *Dairy Farming in Kenya*. Nairobi: ACTS, 1993.

Leo, Christopher. "Failure of the 'Progressive Farmer' in Kenya's Million-Acre Settlement Scheme." *JMAS* 16 (4) (1978): 619–38.

———. *Land and Class in Kenya*. Toronto: University of Toronto Press, 1984.

Leonard, David. *African Successes: Four Public Managers of Kenyan Rural Development*. Berkeley: University of California Press, 1991.

———, ed. *Rural Administration in Kenya*. Nairobi: EALB, 1973.

Little, Peter D. "Absentee Herd Owners and Part-Time Pastoralists: The Political Economy of Resource Use in Northern Kenya." *Human Ecology* 13 (2) (1985): 131–51.

———. *The Elusive Granary: Herder, Farmer, and State in Northern Kenya*. New York: CUP, 1992.

———. "Social Differentiation and Pastoralist Sedentarization in Northern Kenya." *Africa* 55 (3) (1985): 243–61.

Liversage, V. L. "Labour and Land in Native Reserves." *EAAJ* 3 (1938): 37–42.

———. "Some Observations on Farming Economics in Nakuru District." *EAAJ* 4 (1938): 195–204.

Livingstone, Ian. "Re-Assessment of Kenya's Rural and Urban Informal Sector." *WD* 19 (6) (1991): 651–70.

———. *Rural Development, Employment, and Incomes in Kenya*. Aldershot, UK: Gower, 1986.

Lofchie, Michael F. "Kenya's Agricultural Success." *Current History* 511 (1986): 221–25.

————. *The Policy Factor: Agricultural Performance in Kenya and Tanzania.* Boulder, CO: Lynne Rienner Publishers, 1989.

Luckham, M. E. "Early History of the Kenya Department of Agriculture." *EAAJ* 25 (2) (1959): 97–105.

McCabe, J. T. "Land Use Among the Pastoral Turkana." *RA* (15/16) (1983): 69–77.

Mackenzie, Fiona. "Land and Labour: Women and Men in Agricultural Change, Murang'a District, Kenya, 1880–1984." Ph.D. diss., University of Ottawa, 1986.

————. "Land and Territory: The Interface between Two Systems of Land Tenure, Murang'a District, Kenya." *Africa* 59 (1) (1989): 91–109.

McMahon, Gary J. "Income Distribution Effects of the Kenyan Coffee Marketing System." *Journal of Development Economics* 23 (2) (1989): 297–326.

————. "International Commodity Agreements and a Small Developing Country: The Case of Kenya and the International Coffee Agreement." Ph.D. diss., University of Western Ontario, 1984.

McWilliam, M. D. "East African Tea Industry, 1920–1956." D.Phil. diss., Oxford University, 1957.

————. "Kenya Tea Industry." *EAER* 6 (1) (1959): 32–48.

MacWilliam, S., et al. *Domestic Food Production and Political Conflict in Kenya.* Perth: Indian Ocean Centre for Peace Studies, 1995.

Maher, C. "African Labour on the Farm in Kenya Colony." *EAAJ* 8 (1942): 228–35.

————. "The People and the Land: Some Problems." *EAAJ* 7 (1941): 63–9; 7 (1942): 146–51.

Maitha, J. K. *Coffee in the Kenya Economy.* Nairobi: EALB, 1974.

Martin, C. J. "The Agrarian Question and Migrant Labor: The Case of Western Kenya." *JAS* 12 (4) (1985): 164–74.

Martin, David. "The Transition in Smallholder Banking in Kenya: Evidence from Rural Branch Bank Laws." *JDA* 16 (1) (1981): 71–85.

Martin, J. H. *Problem of the Squatter: Economic Survey of Resident Labour in Kenya.* Nairobi: GP, 1947.

Maxon, Robert M. "Early Years of the Gusii Coffee Industry in Kenya, 1933–1946." *JDA* 6 (3) (1972): 365–82.

————. "John Ainsworth and Agricultural Innovation in Kenya." *KHR* 1 (1973): 151–62.

————. "Stifling Capitalism in Rural Africa: The Gusii Coffee Industry in Kenya, 1932–1949." *Journal of Third World Studies* 11 (2) (1994): 317–50.

Mbeche, I. M. "Strategic Management of Kenyan Agricultural Development Projects: Options for the Effective Involvement of Operational Research/Management Science Methodology." Ph.D. diss., University of Lancaster, 1993.

Mbithi, Phillip. *Rural Sociology and Rural Development: Its Application in Kenya.* Nairobi: EALB, 1974.

Mbogoh, Stephen G. "Economic Analysis of Kenya's Sugar Industry with Special Reference to the Self-Sufficiency Production Policy." Ph.D. diss., University of Alberta, 1980.

Melkote, Srinivas R. "Agricultural Extension and the Small Farmer: Revealing the Communication Gap in an Extension Project in Kenya." *JDA* 22 (2) (1988): 239–52.

Miller, Norman N. *Politics of Agriculture in Kenya.* Hanover, NH: American Universities Field Staff Reports, 1971.

Mitchell, Philip E. *Agrarian Problem in Kenya: A Note by the Governor.* Nairobi: GP, 1947.

Mkangi, George C. *Social Cost of Small Families and Land Reform: A Case Study of the Wataita of Kenya.* New York: Pergamon Press, 1983.

Molla, M. R. I., et al. "Economics of Beef Cattle Policy in a Developing Country: The Case of Kenya." *EAJRD* 1/2 (1980): 92–112.

Moock, J. L. "The Migration Process and Differntial Economic Behavior in South Maragoli, Western Kenya." Ph.D. diss., Columbia University, 1976.

Moock, Peter. "Managerial Ability in Small-Farm Production: An Analysis of Maize Yields in the Vihiga Division of Kenya." Ph.D. diss., Columbia University, 1973.

Morgan, W. T. W. "Altitude and Crop Zones: A Transect in the Kenya Highlands." *Die Erde* 1/2 (1977): 124–28.

———. "Role of Temperate Crops in the Kenya Highlands." *Acta Geographica* 19 (1968): 273–78.

Moris, Jon R. "Agrarian Revolution in Central Kenya: A Study of Farm Innovation in Embu District." Ph.D. diss., Northwestern University, 1970.

———. *Rural Development in Kenya.* Nairobi: EAPH, 1971.

Mott, Frank L., and David Shapiro. "Seasonal Variations in Labor-Force Activity and Intrahousehold Substitution of Labor in Rural Kenya." *JDA* 18 (4) (1984): 449–64.

Muga, E. "Problems of Rural Development in Kenya—A Sociological Case Study of Social Change in the Kano Plains." *JEARD* 1 (1971): 41–68.

Mulinge, Munyae Masai. "Job Satisfaction and Organizational Attachment among Agricultural Professionals in Kenya." Ph.D. diss., University of Iowa, 1994.

Mutoro, Basilida Anyona. *Women Working Wonders: Smallscale Farming and the Role of Women in Vihiga District, Kenya.* Amsterdam, Netherlands: Thela Publishers, 1997.

Mwangi, Lucy Ngendo. "Optimization of Pastoral Subsistence Strategies Under Drought and Marketing Risks: Maasai Model Ranch Study." Ph.D. diss., Colorado State University, 1994.

Mwanthi, Mutuku A., and Violet N. Kimani. "Patterns of Agrochemical Handling and Community Response in Central Kenya." *Journal of Environmental Health* 7 (1993): 11–16.

Myers, Richard L. *Sociological Approach to Farming Systems in Kenya.* Ithaca, NY: Program in International Agriculture, Cornell University, 1982.

Newiger, Nicholaus. *Cooperative Farming in Kenya and Tanzania.* Munich: Institute für Wirtschaftsforschung, 1967.

Ngunjiri, Peter. *In a Dry Land: A Report on the Turkana Rural Development Programme, Kenya.* London: Panos, 1987.

Njonjo, Apollo. "Africanization of the 'White Highlands': A Study in Agrarian Class Struggles in Kenya, 1950–1974." Ph.D. diss., Princeton University, 1977.
———. "Kenya Peasantry: A Reassessment." *ROAPE* 20 (1981): 27–40.
Njoroge, J. M., and J. K. Kimemia. "Current Intercropping Observations and Future Trends in Arabica Coffee, Kenya." *Outlook on Agriculture* 22 (1) (1993): 43–48.
———. "Economic Benefits of Intercropping Young Arabica and Robusta Coffee with Food Crops in Kenya." *Outlook on Agriculture* 24 (1) (1995): 27–34.
Nottidge, C. P. R., and J. R. Goldsack. *Million Acre Settlement Scheme, 1962–1966.* Nairobi: Department of Settlement, 1966.
Nyangira, Nicholas. *Relative Modernisation and Public Resource Allocation in Kenya.* Nairobi: EALB, 1975.
Nyong'o, Anyang' P. "Development of a Middle Peasantry in Nyanza." *ROAPE* 20 (1981): 108–20.
———. "What 'The Friends of the Peasants' Are and How They Pose the Question of the Peasantry." *ROAPE* (20) (1981): 17–26.
Odingo, Richard S. *Kenya Highlands.* Nairobi: EAPH, 1971.
———. "Post-Independence Agricultural Changes in the Kenya Highlands." *Geographica Polonica* (1970): 207–26.
Ogutu, M. A. "Dualism and the Development of Coffee in Meru, Kenya, in 1930s." *TJH* 8 (2) (1979): 140–59.
O'Leary, Michael F. *Kitui Akamba: Economic and Social Change in Semi-Arid Kenya.* Nairobi: Heinemann Educational Books, 1984.
Ongaro, Wilfred Abuom. *Adoption of New Farming Technology: A Case Study of Maize Production in Western Kenya.* Göteborg, Sweden: Handelshögskolan, 1988.
Orvis, Stephen. *The Agrarian Question in Kenya.* Gainesville, FL: University Press of Florida, 1997.
———. "Kenyan Agrarian Debate: A Reappraisal." *ASR* 36 (3) (1993): 23–48.
Ouma, Sylvester J. *History of the Cooperative Movement in Kenya.* Nairobi: Bookwise Ltd., 1980.
Oyugi, W. O. *Rural Development Administration: A Kenyan Experience.* New Delhi: Vikas Publishing House Pvt., Ltd., 1981.
Paterson, Douglas. "Kinship, Land and Community: The Moral Foundation of the Abaluhya of East Bunyore (Kenya)." Ph.D. diss., University of Washington, 1984.
Pearson, Scott, et al. *Agricultural Policy in Kenya.* Ithaca, NY and London: Cornell University Press, 1995.
Pedraza, G. J. W. "Land Consolidation in the Kikuyu Areas." *JAA* 8 (2) (1956): 82–87.
Pischke, J. D. von. "Political Economy of Farm Credit in Kenya." Ph.D. diss., University of Glasgow, 1977.
———. *Smallholder Agricultural Credit Programs and Performance in Kenya.* Nairobi: Institute for Development Studies, 1974.

Raikes, P. "Business as Usual: Some 'Real' Food Markets in Kenya." *Sociologica Ruralis* 34 (1) (1994): 26–44.

Rasmusson, Peter. *Kenyan Rural Development and Aid.* Stockholm: Swedish International Development Authority, 1972.

Remole, R. A. "Foundation of European Agricultural Settlement in Kenya." Ph.D. diss., Harvard University, 1959.

Republic of Kenya. *Integrated Rural Survey.* Nairobi: GP, various years.

———. *Report of the Maize Commission of Inquiry.* Nairobi: GP, 1966.

Ruthenberg, Hans. *African Agricultural Production Development Policy in Kenya, 1952–1965.* Berlin: Springer-Verlag, 1966.

Schapiro, M. O., and S. Wainaina. "Kenya's Export of Horticultural Commodities." *Public Administration and Development* 11 (3) (1991): 257–61.

Scheer, S. J. "Economic Factors in Farmer Adoption of Agroforestry: Patterns Observed in Western Kenya." *WD* 23 (5) (1995): 787–804.

Sharpley, Jennifer. *Economic Policies and Agricultural Performance: The Case of Kenya.* Paris: Development Centre, Organization for Economic Cooperation and Development, 1986.

Shipton, Parker. "Luo Entrustment: Foreign Finance and the Soil of the Spirits in Kenya." *Africa* 65 (2) (1995): 165–96.

Silberfein, Marilyn. *Rural Change in Machakos, Kenya: A Historical Geography Perspective.* Lanham, MD: University Press of America, 1989.

Simpson, M. C. *Alternative Strategies for Rangeland Development in Kenya.* Leeds: Leeds University Press, 1973.

Smoke, Paul J. *Local Government Finance in Developing Countries: Case of Kenya.* Nairobi: OUP, 1994.

———. "Local Government Fiscal Reform in Developing Countries: Lessons from Kenya." *WD* 21 (6) (1993): 901–23.

———. "Rural Local Government Finance in Kenya: The Case of Murang'a County Council." *Public Administration and Development* 12 (1) (1992): 87–96.

———. "Small Town Local Government Finance in Kenya: The Case of Karatina Town Council." *Public Administration and Development* 12 (1) (1992): 71–85.

Sobania, Neal. "Fisherman Herders: Subsistence, Survival and Cultural Change in Northern Kenya." *JAH* 29 (1) (1988): 41–56.

Sorrenson, M. P. K. *Land Reform in the Kikuyu Country.* Nairobi: OUP, 1967.

Staudt, Kathleen A. "Administrative Resources, Political Patrons, and Redressing Inequities: A Case From Western Kenya." *JDA* 12 (4) (1978): 399–414.

———. *Agricultural Policy Implementation: A Case Study from Western Kenya.* West Hartford, CT: Kumarian Press, 1985.

Steeves, Jeffrey S. "Class Analysis and Rural Africa: The Kenya Tea Development Authority." *JMAS* 16 (1) (1978): 123–32.

———. "Politics and Administration of Agricultural Development in Kenya: The Kenya Tea Development Authority." Ph.D. diss., University of Toronto, 1975.

Stern, N. H. *Appraisal of Tea Production on Small-Holding in Kenya.* Paris: Organisation for Economic Co-operation and Development, 1972.

Strobel, Herbert, ed. *Economic Analysis of Smallholder Agriculture in the Kericho District (Kenya)*. Berlin: Institute of Socio-economics of Agricultural Development, 1973.

Suda, Collette. "Agricultural Development Policies and Institutional Support Systems in Post-Colonial Kenya and Tanzania." *JEARD* 20 (1990): 104–26.

Swift, J. "Local Customary Institutions As the Basis for Natural Resource Management among the Boran Pastoralists in Northern Kenya." *I.D.S. Bulletin* 4 (1991): 34–37.

Swynnerton, R. J. M. "Agricultural Advances in Eastern Africa." *AA* 61 (244) (1962): 201–15.

———. "Kenya's Agricultural Planning." *AA* 56 (224) (1957): 209–15.

———. *A Plan to Intensify the Development of African Agriculture in Kenya*. Nairobi: GP, 1954.

Talbott, I. D. *Agricultural Innovation in Colonial Africa: Kenya and the Great Depression*. Lewiston, ME: Edwin Mellen, 1991.

Taylor, D. R. F. "Agricultural Change in Kikuyuland." In *Environment and Land Use in Africa*, edited by M. F. Thomas and G. W. Whittington, 463–93. London: Methuen, 1969.

———. "Land Reform in Kenya: A Reappraisal." *RA* 23 (1974): 79–90.

———. "New Tea-Growing Areas in Kenya." *Geography* 4 (1965): 373–75.

———. "Rural Development in Kenya." *Newstatements* 1 (1) (1971): 78–84.

Thirtle, C. "Agricultural Research and Institution Building in Sub-Saharan Africa: The Kenyan Example." *Journal of International Development* 1 (1) (1989): 83–111.

Thomas, B. P. "Development Through Harambee Donations: Who Wins and Who Loses? Rural Self-Help in Kenya." *WD* 15 (4) (1987): 463–81.

Thurmann, Ulrick, ed. *Rural Development Administration in Bugoma District, Kenya*. Berlin: German Development Institute, 1968.

Thurston, Anne. *Smallholder Agriculture in Colonial Kenya: The Official Mind and the Swynnerton Plan*. Cambridge: University of Cambridge, African Studies Centre, 1982.

Trapman, Christopher. *Change in Administrative Structures: A Case Study of Kenyan Agricultural Development*. London: ODI, 1974.

Uchendu, Victor C., and Kenneth R. M. Anthony. *Agricultural Change in Kisii District, Kenya*. Nairobi: EALB, 1975.

Vasthoff, Josef. *Small Farm Credit and Development: Some Experiences in East Africa with Special Reference to Kenya*. Munich: Weltforum-Verlag, 1968.

Waaijenberg, H. *Mijikenda Agriculture in Coast Province of Kenya: Peasants Between Tradition, Ecology, and Policy*. Amsterdam: Royal Tropical Institute, 1994.

Wainwright, H. "Export Diversification Through Horticulture: Kenya, A Case Study." *Outlook on Agriculture* 23 (1) (1994): 41–45.

Wallace, I. R. "Agricultural Education and Rural Development: Some Problems and Approaches in Kenya." *EAJRD* 1/2 (1980): 1–25.

Wallis, M. "District Planning and Local Government in Kenya." *Public Administration and Development* 10 (4) (1990): 437–52.

Wallis, M. A. H. *Bureaucrats, Politicians, and Rural Communities in Kenya.* Manchester: University of Manchester, U.K., 1982.

Wang Ombe, Joseph K., and Germano M. Mwabu. "Agricultural Land Use Patterns and Malaria Conditions in Kenya." *SSM* 29 (9) (1993): 1121–30.

Waters, Alan Rufus. "Change and Evolution in the Kenya Coffee Industry." *AA* 71 (282) (1972): 163–75.

———. "Change and Evolution in the Structure of the Kenya Coffee Industry." *History of Agriculture* 1 (4) (1974): 81–105.

Watts, E. Ronald. "Agricultural Extension in Embu District of Kenya." *EAJRD* (1969): 63–81.

Widner, Jennifer A. "Single Party States and Agricultural Policies: The Cases of Ivory Coast and Kenya." *Comparative Politics* 2 (1994): 127–47.

Wiggins, S. "The Planning and Management of Integrated Rural Development in Drylands: Early Lessons from Kenya's Arid and Semi-Arid Lands Programmes." *Public Administration and Development* 5 (2) (1985): 91–108.

Wilson, Gordon M. *Rural Development Survey in Three Areas of Kenya.* Nairobi: Ministry of Co-operatives and Social Sciences, 1968.

Wilson, R. G. "Land Consolidation in the Fort Hall District." *JAA* 8 (3) (1956): 144–51.

Wilson, Rodney J. A. "Land Control in Kenya's Smallholder Farming Areas." *EAJRD* 1/2 (1972): 123–40.

Youé, Christopher P. "Agrarian Change and Conflict in Kenya." *CJAS* 25 (1) (1991): 122–28.

Zeleza, Tiyambe. "Development of the Cooperative Movement in Kenya since Independence." *JEARD* 20 (1990): 68–94.

Zwanenburg, Roger van. *Agricultural History of Kenya to 1939.* Nairobi: EAPH, 1972.

———. "Development of Peasant Commodity Production in Kenya 1920–40." *Economic History Review* 27 (3) (1974): 442–54.

L. FOREIGN AFFAIRS

Adanalian, Alice A. "Horn of Africa." *World Affairs* 131 (1) (1968): 38–42.

Adar, Korwa G. "Kenya–US Relations: A Recapitulation of the Patterns of Paradigmatic Conceptualization, 1960–1990s." In *United States and Africa: From Independence to the End of the Cold War*, edited by Macharia Munene, J.D. Olewe Nyunya, and Korwa Adar, 89–104. Nairobi: EAEP, 1995.

———. *Kenyan Foreign Policy Behavior towards Somalia, 1963–1983.* Lanham, MD: University Press of America, 1994.

Africa Watch. *Seeking Refuge, Finding Terror: The Widespread Rape of Somali Women Refugees in North Eastern Kenya.* New York: Africa Watch, 1991.

African Rights. *The Nightmare Continues: Abuses Against Somali Refugees in Kenya*. London: African Rights, 1993.

Al-Safi, Mahasin A. G. H. "Kenya Somalis: The Shift From 'Greater Somalia' to Integration with Kenya." *Nordic Journal of African Studies* 4 (2) (1995): 34–41.

Attwood, William. *The Reds and the Blacks: A Personal Adventure*. New York: Harper and Row, 1967.

Barve, Arvind G. *Foreign Trade of Kenya*. Nairobi: Transafrica, 1984.

Bennett, George. "Kenya and Tanzania." *AA* 66 (265) (1967): 329–35.

Biswas, Aparajita. "India-Kenya Relations 1947–1977." *African Currents* 13 (1991): 18–43.

————. "Role of Production Co-operation in India-Kenya Economic Relations." *Africa Quarterly* 30 (1/2) (1990): 34–49.

Bonner, Raymond. "Sad Misuse of Influence." *Spectator* 8568 (26 September 1992): 15–18.

Burkhalter, Holly. "Kenya: Dances with State." *AR* 36 (3) (1991): 53–55.

————, and Rakiya Omaar. "Human Rights: Failures of State." *AR* 35 (6) (1990): 27–29.

Capenny, S. H. F. "Proposed Anglo-Abyssinian Boundary in East Africa." *Scottish Geographical Magazine* 11 (1905): 260–63.

Castagno, A. A. "Somali-Kenya Controversy: Implications for the Future." *JMAS* 2 (2) (1964): 165–88.

Charlier, T. "A Propos des Conflits de Frontières entre la Somalie, l'Ethiopie et la Kenya." *Revue Française de Science Politique* 16 (2) (1966): 310–19.

Cohen, J. M. "Foreign Advisors and Capacity Building: Case of Kenya." *Public Administration and Development* 12 (5) (1992): 493–510.

Collinson, S. "Constraints on the Transfer of Manufacturing Technology: A British-Kenyan Comparison." *Science, Technology and Development* 11 (2) (1993): 113–43.

Doob, Leonard W., ed. *Resolving Conflict in Africa: The Fermeda Workshop*. New Haven, CT: YUP, 1970.

"Dr. Munyua Waiyaki, Kenyan Minister of Foreign Affairs." *AR* 22 (2) (1977): 37–40.

El-Safi, Mahassin Abdel Gadir Hag. "Position of 'Alien' Somalis in the East Africa Protectorate and Kenya Colony 1916–1963." *JAS* 8 (1) (1981): 38–45.

Gitelson, Susan Aurelia. "Policy Options for Small States: Kenya and Tanzania Revisted." *Studies in Comparative International Development* (1977): 30–57.

Goldsmith, Paul. "Somali Impact on Kenya, 1990–1993." In *Mending Rips in the Sky*, edited by Hussein M. Adam and Richard Ford, 461–83. Lawrenceville, NJ: Red Sea Press, 1997.

Good, Kenneth A. "Kenyans and Their Foreign Policy Pressures, Images, and Decisions." Ph.D. diss., McGill University, 1969.

Gordon, David F. "Anglophonic Variants: Kenya Versus Tanzania." *Annals of the American Academy of Political and Social Science* 489 (1987): 88–102.

———. "Foreign Relations: Dilemmas of Independence and Development." In *Politics and Public Policy in Kenya and Tanzania*, edited by Joel Barkan, 297–335. Nairobi: Heinemann, 1984.

Holtham, Gerald, and Arthur Hazlewood. *Aid and Inequality in Kenya: British Development Assistance to Kenya*. New York: Africana, 1976.

Hoskyns, Catherine. *Case Studies in African Diplomacy: The Ethiopia-Somali-Kenya Dispute, 1960–1967*. Dar-es-Salaam, Tanzania: OUP, 1969.

Howell, John. "Analysis of Kenya's Foreign Policy." *JMAS* 6 (1) (1968): 29–48.

Johns, Michael. "Strengthening U.S. Ties with Kenya." *Backgrounder* 766 (24 April 1990): 1–16.

Kagombe, Maina. "The Impact of Foreign Governments on Kenya's Domestic Policies." *Pan-African Journal* 3 (2) (1970): 50–65.

———. "Somali-Kenya Diplomacy and the Conference on Education." *Pan-African Journal* 1 (1968): 172–74.

Kenya and the OAU. Nairobi: Space Publications, 1981.

Khainza, Mary Margaret. *Illicit Trade: South Mbale District, Kenya-Uganda Border*. Kampala, Uganda: Makerere University, 1981.

Khapoya, Vincent B. "Kenya," in *Political Economy of African Foreign Policy: Comparative Analysis*, edited by Timothy Shaw and Olajide Aluko, 145–64. Aldershot, UK: Gower, 1984.

———. "Political Economy and Foreign Policy of Kenya." *African Studies Association Papers* 24 (47/49) (1981): 1–18.

Kiano, Julius Gikenyo. "Foreign Policy of East African Nations." In *Foreign Policies in a World of Change*, edited by J. E. Black and K. W. Thompson, 407–23. New York: Harper and Row, 1963.

Leighton, Marian. *The USSR, Kenya, and the Horn of Africa*. Munich: Radio Liberty Research, 1977.

Lewis, I. M. "The Problem of the Northern Frontier District of Kenya." *Race* 5 (1) (1963): 48–60.

Makinda, Samuel M. "Conflict and Accommodation in the Horn of Africa: Kenya's Role in the Somali-Ethiopian Dispute." *Australian Outlook* 1 (1983): 34–39.

———. "From Quiet Diplomacy to Cold War Politics: Kenya's Foreign Policy." *Third World Quarterly* 5 (2) (1983): 300–19.

Marcus, Harold. "A History of Negotiations Concerning the Border Between Ethiopia and British East Africa, 1897–1914." In *Boston University Papers on Africa*. Vol. 2, edited by Jeffrey Butler, 239–65. Boston: Boston University Press, 1966.

Martin, Denis. "L'Occident, l'Océan et le Kenya." *Annuaire des Pays de l'Océan Indien* (2) (1975): 229–42.

Mbogua, J.P. "Tour of Duty as Kenya's Ambassador to the United States; Experiences and Impressions." In *United States and Africa: From Independence to the*

End of the Cold War, edited by Macharia Munene, J.D. Olewe Nyunya, and Korwa Adar, 276–91. Nairobi: EAEP, 1995.

Mungai, Njoroge. "Kenya's Foreign Policy on Southern Africa." *Pan-African Journal* 4 (2) (1971): 218–22.

Nzomo, Maria. "External Influence on the Political Economy of Kenya: The Case of MNCs." In *Politics and Administration in East Africa*, edited by Walter Oyugi, 429–67. Nairobi: EAEP, 1994.

————. Foreign Policy of Kenya and Tanzania: The Impact of Dependence and Underdevelopment." Ph.D. diss., Dalhousie University, 1981.

Odinga,Oginga. "Kenya at the United Nations." *African Communist* 16 (1964): 93–105.

Ododa, Harry. "Continuity and Change in Kenya's Foreign Policy from the Kenyatta to the Moi Government." *JAS* 13 (2) (1986): 47–57.

Okoth, Godfrey P. "The Foreign Policy of Uganda Toward Kenya and Tanzania." In *Politics and Administration in East Africa*, edited by Walter O. Oyugi, 359–94. Nairobi: EAEP, 1994.

————. "Intermittent Tensions in Uganda-Kenya Relations: Historical Perspectives." *TJH* 21 (1992): 69–92.

————. "Uganda-Kenya Relations, 1971–1979." *African Studies Association Papers* 29 (71) (1986): 1–19.

————. *United States of America's Foreign Policy towards Kenya 1952–1969*. Nairobi: Gideon S. Were Press, 1992.

Okumu, John J. "Kenya's Foreign Policy." In *Foreign Policies of African States*, edited by O. Aluko, 136–62. London: Hodder and Stoughton, 1977.

————. "Some Thoughts on Kenya's Foreign Policy." *TAR* 3 (2) (1973): 263–90.

Orwa, D. Katete. "Change and Continuity in Kenya's Foreign Policy from Kenyatta to Moi." In *Politics and Administration in East Africa*, edited by Walter O. Oyugi, 297–330. Nairobi: EAEP, 1994.

————. "Kenya's Relations with its Neighbors: The Search for a Regional Equilibrium." *Jerusalem Journal of International Relations* 11 (4) (1989): 106–28.

Orwenyo, Jason Nyariki. "The Soviet Union and Communism as Factors Among Kenyan Intelligentsia in Kenya's Internal Problems, 1957–1966." Ph.D. diss., Georgetown University, 1973.

Overseas Development Administration. *British Aid to Kenya*. London: Overseas Development Administration, 1986.

Ramchandani, R. R. and A. Biswas. "India-Africa Economic Relations: The Case of Bilateral Relations between India and Kenya." *African Currents* 11 (1990): 58–85.

Republic of Kenya. *Kenya-Somali Relations: Narrative of Four Years of Inspired Aggression and Direct Subversion Mounted by the Somali Republic Against the Government and People of the Republic of Kenya*. Nairobi: GP, 1967.

Rodgers, W. M. "Significance of Access to Land as a Determinant of Kenya's Interregional Migration." *WD* 19 (7) (1991): 921–26.

Rothchild, Donald. "From Hegemony to Bargaining in East African Relations." *JAS* 1 (4) (1974): 390–416.

Shaw, Timothy M. "Kenya and South Africa: 'Subimperialist' States." *Orbis* 21 (2) (1977): 375–94.

Smith, C. S. "The Anglo-German Boundary in East Equatorial Africa. Proceedings of the British Commission, 1892." *GJ* (1894): 424–37.

Stephens, Robert Fyfe. "An Analysis of the Foreign Relations of Tanzania and Kenya: A Comparative Study." Ph.D. diss., University of Michigan, 1973.

Tandon, Y. "Ugandan Refugees in Kenya: A Community of Enforced Self-Reliance." *Disasters* 8 (4) (1984): 267–71.

Thompson, Vincent B. "Conflict in the Horn of Africa: The Kenya-Somalia Border Problem." Ph.D. diss., University of London, 1985.

———. "Phenomenon of Shifting Frontiers: The Kenya-Somalia Case in the Horn of Africa, 1880s-1970s." *Journal of Asian and African Studies* 1/2 (1995): 1–40.

Throup, David. "Kenya's Relations with Museveni's Uganda." In *Changing Uganda: The Dilemmas of Structural Adjustment and Revolutionary Change*, edited by H. B. Hansen and Michael J. Twaddle, 187–96. London: James Currey, 1991.

Turton, Edmond Romilly. "Impact of Mohammad Abdille Hassan in the East Africa Protectorate." *JAH* 10 (4) (1969): 641–57.

———. "Isaq Somali Diaspora and Poll-Tax Agitation in Kenya, 1936–41." *AA* 73 (292) (1974): 325–46.

———. "Somali Resistance to Colonial Rule and the Development of Somali Political Activity in Kenya, 1893–1960." *JAH* 13 (1) (1972): 119–43.

United Kingdom. Ministry of Overseas Development. *Aid Policy in One Country: Britain's Aid to Kenya, 1964–68*. London: Mimeographed, 1970.

United States. Department of State. Office of the Geographer. *Kenya-Somalia Boundary*. Washington, D.C.: Department of State, 1973.

———. *Kenya-Tanzania Boundary*. Washington, D.C.: Department of State, 1966.

———. *Kenya-Uganda Boundary*. Washington, D.C.: Department of State, 1973.

———. *Maritime Boundary: Kenya-Tanzania*. Washington, D.C.: Department of State, 1981.

Waller, Peter P. "Aid and Conditionality: The Case of Germany, with Particular Reference to Kenya." In *Aid and Political Conditionality*, edited by Olav Stokke, 110–28. London: Frank Cass, 1995.

Wanjohi, N. Gatheru. "Politics of Foreign Aid in Kenya Since Independence, 1963–1977." Ph.D. diss., University of Nairobi, 1980.

Wilkin, David. "Refugees and British Administrative Policy in Northern Kenya, 1936–1938." *AA* 79 (317) (1980): 510–30.

Woodward, Peter. "Relations between Neighbouring States in North-East Africa." *JMAS* 22 (2) (1984): 273–85.

Wright, S. J. "Foreign Policy of Kenya, 1963–1978." Ph.D. diss., University of London, 1980.

M. WOMEN'S AFFAIRS

Achola, P., et al., eds. *Participation of Women in Kenyan Society.* Nairobi: KLB, 1983.

Adams, Bert N., and Edward Mburugu. "Kikuyu Bridewealth and Polygyny Today." *Journal of Comparative Family Studies* 25 (2) (1994): 159–66.

Ahawo, D. O. *Kenyan Women in Socioeconomic Development.* Nairobi: Women's Bureau, 1990.

Ahlberg, Beth Maina. *Women, Sexuality and the Changing Social Order: The Impact of Government Policies on Reproductive Behavior in Kenya.* Philadelphia: Gordon and Breach, 1991.

Amisi, B., ed. *Women and Democracy in Kenya.* Nairobi: AFARD, 1992.

Amnesty International. *Women in Kenya: Repression and Resistance.* New York: AI, 1995.

Ayodo, Awuor. "Definitions of the Self in Luo Women's Orature." *Research in African Literatures* 25 (3) (1994): 121–29.

Ayot, Theodora O. *Women and Political Leadership in Pre-Colonial Period: Case Study of Chief Mang'ana of Kadem in Western Kenya.* Nairobi: Kaswanga Press, 1994.

Baker, Jean, and Shanyisa Khasiani. "Induced Abortion in Kenya: Case Histories." *Studies in Family Planning* 1 (1992): 34–44.

Baksh, Michael, et al. "Influence of Reproductive Status on Rural Kenyan Women's Time Use." *SSM* 39 (3) (1994): 345–54.

Barret, Minna. "Women's Income-Generating Initiatives in Kenya: Self-Report Perceptions of the Need for and Value of Women's Groups." *African Urban Quarterly* 2 (4) (1987): 435–42.

Bifani, Patricia, Kavetsa Adagala, and Priscilla W. Kariuki. *Impact of Development on Women in Kenya.* 2 vols. Nairobi: University of Nairobi, 1982.

Bissmarck, Ann. *Savings and Credit Project for Rural Women in Kenya: Report of a Feasibility Study.* Stockholm: Swedish Savings Bank Association, 1986.

Bradley, Candice. "Women's Empowerment and Fertility Decline in Western Kenya." In *Situating Fertility: Anthropology and Demographic Inquiry*, edited by Susan Greenhalgh, 157–78. Cambridge: CUP, 1995.

Brantley, Cynthia. "Mekatalili and the Role of Women in Giriama Resistance." In *Banditry, Rebellion and Social Protest in Africa*, edited by Donald Crummey, 333–50. London: James Currey, 1986.

Bujra, Janet M. "Women 'Entrepreneurs' of Early Nairobi." *CJAS* 9 (2) (1975): 213–34.

Bülow, Dorthe von. "Bigger Than Men? Gender Relations and Their Changing Meaning in Kipsigis Society, Kenya." *Africa* 62 (4) (1992): 523–46.

————. *Reconsidering Female Subordination: Kipsigis Women in Kenya.* Copenhagen: Centre for Development Research, 1991.

————. *Transgressing Gender Boundaries: Kipsigis Women in Kenya.* Copenhagen: Centre for Development Research, 1991.

Byamukama, James. *Land Law Reform and Women's Property Rights in Land in Kenya.* Toronto: African Human Rights Research Association, 1985.

Caplan, Pat. "Perceptions of Gender Stratification." *Africa* 59 (2) (1989): 196–208.

Carlebach, Julius. *Juvenile Prostitutes in Nairobi.* Kampala: East African Institute of Social Research, 1962.

Chege, J. N. "Politics of Gender and Fertility Regulation in Kenya: A Case Study of the Igembe. Ph.D. diss., University of Lancaster, 1993.

Chitere, Preston O. "Women's Self-Help Movement in Kenya: A Historical Perspective, 1940–80." *TJH* 17 (1988): 50–68.

Ciekway, Diane. "Witchcraft Eradication as Political Process in Kilifi District, Kenya, 1955–1988." Ph.D. diss., Columbia University, 1992.

Clark, Carolyn M. "Land and Food, Women and Power in Nineteenth Century Kikuyu." *Africa* 50 (4) (1980): 357–70.

Cubbins, L. A. "Women, Men and the Division of Power: A Study of Gender Stratification in Kenya." *Social Forces* 69 (4) (1991): 1063–85.

Davison, Jean. "School Attainment and Gender: Attitudes of Kenyan and Malawian Parents toward Educating Girls." *International Journal of Educational Development* 13 (4) (1993): 331–38.

————. *Voices from Mutira: Lives of Rural Gikuyu Women.* Boulder, CO: Lynne Rienner, 1989.

————. "'Without Land We Are Nothing': The Effect of Land Tenure Policies and Practices Upon Rural Women in Kenya." *RA* 27 (1987): 19–33.

Duncan, M. E. "A Socioeconomic, Clinical and Serological Study in an African City of Prostitutes and Women Still Married to Their First Husband." *SSM* 39 (3) (1994): 323–33.

Eshiwani, George S. "Women's Access to Higher Education in Kenya: A Study of Opportunities and Attainment in Science and Mathematics Education." *JEARD* 15 (1985): 91–110.

Feldman, Rayah. "Women's Groups and Women's Subordination: An Analysis of Policies Toward Rural Women in Kenya." *ROAPE* 27/28 (1984): 67–85.

Francis, Elizabeth. "Migration and Changing Divisions of Labour: Gender Relations and Economic Change in Koguta, Western Kenya." *Africa* 65 (2) (1995): 197–216.

Fratkin, Elliot, and Kevin Smith. "Women's Changing Roles with Pastoral Sedentarization: Varying Strategies in Alternate Rendille Communities." *Human Ecology* 23 (4) (1995): 433–54.

Frederiksen, Bodil Folke. "Gender, Ethnicity and Popular Culture in Kenya." *European Journal of Development Research* 6 (2) (1994): 52–62.

Friedman, Ariella, and Judith Todd. "Kenyan Women Tell a Story: Interpersonal Power of Women in Three Subcultures in Kenya." *Sex Roles: A Journal of Research* 32 (9/10) (1994): 533–46.

————, and Priscilla Wanjiru. "Cooperative and Competitive Behavior or Urban and Rural Children in Kenya." *Journal of Cross-Cultural Psychology* 4 (1995): 374–83.

Gakuo, M. "Kenyan Women and Situation and Strategies for Improvement." *Women's Studies International Forum* 8 (4) (1985): 373–79.

Gakure, Roselyn Wangui. "Factors Affecting Job Creating and Low Job Creating Firms Owned by Women in Kenya." Ph.D. diss., University of Illinois, 1995.

Goldfarb, Alan. "A Kenyan Wife's Right to Bury Her Husband: Applying the Convention on the Elimination of All Forms of Discrimination against Women." *ILSA Journal of International Law* 14 (1990): 1–21.

Gordon, April. "Gender, Ethnicity, and Class in Kenya: 'Burying Otieno' Revisited." *Signs: Journal of Women in Culture and Society* 20 (4) (1995): 883–912.

Government of Kenya and United Nations Children's Fund. *Situation Analysis of Children and Women in Kenya*. Nairobi: United Nations Children's Fund, Kenya Country Office, 1989.

Gutto, Shadrack B. O. *Status of Women in Kenya: A Study of Paternalism, Inequality and Underprivilege*. Nairobi: University of Nairobi, Institute for Development Studies, 1976.

Gwakop, Edwins Laban Moogi. "Continuity and Change in the Practice of Clitoridectomy in Kenya: A Case Study of the Abagussi." *JMAS* 33 (2) (1995): 333–37.

Håkansson, Thomas N. *Bridewealth, Women and Land: Social Change Among the Gusii of Kenya*. Uppsala, Sweden: University of Uppsala, 1988.

————. "Detachability of Women: Gender and Kinship in Processes of Socioeconomic Change Among the Gusii of Kenya." *American Ethnologist* 21 (3) (1994): 516–38.

————. *Landless Gusii Women: A Result of Customary Land Law and Modern Marriage Patterns*. Uppsala, Sweden: University of Uppsala, 1986.

————. "Why Do Gusii Women Get Married? A Study of Cultural Constraints and Women's Strategies in a Rural Community in Kenya." *Folk* 27 (1985): 89–114.

Harris, Joan. "Women in Kenya: Revolution or Evolution?" *AR* 30 (2) (1985): 30–32.

Hay, Margaret Jean. "Luo Women and Economic Change During the Colonial Period." In *Women in Africa: Studies in Social and Economic Change*, edited by Nancy J. Hafkin and Edna G. Bay, 87–109. Stanford, CA: Stanford University Press, 1976.

Herz, B. "Women in Development: Kenya's Experience." *Finance and Development* 26 (2) (1989): 43–45.

Hinga, T. M. "Women, Power and Liberation in an African Church: A Theological Case Study of the Legio Maria Church in Kenya." Ph.D. diss., University of Lancaster, 1990.

Hoddinott, John. "Rotten Kids or Manipulative Parents: Are Children Old Age Security in Western Kenya?" *Economic Development and Cultural Change* 3 (1992): 545–65.

Hoehler-Falton, Cynthia Heyden. "Women of Fire and Spirit: History, Faith and Gender in Roho Religion in Nyanza [Kenya]." Ph.D. diss., University of Virginia, 1993.

Hollander, Roberta Beth. "Out of Tradition: The Position of Women in Kenya and Tanzania During the Pre-Colonial, Colonial and Post-Colonial Eras." Ph.D. diss., American University, 1979.

Horton, Susan R. *Difficult Women, Artful Lives: Olive Schreiner and Isak Dinesen, In and Out of Africa.* Baltimore and London: Johns Hopkins University Press, 1995.

House-Midamba, Bessie. *Class, Development and Gender Inequality in Kenya, 1963–1990.* Lewiston, ME: Edwin Mellen Press, 1990.

———. "Gender, Democratization, and Associational Life in Kenya." *AT* 43 (3) (1996): 289–306.

———. "United Nations Decade: Political Empowerment or Increased Marginalization for Kenyan Women." *AT* 37 (1) (1990): 37–48.

Joekes, S., et al. "Gender, Environment and Population." *Development and Change* 25 (1) (1994): 137–65.

Jules-Rosette, Bennetta. "Women and New Technologies in Comparative Perspective: Case Studies in Ivory Coast and Kenya." *African Urban Studies* 21 (1985): 25–37.

Kabira, W. M., and E. A. Nzioki. *Celebrating Women's Resistance: A Case Study of Women's Groups Movement in Kenya.* Nairobi: African Women's Perspective, 1993.

Kane, K., et al. "Case for Business Training with Women's Groups." *Small Enterprise Development* 2 (1) (1991): 13–19.

Karega, R. G. M. "Women's Groups: From Welfare to Small-Scale Business in Kenya." *Small Enterprise Development* 7 (1) (1996): 31–41.

Kennedy, Dane. "Isak Dinesen's African Recovery of a European Past." *Clio* 1 (1987): 37–50.

Kershaw, Greet. "The Changing Roles of Men and Women in the Kikuyu Family by Socio-Economic Strata." *RA* 29 (1975/1976), 173–94.

Kibwana, Kivutha, ed. *Women and Autonomy in Kenya: Policy and Legal Framework.* Nairobi: Claripress, 1995.

———. "Women and the Constitution in Kenya." *Verfassung und Recht in Übersee* 25 (1) (1992): 6–20.

Kiteme, Kamuti. "Socioeconomic Impact of the African Market Women Trade in Rural Kenya." *Journal of Black Studies* 23 (1) (1992): 135–51.

Knotts, Mary Ann. "Social and Economic Factors Associated with the Rural-Urban Migration of Kenyan Women." Ph.D. diss., Johns Hopkins University, 1977.

Kratz, C. A. *Affecting Performance: Meaning, Movement, and Experience in Okiek Women's Initiation.* Washington, D.C.: Smithsonian Institution Press, 1994.

———. "Sexual Solidarity and the Secrets of Sight and Sound: Shifting Gender

Relations and Their Ceremonial Constitution." *American Ethnologist* 17 (3) (1990): 449–69.

Krhoda, G. O. "Women, Water Supply and Sanitation in Kenya." *African Urban Quarterly* 5 (3/4) (1990): 247–54.

Landau, Loren B. "What Role Can History Play for the Newly Urbanized Women of Kenya and Tanzania?" *Ufahamu* 23 (2) (1995): 29–54.

Leakey, Louis Seymour Bazett. "Kikuyu Problem of the Initiation of Girls." *JRAI* 90 (1931): 277–85.

Leslie, Paul W., Kenneth L. Campbell, and Michael A. Little. "Pregnancy Loss in Nomadic and Settled Women in Turkana, Kenya: A Prospective Study." *Human Biology* 2 (1993): 237–54.

Likimani, Muthoni Gachanja. *Women of Kenya: Fifteen Years of Independence.* Nairobi: Giant Printers, 1983.

———. *Women of Kenya in the Decade of Development.* Nairobi: Noni's Publicity, 1985.

———. *Women of Kenya: Twenty-Seven Years of Development.* Nairobi: Noni's Publicity, 1991.

Maas, Maria. *Women's Groups in Kiambu, Kenya: It Is Always a Good Thing to Have Land.* Leiden, Netherlands: African Studies Centre, 1986.

McCormick, D. "Gender and Work: Women in Nairobi's Small Enterprise." *Wajibu* 7 (4) (1992): 12–15.

Mackenzie, Fiona. "'A Farm Is Like a Child Who Cannot Be Left Unguarded': Gender, Land and Labour in Central Province, Kenya." *IDS Bulletin* 26 (1) (1995): 17–23.

———. "Gender and Land Rights in Murang'a District, Kenya." *Journal of Peasant Studies* 17 (4) (1990): 609–43.

———. "Land and Territory: The Interface between Two Systems of Land Tenure, Murang'a District, Kenya." *Africa* 59 (1) (1989): 91–109.

———. "Local Initiatives and National Policy: Gender and Agricultural Change in Murang'a District, Kenya." *CJAS* 20 (3) (1986): 377–401.

———. "Political Economy of the Environment, Gender, and Resistance under Colonialism: Murang'a District, Kenya, 1910–1950." *CJAS* 25 (2) (1991): 226–56.

Maina, W. "Women Participation in Public Affairs in Kenya." *NLM* 40 (1992): 34–37.

Mazire, D. "Une Organisation des Femmes au Kenya." *Politique Africaine* (53) (1994): 139–43.

Mbeo, Mary Adhiambo, and Oki Ooko-Ombaka, eds. *Women and Law in Kenya: Perspectives and Emerging Issues.* Nairobi: Public Law Institute, 1989.

Meghji, Z., R. Meghji, and C. Kwayu. *The Woman Co-operator and Development: Experiences from Eastern and Central and Southern Africa.* Nairobi: Maarifa, 1985.

Michaelson, Marc. "Wangari Maathai and Kenya's Green Belt Movement: Exploring the Evolution and Potentialities of Consensus Movement Mobilization." *Social Problems* 4 (1994): 540–61.

Mirza, S., and Margaret Strobel, eds. *Three Swahili Women: Life Histories from Mombasa*. Bloomington: Indiana University Press, 1989.

Monsted, Mette. *Women's Groups in Rural Kenya and Their Role in Development*. Copenhagen: Centre for Development Research, 1978.

Moore, Henrietta. *Space, Text, and Gender: An Anthropological Study of the Markawet of Kenya*. Cambridge: CUP, 1986.

Mulder, M. B. "Kipsigis Women's Preference for Wealthy Men: Evidence for Female Choice in Mammals?" *Behavioral Ecology and Sociobiology* 27 (4) (1990): 255–64.

Murray, J. M. "Kikuyu Female Circumcision Controversy with Special Reference to the Church Missionary Society's 'Sphere of Influence,'" Ph.D. diss., University of California, Los Angeles, 1974.

Mutiso, Roberta. "Poverty, Women and Cooperatives in Kenya." *African Studies Association Papers* 28 (92) (1985): 1–18.

Mwaniki, Nyaga. "Against Many Odds: The Dilemmas of Women's Self-Help Groups in Mbeere, Kenya." *Africa* 56 (2) (1986): 210–28.

Nasimiyu, Ruth. "Women and Children's Labour in a Rural Economy: A Case Study of Western Province, Kenya, 1902–1985." Ph.D. diss., Dalhousie University, 1991.

———. "Women in the Colonial Economy of Bungoma: Role of Women in Agriculture, 1902–1960." *JEARD* 15 (1985): 56–73.

Neitzert, M. "A Women's Place: Household Labour Allocation in Rural Kenya." *Canadian Journal of Development Studies* 15 (3) (1994): 401–27.

Ngau, Margaret. "Women's Participation in Education and National Development: The Dilemma of Institutional Bias in Kenya." *Ufahamu* 16 (2) (1988): 3–20.

Njau, E., and G. Mulaki. *Kenyan Women Heroes and Their Mystical Power*. Nairobi: Risk, 1985.

Njonjo, A.L., et al. *Study on an Integrated Approach to Women's Programmes in Kenya*. Nairobi: Business and Economic Research Company Ltd., 1985.

Nzomo, Maria. "The Gender Dimension of Democratisation in Kenya: Some International Linkages." *Alternatives* 18 (1) (1993): 61–73.

———. "Impact of the Women's Decade on Policies, Programs and Empowerment of Women in Kenya." *Issue: A Journal of Opinion* 17 (2) (1989): 9–17.

———. "Status of Women's Human Rights in Kenya." *Issue: A Journal of Opinion* 22 (2) (1994): 17–20.

———, and Kivutha Kibwana. *Women's Initiatives in Kenya's Democratization: Capacity Building and Participation in the December, 1992, Multiparty General Election*. Nairobi: The National Committee on the Status of Women, 1993.

O'Barr, Jean F. "Feminist Issues in the Fiction of Kenya's Women Writers." *African Literature Today* (15) (1987): 55–70.

Oboler, Regina Smith. "Is the Female Husband a Man? Woman/Woman Marriage among the Nandi of Kenya." *Ethnology* (1) (1980): 69–88.

———. *Women, Power, and Economic Change: The Nandi of Kenya*. Stanford, CA: Stanford University Press, 1985.

Obura, Anna P. *Changing Images: Portrayal of Girls and Women in Kenyan Textbooks*. Nairobi: ACTS Press, 1991.

Oduol, Wilhemina A. "Kenyan Women in Politics: An Analysis of Past and Present Trends." *TJH* 22 (1993): 166–81.

Ogutu, M. A. "Changing Role of Women in the Commercial History of Busia District in Kenya, 1900–1983." *JEARD* 15 (1985): 74–90.

Omide, Simeon H. *The Luo Girl: From Infancy to Marriage*. London: Macmillan, 1952.

Opondo, Patricia Achieng. "Dodo Performance in the Context of Women's Associations amongst the Luo of Kenya." Ph.D. diss., University of Pittsburgh, 1996.

Otieno, Wambui Waiyaki (edited by Cora Ann Presely). *Mau Mau's Daughter: The Life History of Wambui Waiyaki Otieno*. Boulder, CO: Lynne Rienner, 1998.

Pala, Achola O., T. Awori, and A. Krystal, eds. *Participation of Women in Kenya Society*. Nairobi: KLB, 1983.

Pedersen, Susan. "National Bodies, Unspeakable Acts: The Sexual Politics of Colonial Policy-Making." *Journal of Modern History* (4) (1991): 647–80.

Potash, Betty. *Female Farmers, Mothers-in-Law and Extension Agents: Development Planning and a Rural Luo Community*. East Lansing: Michigan State University Press, 1985.

———. "Some Aspects of Martial Stability in a Rural Luo Community." *Africa* 48 (4) (1978): 380–97.

Presley, Cora Ann. "Labour Unrest among Kikuyu Women in Colonial Kenya." *African Studies Association Papers* 24 (100) (1981): 1–22.

Raikes, P. "Monogamists Sit by the Doorway: Notes on the Construction of Gender, Ethnicity and Rank in Kisii, Western Kenya." *European Journal of Development Research* 6 (2) (1994): 63–81.

Riria-Ouko, J. V. N. "Women's Organizations in Kenya." *JEARD* 15 (1985): 188–97.

Robertson, Claire. "Grassroots in Kenya: Women, Genital Mutilation, and Collective Action, 1920–1990." *Signs: Journal of Women in Culture and Society* 21 (3) (1996): 615–42.

———. "Traders and Urban Struggle: Ideology and the Creation of a Militant Female Underclass in Nairobi, 1960–1990." *Journal of Women's History* 4 (3) (1993): 9–42.

Robinson, W. C. "Kenya Enters the Fertility Transition." *Population Studies* 46 (3) (1992): 445–57.

Romero, Patricia. "Possible Sources for the Origin of Gold as an Economic and Social Vehicle for Women in Lamu (Kenya)." *Africa* 57 (3) (1987): 364–76.

Shaw, Martin. *Colonial Inscriptions: Race, Sex, and Class in Kenya*. Minneapolis and London: University of Minnesota Press, 1995.

Silberschmidt, Margrethe. "Have Men Become the Weaker Sex? Changing Life Situations in Kisii District, Kenya." *JMAS* 30 (2) (1992): 237–53.

Smith, Sidonie. "Other Women and the Racial Politics of Gender: Isak Dinesen and Beryl Markham in Kenya." In *De/Colonizing the Subject: The Politics of*

Gender in Women's Autobiography, edited by Sidonie Smith and Julia Watson, 410–35. Minneapolis: University of Minnesota Press, 1992.

Smock, A. *Women's Education and Roles in Kenya*. Nairobi: Institute for Development Study, University of Nairobi, 1977.

Sorensen, Anne. "Women's Organisations Among the Kipsigis: Change, Variety and Different Participation." *Africa* 62 (4) (1992): 547–66.

———. *Women's Organisations and Changing Gender Relations Among the Kipsigis of Kenya*. Copenhagen: Centre for Development Research,1990.

———, and Dorth von Buello. *Gender and Contract Farming in Kericho, Kenya*. Copenhagen: Centre for Development Research, 1990.

Stamp, Patricia. "Burying Otieno: The Politics of Gender and Ethnicity in Kenya." *Signs: Journal of Women in Culture and Society* (4) (1990/91): 808–45.

Staudt, Kathleen A. "Sex, Ethnic, and Class Consciousness in Western Kenya." *Comparative Politics* 14 (2) (1982): 149–68.

Stichter, Sharon. "Middle Class Family in Kenya: Changes in Gender Relations." *African Urban Studies* 21 (1985): 39–52.

———. "Women and the Labour Force in Kenya, 1895–1964." *RA* 29 (1975/76): 45–67.

Strobel, Margaret. "From Lelemama to Lobbying: Women's Associations in Mombasa, Kenya." In *Women in Africa: Studies in Social and Economic Change*, edited by Nancy J. Hafkin and Edna G. Bay, 183–211. Stanford: Stanford University Press, 1976.

———. *Muslim Women in Mombasa, 1890–1975*. New Haven, CT and London: YUP, 1979.

———. "Slavery and Reproductive Labor in Mombasa." In *Women and Slavery in Africa*, edited by C. Robertson and M. Klein, 111–29. Madison: University of Wisconsin Press, 1983.

Suda, Collette A. "Division of Labour by Gender and Its Implications for the Status of Women in Siaya District, Western Kenya." *African Urban Quarterly* 5 (3/4) (1990): 256–67.

———. "Impact of Changing Family Structures on Nairobi Children." *African Study Monographs* 14 (2) (1993): 109–21.

Talle, Aud. "Women as Heads of Houses: The Organization of Production and the Role of Women among the Pastoral Maasai in Kenya." *Ethnos* 52 (1/2) (1987): 50–80.

Thomas, Barbara P. "Household Strategies for Adaptation and Change: Participation in Kenyan Rural Women's Associations." *Africa* 58 (4) (1988): 401–22.

Thomas-Slayter, Barbara P. "Politics, Class, and Gender in African Resource Management: The Case of Rural Kenya." *Economic Development and Cultural Change* 40 (4) (1992): 809–28.

———. *Politics, Class and Gender in African Resource Management: Examining the Connections in Rural Kenya*. Boston: African Studies Center, Boston University, 1989.

————, and Dianne Rocheleau. *Gender, Environment, and Development in Kenya: A Grassroots Perspective.* Boulder, CO: Lynne Rienner, 1995.

Tibbetts, A. "Mamas Fighting for Freedom in Kenya." *AT* 41 (4) (1994): 27–48.

Udvardy, Monica. "Women's Groups Near the Kenyan Coast: Patron-Clientship in the Development Arena." In *Anthropology of Development and Change in East Africa*, edited by Peter Little and David Brokensha, 217–35. Boulder, CO: WP, 1988.

Von Bülow, D. "Bigger Than Men? Gender Relations and Their Changing Meanings in Kipsigis Society, Kenya." *Africa* 62 (4) (1992): 522–46.

Wainaina, Njoki. *Indigenous Savings and Credit Schemes for Women in Kenya.* Nairobi: SIDA, 1989.

Wasow, Bernard. "The Working Age Sex Ratio and Job Search Migration in Kenya." *JDA* 15 (3) (1981): 435–44.

Watson, C. "Kenya: Turkana: Women Coping." *Rural Extension Bulletin* 4 (1994): 23–28.

Were, Gideon S., ed. *Women and Development in Kenya: Kakamega District.* Nairobi: University of Nairobi, Institute of African Studies, 1990.

White, Luise. "Bodily Fluids and Usufruct: Controlling Property in Nairobi, 1917–1939." *CJAS* 24 (3) (1990): 418–38.

————. *Comforts of Home: Prostitution in Colonial Nairobi.* Chicago and London: University of Chicago Press, 1990.

————. "Prostitution, Identity, and Class Consciousness in Nairobi During World War II." *Signs: Journal of Woman and Culture in Society* 11 (2) (1986): 255–73.

————. "Separating the Men from the Boys: Constructions of Sexuality, Gender, and Terrorism in Central Kenya, 1939–1959." *IJAHS* 23 (1) (1990): 1–26.

Wijeyeratne, Pandu, ed. *Gender, Health and Sustainable Development: Proceedings of a Workshop Held in Nairobi, Kenya 5–8 October 1993.* Ottawa: International Development Research Centre, 1994.

Wipper, Audrey. "Equal Rights for Women in Kenya?" *JMAS* 9 (3) (1971): 429–42.

————. "Kikuyu Women and the Harry Thuku Disturbances: Some Uniformities of Female Militancy." *Africa* 59 (3) (1989): 300–37.

————. "Maendeleo ya Wanawake [Women's Progress] Organization: The Co-optation of Leadership." *ASR* 18 (3) (1975): 99–120.

————. "Politics of Sex: Some Strategies Employed by the Kenyan Power Elite to Handle a Normative-Existential Discrepancy." *ASR* 14 (3) (1971): 463–82.

World Bank. *Kenya: The Role of Women in Economic Development.* Washington, D.C.: World Bank, 1989.

Zeleza, Tiyambe. "Women and the Labour Process in Kenya Since Independence." *TJH* 17 (1988): 69–107.

N. ARTS, ARCHITECTURE, AND MUSIC

Abdulaziz, M. H. *Muyaka: Nineteenth Century Swahili Popular Poetry*. Nairobi: KLB, 1979.

Allen, James de Vere. "Swahili Culture Reconsidered: Some Historical Implications of the Material Culture of the Northern Kenya Coast in the Eighteenth and Nineteenth Centuries." *Azania* (1974): 105–38.

Barbour, J., and S. Wandibba. *Kenyan Pots and Potters*. Nairobi: OUP, 1991.

Brown, Jean. "Traditional Sculpture in Kenya." *African Arts* 6 (1) (1972): 17–20, 58, 88.

Burt, Eugene Clinton. "Towards an Art History of the Baluyia of Western Kenya." Ph.D. diss., University of Washington, 1980.

Cham, Mbye Baboucar. "African Women and Cinema: A Conversation with Anne Mungai." *Research in African Literatures* 25 (3) (1994): 93–104.

Cole, Herbert M. "Vital Arts in Northern Kenya." *African Arts* 7 (2) (1974): 12–23.

Fuglesang, Minou. *Veils and Videos: Female Youth Culture on the Kenya Coast*. Stockholm: Department of Anthropology, Stockholm University, 1994.

Gecau, Kimani. "Popular Song and Social Change in Kenya." *Media, Culture and Society* 17 (4) (1995): 557–75.

Ghaidan, Usam I. "Swahili Art of Lamu." *African Arts* 5 (1) (1971): 54–57, 84.

Hirst, Terry. "Samuel Wanjau: Kenyan Carver." *African Arts* 3 (3) (1970): 48–51.

Hyslop, Graham. "African Musical Instruments in Kenya." *African Music Society Newsletter* 1 (1958): 31–36.

———. "More Kenya Musical Instruments." *African Music Society Newsletter* 2 (1959): 24–28.

———. *Musical Instruments of East Africa: Kenya*. London: Nelson Africa, 1975.

———. "Some Musical Instruments of Kenya." *African Arts* 5 (4) (1972): 48–55.

Jones, A. M. "Luo Music and Its Rhythm." *African Music* 5 (3) (1973/1974): 43–54.

Jules-Rosette, Bennetta. "Aesthetics and Market Demand: The Structure of the Tourist Art Market in Three African Settings." *ASR* 29 (1) (1986): 41–59.

Kahana, Yoram. "Carved Doors of Lamu." *Mankind* 7 (1974): 30–35.

Kavyu, Paul Ndilya. *Introduction to Kamba Music*. Nairobi: EALB, 1977.

———. *Traditional Music Instruments of Kenya*. Nairobi: KLB, 1980.

Kidd, R. "Popular Theatre and Popular Struggle in Kenya: The Story of Kamiriithu." *Race and Class* 24 (3) (1983): 287–304.

Mumma, O. J. "In Search of a Kenyan Theatre: The Theory and Practice of Educational Drama and Its Potential for Kenya." Ph.D. diss., University of Manchester, 1994.

Osotsi, Ramenga Mtaali. "Performance Analysis of the Tsing'ano of the Abanyore and Avalogooli of Western Kenya." Ph.D. diss., Indiana University, 1995.

Parrot, Fred J. *Introduction to African Arts of Kenya, Zaire, and Nigeria.* New York: Arco, 1972.

Sassoon, Hamo. *Siwas of Lamu: Two Historic Trumpets in Brass and Ivory.* Nairobi: Lamu Society, 1975.

Senoga-Zake, George. *Folk Music of Kenya.* Nairobi: Uzima, 1986.

Tracy, Andrew. "Kamba Carvers." *African Music Society Journal* 2 (3) (1960): 55–58.

Ukadike, N. Frank. "Representative Native Kenya on Film: *Lorang's Way* and the Turkana People." *Ufahamu* 17 (1) (1988): 3–14.

Wolfe, E. *Introduction to the Arts of Kenya.* Washington, D.C.: Smithsonian Institution, 1979.

O. EDUCATION

Abagi, Jared O. "Primary Schooling and Agricultural Education in Kenya: Can Principles of 'Modern' Agriculture Be Taught Effectively in Schools?" Ph.D. diss., McGill University, 1990.

Abbot, Sally. "Education Policy of the Kenya Government, 1904–1935." M.Phil. diss., University of London, 1970.

Abreu, Elsa. "Challenge in Kenya's Colonial History: The Role of Voluntary Organisations in Education with Special Reference to African and Asian Communities." *KHR* 4 (2) (1976): 207–22.

———. *Role of Self-Help in the Development of Education in Kenya, 1900–1973.* Nairobi: KLB, 1982.

Adebola, A. S. "History of Western Education Among the Kikuyu, 1898–1952." Ph.D. diss., University of Ibadan, 1978.

———. "London Connections: A Factor in the Survival of the Kikuyu Independent Schools' Movement, 1929–1939." *JAS* 10 (1) (1983): 14–24.

"Alliance High School, Kikuyu." *East African Teachers Journal* 1 (1953): 22–33.

Anderson, John D. "Kenya Education Commission Report 1964: An African View of Educational Planning." *Comparative Education Review* 9 (2) (1965): 201–7.

———. *Organization and Financing of Self-Help Education in Kenya.* Paris: UNESCO, 1973.

———. "Self-Help and Independency: The Political Implications of a Continuing Tradition in African Education in Kenya." *AA* 70 (278) (1971): 9–22.

———. *Struggle for the School: The Interaction of Missionary, Colonial Government and Nationalistic Enterprise in the Development of Formal Education in Kenya.* London: Longman, 1970.

Anthony, Wilhelmina E. "Nairobi College: A Case Study, Faculty Recruitment and Turnover." Ph.D. diss., Claremont Graduate School, 1974.

Arap-Martin, E. K. "The Predictive Validity of the Twelfth-Grade Achievement Test for Primary School Teacher Trainees in Kenya." *Perceptual and Motor Skills* 63 (1) (1986): 103–8.

Askwith, Tom G. *Adult Education in Kenya*. Nairobi: The Eagle Press, 1961.

Barkan, Joel D. "What Makes the East African Student Run?" *Transition* 29 (1968): 26–31.

Barker, David, and Alan Ferguson. "Craft Training Center As a Rural Mobilization Policy in Kenya." *RA* 12/13 (1981/1982): 75–90.

Beck, Ann. "Colonial Policy and Education in British East Africa 1900–1950." *Journal of British Studies* 5 (2) (1966): 115–38.

Beecher, L. J. "Education in Kenya Today." *East and West Review* (1954): 110–17.

Bennell, Paul. "Engineering Technicians in Africa: A Kenyan Case-Study." *JMAS* 21 (2) (1983): 273–91.

Bigsten, Arne. *Education and Income Determination in Kenya*. Aldershot, UK: Gower, 1984.

Bogonko, Sorobea Nyachieo. "Africans and the Politics of Their Education in Kenya, 1910–1934." *JEARD* 14 (1984): 19–38.

————. "Colonial Chiefs and African Development in Kenya with Special Reference to Secular Education." *TJH* 14 (1985): 1–20.

————. *History of Modern Education in Kenya, 1895–1991*. Nairobi: Evans Brothers, 1992.

————. *Reflections on Education in East Africa*. Nairobi: OUP, 1991.

Bradshaw, York W. "State Limitations, Self-Help Secondary Schooling, and Development in Kenya." *Social Forces* 72 (2) (1993): 347–78.

Brownstein, Lewis. *Education and Development in Rural Kenya: A Study of Primary School Graduates*. New York: Praeger, 1972.

Cameron, John. *Development of Education in East Africa*. New York: Teachers College Press, 1970.

Carron, Gabriel. "Functioning and Effects of the Kenya Literacy Program." *ASR* 33 (3) (1990): 97–120.

Carter, Roger. *Legal Framework of Educational Planning and Administration in East Africa: Kenya, Tanzania, Uganda*. Paris: UNESCO, 1967.

Castle, Edgar Bradshaw. *Growing up in East Africa*. Oxford: OUP, 1966.

Cheru, Fantu. *Dependence, Underdevelopment and Unemployment in Kenya: School Leavers in a Peripheral Capitalist Political Economy*. Lanham, MD: University Press of America, 1987.

Cleghorn, Alie, Marilyn Merrit and Jared O. Abagi. "Language Policy and Science Instruction in Kenyan Primary Schools." *Comparative Education Review* 33 (1) (1989): 21–39.

Clemson, D. W. "Supporting Evaluation in Kenya: Reflections on Experiences with the Kenyan Adult Literacy Programme." *International Journal of Educational Development* 5 (3) (1985): 245–48.

Committee for the Release of Political Prisoners in Kenya. *University Destroyed: Moi Crowns Ten Years of Government Terror in Kenya*. London: Committee for the Release of Political Prisoners in Kenya, 1983.

Corry, Joseph. "History of Agricultural Education in Kenya 1922–54." Ph.D. diss., University of Wisconsin, 1971.

Court, David. "Education System As a Response to Inequality in Tanzania and Kenya." *JMAS* 14 (4) (1976): 661–90.

————. "Village Polytechnic Leavers: The Maseno Story." *RA* 25 (1974): 91–100.

————, and Dharam P. Ghai, eds. *Education, Society, and Development: New Perspectives from Kenya*. Nairobi: OUP, 1976.

Cowan, Laing Gray. *Cost of Learning: The Politics of Primary Education in Kenya*. New York: Columbia Teacher's College Press, 1970.

Cumming, Christopher. *Practical Subjects in Kenyan Academic Secondary Schools: Background Papers*. Stockholm: SIDA, 1985.

D'Souza, Henry. "Some Problems in Technical Education in Kenya." *EEA* 6 (2) (1976): 135–50.

————. "Technical Education in Kenya: Some Problems." *ASR* 19 (3) (1976): 33–41.

Dain, R. "Protestant Contribution to Kenya Education." *Kenya Education Journal* 6 (1960): 16–19.

Dey, I. "Failure of Success and the Success of Failure: The Youth Polytechnic Programme in Kenya." *Public Administration and Development* 10 (2) (1990): 179–98.

Digolo, O. O. "Education Through the Third Channel." *Basic Education Forum* (1993): 23–30.

Duggan, Hayden A. "Village Polytechnic in Kenya." *RA* 9 (1969): 41–48.

East Africa Protectorate. Education Commission. *Report of the Education Commission of the East Africa Protectorate*. Nairobi: Swift Press, 1919.

Eisemon, Thomas Owen. *Benefiting from Basic Education, School Quality and Functional Literacy in Kenya*. Oxford: Pergamon Press, 1988.

————. "Foreign Training and Assistance for University Development in Kenya: Too Much of a Good Thing?" *International Journal of Educational Development* 6 (1) (1986): 1–13.

————. "Primary School Literature and Folktales in Kenya: What Makes a Child's Story Africa?" *Comparative Education Review* 30 (2) (1986): 232–46.

Elkan, Walter. "'Out-of-School' Education and Training for Primary School Leavers in Rural Kenya: A Proposal." *International Labour Review* 104 (3) (1971): 205–16.

Ergas, Z., and F. Chege. "Primary Schools Education in Kenya: An Attempt at Evaluation." *EEA* 4 (2) (1974): 235–49.

Erozer, Savas. "Planning and Development of Extension Training in Rural Development at the Bukura Institute of Agriculture, Kenya." Ed.D. diss., Harvard University, 1978.

Eshiwani, George S. *Education in Kenya Since Independence*. Nairobi: EAEP, 1993.

————. "Educational Reform and Development in Kenya Since 1963: A Critical Appraisal." *Africana Journal* (1994): 174–91.

————. *Implementing Educational Policies in Kenya*. Washington, D.C.: World Bank, 1990.

————. *Research in Education: The Kenya Register 1963–1980*. Nairobi: Bureau of Educational Research, Kenyatta University College, 1982.

Evans, Emmit B. "Sources of Socio-Political Instability in an African State: The Case of Kenya's Educated Unemployed." *ASR* 20 (1) (1977): 37–52.

Fine, J. "Financial Crisis in Kenya Education: Some Perspectives on Policy." *Kenya Education Review* 3 (1974): 47–52.

Ford, R. J. C. "Village Polytechnic Programme in Kenya." *International Labour Review* 111 (4) (1975): 307–20.

Francis, Edward Carey. "Kenya's Problems as Seen by a Schoolmaster in Kikuyu Country." *AA* 54 (216) (1955): 186–96.

Furley, O. W. "Education and the Chiefs in East Africa in the Inter-War Period." *TJH* 1 (1) (1971): 60–83.

————. "The Struggle for Transformation in Education in Kenya since Independence." *EAJ* 9 (8) (1972): 14–24.

————, and Tom Watson. *History of Education in East Africa*. New York: NOK Publishers, 1977.

Gitau, Wangui Nyakioi. "Modernity and its Discontents: An Exploratory Study of Kenyan Elite's Perceptions of the Effects of Modernization of Individual and Family Life." Ed.D. diss., Harvard University, 1995.

Godfrey, Edward Martin. *Education, Training, Productivity, and Income: A Kenyan Case-Study*. Brighton, UK: University of Sussex, 1976.

————, and G. C. M. Mutiso. "Political Economy of Self-Help: Kenya's 'Harambee' Institutes of Technology." *CJAS* 8 (1) (1974): 109–33.

————. *Politics, Economics and Technical Training: A Kenyan Case Study*. Nairobi: KLB, 1979.

Gorman, Thomas Patrick. "Bilingualism in the Educational System of Kenya." *Comparative Education* 4 (3) (1968): 213–21.

Gould, W. T. S. "Migration and Development in Western Kenya, 1971–82: A Retrospective Analysis of Primary School Leavers." *Africa* 55 (3) (1985): 262–85.

————. "Technical Education and Migration in Tiriki, Western Kenya, 1902–1987." *AA* 88 (351) (1989): 253–71.

Hagberg, Gordon. "Kenya." In *Educated Africa: A Country-by-Country Survey of Educational Development in Africa*, edited by Helen Kitchen, 128–44. London: Heinemann, 1962.

Hagglund, George. "Trade Unions and Labor Education in East Africa." *Labor Studies Journal* 19 (1) (1994): 72–91.

Hall, Robert Louis. "Education and National Development: The Kenyan Example." Ed.D. diss., University of Tennessee, 1977.

Hatfield, Vidler. "New Emphasis on English in Kenya African Primary Schools." *Overseas Education* 21 (3) (1950): 1061–65.

Hazlewood, Arthur, Jane Armitage, Albert Berry, and Jon Knight. *Education, Work and Pay in East Africa*. Oxford: Clarendon, 1989.

Hill, Martin J. D. *Harambee Movement in Kenya: Self-Help, Development and Education Among the Kamba of Kitui District*. London: Athlone Press, 1991.

Hooper, H. D. *Leading Strings: Native Development and Missionary Education in Kenya Colony.* London: CMS, 1922.

Hughes, Rees. "Examining the Roots of Educational Demand: The Case Supporting Rural Agrarian Development." *WD* 19 (2/3) (1991): 213–23.

———. "Legitimation, Higher Education, and the Post-Colonial State: A Comparative Study of India and Kenya." *Comparative Education* 30 (3) (1994): 193–204.

———, and K. Mwiria. "Kenya Women, Higher Education and the Labour Market." *Comparative Education* 25 (2) (1989): 178–95.

Hyatt, D. E., and W. J. Milne. "Determinants of Fertility in Urban and Rural Kenya: Estimates and a Simulation of the Impact of Education Policy." *Environment and Planning* 25 (1) (1994): 137–65.

Indire, Filemona F., and John W. Hanson. *Secondary Level Teachers: Supply and Demand in Kenya.* East Lansing: African Studies Center, Michigan State University, 1971.

Juma, M. N. "Some Factors Determining Women Participation in Non-Formal Education: A Study of Mombasa North, Kenya." *Kenya Journal of Education* 5 (1) (1991): 46–74.

Kanyike, Lawrence K. "Ideology and Schooling in Kenya, 1965–1968." Ph.D. diss., University of Calgary, 1986.

Karioki, James N. "University of Nairobi and the Demise of Democracy in Kenya." *Transafrica Forum* 7 (3) (1990): 83–93.

Kawasonga, Marcellus Auja. "Pastoral Role of Catholic High School Teachers as Perceived by Priests and Teachers in the Archdiocese of Kisumu, Kenya." Ed.D. diss., University of San Francisco, 1995.

Kay, Stafford. "African Roles, Responses, and Initiatives in Colonial Education: The Case of Western Kenya." *Paedagogica Historica* 16 (2) (1976): 272–93.

———. "Local Pressures on Educational Plans in Colonial Kenya: Post-Second World War Activity among the Southern Abaluyia." *IJAHS* 11 (4) (1978): 689–710.

———. "The Southern Abaluyia, the Friends Africa Mission, and the Development of Education in Western Kenya, 1902–1965." Ph.D. diss., University of Wisconsin, 1973.

Kazimi, Ali Akbar. *Inquiry into Indian Education in East Africa.* Nairobi: GP, 1948.

Keino, Ester Rose Cherono. "Contribution of Harambee (Self-Help) to the Development of Post-Primary Education in Kenya: The Case of Sosiot Girls' High School, 1969–1978." Ed.D. diss., Harvard University, 1980.

Keller, Edmond J. "Education, Ethnicity, and Political Socialization in Kenya." *Comparative Political Studies* 12 (4) (1980): 442–69.

———. "Harambee! Educational Policy, Inequality, and the Political Economy of Rural Community Self-Help in Kenya." *JAS* 4 (1) (1977): 86–106.

———. "The Political Socialization of Adolescents in Contemporary Africa: The Role of the School in Kenya." *Comparative Politics* 10 (2) (1978): 227–50.

Kenya. Ministry of Education. *Development of Education, 1993 to 1994: National Report from Kenya.* Nairobi: Ministry of Education, 1994.

Khan, O. R. "Sample Study of Students Evaluation of Teaching at Kenyatta University." *International Journal of University Adult Education* 33 (1) (1994): 77–90.

Kiano, Jane. *Causes and Effects of Secondary School Drop-Out in Nairobi, Kenya.* Nairobi: ACOP, 1983.

Kibera, Lucy Wairimu. "Effects of School Stratification on the Career and Educational Aspirations of Girls in Kenya's Secondary Schools." *Journal of Third World Studies* 12 (1) (1995): 59–79.

King, Kenneth J. *African Artisan: Education and the Informal Sector in Kenya.* London: Heinemann, 1977.

————. "Development and Education in the Narok District of Kenya: The Pastoral Maasai and Their Neighbours." *AA* 71 (285) (1972): 389–407.

————. "Education and Ethnicity in the Rift Valley: Masai, Kipsigis and Kikuyu in the School System." *EEA* 5 (2) (1975): 197–217.

————. "Politics of Agricultural Education for Africans in Kenya." *EEA* 7 (2) (1977): 165–76.

————. *Technical and Vocational Education and Training in Kenya: The Movement towards a Comprehensive National System.* Edinburgh: Centre of African Studies, Edinburgh University, 1989.

————, and C. Abuodha. "Education, Training and Technological Development in the Informal Sector of Kenya." *Science, Technology and Development* 2 (1995): 175–202.

Kinyanjui, Kabiru. "Opportunities for School Leavers Outside the Major Towns of Kenya." *RA* 25 (1974): 81–90.

————. "Political Economy of Educational Inequality: A Study of the Roots of Educational Inequality in Colonial and Post-Colonial Kenya." Ph.D. diss., Harvard University, 1979.

Kinyanjui, Peter. "Education, Training, and Employment of Secondary School Leavers in Kenya." *Education in Eastern Africa* 2 (1) (1971): 3–21.

Kipkorir, B. E. "Alliance High School and the Origins of the Kenya African Elite." Ph.D. diss., Cambridge University, 1969.

Kithinji, C. T. "Education of Women in Kenya Before and After the Women's Decade." *Wajibu* 7 (4) (1992): 5–8.

Kivilu, Joseph Mbithi. "Perceived Casual Attribution Factors to Academic Performance: A Multi-Level Analysis." Ph.D. diss., University of Alberta, 1994.

K'olewe, Ochieng Olewe. "The Search for Relevance in the Kenyan Secondary School History: A Case Study of How the Struggle for Kenyan Independence Is Examined." Ed.D. diss., West Virginia University, 1996.

Konana, Lois S. "Diversified Secondary School Curriculum: The Kenyan Case." Ph.D. diss., McGill University, 1992.

Kovar, Michael Harry. "Kikuyu Independent Schools Movement: Interaction of Politics and Education in Kenya (1923–1953)." Ph.D. diss., University of California, Los Angeles, 1970.

Lake, R. A. "A Government African School in 1948." *Overseas Education* 21 (2) (1950): 1004–8.

Lauglo, Jon. *Practical Subjects in Kenyan Academic Secondary Schools: General Report.* Stockholm: SIDA, 1985.

———. *Technical Secondary Schools in Kenya: An Assessment.* Stockholm: SIDA, 1985.

Liehardt, P. "The Mosque College of Lamu and its Social Background." *Tanganyika Notes and Records* 53 (1959): 228–42.

Lillis, Kevin M. "Africanizing the School Literature Curriculum in Kenya: A Case Study in Curriculum Dependency." *Journal of Curriculum Studies* 18 (1) (1986): 63–84.

———. "Processes of Secondary Curriculum Innovation in Kenya." *Comparative Education Review* 29 (1) (1985): 80–96.

Lindsay, Beverly. "Educational Testing in Kenya." *Journal of Negro Education* 3 (1980): 274–88.

Linné, Olga. *An Evaluation of Kenya Science Teacher's College, 1970–71.* Uppsala, Sweden: SIAS, 1971.

———. *An Evaluation of Kenya Science Teacher's College: Phase II 1970–71.* Uppsala, Sweden: Nordiska Afrikainstitutet, 1975.

Lohrentz, Kenneth Peter. "Politics of Educational Development in Central and Southern North Nyanza, Kenya, 1904–1939." Ph.D. diss., Syracuse University, 1977.

McGlashan, Neil. "Indigenous Kikuyu Education." *AA* 63 (250) (1964): 47–57.

McKown, Robert. "Kenya University Students and Politics." In *University Students and African Politics,* edited by William J. Hannah, 215–55. New York: Praeger, 1985.

Mahlmann, J. M., and M. arap Korir Asembo. "An Analysis of Sports in Kenyan Educational Institutions." *JEARD* 23 (1993): 160–75.

Mambo, Robert Makonde. "Challenges of Western Education in the Coast Province of Kenya, 1890–1963." Ph.D. diss., Columbia University, 1980.

———. "Local Native Councils and Education in Kenya: Case of the Coast Province, 1925–1950." *TJH* 10 (1/2) (1981): 61–86.

Maundu, John N. "Student Achievement in Science and Mathematics: A Case Study of Extra-Provincial, Provincial, and Harambee Secondary Schools in Kenya." Ph.D. diss., McGill University, 1986.

Mbiriru, M. W. N. K. *Problems of Teaching Junior Secondary Mathematics in Kenya.* Nairobi: ACOP, 1983.

Mebo, P. "Class Size and Student Behaviour: A Comparison of the Strategies Employed in Different Size Classes by Students Studying Communication Skills in the Kenyan State Universities." Ph.D. diss., University of Leeds, 1995.

Moock, Peter R. "Education and Technical Efficiency." *Economic Development and Cultural Change* 29 (4) (1981): 723–39.

Mukwa, Christopher Wekesa. "Toward a Systematic Approach to Educational Media Use in the Secondary School Education of the Republic of Kenya: A Field

Survey of Tools and Technologies for Learning." Ph.D. diss., Michigan State University, 1979.

Mutiso, G. C. M. "Technical Education and Change in Kenya." *EAJ* 8 (8) (1971): 28–39.

Mutua, Rosalind W. *Development of Education in Kenya, 1846–1963.* Nairobi: EALB, 1975.

Mutunga, Peter Kiilu. "Current Practices in the Recruitment, Selection, Training and Retainment of Kenyan Secondary School Heads: A Case Study of Kenya's Government Maintained Secondary Schools." Ph.D. diss., Claremont Graduate School, 1977.

Mwiria, Kilemi. "Education for Subordination: African Education in Colonial Kenya." *History of Education* 3 (1991): 261–73.

————. "Kenyan Women Adult Literacy Learners: Why Their Motivation Is Difficult to Sustain." *International Review of Education* 39 (3) (1993): 183–92.

Nabanja-Makumbi, Elizabeth Roselyn. *Development of Improved Instructional Units on Ecology in Secondary Form II in Kenya.* Nairobi: ACOP, 1981.

Närmon, Anders. *Practical Subjects in Kenyan Academic Secondary Schools: Tracer Study.* Stockholm: SIDA, 1985.

————. "Technical Secondary Schools and the Labour Market: Some Results from a Tracer Study in Kenya." *Comparative Education Review* 24 (1) (1988): 19–35.

Natsoulas, Theodore. "Rise and Fall of the Kikuyu Karing'a Education Association of Kenya, 1929–1952." *Journal of Asian and African Studies* 23 (3/4) (1988): 219–33.

Ndegwa, L. W. "Extending Museum Education in Kenya." *Museum* 36 (4) (1984): 228–32.

Ngau, Margaret. "Gap between Promise and Performance: Educational Policy-Making and Implementation in Kenya." *Ufahamu* 18 (3) (1990): 3–20.

Njoroge, Nganga. "An Outline of the Historical Development of Primary Education in Kenya, 1844–1970." Ph.D. diss., Ohio University, 1972.

Njunji, A. "Transformation of Education in Kenya Since Independence." *EEA* 4 (1) (1974): 107–25.

O'Connor, E. "Contrasts in Educational Development in Kenya and Tanzania." *AA* 73 (290) (1974): 67–84.

Odhiambo, Douglas. "What Is Kenya's Educational Goal?" *EAJ* 10 (1965): 22–25.

O'Hagan, Charles. "English Medium Teaching in Kenya." *Overseas Education* 32 (1962): 99–106.

Olembo, Jotham Ombisi. "Financing Primary School Facilities in Kenya." Ed.D. diss., Ball State University, 1974.

Olson, Jerry B. "Secondary School and Elites in Kenya: A Comparative Study of Students in 1961 and 1968." *Comparative Education Review* 16 (1) (1972): 44–53.

O'Meara, John. "Catholic Contribution to Kenya Education." *Kenya Education Journal* 5 (1960): 21–24.

Orora, John H. O. "School Culture and the Role of the Principal: A Study of Basic Cultural Assumptions of a Kenyan Secondary School and the Influence on the Principal's Role." Ph.D. diss., Dalhousie University, 1988.

Owigar, Ester Agutu. *Study of Attitudes of Teachers and Pupils Toward History Teaching by Radio in Nairobi Primary Schools*. Nairobi: ACOP, 1981.

Oyugi, E. *National Civic Education Programme: An Evaluation*. Nairobi: NCCK, 1993.

Phelps Stokes Commission. *Education in East Africa*. New York: Phelps Stokes Fund, 1924.

Porozny, G. "Development of Business Teacher Education Programme at Kenyatta University College." *EEA* 6 (1) (1976): 85–93; and 2 (1976): 113–21.

Raju, Beulah M. *Education in Kenya*. London: Heinemann, 1973.

Rathgeber, Eva M. "Education and Employment in the Informal Sector: A Review of Some Recent African Research." *CJAS* 22 (2) (1988): 272–86.

Riak, Isaac Cuir. *Economics of Costing and Financing of Education for Development in Kenya: A Research Agenda in the 1980s and Beyond*. Nairobi: Institute for Development Studies, University of Nairobi, 1987.

Roth, E. A. "Education, Tradition and Household Labour among Rendille Pastoralists of Northern Kenya." *Human Organisation* 50 (2) (1991): 136–41.

Sabar-Friedman, Galia. "Church and State in Kenya, 1986–1992: The Churches' Involvement in the 'Game of Change.'" *AA* 96 (382): 25–52.

Sarone, Ole S. "Pastoralists and Education: School Participation and Social Change Among the Massai." Ph.D. diss., McGill University, 1986.

Savage, Donald C., and Cameron Taylor. "Academic Freedom in Kenya." *CJAS* 25 (2) (1991): 308–21.

Schilling, Donald Gilmore. "British Policy for African Education in Kenya, 1895–1939." Ph.D. diss., University of Wisconsin, 1972.

———. "Dynamics of Education Policy Formation: Kenya 1928–1934." *History of Education Quarterly* 20 (1) (1980): 51–76.

———. "Local Native Councils and the Politics of Education in Kenya, 1925–1939." *IJAHS* 9 (2) (1976): 218–47.

Sheffield, James R. *Education, Employment, and Rural Development: The Proceedings of a Conference Held at Kericho, Kenya in September 1966*. Nairobi: EAPH, 1967.

———. *Education in Kenya: An Historical Study*. New York: Teachers College Press, 1973.

———. *Education in the Republic of Kenya*. Washington, D.C.: USGPO, 1971.

Sifuna, Daniel N. *Development of Education in Africa: The Kenyan Experience*. Nairobi: Initiatives, 1990.

———. "Diversified Secondary Education: A Comparative Survey of Kenya and Tanzania." *Genéve Afrique* 28 (2) (1990): 95–103.

———. "European Settlers As a Factor Influencing Government Policy and Practice in African Education in Kenya, 1900–1963." *KHR* 4 (1) (1976): 63–83.

————. "Indigenous Education in Nomadic Communities: A Survey of the Samburu, Rendille, Gabra and Boran of Northern Kenya." *Présence Africaine* (131) (1984): 66–88.

————. "Mill Hill Fathers and the Establishment of Western Education in Western Kenya 1900–1924: Some Reflections." *TJH* 6/7 (1977/1978): 112–28.

————. "Observations on Some Aspects of Non-Formal Education in Kenya." *EEA* 5 (1) (1975): 95–102.

————. *Short Essays on Education in Kenya.* Nairobi: KLB, 1980.

————. "Some Factors Affecting the Quality of Teaching in the Primary Schools of Kenya." *EEA* 4 (2) (1974): 215–22.

————. "Universal Education and Social Class Formation in Kenya." *Ufahamu* 15 (1/2) (1986): 164–81.

————. *Vocational Education in Schools: A Historical Survey of Kenya and Tanzania.* Nairobi: EALB, 1976.

————, and J. O. Shiundu. "Education for Production in Kenya: Report on the National Seminar, November 1988." *Education Production* (1989): 42–61.

Smith, J. S. *History of Alliance High School.* Nairobi: Heinemann, 1973.

Smith, M. I. "The East African Airlifts of 1959, 1960 and 1961." Ph.D. diss., Syracuse University, 1966.

Snehlata, R. Shah. "History of Asian Education in Kenya, 1886–1963." M.A. thesis, University of East Africa, 1968.

Southall, Roger. *Federalism and Higher Education in East Africa.* Nairobi: EAPH, 1974.

Spitzberg, Irving J. "Educational Planning: Politics, Ideology, and Development." *ASR* 21 (3) (1978): 101–10.

Ssekamwa, J. C. *Readings in the Development of Education in East Africa.* Kampala: Makerere University, 1971.

Stabler, Ernest. *Education Since Uhuru: The Schools of Kenya.* Middletown, CT: Wesleyan University Press, 1969.

————. "Kenya and Tanzania: Strategies and Realities in Education and Development." *AA* 78 (310) (1979): 33–56.

Tignor, Robert L. "Continuities and Discontinuities in East African Education." *History of Education Quarterly* 13 (4) (1973): 409–13.

Truman, Robert Hayward. "Origins and Development of Racial Pluralism in the Educational System of Kenya from 1895 to 1925." Ph.D. diss., University of Illinois, 1973.

Turton, Edward R. "Introduction and Development of Educational Facilities for the Somali in Kenya." *History of Education Journal* 14 (3) (1974): 347–66.

Twoli, N. W., and C. N. Power. "Major Influences on Science Achievement in a Developing Country." *International Journal of Science Education* 11 (2) (1989): 203–11.

Urch, George E. "The Africanization of the Curriculum in Kenya." *Educational Forum* 34 (3) (1970): 371–77.

Varghese, N. V. "Education in Kenya: A Study of the Education System of Kenya, With Special Reference to Its Need for Unity in the Plural Society." M.A. thesis, University of Birmingham, 1961.

Walji, P., and P. Dzvimbo. "Two Contrasting African Cases: Kenya and Zimbabwe." In *Towards a Commonwealth of Scholars*, edited by L. Brown, 190–206. London: Commonwealth Secretariat, 1994.

Walker, Phillip Ray. "Institution Building and Theological Education: An Assessment of a Nontraditional Theological Seminary in Kenya, East Africa." Ph.D. diss., Walden University, 1995.

Wanjala, Edward A. "Village Polytechnic Movement in Kenya." *EEA* 3 (1) (1973): 21–24.

Wanyoike, E. N. *Teacher Training Reading Methodology Manual in Kiswahili for Lower Primary Classes in Kenya.* Nairobi: ACOP, 1982.

Ward, Kevin. "Evangelism or Education? Mission Priorities and Educational Policy in the African Inland Mission 1900–1950." *KHR* 3 (2) (1975): 243–60.

Ward, W. E. F. "Beecher Report on African Education in Kenya." *Overseas Education* 23 (4) (1953): 13–19.

Wass, P. "Development Research Skills in Professional Staff: A Study of Adult Education Training in Kenya." *EEA* 6 (1) (1976): 1–11.

Waters, Alan Rufus. "Rewards and Incentives in Kenya's Educational System." *Universities Quarterly* 29 (2) (1975): 204–11.

Waweru, Julius Macharia. *Social-Economic Background as an Influence Factor in Pupils' Achievement in Primary Schools in Embu District.* Nairobi: African Curriculum Organization, 1982.

Weeks, S. *Divergence in Educational Development: The Case in Kenya and Uganda.* New York: Teachers College Press, 1967.

Were, Gideon S. "Making of Kakamega High School: A Tribute to Harold Arthur Waterloo Chapman." *TJH* 17 (1988): 186–92.

Were, Nereah. *Examination of the Problems Relating to the Teaching of History in Secondary Schools in Kenya.* Nairobi: ACOP, 1982.

Were, P. *The Kenyan We Want: An Approach to Social Education and Ethnics.* Nairobi: Heinemann Kenya, 1987.

Whisson, M.G. "The Place of the School in the Present Day Luo Society." Ph.D. diss., Cambridge University, 1963.

Whitehead, Clive. "Education for Subordination? Some Reflections on Kilemi Mwiria's Account of African Education in Colonial Kenya." *History of Education* 1 (1993): 85–93.

Woodhead, E. W., and G. C. Harper. *Report on Asian and European Education in Kenya, 1958.* Nairobi: GP, 1958.

Zamberia, Agostino M. "Self-Help Secondary Education in Kenya." *International Journal of Comparative Sociology* 37 (1/2) (1996): 47–71.

P. ENVIRONMENT AND GEOGRAPHY

Adams, W. M. "How Beautiful Is Small? Scale, Control and Success in Kenyan Irrigation." *WD* 18 (10) (1990): 1309–23.

Adamson, George. *Bwana Game*. London: Collins Harvill Press, 1968.

————. *My Pride and Joy*. London: Collins Harvill Press, 1986.

Adamson, Joy. *Born Free*. London: Collins Harvill Press, 1960.

————. *Elsa's Pride*. London: Collins, 1962.

————. *Forever Free*. London: Collins, 1972.

————. *Living Free: The Story of Elsa and Her Cubs*. London: Collins Harvill Press, 1961.

————. *Queen of Shaba: The Story of an African Leopard*. London: Collins, 1980.

————. *Searching Spirit*. London: Collins Harvill Press, 1978.

————. *Spotted Sphinx*. New York: Harcourt and Brace, 1969.

Agnew, Andrew D. Q. *Upland Kenya Wild Flowers: Flora of Ferns and Herbaceous Flowing Plants of Upland Kenya*. Nairobi: East Africa Natural History Society, 1994.

Akama, J. S., et al. "Conflicting Attitudes toward State Wildlife Conservation Programmes in Kenya." *Society and Natural Resources* 8 (2) (1995): 133–44.

Akatch, Samuel O., ed. *Dying Lake Victoria: A Community-Based Prevention Programme*. Nairobi: Initiative Publishers, 1996.

Alexander, Shana. "Serengeti: The Glory of Life." *NGM* 5 (1986): 584–601.

Allan, Iain, ed. *Guide to Mount Kenya and Kilimanjaro*. Nairobi: Mountain Club of Kenya, 1981.

Altmann, Jeanne. *Baboon Mothers and Infants*. Cambridge, MA: Harvard University Press, 1980.

Amin, Mohamed, and Ian Parker. *Ivory Crisis*. London: Chatto and Windus, 1983.

Amundson, R. G., A.R. Ali, and A. J. Belsky. "Stomatal Responsiveness to Changing Light Intensity Increases Rain-Use Efficiency of Below-Crown Vegetation in Tropical Savannas." *Journal of Arid Environments* 22 (2) (1995): 139–53.

Anderson, David M. "Managing the Forest: The Conservation History of Lembus, Kenya, 1904–63." In *Conservation in Africa*, edited by David Anderson and R. Grove, 249–69. Cambridge: CUP, 1987.

Anderson, Gordon Henry. *African Safaris*. Nakuru, Kenya: Nakuru Press, 1952.

Bachman, Phillip. *Tourism in Kenya: A Basic Need for Whom?* Berne: Peter Lang, 1988.

Baker, Randall, and David N. Kinyanjui. *Recommendations on the Institutional Framework for Environmental Management in Kenya*. Norwich, UK: School of Development Studies, University of East Anglia, 1980.

Baker, Richard St. Barbe. *Africa Drums*. Oxford: G. Ronald, 1951.

————. *I Planted Trees*. London: Lutterworth Press, 1945.

————. *Men of the Trees: In the Mahogany Forests of Kenya and Nigeria*. New York: Dial Press, 1931.

Barnes, Carolyn, ed. *Wood, Energy and Households: Perspectives on Rural Kenya.* Uppsala, Sweden: SIAS, 1984.

Barrow, E. G. G. *Tree Rights in Kenya: The Case of Turkana.* Nairobi: ACTS Press, 1992.

————. "Usufruct Right to Trees: The Role of Ekwar in Dryland Central Turkana, Kenya." *Human Ecology* 18 (2) (1990): 163–76.

Bartelmus, Peter. *Economic Development and the Human environment: A Study of Impacts and Repercussions with Particular Reference to Kenya.* Munich: Weltforum-Verlag, 1980.

Battiscombe, Edward. *Trees and Shrubs of Kenya Colony.* Nairobi: GP, 1936.

Beard, Peter. *End of the Game.* New York: Viking, 1965.

Beaton, Ken de P. *A Warden's Diary.* 2 vols. Nairobi: East African Standard, 1949.

Beentje, Henk J. *Kenya Trees, Shrubs, and Lianas.* Nairobi: National Museums of Kenya, 1994.

Bennet, Edward. *Shots and Snapshots in British East Africa.* London: Longman, 1914.

Blundell, Sir Michael. *Collins Photo Guide to the Wild Flowers of East Africa.* London: W. Collins, 1992.

————. *Wild Flowers of Kenya.* London: Collins, 1982.

Brown, Leslie H. *East African Mountains and Lakes.* Nairobi: EAPH, 1971.

Bull, Bartle. *Safari: A Chronicle of Adventure.* New York: Viking, 1988.

Buxton, Edward North. *Two African Trips with Notes and Suggestions on Big Game Preservation in Africa.* London: Edward Stanford, 1902.

Caldwell, Keith. *Report on a Faunal Survey in Eastern and Central Africa.* London: Society for the Preservation of the Fauna of the Empire, 1948.

Campbell, David J. "Prospect for Desertification in Kajiado District, Kenya." *GJ* 152 (1) (1986): 44–55.

Cass, Caroline. *Joy Adamson: Behind the Mask.* London: Weidenfeld and Nicolson, 1992.

Castro, Alfonso Peter. *Facing Kirinyaga: A Social History of Forest Commons in Southern Mount Kenya.* London: Intermediate Technology Publications, 1995.

————. "Indigenous Kikuyu Agroforestry: A Case Study of Kirinyaga, Kenya." *Human Ecology* 19 (1) (1991): 1–18.

————. "Kikuyu Agroforestry: An Historical Analysis." *Agriculture, Ecosystems and Environment* 46 (1/4) (1993): 45–54.

————. "Njukiine Forest: Transformation of a Common-Property Resource." *Forest and Conservation History* 4 (1991): 160–68.

————. "Southern Mount Kenya Forest Since Independence: A Social Analysis of Resource Competition." *WD* 19 (12) (1991): 174–84.

Chapman, Abel. *On Safari: Big-Game Hunting in British East Africa.* London: Edward Arnold, 1908.

Cloudsley-Thompson, J. L. *Animal Twilight: Man and Game in Eastern Africa.* London: Dufour, 1967.

Coe, Malcolm James. *The Ecology of the Alpine Zone of Mount Kenya.* The Hague: W. Junk. 1967.

————, and Hank Beentje. *Field Guide to the Acacias of Kenya.* Oxford: OUP, 1991.

Cole, Sonia M. *Outline of the Geology of Kenya.* London: Pitman, 1950.

Copely, Hugh. *Small Mammals of Kenya.* London: Longman, 1950.

Corebett, Jim. *Tree Tops.* London: OUP, 1955.

Cowie, Mervyn. *I Walk with Lions.* New York: Macmillan, 1964.

————. "The Royal National Parks." In *The Lion and the Lily: A Guide to Kenya,* edited by Kenneth Bolton, 158–71. London: Geoffrey Bles, 1962.

Cullen, Anthony, and Syd Downey. *Syd Downey's Africa.* London: Cassell and Company, 1959.

————. *Saving the Game.* London: Jarrolds, 1960.

Dale, Ivan R., and P. J. Greenway. *Kenya Trees and Shrubs.* Nairobi: Buchanan's Kenya Estates and Hatchards, 1961.

Dalleo, Peter T. "Somali Role in Organized Poaching in Northeastern Kenya, c. 1909–1939." *IJAHS* 12 (3) (1979): 472–82.

Daly, Marcus. *Big Game Hunting and Adventure 1897–1936.* London: Macmillan and Company, 1937.

Darkoh, M. B. K. "Kenya's Environment and Environmental Management." *JEARD* 20 (1990): 1–40.

————. "Land Degradation and Resource Management in Kenya." *Desertification Bulletin* 19 (1991): 61–72.

Davis, R. K. "Trade-Off Between Wildlife and Livestock in One Ranching Area of Kenya." *JEARD* 1/2 (1972): 73–80.

Dewes, Peter A. "Trees and Farm Boundaries: Farm Forestry, Land Tenure, and Reform in Kenya." *Africa* 65 (2) (1995): 217–35.

Downing, Thomas E., Kangethe W. Gitu, and Crispin M. Kamau, eds. *Coping With Drought in Kenya: National and Local Strategies.* Boulder, CO and London: Lynne Rienner, 1989.

Doyle, Mark. "Wildlife and Politics." *AR* 39 (2) (1994): 64–66.

Dublin, Holly T. "Decline of the Mara Woodlands: The Role of Fire and Elephants." Ph.D. diss., University of British Columbia, 1987.

DuBois, C. G. B. *Minerals of Kenya.* Nairobi: GP, 1966.

Dugmore, Arthur Radclyffe. *Autobiography of a Wanderer.* London: Macmillan, 1930.

————. *Camera Adventures in the African Wilds.* New York: Doubleday, 1910.

————. *Wonderland of Big Game.* London: Arrowsmith, 1925.

Dutton, E. A. P. *Kenya Mountain.* London: Jonathan Cape, 1930.

Dyer, Anthony. *East African Hunters: The History of the East African Professional Hunters' Association.* Clinton, NJ: Amwell Press, 1979.

————. *Men for All Seasons: The Hunters and Pioneers.* Agoura, CA: Trophy Room Books, 1996.

Elkan, Walter. "Relations between Tourism and Employment in Kenya and Tanzania." *Journal of Development Studies* 11 (2) (1975): 123–30.

Engelskjn, K. *Tsetse Fly Control in a Maasai Pastoralist Society in Nguruman, Southwest Kenya.* Oslo: Noragric, 1990.

Fane, Rebecca. "Forest Development in Kenya." *AA* 47/189 (1948): 242–45.

Foran, W. Robert. *A Breath of the Wilds.* London: Robert Hale, 1958.

————. *A Hunter's Saga.* London: Robert Hale, 1961.

————. *Kill or Be Killed: The Rambling Reminiscences of an Amateur Hunter.* New York: St. Martin's Press, 1988.

————. *Legends of the Field: More Early Hunters in Africa.* Agoura, CA: Trophy Room Books, 1997.

Fordham, Paul, and Peter Kinyanjui. *Geography of Kenya.* Nairobi: EALB, 1967.

Fratkin, Elliot. "Drought and Development in Marsabit District, Kenya." *Disasters* 16 (2) (1992): 119–30.

Georgiadis, N. J. "Microhabitat Variation in an African Savanna: Effects of Woody Cover and Herbivores in Kenya." *Journal of Tropical Ecology* 5 (1) (1989): 93–108.

Gore, Michael. *On Safari in Kenya: A Pictorial Guide to the National Parks.* Nairobi: Kenway, 1984.

Graham, Alistair, and Peter Beard. *Eyelids of Morning: The Mingled Destinies of Crocodiles and Men.* San Francisco: Chronicle Books, 1990.

Gregory, J. W. *Great Rift Valley and Geology of East Africa.* London: Frank Cass, 1968.

————. *The Rift Valley and the Geology of East Africa.* London: Seeley Service, 1921.

Hall, J. E. "Managing Intervention for the Sustainable Development of the Natural Tropical Forest: An East African Perspective." D.Phil. diss., University of Oxford, 1994.

Hedges, Norman G. *Reptiles and Amphibians of East Africa.* Nairobi: KLB, 1983.

Hemsing, Jan. *Ker and Downey Safaris Ltd.: The Inside Story.* Nairobi: Sealpoint Publicity, 1989.

Henry, Wesley. "Relationships Between Visitor Use and Tourist Capacity for Kenya's Amboseli National Park." Boulder: Colorado State University, 1980.

Hogg, Richard. "Development on Kenya: Drought, Desertification and Food Scarcity." 86 *AA* (1987): 47–58.

Holman, Dennis. *Elephant People.* London: John Murray, 1967.

————. *Elephants at Sundown: The Story of Bill Woodley.* London: W. H. Allen, 1978.

————. *Inside Safari Hunting.* New York: G.P. Putnam's Sons, 1969.

Homewood, Katherine. "Development, Demarcation and Ecological Outcomes in Maasailand." *Africa* 65 (3) (1995): 331–50.

Honore, E. J. "Forestry in East Africa: Kenya." In *Natural Resources of East Africa,* edited by E. W. Russell, 117–21. Nairobi: EALB, 1962.

House, Adrian. *Great Safari: The Lives of George and Joy Adamson, Famous for Born Free.* New York: William Morrow and Company, 1993.

Hughes, Francine. "Conflicting Uses for Forest Resources in the Lower Tana River Basin of Kenya." In *Conservation in Africa: People, Policies, and Practice*, edited by David Anderson and Richard Grove, 211–28. Cambridge: CUP, 1987.

Hughes, Ian Meredith. *Black Moon, Jade Sea*. London: Clifford Frost, 1988.

Hunter, John A. *Hunter*. New York: Harper, 1952.

————. *Hunter's Tracks*. New York: Appleton-Century-Crofts, Inc., 1957.

————. *White Hunter: The Adventures of a Big Game Hunter in Africa*. London: Seeley, Service and Company, Ltd., 1938.

Huxley, Elspeth, and Hugo van Lawick. *Last Days in Eden*. New York: The Amaryllis Press, 1984.

Huxley, Julian. *The Conservation of Wild Life and Natural Habitats in Central and East Africa*. Paris: UNESCO, 1961.

Imperato, Pascal James, and Eleanor M. Imperato. *They Married Adventure: The Wandering Lives of Martin and Osa Johnson*. New Brunswick: Rutgers University Press, 1992.

Jackman, Brian. *Marsh Lions: The Story of an African Pride*. Boston: David R. Godine, 1983.

Jackson, Sir Frederick. *Birds of Kenya and Uganda*. 3 vols. Edinburgh: Oliver and Boyd, 1938.

Jackson, R. T. "Problems of Tourist Industry Development on the Kenyan Coast." *Geography* 58 (1) (1973): 62–65.

Jernelov, Arne, and Uri Marinov. *Approach to Environmental Impact Assessment for Projects Affecting the Coastal and Marine Environment*. Nairobi: UNEP, 1990.

Jex-Blake, Muriel. *Some Wild Flowers of Kenya*. London: Longman, 1948.

Johansson, S., et al. *Forestry in Irrigation Schemes 1: Research Activities at Bura, Kenya 1984–87*. Helsinki: Helsinki University, Department of Siviculture, 1990.

Johnson, Osa. *Four Years in Paradise*. New York: J. B. Lippincott, 1941.

Jommo, Rosemary B. *Indigenous Enterprise in Kenya's Tourism Industry*. Geneva: Institut Universitaire d'Études du Développement, 1987.

Kaarakka, V., et al. *Forestry in Irrigation Schemes 2: Research Activities at Bura, Kenya 1988–89*. Helsinki: Helsinki University, Department of Siviculture, 1990.

Kakamega Forest Conservation Project Proposal. 2 vols. Nairobi: KIFCON, Karura Forest Station, 1992.

Karmali, John. *Beautiful Birds of Kenya*. Nairobi: Westlands Sundries, 1985.

————. *Beautiful Plants of Kenya*. Nairobi: Westlands Sundries, 1986.

Kelly, Nora. "In Wildest Africa: The Preservation of Game in Kenya, 1895–1933." Ph.D. diss., Simon Fraser University, 1978.

Kilewe, A. M., K. M. Kealey, and K.K. Kebaara, eds. *Agroforestry Development in Kenya: Proceedings of the Second National Seminar on Agroforestry*. Nairobi: International Council for Research in Agroforestry, 1989.

Kilewe, A. M., and D. B. Thomas. *Land Degradation in Kenya: A Framework for Policy and Planning*. London: Commonwealth Secretariat, 1992.

Kisovi, L. M. "Population Pressure and Human Carrying Capacity in Kitui District Kenya." *Eastern and Southern Africa Geographical Journal* (1993): 23–33.

Kittenberger, K. *Big Game Hunting and Collecting in East Africa, 1903–1926.* London: Edward Arnold and Company, 1929.

Knowles, Joan N., and D. P. Collett. "Nature as Myth, Symbol and Action: Notes Towards a Historical Understanding of Development and Conservation in Kenya Maasailand." *Africa* 59 (4) (1989): 433–60.

Larsen, Torben B. *Butterflies of Kenya and Their Natural History.* Oxford: OUP, 1991.

Laxen, J., et al. eds. *Proceedings of the Bura Fuelwood Project: Research Seminar.* Helsinki: Helsinki University, Department of Siviculture, 1993.

Ledje, H. *Water for Health and Wealth: A Study on Popular Participation in Tharaka Water and Sanitation Project, Eastern Province, Kenya.* Stockholm: Stockholm University, Development Studies Unit, 1994.

Lindsay, W. K. "Integrating Parks and Pastoralists: Some Lessons from Amboseli." In *Conservation in Africa: People, Policies, and Practice*, edited by David Anderson and Richard Grove, 149–68. Cambridge: CUP, 1987.

Logie, J. P., and W. G. Dyson. *Forestry in Kenya: A Historical Account of the Development of Forest Management in the Colony.* Nairobi: GP, 1962.

Loveridge, Arthur. *Forest Safari.* London: Lutterworth Press, 1956.

———. *Tomorrow's a Holiday.* New York and London: Harper and Brothers Publishers, 1947.

Lusigi, Walter J. "New Approaches to Wildlife Conservation in Kenya." *Ambio* 2/3 (1981): 87–92.

Lyell, Denis D. *African Adventures: Letters from Famous Big Game Hunters.* New York: E. P. Dutton, 1935.

Maathai, Wangari. *The Bottom Is Heavy Too: Even with the Green Belt Movement.* Edinburgh: Edinburgh University Press, 1994.

———. "Kenya: The Green Belt Movement." *IFDA Dossiers* 49 (1985): 3–12.

MacDonald, Malcolm. *Treasure of Kenya.* London: Collins, 1966.

Maforo, David Dhlalangami. "Black-White Relations in Kenya Game Policy: A Case Study of the Coast Province, 1895–1963." Ph.D. diss., Syracuse University, 1979.

Martin, G. H. G. "Small Mammals of Arid Savanna and Montane Sites in Northern Kenya." *Journal of Arid Environment* 11 (2) (1986): 173–80.

Mathu, Winston J. "Growth, Yield and Silvicultural Management of Exotic Timber Species in Kenya." Ph.D. diss., University of British Columbia, 1983.

Mbithi, P. M., and B. Wisner. "Drought and Famine in Kenya: Magnitude and Attempted Solutions." *JEARD* 4 (2) (1974): 161–88.

Medley, K. F. "Patterns of Forest Diversity along the Tana River." *Journal of Tropical Ecology* 8 (4) (1992): 353–71.

Michaelson, M. "Wangari Maathai and the Kenyan Green Belt Movement: Exploring the Evolution of Arid Potentialities of Consensus Movement Mobilisation." *Social Problems* 41 (4) (1994): 540–61.

Miller, Norman N. *Wild Life—Wild Death: Kenya's Man-Animal Equation.* Hanover, NH: Universities Field Staff International, 1982.

Moore, R. *Where to Watch Birds in Kenya*. Nairobi: Transafrica, 1984.

Moorjani, Shakuntala. *Seaweeds of the Kenya Coast*. Nairobi: OUP, 1988.

Morgan, W. T. W. *East Africa: Its People and Resources*. Nairobi: OUP, 1966.

Mortimore, M. *Environmental Change and Dryland Management in Machakos District, Kenya: Tree Management*. London: ODI, 1992.

Moss, Cynthia. *Echo of the Elephants: The Story of an Elephant Family*. New York: William Morrow, 1992.

Munene, M. J. "Grass-Roots Environmental Research in Kenya." *Nature and Resources* 28 (2) (1992): 14–21.

Murimi, S. K. "The Drying up of the East African Rift Valley Lakes in Recent Times: The Case of Lake Elmenteita." *JEARD* 23 (1993): 40–62.

Mwaura, F., and T. R. Moore. "Forest and Woodland Depletion in the Lake Elmenteita Basin, Kenya." *Geoforum* 22 (1) (1991): 17–27.

Oba, Gufu. "Perception of Environment Among Kenyan Pastoralists: Implications for Development." *Nomadic Peoples* 19 (1985): 33–57.

————. *Role of Indigenous Range Management Knowledge for Desertification Control in Northern Kenya*. Uppsala, Sweden: EPOS, 1994.

Obiri, J. A. F., G. Giathi, and A. Massawe. "Effect of Cypress Aphid on Cupressus Lusitanica Orchards in Kenya and Tanzania." *East African Agricultural and Forestry Journal* 3 (1994): 227–34.

Obura, David Obare. "Environmental Stress and Life History Strategies: A Case Study of Corals and River Sediment from Malindi, Kenya." Ph.D. diss., University of Miami, 1995.

Odegi-Awuondo, Casper. *Life in the Balance: Ecological Sociology of Turkana Nomads*. Nairobi: ACTS, 1990.

Odum, Howard T. *Energy, Environment, and Public Policy: A Guide to the Analysis of Systems*. Nairobi: UNEP, 1988.

Ofcansky, Thomas P. "Kenya Forestry under British Colonial Administration, 1895–1963." *Journal of Forest History* 28 (3) (1984): 136–43.

Ogutu, Z. A. "Responding to Population Pressure in Kenya." *Geojournal* 30 (4) (1993): 409–19.

Ojany, F. F. "Mount Kenya and Its Environs: A Review of the Interaction Between Mountain and People in an Equatorial Setting." *Mountain Research and Development* 13 (3) (1993): 305–9.

————, and R. B. Ogendo. *Kenya: A Study in Physical and Human Geography*. Nairobi: Longman Kenya, 1973.

Ojiambo, J. A. *Trees of Kenya*. Nairobi: KLB, 1978.

Olson, John Douglas. "Digital Model of Pattern and Productivity in an Agroforestry Landscape." D.Des. diss., Harvard University, 1995.

Omoro, Ben. *Marginal Soil, Marginal Farms: A Report on the Mutomo Soil and Water Conservation Programme, Kenya*. London: Panos, 1987.

————. *Why Kenyans Save Their Soil: A Report on the Soil Conservation Programme in Nyeri District*. London: Panos, 1987.

Östberg, Wilhelm. *We Eat Trees: Tree Planting and Land Rehabilitation in West Pokot District, Kenya: A Baseline Study.* Uppsala, Sweden: SLU, 1981.

Otsamo, A., et al. *Forestry Research at Bura Kenya 1984–1993: Final Report of the Research Component in the Bura Fuelwood Project.* Helsinki: Helsinki University, Department of Siviculture, 1993.

Ouma, Joseph P. B. M. *Evolution of Tourism in East Africa (1900–2000).* Nairobi: EALB, 1970.

Pagiola, Stefano. *Quantifying the Returns to Soil Conservation in Kitui and Machakos, Kenya.* Stanford, CA: Stanford University, Food Research Institute, 1993.

Pearson, John. *Wildlife and Safari in Kenya.* Nairobi: EAPH, 1970.

Peluso, N. L. "Coercing Conservation? The Politics of State Resource Control." *Global Environmental Change* 3 (2) (1993): 199–217.

Percival, A. Blayney. *Game Ranger on Safari.* London: Nisbet and Company, 1928.

———. *Game Ranger's Note Book.* New York: George H. Doran Company, 1924.

Petrides, George. *Kenya's Wild Life Resource and the National Parks.* Nairobi: Trustees of the Royal National Parks of Kenya, 1955.

Prickett, R. J. *African Ark.* Newton Abbot, UK: David and Charles, 1974.

Pulfrey, William. *Geology and Mineral Resources of Kenya.* Nairobi: GP, 1960.

Rayner, M. J. *Economies of Forest Conservation.* Nairobi: KIFCON, Karura Forest Station, 1991.

Reader, John. *Mount Kenya.* London: Elm Tree Books, 1989.

Richards, Dave. *Birds of Kenya: A Celebration.* London: Hamish Hamilton, 1991.

Robinson, W. C. "Kenya Enters the Fertility Transition." *Population Studies* 46 (3) (1992): 445–57.

Robson, Peter. *Mountains of Kenya.* Nairobi: EAPH, 1969.

Rocheleau, Dianne E., Philip E. Steinberg and Patricia A. Benjamin. "Environment, Development, Crisis, and Crusade: Ukambani, Kenya, 1890–1990." *WD* 23 (6) (1995): 1037–51.

Roosevelt, Theodore. *African Game Trials.* New York: Charles Scribner's Sons, 1910.

Scherr, Sara J. "Economic Factors in Farmer Adoption of Agroforestry: Patterns Observed in Western Kenya." *WD* 23 (5) (1995): 787–804.

Sheldrick, Daphne. *Animal Kingdom: The Story of Tsavo, The Great African Game Park.* Indianapolis, IN: Bobbs Merrill, 1973.

———. *Orphans of Tsavo.* London: Collins and Harvill Press, 1966.

———. *Tsavo Story.* London: Collins and Harvill Press, 1973.

Shisanya, Chris A. "The 1983–1984 Drought in Kenya." *JEARD* 20 (1990): 127–48.

Simon, Noel. *Between the Sunlight and the Thunder: The Wildlife of Kenya.* Boston: Houghton Mifflin, 1963.

Sindiga, I. "Environmental Studies in Kenya." *Professional Geographer* 41 (4) (1989): 492–93.

Smith, David Lavatt. *Amboseli: Nothing Short of a Miracle*. Nairobi: EAPH, 1986.

Someren, V. D. van. *Bird Watcher in Kenya*. London: Oliver and Boyd, n.d.

Spectrum Guide to Kenya. Edison, NJ: Hunter Publishing, 1992.

Steinhart, Edward I. "Hunters, Poachers and Gamekeepers: Towards a Social History of Hunting in Colonial Kenya." *JAH* 30 (2) (1989): 247–64.

———. "National Parks and Anti-Poaching in Kenya, 1947–1957." *IJAHS* 27 (1) (1994): 59–76.

Stelfox, John B. "Mixed-Species Game Ranching on the Athi Plains, Kenya." Ph.D. diss., University of Alberta, 1985.

Stigand, C. H. *The Game of British East Africa*. London: Horace Cox, 1909.

Storey, William K. "Big Cats and Imperialism: Lion and Tiger Hunting in Kenya and Northern India, 1898–1930." *Journal of World History* 2 (2) (1991): 135–73.

Talbot, L. M. "Ecology of Western Maasailand, East Africa." Ph.D. diss. University of California, Berkeley, 1963.

Thomas, D. B., and W. M. Senga, eds. *Soil and Water Conservation in Kenya: Proceedings of the Second National Workshop, Nairobi, 10–16 March, 1982.* Nairobi: University of Nairobi, Institute for Development Studies, 1983.

———, et al., eds. *Soil and Water Conservation in Kenya*. Nairobi: University of Nairobi, Department of Agricultural Engineering, 1989.

Thorbahn, P. F. "The Precolonial Ivory Trade of East Africa: Reconstruction of a Human-Elephant Ecosystem." Ph.D. diss., University of Massachusetts, 1979.

Thouless, C. R. "Conflict Between Humans and Elephants on Private Land in Kenya." *Oryx* 28 (2) (1994): 119–27.

Tiffen, Mary, ed. *Environmental Change and Dryland Management in Machakos District, Kenya: Institutional Profile*. London: ODI, 1992.

———. "Productivity and Environmental Conservation Under Rapid Population Growth: A Case Study of Machakos District." *Journal of International Development* 2 (1993): 297–323.

Tiffen, M., et al. *More People, Less Erosion: Environmental Recovery in Kenya*. Chichester, UK: Wiley, 1994.

Walker, Eric Sherbrooke. *Treetops Hotel*. London: Robert Hale and Company, 1969.

Wandiga, S. O., and N. L. Abuodha, eds. *Environment and Development in Kenya*. Nairobi: Kenya National Academy of Sciences, 1996.

Western, David. *In the Dust of Kilimanjaro*. Covelo, CA: Island Press, 1997.

Wienpahi, Jan. "Turkana Herds under Environmental Stress." *Nomadic Peoples* 17 (1985): 59–87.

Wildlife and Safari in Kenya. Nairobi: EAPH, 1967.

Williams, J. G. *Field Guide to the National Parks of East Africa*. London: Collins, 1967.

Willoughby, Sir John C. *East Africa and Its Big Game: A Narrative of a Sporting Trip from Zanzibar to the Borders of the Masai*. London: Longmans, Green, and Company, 1889.

Wimbush, S. H. *Catalogue of Kenya Timbers.* Nairobi: GP, 1957.

Yeager, Rodger, and Norman N. Miller. *Wildlife, Wild Death: Land Use and Survival in Eastern Africa.* Albany: State University of New York Press, 1986.

Zimmerman, Dale A., Donald A. Turner, and David J. Pearson. *Birds of Kenya and Northern Tanzania.* Princeton, NJ: Princeton University Press, 1996.

Zobisch, M. A. "Erosion Susceptibility and Soil Loss on Grazing Lands in Some Semi-Arid and Subhumid Locations of Eastern Kenya." *Journal of Soil and Water Conservation* 48 (5) (1993): 445–48.

Q. LEGAL AFFAIRS

Agbor-Tabi, P. *Divide and Rule: State-Sponsored Ethnic Violence in Kenya.* New York: Africa Watch, 1993.

———. "International Law and Functional Integration: The East African Community Revisited." *African Review* 16 (1/2) (1989): 16–28.

Africa Watch. *Kenya: Political Crackdown Intensifies.* New York: Africa Watch, 1990.

———. *Kenya: Screening of Ethnic Somalis: Cruel Consequences of Kenya's Passbook System.* New York: Africa Watch, 1990.

———. *Kenya: Taking Liberties.* New York: Africa Watch, 1991.

———. *Multipartyism Betrayed in Kenya: Continuing Rural Violence and Restrictions on Freedom of Speech and Assembly.* New York: Africa Watch, 1994.

Amnesty International. *Kenya: Government Fails to Take Action Against Torture.* London: AI, 1997.

———. *Kenya: Silencing the Opposition to One-Party Rule.* London: AI, 1990.

———. *Kenya: Torture, Political Detention, and Unfair Trials.* New York: AI, 1987.

"Arrest and Detention in Kenya." *Index on Censorship* 16 (1) (1987): 23–29.

Bhalla, R. S. *Property Relations in Kenyan Constitutional Law.* Nairobi: ACTS, 1993.

Brown, Douglas. *Criminal Procedure in Uganda and Kenya.* London: Sweet and Maxwell, 1965.

Bundeh, Benjamin Garth. *Birds of Kamiti.* Nairobi: Heinemann Kenya, 1991.

Butt, Safdar Ali. *An Introduction to Taxation in Kenya.* London: Cassell, 1978.

Bwonwong'a, M. *Procedures in Criminal Law in Kenya.* Nairobi: EAEP, 1994.

Carneiro, Jeannette. *The Forgotten People: Human Rights Violations in Moyale and Marsabit Districts.* Nairobi: Kenya Human Rights Commission, 1997.

Carson, J. B. "Further Notes on the African Courts System in Kenya." *JAA* 10 (1) (1958): 34–38.

Ciekawy, Diane. "Constitutional and Legal Reform in the Postcolony of Kenya." *Issue: A Journal of Opinion* 35 (1) (1997): 16–18.

———. "Human Rights and State Power on the Kenya Coast." *Humanity and Society* 21 (2) (1997): 130–47.

Cockar, Saeed R. *Kenya Industrial Court: Origin, Development, and Practice.* Nairobi: Longman, 1981.

Coldham, Simon F. R. "Comparative Study of Land Tenure Legislation in Africa." *Acta Juridica* (1985): 189–212.

———. "Effect of Registration of Title Upon Customary Land Rights in Kenya." *JAL* 22 (2) (1978): 91–111.

———. "Land Control in Kenya." *JAL* 22 (1) (1978): 63–77.

———. "Land Tenure Reform in Kenya: The Limits of the Law." *JMAS* 17 (4) (1979): 615–27.

———. "Registration of Title to Land in the Former Special Areas of Kenya." Ph.D. diss., University of London, 1977.

———. "Settlement of Land Disputes in Kenyan Historical Perspective." *JMAS* 22 (1) (1984): 59–71.

Conboy, Kevin. "Detention without Trial in Kenya." *Georgia Journal of International and Comparative Law* 8 (1978): 441–61.

Cotran, Eugene. *Casebook on Kenya Customary Law.* Abingdon, UK: Professional Books, 1987.

———. "Development and Reform of the Law in Kenya." *JAL* 27 (1) (1983): 42–61.

———. *Report on Customary Criminal Offenses in Kenya.* Nairobi: GP, 1963.

Days, Drew S., et al. *Justice Enjoined: The State of the Judiciary in Kenya.* New York: Robert F. Kennedy Memorial Center for Human Rights, 1992.

Duodu, C. "Secret Party Leads to Arrests: Ngugi wa Thiong'o Named as Leader of Secret Party by Kenyan MP." *Index on Censorship* 15 (6) (1986): 18, 35–36.

Errington, Kathleen. *Digest of the East African and Kenya Law Reports.* Nairobi: GP, 1953.

Evans, Emmit B. "Education, Unemployment and Crime in Kenya." *JMAS* 8 (1) (1975): 55–66.

Franck, Thomas M. *East African Unity through Law.* New Haven, CT: YUP, 1964.

Gathii, James Thuo. *The Dream of Judicial Security of Tenure and the Reality of Executive Involvement in Kenya's Judicial Process.* Nairobi: Kenya Human Rights Commission, 1994.

Gavron, Jeremy. *Darkness in Eden: The Murder of Julie Ward.* London: HarperCollins, 1991.

Ghai, Y. P., and J. P. W. B. McAuslan. *Public Law and Political Change in Kenya: A Study of the Legal Framework of the Government from Colonial Times to the Present.* Nairobi: OUP, 1970.

Gicheru, H. B. *Parliamentary Practice in Kenya.* Nairobi: TransAfrica, 1976.

Gillies, D. W., and Makau wa Mutua. *Long Road to Uhuru: Human Rights and Political Participation in Kenya.* London: Westminster Foundation for Democracy, 1993.

Hannan, Lucy. "Kenya: Sedition by Edition." *AR* 36 (3) (1991): 49–52.

———. *Kenya: Shadow Justice.* London: African Rights, 1996.

Hayanga, C. A. "Loans to Agriculture in Kenya." *JAL* 19 (1/2) (1975): 105–11.

Hiltzik, Michael. *Death in Kenya: The Murder of Julie Ward*. New York: Delacorte Press, 1991.

Holland, D. C. "Law and Order in Kenya." *Anti-Slavery Reporter* 20 (1) (1955): 8–16.

Hopkins, Raymond F. *The Kenya Legislature: Political Functions and Citizen Perceptions*. Bloomington. IN: International Development Research Center, 1973.

House-Midamba, Bessie. "The Legal Basis of Gender Inequality in Kenya." *African Journal of International and Comparative Law* 5 (4) (1993): 854–68.

———. "Legal Pluralism and Attendant Internal Conflicts in Martial and Inheritance Laws in Kenya." *Africa* 49 (3) (1994): 375–92.

Hussain, Ashiq. *Textbook of Company Law in Kenya*. Nairobi: Heinemann Educational Books, 1980.

Jackson, Tudor. *Guide to the Legal Profession of Kenya*. Nairobi: Kenya Africa Book Services, 1980.

———. *Law of Kenya*. 3rd ed. Nairobi: KLB, 1988.

———. *Law of Kenya: An Introduction*. Nairobi: EALB, 1970.

———. *Law of Kenya: An Introduction, Cases and Statutes*. Nairobi: KLB, 1986.

Jones, George. *Kenya Prisons*. New York: Institute of Current World Affairs, 1975.

Kahonge, Patrick. "Independence and Impartiality of the Judiciary: A Critical Analysis of the Mode of Appointment of Judges in Kenya." *University of Nairobi Law Journal* 1 (1) (1994): 57–61.

Kanyana, D. N. *Commercial Laws of Kenya*. Kisumu, Kenya: Lake Publishers, 1987.

Kapinga, Wilbert B. L. "Legal Profession and Social Action in the Third World: Reflections on Tanzania and Kenya." *African Journal of International Comparative Law* 4 (4) (1992): 874–91.

Kenya. *The Constitution of Kenya*. Nairobi: GP, 1979.

———. *Human Rights Situation in Kenya. The Way It Is*. Nairobi: GP 1996.

———. *Laws of Kenya*. Nairobi: GP, 1970.

Kenya Human Rights Commission. *Death Sentence: Prison Conditions in Kenya*. Nairobi: Kenya Human Rights Commission, 1996.

———. *Independence without Freedom: The Legitimation of Repressive Laws and Practices in Kenya*. Nairobi: Kenya Human Rights Commission, 1994.

———. *Licensed to Kill: Police Shootings in Kenya: An Investigative Report into the Deaths of James Nomi Kangara, Abel Mwaura Kimani and Francis Njoroge Chiira*. Nairobi: Kenya Human Rights Commission, 1995.

Kenya Institute of Administration. *Guide to the Constitutional Development of Kenya*. Nairobi: GP, 1970.

———. *Introduction to Kenya Law*. 2nd ed. Nairobi: GP, 1975.

Kenya Tuitakayo (The Kenya We Want): Proposal for a Model Kenya Constitution. Nairobi: Kenya Human Rights Commission and the International Commission of Jurists (Kenya Section), 1996.

Kercher, Leonard Clayton. *Kenya Penal System: Past, Present, and Prospect.* Lanham, MD: University Press of America, 1981.

Kibwana, Kivutha. "Critical Aspects Regarding the Legal Regulations in the Informal Sector." *Lesotho Law Journal* 2 (1989): 357–87.

———. *Fundamental Rights and Freedoms in Kenya.* Nairobi: OUP, 1990.

———, ed. *Law and the Administration of Justice in Kenya.* Nairobi: International Commission of Jurists, Kenya Section, 1992.

Kuria, Gibson Kamau. "Independence of the Legal Profession and the Judiciary. In International Commission of Jurists (Kenya Section). *Law and Society: Selected Papers from a Seminar, November 24–26, 1988.* Nairobi: English Press, 1989: 37–47.

———. *Majimboism, Ethnic Cleansing and Constitutionalism in Kenya.* Nairobi: Kenya Human Rights Commission, 1994.

———. "Restructuring the Kenyan Constitution." *NLM* 44 (1992): 34–43; 45 (1992): 30–36.

———. "Rule of Law in Kenya and the Status of Human Rights." *Yale Journal of International Law* 16 (1) (1991): 217–33.

———, and A. M. Vazquez. "Judges and Human Rights: The Kenyan Case." *JAL* 35 (1/2) (1991): 142–73.

Law as a Tool of Political Repression in Kenya. London: Committee for the Release of Political Prisoners in Kenya, 1982.

Lewis, Joanna, Peggy Owens, and Louise Pirouet, eds. *Human Rights and the Making of the Constitutions: Malawi, Kenya, Uganda.* Cambridge: African Studies Centre Publications, 1995.

Macharia, Rawson. *The Truth About the Trial of Jomo Kenyatta.* Nairobi: Longman, 1991.

Maina, K.M. *Land Law in East Africa.* London; OUP, 1967.

"Maina Wa Kinyatti: Prisoner of Conscience." *Index on Censorship* 16 (6) (1987): 22–25.

Mazrui, Ali A. "Human Rights in Kenya." *African Journal of International Law* 1 (1) (1988): 92–98.

Mbaya, William. *Commercial Law of Kenya.* Nairobi: Petrans, 1991.

Mburu, C. "Julie Ward Murder Cover-Up: A Father's Search for Elusive Justice." *NLM* 44 (1992): 14–20, 22, 30.

M'Inoti, K. "Enforcement of Fundamental Rights in Kenya: Righting Some of the Initial Wrongs." *NLM* (42) (1992): 33–38.

Moore, S. F. *Social Facts and Fabrications: Customary Law on Kilimanjaro, 1880–1980.* Cambridge: CUP, 1986.

Morris, Henry F. "Some Developments in the Administration of Justice in East Africa since Independence." *South African Journal of African Affairs* 2 (1973): 7–21.

Muga, Erasto. *Crime and Delinquency in Kenya.* Nairobi: EALB, 1975.

———. *Crime in a Kenyan Town: A Case Study of Kisumu.* Kampala, Uganda: EALB, 1977.

————. *Robbery with Violence.* Nairobi: KLB, 1980.

Mumma, Albert. "Preservation of Public Security Through Executive Restraint of Personal Liberty: A Case Study of the Kenyan Position." *Verfassung und Recht in Übersee* 21 (4) (1988): 445–63.

Munrou, C. G. S. "The Development of the Kenya Legal System, Legal Education, and Legal Profession." *East African Law Journal* 9 (1) (1973): 1–10.

Murungi, Kiraitu. "Role of the International Commission of Jurists (Kenya Section) in Promoting the Rule of Law and Protecting the Enjoyment of Human Rights." *NLM* 12/13 (1988/1989): 48–51.

Mutua, Makau wa. "Human Rights and State Despotism in Kenya: Institutional Problems." *AT* 41 (4) (1994): 50–56.

Mutunga, Willy. "Commercial Law and Development in Kenya." *Ufahamu* 12 (1) (1982): 19–50.

Mutungi, Onesmus Kimweh. *Legal Aspects of Witchcraft in East Africa, With Particular Reference to Kenya.* Nairobi: EALB, 1977.

Mwalimu, Charles. *Kenyan Legal System: An Overview.* Washington, D.C.: Library of Congress, Law Library, 1988.

Mwangi, Muriithi. *Aspects of Criminal Law in Kenya.* Nairobi: OUP, 1992.

Nowrojee, P. "Fundamental Questions Regarding Fundamental Rights: The Kenyan Experience." *Legal Forum* 7 (1) (1995): 39–43.

Odek, James Otieno. "Kenyan Patent Law: Promoting Local Inventiveness or Protecting Foreign Patentees?" *JAL* 38 (2) (1994): 79–103.

Odenyo, Amos O. "Conquest, Clientage, and Land Law Among the Luo." *Law and Society Review* 7 (4) (1973): 767–78.

————. "Professionalization Amidst Change: The Case of the Emerging Legal Profession in Kenya." *ASR* 22 (3) (1979): 33–44.

Ogolla, Bondi D. "Legal Regime and the Peasantry: The Case of Land Tenure Reform in Kenya." *African Studies Associations Papers* 29 (70) (1986): 1–20.

Ojwang, J. B. *Constitutional Development in Kenya: Institutional Adaption and Social Change.* Nairobi: ACTS, 1990.

————. "Constitutional Law and Political Change: Recent Developments in Zambia and Kenya." *African Journal of International and Comparative Law* 4 (2) (1992): 325–52.

————. *Environmental Law and the Constitutional Order.* Nairobi: ACTS Press, 1993.

————. *Environmental Law and Political Change in Kenya.* Nairobi: ACTS Press, 1992.

Okech-Owiti, M. D. "Socio-Legal Aspects of Contract-Farming: An Overview of Kenyan Case Study." *Zimbabwe Law Review* 9/10 (1991/1992): 82–95.

Okondo, P. H. *Commentary on the Constitution of Kenya.* Nairobi: Phoenix Publishers, 1995.

Okoth-Ogendo, H. W. O. "Development and the Legal Process in Kenya: An Analysis of the Role of Law in Rural Development Administration." *International Journal of the Sociology of Law* 12 (1) (1984): 59–83.

————. *Tenants of the Crown: Evolution of Agrarian Law and Institutions in Kenya.* Nairobi: ACTS, 1991.

Onalo, P. L. *Land Law and Conveyancing in Kenya.* Nairobi: Heinemann, 1986.

Ooko-Ombaka, O. "Political Justice in Kenya: Prolegomena to an Inquiry into the Use of Legal Procedures for Political Purposes in Post-Kenyatta Era." *Verfassung und Recht in Übersee* 15 (4) (1982): 393–442.

Pfeiffer, Steven B. "Judiciary Constitutional Systems of Kenya, Tanzania, Uganda." *Legal History* 2 (2) (1976): 27–72.

————. "Role of the Judiciary in the Constitutional Systems of East Africa." *JMAS* 16 (1) (1978): 33–66.

Phillips, Arthur. "African Court System in Kenya." *JAA* 4 (4) (1952): 135–38.

Pritt, D. N. *The Defence Accuses.* London: Lawrence and Wishart, 1966.

"Remembering J. M. Kariuki." *NLM* 41 (1992): 27–36.

Republic of Kenya. *Report of Judicial Commission Appointed into Allegations Involving Charles Mugane Njonjo.* Nairobi: GP, 1984.

"Right to a Fair Trial in East Central Africa." *AT* 36 (3/4) (1989): 98–103.

Rogers, Margaret. "A Note of Hire Purchase and Chattels Mortgage in Kenya." *JAL* 19 (1/2) (1975): 154–62.

Ross, Stanley D. "Comparative Study of the Legal Profession in East Africa." *JAL* 17 (3) (1973): 279–99.

————. "Rule of Law and Lawyers in Kenya." *JMAS* 30 (3) (1992): 421–42.

Salter, D. R., and J. B. Ojwang. "Law Reform in Africa: A Comparative Study of the Tanzanian and Kenyan Experiments." *Verfassung und Recht Übersee* 18 (2) (1985): 123–38.

Sevareid, Peter. *An Introduction to Administrative Law in Kenya: Cases and Materials.* Nairobi: Kenya Institute of Administration, 1969.

Shields, Todd. "Kenya: Lawyers vs. the Law." *AR* 35 (5) (1990): 13–16.

Simon, H. J. "Criminal Law and Its Administration in South Africa, Southern Rhodesia and Kenya." Ph.D. diss., University of London, 1936.

Singh, Chanan. "Republican Constitution of Kenya: Historical Background and Analysis." *International and Comparative Law Quarterly* 3 (1965): 878–49.

Slater, Montagu. *Trial of Jomo Kenyatta.* London: Secker and Warburg, 1965.

Sockett, Albert E. *Law of the British East Africa Protectorate.* 2 vols. Nairobi: GP, 1917/1918.

Spencer, Leon P. "Toward Africans As Defenders of Their Own Interests: The Translation of Laws into Swahili in Kenya, 1920–1927." *KHR* 3 (1) (1975): 46–54.

Spurling, A. C. *Digest and Guide to the Criminal Law of Kenya.* Nairobi: GP, 1954.

Sullivan, David Bryan. "Kenya: The Trial of Koigi wa Wamwere et al." *ROAPE* 64 (1995): 262–67.

————. *Kenyan Justice on Trial in Nakuru: Notes from the Trial of Koigi wa Wamwere et al.* New Haven, CT: Orville Schell Centre for International Human Rights, Yale Law School, 1995.

Sure, Kembo. "Language, Law and Pluralism in Kenya." *AQ* 31 (3/4) (1991/1992): 60–72.

Swartz, Marc J. "Religious Courts, Community, and Ethnicity among the Swahili of Mombasa: An Historical Study of Social Boundaries." *Africa* 49 (1) (1979): 29–41.

Tanner, Ralph E. "Crime and Punishment in East Africa." *Transition* 26 (1965): 35–38.

Thiong'o, Ngugi wa. *Detained: A Writer's Prison Diary.* London and Nairobi: Heinemann, 1981.

Thomas, Anthony E. "Oaths, Ordeals, and the Kenyan Courts: A Policy Analysis." *Human Organization* 33 (1) (1974): 59–70.

Thompson, Dudley. *From Kingston to Kenya: The Making of a Pan-Africanists Lawyer.* Dover, MA: Majority Press, 1993.

Unfulfilled Promise: Human Rights in Kenya After the December 1992 Elections. Washington, D.C.: Robert F. Kennedy Memorial Center for Human Rights, 1993.

Wacker, U. *Der Konflikt Verschiedener Rechtssysteme vor, Während und Nach der Kolonialzeit in Kenia.* (Frankfurt am Main: Peter Lang, 1976).

Wamwere, Koigi wa. *Conscience on Trial: Why I Was Detained, Notes of a Political Prisoner.* Trenton: Africa World Press, 1988.

Wandai, K. *Mayor in Prison.* Nairobi: EAEP, 1993.

Waruhiu, S. N. *Affiliation Law in Kenya.* Kampala, Uganda: Eagle Press, 1962.

Wasikhongo, Joab Meshak. "Armed Robbery and the Developmental Process in Africa: Trends in Nairobi, Mombasa, and Abidjan, and Criminal Processes in Nairobi." Ph.D. diss., University of Wisconsin, 1979.

Watkins, Elizabeth. *Jomo's Jailer: Grand Warrior of Kenya.* Calais, France: Mulberry Press, 1993.

Werunga, M. "The Transition Decades: Kenya's Constitution Comes of Age." *Parliamentarian* 67 (1986): 55–58.

Willis, Justin. "Thieves, Drunkards and Vagrants: Defining Crime in Colonial Mombasa, 1902–32." In *Policing the Empire: Government, Authority and Control, 1830–1940,* edited by David Anderson and David Killingray, 219–35. Manchester, UK: Manchester University Press, 1991.

R. MAU MAU

Adebola, A. S. "Kikuyu Independent Schools Movement and the Mau Mau Uprising." *Journal of the Historical Society of Nigeria* 4 (1981): 53–70.

Adekson, J. Bayo. "Algerian and Mau Mau Revolts: A Comparative Study in Revolutionary Warfare." *Comparative Strategy* 1 (1981): 69–92.

Alport, C. J. M. "Kenya's Answer to the Mau Mau Challenge." *AA* 53 (212) (1954): 241–48.

Atieno Odhiambo, E. S. "Kenyatta and the Mau Mau." *Transition* 53 (1991): 147–52.

—————. "Production of History in Kenya: The Mau Mau Debate." *CJAS* 25 (2) (1991): 300–07.

Baldwin, William. *Mau Mau Man-Hunt*. New York: E.P. Dutton, 1957.

Baring, Sir Evelyn. *The Kenya Emergency and the Future*. London: Central Office of Information, 1953.

—————. "Kenya Today and Tomorrow." In *Rhodesia and East Africa*, edited by F. S. Joelson, 164–68. London: East Africa and Rhodesia, 1958.

Barnett, Donald L., and Karari Njama. *Mau Mau from within: Autobiography and Analysis of Kenya's Peasant Revolt*. London: MacGibbon and Kee, 1966.

Bates, Robert H. "Agrarian Origins of Mau Mau." *Agricultural History* 61 (1) (1987): 1–28.

Beecher, Leonard J. "After Mau Mau, What?" *IRM* 44 (174) (1955): 205–11.

—————. "Christian Counter-Revolution to Mau Mau." In *Rhodesia and East Africa*, edited by F. S. Joelson, 82–92. London: East Africa and Rhodesia, 1958.

Berman, Bruce J. "Nationalism, Ethnicity, and Modernity: The Paradox of Mau Mau." *CJAS* 25 (2) (1991): 181–206.

—————, and John M. Lonsdale. "Louis Leakey's Mau Mau: A Study in the Politics of Knowledge." *History and Anthropology* 5 (2) (1991): 143–204.

Buijtenhuijs, Robert. *Essays on Mau Mau: Contributions to Mau Mau Historiography*. Leiden: African Studies Center, 1982.

—————. *Le Mouvement Mau Mau: Une Révolte Paysanne et Anti-Coloniale en Afrique Noire*. The Hague: Mouton and Company, 1971.

—————. *Mau Mau: Twenty Years After the Myth and the Survivors*. The Hague: Mouton and Company, 1973.

Carothers, J. C. *The Psychology of Mau Mau*. Nairobi: GP, 1954.

Castle, Barbara. "Justice in Kenya." *New Statesman and Nation* (17 December 1955): 821–22.

Castro, Alfonso Peter, and K. Ettenger. "Counter-Insurgency and Socioeconomic Change: The Mau Mau War in Kirinyaga, Kenya." *Research in Economic Anthropology* 15 (1994): 63–101.

Clayton, Anthony. *Counterinsurgency in Kenya: A Study of Military Operations against the Mau Mau, 1952–1960*. Manhattan, KS: Sunflower University Press, 1984.

Cleary, A. S. "Myth of Mau Mau in Its International Context." *AA* 89 (355) (1990): 227–45.

Cloete, Stuart. *Storm over Africa: A Study of the Mau Mau Rebellion, Its Causes, Effects and Implications on Africa South of the Sahara*. Cape Town: Culemborg Publishers, 1956.

Clough, Marshall S. *Mau Mau Memoirs: History, Memory, and Politics*. Boulder, CO: Lynne Rienner, 1998.

Cooley, John K. "From Mau Mau to Missiles." *African Forum* 2 (1) (1966): 42–56.

Cooper, Frederick. "Mau Mau and the Discourses of Decolonization." *JAH* 29 (2) (1988): 313–20.

Corfield, F. D. *Historical Survey of the Origins and Growth of Mau Mau*. London: HMSO, 1960.

Cowen, Michael. "Before and After Mau Mau in Kenya." *Journal of Peasant Studies* 16 (2) (1989): 269–75.

Croker, G. W. "Mau Mau." *Journal of the Royal United Service Institute for Defence Studies* 100 (597) (1955): 47–53.

Crossman, R. H. S. "Report on Mau Mau." *New Statesman and Nation* (23 January 1954): 88–89.

Durrani, Shiraz. *Kimaathi: Mau Mau's First Prime Minister of Kenya*. Wembley, UK: Vita, 1986.

Edgerton, Robert. *Mau Mau: An African Crucible*. New York: Free Press, 1989.

Erskine, General Sir George. "Kenya-Mau Mau." *Royal United Service Institution Journal* 101 (601) (1956): 11–22.

———. "Kenya—What Is It All About?" *Journal of the Royal Artillery* (1956): 99–117.

Esmonde-White, D. C. B. L. "Violence in Kenya." *Army Quarterly*, 66 (2) (1953): 183–88.

Etschmann. Wolfgang. "Der 'Mau Mau' Krieg in Kenia 1952–1956." *Truppendienst* (1990): 23–28.

Evans, P. *Law and Disorder: Scenes of Life in Kenya*. London: Secker and Warburg, 1956.

Farrell, Christopher. "Mau Mau: A Revolt or a Revolution?" *KHR* 5 (2) (1977): 187–99.

Furedi, Frank. *Mau Mau War in Perspective*. London: James Currey, 1989.

———. "Social Composition of the Mau Mau Movement in the White Highlands." *Journal of Peasant Studies* 1 (4) (1974): 486–505.

Gikoyo, Gucu G. *We Fought for Freedom*. Nairobi: EAPH, 1979.

Githumo, Mwangi wa. "Truth about the Mau Mau Movement: The Most Popular Uprising in Kenya." *TJH* 20 (1991): 1–18.

Gordon, David F. "Mau Mau and Decolonization: Kenya and the Defeat of Multi-Racialism in East and Central Africa." *KHR* 5 (2) (1977): 329–48.

Great Britain. Army. East Africa Command. *Handbook on Anti-Mau Mau Operations*. Nairobi: GP, n.d.

Great Britain. Colonial Office. *Documents Relating to the Deaths of Eleven Mau Mau Detainees at Hola Camp in Kenya*. London: HMSO, 1959.

———. *Further Documents Relating to the Death of Eleven Mau Mau Detainees at Hola Camp in Kenya*. London: HMSO, 1959.

———. *Record of Proceedings and Evidence into the Death of Eleven Mau Mau Detainees at Hola Camp in Kenya*. London: HMSO, 1959.

Green, Maia. "Mau Mau Oathing Rituals and Political Ideology in Kenya: A Re-Analysis." *Africa* 60 (1) (1990): 69–87.

Greenidge, C. W. W. "Memorandum on Kenya." *Anti-Slavery Reporter* 9 (1) (1953): 3–10.

Hatch, John. "Kenya and the Mau Mau." *Jewish Frontiers* (1954): 18–21.

Heather, Randall W. "Counter-Insurgency and Intelligence in Kenya, 1952–56." Ph.D. diss., Cambridge University, 1994.

————. "Intelligence and Counter-Insurgency in Kenya, 1952–56." *Intelligence and National Security* 5 (3) (1990): 57–83.

Henderson, Ian, and Philip Goodhart. *Hunt for Kimathi*. London: Hamish Hamilton, 1958.

Holman, Dennis. *Bwana Drum: The Unknown Story of the Secret War against Mau Mau*. London: W. H. Allen, 1964.

Huxley, Elspeth. "Kenya After Mau Mau." *Optima* 7 (3) (1957): 101–10.

Itote, Waruhiu. *"Mau Mau" General*. Nairobi: EAPH, 1967.

————. *Mau Mau in Action*. Nairobi: Transafrica, 1979.

Kamunchuluh, J. T. Samuel. "Meru Participation in Mau Mau." *KHR* 3 (2) (1975): 183–216.

Kanogo, Tabitha M. J. "Rift Valley Squatters and Mau Mau." *KHR* 5 (2) (1977): 243–52.

————. *Squatters and the Roots of Mau Mau 1905–63*. Athens, OH: Ohio University Press, 1987.

Kariuki, Josiah Mwangi. *"Mau Mau" Detainee: The Account by a Kenyan African of His Experiences in Detention Camps 1953–1960*. London: OUP, 1963.

Kauffman, Dick. "Mau Mau: Peasant War or Revolution?" *KHR* 5 (2) (1977): 173–86.

Keller, Edmond J. "Twentieth-Century Model: The Mau Mau Transformation from Social Banditry to Social Rebellion." *KHR* 2 (1973): 189–205.

Kennedy, Dane. "Constructing the Colonial Myth of Mau Mau." *IJAHS* 25 (2) (1992): 241–60.

"Kenya after the Storm (Effects of the Mau Mau Rebellion: Economic and Racial Prospects)." *British Survey* (1957): 1–16.

Kenya Colony and Protectorate. *Report on the General Administration of Prisons and Detention Camps in Kenya*. Nairobi: GP, 1956.

"Kenya: Mau Mau and the Kikuyu Problem." *British Survey* (1954): 1–25.

Kenya War Council. *Kenya Emergency*. London: Central Office of Information, 1954.

Kerby, M.H. "Unhappiness of the Kikuyu, or the Seeds of Mau Mau." *EAMJ* 36 (10) (1959): 529–32.

Kershaw, Greet. *Mau Mau from Below*. Athens, OH: Ohio University Press, 1997.

————. "Mau Mau from Below: Fieldwork and Experience, 1955–57 and 1962." *CJAS* 25 (2) (1991): 274–97.

Kiano, Gikonyo. "Mau Mau in Africa: An African's View." *Saturday Review of Literature* (3 May 1953): 17–19, 41–42.

Kilson, Martin L. "Behind the Mau Mau Rebellion." *Dissent* 3 (3) (1956): 264–75.

————. "Land and Politics in Kenya: An Analysis of African Politics in a Plural Society." *Western Political Quarterly* 10 (3) (1957): 559–81.

————. "Land and the Kikuyu: A Study of the Relationship Between Land and Kikuyu Political Movements." *Journal of Negro History* 40 (2) (1955): 103–53.

Kinyatti, Maina wa. *Kenya's Freedom Struggle: The Dedan Kimathi Papers.* London: Zed Press, 1987.

————. *Mau Mau: A Revolution Betrayed.* New York: Mau Mau Research Center, 1993.

————. "Mau Mau: The Peak of African National Organization in Colonial Kenya." *KHR* 5 (2) (1977): 287–311.

————. "Mau Mau: The Peak of African Political Organization and Struggle for Liberation in Colonial Kenya." *Ufahamu* (3) (1982/1983): 90–123.

————. *Thunder from the Mountains, Mau Mau Patriotic Songs.* London: Zed Press, 1980.

Kipkorir, B. E. "'Mau Mau' and the Politics of the Transfer of Power in Kenya, 1957–1960." *KHR* 5 (2) (1977): 313–28.

Kitson, Frank E. *Bunch of Five.* London: Faber and Faber, 1977.

————. *Gangs and Counter Gangs.* London: Barrie and Rockliff, 1960.

Koinange, Mbiyi. *People of Kenya Speak for Themselves.* Detroit, MI: Kenya Publication Fund, 1955.

Krug, W. G. "Terror and Counter-Terror in British East Africa." *Aussenpolitik* (1953): 589–94.

Kushner, Gilbert. "African Revitalization Movement: Mau Mau." *Anthropos* 60 (1/6) (1965): 763–802.

Lander, Cherry. *My Kenya Acres: A Woman Farms in Mau Mau Country.* London: George G. Harrap and Company, 1957.

Lathbury, Gerald. "Security Forces in the Kenya Emergency." In *Rhodesia and East Africa*, edited by F. Joelson, 36–47. London: East Africa and Rhodesia, 1958.

Lavers, Anthony. *Kikuyu Who Fight Mau Mau.* Nairobi: Eagle Press, 1955.

Leakey, Louis Seymour Bazett. *Defeating Mau Mau.* London: Methuen, 1954.

————. *Mau Mau and the Kikuyu.* London: Methuen, 1952.

Leigh, Ione. *In the Shadow of the Mau Mau.* London: W. H. Allen, 1954.

Likimani, Muthoni. *Passbook Number F.47927: Women and Mau Mau in Kenya.* New York: Praeger, 1986.

Lonsdale, John. "Constructing Mau Mau." *Transactions of the Royal Historical Society* 40 (1990): 239–60.

————. "Explanations of the Mau Mau Revolt." In *Resistance and Ideology in Settler Societies*, edited by Tom Lodge, 168–78. Johannesburg: Raven, 1986.

————. "Mau Mau's of the Mind: Making Mau Mau and Remaking Kenya." *JAH* 31 (3) (1990): 393–421.

————. "Mau Mau Through the Looking Glass." *Index on Censorship* 15 (2) (1986): 19–22.

————. "La Pense Politique Kikuyu et les Ideologies du Mouvement Mau-Mau." *Cahiers d'Études Africaines* 27 (1987): 329–57.

Lorents, Yngve Samuel. *Mau Mau.* Stockholm: Utrikespolitiska Institutets, 1954.

Maina, Paul. *Six Mau Mau Generals.* Nairobi: Gazelle Books, 1972.

Majdalany, Fred. *State of Emergency: The Full Story of Mau Mau*. London: Longman, 1966.

Maloba, Wunyabari O. *Mau Mau and Kenya: An Analysis of a Peasant Revolt*. Bloomington: Indiana University Press, 1993.

————. "Media and Mau Mau: Kenyan Nationalism and Colonial Propaganda." In *Africa's Media Image*, edited by Beverly G. Hawk. New York: Praeger, 1992.

Mathu, Mohamed. *The Urban Guerrilla*. Richmond, B.C.: LSM Information Center, 1974.

"Mau Mau after Twenty Years." *Race and Class* 24 (1983): 259–66.

"Mau Mau and the New Society." *Correspondence* (2 April 1955): 1–12.

Mazrui, Ali. "Ideology, Theory, and Revolution: Lessons from the Mau Mau of Kenya." *Monthly Review* 39 (4) (1987): 20–30.

Mbabu, Elishu. *From Home Guards to Mau Mau*. Nairobi: EAEP, 1996.

Medjigbodo, Nicole. "Dedan Kimathi: Héros de la Lutte de Liberation Kenyanne." *Presence Africaine* 111 (1979): 70–79.

Middleton, John. *Les Kikouyou et les Kamba du Kenia: Étude Scientifique sur les Mau Mau*. Paris: Payoy, 1954.

Millner, Ralph. *Right to Live*. London: Kenya Committee, 1955.

Mitchell, Sir Philip. "Mau Mau." In *Africa Today*, edited by Charles Grove Harris, 485–93. Baltimore: Johns Hopkins University Press, 1955.

————. "Report on Mau Mau." *New Statesman and Nation* (28 May 1955): 739–40.

Monfried, Henry de. *Sous le Masque Mau Mau*. Paris: Bernard Grasset, 1956.

Mukenge, Muadi. "Sensationalism at Work: Creating the Myth of the Mau Mau." *Ufahamu* 21 (1/2) (1993): 14–26.

Muriithi, Kiboi. *War in the Forest*. Nairobi: EAPH, 1971.

Muroria, Henry. *I, The Gikuyu and the White Fury*. Nairobi: EAEP, 1994.

Murra, John V. "Kenya and the Emergency." *CH* 30 (177) (1956): 279–84.

National Council of Civil Liberties. *Civil Liberties in Kenya: A Memorandum*. London: National Council for Civil Liberties, 1953.

Neubauer, Carol E. "One Voice Speaking for Many: The Mau Mau Movement and Kenyan Autobiography." *JMAS* 21 (1) (1983): 113–31.

Newsinger, John. "Counter-Insurgency Tale: Kitson in Kenya." *Race and Class* 31 (4) (1990): 61–72.

————. "Mau Mau—30 Years Later." *Monthly Review* 37 (1) (1985): 12–21.

————. "Minimum Force, British Counter-Insurgency and the Mau Mau Rebellion." *Small Wars and Insurgencies* 1 (1992): 47–57.

————. "Revolt and Repression in Kenya: The 'Mau Mau' Rebellion, 1952–1960." *Science and Society* 45 (2) (1981): 159–85.

Ng'ang'a, D. Mukaru. "Mau Mau: Loyalists and Politics in Murang'a 1952–1970." *KHR* 5 (2) (1977): 365–84.

Ngunjiri, Ngari wa Ndirangu. "Role of the Gikuyu Land Grievance in the Outbreak of Mau Mau." Ph.D. diss., St. John's University, 1984.

Njagi, David. *Last Mau Mau Field Generals: Kenya's Freedom War 1952–63 and Beyond: Their Own Story*. Meru, Kenya: Ngwataniro Self Help Group, 1993.

Ogot, Bethwell. "Politics, Culture and Music in Central Kenya: A Study of Mau Mau Hymns, 1951–1956." *KHR* 5 (2) (1977): 275–86.

Omosule, Monone. "Kiama kia Muingi: Kikuyu Reaction to Land Consolidation in Kenya, 1955–59." *TJH* 4 (1/2) (1974): 115–34.

Osmunson, Rosemarie. *Njoki and Mau Mau Terror.* Nashville, TN: Southern Publishing Association, 1959.

Padmore, George. "Behind the Mau Mau." *Phylon* 14 (4) (1953): 355–72.

Pavlis, Paul A. "Maasai and the Mau Mau Movement: Avenues for Future Research." *KHR* 5 (2) (1977): 253–73.

Perkins, Robert C. "Independence for Kenya: A Study in the Development of British Colonial Policy, 1955–1963." Ph.D. diss., University of South Carolina, 1968.

Peverett, Allan. *Death Stalks in Kenya.* Ilfracombe, UK: Arthur H. Stockwell, 1957.

Phillips, Kenneth Norman. *From Mau Mau to Christ.* London: Stirling Tract Enterprise, 1958.

Pirouet, M. Louise. "Armed Resistance and Counter-Insurgency: Reflections in the Anya Nya and Mau Mau Experience." *Journal of Asian and African Studies* 11 (1/4) (1977): 197–214.

Presley, Cora Ann. "Kikuyu Women in the Mau Mau Rebellion." In *In Resistance: Studies in African, Caribbean, and Afro-American History*, edited by Gary Y. Okihiro, 54–69. Amherst: University of Massachusetts Press, 1986.

———. *Kikuyu Women: The Mau Mau Rebellion and Social Change in Kenya.* Boulder, CO: Westview Press, 1992.

———. "Mau Mau Rebellion, Kikuyu Women and Social Change." *CJAS* 22 (3) (1988): 502–27.

Prunier, Gérard A. "Mythes et Histoire; Les Interprétations du Mouvement Mau Mau de 1952 à 1986." *Review Française d'Histoire d'Outre-Mer* 74 (277) (1987): 401–29.

Rawcliffe, Donovan Hilton. *Struggle for Kenya.* London: Victor Gollancz, 1954.

Retif, Andre. "Retroactes Juridiques et Économiques du Mouvement Mau Mau." *La Vie Économiques et Sociale* 1/2 (1954): 78–83.

Rosberg, Carl G., and John Nottingham. *Myth of 'Mau Mau': Nationalism in Kenya.* New York: Praeger, 1966.

Rosenstiel, Annette. "Anthropological Approach to the Mau Mau Problem." *Political Science Quarterly* 68 (3) (1953): 419–32.

Sabar-Friedman, G. "The Mau Mau Myth: Kenyan Political Discourse in Search of Democracy." *Cahiers d'Études Africaines* 35 (1995): 101–32.

Santilli, Kathy. "Kikuyu Women in the Mau Mau: A Closer Look." *Ufahamu* 8 (1) (1977/1978): 143–59.

Santoru, Marina E. "The Colonial Idea of Women and Direct Intervention: The Mau Mau Case." *AA* 95 (379) (1996): 253–67.

———. "Nuove Tendenze Storiografiche nell'Interpretazione del Movimento Mau-Mau." *Africa* 44 (2) (1989): 256–62.

———. "Politica Coloniale e Repressione in Kenya: Il Caso del Movimento Mau Mau." *Storia Contemporanea* 25 (1) (1994): 83–101.

————. "La Visione Coloniale del Nazionalismo Kikuyu: Il Movimento Mau Mau." *Africa* 48 (4) (1993): 528–48.

Schutte, A. G. "Mau-Mau: The Cognitive Restructuring of Socio-Political Action." *African Studies* 32 (4) (1973): 215–27.

Shannon, Mary I. "Rebuilding the Social Life of the Kikuyu." *AA* 56 (225) (1957): 276–84.

————. "Rehabilitating the Kikuyu." *AA* 54 (215) (1955): 129–37.

Slane, P. M. "Tactical Problems in Kenya." *Army Quarterly* (1954): 45–52.

Spencer, John. *James Beauttah: Freedom Fighter.* Nairobi: Stellascope Publishing, 1983.

————. "KAU and 'Mau Mau': Some Connections." *KHR* 5 (2) (1977): 201–24.

Stanner, W. E. H. "Kenya and Mau Mau." *Australian Outlook* 7 (2) (1953): 92–106.

Stichter, S. B. "Workers, Trade Unions, and the Mau Mau Rebellion." *CJAS* 9 (2) (1975): 259–75.

Stoneham, Charles Thurley. *Mau Mau.* London: Museum Press, 1953.

————. *Out of Barbarism.* London: Museum Press, 1955.

Sykes, John P. *Slaves Uprooted and the Mau Mau Massacre.* Hicksville, NY: Exposition Press, 1978.

Tamarkin, Mordechai. "Failure in the British Colonial Counter-Revolution to Mau Mau: The Case of Moderate African Politics in Nakuru." *Asian and African Studies* 18 (3) (1984): 231–47.

————. "Loyalists in Nakuru during the Mau Mau Revolt and Its Aftermath, 1953–1963." *Asian and African Studies* 12 (2) (1978): 247–61.

————. "Mau Mau in Nakuru." *JAH* 17 (1) (1976): 119–34.

Thiong'o, Ngugi wa. "Mau Mau Is Coming Back: The Revolutionary Significance of 20th October 1952 in Kenya Today." *Journal of African Marxists* 4 (1983): 18–44.

————, and Micere Githae Mugo. *Trial of Dedan Kimathi.* London: Heinemann, 1976.

Three African Officers. "Mau Mau into Citizens." *Corona* (8) 5 (1956): 170–72.

Throup, David W. *Economic and Social Origins of Mau Mau, 1945–53.* Athens, OH: Ohio University Press, 1988.

————. "Origins of Mau Mau." *AA* 84 (336) (1985): 399–434.

Ulin, R. C. "Peasant Politics and Secret Societies: The Discourse of Secrecy." *Anthropological Quarterly* 59 (1) (1986): 28–39.

Venys, Ladislaw. *History of the Mau Mau Movement in Kenya.* Prague: Studia Orientalia Pragensia, Charles University, 1970.

Wachanga, Henry Kahinga. *Swords of Kirinyaga: The Fight for Land and Freedom.* Nairobi: EAPH, 1975.

Wachira, G. *Ordeal in the Forest.* Nairobi: EAPH, 1968.

Wamweya, Joram. *Freedom Fighter.* Nairobi: EAPH, 1971.

Wanjau, Gakaara wa. *Mau Mau Author in Detention: An Author's Detention Diary.* Nairobi: EAEP, 1988.

Watene, Kenneth. *Dedan Kimathi*. Nairobi: Transafrica, 1974.
———. *My Son for My Freedom*. Nairobi: Transafrica, 1973.
Waters, Alan Rufus. "Cost of Air Support in Counter-Insurgency Operations: The Case of the Mau Mau in Kenya." *Military Affairs* 37 (3) (1973): 96–100.
Welbourn, F. B. "Comment on Corfield." *Race* 2 (2) (1961): 7–27.
Whately, Monica. "Real Terrorists in Kenya." *Labour Monthly* (1954): 38–41.
Whittlesey, Derwent. "Kenya, the Land and Mau Mau." *Foreign Affairs* 32 (1) (1953): 80–90.
Wilkinson, John. "The Mau Mau Movement: Some Central and Medical Prospects." *EAMJ* 31 (7) (1954): 295–314.
Wills, Colin. *Who Killed Kenya?* London: Dobson, 1953.
Wilson, Christopher J. *Kenya's Warning: The Challenge to White Supremacy in Our British Colony*. Nairobi: The English Press, 1954.
Wiseman, Edith Martin. *Kikuyu Martyrs*. London: The Highway Press, 1958.
Wiste, Michel. "La Revolte des Mau-Mau au Kenya." *Problemes d'Afrique Centrale* 21 (1953): 190–99.
World Federation of Trade Unions. *Terror in Kenya: The Facts Behind the Present Crisis*. London: W. F. T. U. Publications Ltd., 1952.
Wyatt, E. G. "Mau Mau and the African World." *Contemporary Review* 184 (1953): 206–11.
Yankwich, Richard. "Continuity in Kenya History: Negative Unity and the Legitimacy of the Mau Mau Rebellion." *KHR* 5 (2) (1977): 349–63.

S. MEDICINE, HEALTH, AND SOCIAL SERVICES

Abilla, W. D. "Alternatives and Additional Medical and Sociological Control Measures to Malaria Prevention in Rural and Urban Kenya." *Medicus* 12 (3) (1993): 83–84.
Adams, Elizabeth J., et al. "Physical Activity and Growth of Kenyan School Children with Hookworm, Trichuris Trichiura and Ascaris Lumbricoides Infections Are Improved after Treatment with Albendazole." *Journal of Nutrition* 8 (1994): 1199–1206.
AIDS in Kenya: Socioeconomic Impact and Policy Implications. Nairobi: USAID; Arlington, VA: Aidscap/Family Health International, 1996.
Airey, Tony. "Impact of Road Construction on Hospital In-Patient Catchments in the Meru District of Kenya." *SSM* 29 (1) (1989): 95–106.
———. "Impact of Road Construction on the Spatial Characteristics of Hospital Utilisation in the Meru District of Kenya." *SSM* 32 (1992): 1135–146.
———. "Influence of Road Construction on the Health Care Behaviour of Rural Households in the Meru District of Kenya." *Transport Review* 11 (3) (1991): 273–91.
Ajode, K., et al. *Maintaining Health: An Evaluation/In-Depth Review of the Maintenance Project for Rural Health Facilities in Kenya*. Stockholm: SIDA, 1992.

Alger, Bernard Carl. "Rural Health Services in Kenya Since 1946: Implications of a Development Perspective." Ph.D. diss., University of Iowa, 1973.

Ambler, Charles H. "Drunks, Brewers, and Chiefs: Alcohol Regulation in Colonial Kenya, 1900–1939." In *Drinking: Behavior and Belief in Modern History*, edited by Susanna Barrows and Robin Room, 165–83. Berkeley and Los Angeles: University of California Press, 1991.

Amnesty International. *Kenya: Torture, Compounded by the Denial of Medical Care*. New York: AI, 1995.

Amuyunzu, M. K. "Management of Illness in a Plural Health Care Setting: A Case Study of the Duruma of Coastal Kenya." Ph.D. diss., Cambridge University, 1994.

Anderson, David L. "Intra-Programme Resource Allocation: The Case of Hospitals in Kenya." In *Planning African Development*, edited by Glen Norcliffe and Tom Pinfold, 129–47. Boulder, CO: WP, 1981.

————. "Statistical Cost Function Study of Public General Hospitals in Kenya." *JDA* 14 (2) (1980): 223–35.

Anker, Richard, and James C. Knowles. *Fertility Determinants in Developing Countries: A Case Study of Kenya*. Liege, Belgium: Ordina, 1982.

Barnett, T., and P. Blaikie. *Simple Methods for Monitoring the Socio-Economic Impact of AIDS: Lessons from Research in Uganda and Kenya*. Norwich, UK: University of East Anglia, School of Development Studies, 1992.

Beck, Ann. "East African Community and Regional Research in Science and Medicine." *AA* 72 (288) (1973): 300–8.

————. *History of the British Medical Administration of East Africa, 1900–1950*. Cambridge, MA: Harvard University Press, 1970.

————. "Medical Administration and Medical Research in Developing Countries: Remarks of Their History in Colonial East Africa." *Bulletin of the History of Medicine* 46 (4) (1972): 349–58.

————. *Medicine, Tradition, and Development in Kenya and Tanzania, 1920–1970*. Waltham, MA: Crossroads Press, 1981.

————. "Problems of British Medical Administration in East Africa between 1900 and 1930." *Bulletin of the History of Medicine* 36 (3) (1962): 275–83.

Beckerleg, S. "Medical Pluralism and Islam in Swahili Communities in Kenya." *Medical Anthropology Quarterly* 8 (3) (1994): 299–313.

Bennet, F. J., S. A. Hall, J. S. Lutwama, and E. R. Rado. "Medical Manpower in East Africa: Prospects and Problems." *EAMJ* 42 (4) (1965): 149–61.

Bollom G., et al. *Expenditure and Financing of the Health Sector in Kenya: Abridged Report of a Study Performed for the Ministry of Health and the World Bank*. Brighton, UK: IDS, 1993.

Bowman, Martin. "Kenya's Flying Doctors." *Air Progress* (9) (1993): 52–55.

Brainard, J. M. *Health and Development in a Rural Kenyan Community*. New York: Land, 1991.

Carman, John Ambrose. *Medical History of the Colony and Protectorate of Kenya: A Personal Memoir*. London: Rex Collings, 1976.

Chaiken, Miriam S. "Anthropology, Nutrition, and the Design of a Health Intervention Program in Kenya." In *Anthropology of Development and Change in East Africa*, edited by Peter Little and David Brokensha, 237–54. Boulder: WP, 1988.

Christie, James. *Cholera Epidemics in East Africa*. London: Macmillan and Company, 1876.

Currie, Kate, and Larry Ray. "Going up in Smoke: The Case of British American Tobacco in Kenya." *SSM* 19 (11) (1984): 1131–39.

Dahlgren, G. "Strategies for Health Financing in Kenya: The Difficult Birth of a New Policy." *Scandinavian Journal of Social Medicine* 46 (1991): 67–81.

Davies, J. N. P. "James Christie and the Cholera Epidemics of East Africa." *EAMJ* 36 (1) (1959): 1–6.

Dawson, Marc H. "The 1920s Anti-Yaws Campaigns and Colonial Medical Policy in Kenya." *IJAHS* 20 (3) (1987): 417–35.

Dean, Nicola R. "Community Study of Child Spacing, Fertility and Contraception in West Pokot District, Kenya." *SSM* (1994): 1575–84.

DeBoer, Cornelis N. and Malcolm McNeil. "Hospital Outreach Community-Based Health Care: The Case of Chogoria, Kenya." *SSM* 28 (10) (1989): 1007–17.

Deolalikar, A. B. "Child Nutritional Status and Child Growth in Kenya: Socio-Economic Determinants." *Journal of International Development* 8 (3) (1996): 375–93.

Dhadphale, Manohar, Graham Cooper and Lesley Cartwright-Taylor. "Prevalence and Presentation of Depressive Illness in a Primary Health Care Setting in Kenya." *American Journal of Psychiatry* 146 (5) (1989): 659–61.

Echessah, P. N., et al. "Willingness to Contribute Labor and Money to Tsetse Control: Application of Contingent Valuation in Busia District, Kenya." *WD* 25 (2) (1997): 239–53.

Esamai, F., and G. M. Buku. "HIV Seropositivity in Children Admitted with Diarrhea at Eldoret District Hospital, Kenya." *EAMJ* 71 (10) (1994): 631–34.

Ethangatta, L. K., M. I. Gee, and Z. J. Hawrysh. "Protein-Energy Malnutrition in Low Income Elderly Nairobi Women." *International Journal of Food Sciences and Nutrition* 47 (2) (1996): 147–57.

Fendall, N. R. E. "Health Centres in Kenya." *EAMJ* 37 (3) (1960): 171–236.

Ferguson, Alan G. "Fertility and Contraceptive Adoption and Discontinuation in Rural Kenya." *Studies in Family Planning* 4 (1992): 257–67.

————. "Women's Health in a Marginal Area of Kenya." *SSM* 23 (1) (1986): 269–76.

Ford, J. *Role of Trypanosomiases in African History*. Oxford: The Clarendon Press, 1971.

Fortin, Alfred J. "Politics of AIDS in Kenya." *Third World Quarterly* 9 (3) (1987): 906–19.

Garland, M., et al. "Knowledge of AIDS and Other Sexually Transmitted Diseases among Women Attending a Family-Planning Clinic in Nairobi, Kenya." *American Journal of Preventive Medicine* 9 (1) (1993): 1–5.

Gikaru, J. "Tragedy of AIDS Orphans." *Echo* (October 1991): 26–30, 32–34.

Good, Charles. *Ethnomedical Systems in Africa: Patterns of Traditional Medicine in Rural and Urban Kenya.* New York: Guilford, 1987.

Gregory, J. R. *Under the African Sun: A Memoir of Dr. R. W. Burkitt of Kenya.* Nairobi: Colourprint Ltd., 1977.

Gyepi-Garbrah, Benjamin. *Adolescent Fertility in Kenya.* Boston: Pathfinder Fund, 1985.

Haq, M. A., and A. Haq. "Pressure Therapy in Treatment of Hypertrophic Scar, Burn Contracture, and Keloid: The Kenyan Experience." *EAMJ* 67 (11) (1990): 785–94.

Hanjari, G. B. "Health Services for Kilifi District in Kenya." Ph.D. diss., University of London: 1977.

Harthoorn, A. M. *Flying Syringe.* London: Geoffrey Bles, 1970.

Hartwig, Gerald Walter. "Economic Consequences of Long-Distance Trade in East Africa: The Disease Factor." *ASR* 18 (2) (1975): 63–73.

Hawken, Mark, et al. "Increased Recurrence of Tuberculosis in HIV-1 Infected Patients in Kenya." *Lancet* (7 August 1993): 332–37.

Hoorweg, Jan C., and Rudo Niemeijer. *Impact of Nutrition Education at Three Health Centres in Central Province, Kenya.* Leiden: African Studies Center, 1980.

Hornsby, V. P. L. "An Experience in Family Planning in Nairobi." *EAMJ* 49 (10) (1972): 714–24.

Huber, Joyce H. "Ensuring Access to Health Care with the Introduction of User Fees: A Kenyan Example." *SSM* (1993): 485–94.

Imperato, Pascal James. "Early Modern Medical Services at Marsabit, Kenya." *EAMJ* 58 (1) (1981): 769–76.

Jacobson, Mark L., Miriam H. Labbok, et al. "Case Study of the Tenwek Hospital Community Health Programme in Kenya." *SSM* 28 (10) (1989): 1059–62.

James, A. E. "The National Teaching Hospital of the University of Nairobi School of Medicine." *Journal of the Royal Society of Health* 105 (5) (1985): 160–62.

Janovsky, Gerlinde Katarina. "Planning as Organizational Transaction and bargaining: The Case of Health in Kenya." Ed.D. diss., Harvard University, 1979.

Johnson, K. E., et al. "Community Based Health Care in Kibwezi, Kenya: 10 Years in Retrospect." *SSM* 28 (10) (1989): 1039–51.

Johnson, M. "AIDS and the Implications for Life Assurance in East Africa. *Kenya Underwriter* 18 (1990): 11–13, 16.

Kaendi, J. Munguti. "Coping with Malaria and Visceral Leishmaniasis (Kala-Azar) in Baringo District, Kenya: Implications for Disease Control." Ph.D. diss., University of California, Los Angeles, 1994.

Kaimenyi, J. T., and F. L. Ndung'u. "Knowledge, Practices and Attitudes towards HIV Positive and AIDS Patients Among Dental Auxiliaries." *EAMJ* 71 (5) (1994): 304–10.

Karechio, Boniface. *Drug Abuse in Kenya.* Nairobi: Uzima Press, 1994.

Kaseje, Dan C. Owino, and Ester K. N. Sempebwa. "Integrated Rural Health Project in Saradidi, Kenya." *SSM* 28 (10) (1989): 1063–71.

Katisivo, M. N., and L. N. Muthami, "Social Characteristics and Sexual Behaviour of Women at High Risk of HIV." *EAMJ* 68 (1) (1991): 34–38.

Katz, Sydney, and Selig Katz. "Evolving Role of Traditional Medicine in Kenya." *African Urban Studies* 9 (1981): 1–12.

"Kemron Comes to Market." *Industrial Review* 24 (1990): 30–31.

Khaemba, B. M., A. Mutani, and M. K. Bett. "Studies of Anopheline Mosquitoes Transmitting Malaria in a Newly Developed Highland Urban Area: A Case Study of Moi University and its Environs." *EAMJ* 71 (3) (1994): 159–64.

Kiarie, J. N., et al. "Acceptability of Prenatal Screening for HIV." *Medicus* 13 (1) (1994): 3–6.

Kibwana, K. "HIV/AIDS and the Law in Kenya: Preliminary Observations." *Eastern Africa Law Review* 1 (1991): 1–45.

Klauss, V., and H. A. Adale. "Traditional Herbal Eye Medicine in Kenya." *World Health Forum* 15 (2) (1994): 138–43.

K'Okul, R. N. O. *Maternal and Child Health in Kenya.* Uppsala, Sweden: SIAS, 1992.

Kokwaro, J. O. *Medicinal Plants in East Africa.* Nairobi: EALB, 1976.

Kreiss, Joan, et al. "Efficacy of Nonoxynol 9 Contraceptive Sponge Use in Preventing Heterosexual Acquisition of HIV in Nairobi Prostitutes." *Journal of the American Medical Association* (22 July 1992): 477–82.

Kwasa, T. O., et al. "Behavioural Mechanisms in AIDS Patients Under Stress." *EAMJ* 70 (1) (1993): 43–45.

Lackritz, Eve M., et al. "Effect of Blood Transfusion on Survival among Children in a Kenyan Hospital." *Lancet* (29 August 1992): 524–28.

Lamba, N. "Forgotten Half: Environmental Health in Nairobi's Poverty Area." *Environment and Urbanisation* 6 (1) (1994): 164–73.

Lanegran, K., and Goren Hyden. "Mapping the Politics of AIDS: Illustrations From East Africa." *Population and Environment* (3) (1993): 245–63.

Lema, Valentino M. *Knowledge, Attitudes, and Practices Related to AIDS and HIV Infection among Adolescents in Kenya.* Nairobi: Centre for the Study of Adolescence, 1992.

———, and M. A. Hassan. "Knowledge of Sexually Transmitted Diseases, HIV Infection and AIDS among Sexually Active Adolescents in Nairobi, Kenya and Its Relationship to Their Sexual Behaviour and Contraception." *EAMJ* 71 (2) (1994): 122–28.

Luijk, J. N. van. *Utilization of Modern and Traditional Medical Care by the Kamba of Machakos, Kenya.* Amsterdam: Royal Tropical Institute, 1983.

Mang'ombe, J. K., and G. M. Mwabu. "Agricultural Land Use Patterns and Malaria Conditions in Kenya." *SSM* (1993): 1121–30.

Mbai, Crispine V. "Implementation and Management of Health Care Programmes in Kenya: The Case of the Expanded Programme on Immunization." Ph.D. diss., University of Toronto, 1992.

Mburu, Francis Mwichigi. "Health Behavior in Kenya: A Comparative Multivariate Analysis of Factors Associated with Child Health in Rural Communities." Ph.D. diss., University of Mississippi, 1976.

Miller, Norman N. *Traditional Medicine in East Africa.* Hanover, NH: American Universities Field Staff Reports, 1980.

Milne, A. D. "Rise of a Colonial Medical Service." *Kenya and East African Medical Journal* 5 (1928): 50–58.

Moses, Stephen, et al. "Impact of User Fees on Attendance at a Referral Centre for Sexually Transmitted Diseases in Kenya." *Lancet* (22 August 1992): 463–66.

————. "Sexual Behaviour in Kenya: Implications for Sexually Transmitted Disease Transmission and Control." *SSM* (1994): 1649–56.

Mosley, Wiley Henry. *Dynamics of Birth Spacing and Martial Fertility in Kenya.* London: World Fertility Survey, 1982.

Mott, Frank. *Infant Mortality in Kenya: Evidence from the Kenya Fertility Survey.* London: World Fertility Survey, 1982.

Muhangi, J. *Psychiatry in Kenya: New Horizons in Medical Care.* Nairobi: University of Nairobi, 1980.

Mulindi, S. A. Z. "Health Education Strategies on AIDS." *Wajibu* 2 (1991): 4–6.

————. "Strategies for HIV Infection Prevention in a Developing Country: Case Example of Kenya." *Scandinavian Journal of Development Alternatives* 11 (1) (1992): 53–62.

Mutema, Alfred A. "Interorganizational Linkages and the Effectiveness of Clinical Practice in Two Allied Health Professions in Kenya." Ph.D. diss., University of Alberta, 1981.

Mutero, C. M., et al. "Visceral Leishmaniasis and Malaria Prevalence in West Pokot District, Kenya." *EAMJ* 69 (1) (1992): 3–8.

Mwabu, Germano M. "The Effect of Ownership of Health Care Systems on Distribution and Quality of Health Services." *EAER* 2 (1) (1986): 77–84.

————. "Health Care Decisions at the Household Level: Results of a Rural Health Survey in Kenya." *SSM* 22 (3) (1986): 315–19.

————. "Nonmonetary Factors in the Household Choice of Medical Facilities." *Economic Development and Cultural Change* 37 (2) (1989): 383–92.

————, Martha Ainsworth, and Andrew Nyamete. "Quality of Medical Care and Choice of Medical Treatment in Kenya: An Empirical Analysis." *Journal of Human Resources* 28 (4) (1993): 838–62.

Mwangi, W. M., and G. M. Mwabu. "Economics of Health and Nutrition in Kenya." *SSM* 22 (7) (1986): 775–80.

Mwenesi, Halima, Trudy Harpham, and Robert W. Snow. "Child Malaria Treatment Practices Among Mothers in Kenya." *SSM* (1995): 1271–77.

Nathan, Martha A. "Sedentism and Child Health Among Rendille Pastoralists of Northern Kenya." *SSM* (1996): 503–15.

Ndege, George Oduor. "Disease and Socio-economic change in the Politics of Colonial Health Care in Western Kenya, 1895–1939." Ph.D. diss., West Virginia University, 1996.

Ndirangu, S. *History of Nursing in Kenya*. Nairobi: KLB, 1982.

Njenga, F. G. "AIDS, the Doctor and the Lawyer." *Medicus* 11 (6) (1992): 11–13.

Njogu, W. "Trends and Determinants of Contraceptive Use in Kenya." *Demography* 28 (1) (1991): 83–99.

Nordberg, E., et al. "Rapid Assessment of an African District Health System: Test of a Planning Tool." *International Journal of Health Planning and Management* 8 (3) (1993): 219–33.

Nzyuko, S., et al. "AIDS and Condoms: Some Notes on the 'Invisible Disease.'" *African Urban Quarterly* 6 (1/2) (1991): 59–73.

Oduol, Elly. "Alcohol Use and Abuse: Strategies for Prevention-Some Experiences in Kenya." *Contemporary Drug Problems* 1 (1989): 95–104.

Ojwang, A. W., V. M. Lema, and S. H. M. Wanjala. "HIV Infection Among Patients with Acute Pelvic Inflammatory Disease at the Kenyatta National Hospital, Nairobi, Kenya." *EAMJ* 70 (8) (1993): 506–11.

Oloo, A. J., et al. "Sensitivity of Falciparum Malaria to Chloroquine and Amodiaquine in Four Districts of Western Kenya (1985–1987)." *EAMJ* 68 (8) (1991): 606–10.

Oranga, H. M., and E. Nordberg. "Delphi Panel Method for Generating Health Information." *Health Policy and Planning* 8 (4) (1993): 405–12.

Owino, P. "Kenyan Pharmaceutical Industry." M.A. thesis, University of Nairobi, 1985.

Oyugi, W. "Bureaucracy and the Management of Health Services in Kenya." In *Bureaucracy and Developmental Policies in the Third World*, edited by H. K. Asmerom, et al., 221–36. Amsterdam: University of Amsterdam Press, 1992.

Partnanen, Juha. *Sociability and Intoxication: Alcohol and Drinking in Kenya*. Helsinki: Finnish Foundation for Alcohol Studies, 1991.

Pattullo, A. L. S. "Survey of Knowledge, Behaviour and Attitudes Relating to HIV Infection and Institute of Development Studies Among Kenyan Secondary School Students." *Institute of Development Studies Care* 6 (2) (1994): 173–81.

Poweska, Halina. "Development of Medical Services in Kenya." *Africana Bulletin* 39 (1991): 97–108.

Raikes, Alanagh. *Pregnancy, Birthing and Family Planning in Kenya*. Copenhagen: Center for Development Research, 1990.

———. "Women's Health in East Africa." *SSM* 28 (5) (1989): 447–59.

Rathgeber, Eva M. "Cultural Production in Kenyan Medical Education." *Comparative Education Review* 29 (1985): 299–316.

Sindiga, Isaac. "The Persistence of High Fertility in Kenya." *SSM* 20 (1) (1985): 71–84.

———. "Sleeping Sickness in Kenya." *Erdkunde* 14 (1987): 133–45.

———. "Sleeping Sickness in Kenya Maasailand." *SSM* 18 (2) (1984): 183–87.

———, and M. Lukhando. "Kenya Universities Students' Views on AIDS." *EAMJ* 70 (11) (1993): 713–16.

Snow, Robert W., et al. "Factors Influencing Admission to Hospital During Terminal Childhood Illnesses in Kenya." *International Journal of Epidemiology* 23 (5) (1994): 1013–19.

Some, E. S. "Effects and Control of Highland Malaria Epidemic in Uasin Gishu District, Kenya." *EAMJ* 71 (1) (1994): 2–8.
Suda, Colette A. "Sex Behaviour, Cultural Practices and the Risk of HIV/AIDS in South Nyanza District, Kenya." *Kenya Journal of Sciences* (1993): 5–18.
Tyndall, M. W., et al. "Sexual Behaviour and Perceived Risks of AIDS among Men Attending a Clinic for Sexually Transmitted Diseases." *Clinical Infectious Diseases* 19 (3) (1994): 441–47.
Vogel, L. C., ed. *Health and Disease in Kenya (1900–1950).* Nairobi: EALB, 1974.
Waller, Richard D. "Tsetse Fly in Western Narok, Kenya." *JAH* 31 (1) (1990): 81–101.
Wang'ombe, J. K. "Economic Evaluation in Primary Health Care: The Case of Western Kenya Community Based Health Care Project." *SSM* 18 (5) (1984): 375–85.
Way, P. O., and K. Stanecki. "How Bad Will It Be: Modelling the AIDS Epidemic in Eastern Africa." *Population and Environment* 3 (1993): 265–78.
Wellde, et al. "History of Sleeping Sickness in Kenya." *Annals of Tropical Medicine and Parasitology* 83 (1) (1989): 1–11.
Westoff, C. F., and G. Rodriguez. "Mass Media and Family Planning in Kenya." *International Family Planning Perspectives* 21 (1) (1995): 26–31.
Willms, Dennis G. "Epistemological Relevances in Community-Based Health care Programmes in the Republic of Kenya." Ph.D. diss., University of British Columbia, 1983.
Wood, Michael. *Different Drums: A Doctor's Forty Years in Eastern Africa.* New York: Clarkson N. Potter, 1987.
———. *Go an Extra Mile: Adventures and Reflections of a Flying Doctor.* London: Collins, 1978.
Wynne, Barry. *Angels on Runway Zero 7: The Story of the East African Flying Doctor Service.* London: Souvenir Press, 1968.
Zeller, D.C. "Medicine in East Africa: The Introduction and Effects of Western Medicine on the Traditional Societies of Kenya and Uganda until 1938." Ph.D. diss., Columbia University, 1968.

T. LITERATURE AND LANGUAGE

Abdulaziz, M. H. *Muyaka: Nineteenth-Century Swahili Popular Poetry.* Nairobi: KLB, 1979.
Adagala, K., and W. Mukabi. *Kenyan Oral Literature.* Nairobi: Heinemann Kenya, 1987.
Allen, James de Vere. "Swahili Culture Reconsidered: Some Historical Implications of the Material Culture of the Northern Kenya Coast in the Eighteenth and Nineteenth Centuries." *Azania* (1974): 105–38.
Anoby, John. "Theological Reflections on the Novels of Ngugi wa Thiong'o." *East African Journal of Evangelical Theology* (1986): 16–21.

Awuyah, Christian K. "Aesthetics and Commitment: A Study of Ngugi wa Thiong'o's Novels." M.A. thesis, University of Guelph, 1984.

Balogun, F. Odun. "Ngugi's Devil on the Cross: The Novel as Hagiography of a Marxist." *Ufahamu* 17 (2) (1988): 76–92.

Barlow, A. R. *Studies in Kikuyu Grammar and Idiom.* Edinburgh: William Blackwood and Sons, 1951.

Barra, G., ed. *1,000 Kikuyu Proverbs.* Nairobi: KLB, 1960.

Bennett, P. R. "Grammar in the Lexicon: Two Bantu Cases [i.e. Swahili and Kikuyu]." *Journal of African Languages and Linguistics* 8 (1) (1986): 1–30.

Bertoncini, Elena Zubkova. *Outline of Swahili Literature: Prose Fiction and Drama.* Leiden, Netherlands: E.J. Brill, 1989.

Biersteker, A. "An Alternative East African Voice: The Wa-Nduuta Stories of Gakaara wa Wanjau." *Research in African Literatures* 22 (4) (1991): 63–78.

Binder, R., and G. W. Burnett. "Ngugi wa Thiong'o and the Search for a Populist Landscape Aesthetic." *Environmental Values* 3 (1) (1994): 47–59.

Björkman, I. *'Mother, Sing for Me': People's Theatre in Kenya.* London: Zed Books, 1989.

Bono, James Dennis. "Karen Blixen: Primitivist, Mystic, Nietzschean." Ph.D. diss., University of Kansas, 1978.

Buchanan, K. "The Gun and the School: Reflections on Ngugi wa Thiong'o's *Decolonising the Mind.*" *Race and Class* 30 (2) (1988): 61–69.

Chesaina, Ciarunji. *Oral Literature of the Kalenjin.* Nairobi: Heinemann Kenya, 1991.

————. *Oral Literature of Kenya.* Nairobi: Heinemann Kenya, 1991.

Conte, S. "Ngugi wa Thiong'o il Travaglio Intellettuale di uno Scrittore del Kenya." *Afriche* 23 (1994): 8–32.

Cook, David, and Michael Okenimpke, eds. *Ngugi wa Thiong'o: An Exploration of His Writings.* London: Heinemann, 1983.

Crehan, S. "The Politics of the Signifier: Ngugi wa Thiong'o's *Petals of Blood.*" *World Literature Written in English* 26 (1) (1986): 1–24.

Creider, C. A. *Syntax of the Nilotic Languages: Themes and Variations.* Berlin: Dietrich Reimer, 1989.

Duder, C. J. D. "Love and the Lions: The Image of White Settlement in Kenya in Popular Fiction 1919–39." *AA* 90 (360) (1991): 427–38.

Durrani, Shiraz. "Kiswahili Resistance Publishing at the Kenyan Coast." *Ufahamu* 17 (3) (1988): 26–34.

————. "The Other Kenya: Underground and Alternative Literature." *Collection Building* 16 (2) (1997): 80–87.

Eastman, Carol. "The Emergence of an African Regional Literature: Swahili." *ASR* 20 (2) (1977): 53–61.

Gecau, Kimani. "Popular Song and Social Change in Kenya." *Media, Culture and Society* 17 (4) (1995): 557–75.

Gecau, Rose. *Kikuyu Folktales.* Nairobi: EALB, 1970.

Gikandi, Simon. "On Culture and the State: The Writings of Ngugi wa Thiong'o." *Third World Quarterly* 11 (1) (1989): 148–56.

Glinga, W. "*The River Between* and Its Forerunners: A Contribution to the Theory of the Kenyan Novel." *World Literature Written in English* 26 (2) (1986): 211–28.

Gorman, Thomas Patrick, ed. *Glossary in English, Kiswahili, Kikuyu and Dholuo, etc.* London: Cassell, 1972.

Greenfield, Kathleen. "Self and Nation in Kenya: Charles Mangua's 'Son of Woman.'" *JMAS* 33 (4) (1995): 685–98.

Gugler, Josef. "How Ngugi wa Thiong'o Shifted from Class Analysis to a Neo-Colonialist Perspective." *JMAS* 32 (2) (1994): 329–39.

Haring, Lee. "Gusii Oral Texts." *IJAHS* 7 (1) (1974): 107–19.

Harmon, H. *Black Samson.* London: Hutchinson and Company Ltd., 1965.

———. *Tales Told Near a Crocodile: A Collection of Stories from Nyanza.* London: Hutchinson and Company Ltd., 1962.

Harries, Lyndon. *Poems from Kenya: Gnomic Verses in Swahili by Ahmed Nassir bin Juma Bhalo.* Madison: University of Wisconsin Press, 1966.

———. "Swahili Literature in the National Context." *Review of National Literature* 2 (2) (1971): 38–65.

———. *Swahili Poetry.* New York: OUP, 1962.

———, ed. *Swahili Prose Texts: A Selection from the Material Collected by Carl Velten from 1893 to 1896.* New York: OUP, 1965.

Heine, Bernd. *Non-Bantu Languages of Kenya.* Berlin: Dietrich Reimer, 1980.

———, and Wilhelm J. G. Möhlig, eds. *Language and Dialect Atlas of Kenya.* Berlin: Dietrich Reimer, 1980.

Hower, Edward. "Post-Independence Literature of Kenya and Uganda." *EAJ* 7 (11) (1970): 24–34.

Kabira, Wanjiku Mukabi, and Karega Mutahi. *Gikuyu Oral Literature.* Nairobi: Heinemann Kenya, 1988.

Kalugila, Leonard. *Swahili Proverbs from East Africa.* Uppsala, Sweden: SIAS, 1977.

———, and A. Lodhi. *More Swahili Proverbs from East Africa.* Uppsala, Sweden: SIAS, 1980.

Killam, G. D., ed. *Critical Perspectives on Ngugi wa Thiong'o.* Washington, D.C.: Three Continents Press, 1984.

Kipury, Naomi. *Oral Literature of the Maasai.* Nairobi: Heinemann, 1983.

Knappert, Jan. *Four Centuries of Swahili Verse: A Literary History and Anthology.* London: Heinemann Educational, 1979.

———. *Myths and Legends of the Swahili.* London: Heinemann, 1970.

———. *Proverbs from the Lamu Archipelago and the Central Kenya Coast.* Berlin: Dietrich Reimer, 1986.

———, trans. and ed. *Traditional Swahili Poetry.* Leiden: Brill, 1967.

Laitin, D., and Eastman, C. M. "Language Conflict: Transactions and Games in Kenya." *Cultural Anthropology* 4 (1) (1989): 51–72.

Lepine, Richard. "Swahili Fiction Serial from the Kenya Newspaper *Baraza.*" *Ba Shiru* 13 (1) (1987): 61–74.

————. "Swahili Newspaper Fiction in Kenya: The Stories of James L. Mwagojo." Ph.D. diss., University of Wisconsin, 1988.

Lindfors, Bernth. "East African Popular Literature in English." *Journal of Popular Culture* 1 (1979): 106–15.

Loflin, Christine. "Ngugi wa Thiong'o's Visions of Africa." *Research in African Literatures* 26 (4) (1995): 76–93.

Masilela, Ntongela. "Ngugi wa Thiongo's *Petals of Blood.*" *Ufahamu* 7 (2) (1979): 9–28.

Maughan-Brown, David. *Land, Freedom and Fiction: History and Ideology in Kenya.* London: Zed Press, 1985.

————. "Myths on the March: The Kenyan and Zimbabwean Liberation Struggles in Colonial Fiction." *Journal of Southern African Studies* (1982): 93–117.

Mazimhaka, Jolly R. "'The Heroines of Toil': Women and Struggle in the Novels of Ngugi wa Thiong'o." M.A. thesis, University of Saskatchewan, 1989.

Mazrui, Ali A., and Alamin M. Mazrui. *Swahili State and Society: The Political Economy of an African Language.* Nairobi: EAEP, 1995.

Mazrui, Ali, and L. Mphande. "Historical Imperative in African Activist Literature." *Ufahamu* 18 (2) (1990): 47–58.

Mbaabu, Ireri. *Proverbs, Idioms, and Poetry in Kimeru.* Nairobi: KLB, 1978.

Miruka, Simon Okumba. *Encounter with Oral Literature.* Nairobi: EAEP, 1994.

Moore, Gerald. "Language of Literature in East Africa." *Dalhousie Review* 4 (1973/1974): 688–700.

Mputubwele, Makim Mput-a-nkah. "Ngugi wa Thiong'o and Sembène Ousmane: The African Writer's Commitment to Society." Ph.D. diss., Purdue University, 1995.

Mutahi, E. K. *Sound Change and the Classification of the Dialects of Southern Mt. Kenya.* Berlin: Dietrich Reimer, 1983.

Muthwii, M. J. "Variability in Language Use: A Study of Kalenjin Speakers of English and Kiswahili in Kenya." Ph.D. diss., University of East Anglia, 1994.

Mwanzi, Helen. *Language Policy.* Nairobi: Bureau of Educational Research, Kenyatta University College, 1982.

Naipaul, Shiva. *North of South: An African Journey.* London: Deutsch, 1978.

Narang, H. "Politics of Protest: Subtext in the Novels of Meja Mwangi and Ngugi wa Thiong'o." *AQ* 34 (3) (1994): 242–56.

Nassir, Ahmad bin Jume Bhalo. *Poems from Kenya: Gnomic Verses in Swahili.* Madison and London: University of Wisconsin Press, 1966.

Neubauer, C. E. "Tradition and Change in Charity Waciuma's Autobiography *Daughter of Mumbi.*" *World Literature Written in English* 25 (2) (1985): 211–21.

Njururi, Ngumbu, ed. *Gikuyu Proverbs.* Nairobi: OUP, 1983.

Nurse, Derek. "Language and History on Mount Kilimanjaro, the Pare Mountains, and the Taita Hills." Ph.D. diss., University of Dar-es-Salaam, 1977.

Ochillo, Yvonne H. "*Weep Not Child* and the Need to Believe." *CLA Journal* (3) (1993): 270–79.

Ogot, Grace Emily Akinyi. *The Graduate*. Nairobi: Uzima Press, 1980.

—————. *Island of Tears*. Nairobi: Uzima Press, 1980.

—————. *Land without Thunder*. Nairobi: EAPH, 1968.

—————. *The Other Woman*. Nairobi: Transafrican Publishers, 1976.

—————. *The Promised Land*. Nairobi: EAPH, 1966.

—————. *Short Stories from Kenya*. Stockholm: Brevskolan, 1976.

Onyango-Ogutu, B., and A. A. Roscoe. *Keep My Words: Luo Oral Literature*. Nairobi: EAPH, 1974.

Opoku-Agymang, Naana J. "Milestones: Ngugi's Theory and Practice of Art." Ph.D. diss., York University, 1986.

Osa, Osayimwense. "Novels of Ngugi wa Thiong'o." M.A. thesis, University of New Brunswick, 1979.

Perera, Senath W. "Protest in the English Fiction of Kenya and India: The Novels of Raja Rao, Khushwant Singh, Ngugi wa Thiong'o and Meja Mwangi." M.A. thesis, University of New Brunswick, 1987.

Pugliese, Cristiana. "La Nascita di un Teatro Nazionale in Kenya." *Africa* 2 (1990): 325–35.

—————. "Organic Vernacular Intellectual in Kenya: Gakaara wa Wanjau." *Research in African Literatures* 25 (4) (1994): 177–87.

Ruark, Robert. *Something of Value*. Garden City, NY: Doubleday, 1953.

—————. *Uhuru*. Greenwich, CT: A Crescent Reprint, 1963.

Ruganda, John. "Alienation and Leadership Figures in the Plays of Francis Imbuga [Kenya]." Ph.D. diss., University of New Brunswick, 1990.

Russell, John. *Communicative Competence in a Minority Group: A Sociolinguistic Study of the Swahili-Speaking Community in the Old Town, Mombasa*. Leiden, Netherlands: E.J. Brill, 1981.

Ryanga, Shiela. "Imbalances in the Modernization and Promotion of the Swahili Language in East Africa: The Case of Kenya and Tanzania." *Ufahamu* 18 (3) (1990): 21–34.

Sickerman, Carol M. "Creativity and Political Repression: The Confusion of Fact and Fiction." *Race and Class* 37 (4) (1996): 61–71.

—————. "Ngugi wa Thiong'o and the Writing of Kenyan History." *Research in African Literatures* 20 (3) (1989): 347–70.

—————. "Ngugi's Colonial Education: 'The Subversion...of the African Mind.'" *ASR* 38 (3) (1995): 11–41.

Singh, P. K. "Resisting Neo-Colonialism: The Trial of Dedan Kimathi and I Will Marry When I Want." *AQ* 34 (3) (1994): 120–31.

Stafford, R. L. *An Elementary Luo Grammar with Vocabularies*. Nairobi: OUP, 1967.

Strommer, H. *Comparative Study of Three Southern Oromo Dialects in Kenya: Phonology, Morphology and Vocabulary*. Hamburg: Helmut Buske, 1987.

Thiongo, Ngugi wa. *Barrel of a Pen: Resistance to Repression in Neo-Colonial Kenya*. London: New Beacon Press, 1983.

————. *Black Hermit.* London: Heinemann, 1968.

————. *Decolonising the Mind: The Politics of Language in African Literature.* London: James Currey, 1986.

————. *Devil on the Cross.* London: Heinemann, 1987.

————. *Grain of Wheat.* London: Heinemann, 1968.

————. *Homecoming.* London: Heinemann, 1972.

————. *Matigari.* London: Heinemann, 1989.

————. "*Matigari* as Myth and History: An Interview." *Third World Quarterly* 11 (4) (1989): 241–51.

————. *Moving the Centre: The Struggle for Cultural Freedoms.* Nairobi: EAEP, 1993.

————. *Petals of Blood.* London: Heinemann, 1968.

————. *River Between.* London: Heinemann, 1965.

————. *Weep Not Child.* London: Heinemann, 1964.

————. "The Writer in a Neocolonial State." *Black Scholar* (1986): 2–10.

————. *Writers and Politics: Essays.* London: Heinemann, 1981.

————, and Ngugi wa Mirii. *I Will Marry When I Want.* London: Heinemann, 1982.

Toweett, Taaitta. *Study of Kalenjin Linguistics.* Nairobi: KLB, 1979.

Tucker, A. N., and J. Tompo Ole Mpaayei. *A Maasai Grammar with Vocabulary.* London: Longman, 1955.

Verma, C. "Women in Ngugi wa Thiong'o's Novels." *AQ* 34 (3) (1994): 194–204.

Vitale, Anthony J. "Kisetla: Linguistic and Sociolinguistic Aspects of a Pidgin Swahili of Kenya." *Anthropological Linguistics* 22 (2) (1980): 47–65.

Wamalwa, D. Salituma. "Engaged Artist: The Social Vision of Ngugi Wa Thiong'o." *AT* 33 (1) (1986): 9–18.

Wanjohi, Gerald Joseph. *The Wisdom and Philosophy of the Gikuyu Proverbs.* Nairobi: Paulines Publication, 1998.

Whiteley, Wilfred Howell, ed. *Language in Kenya.* Nairobi: OUP, 1974.

————. *Practical Introduction to Gusii.* Nairobi: EALB, 1956.

————, and M. G. Mulli. *Practical Introduction to Kamba.* London: OUP, 1962.

Wilkinson, Jane. "From 'Shore' to 'Stream': The Development of a Kenyan Novelist." *Africa* 44 (4) (1989): 551–90.

Zetterstein, A., ed. *East African Literature: An Anthology.* London: Longman, 1983.

U. COMMUNICATIONS, MEDIA, AND TRANSPORT

Abuoga, John Baptist, and Absalom Aggrey Mutere. *History of the Press in Kenya.* Nairobi: African Council on Communication Education, 1988.

Africa Watch. *Kenya: Once Again, a Critical Magazine Faces Threat of a Banning Order: The Nairobi Law Monthly and Its Editor Under Fire.* New York: Africa Watch, 1990.

————. *Kenya: Suppression of Press Freedom*. New York: Africa Watch, 1989.

Akahenda, Elijah F. "The Imperative of National Unity and the Concept of Press Freedom: The Case of East Africa." *Gazette* 31 (2) (1983): 89–98.

Akwule, Raymond U. "Telecommunications in Kenya: Development and Policy Issues." *Telecommunications Policy* 7 (1992): 603–11.

Alot, Magaga. *People and Communication in Kenya*. Nairobi: KLB, 1982.

Amin, Mohamed, Duncan Willets, and Alastair Matheson. *Railway Across the Equator: The Story of the East African Line*. London: Bodley Head, 1986.

Article 19. *Censorship in Kenya: Government Critics Face the Death Sentence*. London: Article 19, 1995.

————. *Kenya: Continued Attacks on the Independent Press*. London: Article 19, 1993.

————. *Kenya: Recent Threats to Freedom of Expression*. London: Article 19, 1992.

————. *Kenya: Shooting the Messenger*. London: Article 19, 1993.

Awuondo, C. O. "War Against the Free Press." *Finance* (31 March 1993): 46–47.

Baranson, Jack. "Kenya: Road Construction Equipment for Local Manufacture." *Ekistics* 43 (259) (1977): 369–72.

Beckenham, A. F. *Wagons of Smoke: An Informal History of the East African Railways and Harbours Administration, 1948–1961*. London: Cadogan Publications, 1987.

Bulman, W. E. "Development of Motive Power on the EAR&H Administration." *Journal of the East African Institution of Engineers* (1958): 82–93.

Carter, Felice. "Asian Press in Kenya." *EAJ* 6 (10) (1969): 30–34.

————. "Kenya Government and the Press, 1906–60." In *Hadith 2: Proceedings of the 1968 Conference of the Historical Association of Kenya, 1967*, edited by Bethwell A. Ogot, 245–59. Nairobi: EAPH, 1970.

————. "Press in Kenya." *Gazette* 14 (2) (1968): 85–88.

Chakava, H. "Decade of Publishing in Kenya, 1977–1987: One Man's Involvement." *African Book Publishing Record* 14 (4) (1988): 235–41.

————. "Private Enterprise Publishing in Kenya: A Long Struggle for Emancipation." *Logos* 4 (3) (1993): 130–35.

Charles, Rodney A. "Political Change and Mass Media Development: A Case Study of the *Trinidad Guardian*, the *Daily Gleaner*, and the *East African Standard*." M.J. thesis, Carleton University, 1977.

Chege, J. W. *Copyright Law and Publishing in Kenya*. Nairobi: KLB, 1978.

Committee to Protect Journalists. *Press Conditions in Kenya*. New York: Committee to Protect Journalists, 1991.

Dennis, L. G. "Bill." *Lake Steamers of East Africa*. Egham, UK: Runnymede Malthouse Publishing, 1996.

Fossard, Esta de. *Writing the Instructional Radioscript*. Washington, DC: Academy for Educational Development, 1982.

Gadsen, Fay. "African Press in Kenya, 1945–1952." *JAH* 21 (4) (1980): 515–35.

Gallay, Pierre. "The English Missionary Press of East and Central Africa." *Gazette* 14 (2) (1968): 129–33.

Gathu, Faith W. "Freedom of Expression in Kenya and USA: A Comparison." *Africa Media Review* 9 (3) (1995): 76–89.

George, Nancy A. "Using Radio for Community Mobilization: Experiences in Zimbabwe and Kenya." *Africa Media Review* 7 (2) (1993): 52–67.

Gikaru, L. "National Interest and the Media: Comparison of the Coverage of Kenyan Elections by the *New York Times* and the *Guardian*." *Africa Media Review* 8 (2) (1994): 27–37.

Githii, George. "Press Freedom in Kenya." In *Reporting Africa*, edited by Olav Stokke, 57–64. New York: Africana Publishing, 1971.

Hachten, William A. "Press in a One-Party State: Kenya Since Independence." *Journalism Quarterly* 42/43 (1965): 262–67.

Hamshere, C. E. "The Uganda Railway." *History Today* 28 (3) (1968): 188–95.

Hardy, Robert. *Iron Snake*. London: Collins, 1965.

Heath, Carla W. "Politics of Broadcasting in Kenya: The Case of the Homa Bay Community Radio Station." *African Studies Association Papers* 28 (52) (1985): 1–24.

———. "Private Sector Participation in Public Service Broadcasting: The Case of Kenya." *Journal of Communication* 38 (3) (1988): 96–107.

———. "Structural Changes in Kenya's Broadcasting System: A Manifestation of Presidential Authoritarianism." *Gazette* 50 (1) (1992): 37–51.

Hempstone, Smith. "The Dreams Will Be Realised." *Finance* (28 February 1995): 35–6.

Hill, M. *Permanent Way. Vol. I. The Story of the Kenya and Uganda Railway.* Nairobi: East African Railways and Harbours, 1950.

Hoyle, B. S. *Seaports and Development: The Experience of Kenya and Tanzania.* New York: Gordon and Breach, 1983.

———. "Transport and Economic Development in the Less-Developed Countries: Some Reflections on the Seaports of Kenya and Tanzania." *GeoJournal* 12 (3) (1986): 233–42.

Hughes, Anthony J. "Nairobi Press Notebook." *AR* 26 (5) (1981): 55–57.

Imanyara, G. "Mass Media and Campaign against Corruption." *NLM* 52 (1995): 36–7.

Imhoof, Maurice, Philip R. Christensen, and Kurt Hein. *English by Radio: Implications for Non-Formal Language Education*. East Lansing: Non-Formal Education Center, Michigan State University, 1984.

Jacobs, Francine. *Firesnake: The Railroad that Changed East Africa.* New York: William Morrow and Company, 1980.

Jennings, P. D. T. L. "British Mass Media Coverage of the Late Wars in Cyprus and Kenya in the 1950s." Ph.D. diss., University of Swansea, 1995.

Kabetesi, Kibisu. *Press Law, Information Technology and Freedom of the Press.* Nairobi: Centre for Law Research International, 1994.

———. *Press Law: Some Home Truth.* Nairobi: Centre for Law Research International, 1994.

Kapila, Sunita. *Matatu Mode of Public Transport in Metropolitan Nairobi.* Nairobi: Mazingira Institute, 1982.

Kareithi, Peter. "The Press in Kenya: Persecution and Perseverance." *Voices of the African Diaspora* 7 (3) (1991): 28–32.

Kenya: A Legal Magazine and Its Editor Under Attack—Again: Gitobu Imanyara and the Nairobi Law Monthly. New York: Lawyers Committee for Human Rights, 1991.

"Kenya: Back to Suppression, Corruption as Usual?" *NLM* 58 (1995): 10–12.

"Kenya's Record is Abhorrent." *Finance* (15 August 1993): 42–44.

Kovach, Bill. "Clampdown in Kenya." *Nieman Reports* 44 (4) (1990): 2, 26.

McCormack, R. L. "Imperialism, Air Transport and Colonial Development: Kenya, 1920–46." *JICH* 13 (3) (1989): 323–48.

Maja-Pearce, Adewale. "Press in East Africa." *Index on Censorship* 21 (7) (1992): 50–89.

Makoysi, Ruth, and Lily K. Nyariki. *Publishing and Book Trade in Kenya.* Nairobi: EAEP, 1997.

Marami, D. "Broadcasting in Kenya." In *Making Broadcasting Useful: The African Experience*, edited by G. Wendell, 187–91. Manchester, U.K.: Manchester University Press, 1986.

Marshal, J., and F. Swai. "President Moi Speaks Out on Democracy and Press Freedom." *Society* 2 (1991): 18–20.

Matson, A. T. "A Unique African Journalistic Achievement: Four Decades of 'Coast Causeries.'" *African Research and Documentation* 38 (1986): 31–34.

Maxon, Robert M. "African Production and the Support of European Settlement in Kenya: The Uasin Gishu-Mumias Railway Scheme." *JICH* 14 (1) (1985): 52–64.

"Memorandum Issued by 140 Unnamed 'Academics' to the Press." *NLM* 38 (1991): 27–8.

Miller, Charles. *Lunatic Express.* London: Macdonald, 1960.

M'inoti, Kathurima, and Wachira Maina. "The Press Council of Kenya Bill and the Kenya Mass Media Commission Bill: A Critical and Comparative Review." *NLM* 60 (1996): 15–48.

"Moi Terrorizes the Press." *Finance* (16–31 December 1991): 31–32.

Mutere, Absalom. "Analysis of Communications Policies in Kenya." *Africa Media Review* 3 (1) (1988): 46–63.

Mutula, J. N. "Of Section 70 and 79 of the Constitution of Kenya: A Case of Rape or Defilement." *NLM* 30 (1991): 41–43.

Mwangi, Mary W. "Gender Roles Portrayed in Kenyan Television Commercials." *Sex Roles: A Journal of Research* 34 (3/4) (1996): 205–14.

Mwaura, Peter. *Communications Policies in Kenya.* Paris: UNESCO, 1980.

Nalo, D. S. O. "Adequate Road Maintenance in Kenya: The Need for Appropriate Policies." *International Journal of Transport Economics* 20 (2) (1993): 221–37.

Nastoulas, Theodore. "Harold G. Robertson: An Editor's Reversal from Settler Critic to Settler Ally in Kenya, 1922–1923." *IJAHS* 5 (4) (1972): 610–28.

Ngugi, C., and W. A. Ngaira. "Law of Sedition in Kenya: A Denial of the Right to Information." *Wajibu* 4 (1993): 12–14.

Ng'weno, Hilary. "All Freedom Is at Stake." In *Third World and Press Freedom*, edited by Philip C. Horton, 127–34. New York: Praeger, 1978.

Njuchu, Ruth Rukunga. *Extent to Which Radio Is Used in Teaching of Home Science in Primary Schools in Kenya*. Nairobi: ACOP, 1981.

Njuru, L. D. "Organisation and Management of a Broadcasting Service." In *Making Broadcasting Useful: The African Experience*, edited by G. Wendell, 166–76. Manchester: University Press for the European Institute for the Media, 1986.

"No Respite." *Society* 7 (1992): 34–38.

Nottingham, John. "Establishing an African Publishing Industry: A Study in Decolonization." *AA* 68 (271) (1969): 139–44.

Obiero-On'gan'ga, O. *Evaluation of the Effectiveness of Radio Programmes in Teaching English Language to Class Six Pupils in Primary Schools in South Nyanza, Kenya*. Nairobi: ACOP, 1982.

Ochieng, Mark. "Kenya (with CNN) Unmuffles Its Press and TV." *Intermedia* 21 (4/5) (1993): 59–60.

Ochieng, Philip. *I Accuse the Press: An Insider's View of the Media and Politics in Africa*. Nairobi: Initiatives Publishers, 1992.

Ochilo, Polycarp J. Omolo. "Press Freedom and the Role of the Media in Kenya." *Africa Media Review* 7 (3) (1993): 19–33.

Ochola, A. "On Political Discourse and KANU's Oppression of Freedom of Expression: Need for Moral Change of Mind Journal." *NLM* 35 (1991): 23–24.

Ogonda, R. T. "Regionalisation of the Road Network Systems in Kenya." *Maseno Journal of Education, Arts and Science* 1 (1) (1992): 84–98.

Ogunade, Dele. "Mass Media Systems of Kenya and Tanzania: A Comparative Analysis." *Africa Media Review* 2 (1) (1986): 99–112.

Okoth-Owiro, A. "Law and the Mass Media in Kenya." *Africa Media Review* 4 (1) (1988): 15–26.

Omolo Ochilo, P. J. "Press Freedom and the Role of the Media in Kenya." *Africa Media Review* 7 (3) (1993): 19–33.

Onyango-Obbo, Charles. "East African Doors Unlocking—Except in Kenya." *Nieman Reports* 50 (1) (1996): 69–73.

Opiyo, Baruck A. "The Press and Kenyan Politics: A Study of Newsmaking in a Newly Democratic State." Iowa City: University of Iowa, 1994.

Otieno, S. "Press Censorship: A Contradiction of the Kenyan Constitution. *Kenya Jurist* 2 (1993): 19–21.

Patience, Kevin. *Steam in East Africa: A Pictorial History of the Railways in East Africa 1893–1976*. Nairobi: Heinemann, 1976.

Pugliese, C. "Kenyan Publishers in Vernacular Languages: Gikuyu, Kikamba and Dholuo." *Africa* 49 (2) (1994): 250–59.

Puri, Shamlal. "Editor Pays the Price of Honesty." *IPI Report* 9 (1992): 20–21.

Ramaer, R. *Steam Locomotives of the East African Railways*. London: David and Charles, 1974.

Roberts, John Storm. "Hilary Ng'weno, Publisher and Editor of the *Nairobi Times*." *AR* 23 (4) (1978): 22–24.

Rural Primary Schools Extension Project: Radio Language Arts. Implementation Plan. Washington, D.C.: Academy for Education Development, 1981.

Scotton, James F. "Kenya's Maligned African Press: Time for a Reassessment." *Journalism Quarterly* 52 (1) (1975): 30–36.

————. "The Press in Kenya a Decade after Independence: Pattern of Readership and Ownership." *Gazette* 21 (1) (1975): 19–33.

Sicherman, Carol. "Kenya: Creativity and Political Repression: The Confusion of Fact and Fiction." *Race and Class* 37 (4) (1996): 61–71.

Standa, Everett Maraka. "Systems Approach to Instructional Radio Broadcasting in the Kenya School System: A Model." Ph.D. diss., State University of New York at Buffalo, 1979.

Stein, M. L. "UNESCO Debate Muted in Nairobi." *Quill* 70 (1) (1982): 10–11.

"Trampling on Press Freedom." *Kenya Jurist* 2 (1993): 4–5.

"Tribulation of Kenyan Journalists." *Monthly News* (May 1992): 9–11.

Tyler, Michael, and C. Jonscher. *Telecommunications for Development: The Impact of Telecommunications on the Performance of a Sample of Business Enterprises in Kenya.* Geneva: International Telecommunications Union, 1983.

Ugboajah, Frank Okwu. "Media Habits of Rural and Semi-Rural (Slum) Kenya." *Gazette* 36 (3) (1985): 155–74.

Uzoigwe, G. N. "The Mombasa-Victoria Railway, 1890–1902: Imperial Necessity, Humanitarian Venture or Economic Imperialism." *KHR* 4 (1) (1976): 11–34.

Veen, J. J. de. *Rural Access Roads Programme: Appropriate Technology in Kenya.* Geneva: International Labour Office, 1980.

Wachira, C. "Government Crack-Down on the Press." *Kenya Jurist* 1 (1994): 7–8.

Wanyande, Peter. "Mass Media: State Relations in Post-Colonial Kenya." *Africa Media Review* 9 (3) (1995): 54–75.

"War on Magazines and Their Editors." *Finance* (April 1991): 20–21.

Whitehouse, B. "To the Victoria Nyanza by the Uganda Railway." *Scottish Geographical Magazine* 17 (4) (1902): 169–86.

Zaring, D. T. "Journalist Responses to Ethnic Tensions: A Study of the Press in Kenya." *Africa Media Review* 8 (1) (1994): 57–68.

V. URBAN CENTERS AND URBANIZATION STUDIES

"African Social Welfare in Nairobi." *AA* 49 (1950): 50–56.

Akinola, G. A. "The Mazrui of Mombasa." *Tarikh* 2 (3) (1968): 26–40.

Alikhan, Fatima. *Urbanization in the Third World: An African Experience.* Hyderabad, India: Booklinks, 1987.

Amis, Philip. "Squatters or Tenants: The Commercialization of Unauthorized Housing in Nairobi." *WD* 12 (1) (1984): 87–96.

Askwith, Tom. "Tribalism in Nairobi." *Corona* 2 (8) (1950): 292–96.

Banyikwa, W. F. "Signatures of Four Generations of Urban Planning in Nairobi, Kenya." *JEARD* 20 (1990): 186–201.

Berg, F. S. "Mombasa under the Busaidi Sultanate: The City and Its Hinterland in the 19th Century." Ph.D. diss., University of Wisconsin, 1971.

———. "The Swahili Community of Mombasa, 1500–1900." *JAH* 9 (1) (1968): 35–56.

Blij, Harm J. de. *Mombasa: An African City.* Evanston, IL: Northwestern University Press, 1968.

Boxer, C. R., and Carlos De Azevedo. *Fort Jesus and the Portuguese in Mombasa 1593–1729.* London: Hollis and Carter, 1960.

Brown, W. H. "History of Siu: The Development and Decline of a Swahili Town on the Northern Kenya Coast." Ph.D. diss., Indiana University, 1985.

Bubba, N., and D. Lamba. "Urban Management in Kenya." *Environment and Urbanization* 3 (1) (1991): 37–59.

Carlebach, Julius. *The Jews of Nairobi.* Nairobi: The Nairobi Hebrew Congregation, 1962.

———. *Juvenile Prostitutes in Nairobi.* Kampala, Uganda: East African Institute of Social Research, 1962.

Cassidy, G., and F. Renssen. "Urban Growth and Population Distribution in Kenya." *Journal of the Town Planning Institute* (5) (1970): 175–79.

Cooper, Frederick. *On the Waterfront: Urban Disorder and the Transformation of Work in Colonial Mombasa.* New Haven, CT and London: YUP, 1987.

Curtis, John W. *Opportunity and Obligation in Nairobi: Social Networks and Differentiation in the Political Economy of Kenya.* Münster and Hamburg, Germany: Lit-Verlag, 1995.

Despair and Hope in the Slums of Nairobi. Nairobi: Undugu Society of Kenya, 1980.

Deverell, N. M. "The African Child in an Urban Environment." *EAMJ* 31 (4) (1954): 175–79.

Duchhart, I. "Evaluation and Options for Improvement of the Environment in a Slum Upgrading Project in Nairobi, Kenya." *Landscape and Urban Planning* 18 (2) (1989): 153–74.

Dutto, Carl A. *Nyeri Townsmen, Kenya.* Nairobi: EALB, 1975.

Elkan, Walter. "Is a Proletariat Emerging in Nairobi?" *Economic Development and Cultural Change* 24 (4) (1976): 695–706.

Evans, Hugh Emrys. "National Development and Rural-Urban Policy: Past Experience and New Directions in Kenya." *Urban Studies* 26 (2) (1989): 253–66.

———. "Virtuous Circle Model of Rural-Urban Development: Evidence from a Kenyan Small Town and Its Hinterland." *Journal of Development Studies* 28 (4) (1992): 640–67.

Fair, Denis. "Kenya's Urbanization Policy." *Africa Insight* 16 (1) (1986): 33–35, 41.

Fair, T. J. D. "Urban Growth in Kenya." *Africa Insight* 13 (3) (1983): 183–89.

Ford Foundation. *Urbanisation in Kenya*. 2 vols. New York: Ford Foundation, 1972.

Fox, R. "Impact of Space: Land Division and Urban Development in Kenya and South Africa." *International Regional Science Review* 15 (1) (1992): 39–49.

Frankl, P. J. L. "An Arabic Deed of Sale from Swahili Mombasa Dated 1292/1875." *British Journal of Middle Eastern Studies* 20 (1) (1993): 33–41.

Freeman, Donald B. *City of Farmers: Informal Agriculture in the Open Spaces of Nairobi, Kenya*. Montreal and Kingston: McGill-Queen's University Press, 1991.

Furedi, Frank. "African Crowd in Nairobi: Popular Movements and Elite Politics." *JAH* 14 (2) (1973): 275–90.

Gaile, Gary L. "Choosing Location for Small Town Development to Enable Market and Employment Expansion: The Case of Kenya." *Economic Geography* 64 (3) (1988): 242–54.

Ghaidan, Usam I. *Lamu: A Study of the Swahili Town*. Nairobi: EALB, 1975.

Githumo, Mwangi wa. "Quagmire of the Urban Poor in Nairobi." *JEARD* 13 (1983): 126–49.

Golds, J. M. "African Urbanization in Kenya." *JAA* 13 (1) (1961): 24–28.

Gould, W. T. S. "Urban Bias, Regional Differentiation and Rural-Urban Interaction in Kenya." *African Urban Quarterly* 2 (2) (1987): 122–33.

Great Britain, Foreign Office. *Report on the Mombasa-Victoria Lake Railway Survey*. London: HMSO, 1893.

Groot, Francis. "African Lakeside Town: A Study of Urbanisation in Western Kenya with Particular Reference to Religion." Ph.D. diss., Pontificia Universitas Gregoriana, 1975.

Guide to Nairobi: City in the Sun. Nairobi: East African Standard, 1959.

Hake, Andrew. *African Metropolis: Nairobi's Self-Help City*. London: Chatto and Windus for Sussex University Press, 1977.

Hirst, Terry. *Struggle for Nairobi: Story of an Urban Environment Built at 'the Place of Cold Waters.'* Nairobi: Mazingira Institute, 1994.

House, William J. "Nairobi's Informal Sector: Dynamic Entrepreneurs or Surplus Labor." *Economic Development and Cultural Change* 32 (2) (1983): 277–302.

———, et al. "Urban Self-Employment in Kenya: Panacea or Viable Strategy?" *WD* 21 (7) (1993): 1205–23.

Hutton, John, ed. *Urban Challenge in East Africa*. Nairobi: EAPH, 1972.

Hyder, Kindy. *Life and Politics in Mombasa*. Nairobi: EAPH, 1972.

Ismail, Zahir. "Aiding the Urban Informal Sector: The Case of Nairobi, Kenya." Ph.D. diss., University of Waterloo, 1990.

Janmohamed, K. K. "A History of Mombasa c. 1895–1939: Some Aspects of the Economic and Social Life in an East African Port Town During Colonial Rule." Ph.D. diss., Northwestern University, 1977.

Jewell, John H. A. *Mombasa: The Friendly Town*. Nairobi: EAPH, 1976.

Jones, B. G. "Urban Support for Rural Development in Kenya." *Economic Geography* 62 (3) (1986): 201–14.

Kabagambe, Denis, and Cliff Moughtin. "Housing the Poor: A Case Study in Nairobi." *Third World Planning Review* 5 (3) (1983): 227–48.

Kabecha, W. W., and T. H. Thomas. "The Quality of Informal Sector Manufactures in Nairobi." *Small Enterprise Development* 4 (1995): 43–49.

Kabwegyere, T. B. "Small Urban Centres and the Growth of Underdevelopment in Rural Kenya." *Africa* 49 (3) (1979): 308–15.

Kayongo-Male, Diane, and Philista Onyango. "Child Labour and Delinquency in Nairobi." *JEARD* 13 (1982): 32–44.

Kenya Human Rights Commission. *Behind the Curtain: A Study on Squatters, Slums, and Slum Dwellers.* Nairobi: Kenya Human Rights Commission, 1996.

Kobiah, Samuel Mugwika. "Origins and Squatting and Community Organization in Nairobi." *African Urban Studies* 19/20 (1984/1985): 1–107.

Kimuyu, P. K. "Urbanisation and Consumption of Petroleum Products in Kenya." *Energy Policy* 21 (4) (1993): 403–07.

Kingoriah, G. K. "Causes of Nairobi's City Structure." *Ekistics* 50 (301) (1983): 246–54.

———. "Regions and Regional Delimitation as Aids for Urban and Rural Development in Kenya." *Ekistics* 51 (304) (1984): 18–25.

Kinyanjui, Mary N. "Intra-Urban Distribution of Manufacturing Industries in Thika Town." *JEARD* 18 (1988): 67–87.

Kirkman, James S. *The Tomb of the Dated Inscription at Gedi.* London: Royal Anthropological Institute, 1960.

Kironde, J. M. L. "Creations in Dar-es-Salaam and Extensions in Nairobi: The Defiance of Inappropriate Building Standards." *Cities* 9 (3) (1992): 220–31.

Knappert, J. "Chronicles of Mombasa." *Swahili* 34 (2) (1964): 21–27.

Lamba, D. "Forgotten Half: : Environmental Health in Nairobi's Poverty Area." *Environment and Urbanisation* 6 (1) (1994): 164–73.

Lee-Smith, Diana. "Urban Management in Nairobi: A Case Study of the Matatu Mode of Public Transport." In *African Cities in Crisis: Managing Rapid Urban Growth*, edited by Richard E. Stren and Rodney R. White, 276–304. Boulder,CO: WP, 1989.

———, and Pyar Ali Memon. "Institution Development for Delivery of Low-Income Housing: An Evaluation of the Dandora Community Development Project in Nairobi." *Third World Planning Review* 10 (3) (1988): 217–38.

———, and Richard E. Stren. "New Perspectives on African Urban Management." *Environment and Urbanisation* 3 (1) (1991): 23–36.

Lewis, B. D. "Enquiry into Kenyan Small Town Development Policy." *Economic Geography* 67 (2) (1991): 147–53.

Macharia, Kinuthia. "Housing Policy in Kenya: The View from the Bottom. A Survey of Low-Income Residents in Nairobi and Thika." *African Studies Association Papers* 28 (75) (1985): 1–28.

———. "Slum Clearance and the Informal Economy in Nairobi." *JMAS* 30 (2) (1992): 221–36.

————. *The State and the Informal Sector in Nairobi, Kenya.* Nairobi: IFRA, 1993.

Macoloo, Gervase Chris. "Changing Nature of Financing Low Income Urban Housing Development in Kenya." *Housing Studies* 9 (2) (1994): 281–99.

————. "Housing the Urban Poor: A Case Study of Kisumu Town, Kenya." *Third World Planning Review* 10 (2) (1988): 159–74.

————. "Transformation of the Production and Retail of Building Materials for Low-Income Housing in Mombasa, Kenya." *Development and Change* 22 (3) (1991): 445–73.

McVicar, Kenneth G. "Twilight of an East African Slum: Pumwani and the Evolution of African Settlement in Nairobi." Ph.D. diss., University of California, Los Angeles, 1968.

Malombe, Joyce M. "Impact of Site and Service Projects on Urban Housing Markets: The Case of Dandora, Nairobi." Ph.D. diss., University of Western Ontario, 1990.

Martin, Esmond Bradley. *Malindi: The Historic Town on Kenya's Coast.* Nairobi: Marketing and Publishing, 1975.

Matsuda, M. "Soft Resistance in the Everyday Life: A Life-Strategy of the Maragoli Migrants in Nairobi." *Senri Ethnological Studies* 31 (1992): 1–82.

Memon, Pyar Ali. "Growth of Low-Income Settlements: Planning Response to the Peri-Urban Zone of Nairobi." *Third World Planning Review* 4 (2) (1982): 145–58.

————. "Some Geographical Aspects of the History of Urban Development in Kenya." In *Economic and Social History of East Africa*, edited by Bethwell A. Ogot, 128–53. Nairobi: EALB, 1975.

————, and Diana Lee-Smith. "Urban Agriculture in Kenya." *CJAS* 27 (1) (1993): 25–42.

Milukas, M. V. "Energy for Secondary Cities: The Case of Nakuru, Kenya." *Energy Policy* 21 (5) (1993): 543–58.

Mitullah, W. V. "Hawking as a Survival Strategy for the Urban Poor in Nairobi: The Case of Women." *Environment and Urbanization* (1991): 13–22.

————. *State Policy and Urban Housing in Kenya: The Case of Low Income Housing in Nairobi.* Nairobi: IDS, 1992.

Morgan, W. T. W., ed. *Nairobi: City and Region.* New York: OUP, 1967.

Muller, Maria S. "National Policy of Kenyanisation of Trade: Its Impact on a Town in Kenya." *CJAS* 15 (2) (1981): 293–333.

————. "Self-Employed in Kitale: No Easy Road to Success." *African Urban Studies* 12 (1982): 1–15.

Mwega, F. M. "Informal Entrepreneurship in an African Urban Area." *Small Enterprise Development* 2 (3) (1991): 133–37.

Ngethe, N. and M. Ngunyi. "Role of Small Urban Centres in Kenya's National Development." *African Urban Quarterly* 6 (3/4) (1991): 236–50.

Obudho, Robert A. "Multivariate Analysis of Kenya's Urban System." *GeoJournal* 13 (4) (1986): 385–99.

————. "National Urban and Regional Planning Policy in Kenya." *Third World Planning Review* 6 (4) (1984): 363–88.

————, ed. *Urbanization and Development Planning in Kenya*. Nairobi: KLB, 1981.

————. "Urbanization and Rural Planning in East Africa." *African Studies Association Papers* 26 (102) (1983): 1–46.

————. *Urbanization in Kenya: A Bottom-Up Approach to Development Planning*. Lanham, MD: University Press of America, 1983.

————, and G. O. Aduwo. "Small Urban Centres and the Spatial Planning of Kenya." In *Small Town Africa: Studies in Rural-Urban Interaction*, edited by Jonathon Baker, 51–68. Uppsala, Sweden: SIAS, 1990.

————, and P. P. Waller. *Periodic Markets, Urbanization and Regional Planning: A Case Study from Western Kenya*. Westport, CT: Greenwood Press, 1976.

Olima, Washington H. A. *The Land Use Planning in Provincial Towns of Kenya: A Case Study of Kisumu and Eldoret Towns*. Dortmund, Germany: Projekt-Verlag, 1993.

Oucho, John O. "Rural Orientation, Return Migration and Future Movements of Urban Migrants: A Study of Kisumu, Kenya." *African Urban Quarterly* 1 (3/4) (1986): 207–19.

Owiro, A. Okoth. "Urban Planning and the Law in Kenya." *African Urban Quarterly* 3 (1/2) (1988): 69–78.

Parker, Mary. "Municipal Government and the Growth of African Political Institutions in the Urban Areas of Kenya." *Zaire* 3 (6) (1949): 649–62.

————. "Political and Social Aspects of the Development of Municipal Government in Kenya with Special Reference to Nairobi." Ph.D. diss., University of London, 1944.

Peake, Robert. "Swahili Stratification and Tourism in Malindi Old Town, Kenya." *Africa* 59 (2) (1989): 209–20.

Pearson, Michael N. *Port Cities and Intruders: The Swahili Coast, India, and Portugal in the Early Modern Era*. Baltimore, MD and London: Johns Hopkins University Press, 1998.

Preston, R. O. *Oriental Nairobi*. Nairobi: Colonial Printing Works, 1938.

Rempel, Henry. "Labor Migration into Urban Centres and Urban Unemployment in Kenya." Ph.D. diss., University of Wisconsin, 1970.

Richardson, Harry W. "An Urban Strategy for Kenya." *JDA* 15 (1) (1980): 97–118.

Rodriguez-Torres, D. *Urban Development in Nairobi, Yesterday and Today*. Nairobi: IFRA, 1992.

Romero, Patricia W. *Lamu: History, Society, and Family in an East African Port City*. Princeton, NJ: Markus Wiener, 1996.

————. "Where Have All the Slaves Gone: Emancipation and Post-Emancipation in Lamu, Kenya." *JAH* 27 (3) (1986): 497–512.

Romero Curtin, Patricia W. "Lamu (Kenya) Slave Trade, and British Efforts to Suppress." *Slavery and Abolition* 7 (1986): 148–59.

Ross, Marc Howard. *Grass Roots in an African City: Political Behaviour in Nairobi.* Cambridge, MA: MIT Press, 1975.

————. *Political Integration of Urban Squatters.* Evanston, IL: Northwestern University Press, 1973.

————. "Two Styles of Political Participation in an African City." *American Journal of Political Science* 17 (1) (1973): 1–22.

Rubia, C. W., et al. "City of the Commonwealth: Nairobi." *New Commonwealth* 44 (1966): 335–40.

Sabini, Maurizio. *Architecture of Mombasa.* 2 vols. Vienna: n.p., 1993.

Scholfield, John Frank. "City of Gedi (Kenya)." *South African Archaeological Bulletin* 10 (38) (1955): 35–42.

Seeley, Janet. "Social Welfare in a Kenyan Town: Policy and Practice, 1902–1985." *AA* 86 (345) (1987): 541–66.

Seger, M. "Nairobi: Struktur und Funktion Einer Postcolonialen Primate City." *Geographische Rundschau* 44 (9) (1992): 528–35.

Seierup, S. *Small Town Entrepreneurs and Their Networks in Kenya.* Copenhagen: CDR, 1994.

Senga, William. "Growth Profiles of Small Cities: Thika, Kenya." In *Growth Profiles of Small Cities*, 21–26. Tokyo: United Nations Centre for Regional Development, 1983.

Silberman, Leo. "Social Survey of the Old Town of Mombasa." *JAA* 1 (1) (1950): 14–21.

Smart, J. A. *Jubilee History of Nairobi, 1900–1950.* Nairobi: East African Standard, 1950.

Smoke, P. "Small Town Local Government Finance in Kenya: The Case of Karatina Town Council." *Public Administration and Development* 12 (1) (1992): 71–85.

Stamp, A. P. D. "Governing Thika: Dilemmas of Municipal Politics in Kenya." Ph.D. diss., University of London, 1981.

Stren, Richard E. "Factional Politics and central Control in Mombasa, 1960–69." *CJAS* 4 (1) (1970): 33–56.

————. *Housing the Urban Poor in Africa: Politics, Policy, and Bureaucracy in Mombasa.* Berkeley, CA: Institute of International Studies, 1978.

————. "Urban Policy in Africa: A Political Analysis." *ASR* 15 (3) (1972): 489–516.

Suda, Colette A. "Impact of Changing Family Structures on Nairobi Children." *African Study Monographs* 14 (2) (1994): 109–21.

Survey of Kenya. *City of Nairobi.* Nairobi: Survey of Kenya, 1971.

Tamarkin, Mordechai. "Impact of the First Lancaster House Conference (1960) and the Kenyatta Election (1961) on Urban Politics in Nakuru, Kenya." *TJH* 10 (1/2) (1981): 28–44.

————. "Tribal Associations, Tribal Solidarity, and Tribal Chauvinism in a Kenya Town [Nakuru]." *JAH* 14 (2) (1973): 257–74.

Tolmacheva, Marina. "They Came from Damascus, Syria: A Note on Traditional Lamu Historiography." *IJAHS* 12 (1979): 259–69.

Vasey, Ernest A. *Housing of Africans in the Urban Areas of Kenya*. Nairobi: Kenya Information Office, 1946.

Veda, G. "Social Relations in Urban Petty Production: Market Traders in Nyeri, Kenya." *Science Reports, Tohuku University, Seventh Series: Geography* 42 (2) (1992): 75–106

Walmsley, R. W. *Nairobi: The Geography of a New City*. Kampala: Eagle Press, 1957.

Werlin, Herbert H. *Governing an African City: A Study of Nairobi*. New York: Africana Publishing House, 1974.

———. "Hawkers of Nairobi: The Politics of the Informal Sector," in *Urbanization and Development Planning in Kenya*, edited by R. A. Obudho, 194–214. Nairobi: KLB, 1981.

———. "Nairobi City Council: A Study in Comparative Local Government." *Comparative Studies in Society and History* 8 (1966): 181–98.

———. "Nairobi's Politics of Housing." *African Review* 3 (4) (1973): 611–29.

White, L. W. T. et al. *Nairobi: A Master Plan for a Colonial Capital*. London: HMSO, 1948.

Wilson, Gordon. "Mombasa: A Modern Colonial Municipality." In *Social Change in Modern Africa*, edited by Aiden Southall, 98–112. London: OUP, 1961.

Winterford, David B. "Creative Development: The Political Economy of the Urban Informal Sector in Kenya." Ph.D. diss., University of British Columbia, 1979.

Wood, Barbara. *Green City in the Sun*. New York: Random House, 1988.

World Bank. *Kenya Economic Development and Urbanization Policy*. Washington, D.C.: World Bank, 1985.

Ylvisaker, M. *Lamu in the Nineteenth Century: Land, Trade, and Politics*. Boston: African Studies Center, Boston University, 1979.

Zwanenberg, Roger van. "History and Theory of Urban Poverty in Nairobi: The Case of Slum Development." *JEARD* 2 (2) (1972): 163–203.

W. TRAVEL AND EXPLORATION

Amin, Mohamed. *Journey through Kenya*. London: Bodley Head, 1982.

Arkell-Hardwick, Alfred. *Ivory Trader in North Kenia*. London: Longman, 1903.

Austin, Herbert Henry. *Among Swamps and Giants in Equatorial Africa: An Account of Surveys and Adventures in the Southern Sudan and British East Africa*. London: C. Arthur Pearson, 1902.

———. "From Njemps to Marich, Save and Mumia's (British East Africa)." *GJ* 14 (1899): 307–10.

———. "A Journey from Omdurman to Mombasa via Lake Rudolf." *GJ* 19 (1902): 669–90.

————. "Lake Rudolf." *GJ* 14 (1899): 148–55.

————. *Some Rambles of a Sapper*. London: Edward Arnold, 1928.

————. "Through Sudan to Mombasa via Lake Rudolf." *Scottish Geographical Magazine* 18 (1902): 281–302.

Bell, Walter Dalrymple Maitland. *Karamoja Safari*. London: Gollancz, 1949.

————. *Wanderings of an Elephant Hunter*. London: Country Life, 1923.

Bowermaster, Jon. *Adventures and Misadventures of Peter Beard in Africa*. Boston: Bullfinch Press, 1993.

Bridges, Roy C. "British Exploration of East Africa, 1788–1885." Ph.D. diss., University of London, 1963.

Brooke, J. W. "A Journey West and North of Lake Rudolf." *GJ* 25 (1905): 525–31.

Bullock, Ronald. "Towards an Understanding of the Exploration of the Kenyan Hinterland by Coastmen, 1850–1880." *Terrae Incognitae* 17 (1985): 69–87.

Casada, James Allen. "Imperialism of Exploration: British Explorers and East Africa, 1856–1890." Ph.D. diss., Vanderbilt University, 1972.

Cavendish, Henry Sheppard Hart. "Through Somaliland and Around and South of Lake Rudolf." *GJ* 11 (1898): 372–81.

Champion, A. M. "In Search of Teleki's Volcano." *JEAUNHS* 12 (1935): 118–29.

————. "The Physiography of the Region to the West and South-West of Lake Rudolf." *GJ* 89 (1937): 97–118.

————. "Teleki's Volcano and the Lava Fields at the Southern End of Lake Rudolf." *GJ* 85 (1935): 323–41.

————. "The Volcanic Region around the Southern End of Lake Rudolf, Kenya Colony." *GJ* 89 (1937): 163–72.

Chanler, William Astor. *Through Jungle and Desert: Travels in Eastern Africa*. London: Macmillan, 1896.

"Count Teleki's Discoveries in Eastern Africa." *Scottish Geographical Magazine* 5 (1889): 96–100.

Dawson, Marc H. "The Many Minds of Sir Halford J. Mackinder: Dilemmas of Historical Editing." *HIA* (1987): 27–42.

DeMott, Maddie. "William Chanler." *Africana* 3 (1) (1967): 15–19.

Donaldson-Smith, A. "An Expedition Between Lake Rudolf and the Nile." *GJ* 16 (1900): 600–25.

————. "Expedition Through Somaliland to Lake Rudolf." *GJ* 8 (1896): 120–37, 221–29.

————. *Through Unknown African Countries: The First Expedition from Somaliland to Lake Lamu*. London: Edward Arnold, 1897.

Dracopoli, I. N. *Through Jubaland to the Lorian Swamp*. London: Seeley, Service, 1914.

"Explorations in British East Africa." *Scottish Geographical Magazine* 7 (1891): 195–205.

Fitzgerald, William Walter Augustine. *Travels in the Grasslands of British East Africa and the Islands of Zanzibar and Pemba*. London: Chapman and Hall, 1898.

Gregory, John Walter. *Great Rift Valley: Being the Narrative of a Journey to Mount Kenya and Lake Baringo.* London: Frank Cass, 1968.

————. *The Rift Valleys and Geology of East Africa.* London: Seeley Service, 1921.

Haywood, C. Wightwick. *To the Mysterious Lorian Swamp.* Philadelphia: J. B. Lippincott, 1927.

Heaton, Tom. *In Teleki's Footsteps: An East African Journey.* London: Macmillan, 1989.

Hillaby, John. *Journey to the Jade Sea.* London: Constable, 1964.

Hindlip, Lord. *Sport and Travel: Abyssinia and British East Africa.* London: T. Fisher Unwin, 1906.

Höhnel, Ludwig von. *Discovery of Lakes Rudolf and Stefanie: A Narrative of Count Samuel Teleki's Exploring and Hunting Expedition in Eastern Equatorial Africa in 1887 and 1888.* London: Longman, 1894.

————. "Lake Rudolf Region: Its Discovery and Subsequent Exploration, 1888–1909." *JRAS* 37 (146) (1938): 21–45; and 37 (147) (1938): 206–26.

Huntingford, G. W. B., trans. and ed. *Periplus of the Erythraen Sea.* London: Hakluyt Society, 1980.

Imperato, Pascal James. *Arthur Donaldson Smith and the Exploration of Lake Rudolf.* Lake Success, NY: Medical Society of the State of New York, 1987.

————. *Quest for the Jade Sea: Colonial Competition Around an East African Lake.* Boulder, CO and London: Westview Press, 1998.

Johnson, Harry Hamilton. *The Nile Quest: A Record of the Exploration of the Nile and Its Basin.* New York: Frederick A. Stokes, 1903.

Loftus, E. A. *Thompson: Through Masai Land.* London: Nelson, 1951.

MacKinder, Halford John. *First Ascent of Mount Kenya.* London: Hurst, 1991.

————. "Journey to the Summit of Mount Kenya, British East Africa." *GJ* 15 (5) (1900): 453–86.

McLynn, Frank. *Hearts of Darkness: The European Exploration of Africa.* New York: Carroll and Graf, 1992.

Moorehead, Alan. *White Nile.* London: Hamish Hamilton, 1960.

Neumann, A. H. *Elephant Hunting in East Equatorial Africa.* London: Rowland Ward, 1898.

Norden, Hermann. *White and Black in East Africa.* Boston: Small Maynard, 1924.

Pavitt, Nigel. *Kenya: The First Explorers.* London: Aurum Press, 1989.

Pern, Stephen. *Another Land, Another Sea: Walking Round Lake Rudolf.* London: Victor Gollancz, 1979.

Peters, Carl. *New Light on Dark Africa.* London: Ward Lock, 1891.

Reece, Alys. *To My Wife—50 Camels.* London: Harvill Press, 1963.

Richards, Charles G., and James Place. *East African Explorers.* London: OUP, 1968.

Rotberg, Robert I. *Joseph Thomson and the Exploration of Africa.* London: Chatto and Windus, 1971.

Simpson, Donald H. *Dark Companions: The African Contribution to the European Exploration of East Africa.* London: Paul Elek, 1975.

Stigand, C. H. *To Abyssinia Through an Unknown Land: An Account of a Journey through Unexplored Regions of British East Africa by Lake Rudolf to the Kingdom of Menelik.* Philadelphia: Lippincott, 1910.

———. *Land of Zinj: Being an Account of British East Africa; Its Ancient History and Present Inhabitants.* London: Frank Cass, 1966.

Tate, H. R. "Journey to Rendille Country, British East Africa." *GJ* 23 (1904): 220–28, 230.

Thesiger, Wilfred. *My Kenya Days.* London: HarperCollins, 1994.

Thomson, Joseph. *Through Masai Land: A Journey of Exploration Among the Snowclad Volcanic Mountains and Strange Tribes.* Boston: Houghton Mifflin, 1885.

———. *To the Central African Lakes and Back.* London: Sampson Low, Marston, Searle and Rivington, 1881.

Whitehouse, William F. "To Lake Rudolf and Beyond." In *Book of the Boone and Crockett Club*, edited by George Grinnell and Theodore Roosevelt, 257–340. New Haven, CT: YUP, 1925.

Wightwick Haywood, Cecil Walter Inglefield. *To the Mysterious Lorian Swamp: An Adventurous and Arduous Journey of Exploration Through the Vast Waterless Tracts of Unknown Jubaland.* Philadelphia: Lippincott, 1928.

Young, Roland, ed. *Through Masailand with Joseph Thomson.* Evanston, IL: Northwestern University Press, 1962.

X. ASIANS

Andrews, Charles F. *The Indian Question in East Africa.* Nairobi: The Swift Press, 1921.

Atieno Odhiambo, E. S. "Political Economy of the Asian Problem in Kenya, 1888–1939." *TJH* 4 (1/2) (1974): 135–49.

Balachandran, P. K. "Embattled Community: Asians in East Africa Today." *AA* 80 (320) (1981): 317–25.

Bennett, Charles. "Persistence Amid Adversity: The Growth and Spatial Distribution of the Asian Population of Kenya, 1903–63." Ph.D. diss., Syracuse University, 1976.

Bharati, Agehananda. *Asians in East Africa: Jaihind and Uhuru.* Calcutta: Bookland, 1970.

Cable, Vincent. "Asians of Kenya." *AA* 68 (272) (1969): 218–31.

———. "Help for the Asians of Kenya?" *WT* 25 (3) (1969): 110–16.

Cowen, Michael, and Scott MacWilliam. *Indigenous Capital in Kenya: The Indian Dimension of the Debate.* Helsinki: Interkont Books, 1996.

"Debate over the Role of Kenya Asians." *Weekly Review* (12 November 1982): 3–16.

Delf, George. *Asians in East Africa.* London: OUP, 1963.

Duder, C. J. D. "Settler Response to the Indian Crisis of 1923 in Kenya: Brigadier General Philip Wheatley and 'Direct Action.'" *JICH* 17 (3) (1989): 349–73.

Furedi, Frank. "Development of Anti-Asian Opinion among Africans in Nakuru District, Kenya." *AA* 73 (292) (1974): 347–58.

Ghai, Dharam P., and Yash P. Ghai, eds. *Portrait of a Minority: Asians in East Africa*. Nairobi: OUP, 1970.

Gregory, Robert G. "Co-operation and Collaboration in Colonial East Africa: The Asians' Political Role, 1890–1964." *AA* 80 (319) (1981): 259–73.

———. *India and East Africa: A History of Race Relations within the British Empire, 1890–1939*. Oxford: OUP, 1971.

———. *Quest for Equality: Asian Politics in East Africa 1900–1967*. Hyderabad, India: Orient Longman, 1993.

———. *Rise and Fall of Philanthropy in East Africa: The Asian Contribution*. New Brunswick, NJ: Transaction, 1992.

———. *South Asians in East Africa: An Economic and Social History, 1890–1980*. Boulder, CO: WP, 1993.

Heyer, S. S. "The Asian in Kenya." *Africa South* 5 (2) (1961): 77–84.

Himbara, David. "The 'Asian Question' in East Africa." *African Studies* 56 (1) (1997): 1–18.

Hollingsworth, Lawrence William. *Asians of East Africa*. London: St. Martins, 1960.

Indian Problem in Kenya: Being a Selection from Speeches, Articles and Correspondence Appearing in the East African Press, April-October 1921. Nairobi: East African Standard, 1922.

Indians Overseas Association. *How India Looks at Kenya*. London: Indians Overseas Association, c. 1923.

———. *Indians in East Africa: Is the Segregation Policy to Prevail?* London: Indians Overseas Association, c. 1921.

———. *The Real Kenya Question: A Few Facts*. London: Indians Overseas Association, c. 1923.

Jeevanjee, Alibhoy Mulla. *An Appeal on Behalf of the Indians in East Africa*. Bombay: 1912.

Jones, Susan. "Kenya and the Devonshire White Paper of 1923." *A.N.U. History Journal* 13 (1977): 20–40.

McCormack, Richard T. *Asians in Kenya*. Brooklyn: T. Gaus' Sons, 1971.

Mangat, J. S. *History of Asians in East Africa c. 1886 to 1945*. Oxford: The Clarendon Press, 1969.

Manji, Madatally. *Mandatally Manji: Memoirs of a Biscuit Baron*. Nairobi: Kenways Publications, 1995.

Maxon, Robert M. "Devonshire Declaration: The Myth of Missionary Intervention." *HIA* 18 (1991): 259–70.

Moon, Henry Lee. "What Future for Asians in East Africa." *Crisis* 80 (1) (1973): 6–10.

Morris, H. S. "Indians in East Africa: A Study in a Plural Society." *British Journal of Sociology* 7 (3) (1956): 194–211.

Nanjira, Daniel D. *Status of Aliens in East Africa: Asians and Europeans in Tanzania, Uganda and Kenya.* New York: Praeger, 1976.

Narain, Singh, ed. *Kenya Independence-Day Souvenir: A Spotlight on the Asians of Kenya.* Nairobi: Kenya Indian Congress, 1963.

Naseem, Abdul Waheed. "Nature and Extent of the Indian Enterprise Along the East African Coast and Subsequent Role in the Development of Kenya, 1840–1905." Ph.D. diss., St. John's University, 1975.

Nazareth, J. M. *Brown Man Black Country: A Peep into Kenya's Freedom Struggle.* New Delhi: Tidings, 1981.

Nyaggah, Mougo. "Asians in East Africa: The Case of Kenya." *JAS* 1 (2) (1974): 205–33.

Okoth, P. G. "Partners in Exploitation: The Case of Asians in Kenya." *Makerere Historical Journal* 2 (1989): 20–34.

Pandit, Shanti, ed. *Asians in East and Central Africa.* Nairobi: Panco Publications, 1963.

Pocock, David F. "'Difference' in East Africa: A Study of Caste and Religion in Modern Indian Society." *Southwestern Journal of Anthropology* 13 (1957): 289–300.

———. "Indians in East Africa, with Special Reference to their Social and Economic Situation and Relationship." D. Phil. diss., Oxford University, 1955.

Rai, Kauleshwar. "British Policy Towards Indians in Kenya." In *Journal of Indian History: Golden Jubilee Volume,* edited by T. K. Ravindran, 909–14. Trivandrum, India: University of Kerala, 1973.

———. *Indians and British Colonialism in East Africa, 1883–1939.* Patna, India: B. K. Sinha for Associated Book Agency, 1979.

Ramchandani, R. R. "Indian Emigration to East African Countries during XIX and Early XX Centuries." *Journal of the University of Bombay* 77 (1972): 166–88.

Rice, Stanley. "Indian Question in Kenya." *Foreign Affairs* 2 (2) (1923): 258–69.

Salvadori, Cynthia. *Through Open Doors: A View of Asian Cultures in Kenya.* Nairobi: Kenway Publications, 1983.

———. *We Came in Dhows: Stories of the Indian Pioneers in Kenya.* 3 vols. Nairobi: Paperchase Kenya, 1997.

Seidenberg, Dana April. *Uhuru and the Kenya Indians: The Role of a Minority Community in Kenya Politics, 1939–63.* New Delhi: Vikas Publishing House, 1983.

Singh, D. "Indians in East Africa." *AQ* 1 (4) (1962): 43–45.

Soff, Harvey G. "British Colonial Attitudes towards Indians in East Africa." *Journal of Indian History* 50 (2) (1972): 573–96.

Spencer, I. R. G. "First Assault on Indian Ascendancy: Indian Traders in the Kenya Reserves, 1895–1929." *AA* 80 (320) (1981): 327–43.

Stigger, P. "Asians in Rhodesia and Kenya: A Comparative Political History." *Rhodesian History* 1 (1970): 1–8.

Tangri, Roger K. "Early Asian Protest in East Africa." *AQ* 7 (2) (1967): 153–67.

Varghese, Mary T. "East African Indian National Congress, 1911 to 1939: A Study of Indian Political Activity in Kenya." Ph.D. diss., Dalhousie University, 1976.

Yash P. Ghai, and Dharam P. Ghai, eds. *Asian Minorities of East and Central Africa (up to 1971)*. London: Minority Rights Group, 1971.

Youé, Christopher P. "Threat of Settler Rebellion and the Imperial Predicament: The Denial of Indian Rights in Kenya, 1923." *CJAS* 12 (3) (1978): 347–60.

Zarwan, John Irving. "Indian Businessmen in Kenya during the Twentieth Century: A Case Study." Ph.D. diss., Yale University, 1977.

About the Authors

Thomas P. Ofcansky received a Ph.D. in East African history from West Virginia University (1981). He has held several academic posts and is currently with the Department of State. He has published numerous books and articles about East Africa. Recently, Ofcansky coauthored the second edition of the *Historical Dictionary of Tanzania*. He has also has traveled widely throughout East Africa.

Robert M. Maxon received a B.A. in history from Duke University, and a Ph.D. in African history from Syracuse University. He has considerable experience in Kenya, where he served as education officer, research fellow in history at the University of Nairobi, and visiting professor of history at Moi University. Maxon has published widely on various aspects of Kenya's colonial history. Since 1969, he has been a member of the faculty of West Virginia University.